30117   010814925

D1610006

THE DURHAM MINERS 1919–1960

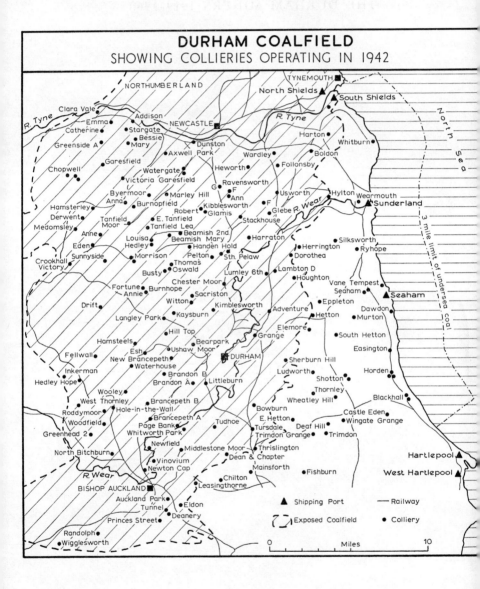

DURHAM COALFIELD
SHOWING COLLIERIES OPERATING IN 1942

NORTHUMBERLAND

TYNEMOUTH
North Shields
South Shields

R. Tyne
Clara Vale
Emma
Catherine
Addison
Stargate
Bessie
Mary
NEWCASTLE
R. Tyne
Harton
Whitburn
Greenside A
Dunston
Wardley
Boldon
Axwell Park
Garesfield
Heworth
Follonsby
Chopwell
Watergate
Victoria Garesfield
Ravensworth
Byermoor
Marley Hill
G F
Usworth
Hylton Wearmouth
Anna
Burnopfield
Ann
F
Sunderland
Hamsterley
Robert
Kibblesworth
Glamis
Glebe R. Wear
Derwent
E. Tanfield
Stackhouse
Tanfield
Medomsley
Moor
Tanfield Lea
Anne
Beamish 2nd.
Harraton
Silksworth
Eden
Louisa
Beamish Mary
Herrington
Ryhope
Hedley
Handen Hold
Dorothea
Crookhall
Sunnyside
Morrison
Pelton
Sth. Pelaw
Victory
Busty
Thomas
Oswald
Lumley 6th.
Lambton D
Houghton
Vane Tempest
Chester Moor
Seaham
Fortune
Burnhope
Sacriston
Eppleton
Dawdon
Annie
Witton
Kimblesworth
Adventure
Seaham
Drift
Kaysburn
Hetton
Murton
Langley Park
Hill Top
Elemore
South Hetton
Hamsteels
Bearpark
Grange
Easington
Fellwall
Esh
Ushaw Moor
DURHAM
Sherburn Hill
Horden
New Brancepeth
Ludworth
Inkerman
Waterhouse
Brandon B
Shotton
Hedley Hope
Brandon A
Littleburn
Thornley
Wooley
Wheatley Hill
Blackhall
West Thornley
Brancepeth B
Bowburn
Castle Eden
Roddymoor
Hole-in-the-Wall
E. Hetton
Wingate Grange
Woodfield
Brancepeth A
Tudhoe
Tursdale
Deaf Hill
Page Bank
Greenhead 2
Whitworth Park
Trimdon Grange
Trimdon
Newfield
Middlestone Moor
Thrislington
North Bitchburn
Vinovium
Dean & Chapter
Hartlepool
Newton Cap
Mainsforth
R. Wear
Chilton
Fishburn
West Hartlepool
BISHOP AUCKLAND
Leasingthorne
Auckland Park
Tunnel
Eldon
Princes Street
Deanery
Randolph
Wigglesworth

North Sea

3 mile limit of undersea coal

▲ Shipping Port
〔 〕 Exposed Coalfield

— Railway
● Colliery

0   Miles   10

THE DURHAM MINERS
1919–1960

BY

W. R. GARSIDE
Lecturer in Economic History, University of Leicester

London
GEORGE ALLEN & UNWIN LTD
RUSKIN HOUSE   MUSEUM STREET

First published in 1971

© George Allen & Unwin Ltd, 1971

ISBN 0 04 942091 7   7201

DR

(331.7622)

20. JAN. 1972

331.881

MINERS

Printed in Great Britain
in 10pt. Times Roman type
by The Aldine Press Letchworth

Foreword

BY J. C. ROBINSON

General Secretary, N.U.M. (Durham Area).

This history is long awaited. It is the fruit of painstaking research
and writing by the author, Dr W. R. Garside, of Leicester University,
the son of a Durham miner.

The Durham Miners' Association, though undoubtedly one of the
most independent and controversial of mining bodies, has no
published history covering the past fifty years. Richard Fynes recorded a faithful account of the struggles of the Northumberland
and Durham miners to achieve union. In the pages of his book we
may read how men like Tommy Hepburn, Tommy Ramsay, Martin
Jude and the redoubtable 'Pitmen's Attorney' (W. P. Roberts) lived
and protested against the binding systems and the squalid conditions
of their day, a day when colliery rows paid homage to the pit and
men lived in the shadows of the Tommy Shops and the Candy Men.
If we have a sensitive ear we may hear the Londonderry lament
mingling with the cries of sacrificed members. These things were
wrought in a time which with patience (said Hepburn) will change the
mulberry leaf to silk.

John Wilson wrote of the Union's infancy and growth to 1904,
and Sidney Webb produced an excellent book in 1921, of which he
remarked, 'It makes no claim to be an exhaustive history of the
Durham Miners.'

Dr Garside commences his volume with the year 1919: the Jubilee
Year of the Association, the year of the Sankey Award. The industry
was on the crest of a post-war boom. It was soon to be tossed into
a trough of trouble. Those who lived through the years of depression
will perhaps be ready for some kind of analysis, and the author is
well equipped for this work. He is an economist and historian, and
has flung his net wide in relating the turmoil in the Durham coalfield
to events of international significance.

We do not need to be reminded that this country, though an island,
has associations and trade, particularly with Europe, which radically
affect our economy. These European connections are fully developed
by Dr Garside. His writing style and his choice of material have
produced an absorbing book which will appeal to the serious student
and the general reader alike. Social conditions, political activity,
trade union finance are amongst the issues which are given an airing
in a book for the curious, the teachable and the experimenters in
what H. G. Wells termed the great adventure of mankind.

7

The present moment in time has been built from the past, minute by minute. Dr Garside has revived the past in an excellent book. It is his story of the Durham miners. I recommend it to anyone who has an interest in the development of the mining community in Durham County.

J. C. ROBINSON
General Secretary

Preface

When I was invited to write the official history of the Durham
miners I had already begun preliminary research into their activities
since 1919 as the basis of a Ph.D. thesis. The Durham Area of the
N.U.M. agreed that though my immediate research interests ignored
the Union's earliest developments it would be appropriate to provide
a volume which not only broke fresh ground, since some published
work is available on the Durham miners' movement before 1921,
but also covered a period of time within the living memory of a great
number of people. The treatment of the early history of the Durham
miners is both superficial and chronologically patchy. It is anticipated that a second volume will be published in the future to add
substance to the existing accounts of the miners' activity in Durham
from 1869 to the end of the First World War.

Since it is unlikely that another full-scale study will be made of the
Durham miners' movement since 1919 I have quoted in detail from
official Union records and made use of as much contemporary
material as possible. The treatment of the subject ends in 1960 because a continuation thereafter would have seriously impinged upon
current economic and social developments within the coalfield and
made historical comment difficult. The chapters on the post-
nationalization period may well suffer from the same hazard but
since none of the existing regional histories of mining trade unions
deal adequately with coal's contrasting fortunes during the fifties it
was felt worth while documenting some of the major developments.

One of the most pleasant aspects of writing this book has been the
opportunity it gave me to work with officials at the miners' headquarters at Red Hill, Durham. I am grateful for their unfailing
courtesy and helpfulness. I particularly wish to express my thanks to
Mr A. Hesler, who retired as General Secretary of the Union in
February 1970, to Mr J. C. Robinson and to Mr W. Dowding and
Mr L. Scollen (now in America) not only for their assistance in
supplying all relevant documents but also for their cheerful encouragement at various stages of my work. I benefited from the
advice of the late Dr Sam Watson and of Professor E. Allen and Mr
G. H. Metcalfe, Director of Education in County Durham, all of
whom gave up much of their spare time on my behalf.

Mr E. H. D. Skinner, a former Chairman of the Board of the
Durham Division of the National Coal Board, willingly co-operated
in answering my many queries and Mr J. Hoare at the Department
of Trade and Industry supplied statistical material often at very short

notice. The staff of the *Durham Chronicle*, Durham County Record
Office and the N.C.B. Library were equally patient and helpful in my
search for primary material.

I am glad to record my gratitude to Dr J. E. Williams who read the
whole of the initial draft many, many times. Without his guidance
and constructive criticism the task of completing this work would
have been infinitely greater. Professor W. H. B. Court read a large
portion of the draft in thesis form and made many helpful comments.
The blemishes which still remain are entirely my responsibility.

Mrs P. Herbert carried most of the burden of typing with great
forbearance and efficiency. Miss J. Watts, Mrs J. Snelling and Mrs
C. Walton kindly assisted in the final stages of preparing the work
for publication. Mr T. Garfield drew the map of the Durham coalfield and my colleague Dr D. H. Aldcroft helped in checking the
proofs.

A special debt is owed to my parents for the many unconscious
ways in which they have helped me during the past few years of
research and writing and to my wife Glen for her patience and good
humour.

Croft
Leicestershire   W. R. GARSIDE

Contents

Illustrations

List of Abbreviations used in the text

D.M.A. Durham Miners' Association
M.F.G.B. Miners' Federation of Great Britain
N.C.B. National Coal Board
N.U.M. National Union of Mineworkers

Prologue

I

The coal measures of the Northumberland and Durham coalfield occupy a triangular area of about 800 square miles, the apex of which is near the mouth of the River Coquet, in Northumberland, and the base along a line extending eastwards from the vicinity of Middleton-in-Teesdale to just north of Hartlepool. The structure of the coalfield is comparatively simple. The rocks lie in the form of a trough or irregular basin of which the longer axis lies in a north–south direction. The coal beds rise towards the north-east or in a seaward direction. The deepest part of the basin is near the mouth of the River Wear, and the eastern limb is mainly under the North Sea. The Durham portion of the coalfield is divided into two parts: a western exposed field and an eastern concealed field.[1]

The sequence of strata in the coalfield is common to both Northumberland and Durham and can be divided into three main divisions: upper coal measures, with relatively few seams, middle or main productive measures, containing all the best coals, and lower measures whose content is relatively unimportant.[2] The Durham portion of the coalfield produces gas, coking, household and steam coal. In west Durham the seams are of low volatile content and produce coking coals of exceptional quality and of particular value for foundry and general metallurgical work. Although coking coals are found in the eastern part of the coalfield they are lower in carbon but higher in volatile content and as such are mainly used for gas and steam purposes. Although gas coals are marketed from almost the whole of the Durham coalfield the most important producing centre is amongst the east Durham collieries in or near to the coastal area. In south Durham the coals tend to be harder and serve as coking, steam and gas coals.[3]

A large tract of the coalfield in south-west Durham is flooded to such an extent that several millions of tons of workable coal have been abandoned and other seams made unworkable unless they can be drained. In 1945 it was estimated that the total flooded resources in working tracts in the region amounted to 73 million tons and that

[1] Sir Arthur Trueman, ed., *The Coalfields of Great Britain*, London 1954, pp. 298, 308; W. Gibson, *Coal in Great Britain*, London 1927 edn, p. 273.
[2] Ministry of Fuel and Power, *Durham Coalfield Regional Survey Report* (*Northern B Region*), 1945, p. 4.
[3] *Ibid.*, pp. 5–7.

three-quarters of the coal remaining unworked was coking coal.[1]
The south-western portion of the coalfield, although one of the
latest sections to be developed because of its distance from the east
coast, was the first to be abandoned. Coal was nearer the surface in
this area than in other districts and was worked with relentless
energy. The resources of the region soon proved insufficient to maintain the long intensive exploitation, while the abandonment of mines
was precipitated by the world-wide industrial depression of the 1920s
and 1930s and the serious problem of waterlogged pits. The clash of
interests between royalty owners and the lessees of mining rights
proved a considerable hindrance to promoting pumping operations
in this area, so much so that by 1935 only eight of the twenty-five pits
normally working had survived, employing at the most only 3,700
men.[2]

In view of the predominance of gas and coking coal close ties exist
within the Durham coalfield between the mining industry and local
iron and steel and gas undertakings. In 1945 a quarter of the total
output of Durham collieries was absorbed in the manufacture of coke
for use in other industries within the region, especially at the iron
and steel works at Consett, Darlington and Middlesbrough. At the
same time roughly half of the gas distributed by public utility undertakings was manufactured at coke-oven plants.[3]

II

Professor Nef, in his valuable study of the rise of the British coal
industry, has shown how the growth in the absolute importance of
Durham and Northumberland as coal-producing and exporting
counties was one of the most striking developments in the industry
during the period 1550–1700.[4] Throughout the eighteenth and nineteenth centuries the coalfields benefited like all other regions from
the increasing demand for coal brought by the industrial revolution,
but from the third quarter of the nineteenth century their relative
importance declined. This was due mainly to the effects of the
expansion of the railway system.

[1] *Ibid.*, p. 18.
[2] T. Sharp, *A Derelict Area: A Study of the South-West Durham Coalfield*, London
1935, pp. 33–4.
[3] Ministry of Fuel and Power, *Durham Coalfield Regional Survey Report* (*Northern
B Region*), 1945, pp. 27–8.
[4] J. U. Nef, *The Rise of the British Coal Industry*, I, London 1932, pp. 19–36.
See also J. U. Nef, 'The Progress of Technology and the Growth of Large-Scale
Industry in Great Britain, 1540–1640', *Economic History Review*, V, 1934–5.

The early supremacy of the Durham and Northumberland coalfield had rested upon its favourable geographical position in relation to markets to the south and east. Up till the third and fourth decades of the nineteenth century, mining enterprise on any significant scale had been limited to producing areas within the immediate vicinity of navigable waterways. The region's advantageous geographical position, its superior coals (screening had been introduced by northern coal owners in 1766) and the powerful influence of London dealers who openly encouraged the development of sea-borne trade all helped to maintain the region's hold on the London market at the time when early improvements in transport—pre-locomotive railways, turnpike roads and canals—helped inland coalfields to expand their immediate markets. In 1805 only 2,580 tons of coal reached London by inland carriage and only 10,742 tons in 1831.[1]

The introduction of railways had more disturbing effects by reducing the ability of the dominant coal-owning interests in the County to administer satisfactorily the Limitation of the Vend—an output and price-controlling combination which had been established in 1772. During the sixty years after its formation the demand for coal continued to expand and provided individual producers with an opportunity to enlarge their already existing enterprises whilst still allowing the Vend to function.[2] The introduction and extension of the railways, however, destroyed the natural barriers to the expansion of coal-bearing areas and brought in its wake a flood of new producers anxious to share the benefits of controlled prices. The opening of the Stockton to Darlington railroad in 1825 connected the inland coal regions of south-west Durham with the coast and within a few years the export trade of the Tees began to expand considerably. Between 1833 and 1844 fourteen new lines were opened up in Durham and Northumberland with a view to entering the coal trade.[3]

Not only did the introduction of railways so alter the competitive situation within the coalfield that members of the Vend could no longer fix prices and regulate trade amongst themselves at their own will[4] but it helped increase competition in the southern market from other coal producing areas. The breakdown of the Vend coincided

[1] T. S. Ashton and J. Sykes, *The Coal Industry of the Eighteenth Century*, Manchester University Press 1964, pp. 194, 238–9.
[2] P. M. Sweezy, *Monopoly and Competition in the English Coal Trade, 1550–1850*, Harvard University Press 1938, pp. 140–6.
[3] *Ibid.*, pp. 47–8.
[4] The Vend ended in May 1845.

with the entry of inland coal, especially from the Midlands, into the London market. The amount of coal sent by rail to London increased by 3,455,000 tons during 1850–70 whilst seaborne supplies fell from 3,500,000 tons to 2,500,000 during 1850–72.[1]

Fortunately just as the railways increased competition in the London market the removal of duties on the export of coal in 1850 opened up new markets for the north-eastern region. Foreign coal exports from Newcastle which had increased from 118,000 tons in 1820 to 594,000 tons in 1840 stood at 2,031,000 tons in 1860. Exports from Sunderland increased from 471,109 tons in 1850 to 1,027,000 tons in 1860.[2] National foreign coal exports continued to increase thereafter at a rapid rate, the largest share of the exports going to Northumberland, Durham and South Wales. In 1895 foreign coal exports (including bunkers) from the Bristol Channel and north-eastern ports together accounted for 75 per cent of total U.K. coal exports and 71 per cent in 1913.[3]

At the same time production and employment gradually expanded, reaching their peak in 1913, as the following table shows: [4]

Output and Employment in the Durham Coalfield 1880–1913

	Output of coal (tons)	Average number of miners employed	
		Below ground	Above ground
1880	28,063,346	57,515	14,237
1885	27,737,324	59,937	15,504
1900	34,800,719	65,001	20,888
1905	37,397,176	71,979	21,640
1910	39,431,598	88,827	24,054
1913	41,532,890	132,661	33,146

III

As the coal industry expanded throughout the eighteenth and nineteenth centuries and developed its own industrial and financial organization the cleavage between capital and labour sharpened. The wage-earner was gradually forced to protect himself by com-

[1] J. H. Clapham, *Economic History of Modern Britain*, Cambridge University Press 1932, II, p. 301.
[2] F. A. Gibson, *The Coal Mining Industry of the United Kingdom, The Various Coalfields Thereof and the Principal Foreign Countries of the World*, Cardiff 1922.
[3] *Ibid.*, pp. 93–4.
[4] *Reports of H.M. Inspectors of Mines*, 1880–1913.

bination and association as greater power passed to the owners of capital. Various writers [1] have already related the story of the early struggles of the Durham miners to establish their own union culminating in the formation in 1869 of the Durham Miners' Association, and it is not the purpose to recount such details here. It is necessary at this stage, however, to discuss in detail the wages and hours situation in Durham prior to 1919 in order to fully understand the nature and significance of changes in these items between the wars.

In August 1890 representatives of the owners and miners in Durham agreed to limit the length of the working day of coal hewers (actual coal getters) to a maximum of seven hours bank-to-bank calculated from the time of the last man going down the mine to the time of the last man coming to the surface.[2] During the same year the working hours of transit hands (classes of labour engaged in connection with the transit of coal from the face to the shaft), which had averaged 12 per shift, were reduced to ten but were still greater than those worked in most other districts where it was customary to work one shift of transit hands with one shift of hewers. The great majority of Durham collieries, however, worked a system of two separate shifts of hewers per day served by one shift of transit hands, while at 'night-shift' pits three shifts of hewers were worked with two of transit hands.

The arrangement of hours concluded in 1890 continued without alteration until the passing of the Coal Mines Regulation Act in 1908, which became operative in Durham on 1 January 1910. Under the terms of this Act it was laid down that 'a workman shall not be below ground in a mine for the purpose of his work, and of going to and from his work, for more than eight hours during any consecutive twenty-four hours'.[3] The Act excluded both winding times and did not, therefore, institute a true eight-hour bank-to-bank shift but established a normal working day of eight hours plus one winding time.

[1] R. Fynes, *The Miners of Northumberland and Durham*, Sunderland 1873; J. Wilson, *A History of the Durham Miners' Association, 1870–1904*, Durham 1907; S. Webb, *The Story of the Durham Miners*, London, Labour Publishing Company, 1921; E. Welbourne, *The Miners' Unions of Northumberland and Durham*, Cambridge University Press 1923; G. H. Metcalfe, 'A History of the Durham Miners' Association, 1869–1915'. Typescript study deposited in the library of the N.U.M. (Durham Area), Red Hill, Durham; W. H. Johnson, 'The North-East Miners' Union (Hepburn's Union) of 1831–2'. M.A. thesis, University of Durham 1959.
[2] Cf. J. F. Rowe, *Wages in the Coal Industry*, London 1923, pp. 11, 114.
[3] 8 Edw. VII, Ch. 57, Sec. I(i).

The hewers in Durham, already working fewer than eight hours, were unaffected by the legislation. Other underground workers in Durham were, prior to the Act, already working an eight-hour bank-to-bank shift and therefore less than eight hours underground,[1] thereby leaving the transit hands the sole beneficiaries of the legal reduction in hours. The Act had another important effect in Durham. To meet the new conditions brought about by the legislation and to limit as far as possible any consequent reduction in output the local coal owners extended the use of the multi-shift system of working. It was customary in the Durham coalfield for hewers to be relieved of certain duties including timbering, except at the coal face, so that they could become specialized coal getters, the other duties being performed by less well paid men. By 1860 it had become almost universal in the County for coal owners to divide the working time of hewers into two short shifts, even at the cost of reducing each man's hours of actual coal getting, leaving the transit hands to work in one long shift. However, as the hours of work of hewers and boys were gradually reduced up to 1890, the tendency to adopt multi-shift working with three shifts of hewers and two shifts of transit hands increased, especially on the coast where pits were deepest and seams thickest.

This tendency was reinforced after 1908. When the maximum working hours for all underground workers, including transit hands, were reduced the system of employing two shifts of transit workers to three of hewers, with sometimes a fourth regular shift of stonemen and shifters doing repairs, was more widely adopted as the easiest way of retaining the shorter working day of hewers.[2] Prior to the Eight Hours Act coming into operation 150 collieries in Durham, employing over 76 per cent of the total hewers in the County, were working under a system of two shifts of hewers with one shift of transit hands and 25 collieries, employing over 23 per cent of total hewers, working three shifts of hewers and two shifts of transit hands. The reduction in hours of work of transit hands from ten to eight per shift made it almost impossible except at great cost to continue the former system except at collieries where conditions allowed for two overlapping shifts of transit hands. Shortly after the Act came into operation in Durham in 1910, 140 collieries out of a total of 175, employing 85 per cent of total hewers, had adopted the three-shift system.[3]

[1] Rowe, op. cit., Appendix V, p. 169.
[2] Webb, op. cit., pp. 64–9.
[3] Coal Industry Commission, 1919, I, Q.7434.

IV

In the period from the establishment of the Durham Miners' Association down to 1917, when the Government took control of the coal industry, district wages in the Durham coalfield were influenced by the selling price of coal either directly by selling-price sliding-scales or indirectly by arbitration and conciliation. Although under conciliation procedures there was no explicit arrangement to link movements in wage rates with movements in coal prices in practice it was the selling value of coal which played a determinate role in the types of settlement eventually reached.[1]

Between 1872 and 1877 general wage questions were settled in Durham by arbitration but as early as 1876 the Durham miners' leaders were supporting the idea of wage regulation by sliding scales providing for the adjustment of wages in a definite relation to changes in the market price of coal. The first sliding scale was introduced for a two-year period in March 1877, South Staffordshire having pioneered the method in July 1874.[2] The Durham coal owners terminated the scale in December 1878 and it was replaced by a new scale in October 1879. This second scale was abandoned by the miners in December 1881 only to be replaced by a third in April 1882. The third scale operated until December 1883, being replaced by a fourth one in June 1884 which regulated wages until July 1889.[3] The fourth scale proved to be the last to operate in Durham since, after the failure of the miners' strike in 1892 against an attempt by the owners to enforce a 10 per cent reduction in wages, a Durham Conciliation Board was established on a temporary basis in February 1895.[4] The Board was eventually terminated in August 1896, only to be re-established in its original form in June 1899.[5]

The payment of wages to miners at the pit for coal won or for work done was accomplished by time-rates and price-lists. These lists outlined specific piece-rates and took account of the variations in the type of coal won and conditions of work. Durham and Northumberland were the only districts with a detailed system of control over

[1] See J. H. Porter, 'Industrial Conciliation and Arbitration, 1896–1914'. Ph.D. thesis, University of Leeds 1968.
[2] Wilson, *op. cit.*, pp. 124–8; S. and B. Webb, *The History of Trade Unionism, 1660–1920*, London 1919, p. 735; H. S. Jevons, *The British Coal Trade*, London 1915, pp. 461–2, 491.
[3] Webb, *op. cit.*, pp. 63–4; Wilson, *op. cit.*, pp. 203–4; S. and B. Webb, *op. cit.*, pp. 735–6.
[4] Wilson, *op. cit.*, pp. 263–6.
[5] *Ibid.*, pp. 271–6; Welbourne, *op. cit.*, pp. 257–9.

fluctuations in earnings at pit level. This control was exercised through a Joint Committee in each County. In Durham the Committee arose out of discussions for the abolition of the yearly bond.[1] The coal owners met Durham miners' representatives on 19 July 1872 and agreed to recommend that six representatives from each side should meet fortnightly to discuss local demands 'except cases of consideration in temporary bad places' which were to be settled by colliery agents.[2] As a result of this recommendation rules of the proposed Joint Committee were agreed to. The Committee, which first met on 16 August 1872, was established:

'... to arbitrate, appoint arbitrators, or otherwise settle all questions (except such as may be termed county questions or questions affecting the general trade) relating to matters of wages, practices of working, or any other subject which may arise from time to time at any particular colliery, and which shall be referred to the consideration of the Committee by the parties concerned.'[3]

In view of the wide definition of its powers it is noteworthy that the Committee acted as an important representative body for the purpose of maintaining industrial peace at pit level. Its control over colliery price-lists was based upon a 'county average' system. The 'county average' wage for any particular class of workmen was the agreed basic wage upon which advances or reductions awarded by either sliding scales, arbitration, or by Conciliation Boards were made. Unlike other districts, however, the rules of the Joint Committee established an *a priori* case for the alteration of price-lists at any colliery if it could be shown that men's earnings in a seam were either 5 per cent more or 5 per cent less than the ruling 'county average' plus the current percentage for the particular class of workmen concerned. This was not an automatic procedure but depended upon either men or owners submitting a claim for alteration.

Up to 1879 percentage additions or reductions in wages at a County level, however determined, were made upon the 'county average' wages ruling in any particular year. Thereafter the piece

---

[1] From at least the early years of the eighteenth-century colliers in the North-East were hired simultaneously by employers once a year. A crude system of collective bargaining developed in connection with the annual hiring or 'binding'. Each colliery had its own 'bond' which each collier signed (or made his mark). By 1826 the terms of the bond had become so similar throughout the coalfield that the owners produced a single document for use at all collieries. See P. E. H. Hair, 'The Binding of the Pitmen of the North-East, 1800–1809', *Durham University Journal*, LVIII, 1965.

[2] Wilson, *op. cit.*, pp. 66–7.

[3] *Ibid.*, p. 68.

work tonnage rates and datal wages prevailing for each class of
workmen in November 1879 became the new 'standard' or 'basis'
upon which future changes in wages were made. This newly-established basis was at a lower level than the rates earned during the
more prosperous period of the early 1870s. In most other districts
the standard represented the rate of wages current in different pits at
the end of a certain year. In Durham the standard was based upon the
'county average' basic rates for different grades of workmen as fixed
for Joint Committee purposes at one particular period of time.[1]

During the early years of the First World War the Miners'
Federation of Great Britain (M.F.G.B.), to which all the district
miners' associations were affiliated, sought to establish new conciliation procedures throughout the districts aimed at providing
wage advances more in line with the prevailing economic conditions
and at effecting a degree of co-ordination amongst the districts which
would strengthen any national demands the Federation might make
on behalf of its constituent membership. A resolution was carried at
the Federation's Annual Conference in Scarborough in 1913 which
provided that all new wage agreements entered into by Conciliation
Boards should terminate at one and the same time and that a new
standard rate of wages should be created in place of the obsolete
standards of 1877, 1879 and 1888 'by merging into the new standard
all bonuses and percentages not less than the existing minimum
percentages and bonuses recognized by the Boards'.[2] Early in 1915
the Federation decided to give notice to terminate all existing Conciliation Board agreements as from 1 April.[3] The Durham Miners'
Association tendered the necessary six months' notice to end its local
agreement but began negotiations with the owners almost immediately to formulate a new conciliation procedure.[4] The period of
notice was subsequently extended with such regularity that negotiations were still in progress in 1919 and were eventually merged with
the M.F.G.B.'s efforts to secure a new method of wage regulation
during the early 1920s.[5]

Throughout the negotiations the Durham Miners' Association
continually stressed the necessity of eliminating the injustices of
regulating wages almost solely in relation to movements in the price
of coal. The Association demanded that in the future a careful
investigation of the methods of ascertaining coal selling prices,

[1] Rowe, *op. cit.*, pp. 42–3; Jevons, *op. cit.*, pp. 340–58.
[2] M.F.G.B., 10 October 1913.
[3] *Ibid.*, 25 February 1915.
[4] *Ibid.*, 22 April 1915.
[5] See Chapters III and IV.

including the costs of production and all money realized from the produce of the industry, should precede any changes in wages in order that the miners might know what were the legitimate costs of working and what wages the industry was in a position to pay.[1] Even with the institution during the 1920s of a system of ascertained costs within the various mining districts, the conflict between the owners' and miners' interpretation of what constituted legitimate costs of production, especially with regard to the proceeds from by-products, antagonized relations between the two parties as each strove to maintain its economic position during a period of long-term industrial depression.[2]

V

Historically the issues of both wages and hours fundamentally affected the relationship of the Durham Miners' Association with other mining associations and, ultimately, with the Miners' Federation of Great Britain. The adoption of sliding-scale procedures in various coalfields throughout the period 1874–80 culminated in a growing dissatisfaction with the device by the 1880s. In 1881 the newly-formed Yorkshire Miners' Association terminated its local sliding-scale agreement. The Lancashire and Cheshire Miners' Federation followed its example and in 1885 a number of smaller local associations in the Midlands formed a Midland Federation with the purpose of abolishing the sliding-scale procedure and promoting a legal eight-hour day.[3]

In 1888 these three organizations, together with Fifeshire, joined forces and established the Miners' Federation of Great Britain with an aggregate membership of only 36,000 miners. The Federation adopted from the outset a definite policy of resistance to sliding scales and a determination to secure an eight-hour day by legislative enactment. On both counts it came into direct conflict with the Durham Miners' Association. The opposition in principle to the sliding-scale determination of wages and the eight-hour day came mainly from the National Union of Miners which had been established in 1863 and contained the Durham Miners' Association, the Northumberland Miners' Mutual Confident Association, the Amalgamated Association of South Staffordshire and the Sliding Scale Associations within the South Wales coalfield. From the

[1] Minutes of the Board of Conciliation for the Durham Coal Trade, 18 March 1918.
[2] See Chapter V.
[3] S. and B. Webb, *op. cit.*, pp. 510–11.

beginning of the 1880s control of the National Union fell almost entirely into the hands of the Durham and Northumberland leaders,[1] and by 1902 only these two latter districts were still members of the Union.

The opposition to the eight-hour day, therefore, sprang mainly from the north-eastern coalfield, and in particular from Durham, largely because a uniform eight-hour day could not easily be established without upsetting the traditional system of working hours. To have introduced a single-shift system in place of the two- and three-shift systems already in operation [2] would have reduced the hours of transit hands (mainly boys), but increased those of hewers. A double shift of men and boys of eight hours would have also entailed a longer working day for hewers whilst it was feared that three shifts of hewers and two of boys would impair competition in the export market by increasing output and reducing price and thus react unfavourably on wages. Furthermore, the miners in Durham feared that there would be an insufficient number of boys available to work an equal number of shifts with the hewers and that an increase in the number of shifts would entail greater domestic and social problems.[3]

The history of the National Union of Miners after 1880 was, according to the Webbs, 'little more than the long drawn-out resistance of the able and respected leaders of the Northumberland and Durham miners to the new ideas of Labour policy which were . . . becoming dominant in the Trades Union Congress, and which were from the first adopted, if not by all the leaders, at least by successive delegate conferences of the Miners' Federation'.[4] As the influence of the National Union declined, that of the Miners' Federation increased, aided by a period of rapid expansion in the coal industry. Membership of the Federation rose from 36,000 in 1888 to over 200,000 in 1893, overshadowing all existing trade unions, and to 363,000 in 1900.[5] Nevertheless it was not until 1908 when Northumberland and Durham joined the M.F.G.B., knowing that their fight against a statutory eight-hour day was no longer of any avail, that all the district miners' associations were affiliated to a national body. With the inclusion of the northern counties the total membership of the Federation in 1908 increased to almost 600,000.[6] The Durham

---

[1] *Ibid.*, pp. 393, 511.
[2] See above, p. 20.
[3] B. McCormick and J. E. Williams, 'The Miners and the Eight-Hour Day, 1863–1910', *Economic History Review*, XII, 1959, pp. 225–6.
[4] S. and B. Webb, *op. cit.*, p. 512.
[5] *Ibid.*, pp. 394, 512.
[6] *Ibid.*, p. 512.

miners had previously been associated with the national Federation
if only for a short period. Members of the Durham Miners' Association had voted in favour of joining the M.F.G.B. in 1892 having received financial aid from it during the dispute with the coal owners
in that year. Unfortunately the Association failed to appreciate that
membership involved accepting majority decisions regarding strike
action. In 1893 the Durham miners refused to support the Federation
in a national strike against the coal owners' demand for a 25 per cent
reduction in wages and were consequently expelled from membership,[1] remaining outside of its ranks for the next fifteen years.

VI

The conditions facing the miners during the inter-war period were
in direct contrast to those experienced before 1914. No longer was the
industry enjoying long-term prosperity. The problems arising from
the revolution in the production and consumption of fuel and power
which had already beset the industry before 1914 were further
aggravated by the First World War. The substitution of other forms
of power for coal and the growth of fuel economy continued but at a
faster rate. The severe industrial depression after 1921 reduced home
and foreign demand for coal. The loss of former exporting markets
proved particularly disastrous to the industry. Never throughout
the inter-war period did the industry ever again equal the record
level of output and coal exports achieved in 1913.

The situation was made more difficult owing to the industry's
failure to appreciate the nature of the long-term problem facing it
and to adopt measures most likely to improve its position. Especially
important in this respect was the effect which the pre-1914 expansion
had had upon the minds of the coal owners. As Professor Court has
pointed out:

'The extraordinary success and activity of that time, the high profits,
the overflowing royalties, implanted standards of what was normal
and natural in the minds of many colliery owners, managements
and royalty owners which were carried over into the post-war
period, where they played an important role.'[2]

To reduce costs and maintain profits in a period of declining trade
coal owners resorted to the traditional palliatives of attempting to

[1] Webb, *op. cit.*, pp. 87–8.
[2] W. H. B. Court, 'Problems of the British Coal Industry between the Wars'
Economic History Review, XV, 1945, p. 3.

reduce wages and/or increase hours of work. The miners' natural resistance to such methods was reinforced as a result of their experience of Government control of the industry during 1917–21. Their success in securing national wage negotiations during those years convinced them of the necessity to dispense with the old method of district wage bargaining dependent, in practice at least, upon the selling price of coal. In exporting districts like Durham, particularly susceptible to the ramifications of the trade cycle, the necessity to remain competitive led coal owners during periods of industrial depression to make relatively more frequent and severe attacks upon miners' wages and hours than those made in districts producing predominantly for the home market. In addition the concentration of older basic industries within the north-eastern region, themselves important coal consumers and similarly depressed after 1921, added to the plight of the coalfield. The magnitude and intensity of the attempts by Durham coal owners to reduce wages and increase hours, especially up to 1930, illustrates most forcibly the relatively weak position of miners in exporting regions and the extent to which they were the real victims of the depression in their industry.

Nationalization of the mines represented to the workmen the most acceptable way of improving the structure and efficiency of the industry so as to provide the means of reducing costs without necessarily resorting to alterations in wages and hours based upon the competitive needs of each coal-producing district. In exporting areas State control was seen as the means of reducing the disparities in wages and hours of work which so often existed between the coalfields but for which there appeared to be no reasonable justification. The demand for a national system of wage regulation, politically less demanding than mines nationalization, represented a similar, but limited, ideal.

The greater part of the activity of the Durham Miners' Association during the period 1919–47 can be explained in terms of the reasons for, and the consequences of, their fight for these ideals both at local and national level. Miners' leaders in Durham were fully aware of the coalfield's vulnerability as a depressed exporting region to alterations in wages and hours made simply to meet the needs of regional competition. The peculiar structure of working hours which already existed in Durham left the miners particularly sensitive to changes in the length of their working day. While hewers in Durham, already working a relatively short shift compared with those in other districts, were unaffected by legislative changes in hours, they were open to the coal owners' attempts to increase the length of shifts within the limits prescribed by law. On the other hand, since large numbers of Durham miners were already working fewer hours than those elsewhere, they were not so easily prepared to accept offers of marginal reductions in working time as miners in areas working the full hours prescribed by law.

Piecemeal intervention in the coal industry by government subsidy, the designation of the North-East as a Special Area during the mid-thirties, without any accompanying long-term economic strategy to help overcome the structural imbalance, and the virtual preoccupation of the Association with maintaining a meagre level of subsistence for those members unemployed or working short-time bore witness between the wars to the slowness with which the basic problems of the industry were being met, and to the paucity of the employers' and Government's anti-depression policies. The demands made upon the coal industry following the outbreak of the Second World War created their own distribution and production problems yet at the same time gave the miners a unique bargaining position from which to campaign, as they had long done, for a structural reorganization of the industry and the abolition of district bargaining.

The transfer of the industry to public ownership in 1947 involved the Association (or the Durham Area of the National Union of Mineworkers, as it became after 1945) in a constant endeavour to prove the worth of the miners' campaign for nationalization. The great disparity in the market situation for coal in the period before and after 1956 proved the most powerful influence upon the nature and outcome of the miners' activity. The continually rising demand for coal in the ten years after 1947 placed a disproportionately heavy burden upon those high-cost and uneconomic pits in Durham which were being pressed to contribute towards meeting home fuel requirements. Though the seller's market for coal could not prevent altogether some pit closures and redundancies within the coalfield, few of the local officials and workmen envisaged the rapidity with which conditions were to change after 1957. As national coal production became concentrated upon low-cost pits in expanding coalfields the Area Union stoically undertook its responsibility to safeguard members' interests in the face of persistent demands for orderly retrenchment within the industry.

The importance of the Association's struggle for an improved standard of life for its membership cannot be fully appreciated only in terms of industrial activity but must be viewed in a wider context embracing organizational, social and political considerations. The facilities available for consultation and bargaining at local level and the financial state of the Association, for example, influenced, in varying degrees, the nature and outcome of union activity. Furthermore, the intensity of the depression within the coal industry during the greater part of the inter-war years is most easily appreciated against a background of the extreme poverty and distress found amongst Durham miners and their families. Poor housing and social facilities were part of the coalfield's heritage, but their effect in increasing the Durham miners' sense of isolation and social injustice was magnified as continued depression in the coal-exporting trade impoverished families to such a degree that their plight became an issue of national importance. During the first decade of national-ization efforts were concentrated at national and local level to ensure that the miners benefited as much as, and sometimes more than, other industrial workers in the improvements in social welfare which were developed with comparative regularity after the end of the Second World War. The responsibility entrusted to the National Coal Board to improve the miners' condition in the widest possible sense involved it in a joint endeavour with the N.U.M. to ensure that the injustice and inadequacy of previous efforts at social improvement were remedied as far as possible.

The miners had long recognized that political as well as industrial action was necessary to effect any lasting improvement in either their social or economic well-being. The very nature of the problems facing the coal industry after 1919 brought it under close political scrutiny. The Durham Miners' Association, therefore, actively en-gaged the support of its membership in sponsoring and supporting local miners' M.P.s in order to strengthen Labour's voice in the House of Commons and to ensure that there existed in Parliament a group of members particularly concerned with improving the condition of the Durham miners as a whole. This effort continued after 1947 and was especially important within an industry publicly accountable to Parliament. The involvement of local miners' M.P.s both with the industry's regional and national problems proved a useful comple-ment to Durham's representation on negotiating bodies at all levels of discussion.

Whatever particular contribution each of these various approaches makes towards a greater understanding of the Durham miners' movement since 1919 it is to the fortunes of the coal industry between the wars that one must first turn to appreciate the extent to which its persistent influence upon the miners' standard of living provided one of the most powerful arguments in favour of mines nationalization.

Chapter I

THE COAL INDUSTRY, 1919–39

I

In order to understand the problems facing the coal industry during the inter-war period it is necessary to distinguish between short-run and long-run tendencies, especially in view of the unstable nature of the years immediately after the war and up to 1925. From a long-term point of view the industry was being forced to adjust itself in the face of shrinking world demand, economies in the use of coal and the introduction of fuel substitutes.[1] Before 1914 world consumption of coal had increased at an annual rate of 4 per cent but in 1929 consumption was only 9 per cent greater than in 1913.[2] Oil was increasingly becoming a serious competitor of coal. During 1913–14 the Royal Navy had consumed 1,900,000 tons of coal but by 1929 total consumption had fallen to 247,000 tons and in 1930 to only 182,000. The total gross tonnage of steamers fitted for burning oil fuel had risen, however, from 1,310,209 in July 1914, to 20,002,307 in July 1931.[3] Even more important in the long term was fuel economy. The average yield of gas per ton of coal increased from about 65 therms to 75 therms during the two decades before 1925,[4] whilst the total consumption of coal by the country's authorized gas undertakings was still only 17·7m. tons in 1930 compared with 16·3m. tons in 1913.[5]

Furthermore, world capacity in the coal industry was increasing. Coal production in Belgium, Netherlands and France [6] had stood at 22·9m. tons, 1·5m. tons and 41·2m. tons respectively on the average of the years 1909–13, but had increased to 26·5m. tons, 11·4m. tons and 52·9m. tons by 1929.[7] Restricted coal exports to Holland during the First World War encouraged her to develop internal supplies.[8] The

[1] A. M. Neuman, *Economic Organization of the British Coal Industry*, London 1934, pp. 69–73; J. H. Jones, G. Cartwright and P. H. Guenault, *The Coal-Mining Industry*, London 1939, p. 22; R.C. on Coal Industry, 1925, I, *Report*, p. 13.
[2] League of Nations Economic and Financial Section, *The Problems of the Coal Industry*, 1929, pp. 6–7.
[3] M.F.G.B., *Memorandum on Part I of the Coal Mines Act, 1930: The Case for Coal Trade Regulation*, February 1932, pp. 1–2.
[4] R.C. on Coal Industry, 1925, I, *Report*, p. 12.
[5] M.F.G.B., *Memorandum, op. cit.*, p. 20.
[6] On a post-war territorial basis.
[7] M.F.G.B., *Memorandum, op. cit.*, p. 4.
[8] M.F.G.B., 15 July 1935.

development of these additional coal resources accompanied by reduced world demand resulted in surplus capacity within the industry. The impact of depression during the 1920s and 1930s served to emphasize those tendencies via a reduction in coal exports and to depress the home market by its effects upon staple coal consuming industries. It was not until after the 1925 dispute that the industry was free to enter upon its task of reconstruction in order to meet the needs of a changed world. The depression lying in wait for the industry had been warded off until then by a series of temporary and fortuitous events in which the North-Eastern coalfield had shared in common with the rest of the country.

The wartime policy of obtaining coal at any price had served to aggravate the long-term tendencies within the industry towards rising costs and declining productivity at work in the decade before 1914 but obscured by high profits and increasing values wrung from an exceptionally favourable market situation.[1] After 1918 rising wages and declining output-per-man made matters worse. The average wage per manshift paid to underground piece-work coal getters in November 1918 had increased by 7s 3·9d in Durham and by 8s 8d in Northumberland from its June 1914 level while total earnings of the same class during the period had increased from £342,441 to £470,891 and from £123,631 to £193,035 respectively. On the other hand the aggregate number of manshifts worked in Durham during the same period had declined from 830,992 to 606,422[2] whilst the average output per shift per person during 1915–19 had declined from 3·4 to 2·7 tons.[3] The five wage advances granted to miners during 1917 to the end of 1920 made the situation even more difficult.

By 1919 the joint coal output of Durham and Northumberland was 14m. tons less than had been achieved in 1913 and foreign coal shipments almost halved to a total of 11·7m. tons.[4] The coal owners were quick to point to the disincentive effect of high wages upon the miners' effort. They argued that the Government flat-rate wage advances granted to workmen in addition to their minimum wage provided a daily wage sufficiently high to discourage piece work. Arthur Pease, Chairman of Pease and Partners,[5] frequently complained to shareholders of precisely this problem,[6] and told the Sankey

[1] A. J. Taylor, 'Labour Productivity and Technological Innovation in the British Coal Industry, 1850–1914', *Economic History Review*, XIV, 1961.
[2] Coal Industry Commission, 1919, III, Appendix 49, p. 88.
[3] *Durham Chronicle*, 15 January 1919.
[4] R.C. on Coal Industry, 1925, III, Appendix I, p. 3.
[5] See below, pp. 55, 57–8.
[6] Pease and Partners Limited, *Report and Accounts for the Year Ending 30 April 1919*, p. 25; and . . . *for the Year Ending 30 April 1920*, p. 23.

1. *Above:* a soup kitchen during the great strike of 1926—miners with families.
Below: Durham Miners' Gala 1954

2. *Left*: Sam Watson and Hugh Gaitskell at Durham Miners' Gala 1961. *Right*: Executive Committee, 20th November 1944

Commission: 'In my district . . . the men coming back from the front do not get as much as they did before they went. . . . Since the minimum wage a great many thousands of men do not try to do a day's work.'[1]

There were other reasons. The condition of the mines had seriously deteriorated during the war and those miners returning to the pits often had to work the less productive parts of the mine which had been left once the demands of war had been satisfied. Furthermore the difficulty of obtaining plant, of workers adjusting to their previous occupations and the shortage of transport above and below ground made matters worse.[2] During 1919 there were numerous complaints in Durham about the shortage of tubs underground which was seriously hindering production.[3]

The operation of government control of the coal industry until March 1921 provided the coal owners with a guaranteed, if restricted, level of profit,[4] whilst the pressure of demand for coal from Europe immediately after the war, acting upon restricted supplies, allowed prices and profits to soar in exporting districts. Although total North-East coal exports[5] fell from 11·7m. tons to 7·5m. during 1919–20 f.o.b. export prices of coal supplied from Sunderland during that period increased from 54s 11d to 79s 9d per ton and from Newcastle from 50s 9d to 82s 9d per ton.[6] During the quarter ended 31 March 1920, the profit per ton of coal commercially disposable earned in Durham amounted to 8s 5d and in Northumberland to 18s 5d compared with only 10d per ton in Yorkshire and a loss of almost 4s 8d in Lancashire during the same period.[7]

During the latter part of 1920 and during 1921 the market situation for coal altered drastically as the long-term tendency of increasing coal supplies began to have effect. Coal output in both France and Belgium began to expand, the United States shipped increasing quantities of coal into Europe and supplies of German reparation coal were stepped up.[8] France fixed maximum prices for British coal through the *Bureau des Charbons* at figures considerably less than the current values—in some cases at levels 30s below previously

[1] Coal Industry Commission, 1919, I. QQ. 7722–7728.
[2] R. A. S. Redmayne, *The British Coal-mining Industry During the War*, Oxford 1923, pp. 222–3.
[3] *Durham Chronicle*, 15 August 1919.
[4] R. H. Tawney, 'The Abolition of Economic Controls, 1918–21', *Economic History Review*, XIII, 1943, p. 21.
[5] i.e. total foreign coal shipments excluding bunkers.
[6] *Colliery Year Book*, 1940, p. 567.
[7] Neuman, *op. cit.*, p. 40.
[8] Redmayne, *op. cit.*, pp. 237–8.

agreed contracts.[1] The illusory prosperity of the coal industry suddenly came to an end. F.o.b. export prices at Sunderland and
Newcastle fell from 79s 9d to 34s 3d per ton and from 82s 9d to
34s 3d per ton during 1920–1 and by the end of the quarter 31 March
1921 both Durham and Northumberland were making a loss per ton
of coal commercially disposable amounting to 9s 7d and 4s 2d
respectively.[2] Home coal prices proved too low to allow production
to pay and the Cabinet, in a frantic effort to cut losses, decided to
decontrol the industry on 31 March 1921, five months earlier than
legislation in 1920 had allowed for—a move described by R. H.
Tawney as the 'classical example of decontrol from fright'.[3] With
the ending of government control the national system of wage
regulation in the coal industry collapsed and district bargaining
re-emerged. Local coal owners, unable to afford the high rates of
wages guaranteed by the Government, sought immediate wage reductions. By February 1922 miners in Durham were working for the
minimum level of wages agreed upon by the 1921 wages settlement.[4]

In the absence of government control and faced with the collapse
of the immediate post-war export boom the industry appeared to be
forced at last to face the depression which had already overtaken
other heavy industries. However a sixteen-week miners' strike in the
United States beginning in August 1921 provided an opportunity of
feeding markets in Germany, France and the Netherlands now partly
depleted of coal supplies.[5] The French occupation of the Ruhr in
January 1923 severely curtailed coal supplies and reparations
deliveries from Germany and provided a temporary windfall for
exporting areas. For the first and last time during the inter-
war period North-East coal exports surpassed their 1913 level,
reaching 25·4m. tons compared with a pre-war level of 23m. tons.
Profits per ton of coal in Durham and Northumberland increased
from 1s 6d and 1s 9d during the quarter ending March 1922 to 4s 1d
and 5s during the quarter ending June 1923. By the end of 1924 the
effect of the French occupation had spent itself; thereafter conditions
worsened. Coal production at German mines recovered from 6·3m.
tons in December 1923 to 11·9m. tons by October 1924—a level
slightly higher than the average monthly output of coal in 1913.[6]
North-East coal exports to Germany, France, Belgium, Netherlands,

[1] Tawney, *loc. cit.*, p. 22.
[2] Neuman, *op. cit.*, p. 40.
[3] Tawney, *loc. cit.*, p. 23; Redmayne, *op. cit.*, pp. 244–7.
[4] See Chapter V, pp. 162–4.
[5] Report of H.M. Inspector of Mines, 1922, p. 3.
[6] *Ibid.*, 1924, p. 3.

Switzerland and the Channel Islands as a group declined from 18·3m. tons in 1923 to only 8·2m. tons in 1925. In the June quarter of 1925 both Northumberland and Durham made a trading loss to the extent of 1s 9d and 1s 5d per ton compared with a profit of 2s and 2s 5d respectively during the March quarter 1925.[1] Total North-East coal exports in 1925 were 4·2m. tons fewer than in 1924, while the average net selling value per ton of coal in Durham declined from 19s 5·8d to 15s 11·25d during 1924–5. Between 1 May 1924 and 31 March 1925, 17 pits in Northumberland and 38 in Durham closed down, affecting 10,000 and 19,000 men respectively compared with only 11 closures involving a total of only 4,000 men in all other districts outside of Scotland.[2]

Coal owners threatened to reduce their costs during this period of declining trade by cutting wages and lengthening hours, but the Government intervened by granting a nine months' subsidy to the industry allowing for the continuation of existing minimum wages and for profits in each district of up to a maximum of 1s 3d per ton. The subsidy, while of immediate advantage, was of doubtful ultimate value since it served to obscure the real fate of the industry in much the same way as the events of the previous years had done. It has been estimated that had the subsidy not operated the profit per ton of coal earned during the quarter ending December 1925 of 0·7s and 0·8s in Durham and Northumberland respectively would have been transformed into a loss of 2·94s and 2·99s. Furthermore, 99 per cent of all coal in Northumberland and 90 per cent of that in Durham had been raised during the same quarter at a loss of more than 1s per ton compared with 60 per cent in the country as a whole.[3] Moreover, the situation was worsening. The appreciation of the £ following Britain's return to the gold standard in 1925 and the subsequent deliberate currency under-valuations by France and Belgium further weakened exporters' competitive strength in foreign markets.[4] By the beginning of 1927 the short-term influences of

---

[1] Neuman, *op. cit.*, p. 40.
[2] R.C. on Coal Industry, 1925, III, Appendix 18, p. 40.
[3] R.C. on Coal Industry, 1925, I, *Report*, p. 226.
[4] R. S. Sayers, 'The Return to Gold' in L. S. Pressnell (ed.), *Studies in the Industrial Revolution*, London 1960, p. 321 *et seq*. Cf. J. M. Keynes, *The Economic Consequences of Mr Churchill*, London 1935, pp. 20–2. The influence of the return to gold upon the fortunes of the coal industry seems to have been unduly minimised by the Samuel Commission which felt that the effect had 'ceased to be of primary importance'—R.C. on Coal Industry, 1925, I, *Report*, p. 9. For a fuller discussion of the impact of the return to gold upon British export performance see D. E. Moggeridge, *The Return to Gold, 1925*, University of Cambridge, Department of Applied Economics, Occasional Papers: 19, Cambridge 1969.

temporary demands and of subsidies had ceased and the real condition of the industry was revealed.

Since 1924 the combined effects of declining coal consumption by local industries and the contraction of the foreign coal market had severely depressed the northern coalfield. Despite its dependence upon foreign coal exports it was the effect of world-wide depression upon other basic industries which proved immediately disastrous. Between 1925 and 1930 North-East coal exports accounted for 38 per cent of the region's total coal output compared with 21 per cent for the country as a whole. The region's other basic industries—shipbuilding, engineering and iron and steel manufacture—were themselves important coal consumers and exerted their own influence upon the nature and extent of the depression in the coal industry. According to the approximations made in Appendix I total consumption of coal for all local purposes amounted to 16·9m. tons (33 per cent of total coal production) in 1924, declined to 11·4m. tons (28 per cent) in 1933 and was 16·7m. tons (35 per cent) in 1937. If it is assumed that the North-East displayed the same stable trend in the quantity of coal consumed per head domestically as was noticeable for the country as a whole after 1913,[1] and discounting the relatively small amounts of coal consumed at collieries, these fluctuations can in large be explained by fluctuations in the coal consumption of local industries. In view of this particular industrial structure, therefore, it is obvious that an examination of the fortunes of the coalfield must of necessity go beyond an account of fluctuations in the export sector alone.

The average annual decline in North-East coal exports during 1925–30 compared with the period 1909–13 amounted to 2·8m. tons whilst, according to estimates in Appendix I, the decline in domestic demand over the same period amounted to 4·7m. tons. Although it is extremely difficult to give an accurate quantitative breakdown of the decline in particular industries it appears that not less than 3·5m. tons of the total decline in consumption was attributable to the decline in the pig-iron industry.[2] Production of pig-iron in the North-East in 1913 amounted to 3·9m. tons (37·7 per cent of the country's total output) but had declined both absolutely and relatively, to 2·1m. tons (30·3 per cent of the country's total output) during the quinquennium 1925–30.[3] The remaining reduction of 1·2m. tons can

[1] R.C. on Coal Industry, 1925, I, *Report*, pp. 10–11.
[2] Assuming an average coal equivalent of 2 tons per ton of pig-iron produced.
[3] i.e. excluding 1926. Board of Trade, *An Industrial Survey of the North East Coast Area*, Armstrong College, Newcastle-upon-Tyne 1932, pp. 93, 103–4, 123. Referred to hereafter as N.E. Industrial Survey.

be attributed largely to reductions in the demand of the shipbuilding, metal and engineering industries.

In the foreign market total coal exports from North-Eastern ports during 1927 were 4·6m. tons fewer than in 1913. The decline was accounted for in the main by the loss of the Russian market due mainly to the dislocation of Russian economic life and a government-imposed prohibition of coal imports into that country. Almost 2m. tons of coal were exported from North-Eastern ports to Russia in 1913. Practically none was taken in any year after the war. Exports to Germany had also declined from 4·7m. tons in 1919 to 2·7m. tons in 1925 and were only 3·1m. tons in 1930 owing mainly to her increased production of lignite from an annual average output of 73·6m. tons in 1903–15 to 138m. tons in 1925, representing an equivalent increase of 15m. tons of bituminous coal.[1] Between 1924 and 1928 German lignite production further increased by over 40m. tons.[2]

The next most important loss for the North-East was in her trade with Norway, Sweden and Denmark, though on account of her more favourable geographical position the loss in these markets was less marked than the decline of the British coal export trade as a whole. Total North-East coal shipments to the Scandinavian countries declined from 4·1m. tons in 1913 to 3·6m. tons in 1925 and to 3·3m. in 1929 (the best post-war year for coal exports) representing a 20 per cent decline from the 1913 level.[3] Before the war Great Britain had held a virtual monopoly in the coal trade with the Scandinavian countries, accounting in 1913 for over 98 per cent of the total foreign coal trade of Norway, 93 per cent of that of Denmark and over 95 per cent of that of Sweden. By 1929 these proportions had declined to 62 per cent, 54 per cent and 47 per cent respectively.[4]

The most important single explanation of declining trade with the Scandinavian countries was the effect of Polish competition especially after 1925. Its origins can be traced to the Treaty of Versailles when a major portion of the Upper Silesian coalfield, hitherto German territory, was transferred to Polish hands. Up to 1925 all coal produced in that region had been consumed either in Germany or Poland, but following a tariff war between the two countries in 1925 restrictions were placed upon all Polish coal imports into Germany, thus forcing Poland to seek alternative markets for the disposal of

[1] R.C. on Coal Industry, 1925, I, *Report*, p. 243.
[2] Jones, Cartwright and Guenault, *op. cit.*, p. 22.
[3] *Report of British Coal Delegation to Norway, Sweden and Denmark*, 1931 (Cmd. 3702), pp. 14–16.
[4] *Ibid.*, p. 4.

her productive surplus. The 1926 stoppage in Britain provided her with an excellent opportunity for gaining a foothold in Scandinavia, now cut off from British supplies—a position she retained even following the resumption of British trade after 1926.[1] Polish coal exports to Denmark and Sweden alone increased from only 0·5m. tons in 1925 to 3·94m. in 1927 and to the Scandinavian group as a whole from 3·99m. in 1928 to 5·39m. tons in 1930.[2]

The success of Polish competition rested mainly upon comparatively low prices, in some cases between 2s and 3s below British prices, due to lower costs of production, the preferential rate payable on coal shipped on State railways to Baltic ports as compensation for the long inland haul, and to a concentrated selling organization within the industry allowing higher charges for inland coal than for export coal[3] amounting in some cases to a difference of 4s 9d per ton for the same class of coal.[4] The preferential freight charges were unable to compare with the extremely low haulage rates in the North-Eastern coalfield where the estimated average rate for coal transport did not exceed 1s although this 2s 4d differential in favour of the coalfield was still insufficient to cover the variation in the cost of production between the two regions, amounting in some cases to between 4s and 6s.[5] In addition the average wage per shift payable to workmen in Polish Silesian collieries during 1926 amounted to only 3s 3d. In Durham the wage per shift of the lowest paid adult workman stood at 6s 8½d. In the case of hewers shift wages could rise to between 11s and 14s 3d whilst the average for all classes amount to about 10s 6d.[6]

In spite of her worsening performance both at home and abroad the North-Eastern coalfield reaped compensation for her losses in the years after 1926 by increasing her volume of coastwise trade, mainly for domestic and gas purposes. Whilst recognition must be given to the probable effect at this time of a revision in railway rates in helping to transfer coal transport from rail to coast—thus strengthening the competitive position of the coalfield in southern markets[7]—

---

[1] Jones, Cartwright and Guenault, *op. cit.*, pp. 238–9; *Daily Telegraph*, special supplement: 'The British Coal-Mining Industry', 16 September 1930, pp. 53–4.
[2] Jones, Cartwright and Guenault, *op. cit.*, p. 256. Cf. *Iron and Coal Trades Review*, 13, 20 January, 9 March 1928; 25 October 1929.
[3] Cmd. 3702, *op. cit.*, pp. 5–6; Jones, Cartwright and Guenault, *op. cit.*, p. 239; *The Times*, 29 October 1927.
[4] *Iron and Coal Trades Review*, 28 October 1928.
[5] N.E. Industrial Survey, *op. cit.*, p. 106.
[6] Pease and Partners Limited, *Report and Accounts for the Year Ending 31 March 1927*, pp. 30–31.
[7] N.E. Industrial Survey, *op. cit.*, pp. 106–7.

the region's greatest comparative advantage in this respect lay in its strong cost position relative to other coalfields. This was largely a direct result of the more onerous wage reductions successfully imposed upon the defeated miners in both counties during 1926–8.[1] These reductions lowered the normal excess of wages costs per ton over wages per shift to a much lower level in Northumberland and Durham than in any other district as the table overleaf shows. As a result of its relatively strong position in this respect the coalfield was able to increase coastwise coal shipments by over 46 per cent between 1924 and 1929, raising the total from 7·8m. tons to 11·4m. tons—3·4m. tons more than had been shipped in 1913. In comparison, during the same period, coastwise coal shipments from the Humber ports declined in total by 40 per cent and from the Bristol Channel ports by 17·6 per cent.

II

In spite of such compensations and a temporary revival in trade in 1929 (when North-East coal exports totalled only 2·3m. tons fewer than in 1913), the onset of world depression shattered any hopes of a lasting recovery within the industry. The exporting regions suffered during the depression to a disproportionate degree compared with other coal-producing districts as the long-standing problems of a declining demand both at home and abroad were intensified in the extreme. By October–December 1934 the average level of pit-head proceeds per ton of coal disposable in Durham had fallen to 12s 5d from 18s 6¼d between October and December 1924.[2] Durham suffered a loss of 4·6d per ton of coal commercially disposable in 1933, which was further reduced to 2·9d per ton in 1934 and stood at 3·6d per ton in 1935 while the profit earned per ton in the country as a whole during the same three years amounted to 2·8d, 5d, and 6·3d respectively.

Despite the fact that the North-East was able during 1929–33 to maintain her export position relative to other districts and even to increase it compared with 1913—contributing 34·3 per cent of total U.K. coal exports in 1933 compared with 31·3 per cent in 1913—it suffered an absolute decline in foreign coal shipments. By 1933 total coal exports stood at only 13·4m. tons compared with 20·7m. in 1929. The greatest loss to the region was in her trade with Germany,

---

[1] Jones, Cartwright and Guenault, *op. cit.*, p. 47; *The Economist*, 21 May 1927. See Chapter VI, pp. 222–4; Chapter VI, pp. 236–43.
[2] M.F.G.B., 15 July 1935. Cf. J. Griffiths, *Between the Wars—Coal*, 1939, p. 22.

Costs of Production in Selected Coalfields *

Year	Durham			Northumberland			Yorks., Notts., Derbyshire, Leics., Cannock Chase, Warwickshire			Lancs., Cheshire, N. Staffs.			Great Britain		
		s d			s d			s d			s d			s d	
	(1)	(2)	(3)	(1)	(2)	(3)	(1)	(2)	(3)	(1)	(2)	(3)	(1)	(2)	(3)
1922	17 3½	11 0¼	9 1	16 9¼	10 11½	8 7¾	17 5	12 4½	11 7¼	20 11½	14 1¾	9 3¾	18 1¾	12 1¾	9 11¾
1924	18 9¼	12 9	10 2	18 2¼	12 6	9 10¾	17 0¾	12 7½	18 8¾	20 4¼	14 7¾	9 6¾	18 7¼	13 3	10 7¾
1927	14 5¼	9 0¼	9 2½	13 6¾	8 7¼	8 7¾	15 5¼	11 0½	11 1	18 8½	13 1½	9 9	15 7	10 7½	10 0¾
1928	12 11½	7 11¼	8 1½	12 0½	7 4	7 6½	13 11½	9 8½	10 1	17 7¼	12 0¾	9 3¼	14 2¼	9 5¾	9 3½

(1) Total cost
(2) Wages cost per ton
(3) Wages cost per shift

* *Reports of H. M. Inspectors of Mines*, 1922–8.

France, Belgium and Italy, which together had taken 12·7m. tons in 1929 but whose combined imports in 1934 were halved to 6·2m. tons.[1] To a large extent these losses can be explained by the adoption in these regions of restrictive trading measures directed against foreign coal imports. In July 1931 France imposed a direct quantitative regulation of coal imports and similar action was soon taken by Belgium and Germany.[2] In France the restrictions were justified as a necessary adjustment to the balance of trade following dumping action as a result of the depreciation of foreign currencies and in Germany as an effort to secure sufficient foreign exhange to pay her outstanding debts to foreign countries. In Belgium the dominant motive was the protection of the home market.[3]

In the North-East home market coal consumption, estimated at 16·9m. tons in 1929, had declined to only 11·4m. tons in 1933 and in 1934 was still 4·7m. tons below its 1924 level.[4] The declining coal consumption of local industries again accounted for a slightly greater share of the depression than the reduced export demand. On the average of the period 1924–33 local coal consumption suffered a decline of 6·5m. tons compared with the period 1909–13 whilst coal exports from the region declined by 5·5m. tons from 21·1m. (1909–13) to 15·6m. (1929–33).[5]

There were some compensations. Although the many factors influencing the course of trade after 1929 make it extremely difficult to assess the effect of the suspension of the gold standard in 1931 upon the fortunes of the coal industry it appears that the expected increase in exports was realized in the North-East 'only to a very limited extent'.[6] Any immediate effect upon the important Scandinavian market was counteracted by the fact that those countries were among the first to follow Britain's example with the result that the change in the value of their currencies, compared with the pre-September 1931 values, proved negligible.[7] On the other hand Poland found it more difficult to compete in Scandinavia since her f.o.b. export charges were made almost identical with those of Northumberland and Durham.[8]

[1] Armstrong College, Newcastle-upon-Tyne, *The Industrial Position of the North-East Coast of England*, London 1935, p. 22. Referred to hereafter as Armstrong College Report, 1935.
[2] Jones, Cartwright and Guenault, *op. cit.*, p. 170.
[3] *Ibid.*, pp. 172–3.
[4] Armstrong College Report, 1935, pp. 21–2.
[5] See Appendix I to this chapter.
[6] N.E. Industrial Survey, *op. cit.*, p. 51.
[7] *Ibid.*, p. 49.
[8] *Ibid.*

Of more importance to the North-East was the effect of the government reciprocal trading agreements made with Norway, Sweden and Denmark during 1933. These arrangements, and others like them, constituted part of the Government's efforts to increase national exports, using the opportunity afforded in February 1932 by the imposition of a 10 per cent *ad valorem* tax upon all imports [1] to secure export concessions in foreign markets.[2] Under the terms of the Agreements Norway agreed to guarantee for Britain 70 per cent of her total coal imports, Denmark 80 per cent and Sweden 47 per cent and thus, by adjusting the relative amounts of coal imported from various producing regions, provide a direct discrimination in favour of Britain.[3] The agreements were of direct benefit to the North-East by virtue of its superior geographical position compared with other exporting areas. North-East cargo exports to the Baltic Region [4] increased from 2·6m. tons in 1932 to 4·2m. tons in 1934 compared with a decline from 3·4m. to 2m. tons during 1929–31.

The net effect of the agreements was to benefit Northumberland, Durham, and to a less extent Yorkshire, at the expense of South Wales since the concessions secured on behalf of east-coast producers forced Poland, a serious competitor in Scandinavia, to seek alternative export outlets in Western Europe and the Italian market—traditionally supplied by South Wales. While Polish exports to Scandinavia declined from 6·4m. tons during August 1932–July 1933 (the first 'pre-Agreement year') to 3·5m. during August 1933—July 1934 (the first 'Agreement-year') her coal exports to Belgium, Italy and the Netherlands doubled from 1·1m. tons to 2·2m. tons between August 1932 and July 1933 and between August 1934 and July 1935.[5]

Nevertheless it must be noted that despite the advantages gained by the North-Eastern coalfield in this respect total cargo exports from the region in 1934 were still only 13·7m. tons compared with 20·7m.

---

[1] Except raw materials and foodstuffs and excluding the Empire.
[2] H. W. Arndt, *The Economic Lessons of the Nineteen Thirties*, London 1963 edn, p. 112.
[3] See *Agreement between the Government of the United Kingdom and the Government of Denmark Relating to Trade and Commerce, 24th April 1933*, Cmd. 4298, p. 14; *Agreement between the Government of the United Kingdom and the Norwegian Government Relating to Trade and Commerce, 15th May 1933*, Cmd. 4323, p. 26; *Agreement between the Government of the United Kingdom and the Government of Sweden Relating to Trade and Commerce, 15th May 1933*, Cmd. 4324, p. 10. For a discussion of the effects of the agreements on British coal exports as a group see Jones, Cartwright and Guenault, *op. cit.*, pp. 174–9.
[4] i.e. Norway, Sweden, Denmark (including Faroe Islands) and Russia.
[5] Jones, Cartwright and Guenault, *op. cit.*, p. 182.

tons in 1929. The advantages reaped from the Scandinavian agreements were not nearly sufficient to offset the decline in foreign
demand, especially in Western Europe.[1] On the other hand Durham
and Northumberland still benefited from the exploitation of the
Southern coal market via increased coastwise trade. Whilst coastwise coal shipments from the North-East had remained at a steady
level between 1929 and 1933 (11·4m. tons compared with 11·3m. tons
respectively) they had risen to 14·7m. tons by 1937, 6·7m. tons more
than their 1913 level.

The condition of the region's heavy basic industries, and therefore
the state of local coal consumption, improved with the gradual
recovery in the home market after 1933. Local coal consumption
by 1937 had risen to 16·7m. tons from its low of 11·4m. tons in 1933
and was only 0·2m. tons below the level reached in 1924.[2]

Foreign coal markets once lost were not easy to regain and since
the stimulus to recovery in Britain after 1933 was largely afforded by
the home market via a building, new industry and re-armament
boom there proved little to stem the decline in foreign coal shipments. In 1937 North-East coal exports totalled 13·3m. tons, only
0·1m. tons more than in 1933 and 7·4m. tons fewer than in 1929.

III

One method of stimulating the coal export trade and obtaining a
favourable level of prices in the home market was for coal owners to
restrict competition amongst themselves and in markets abroad by
co-operative action. In 1925 the Royal Commission on the Coal
Industry (the 'Samuel Commission') argued in favour of the co-
operative marketing of coal which in exporting districts 'would . . .
maintain prices at a remunerative level in those foreign markets
where the competition is not so much between British and foreign
exporters, as among the British exporters themselves'.[3] This recommendation was further supported in July 1926 by the Departmental
Committee on Co-operative Selling which called for the establishment
of local coal-marketing arrangements and selling pools.[4] Representatives of the coal owners, on the other hand, pleaded for a national

[1] Political and Economic Planning (P.E.P.), *Report on the British Coal Industry*,
February 1936, p. 48.
[2] See Appendix I to this chapter.
[3] R.C. on Coal Industry, 1925, I, *Report*, p. 234.
[4] *Report of the Departmental Committee on Co-operative Selling in the Coal Mining
Industry*, 1926 (Cmd. 2770), pp. 24–8.

system of co-operative selling to control output and price in response to severe competition from Germany and Poland.[1]

The report of the Departmental Committee recognized the desirability of cartelization within the industry and argued for the process to be assisted by State intervention. The first effective steps towards combined action to control output and/or prices were, however, voluntary and came during 1928 when the average net selling value of coal in Great Britain reached its lowest level since the war. By the end of 1928 three marketing schemes were in operation covering Scotland and South Wales, the third, the Central Collieries Commercial Association (the 'Five Counties' scheme) involving Cannock Chase, Leicestershire, North Staffordshire and Warwickshire, South and West Yorkshire, Nottinghamshire, Derbyshire, Lancashire and Cheshire.[2] The schemes aimed at encouraging price rises by imposing restrictions on coal output.[3] The Five Counties Scheme had a direct and adverse effect upon the North-Eastern coalfield since, by imposing upon members a levy of not more than 3d per ton, it was able to provide a subsidy in aid of coal exports. Since during the operation of the scheme exports accounted for between only 3 to 8 per cent of total production (estimated at 90m. tons) the subsidy was able to reach amounts ranging from 1s 6d to 4s per ton thus greatly strengthening the competitive position of the Humber ports in foreign markets.[4] The Durham and Northumberland coalfield, supporting an inland tonnage too small to allow for subsidization to the same extent, consequently suffered from competition from Humber ports especially in the Baltic and North Sea areas.[5] Whilst exports from the Humber to the Baltic and North Sea regions increased during 1927–8 from 0·66m. tons to 0·86m. tons and from 1·18m. to 2·12m. tons respectively, North-Eastern coal exports to the Baltic declined from 3·96m. to 2·86 m. tons and increased in the North Sea region from only 9·14m. to 9·46m. tons during the same period. By means of the export levy therefore the Midland producers were able to reap some compensation for the losses incurred through the North-East's invasion of the domestic market in the years after 1926. 'It is feared by colliery owners and coal exporters in the North-East', commented

---

[1] *Ibid.*, pp. 41–4; See above, pp. 37–8.

[2] For a full account of the operation of the schemes see Jones, Cartwright and Guenault, *op. cit.*, Chapter VI.

[3] In the case of S. Wales output regulation only came in 1929 as prices were originally fixed.

[4] Jones, Cartwright and Guenault, *op. cit.*, pp. 93–107; Neuman, *op. cit.*, pp. 161–5.

[5] *Iron and Coal Trades Review*, 25 May 1928.

the *Iron and Coal Trades Review* in 1928, 'that the competition from the Humber will prove even more disastrous than that from Poland.'[1]

At a meeting on 15 October 1928 coal owners in Durham agreed to establish a committee to formulate a scheme for both the regulation of output and fixing of minimum prices [2] and in October of the following year the Durham Collieries Commercial Association was launched. The fixing of minimum prices and members' output quotas ('having regard to the prospects of trade') was entrusted to an Executive Committee with power to impose fines of not more than 3s 6d per ton as a safeguard against contravention of trading regulations. Members were also liable to a levy in aid of exports (excluding coastwise trade).[3] Unfortunately the sponsors failed to secure the support of those firms representing more than half the coal output of Durham in 1928, agreed upon as the necessary prerequisite of the scheme's functioning, despite the fact that over 5 per cent of colliery representatives had offered their support at a meeting on 7 October 1929.[4] S. E. D. Wilson, Chairman of the Derwent Coal Company in Durham, later gave some reasons for the failure of the scheme. In a letter to *The Times* he confessed that 'many of those who voted in favour of adopting a coal-marketing scheme for Durham did so, not from conviction, but for reasons of expediency' since 'a not inconsiderable number' believed that 'any control, with its resulting restriction of output, will increase costs, while price fixing will inevitably lose orders in foreign markets'.[5]

There were real difficulties in establishing output restriction and artificial price regulation while domestic coal-consuming industries struggled for their own existence and whilst competitors such as Germany and Poland enjoyed the advantages of competition in common markets abroad. In addition the variety of coals produced within the North-Eastern coalfield also acted against increased uniformity of prices and output. The demand of foreign customers for anthracite coal from South Wales tended to be less elastic, for example, than for the gas and steam coals produced in Durham and Northumberland because of the varying degrees of internal and

---

[1] *Ibid.*
[2] Durham Coal Owners' Association, *Annual Report*, 1928, p. 12.
[3] Durham Coal Owners' Association, *Durham Collieries Commercial Association, Coal Marketing Organization, Draft Scheme*, 7 October 1929, pp. 2-6; *The Times*, 1 August 1929.
[4] Durham Coal Owners' Association, *Annual Report*, 1929, pp. 15-16; *The Times*, 14 January 1930.
[5] *The Times*, 24 October 1929.

external substitution and sources of alternative supply of the various types of coal.[1]

The coalfield was not completely without some form of co-operative action. In February 1928 Northumberland joined with other exporters in fixing minimum prices for shipment of practically all classes of coal (representing increases on current prices) to compensate for losses in the Scandinavian and Baltic markets. While Durham refused to join in this arrangement the two counties did agree in July 1928 with competitors in other districts to prevent price undercutting in contested markets.[2]

Further voluntary action was suspended once the Labour Government, pledged to legislate in the coal industry, entered the field with a definite view to legally establishing a common regulation of production and marketing.[3] The resulting Coal Mines Act,[4] passed in 1930, was in four parts. Part I, based upon the experience of the 'Five Counties Scheme', aimed at establishing machinery for regulating the 'production, supply and sale of coal'. 'District allocations' (i.e. the maximum permissible output of coal allowed to each district in a specified period) were to be determined by a Central Council representing all the district associations of mineworkers. The scheme was to be administered in each district by an Executive Board empowered to decide the 'standard tonnage' of each mine, the proportion of such which could be raised, i.e. the quota, to fix minimum prices and to impose fines for failure to comply with the regulations. Part II established the Coal Mines Reorganization Commission (the functions of which are discussed later). Part III granted the miners a shorter working day of seven and a half hours underground and Part IV instituted the Coal Mines National Industrial Board to settle disputes covering wages or other conditions of employment. An amendment was made omitting from the Bill a clause providing for a national levy in support of the coal export trade. On the Bill becoming law a marketing scheme for Durham was prepared by the coal owners on the lines of the proposed voluntary agreement which had previously been considered. The amended scheme became operative on 31 October 1930.[5]

Part I of the Coal Mines Act, though originally intended as a temporary measure to offset the financial effects of reduced hours while maintaining prices and spreading employment until the

---

[1] Neuman, *op. cit.*, pp. 121–5.
[2] *Iron and Coal Trades Review*, 25 January 1929; Neuman, *op. cit.*, pp. 167–74.
[3] Cf. Durham Coal Owners' Association, *Annual Report*, 1929, p. 17.
[4] 20 and 21 Geo. V. c. 34.
[5] Durham Coal Owners' Association, *Annual Report*, 1930, pp. 11–12.

industry was reorganized, continued with modifications until 1947. Unfortunately for the industry the ultimate success of the Act was limited at the outset, despite the weaknesses of its own provisions, by the fact that it was forced to operate under conditions markedly different from those envisaged by its architects. No longer was the problem simply one of a slowly declining industry working under conditions of general industrial expansion, as in 1929, but of an industry whose decline had been accentuated in the extreme by the onset of world depression.

Since these conditions were particularly manifest in the exporting areas it was there that the failures of the scheme were most obvious. The control of output soon proved to be ineffective as a means of maintaining prices. In view of the heavy decline in foreign demand during the depression the inevitable result of the distribution among districts of a centrally permitted output according to the ratio of their respective standard tonnages was to leave exporting districts with permitted outputs far exceeding the amount necessary to satisfy the markets they served.[1] The growth of foreign import restrictions and the gradual deepening of the world depression, together with the obvious difficulties in attempting to estimate foreign demand inevitably meant unused coal surpluses—the extent of which seriously hampered the efforts towards output restriction. The percentage by which output in the Durham coalfield fell short of the Central Council allocation ranged from approximately 8 per cent (March quarter 1931) to 19 per cent (March quarter 1932) although the disparity became less pronounced thereafter.[2] 'Supplies for export have been restricted not by the regulation of output but by the unremunerativeness of prices and by embargoes,' commented *The Times* in 1932. 'The Coal Mines Act should not be held responsible for the effects of the general depression of industry or the artificial stimulus of competing supplies.'[3]

Coal owners in Durham and Northumberland faced with unused coal surpluses engaged in widespread evasion of district minimum prices in order to capture the available trade in the home market. Coal was sold at the price of lower qualities; export coal was re-sold for domestic consumption at prices below the minimum and underselling fostered by charging less than the current freight rate charge

[1] J. H. Jones, 'The Coal Mining Industry' in Jones, J. H. (ed.), *Britain in Recovery*, London 1938, p. 241; *The Economist*, 12 March 1932.
[2] Neuman, *op. cit.*, pp. 428–31.
[3] *The Times*, 5 April 1932. Cf. Neuman, *op. cit.*, p. 437; Jones, Cartwright and Guenault, *op. cit.*, p. 157.

on coal shipments.[1] The situation was 'rapidly becoming a farce' reported *The Times*, since minimum prices in Durham 'were being flagrantly evaded'.[2] In the House of Commons it was reported on 1 June 1932, that 'the evasions . . . are reducing the export trade in the North-East to a veritable sink of iniquity. Dishonesty is at a premium'.[3] The ability with which North-Eastern coal producers could capture markets in the Midlands by offering types of coal which were interchangeable with those subject to price restriction illustrated the truth of the coal owners' assertion, made earlier in 1925 before the Departmental Committee on Co-operative Selling, that district and local marketing arrangements were ineffective without a system of national co-ordination.

In August 1933 and November 1934 the Durham Executive Board, established under the 1930 Act, amended its local scheme in an attempt to enforce minimum prices[4] but the evils of inter-district competition had already seriously weakened the structure. From the very beginning of the venture Durham had been at a disadvantage compared with other districts since after South Wales it had formally established district minimum prices in 1930 only to be undersold in local markets by the producers in the Midlands and Scotland who delayed in taking any formal action over prices.[5]

In view of the difficulties in exporting areas and the lack of inter-district co-ordination of minimum prices the Central Scheme was amended in 1935. Henceforth the output of coal for export and inland supply was to be restricted by separate quotas while the Council was authorized to enforce price co-ordination between districts. Whilst Northumberland and Durham gained from the former amendment in so far as the allocation breakdown was based upon the existing distribution of trade amongst the districts—which thereby safeguarded the additional trade they had recently secured in the home market—any further advantage gained from diverting export allocations to the home market was seriously curtailed.[6]

In August 1936 district selling agencies were established in Northumberland and Durham as part of the Government's attempts

---

[1] *Coal Mines Act, Durham District (Coal Mines) Scheme 1930, 1st August 1933*, pp. 1–4; Neuman, *op. cit.*, p. 420.
[2] *The Times*, 8 August 1933.
[3] Quoted in *The Economist*, 31 July 1932.
[4] *Coal Mines Act, Durham District (Coal Mines) Scheme 1930, 1st August 1933*, pp. 1–4; *ibid. . . . for 1934*, p. 5.
[5] Mines Department, *Coal Mines Act 1930, Working Schemes under Part I of the Act During the March quarter 1931* (Cmd. 3905), pp. 4, 7, 10–11; *ibid. . . . for the year 1932* (Cmd. 4224), pp. 8–9; *Durham Chronicle*, 31 July 1931.
[6] Cf. P.E.P. Report, *op. cit.*, p. 75.

both to raise the price of coal in order to meet the miners' demands for increased wages and to secure efficient inter-district co-ordination of coal prices free from evasion. The Central Council issued directions to the districts regarding the terms and conditions for the supply of coal. In Northumberland and Durham a scheme of 'central control of sales' was adopted whereby colliery owners continued to sell their own coal, using their own salesmen and finding their own customers but in amounts, to destinations and at minimum sale prices as prescribed by a Sales Committee. Prices did rise in the Durham coalfield after 1936, the average net selling value of coal rising from 12s 11·5d to 16s 0·2d per ton during 1936–8 under the influence, not only of the selling schemes, but also the rearmament programme and general industrial recovery.

The Durham Miners' Association, like other mining trade unions, expected the selling schemes to bring increased revenue to the coal industry in order to raise the low wages of mineworkers. In 1938, however, the Association complained that the level of pithead selling prices fixed by the Sales Committee was insufficient to increase the volume of revenue so as to lift the Durham miners' wages above the minimum level agreed to in May 1937.[1] Towards the end of 1938 the Central Council's control over coal prices was further extended as it was empowered to issue directions to all districts governing the prices of rail-borne and coastwise coal, the prices and supplies of coal for export and the prices of all coal sold on the inland market outside the immediate neighbourhood of the pits. The possibilities of an international agreement on coal export prices to help reduce the severe fluctuations in prosperity suffered by exporting areas such as Durham were dashed by the outbreak of the Second World War at a time when both Germany and Poland had already displayed considerable interest in the idea.[2]

IV

Of more ultimate value to the industry than attempts to regulate prices and output were proposals for reorganization. Reorganization through amalgamation had long been urged upon the mining industry as a means of increasing efficiency and competitive strength in the absence of nationalization.[3] The 1926 Coal Mines Reorganization

[1] Durham District Committee of Investigation, *Complaints re: Coal Prices*, March 1938. Cf. Chapter VI, pp. 259–61.
[2] Court, *loc. cit.*, p. 17.
[3] Coal Industry Commission, 1919, I, QQ. 5,208, 7,852–7,853; II, QQ. 16,766–16,767, 18,723, 19,795, 20,096, 21,355, 26,293, 26,402–26,411, 26,577; R.C. on Coal Industry, 1925, I, *Report*, p. 233.

Act aimed at encouraging a greater degree of co-operation and integration within the industry but had little effect owing to the rigorous terms it laid down. Colliery owners were enabled to submit schemes to the Board of Trade of total or partial [1] amalgamation while 'absorption schemes', subject to ratification by the Railway and Canal Commission, could compulsorily engage those owners opposed to any generally accepted scheme of amalgamation. The schemes, however, had to be shown to be in the national interest and amalgamations were required to 'promote the more economical and efficient working, treating or disposal of coal', to do no financial harm to the undertakings involved, while the terms had to be fair and equitable to all persons affected.

The Coal Mines Reorganization Commission, appointed by the Board of Trade under the 1930 Coal Mines Act to promote and assist the amalgamation of undertakings in accordance with the provisions of the 1926 Coal Mines Reorganization Act, regarded the schemes of prices and output regulation as no more than 'a stepping stone on the way to scientific reorganization of the industry'.[2] Attempts at scientific reorganization in Northumberland and Durham proved abortive. Originally intent on establishing one large undertaking in Northumberland and several very large concerns in Durham [3] the Commission was forced to seek looser forms of combination in face of opposition from coal owners more intent on spreading employment during the depression than seeking further concentration. In the hope of fostering voluntary enterprise in the Durham coalfield, for example, the Commission suggested in September 1932 that certain undertakings on the eastern side of the coalfield could combine into two groups so that, acting in concert with one another and with other groups already in existence, the problem of the coalfield could be tackled systematically. The response of the coal owners was disappointing and remained so despite further attempts by the Commission during July and August 1933, to persuade them toward a voluntary scheme of total or even partial amalgamation. As a last effort to initiate voluntary effort in the region the Commissioners called upon twenty-three undertakings in December 1933 to prepare within two months a voluntary scheme of amalgamation under the terms of Part II of the 1930 Act.[4]

[1] Defined under the 1926 Mining Industry Act as 'arrangements for the conduct of any business or operations in the common interest of the constituent companies'.
[2] Coal Mines Reorganization Commission, *Colliery Amalgamations*, July 1931.
[3] *Ibid.*, p. 16; *The Times*, 30 March 1931.
[4] *Durham Chronicle*, 16 November 1934.

After the failure to carry out the directive the Commissioners decided in 1934 to call into being its own scheme of partial amalgamation to be supplemented later by total amalgamation among some of the smaller units.[1] Under the proposed scheme a group of otherwise independent units were to establish a central authority to co-ordinate selling policy (by means of a central selling agency or otherwise), to administer a fund, raised by a levy on members, for the purpose of closing 'superfluous' pits, to exercise a general control over the development of the region in the common interest and to supervise other such activities in which duplication and waste would be likely to arise were they left to the uncoordinated conduct of independent undertakings.[2]

Unfortunately a similar scheme of partial amalgamation proposed for West Yorkshire was rejected in May 1935 by the Railway and Canal Commission, on whose decision enforcement of such schemes ultimately lay, on the grounds that among other things no financial fusion was involved. The decision made it clear that the Reorganization Commission had been wrong in assuming that the 1930 Act had empowered it to impose compulsorily a scheme of co-operation between financially independent concerns as a means of securing partial amalgamation. Total amalgamation was now the only objective whereby compulsion could be invoked.[3] Before efforts could be made to evolve an alternative form of total amalgamation for Durham the Commission's work was suspended in July 1935 pending a reconsideration of its powers.[4]

The 1938 Coal Mines Act, which provided for the nationalization of coal royalties, also transferred the functions of the Reorganization Commission to a new Coal Commission. Thereafter proposed amalgamations could take place only after the Commission had satisfied the Board of Trade and Parliament that schemes were desirable on the grounds of efficiency and after the Railway and Canal Commission was satisfied that they were in accordance with the requirements of the 1930 Act.

The Commission's plans for industrial reorganization were circulated amongst the coal-mining districts in June 1939. In Durham various suggestions were made for amalgamations on a geographical basis, e.g. a North-Eastern group (involving a total coal output of 5¾m.

---

[1] Coal Mines Reorganization Commission, *Report to the Secretary of Mines*, December 1933 (Cmd. 4468), p. 15.
[2] *Durham Chronicle*, 16 November 1934.
[3] Coal Mines Reorganization Commission, *Report to the Secretary of Mines*, January 1936 (Cmd. 5609), p. 4.
[4] *Ibid.*, p. 5.

tons) and a South-Eastern group (involving 6¾m. tons). The fate of
the declining south-western sector was left for further discussion.[1]
With the outbreak of the Second World War the Commission's
proposals were held in abeyance and nothing more was heard of
them.

V

In view of the poor record of amalgamation in the North-Eastern
coalfield it seems that neither the recommendations of the Samuel
Commission nor the advice of the Coal Mines Reorganization Commission had convinced local coal owners of the need to secure a
greater unity of control over coal production in the region. In some
respects government policy had hampered the trend towards greater
amalgamation which it sought to encourage after 1926. Granting
subsidies to the industry provided the means under which the inefficient colliery could exist whilst the upper limit set upon the contribution an individual colliery could make towards the district output
quota established under the 1930 Coal Mines Act ensured that each
pit retained a share of the market.

There were other explanations for the reaction against amalgamation. Difficulties in the valuation of coal properties and plants and the
wide differences in the size, productivity and financial strength of the
various collieries were obstacles in the path of a generally accepted
policy of combination. Furthermore, there was doubt amongst coal
owners as to whether large undertakings were necessarily more
efficient than smaller ones.[2] Indeed in Durham where the average size
of mines in terms of output and employment per mine remained
relatively large throughout the inter-war period inasmuch as it
exceeded the size of the average mine in Great Britain as a whole,[3]
productivity, measured in terms of output per man-shift at the face,
remained relatively low rising from only 3·11 tons in 1927 to 3·18
tons in 1938 compared with rises from 2·79 tons to 3·55 tons in

[1] *Colliery Year Book*, 1940, pp. 526–8.
[2] Cf. R.C. on Coal Industry, 1925, III, Appendix 18, pp. 222–3. A 'Durham
Mining Engineer' commenting upon the movement towards greater amalgamation
wrote of the situation in Durham in June 1926, 'It would . . . be folly to exaggerate
the economies likely to be effected in this direction. The cost of working individual
collieries might be tangibly reduced, but spread over the whole country the result
would be very small'. 'The position of the Durham Coalfield: Plain Facts and
Figures', reprinted from the *Northern Echo*, June 1926, p. 12.
[3] *Annual Reports* of H.M. Inspector of Mines, 1919–39.

Yorkshire and from 2·78 tons to 3·76 tons in North Derby and Nottinghamshire during the same period.[1]

Relative efficiency depended not so much upon the size of the productive unit as upon the degree of mechanization within the various collieries. In Scotland, mines of a smaller average size than those found in Durham operated just as efficiently and thus cast doubt upon the contention that mechanization could only be successfully implemented in large-scale undertakings.[2] During the period 1922–38 the percentage of total coal output mechanically cut in Durham increased from 12 to 42 per cent compared with an increase in the nation as a whole from 15 to 59 per cent. The fact that an increasing use of machinery in Durham, albeit below the national average, was unaccompanied by any significant change in output per man shift at the face could be due to the fact that the increase was just sufficient to counter-balance the increasing difficulties of coal getting in an old coalfield.[3]

Durham's performance in the mechanization of the mines was amongst the worst in the country. The percentage of total coal output mechanically conveyed in the coalfield also lagged behind the nation as a whole, the figures rising from 6 per cent and 12 per cent respectively in 1928 to 25 per cent and 54 per cent in 1938.[4] The natural conditions of the coalfield and its age relative to most other fields partly explain this poor performance. In addition the combined effects of declining demand in both the foreign and home markets upon the selling price of coal and the continued necessity for the local coal owners to meet out of total net proceeds the miners' minimum wage,[5] seriously eroded the reserves of capital which might otherwise be available to finance a scheme of heavy capital expenditure. Furthermore many small mines in Durham operated as part of a larger colliery company and were therefore able to reap the commercial economies normally available to the bigger undertakings e.g. in bulk-buying, transport and distribution.[6] The degree of integration already in existence in Durham in 1930 was sufficient to allow many smaller undertakings to benefit in this respect. No less than 81 per cent of

[1] E. C. Rhodes, 'Output, Labour and Machines in the Coal-mining Industry of Great Britain', *Economica*, XII, 1945, p. 103. Cf. Ministry of Fuel and Power, *Coal Mining: Report of the Technical Advisory Committee*, 1945, (Cmd. 6610), paras 44–5.
[2] See N. K. Buxton, 'Entrepreneurial Efficiency in the British Coal Industry between the Wars', *Economic History Review*, XXIII, 1970.
[3] Rhodes, *loc. cit.*, p. 110.
[4] *Reports of H.M. Inspectors of Mines*, 1928–38.
[5] See Chapter V, pp. 164, 174, 177–8.
[6] I owe this observation to Mr N. Buxton.

total coal output in Durham in that year was produced by 15 undertakings each with an output of over 1 million tons per annum.[1] At the same time the number of mines at work in the coalfield was decreasing. From a total of 263 in 1925 the number fell to 242 in 1930 and to 228 by 1934.

In accounting for the coal owners' reluctance to amalgamate attention must also be drawn to prevailing contemporary attitudes which, whilst more difficult to assess, could not have been totally without significance. Lord Gainford, Chairman of Pease and Partners in 1930, argued against amalgamation thus:

'It is impossible to decentralize or delegate work beyond a certain point, and when large amalgamations occur (often overcapitalized) the output per person becomes less, the *esprit de corps* and close touch between owners, officials and workmen disappear, close attention to every detail in business becomes impossible, waste occurs, production and quality suffer, and therefore the loss is greater than any small gain obtained through slight reductions in some overhead charges.' [2]

VI

A survey of the structure and performance of the North-Eastern coalfield would be incomplete without reference to the nature of the major colliery concerns. The coal companies operating within the coalfield were largely of two main types: those dominant concerns, mainly connected with heavy industry, whose directors were often associated with banking and financial houses and coal companies both within and outside of Durham,[3] and those large concerns which maintained a greater degree of independence.

Within the first group two of the most dominant organizations, themselves inter-related, were the Dorman Long Company and Horden Collieries Ltd. In 1939 the eight pits owned by Dorman Long, employing over 9,000 men, had an output capacity of 4 million tons per annum.[4] In addition to mining coal the company owned coke ovens, by-product plants and ironstone mines as well as being an

[1] Coal Mines Reorganization Commission, *Colliery Amalgamations*, 1932, pp. 14–15.
[2] *Daily Telegraph* special supplement, 'The Coal-Mining Industry', 1930, *loc. cit.*, p. 48.
[3] Of the 209 directors of colliery undertakings in Durham in 1925, 105 were directors of another or other coal mining undertakings. R.C. on Coal Industry, 1925, III, Appendix No. 18, p. 182.
[4] W. H. Williams, *Coal Combines in Durham*, Labour Research Department, London 1939, p. 5.

important iron and steel concern. In 1923 the company took over the entire plant of Bell Brothers Ltd,[1] Sir B. Samuelson and Company Ltd, both iron and steel firms, North Eastern Steel Company Ltd, and the Carlton Iron Company Ltd. Its amalgamation six years later with Bolckow, Vaughan & Company, owners of the Dean and Chapter collieries in Durham, established an output capacity of the combined undertaking of 1,750,000 tons of finished steel per year.[2] Dorman Long also owned the constructional engineering business of Redpath Brown & Company Ltd, and jointly with Whitehall Securities Ltd, Pearson and Dorman Long Ltd., which in 1939 owned two pits in the Kent coalfield.[3]

The company's most important connection was with Horden Collieries Ltd, via a directorate association. The latter company was formed in 1900 and owned collieries at Shotton, Blackhall, Horden and Castle Eden.[4] In 1939 the Company held 13,875 acres of leasehold coal, owned 4,007 acres of freehold coal [5] and employed nearly 9,000 miners. The Wearmouth Coal Company formed the remaining section of the Dorman Long combine owning two pits at Wearmouth and Hylton and in 1939 employing over 3,000 miners. The complexity of the interrelationship among the various companies within the combine can be judged from the diagram overleaf.[6]

The nine colliery companies comprising the Furness and Gainford group represented another important combine within the coalfield responsible in 1939 for a total coal output of over 7,550,000 tons. Within this combine were the Weardale Steel Coal and Coke Company Ltd, Pease and Partners Ltd, South Hetton Coal Company, Easington Coal Company, New Brancepeth Colliery Company, Wingate Coal Company, Trimdon Coal Company, Henry Stobart and Company Ltd, and the North Bitchburn Fireclay Company Ltd. The first two companies owned 14 pits between them in 1939 and were responsible for employing over 8,300 men. The Weardale Steel, Coal and Coke Company had important directorate connections with the South Durham Steel and Iron Company, which in turn owned the Cargo Fleet Iron Company, and both of which had substantial

---

[1] *Ibid.*, p. 6; R.C. on Coal Industry, 1925, III, Appendix No. 16, p. 117; *Stock Exchange Year Book*, 1939.
[2] For an account of the early history of the company see Coal Industry Commission, 1919, II, Q. 26,235.
[3] Williams, *op. cit.*, p. 6.
[4] For an account of the early history of the company see Coal Industry Commission 1919, II, QQ. 19,671, 19,892–19,906.
[5] *Stock Exchange Year Book*, 1939.
[6] Williams, *op. cit.*, p. 7.

DORMAN LONG AND HORDEN COLLIERIES

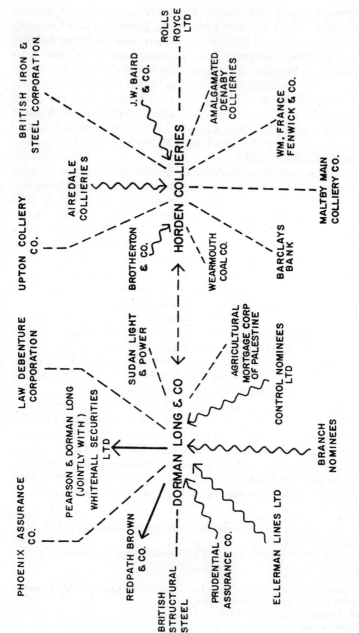

CONTROLLING INTEREST
FINANCIAL INTEREST
DIRECTORATE CONNECTION

controlling interests in the New Brancepeth Colliery, Wingate Coal Company and the Trimdon Coal Company.[1]

Pease and Partners, which apart from producing coal also owned coke-ovens, by-product works, limestone quarries and ironstone mines in Durham, acquired the share capital of Henry Stobart and Company and the North Bitchburn Fireclay Company, both of which owned five mines in Durham, in 1919[2] and in 1925 secured a controlling interest in the Skinningrove Iron Company. Lord Gainford, one of its directors, and for many years a member of the Executive Council of the Mining Association, served on the Board of ten companies in 1939 and was trustee for the debenture stock of the Weardale Steel, Coal and Coke Company thus providing a strong financial link between that concern and Pease and Partners Ltd. Nor were the interconnections between collieries limited to the Durham coalfield. Directors of the Weardale Steel Company and of the South Hetton Coal Company also served on the board of Broomhill collieries which owned two pits in Northumberland.[3]

In 1942 Pease and Partners owned a total of 13 mines employing over 9,000 miners and with an annual output of over 3·3m. tons.[4] The diagram overleaf indicates the important connections which existed among firms in the Furness combine.[5]

Holmside and South Moor Collieries Ltd, which in 1942 owned 11 mines in Durham with a total annual output of 2m. tons and employing over 5,600 miners,[6] was connected to the Dorman Long combine through a directorate association with the Wearmouth Coal Company. The firm of Sir S. A. Sadler Ltd, which owned a number of small mines in Durham and the Bearpark Coal and Coke Company Ltd, which in 1939 owned three mines producing about 360,000 tons of coal per annum and which, through a system of interlocking directorships, had connections with colliery companies in Yorkshire and Derbyshire, joined with the Holmside and South Moor Colliery Company to form the Sadler combine.[7]

Another significant grouping centred around the Streatfield family which was connected with five companies whose six pits produced in 1939 an annual output of over 1,810,000 tons of coal and employed

[1] Williams, op. cit., pp. 11–12.
[2] R.C. on Coal Industry, 1925, III, Appendix No. 16, pp. 120–1; Colliery Guardian, 5 March 1920.
[3] Williams, op. cit., p. 12.
[4] M. Heinemann, Britain's Coal, London 1944, p. 190.
[5] Williams, op. cit., p. 11.
[6] Heinemann, op. cit., p. 194.
[7] Williams, op. cit., pp. 9–10.

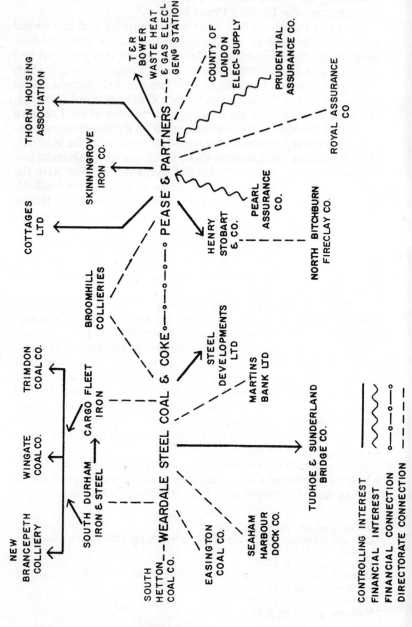

FURNESS AND GAINFORD GROUPS

CONTROLLING INTEREST ——————
FINANCIAL INTEREST ∿∿∿∿∿
FINANCIAL CONNECTION o—o—o—o
DIRECTORATE CONNECTION – – – – –

6,314 men.[1] The companies involved were the Ryhope Coal Company Ltd, the Washington Coal Company Ltd, Levenson's Wallsend Collieries, the Mid-Durham Coal Company Ltd, and the South Pelaw Coal Company Ltd. The 'Priestman Group' of coal owners was centred mainly in Northumberland through connections with the Ashington Coal Company Ltd but had important connections in the Durham coalfield through Priestman Collieries Ltd which in 1942 owned seven mines throughout Northumberland and Durham producing over 1m. tons of coal and employing 3,550 men.[2] A similar connection between Northumberland and Durham was forged within the Cookson group which operated mainly in Northumberland but, through the Consett Iron Company, had interests in 13 mines in Durham with a total annual output of over 2m. tons. In turn the Consett Iron Company, through a system of directorate connections, was linked with the important Bolsover Colliery combine which owned mines in Derbyshire and Nottinghamshire.[3]

The fact that coal combines from outside the Durham coalfield could wield considerable influence within it is well illustrated by the Harton Coal Company, John Bowes and Partners Ltd, and East Hetton Collieries Ltd, all Durham concerns. The Harton Coal Company, which owned seven pits in Durham, had connections with the powerful Powell-Duffryn group in South Wales through directorate associations. Two of the directors of the Harton Coal Company were on the board of John Bowes and Partners which in 1939 owned seven pits in Durham producing annually over 1,500,000 tons of coal.[4] East Hetton Collieries Ltd was linked with the Cadman combine in Staffordshire through an interlocking directorship.

Two of the most notable examples of large independent coal concerns within Durham are afforded by the Londonderry coal company and the Lambton, Hetton and Joicey Collieries Ltd. The latter company owned a group of 20 pits in Durham with an aggregate annual ouput of 5 million tons. The firm first began as a private undertaking under James Joicey, uncle of Lord Joicey, a prominent Durham coal owner during the latter part of the nineteenth century. The firm was formed into a limited company in 1886 and, after the purchase of Lambton Collieries in 1896, assumed a separate form as the Lambton Collieries. In 1911 the Lambton company acquired the pits of the Hetton Coal Company, then producing about 1 million tons per annum, and its name was altered to the Lambton

[1] *Ibid.*, p. 14.
[2] Heinemann, *op. cit.*, p. 180.
[3] Williams, *op. cit.*, pp. 15-16.
[4] *Ibid.*, p. 13.

and Hetton Collieries. In 1924 James Joicey and Company was voluntarily wound up, its collieries transferred to the Lambton company whose title was further changed to the Lambton, Hetton and Joicey Collieries. The Company owned by-product works, coke-works and brick and gas works.[1]

Londonderry Collieries Ltd was a private concern, almost all the shares being owned by the Marquess of Londonderry in his own name or jointly with his wife. The Londonderry family had long established connections with the Durham coalfield since the Marquis' great grandmother, grandfather and father had all been responsible for sinking pits within the region during the nineteenth and early twentieth centuries.[2] In 1919 the company owned pits at Dawdon, Silksworth and Seaham although Silksworth Colliery was sub-sequently bought by Lambton and Hetton Collieries Ltd in 1920. In 1923 the Londonderry company decided to sink a new pit just north of Seaham Harbour. The sinking of the colliery, known as Vane Tempest, was begun on 16 February 1926 and the first coal was drawn on 15 June 1929. By 1938 the three pits were employing a total of 5,500 men and producing 1,781,708 tons of coal.[3]

The rapid deflation which followed the immediate post-war boom in Britain kept company profits at a low level compared with the experience before 1914. Pease and Partners, for example, whose average ordinary dividend during the period 1904–13 had reached 11 per cent,[4] failed to pay a dividend at all during 1925–35 but suc-ceeded in reaching pre-war standards in the years immediately before the outbreak of war. The Consett Iron Company had a similar experience. Its average dividend during the period 1898–1918 reached 38 per cent with a high of 60 per cent in 1913 and a low of 12½ per cent in 1915.[5] By 1922 the Company's ordinary dividend had fallen to 5 per cent, none was paid during 1925–35, and at its highest level between the wars reached 10 per cent in 1937. Horden Collieries Ltd and Weardale Steel Coal and Coke Ltd were among the few com-panies which paid dividends during the 1920s and 1930s.[6] During

[1] Lord Aberconway, *The Basic Industries of Great Britain*, London 1927, pp. 151–2; G. Harvey, *Capitalism in the Northern Coalfield*, Pelaw-on-Tyne 1918, pp. 1–2. Harvey was, at the time he wrote this pamphlet, checkweighman at Follonsby pit, Wardley, had studied at Ruskin College in 1908 and was editor of *The Socialist* during 1911–12.
[2] Londonderry Collieries Ltd, *History of the Londonderry Collieries Ltd*, March 1946; Coal Industry Commission, 1919, II, Q. 15,242.
[3] Londonderry Collieries Ltd, *op. cit.*, p. 1.
[4] Coal Industry Commission, 1919, II, Q. 19,671.
[5] *Ibid.*, I, Q. 4,537; Harvey, *op. cit.*, p. 21.
[6] See Appendix III to this chapter.

short-term periods of prosperity between the wars a number of colliery companies issued out of reserves and undivided profits share bonuses of substantial amounts. Thus in 1924 Holmside and South Moor Collieries issued £654,600 in share bonuses and in the same year Priestman Collieries issued £450,000. In 1937 East Hetton Collieries issued £80,600.[1]

The miners' determination to rid the industry of private ownership sprang from their belief that under nationalization profits could be pooled, uniform rates of wages paid throughout the country and any surplus used for industrial reorganization. In this way the disparities in costs, profitability and living standards between the coalfields could be substantially reduced. In Durham the marked variability in the level of district proceeds, and the tendency towards increased costs and low productivity emphasized the worst evils of district autonomy and strengthened the workmen's resistance to any attempt at economy or reorganization which fell short of public ownership of the mines.

---

[1] Williams, *op. cit.*, p. 21.

Appendix I

PRODUCTION AND DISTRIBUTION OF COAL IN NORTHUMBERLAND AND DURHAM 1924–38 (EXCLUDING 1926)
(MILLION TONS)

Distribution	1909–13 (annual average)	1924	1925	1927	1928	1929	1930	1925–30 (annual average)	1931	1932	1933	1934	1935	1936	1937	1938
EXPORT:																
Cargo	21·1	21·0	17·0	18·5	17·5	20·7	18·1	18·3	14·3	12·6	13·4	13·7	12·9	12·0	13·3	12·0
Bunkers	3·6	3·4	3·1	3·7	3·6	3·3	3·2	3·4	3·2	3·0	2·7	2·7	2·3	2·1	1·8	1·6
COASTWISE																
Cargo	8·1	7·9	7·6	8·9	9·9	11·4	10·8	9·7	10·8	10·8	11·3	12·6	13·4	14·6	14·7	14·1
Bunkers	0·3	0·3	0·3	0·3	0·3	0·4	0·3	0·3	0·4	0·4	0·4	0·4	0·4	0·4	0·4	0·4
TOTAL SHIPMENTS	33·1	32·6	28·0	31·4	31·3	35·7	32·5	31·7	28·7	26·8	27·8	29·4	29·0	29·1	30·2	28·1
TOTAL PRODUCTION	54·4	50·4	43·5	48·1	47·7	53·5	49·0	48·3	42·7	40·1	40·1	42·5	44·3	45·9	47·8	44·7
LOCAL CONSUMPTION*	20·4	16·9	14·6	15·8	15·5	16·9	15·6	15·7	13·1	12·3	11·4	12·2	14·4	15·9	16·7	15·7

* Estimates for local consumption have been corrected to the extent of 0·9m. tons per annum (in accordance with similar calculations made in the Board of Trade, *Industrial Survey* 1932, *op. cit.*) in order to account for the amount of coal carried by rail to districts outside the region.

Source: *Reports of H.M. Inspector of Mines*, 1924–38.

Appendix II

OUTPUT AND PRICE OF COAL 1919–38

	Output		Average net selling value per ton			
	Durham	U.K.	Durham		U.K.	
	m.	m.				
	tons	tons	s	d	s	d
1919	31·0	229·8	n.a.		26	2·97
1920	30·8	229·5	n.a.		34	6·97
1921	21·8	163·2	n.a.		26	2·23
1922	34·9	249·6	17	11·06	17	7·53
1923	38·2	276·0	20	6·01	18	9·86
1924	36·7	267·1	19	5·79	18	10·11
1925	31·5	243·2	15	11·25	16	4·38
1926	14·2	126·3	14	4·93	19	6·50
1927	34·6	251·2	13	6·85	14	7·34
1928	34·7	237·5	12	0·46	12	10·14
1929	39·0	257·9	12	7·18	13	5·21
1930	35·9	243·9	12	10·68	13	7·10
1931	30·2	219·4	12	5·47	13	5·57
1932	27·8	208·7	12	2·46	13	3·11
1933	27·6	207·1	12	0·43	13	0·27
1934	30·6	220·7	11	11·92	12	10·53
1935	30·3	222·2	12	1·48	13	0·08
1936	31·4	228·4	12	11·52	14	0·22
1937	33·5	240·4	14	2·54	15	2·36
1938	31·4	227·0	16	0·20	16	7·62

Source: *Reports of H.M. Inspectors of Mines*, 1919–38.

Appendix III

DIVIDENDS PAID ON ORDINARY SHARES BY SELECTED DURHAM COLLIERY COMPANIES, 1919–39

	Pease and Partners per cent	Consett Iron Company Ltd per cent	Horden Collieries Ltd per cent	Weardale Steel, Coal and Coke Company Ltd per cent	Dorman Long and Company Ltd per cent
1919	18	12½	n.a.	n.a.	n.a.
1920	14	10	14	19⅓	8
1921	5	10	8	6	5
1922	6	5	8	6	—
1923	8	7½	15	14⁸⁄₉	—
1924	1½	2½	12½	7½	—
1925	—	—	6½	10⁴⁄₉	—
1926	—	—	—	6	—
1927	—	—	2½	6	—
1928	—	—	2½	6	—
1929	—	—	7½	6	—
1930	—	—	7½	6	—
1931	—	—	5	6	—
1932	—	—	2	6	—
1933	—	—	2½	6	—
1934	—	—	5	6	—
1935	—	—	5	6	—
1936	5	7½	7½	10⁴⁄₅	6
1937	10	10	10	12⅔	10
1938	12½	7½	10	17½	10
1939	10	7½	10	12⅔	10

Sources: Company Balance Sheets; *Stock Exchange Year Book*.

Chapter II

TRADE UNION ORGANIZATION
AND FINANCE

After half a century's growth in size and scope of activity the Durham Miners' Association had by 1919 become an institution in itself, surrounded by its own bureaucracy and with twice as many rules as it had in 1872.[1] The Association was composed of persons employed in and about the mines in County Durham and was divided into separate Lodges. The objects of the Association, listed in 1919 under Rule 3, read:[2]

'3. The objects shall be to raise funds by contributions, levies, fines, and donations. I. For the purpose of mutual support. II. To obtain legislative enactments for the more efficient management of mines; whereby the lives and health of miners may be preserved. III. To protect all Lodges and members when unjustly dealt with by their employers or managers in any respect whatever. IV. To provide a weekly allowance for support of members who may be locked-out or on strike, or laid idle through no fault of their own. V. To provide a weekly allowance for the support of members injured while following their employment or members sick from natural causes, who may subscribe for the same. VI. To pay a funeral allowance at the death of a member, or of the wife or child of a member, whether caused by accident or sickness, if subscribed for. This fund to be self-supporting. VII. To assist all Associations that have the same objects, namely, the protection of labour and the granting of benevolent support to members. VIII. Generally to regulate the relations between employers and employed. IX. To become federated with the miners of other counties and countries, but before any action is taken it must be submitted to the approval of council or county. X. To seek for a living wage for all workers in and about the mines and for no man or lad to be more than eight hours from bank to bank in one day. XI. To promote and financially support Parliamentary Candidates. Each Candidate must be a member of the Durham Miners' Association, and run solely under the auspices of the National Labour Party, and be subject to its decisions if elected.'

[1] For a guide to the bibliography of the early history of the Association see above, p. 19n.
[2] Rules of the Durham Miners' Association, Revised December 1916, Durham 1917, pp. 5–6.

The supreme government of the Association was vested in a Council, which dealt with all matters relating to the Association's welfare, and which consisted of a President, Treasurer, Secretaries, Joint Committee Agent[1] and one representative from each Lodge with more than 20 members. Each Lodge representative wielded a voting power proportionate to the size of the Lodge from which he was elected. In 1919 representatives from Lodges with from 20 to 150 members had 1 vote; from 150 to 300 2 votes; from 300 to 450 3 votes; from 450 to 600 4 votes; from 600 to 800 5 votes and from 800 to 1,000 6 votes. The greater degree of influence thus given to the larger Lodges had not always been an established part of the Association's structure. Before 1902 each elected Lodge delegate had only one vote.

The President, Treasurer and Secretaries of the Association were permanent officials and known as Agents. They were nominated by the Lodges and elected by the membership at each Annual Council Meeting. Only the President and Secretaries retained the security of at least one year's service since the power of removing the Treasurer from office, without previous notice, rested at all times with the Council.

Any issues concerning the Association which arose between meetings of the Council were dealt with by an Executive Committee, which was also instructed to transact any other business as the Council might direct. In 1919 the Executive consisted of 12 and not more than 17 persons who had been members of the Association for the previous six consecutive months, including the President, Treasurer, Secretaries and Joint Committee Agent. In 1921 the maximum membership was increased to 19. Prior to 1911 it was possible for particular sections of the coalfield not to be represented on the executive since its membership was nominated and elected by the separate Lodges according to their relative voting strength. Thereafter, Lodges were grouped into six wards and elected two representatives from each ward.

The Executive Committee was able to exert a considerable influence upon the Council and hence affect final policy decisions. The Committee could criticize Lodge resolutions placed before the Council and even prevent them from appearing on the Council agenda. Through its power to issue circulars to Lodges the executive was able to readily express its own opinions, criticism, and advice whenever necessary. Although able to stifle the reactions of individual Lodges it could not dictate policy or ignore local feeling altogether since

[1] See below, pp. 68–9.

Lodges were empowered to call a special Council Meeting on any issue if such was requisitioned by 25 collieries within seven days. Ultimately, however, real power was vested, according to rule, in the individual member of the Association since it was he who elected the executive and its agents and who decided upon who should express Lodge opinion at Council level.

Each Lodge of the Association had its own president, secretary, treasurer and committee of not less than five or more than 17 Association members. All Lodges were required to have one general meeting every fortnight and committee meetings whenever necessary to discuss County and local affairs. Lodge representatives to the Council were elected either by a majority of the members present at a general meeting or by a ballot vote of the total Lodge membership.

The miners were brought into contact with other classes of workmen in the coalfield—the mechanics, enginemen and cokemen—through the Durham County Federation Board. The Board, established in October 1878, grew out of the workmen's desire to provide each other with an adequate degree of mutual support in face of attempts to reduce their standard of living and to have a means of promoting their joint interests. By 1919 all agents of the Association were *ex officio* members of the County Federation Board. It was largely the workmen's knowledge of the strength of the coal owners' organization in the County that led to such combined action. The Durham Coal Owners' Association was established in February 1871 to deal with questions of miners' wages and conditions of work and other matters affecting the interests of colliery owners. Until 1920 the Durham and Northumberland coal owners were jointly represented at meetings of the national Mining Association, a federation of coal owners' associations established in 1834, through the North of England United Coal Trade Association. This body, established in 1867, was primarily concerned with dealing with all parliamentary and legal matters affecting coal owners in the North-East and continued that function when in April 1920 it ceased to remain a member of the Mining Association. Thereafter North-East membership of the Mining Association was made through the Durham and Northumberland Coal Owners' Associations separately.[1]

As a result of the growth of negotiations between representatives of employers and employed from 1872 onwards an elaborate system was evolved under which all questions affecting the County in general, individual collieries, or even individual workmen, could be brought forward for consideration and settlement by mutual discussion

[1] Durham Coal Owners' Association, *Annual Report*, 1920, pp. 25–6.

between the parties involved, or, if necessary, by arbitration. Whilst the County Federation Board dealt primarily with County questions disputes at collieries were under the jurisdiction of separate Joint Committees. Recourse was made to the miners' committee, the origins and procedure of which have already been discussed,[1] only when discussions between workmen and management had broken down. Where cases arose which were not within the jurisdiction of the Joint Committee and which could not be settled by the secretaries of the owners' and workmen's associations they were normally dealt with by smaller committees, known as Urgency Committees, representative of both sides but without an independent chairman.

During the First World War all claims submitted to the Joint Committee for reductions in workmen's rates according to the 'county-average system'[2] were suspended whilst other issues in dispute between managers and men continued to be dealt with. The wartime restriction on local wage reductions was still operative when the Joint Committee suspended its operations during the 1921 lock-out. Thereafter, despite a temporary three-month resumption of mutual negotiations, the tribunal procedure became unworkable as the miners determined to resist the owners' attempts to operate the Joint Committee under pre-1914 rules, i.e. allowing local wage reductions.[3] In April 1923, even though the owners agreed to waive the conditions under which they could claim piece-rate reductions, negotiations broke down and the Joint Committee was rendered inoperative.

Representatives of both the Durham Miners' and Coal Owners' Associations met frequently during 1924–5 in an effort to re-establish some form of local disputes procedure, the former seeking to maintain for workmen reasonable conditions of work whilst still refusing local wage reductions, the latter anxious to re-establish a formal means of reducing costs in face of deepening depression in the industry but nothing was achieved.[4] Even though it was agreed as part of the terms of settlement of the 1926 dispute that machinery should be established to adjust piece-work rates and to determine other matters of dispute at the pit,[5] nothing came of the protracted discussions which followed.

[1] See above, pp. 21–3. The existence of established means of joint consultation largely contributed to Durham's reputation for favourable relations between employers and workmen. Cf. K. G. J. C. Knowles, *Strikes—A Study in Industrial Conflict*, Oxford 1952, p. 191.
[2] See above, pp. 22–3.
[3] Durham Coal Owners' Association, *Annual Report*, 1923, p. 50; D.M.A., 24 March, 3 May 1923. Cf. Chapter V.
[4] Durham Coal Owners' Association, *Annual Report*, 1924, pp. 20–1; D.M.A., 14, 22 November 1924; 30 June 1925.
[5] See Chapter V, p. 223.

This was largely due to disagreement over the exact conditions under which each party would be free to claim an alteration in piece-rates and to the owners' persistent refusal to allow a new tribunal to consider matters which had arisen during the interval between the termination of the old Joint Committee and the establishment of the new one.[1] It was not until 1944 that agreement was eventually reached to establish a Disputes Committee within the coalfield.[2]

The rules of the Association were revised four times between 1919 and 1947. Apart from alterations in the amount of financial benefits most of the changes related to the internal organization of the Association, while others reflected its differing industrial and political aspirations. In 1921, for example, the Association resolved 'to seek the Abolition of Capitalism and the substitution of Common Ownership and control of the means of life'; 'To support the Labour Press' and 'To support Education'. As the campaign for a shorter working day in the mines gained momentum between the wars the Association's industrial objectives, as outlined in its rules, were altered accordingly.[3]

An important change in voting procedure was introduced in 1921 which significantly altered the relationship between the Lodges and the Council. Prior to 1921 local delegates to Council meetings were instructed by their particular Lodges exactly how to vote on the resolutions appearing on the programme irrespective of what opinions and explanations were offered during the Council meeting. From 1921 onwards delegates were free to express their individual reaction to resolutions during the course of Council deliberations but were required to report the nature of the discussions to their respective Lodges so that final voting could take place. In effect the agents of the Association, as Council members, were thereafter more able to influence, although not determine, the final outcome of policy decisions by appealing to individual delegates to impress upon Lodges aspects of a situation which might otherwise be ignored. At the same time the voting strength of Lodges was altered to provide one vote for every 100 members, or part thereof, up to a total of 600 with one extra vote for every 200 members, or part thereof, up to a total of 1400 members. The maximum voting strength of the larger

---

[1] Durham Coal Owners' Association, *Annual Report*, 1928, pp. 13–14; *ibid.*, 1929, pp. 28–9; *ibid.*, 1930, pp. 19–21; *ibid.*, 1931, p. 10; *ibid.*, 1933, p. 14. D.M.A., 8 July, 23, 27; August 1927; 1 August 1928; 4 June 1929.
[2] See Chapter IX, pp. 367–8.
[3] Rules of the Durham Miners' Association, Revised February 1921, Durham 1924, p. 4; *ibid.*, Revised December 1925, Durham 1926, p. 8; *ibid.*, Revised October 1937, Durham 1938, p. 2.

Lodges was thereby raised from 6 to 10 votes.[1] In 1927 those Lodges with fewer than 49 members were excluded from representation on the Council. Previously, the lower limit had been fixed at 20 members.[2]

In 1933 the Association began its first moves to define closely the terms and conditions of employment of its agents. Those appointed after June 1933 were required to have had ten years' experience of work in Durham coal mines (twice as many as had been demanded since 1913) and to retire, with pension, on reaching 70 years of age.[3] This rule was subsequently amended in October 1937 to force retirement at 65 years of age with the promise that those affected 'shall not (after such retirement) participate in the affairs of the Association ... and on the date of such retirement shall receive payment out of the Superannuation Fund of a sum calculated on the basis of the contributions to the Fund made by the Association and the agent during his term of office as agent.'[4] At the same time it was laid down that the Association's President was to act also as its Compensation Secretary and that one Agent, normally appointed by the Council, would deal with all cases arising from the Unemployment Acts. If no recommendation was forthcoming from the Council the responsibility would fall automatically to the General Treasurer.[5]

In an effort to promote a close liaison between Lodges and Union headquarters the Association took active steps to keep its membership well informed of the various activities carried out on their behalf. From 1921 Agents were required to issue periodically to Lodges details of the work carried out by the Association's departments [6] and the General Secretary continued the tradition of circulating his own personal quarterly report. A scheme was established to promote at least six meetings throughout the coalfield every year for educational and propaganda purposes,[7] and in 1925 Lodges were permitted to group themselves into local Federation Boards for mutual discussion with other Lodges affiliated to the County Federation Board.[8]

Until 1933 the Association continued the pre-war practice [9] of

[1] Rules of the Durham Miners' Association, Revised February 1921, Durham 1924, p. 4.
[2] Ibid., Revised October 1937, Durham 1938, p. 3.
[3] Ibid., Revised December 1933, Durham 1934, p. 10.
[4] Ibid., Revised October 1937, Durham 1938, p. 5.
[5] Ibid., p. 8.
[6] Ibid., Revised February 1921, Durham 1924, p. 7.
[7] Ibid., p. 31.
[8] Ibid., Revised December 1925, Durham 1926, p. 8.
[9] Cf. Wilson, op. cit., p. 336.

submitting its legal problems to a solicitor who, whilst the guardian of the Union's legal affairs, was not its full-time employee. The rising cost of legal charges led the Association's Executive Committee to recommend in 1933 that a full-time solicitor be appointed on a fixed retaining fee.[1] Ronald W. Williams secured the first post [2] in January 1936 and held it until the formation of the National Union of Mineworkers in 1945.[3]

II

During the period from the formation of the Association in 1869 to the outbreak of the First World War two men dominated the affairs of the union—William Crawford and John Wilson. Crawford was the Association's first General Secretary, having previously been secretary of the Northumberland Miners' Association, and by his energetic yet cautious leadership took credit for consolidating the union during the last quarter of the nineteenth century. Essentially practical and realistic in outlook he preached the virtues of arbitration and conciliation in defiance of ruthless strike action. Possessing both a dominating personality and persuasive use of emotional appeal whenever the occasion demanded it he quickly gained the respect of owners and workmen alike. He was succeeded in 1890 by W. H. Patterson, then Vice-President of the Association. Patterson, a member of the Association's first Executive Committee, failed to show the leadership displayed by Crawford and though he retained office until his death in 1896 rarely dominated the affairs of a Union long geared to leadership from the top. Even before Patterson's death John Wilson, who had been appointed Financial Secretary on the death of Crawford, had achieved immense popularity and following amongst the miners and was eventually elected to succeed Patterson as General Secretary.

Wilson, first elected as an Agent in 1882, was the son of a tramping quarryman and began work in the pits at the age of $16\frac{1}{2}$. In 1856, when he was 19 years old, he went to sea, only to return to the pits in 1860. Two years later he emigrated to America but returned to the Durham mining village of Haswell in 1869 and successfully established a union Lodge there, albeit at the expense of his own job. He became a stationer at Wheatley Hill but soon returned to mining, securing a minor appointment in the Association in 1875.

[1] D.M.A., 9 December 1933.
[2] *Ibid.*, 6 January 1936.
[3] See Chapter IX, pp. 382-5.

Wilson shared Crawford's Liberal, Non-Conformist background, his conviction of the value of industrial peace and his determination to strengthen the Association numerically and financially. Endowed with a forceful character, diplomatic skill and a gift of oratory he managed the Association's affairs until his death in 1915, aided by individuals who were later to share the task of leadership during the difficult inter-war period.

Thomas Cann was the longest serving Agent of the Association in 1919, having first been elected to the office of Treasurer on the death of Patterson in 1896. Cann, born in 1858, was the seventh son of a Cornish tin miner and began working in the coal mines at eight years of age, employed as a surface worker at 3d a day.[1] He was a deputy at Castle Eden Colliery during the 1892 strike,[2] and was sentenced under the Intimidation Act to two months' imprisonment in July 1892, following a disturbance at the colliery when one miner refused to join the strike.[3] A member of the Association's Executive Committee from 1890, he succeeded Wilson as General Secretary in 1915.

By the end of the First World War all of the Agents with whom Cann had worked since 1896 under Wilson's leadership had died. The men who replaced them, with two exceptions, had only become full-time employees of the Association in the period since 1911. James Robson, elected an Agent in 1911, first became a delegate member of the Executive Committee in 1897. Six feet tall and a fluent speaker, he was born at West Auckland in 1860 and began work in the mines at 10 years of age. In 1900 he was elected check-weighman at Broompark Colliery and from there eventually moved to Bearpark Colliery where he worked until his appointment in 1911. William Whiteley took his first job, somewhat reluctantly, as a clerk to the Association in 1894 and remained in that capacity until he was eventually elected an Agent in 1912 only a year before the rules were altered to make service in the mines a necessary prerequisite to holding official status in the Association.

In 1913, because of the pressure of work placed upon Cann as both Financial and Executive Committee Secretary, it was decided to appoint an additional Agent. The position was eventually filled by Thomas Trotter who had first been elected a junior clerk to the Association in May 1886. Trotter, born in Durham city in 1871, attended village school at Fulwell, near Sunderland, but spent the greater part of his life in Durham. Never himself a miner, Trotter

[1] *Durham Chronicle*, 9 April 1915.
[2] See above, p. 21.
[3] Wilson, *op. cit.*, pp. 244–5.

gained a sound knowledge of financial and trade-union affairs under Crawford's and Wilson's leadership and, like Whiteley, secured an Agent's position shortly before it became obligatory to have had practical mining experience. It is noteworthy that during their periods of office both Whiteley and Trotter became self-styled experts in the intricacies and application of involved pieces of social legislation, Whiteley with insurance and Trotter with unemployment, both drawing upon their previous painstaking and methodical disciplines and knowledge of trade-union affairs.

With the death of John Wilson and the resignation in 1915 of Samuel Galbraith, an Agent of the Association since 1900, to become an M.P. it became necessary to appoint a further two Agents. The final selection was made from five candidates, W. P. Richardson, J. Batey, P. Lee, J. Gilliland and R. Richardson. The successful candidates, Richardson (W. P.) and Batey, who became Financial and Joint Committee Secretaries respectively, became the first Agents to be elected by an individual ballot vote of members instead of being subject to the voting of Lodges as a whole.[1] Richardson, son of a Durham miner, was born at Usworth in 1873 and in 1885 began working at the local colliery, only five months after his father had been killed there in an explosion. Appointed Lodge Secretary at Usworth when 25 years old Richardson was still working at the same colliery when appointed an Agent in 1915 although he had become a member of the County Federation Board in 1912.[2] Batey, born at West Moor in Northumberland in 1867, began work in the mine at 12 years of age and, after moving first to Blaydon Main and then to South Shields, was appointed checkweighman there at the St Hilda Colliery, a position he held until 1915.[3]

Following the death in 1917 of William House, President of the Association since 1900, the Executive Committee approached the Lodges to make nominations for the appointment of a new Agent. The Lodges voted against the recommendation and rejected compromise proposals to rearrange the functions of the existing full-time officials.[4] At the time Durham compared unfavourably with other districts in the number of Agents employed. South Wales, for example, with a total membership slightly larger than Durham's had four times as many Agents and Scotland, with fewer members, had three times as many. Northumberland, with only one third of Durham's membership, had four Agents compared with Durham's

[1] D.M.A., 12 August 1915.
[2] *Durham Chronicle*, 17 April 1926.
[3] *Ibid.*, 24 May 1927.
[4] D.M.A., 17 August, 18 September, 20 October 1917.

six.[1] The Association's Executive Committee was finally successful in persuading Lodges to agree to an internal reorganization of staff duties.[2] Robson became President and Whiteley replaced Robson as Joint Committee Secretary. Whiteley assumed responsibility as Financial Secretary. In a circular to members the Executive explained:

'The changes would preserve the continuity of changing Agents round when vacancies occur that has been of immense value to the Association as a whole in enabling the Agents to gather a general knowledge of the work of the Association as represented in the different departments, thereby qualifying them for the general work of the Association much better than they could be by being stereo-typed in any particular department.'[3]

These temporary arrangements were carried out until the end of the First World War but the relative shortage of full-time staff in relation to total membership and the growing pressure of work emphasized the need for the appointment of an additional Agent. Elections were held in October 1919, eight of the eighty-eight nominees being subjected to an individual ballot vote. These included P. Lee, J. Gilliland, J. Herriotts, W. Lawther, J. Ritson, R. Wren, T. Neville and H. James, all but the latter being checkweighmen.[4] Since no candidate secured an absolute majority during the first ballot a second ballot was conducted in December 1919. Lee secured a majority of 31,938 votes over his nearest rival Gilliland, gaining 60,854 votes to 28,916 and was appointed Financial Secretary at the age of 55.[5] Whiteley thereafter concentrated his attention solely upon matters of insurance, having previously combined this activity with his duty as Financial Secretary.

Peter Lee, one of a family of eight, was born in July 1864 at Duff Heap Row, Fivehouses, Trimdon Grange. He began working at the age of 10 in an Oldham cotton mill but within months returned to Durham to work ten hours per day as a pony driver in Littletown Colliery at Sherburn Hill. Physically striking he is described at 21 as 'six foot one and a half, body steeled by hard labour, great straight-looking grey eyes set in a fine face, thick black hair curled round his cap'.[6] From becoming a coal hewer at the age of 16½ he began to drink heavily but at 21 decided to shake off the habits of his youth and began a determined process of self-improvement, devoting a

[1] Ibid., 26 October 1917.
[2] Ibid., 1 December 1917.
[3] Ibid., 16 November 1917.
[4] Ibid., 28 October 1919.
[5] Ibid., 8 December 1919.
[6] J. Lawson, Peter Lee, London 1936, p. 47.

period of hours before the start of each shift towards mastering the art of reading and writing.[1] Inheriting the roving disposition of his parents he emigrated to the U.S.A. in 1886 and as a young man worked in the mines in Ohio, Pennsylvania and Kentucky, returning to England in March, 1887.[2] In the same year he was selected at 23 as Wingate's delegate to the Association's Council and in 1892 as checkweighman at Wingate Colliery.[3] After a short spell in South Africa during 1896-7 he returned to England and was appointed checkweighman at Wheatley Hill Colliery in 1900, Chairman of Wheatley Hill Parish Council in 1903, and in 1909, elected to represent the Thornley division on Durham County Council.[4]

During the inter-war period the Association's leaders had to adapt themselves to an almost totally different situation from that which confronted their predecessors. The long-term depression in the coal industry which followed the brief post-war boom had its own direct effect upon union finance, membership, morale and bargaining power. Furthermore in the early years of the Association's development Agents were, by and large, identified with the ideology and persuasions of those leaders who had pioneered trade-union negotiation within the coalfield and, during the first decade or so of the twentieth century, came under the direct influence of Wilson who personified the Lib.-Lab. tradition and virtues of conciliation. Whilst Cann remained General Secretary the influence of the past lingered on. The remaining Agents, appointed during the period when trade unionism was being influenced away from Liberalism towards Socialism, were already well acquainted with the details of union administration and particularly capable of reorientating their energies towards improving the miners' lot at a time when a love of industrial peace, conciliation and Liberalism seemed scarcely fitted to the circumstances of the time.

The contribution which younger men like Whiteley and Batey could make to the fight for better conditions in the post-1919 period, at least as Agents of the Association, was short-lived. In 1922 both were elected to Parliament [5] and began an equally important task of representing the miners' interest at legislative level. The Association had decided in October 1917 that any agent elected an M.P. had forthwith to resign his post.[6] In view of the union's poor financial

[1] *Durham Chronicle*, 1 May 1926.
[2] Lawson, *op. cit.*, p. 47.
[3] *Ibid.*, pp. 61, 77-83.
[4] *Ibid.*, pp. 106, 108, 142; *Durham Chronicle*, 1 May 1926.
[5] See Chapter VIII, p. 329.
[6] D.M.A., 6 October 1917.

situation[1] the Executive Committee recommended that only one further Agent should be appointed, reducing the total number of full-time officials to six. Whilst desirous to exercise every possible economy the Executive realized the dangers of allowing a mounting pressure of work to be shouldered by a relatively small number of men. In appealing to the Lodges for recommendations for the new post, therefore, the Executive Committee suggested that in the future none of the full-time officials should assume responsibility for matters of insurance as Whiteley had done, for example, between 1917 and 1919. It further recommended that Lee should be transferred to the Joint Committee department and that the new Agent be appointed Financial Secretary.[2]

The Lodges agreed to the recommendations[3] and voting took place in May 1923. W. Lawther, R. Wren and J. Gilliland, who had contested the vacancy for an Agent in 1919, were again amongst the short list of eight candidates which also included J. Hobbs, T. Newton, H. Pearson, G. W. Bloomfield and J. E. Swan.[4] Swan, elected as miners' M.P. for Barnard Castle in 1918 but defeated in the constituency in 1922,[5] was at first disqualified as a candidate for Agent according to Rule 115 of the Association, part of which read:

'Any member leaving the collieries for some other occupation or employment, and being desirous of continuing his membership of this Association, can do so on condition of paying all levies and contributions . . . and adhering to the rules in every respect but shall not be eligible for any office or benefit except sick pay and death benefit . . .'

The attempted disqualification of Swan led the Dawdon and Victory Lodges to demand a Special Council meeting to discuss the matter[6] and on 17 March the Association finally agreed to accept Swan's nomination for the post.[7]

Swan topped the poll during the first ballot with Gilliland second, but as no candidate secured an absolute majority a second ballot was conducted between the top two contestants. Swan eventually secured the post defeating Gilliland by 68,972 votes to 24,487.[8] John

[1] See below, pp. 85-6.
[2] D.M.A., 6 October, 5, 13 December 1922.
[3] *Ibid.*, 27 December 1922.
[4] *Ibid.*, 25 April 1923.
[5] See Chapter VIII, p. 329.
[6] *Durham Chronicle*, 16, 23 February 1923.
[7] D.M.A., 17 March 1923.
[8] *Ibid.*, 9 May 1923.

Swan was born at Dipton in 1877 and began work at the age of eleven as a cattle hand on a farm. Within one year he had turned his attention to coal mining and whilst still a young man was chosen as checkweighman at East Howle Colliery, later being appointed to a similar position at the Delight Pit at Dipton. A previous member of the Association's Executive Committee, he also held positions on the Lanchester Board of Guardians and Annfield Plain Urban District Council.

On 6 May 1924 Cann died at the age of 66. Until a new Agent was appointed the Association recommended to Lodges that Richardson, then Executive Committee Secretary, should become General Secretary, Lee Executive and Joint Committee Secretary and that the Compensation Department, until then under the jurisdiction of Robson the President, should assume separate identity under Swan's leadership. The President and Treasurer would remain in their respective offices, the latter sharing with Swan the problems of running the financial department until a new Agent was appointed. The Lodges agreed to the recommendations.[1]

The Association continued to function in this way for a few months even though it had a greater number of members per Agent (1 to every 25,000 members) than any other district in the Miners' Federation.[2] As pressure upon other departments increased, however, a new appointment became essential. Early in the contest it became evident that the choice of a new Agent lay between James Gilliland,[3] who had fought against Swan for a similar position in 1922, and John Herriotts, ex-Labour M.P. for Sedgefield. Gilliland eventually secured the post defeating Herriotts by 59,531 votes to 33,612.[4] Born at West Rainton, Gilliland was elected as checkweighman at Lintz Green Colliery in 1897 where he worked for ten years during which time he took an active interest in municipal work. He was elected a member of Tanfield Urban District Council in 1899 and for nine years was a member of the Board of the Lintz Co-operative Society. In 1911 he was elected checkweighman at the Ouston 'E' pit at Birtley, a position he retained until his appointment as Agent in 1925.[5]

---

[1] *Ibid.*, 18, 30 June 1924.
[2] *Ibid.*, 18 June 1924.
[3] James Gilliland must not be confused with his brother John Edward Gilliland, who was appointed as one of the Association's Parliamentary Agents in 1915 and who later became Labour Agent in the Chester-le-Street and Blaydon divisions.
[4] *Durham Chronicle*, 3 July 1926.
[5] *Ibid.*, 3 July 1926.

The sudden death of Richardson on 8 August 1930 resulted not in the appointment of a new Agent but in a re-arrangement of the duties of the remaining full-time officials. Peter Lee became General Secretary, Swan Executive and Joint Committee Secretary and Gilliland Compensation Secretary. Robson and Trotter retained their positions as President and Treasurer respectively, Trotter joining Gilliland in supervising the financial department. The pressure of work placed upon the existing staff was further increased in 1932 when the Lodges voted against adopting a further Agent following Trotter's death on 22 November.[1] Lee combined the functions of General Secretary and Treasurer until the end of June 1933,[2] when the Association appointed an unemployed member of its own Executive Committee, E. Moore, as temporary Treasurer.[3] Within two months of Moore's appointment it was decided to appoint an additional Agent.[4] Out of a total of 111 nominees William (later Sir William) Lawther succeeded in securing the vacancy and was elected Treasurer of the Association on 4 December 1933. Lawther was destined to become one of the most well-known personalities in the coal industry as wartime president of the M.F.G.B. and later as the first full-time president of the National Union of Mineworkers.[5] Born at Choppington in Northumberland in 1890 Lawther began work in the coal mines at the age of 12, receiving 1s 0½d for a ten-hour shift. He moved to Chopwell, in County Durham, at 16 and was elected Vice-President of the local miners' Lodge in 1907. A Delegate to the Association between 1908–11 he was eventually elected to its Executive Committee in December 1918 having already studied at the Central Labour College with the aid of a bursary from the Association. His election as an Agent followed upon an inexpectant political career[6] and a local notoriety achieved as a result of his defiance of the authorities during the 1926 dispute.[7] After almost five years' service as Vice-President of the M.F.G.B. Lawther was elected to the presidency in 1939 and received a knighthood in 1947 in recognition of his services on behalf of the British miners.

Within two years of Lawther's appointment the Association suffered the loss of two of its most notable leaders. Robson died in September 1934 and was eventually succeeded by the candidate

[1] D.M.A., 24 November 1932.
[2] Ibid., 14 June 1933.
[3] Ibid., 26 June 1933.
[4] Ibid., 5 August 1933.
[5] See Chapter IX, pp. 384–5.
[6] See Chapter VIII.
[7] See Chapter V, p. 199.

whom Lawther defeated in the final vote for the staff vacancy in 1933. Edward Moore defeated William Pearson and Hubert Tunney to become the Association's new Financial Secretary on 25 January 1935. Moore, who had temporarily held the position of Treasurer of the Association in 1933,[1] was for twenty years Treasurer of Harraton miners' Lodge and from 1928 represented the Lambton division on the Durham County Council. A keen student of economics and well-versed in trade union affairs he was also a member and ex-chairman of the Chester-le-Street Rural Council.[2]

The relatively rapid turnover of the Association's full-time officials compared with the pre-1914 situation was further emphasized by Lee's death on 16 June 1935 only nine months after Robson. The final contest for the vacancy was between Samuel Watson, William Pearson, whom Moore defeated in 1935, and George Harvey. Watson, then secretary of the Boldon miners' Lodge, succeeded in securing the post and on 1 July 1936 began what was to be one of the most distinguished careers within the coal industry. Watson was born at Boldon on 11 March 1898, son of a coal miner, and by the age of 19 was a member of the Boldon miners' Lodge Committee. Secretary of the Boldon branch of the Labour Party at 21 he was elected seven years later to a similar position in the local miners' Lodge. In 1934 he won the Trade Union Congress prize for essay-writing with a study of the social and economic significance of the martyrdom of the Dorsetshire Labourers. Intuitive, industrious and particularly persuasive in argument and negotiation, Watson began his official career as Treasurer and Unemployment Officer, applying to the task the same energy, enthusiasm, and deep concern for the individual which were to make him one of the most influential mining officials in the post-nationalization period. The death of Robson and Lee resulted in a rearrangement of Agents' duties. Lawther became Executive Committee Secretary, Swan General Secretary, Gilliland President, whilst Moore remained Financial Secretary.[3]

There were no further changes in the Association's leadership until 1945 when Lawther was elected full-time President of the newly-established National Union of Mineworkers. Elections for the appointment of an Agent to replace Lawther took place during July. None of the eight candidates for the vacancy, all but two of whom were checkweighmen, secured an absolute majority of votes at the first ballot. J. Kelly and J. Foster, who together had received the highest number of votes in the County, were subjected to a second

---

[1] See above, p. 78.
[2] *Durham Chronicle*, 18 January 1935.
[3] D.M.A., 13 July 1936.

ballot. Kelly finally secured the post by 42,095 votes to Foster's 22,368 and began his duties as Financial Secretary on 6 September 1945.[1]

Kelly, born at Flint Hill in County Durham in October 1896, began work at the age of 12 at the West Shield Row Colliery. In 1920 he was elected checkweighman at the Bessie Pit at Blaydon having already earned a local reputation as an agitator for workmen's rights. After working at the Victoria Garesfield Colliery he became checkweighman at the east coast pit at Blackhall. Particularly interested in local government affairs he was a representative on the Gateshead Board of Guardians, Blaydon Urban District Council and Durham County Council.

Throughout the 1920s there was no compulsory retiring age for Agents of the Association and, apart from the position of Treasurer, no established rules for means of disposing of an Agent. In 1933 a retiring age of 70 had been established, later reduced to 65,[2] but the turnover of officials during the 1930s was due directly to the death of existing leaders. With the establishment of the N.U.M. in 1945, however, no person, according to Rule 19, was eligible for election as a national or area official if over 60 years of age. Swan and Gilliland, 68 years and 79 years old respectively in 1945, were forced to retire from their positions. The names of the eight candidates who had secured the highest number of votes in the County out of the total list of nominations, of whom one, J. Foster, had fought earlier in 1945 for the position of Agent, were submitted to the Lodges for an individual ballot vote under the transferable voting system adopted by the N.U.M. The two new agents were elected only after four and six counts respectively, the votes recorded being transferred to candidates in turn depending upon the particular preferences indicated, until one candidate received an absolute majority over all others. J. Foster succeeded in being elected as General Treasurer and J. Joyce was elected as Financial Secretary,[3] Kelly becoming Committee Secretary.

Joyce, born at Spennymoor in March 1892, spent the whole of his working life at Ushaw Moor Colliery, starting work at the age of 13 and eventually being elected as checkweighman and Compensation Secretary to the local miners' Lodge. Between 1924 and 1945 he served on the Lanchester and Durham Rural District Council. Foster was Secretary of the Easington Colliery miners' Lodge before his appointment as Agent and Secretary of its local Federation Board

[1] D.M.A., 4 September 1945.
[2] See above, p. 70.
[3] D.M.A., 6 January 1946.

during the 1926 dispute. Born at East Hetton in December 1898
he began work at the local colliery at the age of 14 and moved to
Easington three years later. As a young man he was a Methodist
local preacher and took a keen interest in local government. Elected
to the Easington Rural District Council in 1928 he became its
Chairman in 1937.

One of the most distinguished features of the Association's
leadership was its success in achieving high office within the ranks of
the Miners' Federation. All the Association's full-time officials served
at varying intervals in their careers upon the National Executive
Committee of the M.F.G.B. Robson was the Federation's Treasurer
between 1918 and 1924 and was succeeded by Richardson who held
the post until 1930. Peter Lee served in 1931 as Vice-President
and during 1932–33 as President of the M.F.G.B., Lawther being
appointed to these positions during 1934–38 and 1939–44 respectively.

III

Any adult wishing to become a 'financial member' of the Association
in 1919 had to pay an entrance fee of 2s 6d to his local Lodge. Boys
over 16 beginning to work in the mines were allowed to join free of
charge for a period of six weeks after which they were required to pay
a fee of 1s 3d. A fortnightly contribution of 1s to the General Fund
entitled a full member [1] protection 'for his labour in all its branches'
and the following death benefits: death of a full member £7; death of
member's wife £5; death of member's child (under 10) £1; death of
member's son (10–14 years) £3; death of a daughter, over 10 years,
as long as unmarried and unemployed £3 and death of a half-member
under 18 years £4. Any person with fewer than seven fortnightly
contributions received only half the stipulated rates. If a person's
contributions fell six weeks in arrears he forfeited his claim to benefit
until one month after the arrears were fully paid. [2]

Members could insure themselves against sickness and accident by
paying a separate contribution of 1s a fortnight (6d half members) to
a special sick and accident fund. After paying the requisite entrance
fee to the scheme and having contributed thirteen fortnightly payments full members were entitled to sick benefit of 8s per week for the
first 26 weeks, 5s per week for the second 26 weeks and 4s per week

[1] Persons between the ages of sixteen and eighteen, 'half members', paid reduced
contributions and received reduced benefits.
[2] Rules of the Durham Miners' Association, Revised December 1916, Durham
1917, pp. 10–11, 16.

thereafter. Benefits for accidents not covered by compensation payments were of the same amount as those paid for sickness, although by paying an extra weekly contribution of 2d members could receive a higher rate of benefit for accidents for which compensation was paid. Until 1914 sickness and accident benefits had been paid to those members paying a larger contribution to the Association's General Fund than would have ensured payment of death benefit alone. From 1914 the sickness and accident fund was placed upon a self-supporting basis but soon encountered financial difficulty. After the first ten weeks of its operation the fund made a loss of £2,958.[1] The demands which discharged disabled soldiers made upon the fund immediately after the First World War forced the Association's Executive Committee to appeal to members to raise a special levy of 1d per fortnight to meet existing liabilities.[2]

Financial members on strike [3] or who were locked out were allowed payment of 10s per week and a similar payment was made to those unemployed as a consequence of depressed trade, stoppage of collieries or want of pit-room providing they made sufficient efforts to find work.[4] Members who were victimized but not supported by the sympathetic action of their local Lodges were entitled to relief of 18s per week for a period not exceeding 52 weeks. Lodges were free to request permission to collect local levies to help support members dismissed during periods of depression.[5]

The wages of all the Association's officials fluctuated with the County variations in miners' wages and were suspended altogether when a general strike or lock-out took place. Agents also enjoyed the privileges of free house, coal allowance and free lighting. In September 1914 agents received £3 8s 5d a week and in January 1921 £7 18s 1d per week.[6] Following a recommendation by the Executive Committee in 1921 that officials' salaries should be increased a full enquiry was begun in 1922 when it was found that the remuneration of Agents in Durham was comparable with that paid to permanent full-time officials in other county unions.[7] The matter was again raised in 1924 when, as a result of the recommendations of a special Sub-Committee, the Association agreed to establish for Agents a

[1] D.M.A., 12 June 1914.
[2] Ibid., 5 March 1920.
[3] A strike could not be called unless supported by two-thirds majority of the Association's membership.
[4] Rules of the Durham Miners' Association, Revised December 1916, Durham 1917, p. 17.
[5] Ibid., pp. 18–19; 23.
[6] D.M.A., 19 January 1921.
[7] Ibid., 20 January; 4, 11 February 1922.

basic rate of £4 per week in addition to the normal refund of expenses incurred whilst carrying out their duties.[1]

Lodge Secretaries and Treasurers were paid both by the Association and local Lodge committees. In 1919 they were paid 3d per £ by the Association when contributions reached £15 per fortnight; 4d per £ of contributions above £12 but below £15; 5d per £ when above £8 but below £12 and 6d per £ for any amount below £8. In addition the local Lodge committee paid such officials 2½ per cent commission on all subscriptions received for the local Lodge fund.[2]

Provision was made in the Association's rules for safeguarding its general financial position. The General Fund was not allowed to be reduced below £10,000 whilst the Council was empowered at all times to reduce, if necessary, the demands made upon the Fund by lowering the amount of benefits and allowances payable to members.[3] The Council was also responsible for deciding how the Association's funds should be invested amongst the various options authorized in the rules i.e. in government or real securities, public funds, banks, the purchase or building of property; purchase and working of manufactories or mines, trade union or Labour newspapers or in mortgages.[4]

The financial stability of the Association was severely undermined during the twenties by industrial disputes. The three weeks' strike in October and November 1920 occurred just seven months after the Association had agreed to increase members' weekly contributions and, at the same time, the scale of death and relief allowances.[5] Without the advantages of long-term growth in income from increased contributions the Association was obliged to meet the demands for strike allowance—increased from 10s to £1 per week. During the first two weeks of the stoppage over £290,000 was distributed to members and the smaller branches of the Co-operative Bank [6] throughout the coalfield found it impossible to cope with the magnitude of necessary payments. Lodges were forced to arrange for cheques to be cashed at specific centres throughout the County.[7] The Association was ultimately forced to realize some of its investments in order to meet its necessary expenditure. At the beginning of

[1] *Ibid.*, 17 May, 5 July 1924.
[2] Rules of the Durham Miners' Association, Revised December 1916, Durham 1917, pp. 23–5.
[3] *Ibid.*, p. 29.
[4] *Ibid.*, p. 22.
[5] *Ibid.*, 28 February 1920.
[6] From April 1920 the Association conducted its banking business through the Co-operative Wholesale Society Bank and local Lodges were instructed to open a single banking account with the nearest branch.
[7] D.M.A., 27 October 1920.

the strike the union possessed investments to a total nominal value of £427,500, bearing interest at the rate of £20,775 per annum. By the end of 1920 its total investments were worth only £130,000. The Association was only prevented from disposing of all of its investments by obtaining a C.W.S. bank overdraft of £51,688 which allowed it to meet the final demands for relief payment before the strike ended.[1] A total of £400,349 was distributed in strike allowance during the period of the dispute, although by February 1921 the amount of bank overdraft had been reduced to only £12,000.[2]

The 1921 lock-out proved even more disastrous since members' relief payments had to be met out of borrowed money. Without funds to finance strike payments the Association secured an overdraft of £130,000 from the Co-operative Wholesale Society's bank, on the mortgage of the union's property, which allowed one strike payment of £1 per member to be made.[3] Extra relief was provided by outside sources, especially the M.F.G.B., and by 30 June 1921, the last day of the lock-out, the Association had distributed £14,134 to Lodges. By the end of the 1921 dispute the Association's bank overdraft, which had stood at £22,909 at the end of December 1920, had risen to £147,000 with interest charges at the rate of over £9,750 per year.[4]

The aftermath of the lock-out proved an equally unbearable financial strain. Not only had the bank overdraft to be reduced and relief paid to unemployed members but, following a decision made in May 1921, the Association was obliged to pay to all miners living in rented houses 5s per week rent allowance for the duration of the lock-out at an estimate cost alone of £146,250.[5] An emergency weekly levy of 1s 6d per member was inaugurated in July 1921, but by October it had failed even to meet the cost of relief payments. As depression deepened in the industry and pits began working short-time many miners found it increasingly difficult to meet the cost of the special levy. In October 1921 the Executive Committee agreed to relate levy payments to wages earned. Members with gross weekly earnings of less than £1 were no longer obliged to pay the levy; those with £1 and under £1 5s 0d paid 6d per week; those with £1 5s 0d and under £1 15s 0d paid 9d plus an extra 3d per week for every 10s

[1] Ibid., 11 February 1921.
[2] Durham Miners' Association, Statement of Accounts from December 30, 1920 to June 30, 1921, 13 July 1921.
[3] D.M.A., 3 May 1921.
[4] Durham Miners' Association, Statement of Accounts from December 30, 1920 to June 30, 1921, 13 July 1921.
[5] Ibid.

addition to gross earnings. Miners receiving relief were required to pay, in addition to their fortnightly contributions to the General Fund, 6d for every £1 received.[1]

Between July and December 1921 a total of £244,561 was distributed to members in relief, of which £165,733 was met by the special levy and the remainder financed from the Association's General Fund. The relief payments made during these six months were almost £80,000 in excess of the total amount disbursed during the three occasions before 1914 when similar relief funds had been organized i.e. 1877–8; 1884–9 and 1892–6. Between 1 October 1920 and 10 December 1921, when the financial demands of two industrial disputes had to be met, the Association spent over £¾ million in relief and strike allowance, or approximately £6 per member, whilst total income stood at only £450,928. Even by the end of December 1921 the total amount of rent claims still outstanding stood at over £145,000 and the bank overdraft at over £140,000.[2] With over 23,000 members still unemployed it was obvious that the existing rates of benefit could not long be maintained. At the end of 1921 it was decided to halve the amount of weekly relief paid to those miners who had received twelve relief payments since July 1921. Such members were then exempt from paying to the special levy since their income fell to below £1 per week.[3]

Because of trade depression, short-time working, low wages and the rising cost of living the Association was once again compelled in 1922 to carefully consider its financial situation. Hopes for better trade and increased employment had not materialized. Between June 1921 and June 1922 the General Fund had to contribute £139,699 to cover the deficiency between the demands for relief and the funds available from the special levy. By the end of May 1922 the Association was twenty weeks in arrears in distributing relief payments and the Executive Committee anxiously sought some method of establishing financial stability. Although the Executive was in favour of limiting the amount and duration of relief and of replacing the existing graduated levy by a flat rate levy on all members a Special Council Meeting on 24 June 1922 decided to maintain the existing levy and scale of relief but to suspend payments of rent.[4] The financial situation grew worse. By mid-August 1922 relief liabilities exceeded income from both general contributions and the

[1] D.M.A., 19, 25 October 1921.
[2] *Ibid.*, 28 December 1921.
[3] *Ibid.*
[4] *Ibid.*, 24 June 1922.

special levy by £109,000.[1] The Association's officials, only too conscious of the serious financial plight of their organization, constantly drew comfort from their eximious determination to aid their members in times of need. Between 1 October 1920 and 23 March 1922 with a total income from all sources of £658,991, the Association's total expenditure amounted to £1,139,928, of which £961,173 had been spent in relief, strike and lock-out allowance, which prompted Lee and Trotter, Financial Secretary and Treasurer respectively, to write:

'We make the claim, and we do not think that it can be disputed, that there is no single County Organization that from sheer necessity has been compelled, and has actually paid, a sum equal to the above amount. . . . If it proves anything at all, it conclusively proves that in no other district or county is the spirit of brotherhood, with all its financial difficulties, borne in so exemplary a manner as in Durham County.'[2]

Continuing in its efforts to sustain relief payments to members in need the Association's Council decided in December 1922 that since many miners were close to losing their claim to benefit, owing to a resolution of 28 March 1914 which limited a person's right to relief to a maximum of twelve months, the provision should be extended by three months.[3]

The financial situation slowly improved during 1923. The special levy was discontinued in June because so many members were becoming 'unfinancial' owing to the burden of regular contributions.[4] During the same month the Association cleared itself of the liabilities for rent payment during the period of the 1921 lock-out. Even without rent liabilities the union's total expenditure between 27 June 1924 and 30 April 1925 amounted to £499,996 out of a total income of £505,217. In view of the slim margin of resources relief benefits were halved in May 1925 to 10s per week for the first ten weeks and 5s per week thereafter and the maximum period of relief reduced from 52 to 40 weeks.[5] The Executive Committee explained to members:

'We are under the painful necessity of having to draw your attention to the fact that we have practically come to the end of our financial resources. . . . We are at present saddled with the responsibility of paying relief allowance to about 39,000 members,

[1] Ibid., 24 August 1922.
[2] Ibid., 31 March 1922.
[3] Ibid., 16 December 1922.
[4] Ibid., 5, 14 April, 6 June 1923.
[5] Ibid., 4, 5 May 1925.

absorbing a sum of approximately £27,000 each fortnight, and owing to an additional 10,000 having gone off our funds after receiving their full complement of relief,[1] our income is a diminishing one, exceeded by the outlay to the extent of nearly £20,000 per fortnight.'[2]

Because of the slowness with which finances were recovering it was decided in May 1925 to discontinue the separate sick and accident funds because of their persistent tendency to run into deficit. During the first six months of 1921 the funds were making a loss of over £1,100 per month and in June 1924 the balance of income over expenditure stood at only £213.[3]

By the time the outbreak of the 1926 dispute the Association's commitments towards the unemployed had severely strained its financial resources. The first relief payment of 10s per full member was paid during the third week of the dispute.[4] A grant of £36,000 from the M.F.G.B., combined with the balance of the Association's funds, allowed a second payment of 10s per member to be made in June but led Trotter, General Treasurer, to announce:

'We regret to say that this payment will use up all our money, with the exception of a balance that we are compelled to keep in hand for the purpose of meeting the death payments that, seeing no Contributions are coming in,[5] have got to be met from the General Office. Any subsequent payment will depend entirely upon the amount that comes from the Miners' Federation.'[6]

M.F.G.B. contributions allowed seven other relief payments to be made during the period June–November 1926 three of 5s per full member, one of 4s and three of 3s. Out of a total contribution from trade unions and labour supporters throughout the world of £1,813,680 to the M.F.G.B. Relief Fund, £1,793,711 was distributed to mineworkers' organizations, of which Durham received the second largest share of £293,812.[7]

The resilience with which the Association shouldered the financial

[1] The Association depended upon members paying contributions out of the relief allowance granted them.
[2] D.M.A., 26 August 1925.
[3] *Ibid.*, 7 May 1925.
[4] *Ibid.*, 19 May 1926.
[5] Payment of contributions had been suspended during the period of the stoppage. The 4d Death Fund payment was also suspended despite the fact that, according to Rule, the payment was obligatory at all times. D.M.A., 3 December 1926.
[6] *Ibid.*, 5 June 1926.
[7] Miners' Relief Fund, *Settlement of Accounts for the 14 months ending June 30th, 1927*, London 1927, pp. 4–7.

burden of relief and strike payments during the turbulent period of industrial strife between 1919 and 1926 reduced its bargaining strength and resistance to open conflict with the employers but signified, in a commanding way, its adherence to the basic principles of trade unionism.

Not surprisingly, relief payments became the dominant item in the Association's expenditure immediately following the cessation of the 1926 dispute. Liability was again assumed, according to Rule, for the payment of rent to those members forced to spend during the period of the lock-out.[1] Short-time working made matters worse for, in addition to paying relief to the unemployed, the Association was liable, according to a new rule introduced in 1925, to pay an allowance to all miners at collieries working six days or less per fortnight. By October 1927 100 collieries were claiming the new allowance at an estimated total cost of £20,000.[2]

In spite of increasing financial liabilities the Association was hard pressed during 1928 to reduce members' contributions largely as a result of the impact of the reduction in wages imposed during that year.[3] Lodges suggested reducing the scale of benefits; some appealed for the suspension of relief altogether whilst others demanded a cut in the number of staff employed at headquarters in order to facilitate a gradual reduction in fortnightly contributions.[4] Such was the pressure imposed by the rank and file that in November 1928 fortnightly contributions were reduced from 2s to 1s 6d per member and the scale of benefits subsequently altered. In fact the Association saved less money by reduced benefits than it lost by reduced contributions. Until 1928 Lodges retained 2d out of their fortnightly contribution for local and political purposes, whilst thereafter they were allowed to retain 2d per fortnight for local needs and 1d for political purposes reducing the actual cash contribution made by each member to head office from 1s 10d to 1s 3d.[5]

As the depression in the industry deepened after 1929 the financial situation of the Association grew worse largely as a result of its own efforts to widen the scope of relief offered to members. In August 1931 it was decided to reduce from twelve to four months the period after which financial members, having already received their statutory amount of relief, could become eligible for further assistance.[6]

[1] D.M.A., 4 January 1927.
[2] Ibid., 4 March, 17 October 1927.
[3] See Chapter VI, pp. 236–9.
[4] D.M.A., 5 June 1928.
[5] Ibid., 19 November 1928.
[6] Ibid., 15 August, 3 September 1931.

Further concessions were made in 1932. Members who had worked for sixteen weeks or less during the eighteen months ending 12 March 1932 but not eligible for relief from the Association each received a grant of 25s.[1]

The financial strain of granting extra concessions in addition to the Association's statutory liabilities soon began to show. In the seven months after January 1932 total expenditure exceeded total income by £33,184, £63,862 having been paid out in relief.[2] By the end of August 1932 the total amount in the General Fund was reduced below its minimum level of £10,000 [3] largely as a result of the burden of relief payments to those members on short-time working. This special assistance was therefore immediately suspended in order to augment total financial reserves and allow full benefits to be paid according to Rule.[4] In 1937 the lower limit to which the General Fund would be allowed to fall was raised to £20,000.[5]

The extent to which the Association had made financial provision for its membership during periods of dispute and depression was continually stressed during the early years of the 1930s when it became essential to maintain the loyalty of the miners to their union. Membership of the Association had increased from a total of 148,834 in 1919 to a peak of 160,040 in 1924, declined to 155,773 in the following year and in 1931 totalled 21,000 fewer than in 1919.[6] By the mid-1930s the Association's record of financial assistance was certainly impressive. Between June 1920 and June 1934 out of a total income from all sources of £4,583,860, £4,021,581 had been distributed in benefits to members, amounting to 83·37 per cent of total expenditure and equivalent to 16s 8¼d of every £1 spent. £3,321,870, or 68·86 per cent of total expenditure, had been spent in relief and strike allowance alone. During the same period general working expenses amounted to £565,400, equivalent to 11·71 per cent of total expenditure or 2s 3¾d of every £1 spent. The remaining expenditure arose largely from membership of the M.F.G.B. and County Federation Board with relatively small amounts distributed to charities and special appeals.[7]

Despite this praiseworthy financial service the severe contraction in employment during the thirties and the increasing poverty and

[1] *Ibid.*, 2 July 1932.
[2] *Ibid.*, 23 August 1932.
[3] See above, p. 83.
[4] D.M.A., 23 August 1932.
[5] Rules of the Durham Miners' Association, Revised October 1937, Durham 1938, p. 38.
[6] See Appendix I to this chapter.
[7] Durham Miners' Association, Balance Sheets, 1919–39.

poor morale of the miners kept membership of the Association at a low level compared with the early post-war years. By 1934 total membership had declined to 124,445 from a total of 127,976 in 1931 and stood at only 124,783 in 1938, 35,257 fewer than in the peak year of 1924. The decline in membership continued throughout the Second World War period with over 34,000 fewer members in 1947 than there had been in 1919.[1]

The Association's financial commitments were by no means confined only to its members. The responsiveness which the union had long shown towards genuine appeals in aid of the destitute and repressed sharpened significantly as the international political crisis developed after 1935 and became an integral part of its activity during the period of the Second World War. The Association made substantial financial contributions to various organizations and pressure groups throughout the world whenever it felt that, by doing so, it was enhancing the war effort. By January 1943 the total of donations made to various organizations since the outbreak of war totalled £95,394. Of this total, £41,507 had been donated to the Red Cross Fund, £27,627 in aid to Russia, £1,000 each to Finland and Spain, £10,000 for providing the Royal Air Force with two Spitfires and £3,000 in providing six ambulances for the Anglo-French Ambulance Corps.[2] By the end of December 1945 the total of grants-in-aid made by the Association since 1939 had increased to £163,611 and remained quite distinct from the many voluntary levies instituted by Lodges throughout the coalfield for charitable purposes.[3]

IV

The impetus which the First World War gave to the movement towards industrial unionism, i.e. broadening the basis of trade union organization to incorporate various grades of workers, was welcomed by the Durham Miners' Association as an effective means of increasing corporate strength by common organization. The separate Unions comprising the County Federation Board had, since their establishment, catered for all those working in and about the mines in Durham. The Miners' Association, however, had long been forced to protect those of its members who were deputies from the attempted 'poaching' activities of the Durham Deputies' Association, established in 1875 and actively supported by the local coal owners. The

---

[1] See Appendix I to this chapter.
[2] D.M.A., *General Secretary's Review for the Year 1942*, p. 18.
[3] N.U.M., Durham Area, *General Secretary's Review for 1945*, p. 21.

miners' officials feared that since the deputy was directly responsible for the safety of men in the pit his membership of a separate organization or, as the late-nineteenth-century employers wished, his adoption as an agent of the coal owners would reduce his sense of responsibility towards the workman and the degree of control the Miners' Association could exert over his actions.[1]

It was only after a bitter strike at Silksworth Colliery in 1890 that the principle was established that deputies wishing to transfer their membership from the Durham Miners' to the Durham Deputies' Association should be allowed to do so after the issue of a 'clearance card'.[2] The freedom which this gave to workmen to suddenly transfer loyalty to a separate union after having received the benefits of organization in their earlier years was bitterly resented by the miners' officials. Such was the determination of the Miners' Association to assert its influence in the coalfield that, following the results of a County-wide poll of the membership of the two rival unions in October 1918 which revealed the relative popularity of the miners' union,[3] its Executive Committee decided in January 1919 to withhold any further clearance cards from deputies wishing to transfer their union membership.[4]

The Executive's decision encouraged the Deputies' Association to intensify its efforts to secure members from the miners' union. The series of industrial disputes and the onset of depression during the twenties sharpened the rivalry between the two organizations as the Deputies' Association, free from the responsibility of safeguarding the standard of life of the vast proportion of workmen in the coalfield, attracted those employees unprepared to make the personal sacrifices demanded of them as members of the miners' union. Thus, in 1923, 27 deputies employed at Hebburn Colliery left the Durham Miners' Association to join the deputies' union ostensibly as a result of the financial burden of the various levies established in aid of the unemployed.[5] Prior to 1922 only three of the 60 deputies employed at the colliery belonged to the deputies' union despite the fact that one of the three was President both of the County and national Deputies' Association. Although 14 deputies subsequently rejoined the miners' Association an official strike was called at the colliery on 9 June to

---

[1] Cf. Wilson, *op. cit.*, pp. 119–24.
[2] *Ibid.*, pp. 223–7.
[3] It was found that 2,188 deputies belonged to the Durham Miners' Association; 1,731 to the Durham Deputies' Association and six who were in neither organization. D.M.A., 6 February 1919.
[4] *Colliery Guardian*, 17 January 1919.
[5] D.M.A., 4 July 1923.

force the remainder to follow suit.[1] Within a short period after the
pit had been stopped all the remaining deputies except four, who
were reported to have left the district, had rejoined the miners'
Association although work was not resumed at the colliery until
20 August.[2]

Previously, on 2 July 1923, the Durham Deputies' Association had
complained to the General Council of the T.U.C. that the local
miners' union, having succeeded in persuading the deputies at
Hebburn to return to membership, was guilty of 'poaching' activities.
The issue was referred to the T.U.C.'s Disputes Committee. The
Executive Committee of the M.F.G.B., which defended the charge
on behalf of the Durham Miners' Association, succeeded in establishing that the actions of the twenty-seven deputies at Hebburn
Colliery, whilst brought to a head by financial difficulties, were the
direct result of an intensive campaign by the local Deputies' Association to encroach upon its rival's membership and that the subsequent
activities of the Miners' Association could in no way be construed as
'poaching'.[3]

The conflict between the miners' and deputies' organizations continued throughout the inter-war period. Durham and Scotland
remained the only districts in the Federation which refused to recognize the local Deputies' Association. Representatives from the
Durham miners' and deputies' unions met at a conference in April
1936 in an effort to formulate a scheme of joint consultation but failed
to make any progress.[4] Alleged poaching of members by the Deputies'
Association at Murton Colliery in 1937 led to renewed conflict. The
Disputes Committee of the T.U.C. appealed to the Durham miners'
officials to help foster more amicable relationships within the coalfield, but met with stern resistance.[5]

The first visible signs of peaceful co-existence between the rival
unions in Durham came after the outbreak of the Second World War.
In August 1940, following discussions with the Coal Owners' Association to make membership of the appropriate trade union a
necessary condition of employment,[6] the Durham miners' officials
agreed to allow deputies the freedom to transfer their membership

[1] Ibid.
[2] Ibid., 21 August 1923.
[3] M.F.G.B., 10 April 1924.
[4] T.U.C. Report of Proceedings of the 68th Annual Trade Union Congress, London
1936, pp. 101–2.
[5] M.F.G.B., 6 August 1937.
[6] Until 1942 non-union workmen benefited from improvements in conditions of
work mutually agreed upon by the owners' and miners' Associations.

to whichever organization they wished to belong. In 1945, following
an improvement in the wages and status of deputies, agreement was
eventually reached between the two rival organizations which gave
the Deputies' Association the ultimate responsibility for safeguarding
the interests of this class of workman as a whole and which provided
for the transfer of all deputies from the miners' Association within a
period of three months. At the same time all existing members of the
Deputies' Association under 60 years of age who at any time ceased
to retain deputy status were required to transfer their membership
to the Miners' Association.[1] The agreement was made at a time when
the Deputies' Association was already growing in strength. In October,
1944 56·9 per cent of the total number of deputies employed in the
coalfield belonged to the Deputies' Association compared with
42·11 per cent affiliated to the miners' Association. Only 34 (0·99
per cent) were in neither organization.[2]

The deputies did not pose the only problem of trade union
representation in the coalfield. In January 1933 the Disputes Committee of the T.U.C. heard complaints by the Durham Mechanics'
Association that the Electrical Trades Union was actively recruiting
mining electricians into its ranks and weakening the hold which the
Mechanics' Association traditionally had over these workmen. The
E.T.U.'s campaign for increased membership within Durham only
came to an end following the intervention of the M.F.G.B. and
General Council of the T.U.C.[3]

Earlier in 1923 members of the Durham Enginemen, Mechanics
and Cokemen's Associations were reported to have joined the Union
of Winding and General Engineers, known generally as 'Casey's
Union' after its General Secretary, Thomas Casey, Labour M.P. for
Sheffield (Attercliffe) between 1918 and 1922. The union, deprived
of affiliation to the T.U.C. for failing to pay the requisite fees, was
bitterly opposed by the Miners' Association for attempted 'poaching'
of members from organizations attached to the County Federation
Board. Although circulars were issued to workmen throughout the
coalfield during 1923 warning them to ignore appeals to abandon
their existing union membership nothing more was heard of the
matter.[4]

[1] D.M.A., 20 February 1945.
[2] *Ibid.*, 6 November 1944.
[3] M.F.G.B. *Report of the Executive Committee for the Year ending June, 1933*;
T.U.C. *65th Annual Report*, London 1933, p. 94; M.F.G.B. *Report of the
Executive Committee on the Activities of the Mineworkers' Federation of Great
Britain during the Year ended June 30, 1934*, p. 151.
[4] D.M.A., 7 July 1922; 21 August, 2 October 1923; 6 March 1924.

V

The conflicts between the industrial and craft unions were perpetuated to some extent by the district autonomy enjoyed by mining associations affiliated to the M.F.G.B. In the absence of central co-ordination amongst the coal-producing regions conditions of employment varied significantly and the success which sectional interests could have in attracting the loyalty of workmen during times of depression was enhanced. Amalgamation of varying trade union interests such as had occurred after the First World War with the establishment of the Transport and General Workers' Union and the Amalgamated Engineering Union was less easily achieved in the mining industry. Local miners' agents and officers were always anxious to safeguard their personal security whilst districts were keen to retain their own real property, their particular level of benefits and a distinct identity between members and leaders. Whilst it was possible in the prosperous decades before 1914 for a fairly effective national unity to be maintained on the basis of a loose Federation the long-term unemployment and falling prices experienced for most of the inter-war period put the Federation on the defensive but without the collective strength with which to fight.

It is not surprising, therefore, that Durham, particularly conscious of the price of district autonomy, took a leading role in the movement for the reorganization of the Federation launched in 1927. In March 1927 the Association's Executive Committee forwarded a resolution to the M.F.G.B. urging it 'to review the organization and operations of the Federation, with a view to recommending to the districts such reforms and proposals as, in their opinion, are essential to its progress and effective work.'[1] A sub-committee, appointed by the M.F.G.B. in April 1927 to investigate the structure of district organization,[2] condemned the existing diversity of local contributions and benefits. Although uniformity had been established in 1920 in the weekly contributions of districts to the Federation, proposals for standardized benefits were unanimously rejected.[3]

A demand for a new central organization incorporating uniform contributions and benefits was made in July 1931 and referred to the Federation's Executive Committee for further consideration. Peter Lee, as Acting President of the M.F.G.B., joined other members of

[1] D.M.A., 1, 12 March 1927.
[2] M.F.G.B., 13 April 1927.
[3] *Ibid.*, 9 January, 10 March 1920.

the Executive in suggesting that Durham and Northumberland should be amalgamated into one district with similar amalgamations in South Derbyshire and Leicestershire; Yorkshire, N. Derbyshire and Nottinghamshire and in Bristol, Somerset and the Forest of Dean.[1] The variety of resolutions, exhortations and recommendations failed to encourage any positive action due, in part, to the Federation's preoccupation with industrial issues.[2]

In July 1937, however, Watson was instructed by the Federation to join Arthur Horner, from South Wales, in formulating specific proposals for the establishment of one mineworkers' union. Their recommendations, reported to the national Executive Committee in May 1938, were essentially a compromise between district autonomy and central control. Districts were to retain their benefit funds and existing full-time officials but control of strikes and disputes was to become a matter of national policy and direction. The majority of the Durham miners were in favour of a great deal more central organization than Watson had suggested at national level. Indeed, although Durham joined and voted in favour of the proposals as an acceptable basis upon which one mineworkers' union might be established, it submitted lengthy amendments to the suggested scheme aimed at promoting a quicker dissolution of district strength than was being provided for.[3] Before any further progress could be made war broke out and brought considerations of reorganization to a temporary halt.[4]

---

[1] M.F.G.B. *Report on Organization, June 16, 1932*, p. 11.
[2] See Chapter VI.
[3] M.F.G.B., 6 July 1939; D.M.A., 3 August 1939.
[4] The question of the reorganization of the M.F.G.B. was again raised during the period of the Second World War but is best understood against the background of wartime experiences. See Chapter IX, pp. 382–5.

Appendix I

MEMBERSHIP AND FUNDS 1919–1947

Year	Membership	Investments £	Investments per head £	Investments per head at constant prices £ (at 1914 prices)
1919	148,834	434,632	2·92	1·35
1920	151,029	167,019	1·11	0·44
1921	151,253	208,770	1·38	0·61
1922	155,380	214,770	1·38	0·75
1923	158,339	362,774	2·29	1·31
1924	160,040	332,440	2·08	1·18
1925	155,773	141,357	0·91	0·51
1926	149,740	114,767	0·77	0·44
1927	137,853	91,587	0·66	0·39
1928	128,795	100,165	0·78	0·46
1929	132,081	164,704	1·25	0·76
1930	132,801	181,654	1·37	0·86
1931	127,976	162,576	1·27	0·86
1932	125,086	111,403	0·89	0·61
1933	122,824	133,964	1·09	0·77
1934	124,445	166,007	1·33	0·94
1935	124,613	183,876	1·48	1·03
1936	124,647	225,318	1·81	1·24
1937	127,157	282,865	2·22	1·44
1938	124,783	309,073	2·48	1·58
1939	122,031	357,517	2·93	1·85
1940	115,097	328,235	2·85	1·54
1941	110,958	363,624	3·28	1·64
1942	111,569	424,975	3·81	1·90
1943	111,010	460,120	4·14	2·08
1944	112,325	517,687	4·61	2·29
1945	110,194	440,198	3·99	1·96
1946	110,458	471,857	4·27	2·10
1947	114,667	498,353	4·35	2·13

Sources: Durham Miners' Association, Account Books and Balance Sheets; Ministry of Labour, Index of Retail Prices, 1914–1947.

Chapter III

THE SANKEY COMMISSION AND INDUSTRIAL UNREST, 1919–20

I

Long before 1919 the miners had come to accept the notion of national as distinct from district action as the most effective means of improving their standard of living. This was due, in large measure, to the shift in power from the districts towards the Miners' Federation which had occurred before and during the years of the First World War. The 1912 Minimum Wage dispute,[1] the first national strike in the coal mining industry, was a step towards the consolidation of the M.F.G.B. into a united trade-union organization. The formation of the Triple Alliance in 1913 between the M.F.G.B., the National Union of Railwaymen and the National Transport Workers' Federation for the purpose of joint industrial action in support of each other's demands had the same centralizing effect.

The steep rise in the cost of living during the early years of the First World War led the M.F.G.B. in 1915 to seek an immediate national increase in miners' earnings but the move was defeated.[2] With the advent of State control of the mines in 1917, however, the Federation succeeded in securing a flat-rate increase in wages for all grades over all districts, known as the 'war-wage', amounting to 1s 6d a day for all colliery workers 16 years of age and over, and 9d a day for those under 16. In June 1918 the miners secured a second war wage of an equivalent amount.

Before the end of the war the M.F.G.B., encouraged by its success in securing from the Government wage increases on a national scale and by the vague promises of politicians of a 'brave new world', decided to seek a substantial improvement in the standard of living of its entire membership. The M.F.G.B. Annual Conference in 1918 had adopted resolutions calling for a wage increase, a six-hour working day and nationalization of the mines 'with joint control and administration by the workmen and the State.'[3]

The demand for nationalization of the mines had a long history

---

[1] For an account of this strike see R. P. Arnot, *The Miners: Years of Struggle*, London 1953, Chapter IV.
[2] *Ibid.*, pp. 161–3.
[3] M.F.G.B., 10–11 July 1918.

before 1918. Behind this demand, but quite distinct from it, was the old Radical idea that the mines and minerals should belong to the nation. In 1886 John Wilson, a strong advocate of land nationalization, proposed a T.U.C. inquiry into the possibility of nationalizing mineral royalties.[1] Two motions, one for nationalization of mines and another for the resumption of State ownership of minerals, were unanimously accepted by the Trades Union Congress in 1892,[2] but it was not until 1894 that the M.F.G.B. discussed the idea of the actual process of mining being carried on under public ownership. In view of the strong Liberal element within the Federation the resolutions calling for mines nationalization remained little more than expressions of opinion. The first real practical effort came in July 1912 following the appointment of Robert Smillie as the Federation's Acting President and the advent of leadership from the 'Left'. In October 1912 the Federation's Annual Conference approved a draft parliamentary Bill for the nationalization of the mines.[3] The Bill was presented to the House of Commons in 1913 by the miners' M.P.s but was not discussed. The outbreak of war postponed any further attempts to secure nationalization. When the demand was taken up again in 1918 with the publication of a second Federation Bill it provided for the first time for workmen's participation in the control of the mines by Pit Committees, District Councils and a National Board.[4]

The benefits of substituting a system of State control of the mines in place of individual ownership were particularly obvious to miners in Durham. The existing structure of ownership was essentially decentralized and hindered the demand for a national system of wage regulation. The general level of wages in any particular district depended, in normal times, upon the precise relationship between the price of coal and the cost of production. Both of these items were liable to fluctuate and especially so in coal exporting regions such as Durham where the fortunes of the industry were closely linked to movements in the trade cycle. This militated against the establishment of a general uniformity in the level of miners' wages throughout the various districts. The miners in Durham, subject to the same dangers and inconveniences as miners elsewhere, had to suffer greater fluctuations in the capacity of their district to pay adequate wages than those in districts producing mainly for the more stable home market. A system of national rates for every class of labour, such as existed

[1] T.U.C. *Report*, 1886.
[2] *Ibid.*, 1892.
[3] M.F.G.B., 3 October 1912.
[4] Arnot, *op. cit.*, Chapter VIII, Appendix A, pp. 220–3.

for the railwaymen, was not practicable in the coal mining industry where conditions and methods of working varied so much between different districts. Nor did it seem possible to secure the enforcement of standard rates for the principal grades within each coalfield and a general uniformity in wages throughout all the coalfields unless the basic structure of the industry was changed.

The M.F.G.B. did not press its demands for nationalization and improvements in wages and hours until after the signing of the armistice in November 1918 and after the general election during the following month. On 9 January 1919 the M.F.G.B. Executive Committee met Sir Guy Calthrop, Controller of Coalmines, to discuss the proposed wage advance of 30 per cent upon total earnings (exclusive of 'war wage'). Robert Smillie, President of the Federation, explained that the demand was based partly upon the increase in the cost of living and the price of coal but mainly upon:

'. . . the value of the miner's labour, and on the fact that right down through the ages practically the miner has not been adequately or fairly remunerated for his work, and the families of miners have not had the living conditions which they had a right to expect'.[1]

The M.F.G.B. directed its attention to the problems of demobilization whilst the Government considered the demands. The problems of the reinstatement of men to the mines and the unrest amongst the troops, anxious as they were to return to civilian life, pointed to the need for action. Already on 16 December 1918 representatives of the Durham miners and coal owners had met in Newcastle to discuss the procedure for dealing with miners returning from the Forces. A Demobilization Committee had been established consisting of an equal number of owners' and workers' representatives. The Committee sought to ensure the employment of all demobilized miners at their former collieries and at their former class of work. Local arrangements were to be made for miners to undertake alternative work for short periods if there proved insufficient room to accommodate them at their former collieries. If the District Committee failed to secure a miner his former job and failed to secure a place elsewhere in the district his case was passed to the Coal Controller's Advisory Board with a view to finding employment in another district or, in the case of men prevented from occupying their former job due to military disablement, for re-training for another occupation.[2]

[1] M.F.G.B., 9 January 1919.
[2] D.M.A., 6 January 1919.

A special M.F.G.B. conference on 14–16 January decided to put forward a number of demobilization demands. During the discussions Peter Lee reminded delegates:

> 'We owe a duty to these men who have come back and are coming back to see that they are returned to the mines and if places cannot be found to see that they are paid a decent wage until they can.'[1]

The conference consequently demanded the release of miners from the armed forces and their reinstatement in the mines they left at the time of enlistment; payment of wages appropriate to their former grade for miners unable to perform a normal day's work; training for suitable work, with maintenance allowance, for disabled men and payment of unemployment benefits equivalent to miners' wages for men displaced by ex-servicemen. It was also decided to press the Government to amend the Eight Hours Act and substitute 'six hours' in place of 'eight hours' in the Act and to nationalize all mines and minerals.[2]

Representatives of the M.F.G.B. and the Government met on 31 January to discuss these demands. The only outcome of the meeting, however, was a pledge by Sir Robert Horne, Minister of Labour, that all the questions at issue, including the wage demand put forward on 9 January, would be considered by the Cabinet.[3] The Government replied to these various demands on 10 February. It offered an additional 'war wage' of a shilling a day to meet the increased cost of living and to submit the demands for a reduction in hours, a wage increase irrespective of the cost of living and the nationalization of the mines to a committee of inquiry which would also enquire into the general position of the coal trade. All but one of the demobilization demands were rejected on the grounds that they 'would put the miners in an exceptional position compared with the rest of citizens of the country' but the Government agreed to the creation of joint pit committees to help men find work and to administer unemployment benefits.[4] A special conference of the M.F.G.B. held on 12–13 February rejected the proposals, recommended a strike ballot to be taken and urged members to vote in favour of a stoppage. Joseph Batey enquired of the conference whether or not the miners could rely upon the support of the Triple Alliance. Smillie pointed out that as no formal action had been decided upon the miners would have to ballot on the issue on the understanding that they may have

---

[1] M.F.G.B., 14 January 1919.
[2] *Ibid.*, 15 January 1919.
[3] *Ibid.*, 31 January 1919.
[4] *Ibid.*, 10 February 1919; P.R.O., Cab. 23/9.

to fight alone.[1] 'The rapidity with which the decision to reject the Government's terms was arrived at was remarkable,' commented the *Northern Echo*, '. . . it justified the forecast that the Federation would be found in a fighting mood.'[2]

Nor was enthusiasm lacking in the districts. Cann promptly issued a letter to all Lodge members urging them to make speedy arrangements for conducting the ballot the results of which were to be returned to London by 22 February.[3] The Durham Miners' Association offered no direct advice to its members as to how they should vote although suggestions were not lacking from other quarters. The *Northern Echo*, whilst accepting that the Federation had made out a case for a reduction in hours and an increase in wages, continually urged the Durham miners to reconsider the offer with regard to the position of the industry:

'What the miners have not been able to show,' it claimed, 'is that the coal mining industry is in a position to stand the cost of these and other demands without injury to itself or the national industry of which coal is an important raw material. This is a matter which concerns the coal-worker equally as much as it concerns the coal-owners—whether State or individual—and for this reason the miners should welcome the Board of Inquiry which the Government offers.'[4]

The result of the ballot in Durham was a majority in favour of a strike by 76,024 votes to 16,248. The national figures were 615,164 in favour of a stoppage and 105,082 against.[5] Meanwhile Lloyd George took steps to avert the strike. On 21 February he invited the Executive Committee of the M.F.G.B. to meet him at Downing Street. He requested that the miners should delay the expiry of their strike notices, dated for 15 March, and take part in a Commission which would be required to present an interim report by 31 March. The Executive agreed to call a conference to consider the Government's proposals,[6] and a delegate conference met accordingly on 26 February to consider whether the miners should participate in the Commission.

Some delegates feared that an adverse report would prejudice the miners' case and were openly hostile to the Government's proposal.

[1] *Ibid.*, 12–13 February 1919.
[2] *Northern Echo*, 13 February 1919.
[3] D.M.A., 14 February 1919.
[4] *Northern Echo*, 18 February 1919.
[5] M.F.G.B., 26 February 1919.
[6] *Ibid.*, 21 February 1919.

Lee and Whiteley, displaying a touching faith in the usefulness of
Royal Commissions, pleaded for the miners' full participation in the
inquiry:

> 'Are we afraid to put our case before a Commission?', Lee asked
> the delegates. 'Did you ever hear tell of any Government doing
> a thing before some very important evidence was laid before them?
> If we are sure of our ground, and I am myself, I believe we have a
> case, granted an equal opportunity, that we can place before a
> Commission in this country that will prove that the miners are
> justly entitled to all which they seek.'[1]

W. Lowther, another Durham delegate, was more sceptical. Convinced that the recent strike ballot in defiance of the Government's
proposals bound the Federation to the wishes of the rank and file,
he warned delegates against entrusting their demands to a Commission and argued:

> 'We ought to decide to accept the verdict given by the rank and file
> and not accept at this eleventh hour something which is nothing
> more or less than a new political dodge by Lloyd George, because
> we know what our claims are, and we have no right to go back on
> our demands.'[2]

On the following day, however, the Conference resolved unanimously to take part in the inquiry providing the Government agreed
that the Federation had the right of appointment or approval of half
the Commission. It also decided to postpone the expiry of strike
notices until 22 March.[3] On 24 February a Bill was introduced into
the House of Commons giving the proposed Commission full
statutory powers to compel the attendance of witnesses, the giving
of evidence, and the production of relevant documents. A Labour
Party motion urging the Government to concede the miners' demands
on wages and hours without further delay was defeated.[4] The Prime
Minister eventually agreed that the Commission's interim report
should be published by 20 March.[5] The Coal Industry Commission
Act stipulated in its first clause that the Commissioners were to
consist of 'a chairman, who shall be a judge of the Supreme Court,
a vice-chairman, and such other persons as His Majesty may think
fit'. It was eventually agreed that the miners should nominate four
Commissioners directly and two further workers' representatives
to be agreed upon between the miners and the Government, but

---

[1] *Ibid.*, 26 February 1919.
[2] *Ibid.*
[3] *Ibid.*, 27 February 1919.
[4] 112 H.C. Deb. 5s, 1492–6.
[5] 112 H.C. Deb. 5s, 1705–6.

formally nominated by the latter. The Federation nominated Robert Smillie, Herbert Smith, Frank Hodges and Sir Leo Chiozza Money. R. H. Tawney and Sidney Webb were agreed upon between the Government and the M.F.G.B. The employers were represented by three coal owners, Evan Williams, R. W. Cooper and J. T. Forgie and three Government nominees, Arthur Balfour, Sir Arthur Duckham and Sir Thomas Royden. Never before had a Royal Commission been appointed by an Act of Parliament nor had the contesting parties been allowed such direct representation.

Meanwhile in Durham there was continued friction in connection with demobilization despite the fact that the local Demobilization Committee, in theory at least, had power to secure some of the conditions of employment for which the Federation had fought in January. The workmen's representatives on the Committee reported that at several collieries in Durham a considerable number of workmen who had entered the mines since the war had been discharged to make way for returning soldiers.[1] Local efforts were made to ease the situation. The Consett Iron Company decided to re-open a drift around Chopwell and employ about 400 demobilized men and youths.[2] In March a scheme was devised at Seaton Delaval Colliery for placing demobilized miners temporarily on datal work until work of the necessary type became available.[3] Miners at Hebburn Colliery were offered employment at Wallsend Colliery in order to make room for returning soldiers, a move that necessitated crossing the River Tyne, with miners often failing to arrive at work at all during stormy weather.[4] A positive step towards safeguarding wage standards was made on 2 June when the Durham Miners' Association and Durham Coal Owners' Association agreed that putters and hewers displaced from their normal work owing to returning soldiers should be paid the County standard of wages,[5] according to their particular class, whenever they were sent to inferior work.[6]

II

The Coal Industry Commission began its public examination of witnesses on 4 March. Within the first week the evidence of Government officials and representatives of interests linked to the coal

[1] Durham Coal Owners' Association, *Annual Report*, 1919, p. 48.
[2] *Colliery Guardian*, 24 January 1919.
[3] *Ibid.*, 21 March 1919.
[4] *Minutes of the Demobilization Committee*, 7 April 1919.
[5] See above, pp. 22-3.
[6] *Minutes of the Demobilization Committee*, 7 April 1919.

industry weighed heavily against the private enterprise system and provided a sufficiently alarming background to help swing public opinion in favour of the miners. A. L. Dickinson, Financial Adviser to the Coal Mines Department, gave evidence of the financial position of the coal industry down to September 1918 and of the substantial profits earned during the war years.[1] Evidence on behalf of Durham coal owners was presented by R. Guthrie, Secretary of the Durham Coal Owners' Association;[2] S. Hare, Mining Engineer and member of the Durham Coal Owners' Association [3] and A. F. Pease, Chairman of Pease and Partners, Ltd.[4]

The coal owners attempted to show that the effect of the miners' claim would be ruinous to the industry. The effect of further reducing the length of the working day in Durham in light of the existing hours structure, especially of hewers, played an important part in the coal owners' case. Guthrie estimated that the proposed reduction in hours would reduce the effective working time of Durham hewers at the coal face from 5 hours 20 minutes to 4 hours 36 minutes.[5] These estimates were later confirmed by Hare who further concluded that the establishment of a six-hour day in Durham would, assuming no additional trained labour was available underground, reduce total coal output by 19 per cent which in turn, were the demand for a 30 per cent advance on existing earnings to be granted, would increase labour costs by 3s 0·14d per ton.[6] To maintain the existing level of output in the coalfield under a six-hour day, he claimed, would necessitate a 13·75 per cent increase in the total number of hewers employed and a 25 per cent increase in the numbers of all other workers,[7] allowing collieries employing three shifts of hewers and two shifts of transit hands [8] to continue working only 'with disastrous financial results'.[9] The resulting tendency of management to adopt a system of working two shifts of hewers and one shift of transit hands would also create its own problems. Was there a sufficient number of pits already working under a three shift system with enough pit room to allow for the change to a two-shift system? Would the haulage and winding systems at the pits be able to cope with the increase in quantity per hour which would be necessary in

[1] Coal Industry Commission, 1919, I, QQ. 45–69.
[2] Ibid., QQ. 1–21; 6175–6201; 6205–6209.
[3] Ibid., QQ. 7430–7585.
[4] Ibid., QQ. 7661–7889.
[5] Ibid., Q. 6180.
[6] Ibid., QQ. 7434, 7436.
[7] Ibid., Q. 7436.
[8] See above, p. 20.
[9] Coal Industry Commission, 1919, I, Q. 7434.

order to maintain output under the reduced hours available for haulage and winding?

The miners' evidence in support of their claim for increased wages and reduced hours was presented to the Commission not by district witnesses but by Federation delegates. A M.F.G.B. Sub-Committee, under Robson's chairmanship, had decided on 7 March to appoint four witnesses to present the Federation's evidence each dealing with a particular aspect of their claim. J. Potts (Yorkshire) dealt with wages, J. Robertson (Scotland) with the miners' standard of living, V. Hartshorn (S. Wales) with the question of hours and W. Straker (Northumberland) with nationalization.[1] Cann and Richardson had suggested to the Federation on 12 March that a witness from Durham should be included in the syndicate 'in consequence of the references in the Commission to Durham and the evidence as to the effect of the short hours which operate in that district at the present time'. The request was refused.[2]

The substance of the evidence given before the Commission is well known and need not be reiterated here. It is worth noting, however, that much of the strength of the miners' evidence lay in their claim for a higher standard of living and the evidence of the appalling social conditions within the Durham coalfield helped to reinforce their claim.[3]

As the first stage of the Commission's enquiry came to a close it had become abundantly clear that private ownership of the mines was detrimental to the best interests of the nation from whatever standpoint it was viewed. Whilst the Commissioners deliberated over the evidence so far presented others were quick to formulate their own conclusions. Cann, reviewing the situation in March, confessed:

'That the outstanding impression created is that, no matter what the case may have been for an immediate betterment of the wages and conditions of the miners themselves, at any rate an unanswerable case has been made out for the nationalization of the mines.'[4]

Continuing, he asked:

'Why should a man's employment in the production of a commodity which it has taken more than $4\frac{1}{2}$ years of unparalleled warfare to prove to be absolutely an imperative national asset, be at the mercy

[1] M.F.G.B., 7 March 1919.
[2] *Ibid.*, 12 March 1919.
[3] See Chapter VII.
[4] D.M.A., *Monthly Circular*, January–February 1919, p. 6.

of the private speculator? . . . Coal is not the product of a man's brain; and as it is absolutely essential to the welfare of the State, to the State it ought to belong.'[1]

The question of nationalization had to await the second stage of the enquiry although preliminary observations on this issue were contained in two of the Commissioners' interim reports. By 20 March the Commissioners had presented not one but three interim reports—a lack of unanimity which was not surprising considering the partisan composition of the Commission. The Majority Report, signed by Smillie, Hodges, Smith, Money, Tawney and Webb, was in full sympathy with the miners' demands, recognizing their plea as 'essentially one for justice'.[2] It recommended that the miners' claim for a 30 per cent wage advance and a six-hour working day (exclusive of winding times), with 'corresponding reductions' in the hours of surface workers should be granted and that the demobilization demands should be dealt with 'along with the cases of men in other industries'.[3] The Sankey Report' signed by the Chairman, Justice Sankey, Balfour, Duckham and Royden, recommended the introduction of a seven-hour day from 16 July 1919 and, 'subject to the economic position of the industry at the end of 1920', a further reduction in the length of the working day to six hours from 13 July 1921. Surface workers were to have a $46\frac{1}{2}$-hour week, exclusive of meal times, the details to be settled locally. Wages were to be increased by 2s a day 'in the case of the classes of colliery workers, employed in coal mines, whose wages in the past have been regulated by colliery sliding scales'.[4] The three coal owners' representatives recommended a wage increase of 1s 6d a day, a seven-hour day for underground workers and an eight-hour day for surface workers.[5]

The Sankey Report further stated that 'the present system of ownership and working in the coal industry stands condemned' and that 'it is in the interests of the country that the colliery worker shall in the future have an effective voice in the direction of the mine'.[6] The Majority Report recommended that 'nationalization ought to be, in principle, at once determined on'.[7] The coal owners' representatives remained silent on the question of the future organization of the industry.

[1] Ibid.
[2] Coal Industry Commission, 1919, I, p. xiv.
[3] Ibid.
[4] Ibid., p. vii.
[5] Ibid., pp. xii–xxiii.
[6] Ibid., pp. viii–ix.
[7] Ibid., p. xii.

The three reports were discussed in Parliament on 20 March. Bonar Law, speaking for the Cabinet, announced that the Government had adopted the Sankey Report 'in the spirit as well as in the letter'.[1] The Executive Committee of the M.F.G.B. met Bonar Law on 22 March and again on 25 March to press for a number of amendments to the Sankey proposals including a reduction of surfacemen's hours to 45 per week (inclusive of meal times), the introduction of the six-hour day from 12 July 1920, a wage increase of 2s 6d a day, a revision of piece-work rates to prevent any reduction in earnings consequent upon a reduction in hours, the addition of the wage increase to the sixth shift of a 'bonus turn' (i.e. six shifts for five) and the retrospective payment of the wage increase from 9 January 1919.[2] The Government finally agreed to concede the latter three demands but refused to make any further alteration in the recommendations of the Sankey Report.[3] An M.F.G.B. conference on 26 March decided to take a ballot on the Government's proposals on 9–10 April and agreed to recommend their acceptance.[4] The strike notices had expired on 22 March but the Federation had previously decided on 21 March to recommend that the men continue working on day-to-day contracts.

Durham delegates had remained almost silent during the Federations's deliberations following the publication of the interim reports. The Association's Executive Committee, however, took every opportunity to prepare local miners for the forthcoming ballot. They anticipated an overwhelming majority in favour of the Government's proposals but in order to ensure that the miners fully understood what lay behind the provisions of the Government's offer organized six mass meetings throughout the County on 6 April.[5] Meetings were arranged at Blaydon, Monkwearmouth, Hetton, Durham, West Stanley and Bishop Auckland. The following resolution in support of the Government's offer was submitted and carried unanimously at each meeting:

'That this meeting expresses its utmost confidence in our representatives on the Coal Commission, and it further agrees that in view of the valuable results gained as contained in Judge Sankey's Report, coupled with the important fact that the Commission is to continue in its work and deal with nationalization of mines and other important subjects, we strongly recommend our members to vote

[1] 113 H.C. Deb. 5s, 2346. For details see P.R.O., Cab. 23/9.
[2] M.F.G.B., 21 March 1919.
[3] *Ibid.*, 25 March 1919.
[4] *Ibid.*, 26 March 1919.
[5] D.M.A., 28, 31 March 1919.

solidly in favour of accepting the Government's offer as contained in the said Sankey Report.'[1]

As anticipated there was a huge majority in Durham in favour of accepting the terms, 95,648 voting for and only 6,845 voting against. The national figures were 693,084 for and 76,992 against. A special conference of the M.F.G.B. on 16 April decided that all strike notices should be withdrawn.[2]

III

With the acceptance of the Government's terms the Commission was able to enter upon its second stage of enquiry on 23 April. The Commission sat until 23 June and examined a total of 116 witnesses. In the interval between the two stages of inquiry Sir Thomas Royden had resigned owing to ill-health and was succeeded by Sir Allan Smith, Chairman of the Engineering Employers' Federation. Shortly after the second stage began, J. T. Forgie was forced to resign through ill-health and was succeeded by Sir Adam Nimmo, former adviser to the Coal Controller.

The Commission undertook a comprehensive investigation of the various proposals submitted for the future organization of the industry. The Government's acceptance of the Sankey Report—containing a serious condemnation of the existing structure of the coal industry—led the miners to believe that full consideration would be given to the reorganization of the industry. W. P. Richardson chose mines nationalization as the subject of a series of lectures sponsored by the Workers' Educational Association which he delivered at the Miners' Hall in Durham during April. Violently attacking the waste, inefficiency and unfairness of the system of private ownership of the mines and criticizing the structure of royalties and wayleaves (by which one Durham landowner received 4d for every ton of coal that passed over a strip of land not more than 20 yards in dimension) he listed the benefits he believed miners would receive from nationalization. They included the abolition of unemployment, better layout of mines, greater safety, abolition of unfair competition, greater efficiency in workmanship by reason of better hours and wages, a reduction of waste and the greater development of the by-product industry.[3]

Though Richardson, renowned as an advocate of nationalization, may have been convinced in its favour the Coal Commission had yet

[1] *Northern Echo*, 7 April 1919.
[2] M.F.G.B., 16 April 1919.
[3] *Northern Echo*, 16 April 1919.

to make up its mind. The evidence of Durham coal and royalty owners as to the extent of their mineral possessions and royalty incomes was fully exploited by the Labour side of the Commission. John Lambton, Earl of Durham and Lord Lieutenant of the County, confessed that he owned 12,411 acres of coal-bearing land in Durham and that in 1918 he received over £40,522 from royalty rents and wayleaves. During 1913–18 Charles Vane-Tempest-Stewart, seventh Marquis of Londonderry and owner of Londonderry Collieries Ltd., received an income from mineral royalties and wayleaves amounting to over £15,334 or almost 4½d per ton of coal produced. Both Lambton and Stewart were forced to defend their claim to an undisputed right to the ownership and reward from their property in face of the skilful cross-examination of Frank Hodges and Herbert Smith.[1]

The coal owners' determined opposition to nationalization was most clearly expressed by Baron Gainford of Headlam, chief witness of the Mining Association of Great Britain, Vice-Chairman of Pease and Partners Ltd. and a member of the Durham Coal Owners' Association. In his evidence to the Commission he claimed:

'I am convinced, through actual experience as a director of collieries and as a Minister of the Crown [2] that the nationalization of the industry would be nothing less than a disaster to the nation. I believe the nation as a whole . . . is convinced that State management of industrial enterprise means waste, inefficiency and want of progress. State ownership and management should be resorted to only if the peculiar circumstances of the specific undertaking precludes resort to private ownership or management . . . I utterly reject the idea that any such particular circumstances attach to the mining industry.'[3]

In support of his evidence Gainford quoted the history of the development of Horden Collieries Ltd. 'as an example of the necessity of private enterprise in the development of coal mines'.[4] Quoting from a letter from E. R. Whitwell, Managing Director of the Company, dated 2 May 1919, he gave evidence of the company's early difficulties. Criticized as a 'speculative flotation' in its early years it soon ran into financial difficulties and the Company's directors and their friends were forced through lack of public support to raise four-fifths

[1] Coal Industry Commission, 1919, II, QQ. 14,177–14,403; 14,561–14,608; 15,242–15,283.
[2] He had previously been Chancellor of the Duchy of Lancaster, President of the Board of Education and Postmaster-General.
[3] Coal Industry Commission, 1919, II, Q. 19,671.
[4] *Ibid.*

of the required capital. The problems of sinking shafts, pumping water and driving main haulage-ways through stone, especially at the Blackhall and Shotton collieries, involved considerable expense and constituted problems which, Whitwell claimed, would not have been overcome had it not been for the 'indomitable perseverance and courage' of the general manager of Horden Collieries Ltd. Whilst Gainford refused to suggest that such services would not be forth-coming under a system of State Control he added '. . . what I do suggest is that under the system of nationalization he would never have had the chance'.[1]

Before any considered opinon on the nationalization issue could be given evidence had to be heard from the workers' representatives. H. Slesser, standing counsel to the M.F.G.B., submitted a draft Parliamentary Bill outlining the miners' scheme for the nationaliza-tion of the mines ably supported by evidence from W. Straker of the Northumberland Miners' Mutual Confident Association.[2] Miners' wives from Lancashire, South Wales and Scotland gave further evi-dence of the condition of the miner's life.[3] S. Webb and Sir Leo Chiozza Money, both members of the Commission, gave detailed evidence in support of nationalization and submitted individual plans for schemes of ownership and management of the mines.[4]

Whilst the Commission was in session both the coal owners and the miners' leaders sought to influence public opinion in their favour. Shareholders of the Weardale Steel, Coal and Coke Company were urged by letter to contact as many Members of Parliament as possible demanding that they sign a memorandum circulated by the Company protesting against mines nationalization.[5] Representatives of important coal-consuming industries throughout Durham as-sembled at the Commercial Exchange at Newcastle on 26 May demanding adequate consultation of their various interests prior to any decision being made upon the future organization of the coal industry.[6] At its meeting on 27 May the Executive Committee of the Durham Miners' Association strongly protested against this Con-ference and urged authorities not only to refuse the requests put forward but also 'to introduce further enquiries so that the industries with which they have been particularly connected may be subject to the same enquiry, when we feel sure that similar revelations as to

[1] *Ibid.*
[2] *Ibid.*, QQ. 22,041–22,204; 22,619–22,622; 22,853–23,223; 23,224–23,765.
[3] *Ibid.*, QQ. 24,333–24,537.
[4] *Ibid.*, QQ. 11,610–11,935; 12,014–13,071.
[5] *Durham Chronicle*, 28 July 1919.
[6] *Ibid.*, 30 May 1919.

profiteering, exploitation and even waste will be brought to the knowledge of the Country as a whole'.[1] Two weeks later a conference of the Lodges in the eastern part of the coalfield was called for the purpose of reaffirming the Association's stand in favour of nationalization and calling upon an early decision by the Commission in support of that ideal.[2]

The Commissioners eventually reported on 20 June and again presented divergent reports. All agreed in proposing the immediate nationalization of mining royalties, the undertaking of the retail distribution of coal by local government authorities and the establishment of Pit Committees of the workmen and District Councils and a National Board on which both workers and owners would be represented. The Chairman's report proposed the immediate introduction of a system of local administration under the supervision of the Coal Controller with public ownership following after the scheme had been in operation for three years.[3] The six miners' representatives on the Commission, although in substantial agreement with the Chairman's recommendations, drew up a separate report objecting to the proposed procedure for settling disputes by imposing upon the workers a legally binding contract. They also recommended the nationalization of all coke and by-product plants attached to collieries, an immediate enquiry into allegations that miners were responsible for the decline in coal output and a speedy remedy of shortages of tubs, wagons and materials. Hodges, Smith and Smillie further objected to any compensation of royalty owners.[4]

The coal owners' representatives and the Government nominees, with the exception of Duckham, refused to entertain any change in the existing system of private ownership except to agree to the establishment of consultative pit committees.[5] Duckham, in a separate report, offered a scheme for 'district unification' of collieries as an alternative to nationalization. He agreed to the necessity for the abolition of the existing colliery companies and recommended their compulsory union, coalfield by coalfield, into District Trusts. These trusts would be partially controlled by representatives of the miners and the community as a whole, be public in character and carry shares with a minimum rate of dividend guaranteed by the Government.[6]

Since the Government had already committed itself in principle to the adoption of the first 'Sankey Report', initial reaction to the Commission's findings centred upon the possibility or otherwise of

[1] D.M.A., 27 May 1919.
[2] *Northern Echo*, 16 June 1919.
[3] Coal Industry Commission, 1919, II, pp. iv–xiii.
[4] *Ibid.*, pp. xii–xiv.
[5] *Ibid.*, pp. xiv–xxi.
[6] *Ibid.*, pp. xxii–xviii.

the Government submitting to further demands to nationalize the mines. The coal owners in Durham and Northumberland were quick to express their continued opposition to such a move. At their joint meeting in Newcastle on 28 June they resolved:

'That in the event of the Government proposing to introduce legislation to carry out the Chairman's proposals all possible measures will be taken to bring the facts of the situation before Parliament and the public with a view to securing the rejection of any measure intended to carry out nationalization of the coal industry.'[1]

IV

Meanwhile in Durham negotiations had been progressing between representatives of the miners' and coal owners' Associations over the necessary arrangements for implementing the reduction in hours under the 'Sankey award'. The precise effect of this legal reduction was different in Durham from elsewhere owing to the County's existing structure of working hours. As in 1908 not every Durham mineworker benefited to the full extent of the law. The substitution of 'seven hours' for 'eight hours' in the Eight Hours' Act established in effect a normal working day of seven plus one winding time but reduced the maximum time spent underground by one hour. The reduction did not affect Durham hewers, the largest proportion of the underground piece workers employed in the coalfield,[2] as the agreement regarding their hours of work, signed in 1890, had safeguarded them from any change in 1908. The transit hands, already working the full hours prescribed by law, benefited to the full extent of an hour's reduction in time spent underground. Other underground workers, including stonemen, shifters and wastemen, already working an eight hour bank-to-bank shift and therefore spending less than eight hours in their recognized working shift, i.e. excluding winding time,[3] benefited only to the extent of the difference between their existing working time underground and the maximum prescribed by law. It is possible to estimate from statistics supplied to the Sankey Commission[4] the average winding time in Durham during 1919 to be

[1] *Durham Chronicle*, 4 July 1919.
[2] In 1919 out of a total of 51,849 underground piece workers employed in Durham 38,887 were hewers the remainder being accounted for largely by stonemen, shifters and transit workers i.e. putters, onsetters and wagonwaymen. M.F.G.B., 25 July 1919.
[3] See above, pp. 19–20.
[4] Coal Industry Commission, 1919, III, Appendix 25, pp. 44–5.

23 minutes, thus providing an underground working shift for these classes of 7 hours 37 minutes. The difference, therefore, in the maximum time they spent in their working shift as a result of the Seven Hours Act, compared with under an eight-hour bank-to-bank system was only 37 minutes. From less precise figures Durham delegates to the national Federation announced in July 1919 that the reduction in working time for this class of miner varied from 40 to 35 to 30 minutes but averaged 40 minutes.[1]

The detailed local arrangements necessary to implement the change in hours and working conditions were the subject of numerous meetings between owners and men during May–July 1919. During these negotiations it became obvious to the miners' representatives that the owners were prepared to adjust working conditions not only in accordance with the law but in such a way as to provide long-term benefits to the miners as a whole. Before the negotiations opened the Durham Miners' Association had decided to use the occasion for bargaining to the fullest possible advantage by seeking to deal with such long-standing grievances as the need to equalize hours and conditions, to abolish the custom of large collieries on the east coast working a third shift of 7 hours 10 minutes and to terminate once and for all the system of three-shift working.

At a meeting on 3 July the owners agreed to reduce the working time at east coast pits to seven hours 'providing arrangements can be made on all other points' and proposed that at all two-shift pits hewers were to work seven hours bank-to-bank in the 'first shift' and six and three quarters hours bank-to-bank in the 'back shift' while all other underground workers were to work two complete shifts of seven hours bank-to-bank. In three-shift pits, however, hewers' shifts were to remain 'as at present' and the hours of all other classes underground to be the maximum legally provided. The arrangements for the two-shift system of working were to apply equally to those three-shift pits which at any time reverted to a two-shift system.[2]

The Association's Executive quickly realized the potential advantages of the owners' proposals for two-shift pits. Although they increased the average working time of hewers from six and three-quarter hours to 6 hours 52 minutes bank-to-bank, the hours of all other underground workers would be less than those prescribed under the law since their working day would include, rather than exclude, one winding time. The absence of such concessions in three-shift pits, it was hoped, would eventually rid the County of the third shift—

[1] M.F.G.B., 15 July 1919.
[2] D.M.A., 4 July 1919.

the adoption of which had become increasingly popular since 1908.[1] At the time of the negotiations approximately 12,000 hewers were working at two-shift pits but judging from the willingness of colliery managers to revert from a three-shift to two-shift system of working, the Association calculated that within twelve months two-thirds of the total number of hewers in the County could be working under a two-shift system.[2] Hewers, however, numerically the strongest in the Union, would have to work on an average seven and a half minutes longer in order that other underground workers could work for a shorter period.

The miners were left to decide for themselves. Following a vote amongst the Lodges the owners' proposals regarding two and three shift pits were rejected by 433 votes to 304.[3] The result proved a bitter disappointment to the Association's Executive. Cann regarded the rejection as 'nothing more or less than a golden opportunity to improve the condition of the mining community in Durham County frittered away'.[4] In his monthly circular to union members published in July he further bemoaned their rejection of the owners' scheme thus:

'One of the shortcomings of the three shift system that has always appealed to me as being most pernicious in its effects is the most slavish demands it makes upon many of our women-folk. The drudgery of domestic life has always been a pronounced one; but there is no gain-saying the fact that with an increase in the three shift system this already too-acute drudgery was considerably accentuated. ... It was in the earnest hope of minimizing, if not doing away to a large extent with, the sacrifice of these willing slaves that I was profoundly impressed with the scheme. ...'[5]

The will of the majority, or more especially that of the hewers, had prevailed. The Executive Committee of the Miners' Association immediately informed the owners that the rank and file were opposed to any lengthening of hewers' hours even by seven and a half minutes but in addition sought a guarantee that all collieries would be working a two-shift system within five years.[6] On 10 July 1919 the miners' and owners' representatives finally agreed that hewers should continue to work the existing hours per shift and that the hours of all other under-ground workers would be as legally provided, the details of the

[1] See above, p. 20.
[2] D.M.A., 4 July 1919.
[3] Ibid., 14 July 1919.
[4] D.M.A., Monthly Circular, May–June 1919, p. 5.
[5] Ibid., pp. 5–6.
[6] D.M.A., 5 August 1919.

timing of the shifts to be settled locally. Surface workers were to work an 8 hour 5 minute shift including twenty minutes for meal times.[1] It was further agreed that there should be an overall increase of 12½ per cent in piece-work rates to compensate underground workers for the loss of working time suffered through the reduction in hours. All classes of workmen received the same amount of compensation irrespective of the amount of time lost.

Earlier in July Sir Evan Jones, who had been appointed Coal Controller in March following the death of Sir Guy Calthrop, had issued a circular limiting the amount to be paid in any district in compensation for lost working time to 10 per cent.[2] This decision was based upon the Sankey Commission's prediction that there would be a 10 per cent reduction in output following the reduction in working hours. This estimate did not, however, take into account the large numbers of hewers in Northumberland and Durham who were unaffected by the change. The miners were not prepared to accept an addition of only 10 per cent to their piece-work rates even if they accepted that their efficiency was increased. Transit hands alone in Durham would suffer, on the basis of the calculations made of winding times, a reduction in effective working time of over 13 per cent.

An M.F.G.B. conference on 17 July decided to seek from the Government a 14·3 per cent advance for piece workers.[3] Meanwhile miners in Yorkshire had stopped work over the piece-rate controversy and Derbyshire miners came out on strike on 21 July against the advice of their leaders. These counties were still idle when a sub-committee of the M.F.G.B. Executive Committee met the Coal Controller on 24 July to attempt to arrive at a settlement which would satisfy every district. On the following day the M.F.G.B. Executive met the Prime Minister and agreed upon a formula which gave an increase of 14·2 per cent for the loss of an hour's working time. The formula was as follows:[4]

The reduction in output as calculated over the whole country viz. 11·1%	×	The reduction in point of time in respect of any given class of workmen in the district in question

$$\frac{}{47}$$

The constant represented the average reduction in minutes in working time for the whole country. Previously determined to be

[1] *Ibid.*, 11 July 1919.
[2] M.F.G.B., 4 July 1919.
[3] *Ibid.*, 17 July 1919.
[4] *Ibid.*, 25 July 1919.

50 minutes it was eventually adjusted by three minutes to account for the complications of interpreting the change in hours in Yorkshire, Lancashire, Northumberland and Durham. In Yorkshire and Lancashire the one-hour reduction in working time was effective on only five of the six working days while over 51,000 hewers in Northumberland and Durham were not affected at all.[1] The adoption of a uniform $12\frac{1}{2}$ per cent advance for all classes in Durham gave underground workers, except hewers, an advance in piece-rate earnings greater than they would have received according to the formula whilst transit workers, subject to a full hour's reduction, gained less.

During negotiations with the owners over the implementation of the Sankey recommendations the Durham miners' leaders made a further request on behalf of deputies demanding a seven hour bank-to-bank shift instead of the existing seven and a half hours and additional pay for emergency overtime. The issue was not finally settled until August when a shift of seven hours plus one deputy's winding time, equivalent to five minutes, additional payment for overtime and an increase in the basic wage from 4s $8\frac{1}{2}$d to 5s 6d per day were agreed upon. Where deputies had been working longer than seven hours plus one winding since the introduction of the seven-hour day they were to be paid overtime at the old basic rate.[2] The agreement, represented with the current percentage addition to the new basic rate, an increase of over 1s 7d per shift. The Deputies' Association agreed to accept the offer on 22 August by a majority of 527 votes.[3]

V

On the day previous to the settlement of hours and working conditions in Durham the Government suddenly decided to increase the price of coal by 6s a ton. This came as a shock to the miners at large who had been content since the publication of the Commission's reports to await the decision of the Government as to the fate of the coal industry. No attempt had been made to clarify the precise conditions under which the Government would accept the Commission's findings—if it would at all. Nor did the M.F.G.B. do anything to counteract the vigorous campaign launched by the Chamber of Commerce, the coal owners and other industrialists against nationalization.

[1] *Ibid.*, 14, 24, 25 July 1919.
[2] D.M.A., 23 August 1919.
[3] *Ibid.*, 5 September 1919.

The announcement of an increase in coal prices, however, roused them from inactivity. The miners regarded the Government's decision as nothing less than an attempt to turn public opinion against them. The Executive Committee of the Durham Miners' Association at its meeting on 10 July 1919 promptly denounced the increase as 'only one of the many things that are now being done to prejudice the public mind against the nationalization of mines'.[1] The most vicious attack came from Cann. Writing in his monthly circular to members in July he exclaimed:

> 'There isn't the slightest doubt in my mind that this imposition of 6s per ton is one of the methods that has appealed to the Government as being a very potent, even though utterly unscrupulous, method of evading a moral obligation that was imposed upon them by the findings of the Commission they were a party to. . . . To avoid Nationalization the Government have joined the many groups of profiteers who are daily exploiting the consumer, and are being materially assisted by the supporters of private monopoly, who realize that under Nationalization the making of huge fortunes by the coal industry will be a closed door, always with the hope that the consumer can be so gulled as to believe that the tax is directly due to the demands of the miners for that better life so glibly promised them when their services were so urgently required, and so freely given, during the War.'[2]

The M.F.G.B. rejected a suggestion made by Bonar Law in the House of Commons on 14 July [3] that it give a pledge, in return for the post-ponement of the increase in the price of coal, that there should not be any strikes for three months. 'I hope we shall tell the Government . . . that we want something different to the withholding of the 6s', Peter Lee told a meeting of the Federation delegates. 'We want a declaration as to their attitude to the [Sankey] Report. Do they intend to honour that Report, or do they intend to give way to pressure from capitalists?'[4]

It was not until 18 August that Lee's question was answered. Speaking in the House of Commons Lloyd George announced that the Government had accepted State purchase of minerals, decided to establish a fund for improving amenities in the colliery villages and that the unification in the industry was to be promoted 'by amalgamation in defined areas'. Workers would be represented on area govern-

[1] *Ibid.*, 14 July 1919; *Northern Echo*, 11 July 1919.
[2] D.M.A., *Monthly Circular*, May–June 1919, p. 4.
[3] 118 H.C. Deb. 5s, 176.
[4] M.F.G.B., 17 July 1919.

ing boards. The amalgamation schemes were 'subject to the approval of the Government' and had to conform to conditions laid down by the Government 'for the protection of the general body of coal consumers'.[1]

Protest from the coalfields over the rejection of nationalization was as inevitable as it was strong. The reaction of the Durham miners' leaders, however, was by no means uniform. The younger Agents condemned the Government outright. 'In my opinion,' Robson claimed, 'the Prime Minister has been the object of strong solicitations by the coal owners and financiers of the country.'[2] On the other hand Cann, the oldest of the officials, resorted to excusing the Government's action on account of the country's weak financial condition. 'Bearing in mind our perilous position, and remembering the advantages already received from the Sankey Report by increases in wages and shortening of hours,' he claimed, 'I do not think it would be wise, or to the ultimate advantage of any section, to harass the Government unduly at the present juncture.'[3] The Association's Executive Committee did not share his conciliatory feelings and at its meeting on 20 August condemned the Government's rejection of the Sankey recommendations for the nationalization of mines.[4] Certainly the Government's betrayal of the miners' trust was destined to embitter relations between the two parties for many years to come. Mines nationalization in 1919 would not by itself have solved all the coal industry's problems but would probably have avoided the deep mistrust of the Government which miners' leaders nurtured well before the outbreak of the 1926 dispute.[5]

Announcing their intention to organize a series of mass meetings throughout the County in support of mines nationalization the Executive Committee reaffirmed the miners' opposition to private ownership of the industry in no uncertain terms:

'Let the ordinary householder and his wife remember that those who now own the mines desire to keep them. Why? Because they are doing well out of them. When the miners joined the Colours in

[1] 119 H.C. Deb. 5s, 2007.
[2] *Durham Chronicle*, 22 August 1919.
[3] *Ibid.*
[4] D.M.A., 20 August 1919.
[5] A. J. P. Taylor in his study, *English History, 1914–1945*, Oxford 1965, provides a misleading account of the Sankey Commission and its effects upon the miners. He ignores the previous acceptance by the Government of the interim Sankey Report and fails to appreciate the long-term consequences of the subsequent reversal of policy upon relations between the two parties. See J. Saville's critical review of the book in *Bulletin of the Society for the Study of Labour History*, 12, 1966, pp. 49–51.

their thousands they were heroes. When they ask that the land and
the mines should belong to the country they are robbers. "Britain
for the British" is our motto, and this includes the mines for the
people. The miners will respond to their country's need both on the
battlefield and in the coal mine, but they are not prepared to continue to produce wealth for the privileged few.'[1]

Twenty meetings were organized to take place on 27 September and
vigorous attempts made to secure support from the outside public—
especially women who now had the vote. In the meantime the
M.F.G.B. had rejected the Government's scheme of district unification of the industry as 'wholly impracticable', refused to recommend
industrial action to secure nationalization but had resolved to invite
the T.U.C. 'to declare that the fullest and most effective action be
taken to secure that the Government shall adopt the majority report
of the Commission as to the future governance of the industry'.[2] At
the T.U.C. meeting in Glasgow on 10 September the Parliamentary
Committee was instructed, with representatives of the M.F.G.B., to
interview the Prime Minister and insist upon the adoption of the
majority report. In the event of the Government's continued refusal
a Special Congress was to be called to decide upon further action.[3]
The T.U.C.'s decision was welcomed throughout Durham and at
each of the mass meetings held in September miners pledged themselves to loyally carry out such action as either the M.F.G.B. or
T.U.C. should decide upon in furtherance of the miners' demands.[4]
    The Prime Minister refused to alter his previous decision. In
December a special T.U.C. meeting launched 'The Mines for the
Nation' campaign. The campaign, coming as it did almost five
months after the Commission had reported, had little impact and
proved a failure. In January 1920 the M.F.G.B., after consultation
with C. W. Bowerman, secretary of the T.U.C. Parliamentary Committee, agreed to a special congress being held on 11 March to discuss
whether or not a general strike could be used to bring about nationalization of the mines, to be preceded by a Federation conference on 10
March.[5] The campaign for nationalization continued in the meantime
throughout colliery villages in Durham. In December 1919 the
Miners' Association had decided to pledge it full co-operation with
other sections of the Durham Miners' Federation Board, the Divi-

---

[1] D.M.A., 20 August 1919.
[2] M.F.G.B., 3 September 1919.
[3] *Colliery Guardian*, 12 September 1919; E. E. Barry, *Nationalization in British
Politics*, London 1965, p. 240.
[4] *Durham Chronicle*, 3 October 1919.
[5] M.F.G.B., 9 January 1919.

sional Labour Parties and any other organized groups willing to support a campaign for the end of private ownership of the mines.[1] A joint demonstration in favour of nationalization was organized in Durham City on 20 January 1920 by the Durham Labour Party in conjunction with the T.U.C., M.F.G.B., National Labour Party and Co-operative Union Ltd to which Robson was invited as principal speaker.[2]

At a special Council meeting of the Durham Miners' Association on 6 March it was decided to instruct the delegates to the special Federation congress on 10 March to vote in favour of political action to enforce nationalization following the decision of the Lodges, by a narrow majority of only 38 votes, to oppose industrial action.[3] Durham therefore joined six other districts voting against industrial action but was defeated by 524 votes to 344. At the special T.U.C. Congress on the day following the Federation conference the strength of the majority against strike action became apparent. It was decided by 3,732,000 votes to 1,050,000 not to call a general strike but to undertake intensive political propaganda in favour of mines nationalization. Despite the fact that their chances of securing this ideal seemed extremely doubtful the miners continued, at regular intervals, to urge the Government into action. Speaking at the Federation's Annual Conference in July 1920, Robson referred to nationalization as 'the only solution of all the problems connected with the mining industry' and moved a resolution urging the Government 'to bring about this fundamental change in the ownership and management of the industry'.[4]

VI

As the campaign for nationalization lapsed the miners focused their attention increasingly on the question of wages and prices in view of the continuing rise in the cost of living. The Ministry of Labour Index of Retail Prices (July 1914=100) stood at 215 in 1919 and rose to 249 in 1920.[5] At the same time as wages lagged behind the cost of living the immediate post-war boom in the coal export trade drove export prices and proceeds in Durham to unprecedented levels. F.o.b. coal export prices at Sunderland and Newcastle

[1] D.M.A., 31 December 1919.
[2] *Durham Chronicle*, 23 January 1920.
[3] D.M.A., 30 March 1920.
[4] M.F.G.B., 7 July 1920.
[5] B. R. Mitchell and P. Deane, *Abstract of British Historical Statistics*, Cambridge 1962, p. 478.

rose by over three-fifths during 1919–20.[1] The Durham miners, naturally anxious to share in the coalfield's good fortune, put forward a claim in November 1918 for an advance in wages. The realized selling price of coal for the quarter ending 30 September 1918 had reached 19s 11·26d exclusive of the 4s per ton charged by the Coal Controller to meet the liability of the 'war wage,' compared with 16s per ton during the equivalent quarter in 1917, an increase of 3s 11·26d. The miners claimed an advance equal to the full value of the increase in the selling price on the grounds that the 'war wage,' given for the specific purpose of meeting the increased cost of living, might at any time be reduced without in any way providing grounds for an increase in the general level of wages.[2]

The owners refused the request and the issue was brought before the M.F.G.B. At a meeting of the Federation in November, the Durham delegates were reminded of a previous resolution to determine all future wage changes on a national basis on the grounds that restriction of prices and profits under Government control made Conciliation Board procedures 'ineffective in securing further advances in wages in consequence of controlled selling prices'.[3] Since there was no restriction placed upon the price of coal exported to neutrals comparable with that put upon home market sales the Durham miners' leaders pleaded with the Federation to help secure for the miners in the coalfield an increased share of the proceeds from the coal export trade. Their efforts were in vain. The M.F.G.B. was determined to maintain negotiations on a national level. Robert Smillie told the Durham delegates on 27 November 1918, 'If we assist Durham, or Durham insists on going forward because for the moment prices justify their getting an increase, and they got an increase, there is nothing to prevent employers, where there is a reduction of prices, asking for a reduction in wages.'[4] The lag between wages and the cost of living, therefore, was felt most keenly in Durham where, in the particular circumstances of the time, miners were forced to forgo wage advances otherwise justified by the rising price of coal. In August 1919 the Association estimated that had wages been governed by the Conciliation Board the rise in the price of coal between the quarter ended 30 September 1917 and 30 June 1919 would have justified an increase in coal hewers' wages of 4s 6d per shift—6d less than the total flat rate additions actually made to his wages during the same period.[5]

[1] See Chapter I, p. 33.
[2] D.M.A., 11 November 1918.
[3] M.F.G.B., 11 July, 27 November 1918.
[4] *Ibid.*, 27 November 1918.
[5] D.M.A., 14 August 1919. Cf. *Durham Chronicle*, 13 February 1920.

By November 1919, however, the situation was different. Had the existing selling price of coal ruled it was estimated that coal hewers' wages would have stood at 15s 11d per shift compared with the 14s 6½d per shift that was actually paid.[1]

There were other grievances common to miners in all districts. Although the price of household coal had been reduced by 10s per ton from 1 December 1919 the miners felt that the price of industrial coal for home consumers was excessive. Furthermore domestic consumers, they claimed, were unable to obtain their supplies even at its reduced price and the continued high price of coal was seriously affecting the cost of living.[2] The Federation was determined therefore either 'that there should be an immediate and considerable reduction in the price of industrial coal' with a view to lowering the cost of living or, alternatively, that there should be 'an advance in wages consequent upon the high cost of living'.[3]

Following two unsuccessful meetings with the Government on 28 January and 19 February a special conference of the Federation decided on 12 March to demand an increase of 3s a day, dating from 1 March 1920.[4] Lee and Richardson realized that by the time such a demand was granted the majority of Durham miners would, under the conciliation procedure, have been entitled to more than had been asked for by the Federation. By February 1920 the total effect of the increase in the selling price of coal in Durham during the quarters ending 30 September 1919 and 30 December 1919 would have been to increase the wage per shift of coal hewers from 14s 6½d to 17s 3d, and prices were still rising.[5] Nevertheless Durham was bound by the decisions of the Federation and joined in voting in favour of the wage recommendation.

Following meetings between the Executive Committee of the M.F.G.B., the Prime Minister and A. R. Duncan, who had succeeded Sir Evan Jones as Coal Controller in October 1919, the Government made its final offer on 29 March. It proposed a 20 per cent advance on gross earnings, excluding the 'war wage' and the 'Sankey Wage', with a guaranteed minimum flat rate increase of 2s per shift for persons 18 years and over, 1s for those between 16 and 18, and 9d for those under 16. On the same day as the offer was made the M.F.G.B. decided to take a strike ballot, the results of which were to be reported to a special conference on 15 April.

In contrast to the policy of the national Federation which declined

---

[1] *Ibid.*, 12 November 1919.
[2] M.F.G.B., 8 January 1920.
[3] *Ibid.*
[4] *Ibid.*, 12 March 1920.
[5] M.F.G.B., 29 March 1920.

to advise members how to vote, the Executive Committee of the Durham Miners' Association urged its members to vote in favour of accepting the Government's offer.[1] It realized that whilst the offer was not all the miners desired it represented a substantial advance— the largest ever secured at one time. The minimum of 2s per shift advance for adults was of particular value to workmen with gross earnings below 10s. The value of accepting the offer was not limited, however, to pecuniary reward as the Executive Committee explained to members:

'There are more important matters than wages that need our attention, such as further reduction in hours, better houses, the elimination of private enterprise and monopoly from our industry, the right of the workman to have some say in the control and conducting of the mines and last, but not least, to join our comrades in other trades to deal with the high cost of living and the profiteers, who are sucking the life's blood out of the people. We believe that it is in the interests of these things and of our members that we should accept this offer, and thus clear the way for further activities in the interests of the common people.'[2]

Speaking at a meeting of miners in Murton on 4 April Robson declared that it would be 'absolute insanity' and a 'fatal step' if the miners were to vote against the offer.[3] The results of the voting in Durham showed a majority of 33,162 for acceptance. The national figures were 181,009 votes for acceptance and 115,874 against.[4]

No sooner had the miners received their wages than a fresh dispute arose regarding the cost of living. On 10 May 1920 Sir Robert Horne, President of the Board of Trade, announced an increase of 4s 2d in the price of industrial coal and of 14s 2d for domestic coal. The Government aimed at removing the artificial differential between the prices of household and industrial coal—the latter of which was being sold at below its average cost of production but subsidized out of the profits from the coal export trade. The Government had decided, Horne explained, 'that household coal should no longer be sold at less price than coal for industry and that both should be sold at a price sufficient to meet the cost of production and the standard profits allowed by the Coal Emergency Act'.[5] The miners

[1] D.M.A., 3 April 1920.
[2] Ibid.
[3] Auckland and County Chronicle, 8 April 1920.
[4] M.F.G.B., 15 April 1920.
[5] 129 H.C. Deb. 5s, 9. Under the Coal Mines (Emergency) Act the owners received one-tenth of the excess profits of the industry.

believed that the Government were aiming to influence public opinion against them. 'The Government has simply taken the line of least resistance,' stated the *Durham Chronicle*, '. . . neatly including the cost of the miners' rise in a bigger bill to be met by the consumer. The powers that be have thus given one more spin to the merry-go round in its "vicious circle".'[1] Meanwhile the continuing rise in the cost of living was causing grave concern. A resolution passed by the Council Meeting of the Durham Miners' Association on 29 May declared: 'The time has arrived when drastic measures should be taken to force a material reduction in the price of foodstuffs.'[2]

A special conference of the M.F.G.B. on 10 June discussed the increase in the price of inland coal and the feasibility, or otherwise, of demanding a further wage advance. Robert Smillie recognized that the recent price increase, by allowing efficient and inefficient pits alike to make a profit, strengthened the Government's ability to bring an end to State control of the industry. Convinced, therefore, that either a reduction in the price of coal or an increase in wages should make it possible for the Government to decontrol the mines, the conference decided to ask the Federation's Executive Committee to formulate a claim for a substantial advance in wages.[3]

The Executive Committee advised the Federation to demand a reduction in the cost of living as a means of winning public support for their claim. Consequently, on 21 June, the Federation decided to ask for a reduction of 14s 2d in the price of household coal and a wage increase of 2s per day for those over 18, 1s per day for those between 18 and 16 and 9d per day for those under 16.[4] Not all the districts were content with the double-barrelled nature of the claim. The Nottinghamshire miners felt that the largest part of the surplus in the industry, earned mainly from the export trade, should help finance a flat-rate increase in wages of 4s a day and that the miners should reject any proposal to reduce the price of coal. It was easy for export- ing districts such as Durham, Northumberland and South Wales to agree since a single demand for a wage advance, without the com- plications of changes in coal prices, could go some way towards compensating their members for the wage sacrifices already made during the post-war boom.[5] Their sentiments were most clearly expressed by A. J. Cook (South Wales) at the annual conference of the Federation in July when he said:

[1] *Durham Chronicle*, 14 May 1920.
[2] D.M.A., 29 May 1920.
[3] M.F.G.B., 10 June 1920.
[4] *Ibid.*, 21 June 1920.
[5] See above, pp. 121–2.

'I feel that we have been considering this question from a political point of view . . . and not from a Trade Union point of view, whilst other Trade Unions have been going forward. Look at the action taken by the cotton people, the railwaymen and printers. Despite the fact that there is no surplus to be considered they demanded an advance in wages based on the increased cost of living . . . and . . . we, as the most powerful organization, are always considering the the regulation of wages and prices . . . whilst we allow the owners to retain profits to the extent of £26,000,000. . . . The rest of the public . . . have been making use of their organizations . . . in raising their wages relatively to the increased cost of living, we, as miners, ought to have done the same.'[1]

The Durham delegates to the conference, however, refused to seek individual gain alone. W. P. Richardson declared altruistically:

'Our people have decided in favour of the Committee's recommenda-tion and we are prepared to continue to support it, even to the extent of making a sacrifice. . . . We shall show during our negotia-tions that we are out for bigger things than an immediate gain to ourselves by obtaining some advantage to people less organized, less fortunate than ourselves . . . and instead of demanding our full pound of flesh, let us take a more righteous course, and proceed on the lines of the greatest good for the greatest number.'[2]

After considerable discussion the Conference decided by 545 votes to 360 to accept the Executive Committee's recommendations, Durham voting with the majority.[3]

The Government refused the miners' demands, stating on 26 July that 'whatever surplus profits are derived from the sale of coal during the next twelve months should go to the Exchequer'.[4] On 12 August the M.F.G.B. decided to take a strike ballot and recom-mended the members to vote for a stoppage.[5] The Durham Miners' Association played little part in advising its membership which way to vote but at a M.F.G.B. conference on 2 September it was reported that 70 per cent of the Durham votes were cast in favour of a stop-page, the voting being 76,869 for and 32,783 against. The national figures were 606,782 votes for and 238,865 against.[6] It was agreed that work should cease in all the districts on 25 September 1920. The

[1] *Ibid.*, 6 July 1920.
[2] *Ibid.*, 7 July 1920.
[3] *Ibid.*
[4] *Ibid.*, 26 July 1920; P.R.O., Cab. 23/21.
[5] *Ibid.*, 12 August 1920.
[6] *Ibid.*, 2 September 1920.

recent events had also gained for the miners the sympathetic support
of the Triple Alliance and the T.U.C.[1] Feeling was running high
amongst the miners' leaders in Durham. 'I do not think there is much
hope of a settlement if the Government adhere to their decision not
to reduce the price of coal,' Robson told a press conference, 'Unless
they give way I am afraid there will be a collision. The miners are
determined on that point.'[2] Joseph Batey told miners at Shotton:
'The strike is bound to come ... and ... unless the Government
gives way, we are bound to fight. Once the strike commences all other
trade unions will rally to the support of the miners. I hope there will
be no patching up of peace until we have smashed this Government
of profiteers and taken effective means to reduce the cost of living.'[3]

VII

The Executive Committee of the M.F.G.B. met Sir Robert Horne
on four occasions throughout September in an attempt to resolve
the deadlock but without success. The Government refused to consider reducing the price of domestic coal and proposed that any
further advance in wages should be conditional upon arrangements
for higher output. On 15 September the Federation's Executive
decided to recommend to a special conference that the claim for a
reduction in the price of coal should be abandoned since the estimated surplus in the industry in the period from 1 June 1920 to 1
June 1921, upon which their claim was based, appeared from more
recent calculations to be double what could confidently be expected.[4]
Consequently the Executive Committee drafted a revised claim under
which the Government was to be asked to concede the wage claim;
to agree that the cost should not be added to the price of home-
consumed coal; to appoint a competent and representative tribunal
to determine whether in view of the financial position of the industry
a reduction in the price of domestic coal should take place; and agree
to establish a committee to inquire into the causes of declining output.[5] At a M.F.G.B. Special Conference on 21 September delegates
approved the Executive Committee's action in submitting the revised
claim to the Government and at the same time re-asserted their
determination for strike action. 'There is only one path now to try

[1] *Ibid.*, 31 August, 1 September 1920.
[2] *Durham Chronicle*, 17 September 1920.
[3] *Ibid.*
[4] M.F.G.B., 15 September 1920; *Summary of Coal Output, Costs of Production,
etc. for three months to June 30, 1920.* Cmd. 949.
[5] M.F.G.B., 15 September 1920.

and that is to go forward even to a strike,' Lee told the Conference. 'No one will suffer more than the miners' families, and the poor of our land . . . but we must go forward or forever be disgraced before those who are trying to bring better conditions to the people.'[1] Lee's remarks illustrated the general feeling amongst the majority of miners in Durham. Notices had already been served at every colliery in the coalfield save one.[2]

On 22 September a deputation of the Triple Alliance met the Prime Minister to urge the Government to accept the miners' claim. Lloyd George proposed that the dispute should be referred to arbitration or, alternatively, that an advance of miners' wages should be contingent upon an increase in coal production.[3]

The Triple Alliance met again on the following day to consider the report of the deputation. It was decided to adjourn the conference so that the three organizations could discuss the matter individually. 'My own conclusion,' remarked Robson, on behalf of the Miners' Federation, 'is that the Government is refusing this advance because they have made up their minds to fight us.'[4] The main issue at hand was not to assess Government motive but to decide on the action to be taken over its latest proposal. At a special M.F.G.B. conference on the afternoon of the same day Smillie advocated the acceptance of arbitration. This aroused considerable opposition amongst the delegates including Robson. Confident that the Government was able to pay the wages advance ('if there was anything legitimately to arbitrate about I would go') Robson violently attacked Smillie's suggestion. 'I believe . . . as honestly as I stand here on my feet', he asserted, 'that if we go to a court we shall go down. . . . I want to suggest that if we go before a court of arbitration, if we go down, absolutely there is an end of this Federation.'[5] Smillie's proposal was eventually defeated by 545 votes to 360.[6] This decision proved a disappointment to the transport workers and the railwaymen who had both recently accepted arbitration procedures. Later in the same day the Triple Alliance withdrew its sympathetic support from the miners' threatened strike action. On the day before the strike was due to begin the Prime Minister asked the miners' leaders to suspend the strike notices for a week to allow them to meet the coal owners in an attempt to evolve a scheme to increase output.

---

[1] *Ibid.*, 21 September 1920.
[2] *Ibid.*
[3] *Ibid.*, 22 September 1920.
[4] *Ibid.*, 23 September 1920.
[5] *Ibid.*
[6] *Ibid.*

The Federation decided to accede to the Prime Minister's request although some delegates were openly suspicious. 'Does it mean we are going to commit ourselves as a Conference to an investigation of a system for the regulation of wages according to output?' asked Batey. 'I would rather go back to the system of regulating wages under the conciliation boards than this system.'[1]

Negotiations between miners' leaders and the coal owners' representatives began on 25 September. On 27 September the owners submitted their proposals which consisted of the fixing of a datum line from which increases in output and wages could be calculated. They offered a bonus of 1s a day (with 6d for youths and 4½d for boys) if the output in the first fortnight in October increased to the rate of 242 million tons per annum; 2s a day if the rate increased to 250 million tons and 3s a day if it increased to 260 million tons. The miners insisted that the output of the current (September) quarter should be accepted as the datum line. They also demanded an increase of 2s a shift payable from 14 July and a 6d a shift bonus in November if output rose in October to the annual rate of 244 million tons, with a further 6d a shift for an increase to the rate of 248 million tons, in any month thereafter.[2] The negotiations were reported to a special M.F.G.B. conference on 30 September. Smillie, hesitant to enter upon a strike over the issue, urged that the dispute be submitted to a tribunal but again faced strong opposition. 'I believe our county would rather strike than surrender further than we have already done,' said Lee.[3]

On the following day at a tripartite meeting between miners' leaders, owners' representatives and the Prime Minister the owners submitted a final and modified offer which can be summarized thus:[4]

Rate of output of coal million tons per annum	Increase in wages to be given per shift		
	Over 18	16–18	Under 16
	s d	s d	s d
240	1 0	6	4½
244	1 6	9	6¾
248	2 0	1 0	9
252	2 6	1 3	11¼
256	3 0	1 6	1 1½

Lloyd George suggested either that negotiations should continue, a ballot vote be taken on the owners' proposals or that the dispute be

[1] Ibid., 24 September 1920.
[2] Ibid., 30 September 1920.
[3] Ibid.
[4] Ibid., 1 October 1920.

submitted to arbitration. Failing this the only avenue left was a strike which, he claimed, 'would cast a deep gloom throughout the land'.[1] On the same day the M.F.G.B. decided to suspend notices for a fortnight until 16 October to allow a ballot to be taken upon the owners' offer. Durham, which had long argued against any compromise, joined Leicester, Lancashire, South Wales and Forest of Dean in voting against the proposal.

The Federation's decision caused a rift between Cann and the Durham delegates to the national conference. Robson, in a press interview in Durham, openly criticised the Federation's Executive in the handling of the datum-line issue. 'The whole circumstances have been very much complicated by the drifting policy adopted by the Executive Committee,' he claimed. 'The chance of the success of the strike policy lay in it being taken at first. As that was not done men may have been led to believe that there is no chance of its success and that they had better take what is offered than lose the lot.'[2] Cann, who did not attend the Federation conference when the decision to vote was taken, took exception to these remarks and directly accused Robson of being a favourite advocate of accepting the datum line. 'I like individuals to be straight,' he wrote in a letter to the *Durham Chronicle*, 'and, seeing the date is approaching when the ballot will have to be taken, I assert, fearless of contradiction, that he did his utmost to induce the conference to accept the datum line.'[3] The remaining Durham delegates denied this and gave a full report of the negotiations at national level to a special Council Meeting held on 9 October.[4] Consequently the Executive Committee of the Durham Miners' Association, in a letter to local newspapers, strongly denied that any of its members had given support to either the suggestion of a datum-line agreement or to the submission of the dispute to an impartial tribunal.[5] It is probable that Cann confused Durham's support of a separate suggestion to limit the ballot vote to a consideration of the owners' offer alone without considering the feasibility, or otherwise, of the use of an arbitration tribunal with its acceptance of either of these methods as a means of settling the dispute.[6]

Nevertheless Cann refused to drop the issue and published at his own expense a personal letter to all the Association's members describing his treatment at the special Council meeting on 9 October:

[1] *Ibid.*
[2] *Durham Chronicle*, 8 October 1920.
[3] *Ibid.*
[4] *Ibid.*, 15 October 1920.
[5] *Ibid.*
[6] M.F.G.B., 1 October 1920.

'I . . . attempted to say a word or two, when the Chairman [1] immediately ruled me out of order, and told the Council very definitely that
he would not allow me to speak on the subject under discussion
under any consideration. I protested several times, but with his
strident voice and vehement ringing of his bell I was prevented from
obtaining a hearing. . . . I can recall no other instance to compare in
flagrant injustice with this attempt to gag and bind me: and I would
point out that if you abolish the saving grace of open criticism . . .
and allow a domineering clique to agree together to buy and sell you
unchallenged, then you are false to the whole honourable life history
of your Association and deserve the fate that inevitably follows a
suicidal policy like that.'[2]

There appears to be no evidence by which one can judge the response
of the rank and file miners in Durham to Cann's stringent criticism
of the Association's leadership nor is the final outcome of the feud
known.

Whatever the merits or demerits were of submitting the owners'
terms to a ballot vote the Durham miners at least had the opportunity
to reaffirm, or otherwise, their leaders' opposition to the datum line.
The result of the ballot in Durham showed a large majority against
acceptance of the owners' offer: 78,750 votes against and only 17,185
in favour. The national figures, reported to an M.F.G.B. conference
on 14 October, showed 181,428 votes for accepting the offer and
635,098 against.[3] It was consequently resolved that the strike notices
should be allowed to expire and that a strike take place on 16 October.
The decision pleased Peter Lee, who had continually urged the
Federation to take a firm stand without sacrificing any of its demands.
'There have never been, in my opinion, for the last 20 years negotiations carried on where one side has moved more than the other to
make peace', he reminded the Conference on 15 October. 'The
miners have done everything they could to prevent a fight. . . . It is
now war.'[4] Smillie, who had disagreed with the desirability of a
strike, attempted to resign but was persuaded to retain his office for
the sake of maintaining unity within the Federation. 'If we are to
win now', remarked Robson, 'it will only be by unity. . . . This is
not a time for differences amongst either officials or men.'[5]

[1] James Robson.
[2] *Durham Chronicle*, 15 October 1920.
[3] M.F.G.B., 14 October 1920.
[4] *Ibid.*, 15 October 1920.
[5] *Ibid.*

VIII

The 'Datum Line' strike began on 16 October. A notable characteristic of the strike in Durham was the unanimity with which the miners obeyed the order to cease work. 'Around Durham City the miners are taking matters very quietly and are absolutely relying upon their leaders', stated the *Durham Chronicle*. 'Ponies have been brought to bank, and are to be seen grazing happily in the fields.'[1] The general opinon amongst the rank-and-file miners was that the strike would be brief, if not over in a week.[2] *The Times* Special Correspondent in Northumberland and Durham was particularly surprised at the behaviour of the younger miners. 'Many of them struck work in the morning and then travelled 20 or 30 miles in the afternoon to see Newcastle United play Sunderland at football', he reported. 'They seemed much more concerned . . . over the result of that match than the issue of the strike.'[3]

On 16 October the Durham County Mining Federation Board met with the owners and decided to allow pumpmen, horsekeepers, enginemen, mechanics and cokemen to continue working in the interests of the safety and repair of the mines. Sub-Committees representative of each of the four sections on the Board were established at local Lodges and collieries to enforce the arrangements.[4] A number of miners' Lodges refused, however, to recognize the arrangements and either withdrew the men who had started work or refused to arrange meetings with the local colliery management to decide upon the particular classes of workmen to be employed.[5] Arrangements were also made for the payment of strike pay. The Association agreed to pay each full member a fortnight's allowance of £1 per week (10s half members) plus 5s rent allowance for members in rented houses.[6]

Meanwhile the effect of the miners' strike was being felt elsewhere in the County. By 18 October the streets of Consett were reported to be thronged with iron and steel workers idle as a consequence of the strike. One hundred working men at Seaham Dock, dependent upon the coal export trade, were given a week's notice immediately after the strike began. Householders were urged to economize in their use

[1] *Durham Chronicle*, 22 October 1920.
[2] *Ibid.*
[3] *The Times*, 18 October 1920.
[4] D.M.A., 16 October 1920.
[5] *Ibid.*, 21 October 1920.
[6] *Ibid.*, 23 October 1920.

of gas owing to the restricted supplies of coal.[1] Blast furnaces, steel works and rolling mills at Jarrow closed on 17 October. The larger part of the Darlington Forge closed at noon on the first day of the strike.[2]

A change in the situation suddenly occurred on 21 October. A special delegate meeting of the National Union of Railwaymen on that day agreed to inform the Prime Minister that unless the miners' claims were granted or negotiations resumed by 23 October the railwaymen would strike.[3] Lloyd George quickly reopened negotiations with the M.F.G.B. on 24 October in order to postpone the railwaymen's threatened stoppage. After four days of discussion the Executive Committee of the Federation decided to recommend a ballot on the Government's proposals for a settlement. The Government offered as a temporary measure an immediate wage increase of 2s a shift for adults with corresponding amounts for youths and boys guaranteed until 31 December 1920. It was to be continued from 3 January 1921 if the value of export sales for the five weeks ending 18 December 1920 exceeded the value for the September quarter by a sufficient sum to cover the full wage advance. For every £288,000 less than the amount required there was to be a reduction of 6d a shift for adults (and corresponding reductions for youths and boys). For every 6d reduction in wages the owners were to forgo a quarter of the amount by which their profit exceeded the level guaranteed under the Coal Mines (Emergency) Act. For every advance of 6d a shift in wages the owners' profits in excess of their guaranteed standard were to be increased by a quarter. Export prices were to be guaranteed at a level of 72s a ton. This scheme was to continue until a National Wages Board was established. The owners and workmen were required to formulate a permanent scheme not later than 31 March 1921. Joint production committees were to be established locally and nationally.[4]

Robson, speaking at Thornley on 31 October, advised the miners to accept the terms, 'By continuing the strike we shall be drifting further towards chaos,' he explained, 'and there will be great uncertainty as to where the money is coming from to pay the advance. . . . We will not be as favourably circumstanced at the end of another fortnight as we are now.'[5] Although the Association did not make a formal recommendation to its members on which way to vote 51,589 votes were cast in Durham in favour of accepting the terms and

[1] *Durham Chronicle*, 22 October 1920.
[2] *The Times*, 18 October 1920.
[3] M.F.G.B., 23 October 1920.
[4] *Ibid.*, 28 October 1920.
[5] *Durham Chronicle*, 5 November 1920.

39,819 against compared with the national figures of 338,045 and 346,504 respectively.[1] Sixteen districts had voted in favour of the terms but the disproportionately large majorities recorded against the offer in Lancashire and South Wales helped produce a small majority in favour of continuing the strike. Nevertheless it was below the requisite two-thirds majority and on 3 November the M.F.G.B. agreed to instruct men to return to work on the following day.[2] The 'Datum Line' strike was over but only after an estimated loss in coal output of between 13–14 million tons and a loss in wages to miners amounting to £14–15 million.[3]

IX

Despite the predominance of national events in the mining industry during 1919–20 the Durham Miners' Association actively sought to improve local working conditions and terms of employment on behalf of its membership. By mid-1920 large collieries on the east coast of Durham, at Murton, Ryhope, Seaham, Silksworth, Wearmouth and Hylton, were still working a third shift of 7 hours 10 minutes despite the fact that arrangements had been concluded in the County for working a seven-hour day. In July 1919 the Durham miners had rejected an offer of the owners to reduce working times at these pits to seven hours bank-to-bank.[4] In April 1920 the issue was again raised and a sub-committee consisting of representatives from the miners' and coal owners' Associations was appointed to settle the matter. In May it was finally decided that at the six pits in question hewers should work a shift of seven hours bank-to-bank except on 'Baff Saturdays'[5] when both hewers and datal hands would each work six hours bank-to-bank.[6]

By the end of April 1920 agreement had been reached with the owners to increase the basic wages of labourers, screeners and bank hands.[7] On 8 May a further agreement was signed by the two Associations providing for all overtime worked between the start of a Sunday night shift and the end of the following Saturday shift to be paid for at the rate of time and a half.[8] The method of payment was an

[1] M.F.G.B., 5 November 1920.
[2] *Ibid.*
[3] *The Economist*, 13 November 1920.
[4] See above, pp. 113–4.
[5] i.e. the Saturday on which men paid fortnightly received no wages.
[6] D.M.A., 14 April, 31 May 1920.
[7] *Ibid.*, 10 January, 23 April 1920.
[8] *Ibid.*, 17 May 1920.

innovation and was not well received by the miners. Overtime and week-end work had always been regulated by a length of shift and it was not until 31 January 1921 that an agreement of interpretation was reached which gave the results of the time and a third and time and a half principle in a length of shift to be worked for overtime and at week-ends. All overtime worked underground between the start of the Sunday night shift and the end of the following Saturday morning shift was to be paid at the rate of 5 hours 15 minutes per shift and at the surface at the rate of 5 hours 50 minutes per shift exclusive of meal times. All underground persons working from the start of the Saturday afternoon shift to the start of the Sunday night shift were entitled to a payment at the rate of 4 hours 40 minutes per shift and surface workers at the rate of 5 hours 10 minutes per shift exclusive of meal times. Complications arose out of the recognized County custom of allowing certain classes of workmen to work one 'short shift' of six hours in any one fortnight or two 'short shifts' of seven hours. It was agreed to pay such shifts at the rate of 1 1/11 shifts per shift but in the case where the customary two short shifts of seven hours per fortnight had been reduced under the Sankey Award to six and a half hours no extra payment had to be made. Collieries were, however, allowed to revert to working seven hours per shift in which case payment would be made at the stipulated rate.[1]

[1] *Ibid.*, 31 January 1921.

Chapter IV

THE 1921 LOCK-OUT

I

Following the termination of the national strike in November 1920 the Durham County Federation Board, in accordance with the terms of settlement, met representatives of the Durham Coal Owners' Association regarding the arrangements to be made to increase the output of coal. Early in December 1920 a District Committee on Output was established consisting of sixteen representatives on each side (the workmen's representatives consisting of ten from the miners' section of the Federation Board and two from each of the other three sections).[1] W. P. Richardson acted as Secretary to the workmen's representatives on the Committee. During the five weeks ending 18 December the national output of coal reached an average of 5,215,160 tons a week which represented under the terms of the 'Datum Line' agreement an annual rate of 260,758,000 tons. Consequently the miners secured an increase in wages of 1s 6d a day from 3 January 1921 making the total flat rate advances to date 10s 6d.[2] The benefits of increasing output were, however, shortlived. With the collapse of the coal export trade at the end of 1920 conditions gradually deteriorated. As a result of falling output during the four weeks ending 22 January 1921 wages were reduced by 2s a shift in February.[3]

Meanwhile meetings were being held between the M.F.G.B. and the coal owners to prepare a scheme for the future adjustment of wages to be submitted to the Government by 31 March 1921. Substantial progress was made after only a few meetings. Both sides agreed in principle that wages should be governed by the ability of the industry to pay. They further agreed that during the period of the agreement a standard wage should be established for the men, below which there should be no automatic reduction: this was to be the first charge on the industry. Against the standard wage there was to be established a recognized standard of profit to be a charge against the cost of production before the miners were entitled to any advance

[1] Durham Coal Owners' Association, *Annual Report*, 1920, pp. 19–20; D.M.A., 27 November, 16 December 1920.
[2] M.F.G.B., 5 January 1921; *The Economist*, 8 January 1921.
[3] M.F.G.B., 29 January 1921.

upon the standard wage. After standard wages, standard profits and other costs of production had been met, any surplus profits were to be divided in definitely agreed proportions between the workmen and the owners, the workmen's share being expressed by a percentage addition to the standard wage.[1]

Both the coal owners and the M.F.G.B. were anxious to simplify the existing wages structure by consolidating some part of the advances already made into a new standard rate in each district and by determining some uniform method of calculating all future advances or reductions on the new standard. On the question of the amounts to be consolidated into the new standard rates the M.F.G.B. put forward two proposals. Either 70 per cent of the existing wages would be consolidated into a new standard rate and the remaining 30 per cent treated as a floating margin subject to increase or decrease, or all percentage advances made so far could be merged into a new standard leaving the war and Sankey flat-rate advances as a floating margin subject to future alteration. Agreement had also to be reached on whether the floating margin should be treated as a flat-rate addition to the standard and therefore subject to flat-rate additions or reductions in the future or as a percentage addition to the standard subject to future percentages increases or reductions.

Frank Hodges explained the details of the various schemes to a special Council Meeting of the Durham Miners' Association on 5 February. The Association's Executive Committee decided in favour of consolidation by the first of these methods subject to variation by percentage advances or reductions.[2] The Durham leaders realized that whilst percentage advances helped maintain the traditional wage differentials between low and high paid wages by giving the more highly paid workers larger actual advances than the low paid, in a period of declining wages they avoided taking a larger percentage reduction from the low paid than for the more highly paid workers. Furthermore they favoured incorporating as much of the flat-rate advances as possible into any new standard on the grounds that it provided the only effective safeguard against fluctuations in both the cost of living and the selling price of coal.[3] The majority of other districts felt differently. The votes of the district Associations on the various issues arising out of the wages question were reported to a conference of the M.F.G.B. on 22 February. The decision, by

[1] Durham Coal Owners' Association, *Report on Discussions at the Provisional National Committee on the Proposed Scheme for Future Settlement of Miners' Wages* (n.d.), pp. 1–2.
[2] D.M.A., 11 February 1921.
[3] *Durham Chronicle*, 25 February 1921.

572,449 votes to 249,160, was in favour of consolidation by the second of the methods outlined above, subject to future flat-rate advances or reductions. Durham, Northumberland, Somerset and Leicester voted against the scheme.[1] The decision of the districts seriously jeopardized the possibility of any agreement being made with the coal owners on the future structure of wages. Not only did the coal owners themselves favour the percentage system but they had made it clear that they were unwilling to accept any scheme of consolidation which involved the embodiment of more than half the existing wage rates. Instead they proposed that any new standard rate should be the rate which had been actually payable in July 1914 and that all wartime advances, whether percentage or flat rate, should be excluded from the standard.

Apart from these points of dispute there remained the question of the relation of wages to profits, selling prices and costs of production and whether future wage changes should be on a national or local basis. The miners and owners had, during their negotiations, already agreed in principle to a profit-sharing scheme to replace the selling price of coal as the major determinant of the level of miners' wages. A majority of the district associations voted in February in favour of the principle (Durham deciding to leave the question to the Federation's discretion believing it would 'secure the largest possible share . . . for the workers') on the condition that the owners accepted a national system of wage regulation.[2]

The miners proposed the establishment of a National Wages Board to determine, by national agreement between the representatives of the owners and mineworkers, the amount and method of future wage adjustments. They also proposed the creation of a central fund or 'pool' to be formed by a levy on the tonnage of each undertaking for the purpose of smoothing out the inequality in the wage rates between the several districts. To miners in Durham it was a patent injustice that because of the age of their coalfield, the state of the coal export market or the geological peculiarities of their particular district their wages should be lower than in Yorkshire, for example, where the age of the coalfield, the state of the technique and the market for coal worked in favour of the miner. Wages, they claimed, should be adjusted not in relation to each district's ability to pay but to the capacity of the industry as a whole. The miners did not propose an absolute equality of wages throughout all the districts but rather a method of financial unification, realized by the voluntary co-operation of owners and workers, under which all the profits of all the

[1] M.F.G.B., 22 February 1921.
[2] M.F.G.B., 11, 22, 29 February 1921.

collieries would be pooled to allow uniform wage advances and reductions to be made as they had been since 1917. Prosperous districts would thereby subsidize poorer ones. Profits would not be equalized. The differences that existed between the well-managed and the inefficient undertaking would continue but the National Wages Board, which would supervise the distribution of the pool, would watch carefully to discover whether a particular district or colliery was taking from the pool more than it contributed. Pressure would then be put upon the district or colliery to improve its methods or go out of business. The old system of fixing wages and prices so as to perpetuate the life of the worst-situated and ill-managed collieries would thereby be replaced. The coal owners insisted that wages should be determined on a district basis.

The negotiations on these issues were brought to a sudden halt with the Government's decision, announced on 23 February, to decontrol the industry on 31 March, five months earlier than the date laid down in the 1920 Mining Industry Act. Sir Robert Horne, President of the Board of Trade, had raised the question of decontrol in January 1921 and immediately aroused the opposition of the M.F.G.B. 'We cannot acquiesce in any proposal for the decontrol of the coal trade,' it announced, 'until the coal owners and ourselves are able to present to the Government a jointly agreed plan for the national control of the industry which will effectively substitute the present arrangements.'[1] The miners had asserted during the previous crisis, at the end of 1920, that the Government's object of raising the price of coal in May 1920 had been to place each district, and as far as possible each colliery, on a paying basis in preparation for decontrol, but this had been denied by Horne. The miners regarded the latest move as unwarrantable and immoral. The Government simply wished to rid itself of all responsibility for an industry making abnormal losses, having squeezed as much as possible from it when it was making extraordinary profits. The impact of the Government's decision upon the coal owners was immediate and decisive. They announced that under no consideration could they agree to the establishment of either a National Wages Board or a national profits pool. Evan Williams, the President of the Mining Association explained:

'Such decontrol would seriously embarrass the owners and make it impossible for certain districts and collieries to maintain themselves in production. . . . In the absence of financial control the good collieries would have to provide out of their natural profits the means for maintaining the poor collieries in production. . . . The

[1] *Ibid.*, 12 January 1921. Details of Cabinet policy are in P.R.O., Cab. 23/24.

general efficiency of the industry would decline because the incentive to remain efficient or to improve efficiency would disappear once it was established that the skill and energy of the good concerns were to be used to subsidize the inefficiency and indifference of the poor concerns.'[1]

The decision to decontrol provided recalcitrant owners with an opportunity to voice further opposition to the miners' demands. In a statement to their shareholders the directors of Bolckow, Vaughan and Company reiterated their objections to the idea of a national pool of wages or profits which they described as 'a direct attack upon the principles of private ownership and an intolerable interference with the right of the owners to manage their own business and control their own property'.[2]

II

When the Coal Mines (Decontrol) Act received the Royal Assent on 24 March the miners and the owners had only a matter of days to deal with the wages question. The Government's arrangements guaranteeing certain profits to owners and the national system of wage regulation established under control were due to end within a week. It was clear that, without Government assistance, the industry could not afford to continue to pay the rate of wages which had existed during the period of control. The owners had decided that wages were to be determined by the capacity of the district to pay and they began issuing notices in the various coalfields that all contracts of service would end on 31 March. In Durham the employers announced 'that arrangements will be made as to the wages which will be payable on and after 1 April 1921 so as to enable work to be continued without interruption'.[3] Robson optimistically issued a circular to members claiming that there 'was no need for alarm' since 'it is quite easy for us to read into such events a good deal more than all the circumstances would justify'.[4]

On 10 March the owners put forward their wage proposals. A basic rate was to be established consisting of the wages paid in each district in July 1914 together with the percentage addition for the reduction in hours in 1919. The owners' standard profits in each district were to be 17 per cent of the aggregate amount paid in basic

[1] *Ibid.*, 2 March 1921.
[2] *Durham Chronicle*, 27 May 1921.
[3] *Ibid.*, 18 March 1921.
[4] D.M.A., 14 March 1921. *Durham Chronicle*, 1 April 1921.

wages. Any surplus was to be divided between wages and profits in a ratio of 75:25 respectively, the workmen's share being expressed as a percentage upon the standard rate in each district. The level of costs in any particular district and the market price of coal were to be the main determinants of wages. Under this scheme the average wage per week in Durham would have been raised from its existing level of 87s to 88s 10d on the basis of January 1921 prices. This was due in part to the relatively low average minimum cost per ton compared with other districts, both inland and export alike.[1] On the other hand were prices to fall rapidly the situation would be vastly different. Prices per ton of coal in Durham in January 1921 stood at 36s 7·8d. Were they to fall to 19s 8·5d the proposed average wage would have fallen to only 32s 3d per week.[2] The Federation's proposals offered in Durham an average wage per week of 61s 9d for an average minimum cost price of 29s 5·8d per ton.[3] By 11 March the Government had been presented with the rival schemes.

On the instructions of a Special Conference on 18 March the M.F.G.B. submitted the owners' proposals for acceptance or rejection to the district Miners' Associations asking whether or not they were prepared to recommend the temporary abandonment of the demand for a National Pool and the opening up of negotiations for a settlement on a district basis.[4] The Council of Durham Miners' Association decided to take a Lodge vote on the issue. This immediately aroused the opposition of the Newbiggin Lodge. In a resolution passed at a general meeting its members denounced the 'autocratic policy' of the Association's Executive Committee in the handling of its negotiations in support of a national system of wages. Conscious of the fact that until then Durham's reaction to the Federation's policy over wages had been determined solely by the Association's Executive Committee, the Lodge condemned the manner in which the opinion of the rank-and-file was sought only at the most critical stage in the negotiations. 'They now decide to submit the owners' ... demands to the branches,' read part of the resolution. 'Like the Lloyd George autocracy that our leaders condemn, they carry on by secret diplomacy until faced with fight. Then in the hour of defeat the rank-and-file are recognized.'[5]

It is clear, however, that the Association's Council, on the advice of its Executive, felt it more important to secure rank-and-file opinion

[1] M.F.G.B., 17 March 1921.
[2] *Ibid.*
[3] *Ibid.*
[4] *Ibid.*, 18 March 1921.
[5] *Colliery Guardian*, 24 March 1921. Cf. *Durham Chronicle*, 6 May 1921.

on the decision of whether or not to abandon the fight for a national wages structure, even if only temporarily, than to confirm its determination to rid the County of district wage bargaining. Nevertheless, the Executive Committee of the Durham Miners' Association, in a circular to members, openly confessed their wariness of 'a strike', although technically it was a lock-out that was threatening. In this they were aware of the depression that had hit the County. The collapse of the coal export trade had led to the closing of pits, the dismissal of miners and an increase in short-time working. Between 60,000 and 70,000 miners had been dismissed throughout the country. Mines at Rainton, Wingate, North Bitchburn, Low Bitchburn, Cold Knot, Usworth, South Moor, Burnhope, and New Brancepeth had shut down owing to depression.[1] During the quarter ending 31 March 1921 Durham was losing 4s 2·4d on every ton of coal commercially disposable. Against this background the Executive Committee wrote:

'We are . . . face to face with a reduction in wages which could only have been avoided by the Government agreeing to subsidize the trade until the markets revived. This, as you know, they have refused to do. . . . With no money in the industry, and very little in the Miners' Associations, coupled with the vast army of the unemployed and under-employed, we have got to recognize that the tide is against us, and that it is very doubtful whether we could successfully carry through a strike.'[2]

The Durham miners showed in their voting that they were not prepared to abandon their fight for a national wages structure rejecting the acceptance of a temporary agreement on a district basis by 564 votes to 114.[3] The national voting on this proposal, reported to a special M.F.G.B. conference on 24 March, showed 627 votes against and 241 for.[4]

In a final attempt to harness Government support for the industry the M.F.G.B. Executive Committee met Sir Robert Horne on 30 March and urged a subsidy to be made to maintain the wages of the miners. Horne, regarding the offer as 'an absolutely impossible proposal' refused to consider the matter fearing similar demands from other industrial workers.[5] The Miners' Federation immediately instructed all districts 'that all notices should be allowed to expire

[1] Durham Chronicle, 18, 25 February 1921; Colliery Guardian, 18 February, 11 March 1921; D.M.A., 9, 28 February; 11, 14 March 1921.
[2] D.M.A., 19 March 1921.
[3] Ibid., 26 March 1921.
[4] M.F.G.B., 24 March 1921.
[5] Ibid., 30 March 1921.

regardless of occupation'.[1] Robson and Hodges supported an amendment to the instruction, moved by Herbert Smith, who had been
appointed Acting Secretary of the M.F.G.B. on the resignation of
Smillie earlier in the month, that all work necessary to maintain the
safety and condition of the mines should be allowed to continue on
the understanding that no reduction in the prevailing level of wages
should occur. The amendment was defeated by 2 votes.[2] On 31
March Government control of the mines came to an end and on the
same day the notices served by the owners took effect. The national
lock-out had begun.

III

Meanwhile the Durham coal owners had announced the terms on
which pits would be re-opened. In the majority of districts the
amended scales of wages were based upon the most recent ascertainment of the financial position of the industry i.e. February 1921. In
Durham, however, the owners based their offer upon the statistics
available for March 1921. They offered 155 per cent upon the 1879
basis, 55 per cent less than comparable calculations on the figures for
February 1921 would have given. Since prices were falling the owners
claimed they were forced to adjust the scales of wages to such a level
as to meet the changing conditions over time.[3] For this they blamed
a previous decision of the Miners' Federation [4] which prevented any
district association from entering into discussions with the owners
as to the wages to be paid since it would have involved the abandonment of the claim to a national wages system. As the employers
explained:

'It was necessary to fix the wage at such a point that it could be
maintained for some considerable time and allow of [sic] employment being offered to the men for such time. ... The fixing of a
wage based on the February figures would have resulted in a very
serious increase of unemployment. If the owners were in a position
to arrange with the workmen's representatives for a system by
which for some months, and pending a permanent scheme, the
wages should be fixed month by month on the results of the latest
preceding month, for which ascertainments could be obtained, then

[1] *Ibid.*
[2] *Ibid.*
[3] *Colliery Guardian*, 22 April 1921; *Newcastle Daily Journal*, 5 April 1921.
[4] M.F.G.B., 24 March 1921.

the owners would be in a position to offer for April a wage considerably higher than the 155 per cent which they have proposed to apply in the absence of any method of revising the rates at short intervals.'[1]

The effect of the owners' proposals on the wages of particular classes of workmen can be seen from the following table:[2]

Class of workmen	Owners' offer 155 per cent on 1879 basis (per shift)		Money reduction per shift		Percentage reduction per shift
	s	d	s	d	
Hewers	11	11·0	4	7·5	28·0
Labourers and screeners	8	3·4	5	5·5	36·7
Shifters	7	9·7	5	6·5	41·5
Wastemen	7	5·2	5	7·3	43·0

The larger cuts proposed for the lower-paid grades resulted from the return to a percentage basis in the calculation of advances over the new standard rates. Since the coal owners' offers in the various districts depended upon the ability of the district to pay the offers varied widely. Thus, while coal getters and labourers in Durham were likely to suffer reductions of £1 3s 1½d and £1 7s 3d respectively per week of five shifts the weekly wage of colliers and labourers in Northumberland was being reduced by only 10s 4d and 18s 5d respectively.[3]

At a meeting with representatives of the Mining Association in London on 30 March Sir Robert Horne expressed bitter disappointment with the offer and tried in vain to persuade the Durham employers to offer the 210 per cent addition to wages in accordance with the February ascertainment. He even suggested that, rather than depart from the February figures, collieries unable to carry on with the wages so brought about could close down temporarily.[4]

The owners' offer aroused a storm of protest in Durham. The County Federation Board reported to its members: 'We are prepared to assert from our information from other districts that the Durham

---

[1] Durham Coal Owners' Association, *Minutes of the Executive Committee*, 31 March 1921.
[2] *Durham Chronicle*, 8 April 1921.
[3] G. D. H. Cole, *Labour in the Coal-Mining Industry (1914–1921)*, Oxford 1923, p. 197.
[4] Durham Coal Owners' Association, *Minutes of the Executive Committee*, 31 March 1921.

owners have met us in a less favourable spirit, and with a demand that is more exacting than is to be found in any other part of the British coalfield.'[1] 'Some of our men at the price offered would have very little over £2 a week,' Peter Lee explained to a *Durham Chronicle* reporter, '. . . the owners of the Durham mines could have made a better offer if they had wished to be just and fair to the workmen.'[2] At some pits the owners had agreed to withdraw the notices previously served and open the pits on 1 April under the terms outlined in their offer.[3] The miners firmly resisted and prepared themselves for the ensuing conflict.

IV

Already, on 31 March, the Executive Committee of the M.F.G.B. had asked the other members of the Triple Alliance to strike in support of the miners. Both the National Union of Railwaymen and the Transport Workers' Federation asked for an opportunity to discuss the matter. In a statement to the press, however, the N.U.R. declared: 'Our Executive are deeply impressed with the gravity of the situation, and they regard the position as being the prelude to a general attempt to destroy national negotiations and reduce wages.'[4] Judging from similar reports the Transport Workers' Federation were equally sympathetic to the miners' cause.[5] On the same day the Government declared a 'state of emergency', and by 8 April troops had been moved into some coalfields, reservists called up, and a special 'Defence Force' created.

The stoppage in Durham was not attended by any violence or disorder. 'With fine weather prevailing the miners have been hard at work in their gardens and allotments,' reported the *Durham Chronicle*. 'The younger men are indulging in football, while others are practising in their respective cricket fields for the coming season.'[6] The press outside of the coalfields, and especially in London, were less precise in the nature of their reporting. Writing in 1936 J. Lawson recalled the early days of the lock-out in Durham and noted: 'To leave London with its flaming headlines at such times and arrive in Durham to find the whole village at a football match or all the roads leading to a great pony-racing event is an unforgettable ex-

[1] *Newcastle Daily Chronicle*, 6 April 1921.
[2] *Durham Chronicle*, 8 April 1921.
[3] D.M.A., 29 March 1921.
[4] M.F.G.B., 30 March 1921.
[5] *Ibid.*
[6] *Durham Chronicle*, 15 April 1921.

perience.'[1] Relations with the police were reported to be 'perfect'.[2] Soup kitchens were opened in the various mining centres throughout the coalfield. The Labour-controlled County Council in Durham took full advantage of the power given in the 1906 Provisions of Meals Act to organize feeding centres for schoolchildren.[3] Miners at Shotton Colliery were allowed groceries up to a value of £10 from local tradesmen in weekly instalments of not more than £2. Arrangements were made to deduct 5s per week from their post-stoppage earnings until the value of the credit was repaid.[4] Londonderry Collieries Ltd allowed 1 cwt of coal per week to be delivered to all miners working at their collieries.[5] Workmen's clubs, co-operative societies and local tradesmen offered what assistance they could—often by way of credit facilities—while some Lodges agreed to distribute local funds amongst those in most need, arrrangements being made to levy members on their return to work in order to restore the funds.[6]

In the early days of the dispute there was much propaganda in the press and in Parliament against the miners' decision to withdraw all classes of labour from the mine. The dangers of flooding and of ill-treatment to pit ponies were largely overcome in Durham. During the period of the lock-out colliery officials undertook to maintain the pits and in most collieries pit ponies were brought to the surface in accordance with a directive from the M.F.G.B.[7] At some colliery villages, for example Thornley and Wheatley Hill, the domestic supplies of drinking water depended upon the operation of colliery plants. Colliery officials agreed to undertake the necessary work at these villages and were solely responsible for maintaining the water-supply during the period of the lock-out.[8]

On 6 April Lloyd George invited both the miners' and the owners' leaders to meet him on the following day in order to resume negotiations for a settlement. By 8 April, however, deadlock had ensued owing to both the owners' and Government's insistence that the enginemen and pumpmen should return to work as the preliminary to any settlement. The miners were reluctant to surrender their strong bargaining position fully realizing that the owners feared any destruction of their property.[9] On the same day a full conference of the

[1] Lawson, *op. cit.*, p. 233.
[2] *Ibid.*
[3] *Ibid.*, p. 234.
[4] *Durham Chronicle*, 22 April 1921.
[5] *Ibid.*, 13 May 1921.
[6] *Ibid.*
[7] *Ibid.*, 1 April 1921; M.F.G.B., 9 April 1921.
[8] *Durham Chronicle*, 15 April 1921.
[9] M.F.G.B., 9 April 1921; P.R.O., Cab. 23/25.

Triple Alliance decided to issue strike notices in support of the miners taking effect from midnight, 12 April. Following a meeting between representatives of the Government and the railwaymen and transport workers on 9 April, at which the Government impressed upon the other two sections of the Triple Alliance the absolute necessity of maintaining the safety of the mines, the M.F.G.B. sent a telegram to all districts to refrain from any action which could endanger such safety.[1] The Durham County Federation Board, instructed to deal with all negotiations during the period of the lock-out, promptly urged all its members not to interfere in any way with the colliery officials working the pumps or maintaining the pits.[2]

Negotiations continued between the Government and representatives of the Mining Association and the M.F.G.B. from 11 to 12 April. The only new feature to emerge from the discussions was a pledge from the Government that it would 'be willing to give assistance, either by loan or otherwise, during a short period in order to mitigate the rapid reduction in wages in the districts most severely affected'.[3] The M.F.G.B. rejected the offer. Meanwhile the Triple Alliance had agreed to postpone the strike planned for midnight, 12 April but, faced with the breakdown in the negotiations, decided on 13 April to call a strike for 10 p.m. on 15 April.[4] The strike never took place. On 14 April, at a meeting of M.P.s in the Committee rooms of the House of Commons, Frank Hodges, accompanied among others by Robson, was reported to have intimated that the miners would be prepared to accept some temporary settlement of the wages question without the complication of a national pool. Hodges later denied the reports claiming that his references were to a temporary settlement of a national character providing for uniform wage reductions in response to reductions in the cost of living.[5] Nevertheless, the Prime Minister, acting upon the former interpretation, invited M.F.G.B. representatives to a further meeting with the coal owners. The miners refused, reminding him in reply: '. . . the only conditions upon which a temporary settlement can be arrived at is one that must follow the concession of the two principles already made known to you, viz.: a National Wages Board and a National Pool'.[6]

Within the N.U.R. and T.W.F. there was a growing feeling that the M.F.G.B. should have accepted the Prime Minister's invitation. On

[1] Ibid.
[2] D.M.A., 10 April 1921.
[3] M.F.G.B., 12 April 1921.
[4] Durham Chronicle, 15 April 1921.
[5] M.F.G.B., 22 April 1921.
[6] Ibid., 15 April 1921.

15 April, the so-called 'Black Friday', C. T. Cramp, the railwaymen's leader, informed the Executive of the M.F.G.B. that the N.U.R., T.W.F. and the Associated Society of Locomotive Engineers and Firemen had decided to call off their sympathetic strike.[1] The decision, apart from its effects upon the miners, was particularly unfortunate, as the mass of railwaymen and transport workers supported the miners in their fight. Indeed when asked in 1926 whether he had been instrumental in 'selling out' the miners on 'Black Friday', one of the most moderate of the railwaymen's leaders, J. H. Thomas, replied: 'I accept the blame for averting the general strike then.'[2] The Triple Alliance was split. Its breakdown was, to a large extent, the result of its own internal weaknesses. Its creators had never seriously considered the problems of leadership and coordinated action which its existence implied; problems which proved to be all important when the moment of action arrived. Ironically, Richardson had written to the M.F.G.B. in December 1920 requesting a full review of the rules governing the Triple Alliance 'with a view of seeing whether they can be readjusted to more effectively meet the requirements of the three organizations in the event of common action being desirable'. Nothing was done, however, towards this end.[3] The miners were now left to fight alone discouraged and disillusioned. 'We are greatly disappointed by the action of the railwaymen and transport workers,' said Cann. 'The miners are determined to fight to the bitter end, notwithstanding that they have been forsaken by the other two sections of the Triple Alliance.'[4] The same determination was voiced by Batey at a gathering of miners at Ushaw Moor when he claimed: 'In my opinion, there is no fear of the miners being defeated. They may be starved for a week or two, but they cannot be defeated.'[5]

V

Despite the failure of the Triple Alliance the miners remained steadfast in their determination to secure a National Wages Board and a National Pool especially since reports from the various districts

[1] *Ibid.*, 15 April 1921. Cf. *The Economist*, 23 April 1921. By this time other unions had joined the Triple Alliance in support of the miners including not only A.S.L.E.F. but the London District Council of the Electrical Trades Union, Cole, *op. cit.*, p. 210.
[2] *The Times*, 15 November 1926.
[3] M.F.G.B., 7 January 1921.
[4] *Durham Chronicle*, 7 April 1921.
[5] *Ibid.*, 15 April 1921. Cf. G. D. H. Cole, 'Black Friday and Afterwards', *Labour Monthly*, July 1921.

revealed overwhelming support in favour of both demands.[1] At a
meeting of the Durham County Federation Board on 18 April a
resolution was passed recommending the continuance of the lock-
out until these two demands were conceded and at further meetings
with Lodges on 20 April delegates representing each section on the
Board urged their members to maintain their resistance to local
settlements.[2]

Lloyd George successfully brought the owners and miners
together on 22 April to continue negotiations and meetings took
place until 28 April, when both the owners' and the Government's
proposals for settlement were submitted to a delegate conference of
the M.F.G.B. The Government had renewed its offer of a subsidy
but continued to insist upon the district settlement of wages. The
miners rejected the offer since it did not 'concede the fundamental
principle for which we stand'.[3]

Meanwhile the stoppage in Durham dragged on. Soup kitchens
and the efforts of local tradesmen and organizations aimed to reduce
distress to a minimum. Lodges continued to offer credit facilities to
their members. Miners at East Hetton, Bowburn, Mainsforth,
Tursdale, Dean and Chapter, Fishburn and Thrislington were issued
vouchers entitling them to parcels of food to a weekly value of up
to £2.[4] Concerts and sports meetings, predominantly fund-raising
efforts, were organized with a rapidity unknown in normal times.
Reporting on conditions at the colliery village of Fence Houses the
Durham Chronicle stated, 'Another busy week has been spent in this
district, local sports and attractions having been arranged as in the
previous weeks of the crisis. The people are alive to sport, and
eagerly scan the shop windows for any notices announcing the sports
from day to day.'[5] The miners attended meetings and demonstrations
organized by the Durham Miners' Association in support of their
demands for a national wages structure. About 1,000 men attended
a meeting at Langley Moor when a resolution was carried in support
of the demand for a National Wages Board and National Pool. On 2
May, at a May Day demonstration at Houghton-le-Spring, R.
Richardson, the constituency's M.P., emphasized the miners' determination to defeat 'the unholy alliance between the Government and
the mine owners'. 'We won the war,' he declared. 'We are now fighting

[1] M.F.G.B., 22 April 1921.
[2] D.M.A., 18 April 1921; *Durham Chronicle*, 22 April 1921; *Colliery Guardian*,
22 April 1921.
[3] M.F.G.B., 28 April 1921; P.R.O., Cab. 23/25.
[4] *Durham Chronicle*, 6, 13 May 1921.
[5] *Ibid.*, 13 May 1921.

to win the peace.'[1] Not all sections of the public were equally enthusiastic. The Bishop of Durham, assuming his often-played role of miners' critic, urged workmen to seek an end to the stoppage so that the mineworkers' grievances could be 'sifted by an impartial and trustworthy Commission and a permanent settlement agreed upon'.[2] The miners' memory of the efficacy of the Sankey Commission and their growing mistrust of the Government deafened them to such appeals.

The Government initiated a scheme for importing coal and immediately aroused the opposition of the railwaymen and the dockers. The Transport Workers' Federation determined to place an embargo upon such imports and the N.U.R. refused to handle any coal by rail except for household, public service and hospital use. Dockers refused to allow steamers to depart with half-empty bunkers lest they should be filled with coal from overseas.[3] In Durham similar attempts were made to crush any action likely to weaken the miners' cause. Workmen in various parts of the County were producing coal from outcrop seams and selling it to the public at a high price. The County Federation Board promptly denounced such activities:

'It is very little use desiring the railwaymen and transport men not to handle imported coal that would tend to defeat the miners if our members are prepared to produce coal for sale purposes. In addition to this it is having a bad effect upon the public mind.'[4]

Some workmen took the matter into their own hands. On 17 May 400 miners marched from Annfield Plain to Mounsett Fell and blew up a drift where men had been hewing coal and selling it to outsiders during the stoppage.[5]

VI

The Executive Committee of the M.F.G.B. again met the owners and representatives of the Government on 27 May. The Government's proposals were similar to those made in April except for an additional suggestion that if the coal owners and miners could not agree on a permanent scheme for wage regulation the matter should be settled by arbitration.[6] On the following day the Federation submitted the

[1] *Ibid.*, 6 May 1921.
[2] *Ibid.*, 13 May 1921.
[3] *Ibid.*, *The Economist*, 30 April 1921.
[4] D.M.A., 11, 12 May 1921.
[5] *Ibid.*, 20 May 1921.
[6] M.F.G.B., 27 May 1921.

proposals to the districts for their consideration. By 3 June all the districts had reported to the Executive Committee of the M.F.G.B. that they were not prepared to accept the Government's proposals. The Council of the Durham Miners' Association had promptly rejected the proposals as 'lacking the essential ingredients' the Federation was fighting for.[1]

The Government responded to the rejection by threatening to withdraw the offer of the £10 million subsidy if a settlement was not reached within two weeks.[2] The Executive Committee of the M.F.G.B. met the Central Committee of the Mining Association on 6 June for further negotiations. On the following day the Executive Committee decided to call a special conference and recomended a ballot vote to be taken on the owners' and Government's proposals.[3] The recommendation was accepted at a special conference on 10 June by all districts except Durham, Somerset and Kent.[4] Having failed to prevent a ballot being taken the Durham delegates urged the Federation Executive to at least recommend the districts to vote against the terms but again failed. Peter Lee feared that with the Federation reaffirming its determination not to settle for anything less than a National Wages Board and National Pool public opinion could come to regard the proposals of the Government and owners as the ideal formula for a quick settlement. 'I believe . . . if we fail in the struggle this time,' Lee told the delegates, 'the whole process through which we are now going must one day be faced again.'[5] Within five years he was to be proved correct.

The precise nature of the Government's and owners' proposals were printed on the ballot paper, which read as follows:[6]

MINERS' FEDERATION OF GREAT BRITAIN

BALLOT PAPER

Are you in favour of fighting on for the principles of the National Wages Board and National Pool, with loss of Government subsidy of ten million pounds for wages if no settlement by June 18th, 1921? ....

---

[1] *Durham Chronicle*, 3 June 1921.
[2] M.F.G.B., 4 June 1921.
[3] *Ibid.*, 7 June 1921.
[4] *Ibid.*, 10 June 1921.
[5] *Ibid.*
[6] *Ibid.*

Are you in favour of accepting the Government and owners' terms as set forth on the back of this ballot paper ?.......................

Please place your 'X' in the space provided for the purpose.
June 10th, 1921.   FRANK HODGES, General Secretary.

BACK OF BALLOT PAPER

NOTE.—The Government and owners having definitely rejected the principles of the National Wages Board and the National Pool now offer the terms fully set out below. You are now asked to say whether you will continue the fight for the National Wages Board and the National Pool, or accept the terms offered by the Government and owners. The Government offer of ten million pounds grant in aid of wages referred to below is to be withdrawn on June 18th unless an agreement is arrived at by that date.

TEMPORARY PERIOD

Government offers ten million pounds to prevent large reductions in wages where reductions are necessary.

First reductions not to exceed 2s per shift for all workers of 16 years and upwards, and 1s per shift for workers below 16 years.

No further reductions until August 1st.

Further reduction after August 1st to be agreed mutually until Government grant is exhausted.

The temporary agreement will come to an end as soon as Government grant is used up.

Owners' Proposals

National Board to fix principles for guidance of districts. Board to be comprised of equal number of representatives of both sides with independent chairman.

The parties have already agreed the principle that profits shall only be a fixed percentage of wages paid.

The Board to fix the amount of the percentage of profits to wages.

The Board to fix the amount of the new standard wage.

In this connection, the owners have offered as a standard wage the total wages paid in July, 1914, plus district additions to standards, plus the percentage for piece workers caused by the reduction of hours from 8 to 7, and a minimum percentage of 20 per cent added thereto. This minimum percentage to continue until June 30th, 1922.

The Board will also fix the items of cost, which must be taken into account by the district auditors when ascertaining the district revenue.

Wages during permanent scheme to be based upon the capacity of each district to pay.

In the event of a low paid dayworker receiving a wage which does not provide him with a subsistence wage, the District Board will fix a wage which will secure it for that workman.

The decision of the National Board as to the permanent scheme to be binding upon both parties for a period of twelve months and thereafter subject to three months' notice on either side.

The M.F.G.B. estimated that under the proposed settlement wages per shift in Durham would be reduced by 3s 5d on the basis of figures for March 1921 compared with only 1s 3¾d reduction for the combined counties of Yorkshire, Nottinghamshire, Leicestershire, Cannock Chase and Warwickshire.[1]

In Durham, despite the hardships being suffered as a result of the lock-out, the majority of the miners and the Association's officials were determined to resist any proposal for wages to be based upon the capacity of each district to pay. The vulnerability of a coal-exporting region during periods of falling prices and declining trade, together with the low basic rates offered by the employers, stiffened their resistance. A mass meeting of miners from Mainsforth, Chilton, Tursdale, Dean and Chapter, Thrislington and Windlestone met at Ferryhill on 13 June, passed a resolution condemning the nature of the proposals and reaffirmed their willingness to fight for national negotiations.[2] The result of the ballot in Durham showed 69,991 votes in favour of continuing the struggle and only 20,744 for the Government and owners' terms, 72 per cent of the total membership of the miners' Association having voted. The national figures similarly showed a majority in favour of continuing the struggle the voting being 453,614 for and 180,724 against.[3]

On 18 June Lloyd George stated that the Government's offer of financial assistance would be withdrawn on 19 June. Having failed to secure sympathetic support from other unions threatened with wage reductions the Executive Committee of the M.F.G.B. decided to approach the Government and owners with a view to negotiating a satisfactory wage agreement.[4] There was little hope of the owners making any major concessions. Lord Gainford, Vice-President of Pease and Partners, writing in the *Contemporary Review* in June 1921, aptly summarized their viewpoint:

'The coal owners are firmly convinced that the national interests will be best promoted by district settlements. The collieries which could

[1] *Ibid.*
[2] *Durham Chronicle*, 17 June 1921.
[3] M.F.G.B., 17 June 1921.
[4] *Ibid.*, 24 June 1921.

be worked economically and would be self-supporting through the
depressed period in front of us, would then be able to supply coal
in their own areas at the lowest possible price. Thus industries
dependent upon fuel would be able to recommence production, and
thus in each district a gradual development of trade would take
place so as to absorb those who are thrown out of work through
the present trade depression. Any national system, any pooling, any
kind of levy would inevitably prevent the best equipped, the most
efficiently managed, and the best class of colliery from producing coal
at the lowest and most attractive price to the consumer, and it is
therefore only through district settlements that the best national
results will be secured and the highest wages fund provided in the
interest of the workers.'[1]

The duration of the lock-out, the increasing financial difficulties of
many of the district associations and the stubbornness of both the
Government and the owners gave the miners little hope of succeed-
ing in their fight. 'The Federation officials are ... in a hopeless
position,' noted *The Economist*. 'The bankruptcy of their policy is
only a matter of time.'[2]

During the weekend beginning 24 June, Smith, Hodges and
Robson[3] met the Prime Minister at Chequers, during which time
Lloyd George intimated that he would invite his Cabinet to recommend the restoration of the offer of financial assistance to the industry
if the Federation's Executive Committee would recommend the
resumption of work.[4] Consequently, at a meeting between representatives of the miners, owners, and the Government at the Board of
Trade on 27 June, an agreement was proposed to settle the dispute.
The Executive Committee of the M.F.G.B. justified negotiating a
settlement in defiance of the previous ballot, because 'of our certain
knowledge that a National Wages Board, with the National Profits
Pool, could not be secured by the continuation of this struggle. Every
economic and political factor is dead against us'.[5]

According to the terms of agreement wages were to be determined
on a district basis according to the financial ability of each district
to pay. In each district there was to be a standard rate for each grade
defined as the district rate existing on 31 March 1921 plus the
district percentages payable in July 1914 plus, in the case of piece

[1] Lord Gainford, 'The Coal Problem', *Contemporary Review*, 119, June 1921,
p. 726.
[2] *The Economist*, 25 June 1921.
[3] At the time Treasurer of the M.F.G.B.
[4] P.R.O., Cab. 23/26.
[5] M.F.G.B., 28 June 1921.

workers, the percentage additions made consequent upon the reduction in hours from eight to seven in 1919. A minimum wage was established at not less than 20 per cent of the new standard and was to be the first charge upon the proceeds of the industry. Standard profits were to be equivalent to 17 per cent of the cost of standard wages. The surplus revenue of the industry in each district was to be divided in the ratio of 83 per cent to wages and 17 per cent to profits after allowing for standard wages, standard profits and other ascertained costs of production. If during any period revenue was insufficient after paying costs of production and standard wages to meet standard profits, the deficiency was to be carried forward to the next accounting period as the first charge to be met out of any surplus made in subsequent periods. National and District Boards were to be established with provision for the appointment of Independent Chairmen. If at any time the application of the 'profit-sharing' principle resulted in low-paid day workers receiving a wage less than a 'subsistence wage' the District Board, or, if necessary, the impartial district Chairman was to fix the level of a subsistence wage.[1]

As far as the miners were concerned the terms of settlement were those of defeat. The emphasis upon district wage determination, albeit based upon total district profits and not upon the price of coal, was in direct opposition to the miners' demands for national wage regulation via a national wages board and a national profits pool. Whilst the miners secured a minimum wage for all workers many were suspicious of the method of paying wages above the standard. Since the share of the surplus profits going to wages was influenced directly by the cost of both the standard wages and standard profit and by 'costs of production other than wages', and since the two former items were fixed in amount by agreement, wages could be directly influenced by fluctuations in 'other costs of production', the constituent items of which were not specified in the agreement. Other trade unionists were strongly against profit sharing because they believed it endangered the standard trade union rate of wages and divided the loyalty of the workers between their union and their employer. Moreover, the owners had virtually dictated the proportion that profits should bear to wages and the amount of the new standard wage established in each district.

The proposed settlement was accepted by the Durham miners by 437 votes to 278.[2] Every other district in the Federation except Lancashire, Kent, Somerset and the Forest of Dean agreed to accept

[1] See Appendix I to this chapter.
[2] D.M.A., 1 July 1921.

the terms.[1] Consequently the M.F.G.B. decided to recommend the resumption of work. The lock-out was ended. Miners in Durham were back at work within a very short time. For many, however, there was no work to return to. Continued depression in the coal export trade and falling coal prices led many pits to close down temporarily or adopt short-time working. By the end of July 1921 over 22,000 miners, almost one-fifth of the Association's membership, were unemployed and by the middle of August the figure had risen to nearly 60,000.[2] By the end of August 106 collieries in Durham stood idle.[3] The defeat of the M.F.G.B. at the hands of the owners made many miners bitter and some felt that they had been betrayed for the sake of industrial peace. Miners at Leadgate protested against the 'autocratic attitude' of the M.F.G.B. Executive in forgoing the demand for a National Wages Board and Profits Pool without a mandate from the rank and file and called for the resignation of its entire membership.[4]

Since the settlement involved, at least for the time being, the abandonment by the Miners' Federation of the claim to a national system of wage negotiation it led the Federation to reconsider its opposition to the Mining Industry Act, 1920. Under the Act a Department of Mines and a Miners' Welfare Fund were established and welcomed by the miners, but provision was also made for the establishment of a system of Joint Committees and Boards representing owners and workers. The intention behind this system was that wages and conditions of employment should be adjusted on an area and district basis following the national determination of very broad questions of principle. The Federation adamantly refused to support a measure which implied a return to district wage bargaining,[5] but once the 1921 settlement removed its main objection the M.F.G.B. recommended district associations to agree to work the Act.[6]

VII

Before relations between the Durham miners' and coal owners' Associations rapidly deteriorated immediately prior to the start of the lock-out an important agreement was reached on the scale of boys' wages. Until February 1921 there had been no specified scale

[1] M.F.G.B., 1 July 1921.
[2] *Durham Chronicle*, 22 July, 5, 19 August 1921; *Colliery Guardian*, 22 July, 19 August 1921.
[3] *Durham Chronicle*, 26 August 1921.
[4] *Colliery Guardian*, 29 July 1921.
[5] Cf. M.F.G.B., 7 July 1920.
[6] *Ibid.*, 19 July 1921.

of wages applying to boys working either at bank or underground in Durham collieries. Many of the boys, reaching early manhood, were receiving only between 1s 6d and 1s 9d per day as a basic wage. The Durham Miners' Association, therefore, sought to secure a graduated scale of wages for boys aged between 14 years and 21 years old providing for an increase in basic wages every six months. The owners were at first reluctant to agree to such a scale and emphasized the advantage which boys over 16 years had already received from the flat-rate advances granted by the Government. Nevertheless, on 14 March 1921 an agreement was signed which fixed the basic wage of bank lads aged 14 at 1s to be advanced by 2d every six months until the age of 21 when the basic wage of 3s 3d would represent the equivalent adult rate. For boys underground the scale was fixed at a basic rate of 1s 4d at the age of 14 rising to 3s $0\frac{1}{2}$d at $20\frac{1}{2}$ years of age. Six months thereafter the boys would receive the full adult wage corresponding to the particular class of underground work at which they were employed.[1]

On 15 August the County Federation Board decided to approach the owners for the purpose of establishing a District Board under the terms of the National Agreement. It was decided to recommend that the existing members of the Conciliation Board should constitute the new District Board for the purpose of dealing exclusively with wages but that the Conciliation Board should continue in its function of dealing with all general questions affecting workers apart from wages.[2] Following negotiations with the owners an agreement was reached for the constitution and functions of the Board. Entitled 'The District Board for the Coal Industry of Durham' it was to consist of representatives from the County Federation Board and the Coal Owners' Association in 'such number as may be decided from time to time'. Both sides were free, therefore, to alter the membership of the new Board so as to differ from the old Conciliation Board. The Board was directed to deal with all questions referred to it under the terms of the 1921 settlement but no provision was made for the continuance of the old conciliation procedure of dealing with general questions apart from wages. An Independent Chairman was to be appointed every twelve months. Questions were first dealt with by the Board without the Independent Chairman and only referred thus when both parties failed to reach an agreement. The decisions of the Independent Chairman were to be final and binding on each party.[3]

[1] D.M.A., 15 March 1921.
[2] *Ibid.*, 15 August 1921.
[3] District Board for the Coal Industry of Durham, Rules of Procedure, 30 August 1921.

The 1921 Agreement, the essence of which lay in its abolition of the price criterion and the substitution of a profits criterion of wage capacity, was hailed both in this country and abroad[1] as a landmark to better relations between employers and employed. Its actual results did not match up to its aspirations. The Durham miners soon found themselves in dispute with the owners over the operation of the Agreement, especially in the definition of 'costs of production other than wages', and after 1921 a great deal of their time was spent in trying to amend its terms and method of operation.

[1] See *Final Report of the United States Coal Commission*, 1922–3, p. 274.

Appendix I

THE COAL MINING INDUSTRY DISPUTE 1921

TERMS OF SETTLEMENT

1. A National Board shall be constituted forthwith, consisting in equal numbers of persons chosen by the Mining Association of Great Britain and persons chosen by the Miners' Federation of Great Britain.

There shall also be established District Boards, consisting in equal numbers of persons representing owners and workmen in each district.

The National and District Boards shall draw up their own rules of procedure, which shall include a provision for the appointment of an Independent Chairman for each Board.

2. The wages payable in each district shall be expressed in the form of a percentage upon the basis rates prevailing in the district, and shall be periodically adjusted in accordance with the proceeds of the industry as ascertained in such district.

3. The amount of the percentage to be paid in each district during any period shall be determined by the proceeds of the industry in that district during a previous period, as ascertained by returns to be made by the owners, checked by joint test audit of the owners' books carried out by independent accountants appointed by each side.

4. The sum to be applied in each district to the payment of wages above the standard wages as hereinafter defined shall be a sum equal to 83 per cent of the surplus of such proceeds remaining after deduction therefrom of the amounts of the following items during the period of ascertainment:

(a) the cost of the standard wages;

(b) the costs of production other than wages;

(c) standard profits equivalent to 17 per cent of standard wages;

and the share of the surplus applicable to wages shall be expressed as a percentage upon the basis rates prevailing in the district.

Provided that if in any period the ascertained proceeds, after deduction of costs other than wages and the cost of the standard wages, prove to have been insufficient to meet the standard profits, the deficiency shall be carried forward as a first charge to be met out of any surplus, ascertained as above, in subsequent periods.

5. If the rates of wages thus determined in any district do not provide a subsistence wage to low-paid day wage-workers, such additions in the form of allowances per shift worked shall be made for that period to the daily wages of these workers as, in the opinion of the District Board, or, in the event of failure to agree by the parties,

in the opinion of the Independent Chairman, may be necessary for the purpose. Such allowances shall be treated as items of cost in the district ascertainments.

6. For the purpose of these periodical adjustments the units shall be the districts set out in the Schedule hereto, and shall only be varied by the decision of the District Board or Boards concerned, provided that no variation shall take place prior to 1st February, 1922, in the grouping of any district unless it is mutually agreed by the representatives of both sides in the district or districts concerned.

7. The standard wages shall be the district basis rates existing on the 31st March, 1921, plus the district percentages payable in July 1914 (or the equivalents in any district in which there has been a subsequent merging into new standards), plus, in the case of pieceworkers, the percentage additions which were made consequent upon the reduction of hours from eight to seven.

8. In no district shall wages be paid at lower rates than standard wages plus 20 per cent thereof.

9. The National Board shall forthwith consider what items of cost are to be included for the purposes of paragraph 4 (b) above, and in the event of agreement not being arrived at by the 31st July, the matter shall be referred to the Independent Chairman for decision.

10. The Wages payable by the owners up to the 31st August inclusive shall be based upon the ascertained results of the month of March, and the wages payable during September shall be based upon the ascertained results of the month of July. The periods of ascertainment thereafter shall be decided by the National Board.

11. During the 'temporary period', as hereinafter defined, the following special arrangements shall apply in modification of the general scheme set out above:

(a) In calculating the proceeds for March the deduction to be made in respect of costs other than wages shall be the average of such costs during January, February, and March.

(b) In any district in which reductions in wages continue to be made after the first ascertainment, no part of the surplus proceeds shall be assigned to profits if and in so far as this would have the effect of reducing the wages below the level in the preceding month.

When in any district there is a break in the continuity of reductions in wages upon the periodical ascertainments, at that point and thereafter the general scheme shall apply fully in regard to owners' surplus profits.

(c) The proviso to paragraph 4 regarding the carrying forward of deficiencies in standard profits shall not apply, but any net losses shall be so carried forward.

(d) The Government will give a grant not exceeding £10,000,000 in subvention of wages.

(e) The subvention shall be available for making such increases to the wages otherwise payable in any district as may be necessary to prevent the reductions below the March rates of wages being greater than the following amounts:

During July, 2s a shift for persons of 16 years of age and upwards, and 1s a shift for persons under 16.

During August, 2s 6d and 1s 3d respectively.

During September, 3s and 1s 6d respectively, provided that the balance of the subvention is sufficient for this purpose.

(f) If any district in which in any month the proceeds available for wages, calculated in accordance with the terms of this settlement, are sufficient to admit of a rate of wages equal to or higher than the rate payable under the maximum reduction for that month, the wages payable by the owners shall be calculated not in terms of basis plus percentage, but on the same basis as during March, less flat rate reductions uniform throughout the district for persons of 16 years of age and upwards, and persons under 16 years of age respectively.

(g) In any district in which the wages calculated in accordance with the terms of this settlement are less than the wages payable under the maximum reductions aforesaid, the difference shall be met by the owners in that district during September to the extent of the aggregate net profits realized by them on the district ascertainment for July, and during October to the extent of the aggregate net profits realized by them on the district ascertainments for July and August.

(h) The expression 'temporary period' means the period from the date of the resumption of work to the 30th September, 1921.

12. The period of duration of this agreement shall be from the date of resumption of work until the 30th September, 1922, and thereafter until terminated by three months' notice on either side.

13. It is agreed as a principle that every man shall be entitled to return to his place when that place is available for him, and that men temporarily occupying places during the stoppage shall give way to men working in those places before the stoppage.

It is agreed that, on the other hand, there shall be no victimisation of men who have been keeping the collieries open, not in the sense that they are to remain at the jobs they filled during the stoppage, but that they shall not be prevented from going back to their own jobs or from working subsequently at the colliery.

For and on behalf of each member of the Central Committee of the Mining Association of Great Britian and for the Mining Association.

EVAN WILLIAMS, President.

THOMAS R. RATCLIFFE-ELLIS, Secretary.

For and on behalf of each member of the Executive Committee of the Miners' Federation of Great Britain and for the Miners' Federation.

HERBERT SMITH, Acting President.

JAMES ROBSON, Treasurer.

FRANK HODGES, Secretary.

For and on behalf of His Majesty's Government,

WILLIAM C. BRIDGEMAN, Secretary for Mines.

E. A. GOWERS, Under-Secretary for Mines.

Mines Department, July 1st 1921.

Chapter V

THE ORIGINS AND COURSE OF
THE 1926 DISPUTE

I

Wages in Durham under the 1921 National Agreement fell throughout both the temporary and permanent period until in February 1922 they had actually fallen below the minimum percentage addition to basic rates, standing at 72·16 per cent compared with 197·45 per cent in October 1921. Between March 1921 and the end of January 1922 hewers', stonemen's and putters' wages fell by almost 11s per shift.[1] By August 1922 wages in every district within the Federation had fallen to their minimum level. The average wage per shift for all classes of workmen in Durham in November–December 1922 was 45 per cent below its March 1921 level while the index of real wages per shift (June. 1914=100) had fallen from 83·44 to 61·00 during the same period.[2]

The lower paid adult daywagemen in Durham were particularly hard hit by the severe reductions in wages. Under Section 5 of the 1921 agreement any District Board was able to augment the daily wages of low paid workmen by way of allowances payable per shift worked if the rates of wages determined by the ascertainment system did not provide a subsistence wage. Accordingly in October 1922 the Durham County Federation Board approached the owners with a claim for the determination of a subsistence wage for such workers.[3] The owners refused the request for an extra payment to adult daywagemen as a whole but suggested increasing the basic wages of two classes of workmen, shifters and wastemen, on the condition that other miners, notably hewers, 'were prepared to consider the more efficient working of the mine'.[4] More specifically the owners demanded that the working hours of those hewers working less than seven hours bank-to-bank should be increased to the limit imposed by agreement on 10 July 1919[5] before any advance in basic wages was made to shifters and wastemen. The County Federation Board

---

[1] *Durham Chronicle*, 6 January, 3 February 1922.
[2] M.F.G.B., 6 July 1922.
[3] D.M.A., 18 October 1921.
[4] *Ibid.*, 28 December 1921.
[5] See Chapter III, pp. 112-14.

promptly rejected the proposals.[1] The strategy employed by the local coal owners on this occasion marked the beginning of a campaign which they vigorously conducted during the 'twenties to reduce costs at the expense of the miners' standard of living. The attacks were directed largely at enforcing reductions in workmen's piece rates and/ or increases in the length of hewers' hours up to the maximum provided for by agreement with the Durham Miners' Association and eventually in accordance with the strict provisions of the law.[2]

The matter of a subsistence wage for low paid adult wage men still remained to be settled. The issue was eventually put before E. Lewis Thomas, Independent Chairman of the Durham District Board, who announced his award on 22 December 1921. For the period 1–31 December 1921 adult daywage workers were awarded such an allowance as would bring their earnings up to the sum of 7s 1d per shift, exclusive of rent free housing or rent allowance and free coal, the total value of which amounted to 1s 8d per shift.[3] The subsistence wage payable in every month thereafter was to be decided by joint negotiations between the owners and the Federation Board. At a meeting on 6 January 1922 the owners made it clear that any future decisions on the level of the subsistence wage ought to be based upon consideration of fluctuations in the cost of living. The miners' representatives protested against this decision since not only were the owners attempting to influence wages in a manner contrary to the terms of the 1921 Agreement but were asking for a method of wage determination over which the miners would have no control by means of a regular ascertainment of the relevant data. The miners' representatives were unable to press the issue before the Independent Chairman in the district owing to his ill-health. The owners refused to join the Federation Board in requesting a replacement for Thomas. The situation for the adult wagemen gradually worsened and rather than postpone a consideration of their wages until February, when Thomas felt able to consider the case, the Federation Board reluctantly agreed on 23 January to accept the owners' offer of a subsistence wage of 6s 11d per shift for February.[4]

In the joint discussions during the following months the miners were continually pressed by the owners to accept a subsistence wage linked to the cost-of-living index. At a joint meeting on 3 March the workmen's representatives asked that the 6s 11d granted in January should continue during the month of March. The owners referred to

[1] D.M.A., 1 December 1921.
[2] See below, pp. 166–7; 175.
[3] *Ibid.*, 28 December 1921.
[4] *Ibid.*, 23 January 1922.

the Independent Chairman's award of 7s 11d per shift when the cost-of-living index was 99 points above its July 1914 level and, determined to relate the subsistence wage to a similar ratio to the cost-of-living, which then stood at 88 points above July 1914, offered 6s 9d per shift. The workmen's representatives proposed 6s 10d as a basis for agreement which the owners eventually accepted on the distinct understanding:

'. . . that in future consideration of the subject the owners are not committed to a recognition of 6s 10d as the proper rate proportionate to the fall in the cost of living.' [1]

The owners' determination on this point soon became apparent. By the end of March 1922 the cost-of-living index had fallen two points compared with its level at the beginning of the month and at a meeting with the Federation Board on 31 March, to determine the subsistence wage for April, they proposed a wage of 6s 6d per shift. The Federation Board refused to consider the offer and the issue was referred to the Independent Chairman who eventually awarded 6s 8½d per shift.[2] Thereafter, the Federation Board was unable to secure any increase in the level of the subsistence wage but succeeded in preventing the owners from imposing marginal reductions with every monthly fluctuation in the cost-of-living index. The subsistence wage remained at 6s 8½d until May 1924,[3] when it was raised to 7s 6½d, despite the fact that the cost of living continued to fall.

II

In October 1921 the M.F.G.B. asked the Government to use the remaining £3 million balance of its subvention to improve miners' wages, especially in the less profitable districts, but the request was refused.[4] In the meantime miners in Durham were growing impatient with the operation of the 1921 agreement. The 'profit-sharing' element of the agreement was unworkable during its first year of operation since for the most part the majority of districts were being paid minimum wages. In no district did profits receive the agreed share of 'net proceeds'. In Durham miners were on the minimum for seven months during 1922.

[1] Durham Coal Owners' Association, *Minutes of Executive Committee*, 28 February 1922 to 21 January 1923.
[2] D.M.A., 15 April 1922.
[3] See below, p. 172.
[4] M.F.G.B., 19 October, 3 November 1921; P.R.O., Cab. 23/27.

The 1921 agreement was terminable on 30 September 1922 and in June 1922 the Morrison Lodge of the Durham Miners' Association issued a manifesto to all miners in the coalfield explaining why they should seek to terminate the agreement. Part of the manifesto read thus:

'*Fellow Mine-workers,*

In September you may give, if you choose, three months' notice to terminate the existing National Agreement. We urge you to do so for several reasons. First, it is an Agreement which not one of us thoroughly understands. ... Each month our leaders are mystified ... by having all their anticipations upset. No one can say with any degree of certainty what the next month's results will show. The fluctuation of the market does not constitute the only uncertain factor. The cost of production, other than wages, is just as uncertain. We are against the Agreement, not only for this uncertainty of its results, but because we suspect that the intention of the masters is to get the mine workers down, and this agreement plays into their hands. Why has the cost of production other than wages gone up so high? Look around! At almost every pit some kind of improvement is being effected, or money is paid out in some way which enters the account against our wages. How far this sort of thing is going on no one knows. No one will ever know. We have foundation in fact for suspecting that the Masters are "juggling" the figures in the way mentioned. Secondly, the agreement divides us into sectional coalfields and destroys hope of a National Wages Board. It tends to make us think in terms of accounting instead of a national industry. It creates the local feeling that a district must make the best terms for itself. ... The result is that, feeling and thinking this way, we are tempted to "stretch" agreements and lengthen hours because the Masters tell us it is to the advantage of our particular district. ... Thirdly, the principle of the agreement is bad for the Mine-workers. It leaves our wages to the mercy of factors over which we have not the least control. No voice in selling price, no voice in costs other than wages, no voice in management and control or anything else. ... It is said that our Masters are not doing well. ... We are quite prepared to take Durham or any other coalfield and deal with the question as to whether the Masters are merely in the workhouse like unto ourselves, or are doing fairly well out of our labour. We refer to all their concerns, profitable by-product plants included. We also note the privileges of concerns selling in coal and coke to firms composed again, largely of coal owners. ... We must have a new agreement which will scrap all insults such as a bare subsistence wage. We must have an agreement guaranteeing to us wages in keeping with human life and comfort. Our labour must be the first and not the last charge upon industry. Do not forever blame leaders. Express your discontent and show your determination to have better conditions. This is your fight.'[1]

The Lodge succeeded in epitomizing the grievances which miners in other districts had against the agreement although it failed to realize that labour was, in fact, the first charge upon industry. Nevertheless it was fully aware that the final share of total proceeds going to labour was being influenced to a great extent by the owners' own definition of 'costs of production other than wages'. Although the Durham miners' officials remained determined to seek substantial amendments to, and even the termination of, the 1921 agreement they agreed on 18 July to support a recommendation of the M.F.G.B. that the decision as to the future of the agreement should be delayed until the Federation's Executive Committee discussed with the coal owners and the Government 'plans for rendering immediate assistance to the workmen'.[2]

Meanwhile in Durham conditions were improving only very slowly. In November 1922 the percentage addition to basic rates rose above the minimum level for the first time since August 1922 standing at 94·64 per cent. By the end of June 1922 there were over 20,000 miners unemployed in Durham and those who were working, especially if low paid adult wage men, were receiving less than a living wage.[3]

The Durham coal owners persisted in their efforts to lengthen the working day of hewers so as to reduce working costs in face of the continuing depression in the industry. They attempted at first not so much to enforce the full hours prescribed by law, and thereby invoke the agreements on hewers' hours reached in 1890 and in 1919[4] but to abolish the variation in hewers' hours between collieries and between shifts at the same colliery. The hours hewers actually spent winning coal varied from six to six and three quarters although none worked a shift longer than seven hours bank-to-bank. The owners refused to recognize that there was any reason for such local variations, claiming that the imposition of a uniform shift of seven hours bank-to-bank would secure 'the greatest quantity of coal at the least possible cost' and restore the industry's finances which in turn 'would go in

[1] *Durham Chronicle*, 9 June 1922.
[2] M.F.G.B., 20 July 1922.
[3] *Durham Chronicle*, 16 June 1922.
[4] See above, pp. 19–20 and Chapter III, pp. 112–15.

the greater proportion to the workmen'.[1] Furthermore, their demands still meant that Durham piece-work coal getters would be working fewer hours per shift than similar classes of workmen in districts working the full hours prescribed by law. At a meeting between miners' and owners' representatives on 18 December 1922 the owners strongly urged the miners' Association to arrange that at any colliery where the owners required it they should be allowed to request hewers to work the full seven hours bank-to-bank in all shifts.[2] The miners refused to consider the request on the grounds that the agreement reached in 1919 stipulated that the existing hours of hewers were to be maintained.[3] As far as the owners were concerned short hewers' shifts added considerably to costs by preventing the most efficient use of datal hands, whose hours were longer. Individual attempts were made to increase hours. Miners at Auckland Park Colliery had their unemployment pay suspended when they refused to work on the conditions prescribed by the management, which included increasing the length of hewers' shifts.[4] In November 1922 a dispute arose in connection with the length of the hewers' hours at Wooley Colliery. Following the national stoppage the colliery had been re-started under a temporary agreement and without the sanction of the Durham Miners' Association whereby the hewers' hours were lengthened to seven plus one winding. With the expiration of the temporary agreement the workmen requested that the hours worked should be those enforced prior to the national stoppage, i.e. allowing for variations in hewers' hours up to a maximum of seven hours bank-to-bank, but the management instituted a uniform seven hours bank-to-bank shift.[5] The Durham Coal Owners' Association maintained throughout the discussion on hours that since the Seven Hours Agreement in 1919 was only intended to make such alterations as were necessary to meet the reduction of hours from eight to seven they retained the power granted in the Eight Hours Act to fix the length and timing of particular shifts.

During 1923 attention was increasingly focused upon the operation of the national wages agreement, the M.F.G.B. preferring to amend its provisions rather than terminate it altogether. At their Council meeting on 12 May the Association carried a resolution calling for notice to be given to terminate the existing agreement rather than

---

[1] Durham Coal Owners' Association, *Annual Report*, 1922, p. 14.
[2] *Ibid.*, pp. 16–18.
[3] D.M.A., 19 December 1922.
[4] M.F.G.B., 11 April 1922.
[5] Durham Coal Owners' Association, *Annual Report*, 1922, pp. 16–17.

seeking to amend it substantially.[1] The intention was to pave the way
for the drafting of a new agreement under which it would be easier
to demand that the miners had an increased voice in determining the
selling price of coal; fuller information of costs, especially the constituent items of 'costs of production other than wages'; a division
of the miners' surplus to provide a graduated scale allowing workmen 'a more reasonable share than at present' and an immediate
enquiry into the wages conditions of miners as a whole.[2] At a
M.F.G.B. conference on 30 May, however, a resolution was agreed
to by every district except Durham (Forest of Dean and Cumberland
remaining neutral) calling for a postponement of the discussions on
the wages agreement in view of the attempts being made to amend the
Minimum Wage Act, 1912.[3] The M.F.G.B. had earlier sought the
co-operation of the Labour Party in seeking the establishment of a
wage for miners equal to the cost of living after representations to the
Government on this issue had ended in failure.[4] The Amendment
Bill was defeated in its second reading on 21 June.

The Durham delegates to the Annual Conference of the M.F.G.B.
at Folkestone in July continued to fight in favour of terminating the
national wages agreement. In this they were supported by Lancashire
which even submitted a series of alternative proposals as the basis of
a new agreement. 'It is perfectly clear to us,' Robson told the delegates, 'that the agreement has operated absolutely in the interests of
the owners and against the interests of the men.'[5] Peter Lee, anxious
that the Federation should not delay in improving the wages situation, offered his own advice. 'Give the owners notice and tell them
there must be some amendment to the present Agreement,' he stated
dogmatically, 'and bring home to them ... the need for more co-
ordination in helping the poorer districts.'[6] The majority of the
Federation members remained unmoved. A resolution was eventually
carried by 479 votes to 277 outlining a number of proposed amendments to the wages agreement for submission to the National Board
and recommending that no vote should be taken on the question of
ending the agreement. Durham voted in favour of the resolution and
in direct opposition to its County mandate.

This action aroused deep opposition amongst the miners' Lodges
in Durham. Demands were made for the delegates to justify their

[1] D.M.A., 12 May 1923.
[2] Ibid.
[3] M.F.G.B., 30 May 1923.
[4] Ibid., 27 February, 7 March 1923; Durham Chronicle, 22 June 1923.
[5] M.F.G.B., 10 July 1923.
[6] Ibid.

'traitorous action',[1] for their exclusion as representatives to any future conferences up to a period of five years, and, in one case, for their immediate resignation.[2] The action of the delegates was the subject of a Special Council Meeting held on 6 October, the only outcome of which was the acceptance of a resolution which stated in a conciliatory tone: 'that we protest against Delegates sent to the Miners' Conference changing their vote and ask that in future Conferences they vote according to the mandate given by the County'.[3] As far as can be judged from the evidence of newspapers and the official sources of the Durham Miners' Association no adequate explanation of the delegates' conduct was ever given to the County.

Conditions gradually improved in Durham during 1923 mainly as a result of the fortuitous increase in the demand for coal exports following the French occupation of the Ruhr.[4] The percentage addition to basic wages, which had stood at its minimum level between August and October 1922, rose to 97·02 in February 1923 and to 105·16 in June 1923. The improvement in real wages was less encouraging. The average wage per shift of all classes of workmen in Durham during February 1923 was 48·3 per cent higher than that payable in June 1914, while the cost of living had increased by 77 per cent during the same period.[5] On the other hand in the twelve months after February 1922 Durham employers reaped an average profit of 1s 4d per ton of coal, only ¼d per ton less than that earned between 1912 and 1913, the two most prosperous years before 1914.[6]

In July 1923 the Association approached the local coal owners with a proposal to merge the basic wage plus 50 per cent of the existing percentage addition into a new basic wage and to adjust the remaining portion of the percentage so as to leave wages at their existing value. The miners hoped to secure a new basic wage which could be regarded as a permanent minimum and a safeguard against the rising cost of living at a time when percentage additions to wages were increasing under the influence of a short-term coal export boom. The owners, apart from refusing to consider any level of minimum wages except that laid down in the National Agreement, declined even to consider the claim unless the miners reconsidered their position regarding the working of the Joint Committee,[7] the rearrange-

---

[1] D.M.A., 18 August 1923, *Durham Chronicle*, 24 August 1923.
[2] D.M.A., 6 October 1923.
[3] *Ibid.*
[4] See Chapter I, p. 34.
[5] M.F.G.B., *Report of the Executive Committee for the Year Ending June 30th, 1923*, p. 116.
[6] *Durham Chronicle*, 4 May 1923.
[7] See above, pp. 21–2.

ment of hewers' hours[1] and their support of the miners on strike at Hebburn Colliery.[2] It became obvious that the employers were only willing to discuss wages and conditions on their own terms, with an almost singular consideration for making short-term gains in trade, and the negotiations subsequently broke down.[3]

During August and November 1923 the M.F.G.B. negotiated with the coal owners for a revision of the national wages agreement so that the ratio of wages to profits would be 100:13 and the minimum percentage payable on the standard wage be raised from 20 to 40 per cent. In view of the employers' continued refusal to accede their demands the M.F.G.B. resolved on 14 December to recommend its members to take a ballot vote and vote in favour of terminating the agreement.[4] This recommendation was endorsed by a special conference on the following day despite an attempt by Robson to persuade the Federation to tender the necessary three months' notice without the preliminary of a ballot vote.[5] Since the Federation had formulated its own amendment proposals the Durham delegates had, in the meantime, been freed from their Association's previous resolution requiring them to seek an immediate termination of the agreement as a prerequisite to the Durham miners proposing their own series of amendments. The delegates were now free to vote in favour of referring questions back to the districts for consultation whenever necessary.[6] The Durham miners voted by 73,210 to 22,269 in favour of terminating the agreement. The national figures were 510,303 for and 114,458 against.[7] On 17 January the Executive Committee of the M.F.G.B. gave three months' notice to end the agreement.[8]

By March 1924 the coal owners had submitted their own proposed amendments to the agreement. Standard profits were to be 15 per cent of standard wages, the surplus was to be divided in the ratio of 87 per cent to wages and 13 per cent to profits and the minimum percentage on standard wages was to be increased from 20 to 30. They further proposed that men not drawing a subsistence wage should not, nevertheless, work for a wage less than 40 per cent above the standard wages of the lowest-paid class of daywage worker. Furthermore, there was to be a $12\frac{1}{2}$ per cent increase in subsistence

[1] See above, pp. 166–7.
[2] See Chapter II, pp. 91–2.
[3] Durham Coal Owners' Association, *Annual Report*, 1923, pp. 20–23.
[4] M.F.G.B., 14 December 1923.
[5] *Ibid.*, 15 December 1923.
[6] D.M.A., 8 December 1923.
[7] M.F.G.B., 17 January 1923.
[8] *Ibid.*

wages.[1] Had the owners' proposals been effective during the period of the November-December 1923 ascertainment (governing wages payable in March and April 1924) the percentage addition to basic rates would have been increased in Durham from 116·6 to 122·2 and the subsistence wage increased from 6s 8½d to 7s 6½d.[2] The owners' latest proposals were rejected by the M.F.G.B. at a conference on 13 March. Immediately after the conference the miners' leaders were informed by MacDonald, Prime Minister of the newly elected and first Labour Government, that in view of the Party's weak position in the House of Commons the Government was powerless to legislate. During later negotiations between the miners' and coal owners' representatives the Government suggested that a Court of Inquiry should be established to consider the wages situation in the mining industry.[3]

The Federation had to decide whether to accept the employers' terms or a government enquiry. At a special conference on 28 March Robson and Lee tried to persuade the Federation to submit the proposals to the districts with a recommendation for their acceptance while at the same time supporting a government enquiry. 'The offer we are now discussing,' explained Lee, 'whilst not anything like what we would desire, is a great improvement on our present conditions.'[4] The conference decided to recommend the rejection of the owners' proposals and to call for a Government enquiry, the Durham amendment to the Executive Committee's resolution being defeated by 502 votes to 271.[5]

The Durham miners' leaders were anxious that the mining community should share both the rewards of an immediate wage advance and an opportunity for possible future concessions. To them the idea of a strike to enforce an increase in wages was out of the question:

'Nothing could be more disastrous to the mining community of this country,' explained Robson. 'Financially, numerically and from every standpoint we have nothing to hope for from such a course. Our policy is to accept the terms, strengthen our forces and go into an enquiry with sufficient time on hand to review the whole factors that make against wages, and to insist upon Government action in giving effect to the findings of the enquiry.'[6]

[1] *Ibid.*, 12 March 1924.
[2] D.M.A., 18 March 1924. Cf. *Durham Chronicle*, 5 April 1924.
[3] M.F.G.B., 26 March 1924.
[4] *Ibid.*, 28 March 1924.
[5] *Ibid.*
[6] *Durham Chronicle*, 5 April 1924.

The result of the ballot on the owners' proposals in Durham showed 79,619 votes for acceptance and 24,505 against. The national voting figures were, however, in accordance with the Federation's recommendation and showed 338,650 against the terms and 322,392 for.[1]

On 15 April the Minister of Labour appointed a Court of Inquiry under the Chairmanship of Lord Buckmaster (a former Lord Chancellor). The Court rejected the miners' suggestion of a national profits pool as 'a political question' with the merits of which 'we are not concerned'.[2] They regarded the reduction in miners' wages as 'a fate which has been shared with other unsheltered industries, e.g. agriculture, cotton and engineering' but pointed out that 'if 1914 were taken as a measure of the proper wages to be paid to those engaged in the mining industry, practically every class of daywage worker is, in terms of real wages, worse off today than he was then. In some cases this deficiency is most marked'.[3] The Court accepted the miners' contention that the 1921 agreement had allowed certain owners' profits 'substantially in excess of pre-war profits'.[4]

The Court suggested that the employers and workmen should resume negotiations, which they did on 13 May. After four days' discussion the owners published their proposed terms of settlement. Standard profits were to be at the rate of 15 per cent of the amount paid in standard wages, the surplus being divided in the ratio of 88 per cent to wages and 12 per cent to profits. The general minimum percentage on standard wages was to be increased from 20 to $33\frac{1}{3}$ and the subsistence wages increased by one-eighth. In no district were the wages of any adult daywage workmen to fall below 40 per cent above the standard wages of the lowest-paid class of daywage workmen in the district. Only one-third of the surplus accruing from any one ascertainment period was to be used to make good previous deficiencies in standard profits, any balance being carried forward. The effect of the proposals in Durham would have been to raise the minimum percentage addition to basic wages from 89 to 110,[5] which,

---

[1] M.F.G.B., 10 April 1924.
[2] *Report by a Court of Inquiry Concerning the Wages Position in the Coal Mining Industry*, 1924 (Cmd. 2129), p. 14.
[3] *Ibid.*, p. 12.
[4] *Ibid.*, p. 15.
[5] Taking as an example the figures in the August 1921 ascertainment for Durham: Standard wages amounted to £2,737,355 and basic wages £1,738,003. 20 per cent on standard wages equals £547,451 which, expressed as a percentage on basic wages, equals approximately 31·5. The July 1914 percentage was 57·5 making the old minimum percentage addition 89. $33\frac{1}{3}$ per cent on standard wages equals £912,451 which expressed as a percentage upon basic wages equals approximately 52·5 making the new minimum percentage addition 110.

according to M.F.G.B. estimates, would have increased the average standard wage per shift from 7s 3·9d to 8s 3·62d.[1]

The new proposals were discussed at a Special M.F.G.B. conference on 29 May. Supporting the acceptance of the terms Lee told the conference:

'This agreement is undoubtedly in the interests of those districts that have been on the minimum and will be on the minimum in the future, and even on that account I believe we ought to accept and try to keep our forces intact if the owners in any district try to take undue advantage of the weaker districts. ... Don't trouble ... about selling prices remaining in the hands of the owners, because you know we can never have true peace in the coal trade until we have unification or nationalization. This is a step in that direction which will tend to bring it more prominently forward in the future.'[2]

The Conference finally decided to accept the owners' terms and the agreement, to last for twelve months and subject to a month's notice on either side, was signed on 18 June.[3]

III

One of the earliest problems the Durham Miners' Association encountered in working the new wages agreement related to adult day-wage workmen. Under Clause 6 of the agreement district coal owners were empowered to deal with cases of anomalies in the wages of the classes of men at or near the level of the wages of the lowest-paid class of workmen in the district. The Durham coal owners agreed in September 1924 to adopt the subsistence wage, and not the actual wage, as the standard of measure of the wages of the lowest-paid class.[4] This had the effect of reducing the differential which had previously existed between the lowest paid men and other more highly paid adult daywagemen. Datal stonemen, for example, had been earning 8½d per shift more than the lowest paid class of workmen, but with the adoption of the subsistence wage, considerably higher than the actual wage with current percentage, the differential had been reduced to only ½d. The Durham County Federation Board approached the owners to increase the wages of the various classes of workmen thus affected. The owners, anxious to avoid any further

[1] M.F.G.B., 17 May 1924.
[2] *Ibid.*, 29 May 1924.
[3] *Ibid.*
[4] D.M.A., 27 September 1924.

increases in cost, appealed to the Board to withdraw their demands but, being obliged to honour the 1924 agreement, eventually agreed that datal stonemen, screen enginemen, firemen, bellmen, wiremen and platelayers on the surface should be paid not less than 7s 9½d per shift. The offer was accepted by the members of the various branches of the Federation Board.[1]

At the time when the 1921 wages agreement came to an end wage rates in Durham stood at 116·6 per cent above the basis rising to 120·12 per cent in July 1924. From September to December 1924 they stood at the newly-formed minimum level of 110 per cent. Although the total cost per ton of coal in Durham had fallen from 26s 8·5d in July 1921 to 16s 9·19d in July 1924 selling prices per ton during the same period had fallen by almost the same amount from 27s 10·8d to 17s 6·93d. Without any marked increase in the wages fund of the County the main beneficiaries of the decline in selling prices were the public and cognate trades.[2] By July 1924 hewers' wages had increased by 44·46 per cent over their 1914 level, fillers' wages by 42·45 per cent and banksmen's, horsekeepers', picksharpers' and wastemen's wages (all adult datal workers) by just over 39 per cent compared with a 71 per cent rise in the cost of living.[3] By the beginning of 1925, when the coal industry was again faced with continued depression, it had become obvious that the level of miners' wages was being determined by the subsidiary provisions stipulating the payment of the minimum wage and not by the principles of proceeds-sharing.

During January 1925 the Executive Committee of the Durham Miners' Association undertook a close study of the working of the wages agreement and presented its recommendations to a Council meeting on 7 February. The Committee demanded the immediate introduction of a method of wage regulation based not upon a district but a national aggregation of proceeds, the division of surplus proceeds in the ratio 88:12, a minimum wage of 12s per day for all adult workmen in and about the mines and the inclusion in the ascertainments of all proceeds from coke and by-product works.[4] These proposals, together with other district amendments, were discussed at a special M.F.G.B. Conference on 26 February called at Durham's request to consider the modification of the wages agreement. No action was taken, however, except to circularize a full list of proposals to all districts.[5]

[1] *Ibid.*, 27 September, 13 October 1924.
[2] *Ibid.*, 3 September 1924.
[3] *Ibid.*
[4] *Ibid.*, 7 February 1925.
[5] M.F.G.B., 27 February 1925; D.M.A., 20 January 1925.

Meanwhile in Durham the employers persisted in their attempts to enforce widespread reductions in piece rates and increases in hewers' working hours. At a number of meetings with miners' representatives during the early months of 1924 the owners pressed their demand that all hewers should work seven hours bank-to-bank but met with stern opposition.[1] Accordingly on 29 September 1924 Reginald Guthrie, Secretary of the Durham Coal Owners' Association, notified the miners' Association that individual colliery owners would 'no longer be bound by any agreement which prohibits them claiming such alteration in the hours (within the limitation fixed by law) as is necessary to meet the circumstances and enable them to afford employment to the workmen'.[2] The owners' intention was not to terminate all the conditions of the Eight Hours Agreement of 13 December 1909 or the Seven Hours Agreement of 10 July 1919 which governed working hours throughout the coalfield but simply to free individuals from the restriction placed upon them in 1919 to increase hewers' hours to the limit prescribed by law.[3] Individual owners who were not able to carry on their collieries under the existing hewers' hours were now at liberty to approach their workmen and seek some other arrangement. In the extreme some hewers could have the time they spent actually winning coal increased by one hour.[4] The lack of uniformity in hewers' hours throughout the coalfield, proof itself of the miners' resistance to moves to institute a uniform shift of seven hours bank-to-bank, meant that the extent of the potential increases in hours varied from colliery to colliery. In 1925 hewers at 42 collieries (representing 49·2 per cent of the total hewers in the coalfield) were working seven hours bank-to-bank whilst at the remaining 132 collieries hewers were working on an average less than seven hours.[5] Some local coal owners found it difficult to appreciate the Durham miners' resistance to working longer hours. A. F. Pease, Chairman of Pease and Partners Ltd, confessed to shareholders at their Annual Meeting in 1923:

'I cannot understand the great reluctance of the men to work slightly longer hours which would inevitably increase the rate of wage by an increase in the general percentage and in the case of piece workers give them an immediate increase in their pay on account of the extra

[1] Durham Coal Owners' Association, *Annual Report*, 1924, pp. 26–7.
[2] *Ibid.*, p. 27.
[3] Cf. Chapter III, pp. 112–15.
[4] See above, pp. 166–7.
[5] M.F.G.B., 23 September 1925.

tons won per man. I am all for the men having their holidays and having their amusements, but I cannot see why they object so much to working an extra half hour when they have nothing particular to do with the time.'[1]

Whilst the Durham miners fought to maintain the privileged position of its most numerous and influential class of workman the Executive Committee of the M.F.G.B. met the coal owners at national level, at their request, to consider the serious condition of the coal industry and the possible remedies which could be adopted to solve it. The talks began on 29 January 1925 and continued until the end of June. The discussions gave the miners an opportunity to prepare a reasoned account of the nature of the problem facing the industry and to argue that the existing method of organization only aggravated the situation. Viewing the economic position of the industry against the background of a general world depression, the miners drew particular attention to the effects of the use of other sources of power upon the long-term demand for coal and to the harmful effects of reparations coal upon British exports. Anxious to improve the basis upon which wages were determined under the profit-sharing principle they demanded that the workmen should 'share in the results of the industry in the widest sense' and proposed the inclusion in the ascertainments of the profits from coking and by-product plants and all other ancilliary undertakings. The organization of production and distribution and the system of administration in the industry were heavily criticized. The miners asserted that vertically-integrated firms were able to transfer coal to their iron works and other enterprises at low prices and drew attention to the 'inflation of capital and the use of profits in needless new developments'.[2]

The coal owners, on the other hand, continued to view the position of the industry in the light of the high price of coal and urged the necessity of reducing prices either by the direct lowering of wages or by increasing hours of work. The miners were determined as ever to resist both methods and urged strongly in favour of increasing wages to meet the rising cost of living and reducing costs by means of a more efficient system of organization, production and distribution. As the depression in the industry deepened during 1925 these basic antagonisms sharpened. Between 1 January 1924 and the end of May 1925, 79 mines, normally employing 27,406 wage-earners, had closed

[1] Pease and Partners Limited, *Report and Accounts for the Year Ending 31 March 1923*.
[2] Miners' Federation of Great Britain, *The Economic Position of the Coal Industry*, May 1925.

in Durham and never reopened, while only five, employing 257 men, had opened during the same period.[1] The miners' leaders, conscious of the owners' determination to restore the competitive position of the industry even at the expense of the miners' standard of living, sensed the urgency of the situation. Speaking at Wheatley Hill, Peter Lee reminded a group of miners:

'Our funds are going down very rapidly. For every pound you pay into the Association we are paying out more than two in relief alone. We cannot continue to pay at the rate we are paying, and shortly we will have to consider the question of trying to make some arrangement whereby this slump, so far as Durham is concerned, can be checked. There are two facts we must recognize—the men will very likely have to start on new things that are not palatable to us, but the other side will also have to do something which is not very palatable. We have—men and owners—a rough time in front of us.'[2]

A. J. Cook, Secretary of the M.F.G.B., was more precise. Speaking at Ferryhill he prophesied: 'Before 1925 is out . . . we shall be face to face in Britain with the greatest industrial struggle we have ever had, that will involve not only the miners, but the railwaymen, dockers and engineers.'[3]

The subsequent activities of the owners added weight to such prophecies. On 18 June the coal owners stated that they intended to give notice to end the existing wages agreement and that in their view a return to the eight-hour day was essential. The miners' leaders made it clear that they would never agree to longer hours or lower wages.[4] On 30 June the Mining Association formally announced that it wished to end the wages agreement on 31 July 1925. The Directors of the Harton Coal Company reported at their Annual General Meeting on 19 June that the 1924 wages agreement had had 'disastrous results from the owners' standpoint, obliging them to pay a minimum wage far in excess of what the ascertained proceeds alone would provide'.[5] Furthermore in no month since the agreement came into operation in Durham had there been a sufficient balance left, after providing for wages and other costs, to meet the owners' standard profits, and in the three months January, February and

[1] M.F.G.B., 20 May 1925. Cf. *Durham Chronicle*, 14, 28 March, 18 April, 16 May 1925.
[2] *Colliery Guardian*, 3 April 1925. Cf Chapter II, pp. 86–7.
[3] *Durham Chronicle*, 30 May 1925.
[4] M.F.G.B., 19 June 1924.
[5] *Annual General Meeting of the Harton Coal Company*, 19 June 1925.

March 1925 proceeds did not even meet wages and other costs of production. Nor was Durham alone in its experience. During the currency of the 1924 agreement wages in every one of the thirteen districts, with the exception of the Eastern, became rigid at the newly established minimum rates but owners were obliged to pay them irrespective of the amount of district proceeds.[1]

The owners' new proposals radically altered the principles of the 1921 and 1924 agreements. Whilst the main principle of the previous agreements as to the allocation of a definite proportion of the net proceeds of the industry to wages was to continue the separate provisions for the payment of a standard profit corresponding to standard wages were to be abolished. Instead the whole of the proceeds of the industry, after deducting costs of production other than wages, was to be divided between wages and profits in the ratio 87:13. The workmen's share, after deducting subsistence allowances, was to be expressed as a percentage on their basic rates. The minimum percentage addition to basic rates, which the miners had long regarded as the vital part of the previous agreements, was to disappear. In other words it was proposed that a definite portion of the proceeds should be allotted to profits in each ascertainment period, irrespective of the amount of the proceeds and of the position of wages. Wages would thus no longer be a first charge on the industry but would rank equally with profits, each taking a definite share of the proceeds whatever they might be. 'The principle of a national minimum percentage would thus be lost,' stated the M.F.G.B., 'and there would be no limit to the extent to which the wages of the general body of mine workers could be reduced.'[2]

Had the owners' offer been in operation in Durham during the nine months ending 31 March 1925 the wages per shift of hewers would have been reduced from 9s 8d to 7s 5·75d, while wastemen would have suffered a reduction of 2s 8·25d per shift and labourers 2s 1·75d per shift. The percentage addition to basic rates payable in July 1925 would have been reduced from 110 to 66·34. Taking July 1914 as 100, average earnings per man shift in Durham would have fallen from 160·29 in May 1925 to 127·51 in August 1925, when, on the same basis, the cost of living stood at 173. The average wage per man shift

[1] J. A. Bowie, 'A New Method of Wage Adjustment in the Light of the Recent History of Wage Methods in the British Coal Industry', *Economic Journal*, XXXVII, 1927, pp. 386–91.
[2] M.F.G.B., *The Coal Crisis*, 22 July 1925, p. 4. For a full discussion of the workings of the profit-sharing system in the coal industry under the various agreements see A. G. Pool, *Wage Policy in Relation to Industrial Fluctuations*, London 1938, pp. 189–243.

would have been reduced from 9s 11·62d to 7s 11·0d. Owners' profits throughout the country during the nine-month period would have increased by £11,565,478 (at the expense of wages) equivalent to an increase of 1s 3·08d profit per ton raised.[1] The miners' delegates to a special M.F.G.B. conference on 3 July decided unanimously to reject the owners' proposals. Robson urged the Federation to seek the support of the T.U.C. General Council and similar representative bodies to help resist the owners.[2] The proposals were hotly criticized by the Durham miners' leaders. W. P. Richardson described them as 'the most foolish ever offered by any body of capitalists'.[3] Peter Lee, speaking at the Gala meeting of the Durham County Women's Labour Party on 5 July 1925, declared:

'In all seriousness I say to you people that whatever be the consequences we cannot without a struggle accept such conditions. . . . If this reduction is put into operation the wages of the Durham miners will only be 8¾ per cent above 1914.'[4]

IV

Neither Evan Williams, the Chairman of the Mining Association, nor W. C. Bridgeman, the First Lord of the Admiralty, nominated by the Government to act as mediator in the deadlock, was able to persuade the M.F.G.B. to enter into discussions with the owners to discuss the new proposals. Consequently on 13 July the Minister of Labour appointed a Court of Inquiry consisting of H. P. Macmillan as Chairman, W. Sherwood (a trade union official) and Sir Josiah (later Lord) Stamp, 'to inquire into the causes and circumstances of the dispute in the coal-mining industry and to report thereon'. The miners refused to accept the Court of Inquiry 'that has for its object the ascertainment of whether mineworkers' wages can be reduced or their hours extended'. Nothing short of a complete withdrawal of the owners' notices would bring the miners into open conference.[5]

The Court of Inquiry was conducted without the assistance of the M.F.G.B. It issued its report on 28 July and concluded:

'We are satisfied on one point, that the workers are justified in claiming that any wages agreement which they can be asked to accept should provide for a minimum wage.'

[1] M.F.G.B., *The Coal Crisis*, 22 July 1925, pp. 9–15.
[2] M.F.G.B., 3 July 1925.
[3] *Colliery Guardian*, 10 July 1925.
[4] *Durham Chronicle*, 11 July 1925.
[5] M.F.G.B., 15 July 1925.

As for the means of securing a lasting improvement in the miners' standard of living the Court submitted that:

'There is considerable room for improving the efficiency of the industry as a whole, and in this way affording some aid to its economic position. . . . We cannot believe that there is no room for improvement in the management organization and development of the industry, or that no alteration is to be found in these directions.'[1]

Before the termination of the owners' notices on 31 July the Durham miners were informed of the conditions upon which work would be available during August 1925. The owners proposed an 80 per cent addition to basic wages and that adult day-wage workmen should receive not less than 6s 6d per shift (married men) and 6s per shift (single men). They further reasserted their determination to seek changes in the conditions of employment wherever necessary claiming that the proposed arrangement did not preclude owners at individual collieries requiring 'alterations in piece-work rates or arrangements with respect to the hours of work within the limits at present prescribed by Act of Parliament'.[2] The Durham County Federation Board promptly reacted to the owners' terms by appealing to members to resist all attempts to alter conditions of employment and help support the demand for a national wages policy.[3] Not all sections of the Board were as determined as the miners. R. Dobson, President of the Durham County Colliery Enginemen's Association, speaking at Murton, called upon the leaders of the M.F.G.B. to arrange some means of continuing to work the collieries 'even if they have to come down to district arrangements'.[4]

The M.F.G.B. decided on 24 July that the districts should accept the owners' notices and that the necessary safety men should be allowed to continue working at rates of wages and conditions of employment not less favourable than those obtaining before 31 July.[5] Meanwhile on 23 July the T.U.C. assumed full responsibility for conducting the dispute and urged the Prime Minister to bring the miners' and owners' representatives together in an unconditional conference.[6] Negotiations between the Government, the T.U.C., the miners and the owners continued throughout the last week of July. The miners were discouraged by the Government's reaction to the

[1] *Report by a Court of Inquiry concerning the Coal Mining Industry Dispute*, 1925.
[2] *Journal and North Star*, 25 July 1925.
[3] D.M.A., 20 July 1925.
[4] *Durham Chronicle*, 18 July 1925.
[5] M.F.G.B., 24 July 1925.
[6] *Ibid.*, 23 July 1925.

dispute. Baldwin was reported to a special conference of trade union executives on 30 July to have asserted that not only the miners but 'all workers in this country have got to take reductions in wages to help put industry on its feet'.[1] The conference immediately empowered the T.U.C. to issue strike notices if necessary and to financially support strikers. On the same evening the T.U.C. issued instructions for an embargo on coal movements to be enforced after midnight 31 July. This had an immediate effect. On 31 July the Prime Minister announced that the owners had agreed to suspend their notices and that the Government was prepared to guarantee financial assistance to the industry for the payment of existing wages up to 1 May 1926. During the intervening nine months a full enquiry would be conducted into the economic position of the industry. The subsidy was designed to fill the gap between the minimum level of wages established under the 1924 agreement and the level of wages which would have resulted from an acceptance of the owners' proposals made on 1 July. The Government's offer was accepted and the districts were instructed to continue work.[2]

The granting of the Government subvention intensified the antagonism which existed between employers and miners in Durham over conditions of work. The basic assumption underlying the subvention was that existing rates of wages would be maintained but miners at Horden, Bowden and Boldon were pressed after 31 July to accept wages and conditions of employment inferior to those prevailing before the notices were suspended.[3] By September 1925 the attacks upon the Durham miners' standard of living had increased to such an extent that Richardson appealed to the M.F.G.B. for financial assistance to those miners out of work but refused unemployment benefit as a direct result of resisting owners' attempts to alter conditions of employment.[4] The Federation rejected an appeal for a levy but promised to ensure the payment of benefit to men refused work since the granting of the subvention.[5] At a meeting with Federation representatives on 23 September the Prime Minister guaranteed the maintenance of wages at their existing level and undertook to review the whole situation in the face of any further local reductions.[6] At a M.F.G.B. Conference on 9 October Durham supported York-

[1] *Daily Herald*, 31 July 1925. Baldwin later denied the statement. Cf. M.F.G.B., 19 August 1925.
[2] M.F.G.B., 31 July 1925; *Durham Chronicle*, 8 August 1925; P.R.O. Cab. 23/50.
[3] M.F.G.B., 19 August, 8 October 1925; *Durham Chronicle*, 24 October 1925.
[4] M.F.G.B., 23 September 1925.
[5] *Ibid.*
[6] *Ibid.*

shire in trying to persuade the Federation not to participate in the proposed enquiry into the coal industry until a definite assurance was given that no further reductions in wages would occur during the period of the subvention. The suggestion was defeated in favour of a recommendation that the Federation's Executive Committee discussed the issue with the Minister of Labour.[1]

The Durham Miners' Association took action of its own. At its Council meeting on 14 November it was agreed to conduct an individual ballot vote of members in answer to the question, 'Are you prepared to give in 14 days' notice to cease employment to enforce the demand against any further local reductions or increase of hewers' hours?' Resolutions calling for the membership to ballot in favour of the Lodges having power to mutually agree with colliery managers' reductions or revisions in piece rates and for the Executive Committee to meet the owners with a view to unifying the hours of coal hewers to seven hours bank-to-bank were rejected.[2] The resulting vote showed 44,285 in favour and 42,598 against the proposal failing to provide, according to Rule, the necessary two-thirds majority for strike action to occur.[3] By December 1925, 40 collieries had made arrangements for a revision of piece rates on hewers' hours up to a maximum of seven bank-to-bank. Those which remained loyal to the Association's refusal to compromise on either issue did so only in face of increasing hardship. The relief provided by the miners' union to members refused unemployment benefit owing to their rejection of revised conditions of employment had gradually been reduced from £1 to 5s per member and by December 1925 had been suspended altogether, thus leaving the workmen to the mercy of the Board of Guardians.[4] Eventually on 23 December the Executive Committee of the Durham Miners' Association agreed that Lodges should have power to negotiate with local colliery managers for restarting pits by revising piece rates and hewers' hours, always providing that they should not exceed seven hours from bank-to-bank. 'The longer it is put off,' explained the Executive, 'the worse it will be for those collieries that are idle. Time in the present circumstances cannot improve their position.'[5]

The Association remained determined to resist any attempt to increase hewers' working hours to seven plus one winding as the owners were free to demand. In view of the absence of evidence in

[1] Ibid., 9 October 1925; Durham Chronicle, 10 October 1925.
[2] D.M.A., 14 November 1925.
[3] Ibid., 7 December 1925.
[4] D.M.A., 23 December 1925.
[5] Durham Coal Owners' Association, Annual Report, 1925, p. 27.

either official union or coal owners' documents or in the local press
of attempts to impose upon hewers the full statutory provisions of
the law it is reasonable to assume that the majority of individual
colliery owners were prepared to restart work as long as hewers
worked a uniform shift of seven hours bank-to-bank. Certainly any
widespread campaign by local coal owners to impose more severe
terms upon the hewers would have aroused the stern opposition of
the Durham Miners' Association and have figured prominently in its
official records. Nevertheless the Association was fully aware that
the owners had secured an important victory since the threat of even
longer working hours for hewers would always remain a powerful
one especially as the depression in the coal industry deepened. If the
ultimate success of coal owners nationally to enforce widespread
reductions in wages and increases in the length of the working day
had for the moment been delayed by Government intervention,
employers in Durham had succeeded in securing piecemeal reductions in cost at the miners' expense. As the continued depression in
the coal industry served to reinforce the owners' efforts towards cheap
selling it gradually weakened the financial and bargaining strength
of the Durham Miners' Association as short-time working and
unemployment increased.[1] To many Durham miners there was conceivably little more that could be done to reduce their standard of
living. The coal owners and the Government, however, had different
ideas as the subsequent months were to show.

V

The miners, in contrast to the Labour press, were wary of regarding
'Red Friday', the day on which the industry was promised financial
assistance, as a complete victory. The fight had only just begun as
A. J. Cook reminded a gathering at Esh Winning, recalling what
Churchill had said to him: 'Remember, Cook, this is not a gift from
us,' to which Cook had replied, 'You need not tell me that. It is
cheaper than a revolution.'[2] Though the decision to grant a subsidy
and subject the coal industry to yet another extensive inquiry probably sprang from Baldwin's characteristic eagerness to avert a crisis
it seems fairly certain from evidence of contemporary Cabinet and
Departmental Papers and other sources that the nine-month respite
thus afforded was used by the Government to prepare adequately its

[1] Cf. Chapter VII, pp. 268–9.
[2] *Colliery Guardian*, 14 August 1925.

emergency organization to meet the contingencies of a widespread industrial dispute. Churchill gave an early indication of this whilst defending the Government's subvention in the House of Commons on 10 December 1925:

> 'We were . . . impressed by the fact that the country as a whole was not sufficiently informed about the character and immense consequences of such a struggle as that with which it was confronted. . . . We therefore decided to postpone the crisis in the hope of averting it, or, if not averting it, of coping effectually with it when the time came.'[1]

A. J. Cook reminded a mass meeting of miners at Crook that Baldwin had remarked to him: 'You have had us this time; we will be prepared.'[2] The coal owners were more forthright. Lord Londonderry predicted the outcome in no uncertain terms when he said: 'Whatever it may cost in blood and treasure, we shall find that the trade unions will be smashed from top to bottom.'[3] The Durham Coal Owners' Association, with unnerving foresight, regarded the subvention as a 'grave error; the effect of which would be to put off the evil day and give the men the warning that they must prepare at the end of the nine months for a general attack upon the wages' [sic].

The Supply and Transport Service, initially designed to meet wartime emergencies, had been kept in existence until 1921 and was later resurrected by Baldwin.[4] J. C. C. Davidson, Parliamentary Private Secretary to Baldwin during 1921 and 1922, was appointed Chancellor of the Duchy of Lancaster in May 1923 but almost immediately adopted the newly-created role of Chief Civil Commissioner charged with designing 'in strict secrecy' an organization to supply essential services in time of a general stoppage.[5] Such was the Government's subsequent activity in this respect that the Home Secretary reported to the Cabinet in February 1926 that 'little remained to be done before the actual occurrence of an emergency'.[6]

The Organization for the Maintenance of Supplies (O.M.S.), which announced its existence in the newspapers on 25 September 1925, was an unofficial movement which appealed for volunteers

---

[1] 189 H.C. Deb. 5s, 733. Cf. 187 H.C. Deb. 5s, 1684 and the comments of Sir W. Joynson-Hicks, Home Secretary, *The Times*, 3 August 1925.
[2] *Colliery Guardian*, 14 August 1925.
[3] Quoted in W. Hannington, *Unemployed Struggles, 1919–1936*, London 1936, p. 135.
[4] J. Symons, *The General Strike*, London 1957, p. 25.
[5] R. R. James, *Memoirs of a Conservative: J. C. C. Davidson's Memoirs and Papers 1910–37*, London 1969, pp. 178–9.
[6] P.R.O. C.P.81(26). Cf. James, *op. cit.*, p. 230.

to maintain essential services in the event of a general strike.[1] It was handed over to the Government on the eve of the 1926 dispute and was joined by leading members of the British Fascists.[2] At a joint meeting between Government and O.M.S. representatives on 7 December 1925 W. M. Thomson, Chief Civil Commissioner, had emphasized that in the event of an emergency O.M.S. activities would cease and that any O.M.S. volunteers subsequently recruited by the Government would thereafter be under its complete control.[3]

The Organization began its volunteer campaign in Durham during January 1926 but was unable to establish any real footing in the area owing to the opposition of leading industrialists and the Durham Coal Owners' Association which regarded the body as 'undesirable' and which appealed to all colliery managers not to offer their support.[4] By the end of April 1926 the O.M.S. had succeeded in forming a Durham County Committee but still without the support of the public and industry in general. In November 1925 the Ministry of Health issued Circular 636[5] to local authorities outlining schemes for the local administration of the Emergency Powers Act. In the event of a stoppage the country was to be divided into ten divisions under the supervision of Civil Commissioners with whom local authorities were to co-operate to administer and control essential services, road transport, food supplies and to maintain law and order.

Lack of enthusiasm and a too great reliance upon the promised inquiry into the coal industry to provide a panacea for the industry's troubles left the T.U.C. unprepared for a national stoppage. Its General Council were opposed to any plans which entailed even a threat of challenge to the Government. An attempt to revive the idea of the Industrial Alliance was defeated by the slowness with which support could be mustered from the large unions. The Industrial Committee of the T.U.C., which had been established to deal with the July 1925 crisis, was content to issue a statement of policy on 19 February 1926 declaring that 'there was to be no reduction in wages, no increase in working hours, and no interference with the principle

The Times, 25 September 1925.

W. H. Crook, *The General Strike*, Chapel Hill, University of North Carolina Press, 1931, pp. 301–2.

A. Mason, 'The Government and the General Strike', *International Review of Social History*, XIV, 1969, p. 19.

Durham Coal Owners' Association, *Minutes of the Executive Committee*, February 1926.

For the full text of this circular see W. Milne-Bailey, *Trade Union Documents*, London 1929, pp. 352–6.

186   THE DURHAM MINERS

of national agreements'.[1] W. Citrine, Secretary of the Industrial
Committee, had drafted a memorandum on 28 January calling upon
the Committee to 'examine in the closest degree the situation and to
determine upon some form of preparation.' The document was
presented to a joint meeting with the miners on 19 February but
provoked little response.[2]

To the more extreme elements the situation appeared pathetic.
A. J. Cook, who worked constantly to inspire some element of
initiative amongst the miners, toured the coalfields repeating the
famous slogan, 'Not a penny off the pay, not a second on the day'.
At Wheatley Hill he predicted in February 1926 that the coal
industry was going to be 'the cockpit of one of the greatest industrial
crises ever known'.[3] Earlier in December 1925 he had warned the
Durham miners that if they hoped for peace they must be prepared
for the 'emergencies of war'.[4] The Industrial Committee of the T.U.C.
refused to tolerate any action thought to be 'provocative'. The proposals of the Minority Movement to match a Workers' Defence
Corps in opposition to the O.M.S. and the Fascists held out little
hope of success with either the T.U.C., the Labour Party or the trade
union movement as a whole since a large section of the Labour
movement were completely unsympathetic to any form of revolutionary tactics.[5]

Meanwhile on 5 September the Government had appointed Sir
Herbert Samuel (Chairman), Sir Herbert Lawrence, Sir William
Beveridge and Kenneth Lee as members of the Royal Commission.
The Government had insisted that neither the coal owners nor the
miners should be represented to avoid repeating the kind of pro-
ceedings conducted in 1919. Nevertheless the composition of the
Commission was singularly biased towards the capitalist interest
much to the indignation of the M.F.G.B.

The Commission patiently collected evidence between 15 October
1925 and 14 January 1926, publishing its report on 10 March. The
Commissioners were strongly opposed to the idea of a subsidy and
viewed its continuance as 'indefensible'.[6] On the question of wages

[1] T.U.C., *Mining Dispute National Strike, Report of the General Council to the
Conference of Executives of Affiliated Unions, 25 June 1926*, 1927, p. 5.
[2] Lord Citrine, *Men and Work*, London 1964, pp. 145–53. The memorandum
was never published and only members of the Industrial Committee and the
miners' Executive ever saw it.
[3] *Durham Chronicle*, 27 February 1926.
[4] *Ibid.*, 12 December 1925.
[5] Symons, *op. cit.*, p. 30.
[6] R.C. on Coal Industry, 1925, I, Report, p. 235.

and hours, which had now replaced nationalization as the miners'
main concern, the Commissioners asserted:

'If the present hours are to be retained, we think a revision of the
"minimum percentage addition to standard rates of wages", fixed
in 1924 at a time of temporary prosperity is indispensable. A
disaster is impending over the industry and the immediate reduction
in working costs that can be effected in this way, and in this way
alone, is essential to save it. . . . Should the miners freely prefer some
extension of hours with a less reduction in wages, Parliament would
no doubt be prepared to authorize it. We trust, however, that this
will not occur.'[1]

The proposals for the reorganization of the industry[2] could only
affect the miners' standard of living in the long run. In the meantime
the Commissioners recognized the desirability of continuing national
wage agreements but considered it essential 'that there should be . . .
considerable variation in the rates of wages in the several districts'.[3]
    The Commission's findings were naturally disappointing to the
miners. Even Lord Londonderry had hoped—rather surprisingly—
that the Commissioners would indicate that there would be no lowering of wages or lengthening of hours but rather 'that by an increased
output the costs of mining can be reduced to such an extent as would
render possible the sale of coal at a profit'.[4] The Prime Minister made
it clear at a meeting with miners' and owners' representatives on 24
March that both parties would have to agree to accept the Report,
with its inherent assumption of wage reductions, if the Government
was to take any action to help resolve the mining dispute.[5] In this he
continued in his long-established principle of allowing, as far as
possible, both parties to work out their own salvation with the
minimum of interference.[6] The coal owners made it clear, however,
that they were intent on securing not only wage reductions and
district settlements but also a longer working day.[7]
    The intractability of both the miners and employers was patently

---

[1] *Ibid.*
[2] *Ibid.*, p. 233.
[3] *Ibid.*, p. 236.
[4] *Daily Mail*, 28 January 1926.
[5] M.F.G.B., 24 March 1926. Cf. Citrine, *op. cit.*, p. 159.
[6] Although in 1919 Baldwin had subscribed to the idea of nationalization of the
mines he had by 1925 adopted the more orthodox view that industry should be
left as free as possible to solve its own problems. K. Middlemas and J. Barnes,
Baldwin: A Biography, London 1969, pp. 378–80. Cf. S. Baldwin, *On England*,
London 1938 edn, p. 47.
[7] M.F.G.B., 25, 31 March, 1, 8, 9, 13 April 1926.

obvious and the Government's hope that both sides would accept the
Samuel Report as a whole was, to say the least, premature. Certain
members of the Cabinet pleaded for the Government to accept the
Report unconditionally and begin to force a settlement but were
defeated.[1] Though Baldwin's new biographers regard his ultimatum
as 'quite a courageous opening bid'[2] it was destined to prolong the
already bitter recriminations between the two parties to the dispute.

In most districts the employers began issuing notices terminating
all contracts on 30 April, when the subvention would cease, and in
Durham also announced the conditions upon which work would be
available on 1 May 1926. They offered to pay an addition of 53·49
per cent to the existing basic wages plus, where necessary, a subsistence allowance to adult low paid day-wage workmen of 6s 8½d per
shift. The offer was made:

'On the assumption that at collieries requiring it not less than the
legal hours will be worked and that there will be a sympathetic
approach to the abatement of any practices which at present result
in reducing output and increasing costs where such exist, and to the
adoption of improved methods to bring about greater efficiency of
working.'

Furthermore the value of free houses, of rent allowance in lieu of
houses, and of free coal were to be included in the ascertainments as
wages and not as other costs and therefore to the advantage of the
employers and to the detriment of the workers.[3] The effect of the
owners' proposals, if adopted, would have been to reduce the
average wage per shift of Durham miners from 10s to 7s 3d and
hewers' wages per shift from 9s 8d to 6s 10d.[4] In the Midlands the
coal owners decided not to issue notices but to continue working on
existing contracts. Elsewhere coal owners adopted the same hostile
attitude as in Durham which, according to C. L. Mowat, 'simply
confirmed the miners in their belief that the owners did not mean
to negotiate, but only to insist on unconditional surrender'.[5]

An attempt by Baldwin to persuade the coal owners to negotiate
with the miners' representatives on the basis of a national wages
system ended in failure on 22 April. A further attempt was made on
the following day at the request of the Industrial Committee but the

[1] P.R.O., Cab., 11/26, 12/26.
[2] Middlemas and Barnes, *op. cit.*, p. 397.
[3] Durham Coal Owners' Association, *Annual Report*, 1926, pp. 12–13.
[4] M.F.G.B., 28 April 1926; *Colliery Guardian*, 30 April 1926.
[5] C. L. Mowat, *Britain between the Wars, 1918–1940*, London 1964, p. 301.

owners simply responded with a series of wage offers based on an eight-hour day which the M.F.G.B. promptly rejected.[1]

On 30 April, when some of the Durham miners were already locked-out, the coal owners proposed the establishment of a national minimum wage corresponding to that existing in 1921 and the re-introduction of the eight-hour day. The Government stated that it was prepared to introduce temporary legislation permitting the extra hour to be worked while retaining the Seven-Hour Act on the Statute Book.[2] The proposed lengthening of hours was directly contrary to the recommendations of the Samuel Commission. The M.F.G.B. immediately rejected the proposals.[3] The Government remained determined to make the acceptance of wage reductions the necessary preliminary to any settlement and refused an appeal by the Industrial Committee for the continuation of the subsidy for a short period. The negotiations consequently broke down.

On 1 May the Government issued a Royal Proclamation declaring a state of emergency to exist which enabled them, under the Emergency Powers Act, to set in motion all the plans arranged to meet a situation of this kind. The T.U.C. Industrial Committee had reported the breakdown of the negotiations to a conference of trade union executives in London on 30 April which Swan, Gilliland and Richardson attended as representatives of the M.F.G.B. On the following day the conference accepted a scheme, prepared by the General Council of the T.U.C., for co-ordinated action in support of the miners and calling for a cessation of work in selected trades[4] at midnight on 3 May if negotiations were not recommenced. The M.F.G.B. agreed with other unions to surrender their powers to the General Council, the Sailors' and Firemen's Union, led by Havelock Wilson, being the only dissenters. The Federation was intent on preserving a united front against the coal owners and the Government and in submitting to the General Council believed it would receive complete support in a fight to the finish if the coal owners' notices were not withdrawn. The T.U.C., on the other hand, whilst it felt bound to support the miners in their stand against the proposed wage reductions, was anxious to the last for both the miners and the coal owners to reach a settlement. The playing of this double

[1] M.F.G.B., 28 April 1926.
[2] *Ibid.*, 30 April 1926.
[3] *Ibid.*
[4] Described as 'first-line trades' these included transport, iron and steel, other metals, heavy chemicals, industrial building, printing (including the press) and trades ancillary to any of these or to the coal or coal substitute industries. A second series of instructions, covering chiefly engineering and shipbuilding ('second-line' trades) took effect on 12 May.

role of intermediary and a party to the dispute accounts for much of the confusion which prevailed amongst the parties in the days preceding the strike. So reluctant was the General Council to prepare for a strike that, as Ernest Bevin later recalled, it did not begin to draft any plans until 27 April.[1]

Notices were sent out by the unions immediately after the meeting on 1 May. Meanwhile negotiations continued in an attempt to find a formula which would allow a temporary settlement. The M.F.G.B. delegates returned to their districts, leaving A. J. Cook and R. Smillie in London. On the evening of 1 May the T.U.C. Industrial Committee met the Cabinet and on the following day a formula was agreed upon by sub-committees of these two bodies providing for the continuation of negotiations, a withdrawal of the owners' notices and a declaration by the T.U.C. that a settlement would be reached in two weeks along the lines of the Samuel Report. Cook, surprised that negotiations had been continuing without the miners' knowledge, first heard of the formula on 2 May and had to inform the General Council that joint discussions on the proposals were impossible since the miners' delegates had returned to their districts. A second meeting between T.U.C. representatives and the Cabinet took place on the evening of 2 May when the General Council was asked to urge the miners to authorize it to continue negotiations on the understanding that both the miners and the General Council should accept the Samuel Report, together with its proposed wage reductions, as a basis of settlement. Discussions on this formula were interrupted by news that the *Daily Mail* printers, without the knowledge or instruction of the General Council, had refused to print a leading article which implied that a general strike was a revolutionary act. The Government, inflamed by this 'gross interference with the freedom of the press', refused to continue negotiations without 'an immediate and unconditional withdrawal of the instructions for a general strike'.[2]

There is some reason to believe that the *Daily Mail* incident was used simply as a pretext for ending all negotiations until such time as the threat of a general strike was withdrawn and of appeasing the more militant members of the Cabinet, such as Churchill and

---

[1] T.U.C. National Strike Special Conference, *Report of Proceedings at a Special Conference of Executives of All Affiliated Unions to Consider the Report of the General Council on the National Strike Held at the Central Hall, Westminster, on Thursday, 20 January 1927 and the Following Day* (hereafter referred to as *T.U.C. National Strike Special Conference*, January 1927). p. 10.

[2] M.F.G.B., 1–12 May 1926, *Report of Events Leading up to and during the General Strike, and the Conclusion Thereof.*

Joynson-Hicks. It was reported that before the incident seven of the Cabinet had threatened their resignation unless Baldwin took a determined stand against the T.U.C.[1] Even before news of the *Daily Mail* employees had reached the Cabinet a document had been prepared by which negotiations were to be terminated until the threat of a general strike was removed.[2] Certainly it appears that rather than a near-agreement being sadly interrupted relations between representatives of the T.U.C. and the Government were, if anything, worsening by late Sunday evening.[3]

VI

Attempts to achieve a last-minute settlement continued on 3 May but without avail. Neither the Government nor the coal owners were prepared to reopen negotiations. 'It is not wages that are imperilled,' Baldwin declared in the Commons on 3 May. 'It is the freedom of our very Constitution.'[4] Labour leaders tried to dispel the idea that revolution was threatened by appealing for sympathy for what was essentially an industrial dispute. 'I do not believe in spite of all the talk about revolution, that if a ballot was taken of this country, 2 per cent of the people would vote for a revolution,' declared J. H. Thomas, the railwaymen's leader.[5]

The Durham miners were certainly not seeking revolution but were anxious, in spite of suffering long periods of unemployment, to join the battle to resist longer hours and lower wages. By 3 May 200 pits had closed down in Durham and over 150,000 miners were out of work.[6] *The Times* reported on 3 May that the breakdown in negotiations and the threat of a prolonged stoppage had created a feeling of dismay and 'deepest disappointment' in the North.[7] Nevertheless on Tuesday 4 May the vast majority of those workers in the North-East called out on strike in support of the miners responded whole-

---

[1] *Lansbury's Labour Weekly*, 63, 22 May 1926. Cf. H. J. Laski, 'The Coal Strike and Beyond', *The Nation*, 3177, 26 May 1926, p. 579. Citrine, *op. cit.*, p. 197, claims that five members of the Cabinet threatened to resign.

[2] Mason, *loc. cit.*, p. 14.

[3] K. Middlemas (ed.), *Thomas Jones: Whitehall Diary, Volume II: 1926–1930*, Oxford 1969, pp. 34–6; Middlemas and Barnes, *op. cit.*, pp. 406–9; Citrine, *op. cit.*, pp. 167–71; James, *op. cit.*, p. 232.

[4] 195 H.C. Deb. 5s, 72.

[5] *Ibid.*, 81.

[6] *The Times*, 3 May 1926.

[7] *Ibid.*

heartedly.[1] The *Durham Chronicle*, which appeared twice during the nine-day strike, reported on 8 May:

'The commencement of the general strike . . . completely paralysed the commercial and industrial activities of the Durham district. In all the vital industries there was practically a complete withdrawal of labour and citizens devoted their activities to providing for the maintenance of the essential services.'[2]

The engineering and shipbuilding centres in the North-East have been described as 'solid to a man' during the strike period.[3] The majority of manual workers in the power stations decided to strike in sympathy with the miners with the notable exception of power men at South Shields.[4] Coal shipments from ports such as Sunderland and Seaham Harbour were at a standstill while the Government commandeered what stocks remained in port.[5] Even J. Rogers, local organizer of the National Union of Seamen, agreed to recommend his members to join the strike despite the fact that his union had voted against such action at the trade union executives' meeting on 1 May. Rogers was later dismissed for this action.[6]

This kind of response was common throughout the country. The *British Worker*, the official strike bulletin of the T.U.C. published at the head offices of the *Daily Herald*, reported on 5 May:

'The workers' response has exceeded all expectations. . . . All essential industries and all the transport services have been brought to a standstill. The only exception is that the distribution of milk and food has been permitted to continue. . . . Never have the workers responded with greater enthusiasm to the call of their leaders.'[7]

The Government, via its official strike bulletin the *British Gazette*,

[1] For a comprehensive account of the extent and nature of sympathetic support in the North-East and of the activities in Durham and Northumberland during the period of the strike and the ensuing coal stoppage see A. Mason, 'The Miners' Unions of Northumberland and Durham, 1918–1931, with special reference to the General Strike of 1926', Ph.D. thesis, University of Hull 1967. See also 'The General Strike in the North-East', *Our History*, 22, 1965 (issued by the British Communist Party). Referred to hereafter as *Our History*.
[2] *Durham Chronicle*, 8 May 1926.
[3] J. Murray, *The General Strike of 1926*, London 1951, p. 137.
[4] *Daily Express*, 8 May 1926.
[5] *Northern Echo*, 4 May 1926; *Daily Chronicle*, 4 May 1926.
[6] *Our History, op. cit.*, p. 4.
[7] *British Worker*, 5 May 1926.

edited by Winston Churchill, and the B.B.C.[1] took every opportunity to portray the strike as a direct threat to the nation:

'The strike is intended as a direct hold-up of the nation to ransom,' reported the *British Gazette* on 5 May. 'It is a conflict between Trade Union leaders and Parliament . . . and must only end . . . in the decisive and unmistakable victory of Parliament.'[2]

Such accusations were hotly denied by the General Council of the T.U.C. Nevertheless their influence upon public opinion, albeit un-measurable, could not have been without effect. The truth about the strike activities in the regions is extremely difficult to discover since the historian must rely a great deal upon contemporary press reports which were not only relatively scarce but heavily biased in their opinion. Three daily newspapers appeared in the North-East throughout the period of the General Strike in attenuated form. The *Journal and North Star*, owned by the Northern Counties Conservative News-paper Company, was bitterly opposed to organized labour and proved a useful complement to the attacks made upon the miners by the Government in the *Gazette*. The *North Mail and Newcastle Chronicle* and the *Northern Echo*, both Liberal by tradition, were less hostile but refused to condone the stoppage. The *Durham Chronicle*, normally a weekly newspaper and heavily biased in favour of the miners, appeared on 8 and 12 May.[3]

The publication of local strike bulletins helped to counteract hos-tile press reports and boost the morale of the strikers in the absence of official news coverage. One writer maintains that it is doubtful whether very many copies of the *British Worker* circulated in the area south of Gateshead,[4] thus depriving a large proportion of the Durham miners of the psychological benefits of a sympathetic press and of the details of conditions in other parts of the country. On the other hand the *British Gazette* did not appear in the North until 5 May and the first Newcastle edition of the *British Worker* did not appear until 11 May, the day before the strike ended.

[1] The Government's publicity schemes during the strike period, especially the genesis and management of the *British Gazette*, are described by James, *op. cit.*, pp. 223–50. For a discussion of the role of the B.B.C. during the General Strike see A. Briggs, *History of Broadcasting in the United Kingdom*, I, Oxford 1961.
[2] *British Gazette*, 5 May 1926.
[3] For comment on the treatment of the dispute by the press in Durham and Northumberland see A. Mason, 'The Local Press and the General Strike: an example from the North-East', *Durham University Journal*, LXI, 3, June 1969.
[4] Mason, *op. cit.*, p. 285.

The first local strike bulletin to appear was published by the Spen and District Trades and Labour Council based at Chopwell and printed by J. Summerbell, of Sunderland. The bulletin had been printed but not guillotined or folded when the Typographical Association informed the printers on 3 May of the call to a general strike. Due to the efforts of R. Page Arnot, member of the Executive Committee of the Communist Party and also on the staff of the Labour Research Department, and W. Lawther, checkweighman at Victoria Garesfield Colliery, member of the Durham Miners' Association, Durham County Council and National Executive of the Labour Party, Summerbell agreed to complete the work and the first issue appeared on 4 May and sold at 1d.[1]

On the front page the bulletin announced 'Durham and Northumberland Ready for Action' and reported:

'The situation is rapidly developing in the Durham and Northumberland Counties. The trade unionists of the Counties, though utterly unprepared for the unprovoked attack by the Government and its O.M.S. satellites, are rapidly rallying to the appeal of the General Council.'[2]

On the back page, in bold print, was the call:

'Workers of Durham & Northumberland
The General Strike is ALREADY A SUCCESS.
Don't believe the lies put out by the Capitalist press.
The newspapers are trying to dope and deceive you into the belief that the General Strike will fail, and that the Government forces are bound to get the better of the workers. Nothing could be further from the truth.
From centre after centre of industry comes the news of the magnificent response to the call sent out by the General Council of the Trades Union Congress.
On Saturday a million miners were wantonly locked out, and the Government—which is supposed to represent the whole of the nation—put all its forces at the service of a small minority of profiteers and exploiters.
The organized trade unionists of Great Britain cannot suffer the miners to be beaten and starved into submission.
What happens to the miners will happen to you next.

[1] *Our History*, pp. 3–4, 8. There is a single copy of the four-page bulletin in the library of the Communist Party.
[2] Spen and District Trades and Labour Council, *Strike Bulletin* No. 1, Tuesday, 4 May 1926, p. 1.

Your own wages, your livelihood, the welfare of your wife and children, are at stake.
That is why there is a General Strike. That is why you are called out. That is why, fighting in such a cause, you are bound to win.'[1]

The call ended with the words 'Be of good courage, and victory is ours'.[2] Apart from this strike bulletin nothing further was done to issue published material owing to the difficulty of obtaining permits from the printers' unions.[3] Before the appearance of the Newcastle edition of the *British Worker*—for which a permit was never received —workers were, however, able to produce cyclostyled sheets often in the strictest privacy.

The Blaydon and Chopwell District Council of Action produced the *Northern Light* which first appeared on 5 May and was produced intermittently until 17 May. H. Bolton, a local J.P., Labour leader and Chairman of the Blaydon Urban District Council, was reported to have gone to the U.D.C. offices on 3 May, 'went round the numerous staff . . . instructed those whom he did not fully trust to take their holidays that first fortnight of May—immediately—and turned the remaining staff, offices and machinery (including the duplicator) into an organ of the General Strike'.[4] The equipment of the local rent collector's office was used to produce the *Northern Light*, the place of publication being altered each night and the duplicator secretly transferred in a maternity van.[5] Chopwell had long been regarded as a centre of left-wing militancy, a tendency increased by the fact that its three pits had been idle since 22 June 1925 owing to the owners' attempts to alter local wages, and its initiative in producing an unofficial strike bulletin outraged the local press. The *North Mail and Newcastle Chronicle* described the action as 'a practical experiment in Bolshevism' and accused the local Council of Action of creating a 'reign of terror in the neighbourhood'.[6] It is doubtful whether many copies of the bulletin circulated outside the immediate area of North-West Durham. Nevertheless its influence was not without effect since a miner was later sentenced to prison for three months with hard labour accused of committing an act 'likely to cause civil disaffection amongst the civil population' by

[1] *Ibid.* p. 4.
[2] *Ibid.*
[3] T.U.C. Local Collection on the General Strike, Box No. 9, Congress House, London.
[4] R. Page Arnot in a postscript to *Our History, op. cit.*, p. 27.
[5] *Ibid.*
[6] *North Mail and Newcastle Chronicle*, 22 May 1926.

distributing the bulletin.[1] Other strike bulletins included the *Workers'*
Searchlight, published in the Spen and Chopwell area, and the
Workers' Chronicle published in Newcastle.

One notable feature of the General Strike in the North-East was
the attempt that strikers made to organize themselves on a basis
similar to that established under the Government's emergency organization. Equally significant was the lack of support offered by the
Durham Miners' Association to this act of defiance. Durham and
Northumberland had been grouped together into the Northern
Division under the control of Sir Kingsley Wood, Civil Commissioner and Parliamentary Secretary to the Ministry of Health,
with headquarters at Newcastle. The trade unions in the North-East,
in common with those throughout the country, had failed to make
any preparations for the strike during the weekend preceding 3 May.
The impetus given towards establishing an organization to oppose
the Government's strike-breaking machinery came from outside,
namely from R. Page Arnot and W. Lawther. R. Page Arnot recalls
the events of 1 May thus:

'On the Saturday afternoon I was the speaker at a First of May
demonstration at Chopwell, one of the numerous mining villages that
made up the Urban District Council of Blaydon-on-Tyne. After
the open-air demonstration I jotted down headings for a plan of
campaign in the Durham-Northumberland area. . . .

That evening, before a gathering in the Miners' Club, Steve
Lawther [2] and three officials of lodges in the adjacent pits discussed
and agreed on a plan of action. A further proposal was advanced
that a meeting be called at twenty-four hours' notice for Sunday
evening, May 2, of all trade union secretaries and chairmen, all
members of boards of the three or four local co-operative societies
and all local Labour councillors of the county and urban district.
This meeting took place with nearly fifty present, with check-
weigher Will Lawther in the chair and at it the plan of campaign was
discussed and unanimously adopted.[3] It included sending a call for
Councils of Action to be set up all over the huge coalfield. Dozens
of mining lads who never attended a lodge meeting and who were
therefore thought to be of little account turned up the next day
ready to speed throughout the two counties on bicycles and motor-
bikes.'[4]

[1] *Labour Monthly*, 8 June 1926.
[2] Brother of W. Lawther.
[3] For details of the plan see Arnot, *op. cit.*, pp. 436–9.
[4] *Our History*, p. 3.

He further recalls that the proposals for the special joint organization for the two counties and for Councils of Action were elaborated in Blaydon-on-Tyne 'largely by the representatives of half-a-dozen or more D.M.A. Lodges'.[1] The proposals were also discussed at an informal meeting at the offices of the National Union of Distributive and Allied Workers at Newcastle on 3 May. Those present included J. White, Area Secretary of the Transport and General Workers Union, E. Edwards, Financial Secretary of the Northumberland Miners' Association, C. R. Flynn, Northern Divisional officer of the National Union of Distributive and Allied Workers, F. Forster, Organizer of the N.U.D.A.W. and R. Page Arnot. The representatives agreed to meet on the following day in an effort to entice the support of other trade unions.[2]

At neither meeting was the Durham Miners' Association officially represented. Arnot visited the head offices of the Association on 4 May to inform Robson of the proposed strike organization but failed to see him since a Council Meeting was in progress. Will Lawther was present as an unofficial representative of the Durham miners at the meeting of various trade union representatives held on 4 May, again at the Newcastle offices of the N.U.D.A.W. At the meeting it was decided 'to form a local General Council to cover the Northumberland and Durham area with two representatives from each Trade Union' and '. . . in addition to appoint a Strike Committee composed of one representative from each Trade Union or Group of Trade Unions on strike or lock-out'.[3] Will Lawther was co-opted to both bodies as the unofficial representative of the Durham Miners' Association pending an official appointment.[4]

Despite a meeting between Arnot and Robson on 5 May the Association took no action towards appointing representatives to the regional strike committee in Newcastle but promised to raise the matter at the next meeting of the County Federation Board.[5] By 12 May, the day on which the T.U.C. called off the strike, the Association had resolved:

---

[1] Letter to the author, 14 October 1966.
[2] *Account of the Proceedings of the Northumberland and Durham General Council Joint Strike Committee*, May 1926, p. 1. The text of this official report was reprinted in *Labour Monthly*, 8 June 1926. The references given here refer to the original report.
[3] *Account of the Proceedings of the Northumberland and Durham General Council Joint Strike Committee*, May 1926, pp. 2–3.
[4] *Ibid.* p. 5.
[5] *Ibid.*

'That we urge the four Committees comprising the County Federation Board to form a Strike Committee for the County, to cover all
sections of workmen involved in the present crisis, and give our
financial quota towards the same. Further, we suggest that two
members from the County Committee sit on the Strike Committee
now operating in Newcastle and that body be asked to appoint two
representatives on our County Committee.'[1]

The two County Committee representatives were never appointed.[2]
The authority of the regional strike organization had been undermined to the extent that without official links with the miners'
Association few, if any, of the small mining villages in the southern
point of the coalfield were able to share in this act of defiance.

The lethargy of the Durham Miners' Association during the strike
was criticized by the rank and file miners especially in editions of the
Northern Light. It also makes it difficult to portray the strike situation
throughout the Durham coalfield since in the absence of any official
representation the Association's contribution and reaction to the
activities of the Joint Strike Committee was never reported to Lodge
members. Local Councils of Action were undoubtedly established
throughout the coalfield, one estimate putting the total for Durham
and Northumberland at more than 80,[3] and were actively engaged
in resisting the Government's strike-breaking organization but
evidence of their activity is scarce. The activities of the Joint Strike
Committee have been well documented,[4] and it is not the purpose here
to recount such details. A close examination of the strike organization
in the North-East and of its possible effect in co-ordinating and
guiding the policies of the various local strike committees and
Councils of Action established within the area has led one writer to
conclude hesitantly:

'The evidence on this matter is sparse indeed, and what there is
suggests that the Joint Strike Committee had virtually no importance
north of Ashington or south of Gateshead.'[5]

If this estimation is close to the truth then most of the activity which
did take place within the Durham coalfield did so outside of the direct

[1] D.M.A., 13 May 1926; R. Postgate, E. Wilkinson, J. F. Horrabin, *A Workers'
History of the General Strike*, Plebs League 1927, p. 66.
[2] Letter from R. Page Arnot to the author, 14 October 1966.
[3] Mason, *op. cit.*, p. 272.
[4] Symons, *op. cit.*, pp. 127–36; Arnot, *op. cit.*, pp. 436–43; Mason, *op. cit.*,
who critically analyses the various accounts of the Committee's activities
presented so far.
[5] Mason, *op. cit.*, p. 267.

influence of the strike organization in Newcastle. Nevertheless the miners and their local Councils of Action played an important role in the various colliery districts in Durham by frustrating attempts to break the strike. They were particularly successful in stopping traffic. Private car owners and small buses functioned with little effect. Several vehicles were reported to have had their tyres slashed while others had 'blackleg' chalked 'in glaring letters' over them.[1] On 8th May it was reported that intensive picketing had effectively stopped all transport in the mining areas of Annfield Plain, Houghton-le-Spring and Chopwell.[2] The miners' delegates walked to and from the head offices in Durham rather than use the 'buses driven by non-union labour'.[3] The *Northern Light* announced on 5 May that:

'All passenger traffic has been suspended, and the Council of Action has determined to organize mass picketing to deal with commercial vehicles of any description. Permits for the conveyance of milk and other foodstuffs will be issued.'[4]

Most of the disturbances in the Durham coalfield during the strike period were often linked with traffic picketing. One miner was imprisoned for a month after rolling a large stone on to the highway at West Moor in front of a motor-car containing five police officers.[5] W. Lawther and H. Bolton were both tried at Gateshead County Police Court on 13 May accused of interfering with food distribution and police intimidation. They were fined £50 with the alternative of two months' imprisonment. They chose to go to prison.[6] Their arrests aroused a sympathetic demonstration by strikers outside of the police court. The crowd, singing the Red Flag, were only finally dispersed after a number of arrests and baton charges by the police.[7] Attempts by pickets to stop road traffic on the Newcastle to Durham road led to a fight between strikers and police just north of Birtley when three policemen were injured.[8] At Gateshead County Police Court on 20 May 47 offenders, mainly miners from the Chopwell area, were charged with attempting to restrict the use of the highway.

[1] *Durham Chronicle*, 8 May 1926.
[2] *Account of the Proceedings of the Northumberland and Durham General Council Joint Strike Committee*, May 1926, p. 13. Cf. A. Hutt, *Post-War History of the British Working Class*, London 1937, pp. 150–1.
[3] *North Mail and Newcastle Chronicle*, 5 May 1926.
[4] Cited in *North Mail and Newcastle Chronicle*, 22 May 1926.
[5] *Ibid.*, 13 May 1926; Cf. *British Gazette*, 12 May 1926.
[6] *Durham Chronicle*, 15 May 1926.
[7] Symons, *op. cit.*, p. 131. For an account of the incident as portrayed by the *Northern Light* see *Labour Monthly*, 8 June 1926.
[8] *North Mail and Newcastle Chronicle*, 11 May 1926.

Twenty four of them were given prison sentences ranging from one to three months.[1]

Out of a total number of 1,389 cases of actual disorder occurring during the period of the General Strike, 583 occurred in the English Counties of which 183 took place in Durham.[2] The trouble which could have been expected from the employment of voluntary labour was minimized by the fact that although over 21,500 volunteers were claimed to have been recruited throughout the Northern Division by the end of the dispute,[3] only about 1,000 appear to have been given jobs.[4] The Durham Miners' Association followed the T.U.C.'s appeal for orderly conduct in urging its membership to keep the peace.[5] C. Trevelyan (later Sir), who as an independent observer acted as a special emissary of the T.U.C. General Council in the northern area, wrote to the T.U.C. Intelligence Committee about conditions in Durham and Northumberland:

'The general spirit is magnificent. The sense of discipline is strong. The local leaders are imbued with the necessity for keeping the peace if it is possible.'[6]

Despite this encouraging comment, the problems connected with picketing often led to quite serious clashes between strikers and police in colliery villages. However marked was the degree of restraint and social responsibility displayed by the British people as a whole during the nine-day dispute there was little obvious evidence of friendly football matches between police and strikers as occurred at Plymouth. Indeed one writer has concluded that if the situation in Northumberland and Durham during the General Strike period differed in any marked way from the national one it was in the poor relationship which existed between the police and the men on strike.[7]

The Government did not ease the situation, however, with its frequent condemnation of the dispute as subversive to the Constitution. 'Constitutional Government is being attacked,' declared the *British Gazette* on 6 May. 'The General Strike is a challenge to Parliament and is the road to anarchy and ruin.'[8] The response of the

---

[1] *Labour Monthly*, 8 June 1926; *North Mail and Newcastle Chronicle*, 21 May 1926.
[2] 196 H.C. Deb. 5s, 822–825.
[3] *British Gazette*, 12 May 1926.
[4] Mason, *op. cit.*, p. 229.
[5] *Durham Chronicle*, 15 May 1926.
[6] Undated letter from Mr Trevelyan to the T.U.C. Intelligence Committee, T.U.C. General Strike Collection, Box No. 3, Congress House, London.
[7] Mason, *op. cit.*, p. 476.
[8] *British Gazette*, 6 May 1926.

T.U.C. was, as it always had been, to defend the right of workers to withhold their labour in support of a particular class of workmen against attacks upon their standard of living. Nevertheless on 8 May the Government offered its full support to the armed forces in any action they might take 'to aid the Civil Power'.[1]

The Government's declarations of the strike as a revolutionary movement and a threat to constitutional government were supported by Sir John Simon in a speech in the House of Commons on 10 May. Simon, an eminent lawyer of the day, argued that the strike was not a trade dispute within the meaning of the Trades Disputes Act, 1906,[2] and was therefore illegal. His claim was later reinforced by Justice Astbury's *obiter dictum* delivered on 11 May in granting an injunction to the National Sailors' and Firemen's Union to prevent the members of its Tower Hill and Mersey branches supporting the strike, when he said: 'The so-called general strike called by the Trades Union Congress Committee is illegal and contrary to law, and those persons inciting or taking part in it are not protected by the Trades Disputes Act of 1906. ... The orders of the Trade Union Council are . . . unlawful.'[3] These claims of the alleged illegality of the General Strike have been proved to be unfounded[4] but at the time were not without effect in alarming some union leaders, especially those who were not themselves convinced of the value of such an action.

Meanwhile efforts were being made by outside parties to effect a settlement of the dispute. On 7 May, at a meeting of Churchmen and Non-Conformists presided over by Randall Davidson, Archbishop of Canterbury, an appeal was made for a resumption of negotiations suggesting that a cessation of the General Strike, a renewal by the Government of its offer of financial assistance 'for a short indefinite period' and a withdrawal of the coal owners' notices should occur 'simultaneously and concurrently'. The Government refused to allow the appeal to be broadcast by the B.B.C. or to be published in the *British Gazette*.[5] The proposals eventually appeared in diminished form in *The Times* and the *British Worker* on 8 May.[6]

---

[1] *Ibid.*, 8 May 1926.
[2] Section 3 of the Trades Disputes Act, 1906, provided that 'an act done by a person in contemplation or furtherance of a trade dispute shall not be actionable on the ground only that it induces some other person to break a contract of employment'. Cf. Sir John Simon, *Three Speeches on the General Strike*, London 1926, p. 5.
[3] Simon, *op. cit.*, Appendix II, p. 17.
[4] A. L. Goodhart, 'The Legality of the General Strike in England', *Yale Law Journal*, XXXVI, 1927.
[5] G. K. A. Bell, *Randall Davidson*, London 1935, pp. 1306–8.
[6] *The Times*, 8 May 1926; *British Worker*, 8 May 1926.

It was not the churchmen but Sir Herbert Samuel who was to eventually influence the course of negotiations. Having returned uninvited to London from Italy on 6 May he approached J. H. Thomas who agreed to put him in touch with the Negotiating Committee of the T.U.C. The Committee secretly met Samuel during the weekend 7–10 May at the Bryanston Square home of Sir Abe Bailey, the South African millionaire friend of J. H. Thomas.[1] Samuel's intervention only came to the notice of the miners' leaders on 8 May.[2] On the following day at a joint meeting between the miners' Executive and the General Council Industrial Committee the details of the proposed settlement were made known and promptly rejected by the miners' leaders.[3]

On 10 May W. P. Richardson was invited with A. J. Cook and H. Smith to participate in the discussions and on the same evening the Executive Committee of the M.F.G.B. and the General Council met to consider a modified draft of the memorandum. Though the General Council regarded the memorandum as an acceptable basis for the reopening of negotiations the miners refused to accept it. Samuel's proposals for a settlement were framed according to the recommendations of the 1925 Royal Commission and, as such, involved reductions in wages. In accepting the memorandum the General Council were in effect betraying the very principle upon which the miners' resistance was based. The miners had always insisted that there should be no reductions in wages. Furthermore since Samuel was not working in any official capacity there was no assurance that the Government would act upon the proposals were the General Strike to be called off.[4]

The General Council continued to try to persuade the miners' leaders to accept the Samuel Memorandum and was involved in lengthy meetings until midnight on Tuesday 11 May.[5] The miners' rugged determination not to consider wage adjustments angered the Council and, feeling it could no longer be 'tied to a mere slogan',

[1] J. H. Thomas, *My Story*, London 1937, p. 107; J. Bowle, *Viscount Samuel*, London 1957, p. 250; Citrine, *op. cit.*, p. 194.
[2] *Statement of the Miners' Federation of Great Britain on the Occasion of the Conference of Trade Union Executive Committees held to Receive the Report of the General Council of the Trades Union Congress on the Work Entrusted to them in the General Strike of May 1926*, 1927, p. 10.
[3] T.U.C. *Mining Dispute National Strike Report of the General Council to the Conference of Executives of Affiliated Unions, 25 June 1926*, 1927, pp. 16–20.
[4] Cf. Bowle, *op. cit.*, p. 250. For a full discussion of the meetings with Samuel see Citrine, *op. cit.*, pp. 185–96.
[5] T.U.C. General Council, *National Strike Special Conference . . . on Thursday 20 January 1927 and the following day*, 1927, p. 19, Citrine, *op. cit.*, pp.196–201.

the members agreed to end the strike.[1] Attempts on the following day to secure the workmen's support for the Samuel proposals ended in vain. Accordingly a deputation of the T.U.C., headed by A. Pugh, arrived at Downing Street shortly after noon on 12 May and informed the Prime Minister that the strike was over. No discussion took place as to the conditions of settlement nor was the Samuel Memorandum mentioned. It was an unconditional surrender.

In 1927 W. Citrine, General Secretary of the T.U.C., claimed:

'We called off the Strike, definitely and finally made up our minds at the General Council at about ten minutes before we met Mr Baldwin on Wednesday, 12 May.'[2]

The miners' leaders complained that the General Council had made up its mind to end the strike well before midnight on Tuesday, 11 May. Herbert Smith claimed that the decision had been reached 'before half-past nine on Tuesday night'.[3] G. Hicks, Chairman of the General Committee, denied this claiming that the decision had been made 'well after midnight'.[4] Mr Symons claims that 'there is an overwhelming weight of evidence' that the decision had been reached by 9.30 p.m. on Tuesday, 11 May.[5]

News of the surrender was received in the North-East 'with incredulity which changed to fury'.[6] The Newcastle *Workers' Chronicle* exclaimed:

'Never in the history of workers' struggles—with one exception of the treachery of our leaders in 1914—has there been such a calculated betrayal of working-class interests.'[7]

[1] *T.U.C. Mining Dispute National Strike Report of the General Council to the Conference of Executives of Affiliated Unions, 25 June 1926*, 1927, p. 21; Bowle, *op. cit.*, p. 253; Symons, *op. cit.*, pp. 202–3. Since the Government clearly rejected the Samuel Memorandum the miners' stubbornness does, on reflection, appear premature. As Dr Mason has noted: 'Had the miners' leaders been a little more flexible in their tactics and accepted the Memorandum themselves as a basis for settlement, the government, and those members of the General Council who wanted an end of the dispute, would have been placed in an awkward situation. A refusal by the Government to accept the Memorandum might have united the splintering trade unions and government acceptance would have almost certainly necessitated coercion of the owners.' A. Mason, 'The General Strike', *Bulletin of the Society for the Study of Labour History*, 20, 1970, p. 49.
[2] T.U.C., *General Council, National Strike Special Conference . . . on Thursday 20 January 1927 and the following day*, 1927, p. 40.
[3] *Ibid.*, p. 19.
[4] *Ibid.*, p. 8.
[5] Symons, *op. cit.*, p. 205.
[6] Postgate, Wilkinson and Horrabin, *op. cit.*, p. 69.
[7] *Ibid.*

The *Northern Light* said: 'There is only one explanation for this treachery—our leaders do not believe in Socialism.'[1]

The nature of the collapse of the strike can be more clearly understood in terms of the General Council's own weaknesses. The leaders themselves were mentally unprepared for a General Strike and openly feared its consequences. At a speech at Hammersmith on 9 May J. H. Thomas, who more than anyone was responsible for effecting a hasty end to the dispute, declared, 'I have never disguised, and I do not disguise now, that I have never been in favour of the principle of the General Strike.'[2] The miners' obstinacy in refusing to negotiate on the basis of possible reductions in wages and their lack of fear as to what the consequences of continuing the stoppage would be brought them into almost direct conflict with the more Right-wing elements of the General Council. As Mr Symons points out: 'A General Strike can be used only as a political, indeed a revolutionary instrument; and for such a use the General Council and the great majority of strikers were not prepared.'[3] The T.U.C., faced with the outbreak of a national stoppage after hoping for last-minute salvation through government intervention, was forced unprepared into a fight which it almost immediately sought to bring to an end. Nor was the conflict of interests between the miners and the T.U.C. General Council ever completely resolved. Whilst the miners agreed to place the matter of the conduct of the strike in the hands of the General Council they continued to assume that the final right to take any decision about the outcome of the dispute should be theirs. The General Council refused to allow its policy to be dominated by the considerations of one union. The absence of authority invested exclusively in a directing body only added to the confusion and played a large part in determining the nature of the collapse of the strike. This major defeat for labour successfully discredited the future use of large-scale industrial action and helped predetermine labour's reaction to the widespread industrial depression awaiting it.

VII

Without sympathetic support the miners were left to continue their desperate struggle alone. The publication of the Prime Minister's proposals for the settlement of the dispute quickly reassured them of the justice of their fight. The Government proposed a subsidy of

[1] *Ibid.*
[2] *British Gazette*, 11 May 1926. Cf. Citrine, *op. cit.*, p. 157.
[3] Symons, *op. cit.*, p. 231. Cf. Citrine, *op. cit.*, pp. 188–91.

£3,000,000 to enable the miners to return to work at a reduction of 10 per cent in minimum wages for three weeks. Meanwhile a National Wages Board was to formulate a national wages and hours agreement. The wages of the lowest paid men were no longer to be guaranteed if they exceeded 45s a week. An assurance was given that the Government would introduce a number of Bills to give effect to the Samuel Commission's recommendations for the reorganization of the industry but only after such legislative proposals were laid before the Coal Advisory Committee of the Secretary for Mines.[1] The proposals involved important modifications to those made by the Samuel Commission. The temporary subsidy was no longer to guarantee that men resumed work at their previous rate of wages nor were the wages of the lowest-paid men to be safeguarded. More important wage reductions were now to *precede* any reorganization of the industry rather than follow it.

Neither the miners nor the coal owners were ready to accept such terms. The M.F.G.B. rejected them at a conference on 20 May.[2] The Durham Coal Owners' Association had decided two days previously that the proposals were 'unacceptable'.[3] In the face of the obvious consternation of both parties the Government made preparations for a long struggle. It arranged for the importation of foreign coal, restriction of domestic coal allowances and, on the last day of May, once again proclaimed a state of emergency. Attempts by the M.F.G.B. to elicit the aid of other trade unions ended in failure.

Meanwhile in Durham the miners continued their peaceful resistance but in the face of increasing hardship. Local schemes of self-help could not prevent many families from being almost solely dependent upon the Boards of Guardians nor could sporadic aid from outside sources even begin to substantially ease the situation.[4] In an effort to maintain solidarity among its ranks the Durham Miners' Association organized 27 mass meetings throughout the County on 2 June.[5] There was a growing feeling amongst the rank and file that they should have been consulted on many more occasions than they had been for their opinions on the issues facing both the County and the nation. As one miner remarked to a *Newcastle Chronicle* reporter: 'The business seems to be done in London. You

---

[1] M.F.G.B., 15, 20 May 1926.
[2] *Ibid.*
[3] Durham Coal Owners' Association, *Executive Committee Minutes*, 18 May 1926.
[4] See Chapter VII, pp. 271–3.
[5] D.M.A., 28 May 1926.

would think we had lost our voices.'[1] At each of the gatherings a resolution was passed expressing strong support for the unconditional policy adopted by the national Miners' Executive. Peter Lee, speaking at Tyne Dock, aroused a storm of protest when, pointing to a banner bearing the inscription 'No reductions, no increased hours and no district settlements', he exclaimed: 'That will never be in my case. Anyone can shout that motto. What we want is thinking.' Angry exchanges followed between the platform and the crowd and he was unable to finish his speech.[2] The majority of miners were intent to support their case. By the end of June the only sign of activity in the pits was at four small collieries whose owners were not members of the Durham Coal Owners' Association.

In the absence of any formal discussion towards reaching a settlement of the dispute Lord Londonderry wrote a letter to the *Colliery Guardian* in June proposing a basis for agreement between the parties. Pleading for 'co-partnership and co-operation' he called upon both the owners and the miners to make sacrifices for the sake of industrial peace and for the Government to legislate to establish a national wages board, pit head baths, pit committees and to modify the Seven Hours Act:

'A resumption of work on the scale of wages and hours in operation before May 1 would necessitate the closing of a large number of pits. This closing down could be modified by the assistance of the Government covering losses to a certain specified figure; and, of course, would be further modified by an extension of hours. . . . By certain adjustments the rate of the lower paid men could be maintained at the present figure and probably increased, *while an elasticity in the hours of working could certainly have no effect in depressing the standard of living.*'[3] (My italics.)

The suggestion of a longer working day as a basis for settlement could hardly be expected to be welcomed by the miners as a basis for settlement nor could the assurance of stability in the miners' standard of living in face of increased coal output be taken seriously.[4]

Nevertheless the Government's programme of legislation, announced on 15 June, confirmed the miners' worst suspicions. A Bill was to be introduced permitting a lengthening of the working day to eight hours exclusive of winding times, followed by measures for the

[1] *Newcastle Chronicle*, 31 May 1926.
[2] *Durham Chronicle*, 5 June 1926.
[3] *Colliery Guardian*, 18 June 1926. The exact date of the letter is not known except that it was written before 15 June.
[4] Cf. Chapter I, pp. 31–43.

re-organization of the industry. There was to be legislation to facilitate amalgamations and the development of new mines, to double the mineral rights duty to help finance amenities such as pit head baths and to restrict employment for men over 18 years of age to those already working in the mines.[1]

The decision to lengthen the working day was in direct contravention of the advice of the Samuel Commission and was bitterly resented by the miners, especially in Durham. In the first place the effect of long-term depression in the coal export market meant that the estimated savings in cost-per-ton of commercially disposable coal under an eight-hour day in Durham could by no means match the losses incurred during the previous months. Some inland coalfields, as the estimates below show, were expected to reap savings to more than balance their previous losses:[2]

District	Deficit or credit balance in February 1926 (per ton of coal)		Estimated savings under an eight-hour day (per ton of coal commercially disposable		
	s	d	s	d	
Durham	−3	2·1	1	7	
Northumberland	−2	5·5	1	6	
Scotland	−1	9·2	1	10	
S. Wales	−3	3·49	3	0	
Eastern Federated Area	+0	7·71	2	0	estimated surplus
Lancashire, Cheshire	−1	3·58	2	0	L. & C.
and N. Staffs.			2	6	N. Staffs.
Cumberland	−4	1·44	2	2	
Forest of Dean	−2	0·09	2	9	
S. Staffs. and Salop	−0	7·65	1	10	

Furthermore, the adoption of an eight-hour day exclusive of windings for all workers promised to upset the traditional working time of hewers, the most important single group of workmen in the County, as well as involving increases for other classes of workmen. The working hours of hewers in Durham had been unaffected by legislation or agreement since 1890 and since then had been the lowest for any class of underground mineworker in the country. The Government's proposals involved an increase in actual time spent underground per shift of Durham hewers from between six and six and three-quarter hours to a maximum of eight. Whilst the grievances of other classes of workmen in Durham against a permitted

[1] 195 H.C. Deb. 5s, 2137–2151; P.R.O., Cab. 23/53.
[2] Adapted from *The Economist*, 19 June 1926.

eight-hour day were similar to those of men in other coalfields, no other district faced the possibility of such a prodigious increase in the length of the working day of its most numerous and dominant class of workmen. In his recent study of the 1926 dispute in the Durham coalfield A. Mason points, quite correctly, to the solidarity of the rank and file miners in Durham as one of the most important characteristics of the coal stoppage in the region but lays insufficient emphasis upon the question of hours of work as an explanation of this state of affairs. Of all the influences which strengthened the Durham miners in their struggle during the summer of 1926 the threatened eight-hour day was perhaps the greatest. The adoption of an eight-hour day for hewers never, in fact, occurred but the determination of the local coal owners to seek such a change provided the Durham Miners Association and its membership with a power of resistance sufficient to help overcome the distress encountered by the majority of miners and their families.

The Durham County Federation Board, at a meeting on 15 June, resolved to send letters of protest against the Prime Minister's statement in the House of Commons on that day to the Leader of the Opposition, the M.F.G.B., Members of Parliament and the Prime Minister himself.[1] The T.U.C. and the M.F.G.B. agreed temporarily to disregard the quarrel between them and issued a joint appeal for unity in resistance to the Government.[2] The Government's Bill, which suspended the Seven Hours Act for five years while leaving it on the Statute Book and which made an eight-hour day permissible, passed through the House of Commons on the last day of June and was given its third reading on 1 July. During its second reading it was vehemently attacked by Durham miners' M.P.s.

'This measure will throw back my County 50 years at the very least,' exclaimed R. Richardson, M.P. for Houghton-le-Spring, 'and you are asking us to do something we have never done before, and do you think we are going to accept this sort of thing lying down?'[3]

J. Lawson, M.P. for Chester-le-Street, declared:

'So far as this Bill is concerned, terrible as the prospect is before us, our men and women are going through with this thing to the end. They realize that the Government, in this Bill, are not asking or praying for peace. This is a declaration of war.'[4]

[1] D.M.A., 16 June 1926.
[2] M.F.G.B., 29 June 1926.
[3] 197 H.C. Deb. 5s, 938.
[4] Ibid., 1038.

J. Ritson, M.P. for Durham, solemnly announced that in introducing the Bill the Prime Minister 'had made the greatest mistake, politically and industrially, that he has ever made in his life'.[1] On the day following the third reading of the Bill the General Council of the T.U.C. issued a manifesto calling for financial support for the miners but refused to impose a levy on the affiliated unions or to place an embargo on the movement of coal.

On 21 June the Durham Coal Owners' Association appointed three separate committees to examine the implications of operating an eight-hour day in Durham.[2] On 6 July, two days before the Eight Hours Bill received the Royal Assent, it informed Robson, Secretary of the County Federation Board, of the terms for a resumption of work based on an increase in the length of the working day. From 12 July work was to be available on the basis of an eight-hour day plus one winding for all classes employed underground. Surfacemen's hours were to be the same as those prevailing before the reduction to $46\frac{1}{2}$ in 1919. The minimum percentage addition to basic rates was to be reduced by 21 per cent to 89 per cent and the subsistence allowance for adult low paid daywagemen reduced by 10d to 6s $8\frac{1}{2}$d per shift in addition to the usual allowances for houses or rent and coals. The exisiting addition to the basic rates of piece workers given on the reduction of hours to seven plus one winding in 1919 was no longer to apply. The new percentage addition to basic rates was to apply until 30 September 1926 after which time it was to be determined by the ascertainment of net proceeds until some other arrangement was made. The difference between proceeds and the costs other than wages was to be divided in the ratio of 87 to wages and 13 to profits subject to a minimum 89 per cent addition to basic rates. The value of house or rent and coals allowances, amounting to almost 2s per shift, and the allowances made to make wages up to subsistence level were to be included in the ascertainment as wages and not as other costs. The owners also stipulated that:

'Certain modifications of old arrangements should be made which would have the effect of removing the restriction on production and increasing the efficiency in the working of the mines which are essential to secure reductions of cost.'

Individual owners also retained the right to impose alterations in piece-work rates.[3]

[1] *Ibid.*, 1235.
[2] Durham Coal Owners' Association, *Executive Committee Minutes*, 21 June 1926.
[3] M.F.G.B., *Terms Offered in the Districts on the Basis of an Eight Hour Day*, pp. 6–11.

The effect of the owners' proposals upon wages per shift can be seen from the following table:[1]

Class of workmen	Wage at basis plus 110 per cent		Wage at basis plus 89 per cent		Reduction	
	s	d	s	d	s	d
Hewers	9	8	8	7	1	1
Labourers	6	10	6	2		8
Stonemen (datal)	7	7	6	10		9

The Durham owners offered to meet the County Federation Board in order to discuss the 'certain modifications of old arrangements' necessary to reduce working costs but were promptly refused a meeting.[2] 'Our duty at present,' Robson wrote in a circular on behalf of the Board, 'is not to subject these proposals to a careful analysis, as they are impossible; at a glance we can see they cut across all for which we have been standing for the last 10 weeks.'[3] The Durham miners needed no persuasion to resist such terms. A rally of workmen at Sunderland on 8 July denounced the terms and resolved to oppose the adoption of the eight-hour day.[4] A. J. Cook, speaking at a gala meeting organized by the Burnhope Lodge, condemned any supporter of the eight-hour day as a 'traitor' who ought to be 'treated as a leper'.[5] The extent of the sacrifice which miners in Durham would have undergone had the owners' terms been accepted was scarcely realized at national level nor, indeed, by miners in other coalfields. The activities of outside bodies to achieve a blanket settlement of the dispute and the later willingness of individual districts to assess the feasibility of opposition in terms only of their own economic situation served to emphasize the potential weaknesses of the miners' struggle and to outrage leaders of the Durham Miners' Association.

VIII

Representatives of the Christian Churches again intervened in the hope of reaching a settlement in the industry. On 28 June they invited M.F.G.B. representatives to a joint meeting to discuss a method of settlement based upon the adoption of the Samuel Report 'in its

[1] *Ibid.*, p. 7.
[2] D.M.A., 8 July 1926.
[3] *Durham Chronicle*, 10 July 1926.
[4] *Ibid.*
[5] *Colliery Guardian*, 23 July 1926. The traditional Gala had been abandoned.

entirety'.[1] At the joint meeting on 15 July the M.F.G.B. accepted a memorandum which proposed an immediate resumption of work with wages and hours as they were before the stoppage. The Government was to grant a subsidy for a period not exceeding four months, under a scheme to be prepared by the Samuel Commission, to provide a basis for a national settlement to be reached. If, at the end of four months, agreement was still not reached there was to be a Joint Board established to appoint an Independent Chairman, whose award was to be final. The Samuel Commissioners were also to prepare Bills for the reorganization of the industry, which the Government was to act upon as quickly as possible.[2] The Prime Minister promptly rejected the proposals on 19 July on the ground that no subsidy could be granted.[3]

The Durham miners were also disturbed about the memorandum but for different reasons. The Executive Committee of the Durham Miners' Association feared that the provision for the appointment of an Independent Chairman involved 'accepting the principle of compulsory arbitration which the miners had already refused' and which was in itself 'subversive to the policy of the Federation'.[4] The whole issue was discussed at a special conference of the M.F.G.B. on 30 July. The Durham delegates, convinced that the deadlock between the parties would not be resolved within four months and that the depression in the industry would continue, warned the Federation that acceptance of the proposals would be tantamount to submitting to lower wages and longer hours. The matter was referred to the districts.[5] The Lodges of the various sections of workmen represented on the Durham County Federation Board voted by 561 votes to 535 to accept the proposals, a majority for acceptance of only 26 but significant in view of the determined opposition of the miners' leaders to the proposals. Nationally, the voting resulted in 367,650 against the proposals and 333,036 for, the combined forces of Yorkshire, South Wales, Lancashire, Cumberland and the Forest of

---

[1] M.F.G.B., 29 June 1926.
[2] *Ibid.*, 15 July 1926.
[3] After submitting the proposals to the Prime Minister on 19 July one of the Church representatives, William Temple, Archbishop of Canterbury, wrote to his wife: 'Baldwin was very nice personally, but not disposed to budge. He attributes the perpetual trouble with coal to past readiness of Governments to intervene; he says the industry has to be taught not to expect public money whenever it howls.' F. A. Iremonger, *William Temple: His Life and Letters,* London 1948, p. 339.
[4] M.F.G.B., 30 July 1926. Cf. *The Times,* 22 July 1926; *Durham Chronicle,* 24 July 1926.
[5] M.F.G.B., 30 July 1926.

Dean resulting in the rejection of the 'Bishop's Memorandum'.[1]

The Bishop of Durham condemned the further intervention of the Church as a means of prolonging dissension amongst the parties to the dispute. In a letter to *The Times* on 13 August Henson wrote:

'Whatever the final settlement be, I am sure that the intervention of the Ten Bishops has done much harm. It has prolonged the crisis, obscured the true issue for the miners and stimulated their natural but unfortunate disposition to think of themselves as the victim, not of economic conditions, but of oppression.'[2]

The Dean of Durham, Bishop Welldon, had expressed similar sentiments in a letter to *The Times* on 5 August, emphasizing the danger of the Church acting as the guardian of the miners against the coal owners and Government inasmuch as any rejection of their proposals could be construed as an 'immoral act'.[3]

Meanwhile in Durham the miners and their families continued in their vigilance against the attack upon their standard of living. Despite the increasing distress suffered by many families and the small hope of immediate improvement in their condition (in July Bolckow, Vaughan and Co. announced that five of their pits would not re-open after the stoppage),[4] the resistance of the miners, especially against the eight-hour day, remained steadfast. Writing in the *Labour Monthly* in August, W. Lawther declared of the situation in Durham:

'The oldest miners here have never known the spirit that exists today against the latest offer of the coal owners. . . . Go where you care, nothing but the most grim determination to resist exists. Despite the efforts and wealth of your opponents the North remains impregnable. Not because of any leaders, but because the men realize that to submit would be a living death.' [5]

At meetings at Rainton and Murton during the same month A. J. Cook was met by miners bearing lamps with the inscription 'This lamp will not burn more than seven hours.'[6] W. P. Richardson

---

[1] *Ibid.*, 16 August 1926.

[2] *The Times*, 13 August 1926; Cf. Iremonger, *op. cit.*, pp. 340–1; *Industrial Peace*, XVIII, August 1926; K. Martin, *The British Public and the General Strike* London 1926, pp. 42–5.

[3] *The Times*, 5 August 1926.

[4] *Ibid.*, 23 July 1926.

[5] W. Lawther, 'The Miners' Struggle in the North', *Labour Monthly*, 8, August 1926, p. 471.

[6] *Colliery Guardian*, 13 August 1926.

told a M.F.G.B. conference on 30 July that in Durham only about 200–250 men were reported to be working out of a total of approximately 40,000.[1] At a further conference on 16 August he reported:

'There is no breaking away. Our men are loyal and where they are working are only little concerns. The number of safety men working is very small.'[2]

Peter Lee explained:

'I come from a County where you don't need any intensive propaganda. All you have to do in Durham is to put the owners' proposals on a piece of paper, and circulate them amongst the people—eight hours a day where we have been working six and a half. 21 per cent off the wages. You need no more propaganda. That is sufficient for Durham.'[3]

For the few who did work in Durham their position was made difficult. There were complaints of officials hewing coal at particular collieries and the Durham Miners' Association threatened to withdraw all safety men if the practice did not cease.[4] At a meeting at Rainton in August, where 40 men had restarted at the Adventure Pit, A. J. Cook confessed that he was collecting names and addresses of all those working in the hope that their wives and families would be 'ostracized'.[5]

By the end of August the coal owners in the Midlands had succeeded in enticing large numbers of men back to work. In the inland coalfields, where there was less necessity to maintain a highly competitive bargaining position in the coal market compared with coal exporting regions and where the relative stability of the domestic market allowed tempting wage offers to be made, the miners lacked the degree of solidarity and unity of purpose shown in Durham. Nor was any other district threatened with a change in working hours to the extent of hewers in Durham. Nevertheless the drift back to work had begun with important consequences for the relations between member districts of the Federation.

[1] M.F.G.B., 30 July 1926. Cf. *The Times*, 23, 24 August 1926.
[2] M.F.G.B., 16 August 1926.
[3] *Ibid.*
[4] D.M.A., 5, 8, 26 July, 21 September, 5 October 1926. Cf. M.F.G.B., 21 April 1926.
[5] *Durham Chronicle*, 14 August 1926; *Colliery Guardian*, 13 August 1926.

IX

The Executive Committee of the M.F.G.B. had been instructed on
16 August to reopen negotiations with the coal owners and the
Government. The Executive met the Central Committee of the
Mining Association on 19 August and Government ministers a week
later but failed to make any progress.[1] The owners insisted on district
settlements and refused to negotiate on the basis of a national agreement. The Government refused to alter its position or make any
offer of financial aid towards a settlement. The situation in Durham
did not alter substantially even in the face of such opposition and
obstinacy. W. P. Richardson emphasized the determination of the
Durham miners to continue the struggle 'until we can get . . . an
honourable settlement'.[2]

A special conference of the M.F.G.B. decided on 2 September to
instruct its Executive Committee to continue in its efforts to negotiate
a national settlement. The Federation informed Winston Churchill
on the following day that it was prepared 'to enter into negotiations
for a new national agreement with a view to a reduction in labour
costs to meet the immediate necessities of the industry'.[3] The Mining
Association refused to consider a national agreement on the grounds
that it was incompatible with the Government's previous exhortations
to the owners to offer relatively high terms in certain districts in order
to facilitate 'a breakaway, piecemeal, district by district'.[4]

The Durham miners were left in no doubt as to how local coal
owners intended to meet the 'immediate necessities of the industry'.
Writing in *The Times* on 28 September Lord Joicey, a prominent
Durham coal owner, declared:

'The only way that costs can be reduced to such a figure as will
enable ourselves and the industries depending upon cheap coal to
recover our position is by increasing the hours and lowering the
wages. Conditions of working vary so much that it is absolutely
necessary that all agreements should be controlled by independent
districts, as they were before the war.'[5]

[1] M.F.G.B., 16, 19, 26 August 1926.
[2] *Ibid.*, 2 September 1926.
[3] *Ibid.*, 3 September 1926.
[4] Miners' Federation of Great Britain, *The Coal Situation, Note of a Meeting between His Majesty's Ministers and the Mining Association*, 6 September 1926, pp. 14–15.
[5] *The Times*, 28 September 1926. Similar sentiments were expressed by another Durham coal owner, Sir Hugh Bell, in 'The Dispute in the Coal Trade', *Contemporary Review*, CXXX, October 1926.

The district affiliates of the Mining Association refused to empower it to enter into negotiations with the miners and the Government on a national basis.[1] At a meeting on 11 September the Durham Coal Owners' Association determined that 'all questions as to wages (including minimum percentage), hours, and conditions of work in each district shall be discussed and settled by the employers and workmen in that district.'[2] It was obvious to the Durham Miners' Association that despite, or even because of, the incessant demands of the miners for a national system of wages to help counteract the indiscriminate attacks made upon hours and wage rates in the cause of reducing costs, the coal owners were determined to safeguard the supremacy of individual mining districts. The Prime Minister, on the other hand, suggested a compromise. On 17 September he forwarded a series of proposals to the M.F.G.B. for negotiating district settlements 'with national supervision'. The Government would establish a statutory National Arbitration Tribunal to confirm or modify the local agreements at the request of either party where there was any increase in hours.[3]

The M.F.G.B. Executive Committee rejected these proposals on 21 September since they involved the entire surrender of the principle of national agreements.[4] On the same evening the miners' leaders told the Prime Minister that they were prepared to recommend an immediate resumption of work temporarily at wages prevailing under the 1921 agreement and that they were prepared to submit the terms of a national wages agreement to an independent tribunal, which should also consider putting into effect the recommendations of the Samuel Commission.[5] Three days later the Prime Minister rejected the miners' proposals,[6] which proved sufficient to convince Peter Lee of the Government's desire to 'fight to the finish'.[7]

The Government's proposals were submitted to the districts on 29 September. The Durham miners rejected them by 1,067 votes to 15. Only Derbyshire and Leicestershire supported the acceptance of the terms.[8] An adjourned M.P.G.B. conference on 7 September

[1] Miners' Federation of Great Britain, *The Coal Situation, Note of a Meeting between His Majesty's Ministers and the Mining Association*, 6 September 1926, pp. 25–6.
[2] *Durham Chronicle*, 18 September 1926.
[3] Miners' Federation of Great Britain, *The Coal Situation, Note of a Meeting . . .*, 6 September 1926, p. 28.
[4] *Ibid.*, p. 29.
[5] *Ibid.*, p. 30.
'P.R.O., Cab. 23/53.
[7] *Durham Chronicle*, 16 October 1926.
[8] M.F.G.B., 7 October 1926.

decided on the next course of action. Durham supported a militant resolution from South Wales which called for a return to 'the *status quo* conditions'. To this end safety men were to be withdrawn, efforts were to be made to secure an embargo on all imported coal and to bring an end to outcrop working; a special congress of the trade unions was to be asked to arrange a levy in support of the miners and there was to be an intensive propaganda campaign. The Executive Committee recommended that the Welsh resolution be referred to the districts.[1] *The Economist* regarded the South Wales proposals as futile and likely to lead to 'violent antagonisms in the coalfields'.[2] The threatened withdrawal of safety men was not likely to have much effect in Durham since for the greater part of the stoppage colliery officials had been carrying out maintenance duties. Furthermore, it was estimated that 70 per cent of the safety men as a whole were outside the direct influence of the Miners' Federation and that the organizations representing them had already condemned the suggested withdrawal.[3]

Nevertheless the Durham miners decided by a Lodge vote of 691 to 387 to accept the South Wales proposals for the continuation of the struggle.[4] The national voting figures were 460,150 votes for and 284,336 against.[5] The M.F.G.B. immediately made arrangements to put the proposals into affect. It resolved to approach the National Federation of Colliery Enginemen and Boiler Firemen in order to withdraw all safety men; a meeting was to be arranged simultaneously with the T.U.C. General Council to attempt to enforce an embargo on all foreign coal and to impose a levy upon affiliated trade unions and future meetings of the Federation were to be held in the coalfields as part of the propaganda campaign.[6]

In the meantime the Durham owners' offer of the terms of employment under the eight-hour day, scheduled to last until 30 September pending further arrangements, had nominally expired. Although the Durham miners had refused even to consider the proposals the owners made further attempts in October to induce the County Federation Board to agree to a resumption of work on the same terms.[7] The Board promptly rejected the suggestion.[8] By this time, however,

---

[1] *Ibid.*
[2] *The Economist*, 9 October 1926.
[3] *Durham Chronicle*, 9, 16 October 1926.
[4] D.M.A., 22 October 1926.
[5] M.F.G.B., 13 October 1926.
[6] *Ibid.*, 15, 19 October 1926.
[7] Durham Coal Owners' Association, *Executive Committee Minutes*, 11 October 1926.
[8] D.M.A., 13 October 1926.

there had occurred a sudden, yet limited, breakaway in the coalfield. Men began to return to work. On 23 October the *Durham Chronicle* reported:

'There has been a marked weakening in the miners' position during the past week, men returning to work in considerable numbers in various parts of the coalfield. . . . In Durham County . . . the men are showing their eagerness to resume.'[1]

It is difficult to determine exactly the extent of the return to work since the figures supplied by the press are both scanty and, in many cases, exaggerated. On 4 October the Durham Miners' Association reported about 250 men at work while two days previously the *Northern Echo* estimated the total number of men at work in Northumberland and Durham to be over 4,000.[2] The inclusion of estimates for Northumberland in the latter figure cannot reasonably explain such a wide discrepancy in the figures. The number of miners resuming work in Durham in no way compared with the numbers working in other districts, especially in Derbyshire and Nottinghamshire. The *Durham Chronicle* reported that by 21 October 650 miners had resumed work at the St Hilda pit and that work had been resumed 'on a limited scale' at Silksworth, North Bitchburn, Willington, Browney and Esh Winning.[3]

The colliery owners took every advantage to exploit the situation. Local colliery owners in the Chester-le-Street area offered men a 3s per day bonus for a fortnight if they would resume work.[4] By 10 November Richardson reported to a M.F.G.B. conference that 3,018 members of the Durham Miners' Association had returned to work in the County out of a total of over 140,000. 1,846 men had returned to the collieries under the direct influence of the Association, 621 to working on outcrops and 551 to small collieries unable to support Lodges.[5] In Nottinghamshire and Derbyshire over 40,000 men had returned to work by mid-November leaving about 7,000 still on strike. Altogether 58,000 of the 97,000 men who worked in the seven districts of the Midland Federation had resumed work.[6]

Although the numbers of men at work in Durham remained relatively small they were sufficient to arouse the anger of those miners loyal to both the Durham Miners' Association and the M.F.G.B.

---

[1] *Durham Chronicle*, 23 October 1926.
[2] *Northern Echo*, 2 October 1926; cited in Mason, *op. cit.*, p. 429.
[3] *Durham Chronicle*, 23 October 1926.
[4] *Ibid.*
[5] M.F.G.B., 10 November 1926.
[6] *Ibid.*

Only three men resumed work at the Silksworth Colliery during October but they were constantly faced with demonstrations by angry miners. At a gathering on 26 October, during which 'there were cries of "Blacklegs", hisses and cat calls', the seventy policemen protecting the three workers turned and charged the crowd injuring several people.[1] The sixty miners working at the Ouston 'E' pit near Birtley, owned by Pelaw Main Collieries, had to be conveyed in two furniture vans and 'a boarded, canvas-covered lorry'.[2] Nor were they safe at home. Incidents were reported of miners throwing stones at the police and at the houses of the men who had resumed work. A number of miners were later imprisoned and sentenced to a period of hard labour as a result of the disturbances at Ouston.[3] The demonstrations were not without effect since W. Hornsby, general manager of Pelaw Main Collieries, commented that the breakaway at Ouston 'would have been even longer but for the intimidation practised in this area'.[4]

Those miners who returned to work forfeited their right to normal union benefits. At Rainton Colliery, however, the 57 miners, out of a total of 260, who resumed work organized the Rainton Colliery Employees' Thrift Fund 'to promote closer working and a better understanding between the management and the men.' The working miners subscribed not less than 1s per week from their wages and an equal amount was contributed by the employers. The miners were guaranteed a payment equal to 80 per cent of their outstanding credit in case of sickness or 'exceptional circumstances' and, in the case of death, the payment of all credits to their closest survivors.[5]

The Durham Miners' Association joined local miners' M.P.s in helping to stem the return to work, small in numbers though it was. A. J. Cook also toured the coalfield urging men to remain loyal to their Association.[6] Speaking to miners at Esh Winning Robson pleaded:

'If there is any feeling that we are done and if there is going to be any going back, for God's sake let's get back to the Miners' Hall at Durham, and let us all go back together.'[7]

Apart from weakening the miners' cause the return to work gradually antagonized relationships between the miners and the police throughout the coalfield. The miners protested against police being drafted

---

[1] *Durham Chronicle*, 30 October 1926.
[2] *Ibid.*
[3] *Ibid.*, 6, 20 November 1926.
[4] *Ibid.*, 30 October 1926.
[5] *Ibid.*, 23 October 1926.
[6] *Ibid.*
[7] *Ibid.*

into the County from other areas in numbers disproportionate to the number of workers felt to be in need of protection. A total of 243 extra police from Newcastle, Hull and the North Riding of Yorkshire were drafted into County Durham between 25 October and 7 November.[1] W. Whiteley, M.P. for Blaydon, accused the Home Secretary of being responsible for drafting police into County Durham 'with no numbers, so that no one can report them', suggesting that in most cases it was they who were directly responsible for inciting trouble amongst the miners.[2] Nor was the problem simply one of imported police. In a discussion in the House of Commons on 26 October on the Emergency Powers Regulations R. Richardson, M.P. for Houghton-le-Spring, cited instances of workmen being brought from other areas to work in Durham collieries to help support those members of the Durham Miners' Association who had resumed work voluntarily. Local colliery agents claimed that the men were *bona fide* officials and working with the consent of the other miners.[3]

X

Despite the determination of particular districts to fight on, the position of the miners slowly deteriorated in the absence of sympathetic and financial support. The General Council of the T.U.C. failed to persuade the transport unions to impose an embargo on the movement of coal, and, for its own part, declined to impose a compulsory levy in support of the miners. Affiliated unions were recommended to encourage a voluntary contribution from their membership of a penny a day.

By 12 November the M.F.G.B. received further proposals from the Government for ending the dispute. They included an immediate resumption of work by means of district settlements, 'the hours to be worked not being excluded from the district negotiations'. Men were to be reinstated 'as opportunity offers without prejudice to the men at present at work'. District agreements were to be regarded as 'standard' and operative for three years if they provided for a district board with an independent Chairman, ascertainments, a ratio of wages to profits of between 87:13 and 85:15, a minimum of 20 per cent above the standard wage, and payment of subsistence wages at the previous rates. The Northumberland, Durham, Cumberland and North Wales coal owners refused to agree to pay temporarily a

[1] *Northern Echo*, 3 February 1927; cited in Mason, *op. cit.*, p. 433.
[2] 199 H.C. Deb. 5s, 2072.
[3] 199 H.C. Deb. 5s, 778–780.

general district percentage on basic rates not less than that prevailing on 30 April (equivalent in Durham to a 110 per cent addition to basic rates). The Government agreed to establish a national arbitral authority for six months to consider appeals by either party against all agreements which were not 'standard' providing they were based on a longer working day.[1]

The proposals, if accepted, would have instituted the very conditions of work against which the miners in every district had been fighting for over six months. The proposals had been made, however, when the resistance of the miners was rapidly weakening.[2] The Federation conference decided on 12 November to recommend the acceptance of the Government's proposals.[3] Durham delegates voted in favour of the decision in spite of their public condemnation of longer hours, lower wages and district settlements. Only the day before Richardson had told the conference that, as far as Durham was concerned, negotiations with the Government were futile if they threatened to establish a longer working day and disrupt the traditional hours of work of hewers in the coalfield.[4]

The Durham delegates' support of the Government's latest terms aroused a storm of protest amongst miners in the coalfield who openly condemned the action and accused their representatives of betraying the rank and file. The Executive Committee of the Durham Miners' Association fully realized that the willingness of the majority of the Durham miners to continue the fight rested predominantly on their knowledge of the price of defeat, especially in relation to hours. Yet in a desperate attempt to justify their action the Executive stressed the plight which the Federation as a whole had reached by mid-November explaining:

'Our Army . . . was breaking up and already . . . large numbers of men had returned to work in other areas on the Owners' terms.

True, the men in our County, with small exceptions, stood as solid as ever . . . but even there the discerning man could see cracks and an anxiety for something to be done. Is not this what we might expect after 30 weeks of heroic struggle? The marvel to all men throughout the world is that this Army of over one million men, with their women and children, have stood so long and endured the sacrifice forced upon them by a ruthless and relentless foe. If, therefore, the people who condemn us would be less parochial, and take

[1] M.F.G.B., 12 November 1926.
[2] See above, pp. 216–17.
[3] M.F.G.B., 10–13 November 1926.
[4] *Ibid.*, 11 November 1926.

a wider outlook, they would stop their carping and sniping, and realize that what had happened in other areas as to breaking away was inevitable in ours; it would have been clear to them as it was to us that District negotiations were inevitable; and that, therefore, it was in the interests of the Durham men that we negotiate while our Army was unbroken, for, as we informed you at the commencement of the fight, Durham had more to lose than any other County. Judging from things as they are, it would appear that our hope of negotiating with our men solid is gone; and, therefore, our crime is not that we acted too soon, but too late.

The forces of reaction have forced their will upon the nation. The power of the press, the Government, the coal owners and federated capitalism has proved too strong for us. In spite of their declarations they are enforcing slave conditions upon the miners, and the same spirit prevails amongst the Durham coal owners, who are enforcing their will in a ruthless way upon our people. Let them do their worst. This is not the end, and it must for us be a beginning. Your task—our task—is to rebuild so that we may recover not only what we have lost, but make sure that the power that has been used to crush the miners is wrested from those who possess it and put into hands who will organize and run industry for the benefit of the human race, and not for the selfish idea of profits.'[1]

Apart from their final exhortations the Executive Committee portrayed the same spirit of inevitable defeat as was obvious amongst the remaining districts in the Federation. Whether the Association negotiated with the Durham coal owners with its membership largely intact or split amongst themselves proved to be of little consequence. At this stage in the dispute few, if any, of the coal owners were prepared to negotiate; for them the price of the miners' defeat was to be unconditional surrender.

The Lodges of the Durham Miners' Association decided by 742 votes to 359 to reject the Government's proposals. The national figures, reported to a M.F.G.B. conference on 19 November, showed that the terms had been rejected by 480,806 votes to 313,200.[2] The refusal of the miners to settle the dispute by adopting the Government's suggestions aroused the indignation of certain sections of the press. *The Times* accorded the voting in Durham to 'the well-known antipathy of the younger Durham miners to any sort of settlement short of full concession of the old terms'.[3] The *Yorkshire Post*

[1] D.M.A., 25 November 1926.
[2] M.F.G.B., 19 November 1926.
[3] *The Times*, 18 November 1926.

stressed the apathy of the miners in Durham on the one hand, and the influence of Communism amongst the younger workmen on the other.[1] Peter Lee added some weight to the latter accusation when he told Federation delegates on 19 November of the interference of the national Communist Party in Durham during the period of voting. He claimed that the Communists had issued miners with a circular containing a statement by A. J. Cook, initially printed in the *Sunday Worker* on 14 November, which read: 'My advice is to the men to reject the Government's terms. The T.U.C. have acted as mediators for the coal owners urging us to accept first lower wages, then longer hours, and now district settlements.' The circular ended with 'Stand by Cook and reject the terms' printed in bold type. A. J. Cook denied having anything to do with the statement and nothing more was heard of the issue.[2]

After a great deal of discussion the M.F.G.B. finally decided to recommend the districts to open negotiations with the owners according to general principles laid down by the Executive Committee. These were:

1. The method of ascertaining the district percentage on basis rates to be as provided by the National Wages Agreement of 1924.
2. The ratio of division of net proceeds to be 87:13.
3. The minimum percentage to be provided of not less than 20 per cent upon the standard wages prevailing on April 30 1926.
4. The payment of April 1926 subsistence wages to low paid day-wagemen.
5. All agreements to be terminable by one month's notice from either side.
6. District to endeavour to effect the complete reinstatement of all men and boys employed at April 30 1926, on the lines provided by Clause 13 of the National Wages Agreement of 1921.

No district was to enter into a final settlement until a further conference had received reports of all the negotiations.[3]

Immediately after the decision in favour of district bargaining had been made the Durham County Federation Board approached the owners to secure a meeting. On receipt of their application the Durham Coal Owners' Association appointed a special Negotiating Committee of fifteen members with full power to arrange terms of settlement. The Negotiating Committee met representatives of the miners on 23, 25 and 27 November. The terms submitted by the

[1] *Yorkshire Post*, 19 November 1926.
[2] M.F.G.B., 19 November 1926.
[3] *Ibid.*, 19, 20 November 1926.

owners proposed that a District Board, representative of the coal owners and members of the County Federation Board, should be established with an Independent Chairman. Wages were to be determined in relation to the district ascertainment of proceeds subject to a minimum percentage addition to basic rates of not less than 89. Wages payable from the resumption of work until 28 February 1927 were to be at the minimum rate. The wages payable in March 1927 were to be determined by the ascertained proceeds for the months of January 1927; for the month of April by the proceeds for the month of February and so on. The method of ascertainment was to be determined by the parties but the value of the allowances payable for free houses, rent and free coals were to be treated as wages paid and not as other costs. Net proceeds were to be divided in the ratio 87:13. Low paid adult day-wage workers were to be paid a subsistence allowance of 6s 8½d per shift. The arrangements for the payment of wages were conditional upon all classes, except hewers and deputies, working a shift of eight hours plus one winding. Hewers and deputies were to work seven and a half hours plus one winding. Surface workers were to work 49 hours per week, exclusive of mealtimes, and piece workers other than hewers were to forgo the 12½ per cent addition to wages granted in 1919 as a consequence of the reduction in working hours. Changes in local working conditions were also stipulated and a requirement made that machinery should be established for the adjustment of piece-work rates and other matters of dispute continually arising at the pit. The agreement was to continue for one year and thereafter be subject to one month's notice by either party.[1] The terms involved a reduction in the percentage addition to basic rates from 110 to 89 and a reduction in subsistence wages from 7s 6½d to 6s 8½d per shift. The inclusion of allowances payable to workmen in wages paid and not in costs other than wages, infringed the method of ascertaining the district percentage addition to basic rates as provided in the 1924 National Agreement. On this ground, therefore, as well as by the reduction in subsistence wages, the proposed terms were contrary to the 'guiding principles' as defined by the Executive Committee of the M.F.G.B. on 20 November.[2]

On the other hand the miners gained one major concession. The terms offered by the owners were precisely those made on 6 July[3] with one important exception. Hewers were no longer required to work an eight-hour shift plus one winding. No indication was given in the terms offered or in the official reports of the negotiations with

[1] See Appendix I to this chapter.
[2] See above, p. 222.
[3] See above, p. 209.

the Federation Board as to why the concession had been made. The Durham owners could not fail to be unaware of the reaction previously made by the miners to the suggestion of an eight-hour day for all classes. The decision to institute a seven and a half hour shift exclusive of windings for hewers was, furthermore, directly opposed to the recommendations of the Committee established by the owners to investigate the implications of a universal eight-hour day in the Durham coalfield.[1] The Committee estimated that the total savings in cost per ton of coal of establishing a system of eight hours plus one winding for all classes and 49 hours per week for surface hands amounted to 1s 3·29d compared with 1s 0·44d with a system of seven and a half hours plus one winding for hewers and eight hours plus one winding for all other classes and 9·8d for a system of seven and a half plus one winding for all classes, surface hands working 49 hours per week in both cases. These estimates were exclusive of the saving (amounting to 1s 1d per ton) expected to be derived from the reduction in the percentage addition to basic rates and in the level of the subsistence wage.[2] The increase in hewers' working hours, if not as large as might have been, was nevertheless the most damaging of all the proposals and calculated to perpetuate the conflict between owners and men for a long time to come. During the 1920s the hewers in Durham had been increasingly urged to work a complete shift of seven hours bank-to-bank and threatened with the possibility of working the full hours prescribed by law. The acceptance of the owners' proposals in 1926 entailed a far more important change in the structure of working hours in providing, for the first time since 1890, an all-round increase in the length of the hewers' working day above the level of seven hours bank-to-bank.

The miners' representatives had also secured an agreement from the owners, before the terms were finally agreed upon, that the standard basic wage of hewers and fillers should be increased to 4s 8d from its previous level of 4s 2d and 4s 6d respectively, in strict proportion to the proposed increase in hours.[3] Furthermore the owners had stated in clause 18 of the proposed agreement that:

'There is no disposition on the part of the owners to victimize any man on account of his action during the stoppage.

With regard to the reemployment of men, the owners are prepared to engage them as they are required subject to the condition

[1] See above, p. 209. Although three committees were originally established only one published a report.
[2] Durham Coal Owners' Association, *Executive Committee Minutes*, 8 October 1926.
[3] Durham Coal Owners' Association, *Annual Report*, 1926, pp. 46–7.

that the owners cannot consent to discharge any man who was employed during the stoppage.'[1]

The County Federation Board reviewed the proposed terms of settlement and reluctantly instructed its members to accept the terms commenting:

'Never in a struggle in the history of the country have proposals so exacting, so unjust and inhuman, been offered to any body of workers, and they can in no way mean that the men will return to work under that sense of justice that will lay the foundation for peace in industry, but must fill them with resentment and urge them to great endeavour ... to revoke the abominable conditions that have been imposed.'[2]

Without any hope of gaining further concessions from the owners the Board realized that to recommend the workmen to reject the terms was simply to ask them to continue making sacrifices without the slightest hope of any advantage to themselves. Accordingly a ballot was organized on 29 November the results of which were as follows:

	For	Against
Miners	33,916	48,435
Enginemen	3,186	399
Mechanics	3,481	383

Majority against the proposals: 8,634[3]

Only 63 per cent of the miners in the County voted. Their final attempt to secure the rejection of the terms failed to provide the two-thirds majority required for prolonging the stoppage.[4] The County Federation Board issued instructions that work was to be resumed.[5]

The loyalty and determination of the Durham miners in seeking improved conditions had been widely acclaimed by the fact that the coalfield was the last to resume work after the stoppage[6] and it was not surprising, therefore, that there was a marked feeling of resentment amongst many of the members of the Durham Miners' Association over the outcome of the struggle. Over 100 miners left Ryhope in

[1] *Ibid.*, pp. 45–6.
[2] *Durham Chronicle*, 4 December 1926.
[3] *Ibid.*
[4] *Ibid.*
[5] *Ibid.*
[6] Mason, *op. cit.*, p. 443. By November 29 work had restarted in all important cities except Durham, South Wales, and Yorkshire.

charabancs for Rotherham being 'so disgusted' with the terms of settlement.[1] Others looked hopefully to the future already planning their revenge. W. P. Richardson remarked to a *Durham Chronicle* reporter on 10 December:

'The miners are on the bottom and have been compelled to accept dictated and unjust terms. The miners will rise again and will remember because they cannot forget. The victors of today will live to regret their unjust treatment to the miners.'[2]

Without adequate financial and sympathetic support the miners had little hope of victory. Unlike workers in Nottinghamshire and Derbyshire miners in Durham had never been seriously tempted to return to work by offers of comparatively favourable terms since, under the prevailing economic conditions, owners in the northern coalfield were unable to increase their proceeds significantly without reducing costs which, to their mind, meant reducing wages and/or increasing the length of the working day. Durham did share, however, severe financial weaknesses common to most other areas.[3]

However strong their sense of principle and justice might have been the miners were unable to combat the combined forces of the coal owners and the Government. With the institution of district bargaining and the continuing depression in the coal industry there was little hope of expecting any early or substantial improvement in their standard of living. The miners in Durham feared the worst as the coal owners, conscious of the increase in the length of the working day and intent on reducing costs in an effort to gain a footing in foreign markets, embarked upon a policy of cheap selling. The deepening depression in the industry after 1929, especially in the export sector, and the further attacks made upon the Durham miners' wages confirmed that such fears were not without foundation.

[1] *Durham Chronicle*, 4 December 1926.
[2] *Ibid.*, 11 December 1926.
[3] See Chapter II, pp. 86–7.

Appendix I

TERMS OF SETTLEMENT, 1926

The following conditions with respect to the wages and conditions of employment of persons employed at the coal mines in the County of Durham are agreed between the Durham Coal Owners' Association and the Durham County Mining Federation hereinafter referred to as 'the parties':

1. There shall be established a District Board consisting of such number of members as may be determined by the parties.

2. The rules of procedure shall include a provision for the appointment of an Independent Chairman and for the voting to be by sides.

3. The wages payable in the district up to the 28th February, 1927, shall be at the rate of 89 per cent above basis rates. There shall in addition be the payments specified in Clause 6 hereof.

4. The wages payable in the district in subsequent periods other than the payments specified in Clause 6 hereof, shall be expressed in the form of a percentage of the basis rates prevailing at the collieries at the time of adjustment, and shall be periodically adjusted in accordance with the results of the industry in the district as ascertained from time to time. The amount of the percentage to be paid in the district during any period shall be determined by the results of the industry during a previous period as ascertained from returns to be made by the owners. Such returns to be forwarded to independent accountants appointed by each of the parties, and to be checked by test audits of the owners' books carried out jointly by these accountants as arranged by them. The independent accountants shall be entitled to refer any questions arising out of the test audits to the District Boards.

5. The sum to be applied in the district to the payment of wages shall be equal to 87 per cent of the surplus of the proceeds remaining after deduction therefrom of the costs of production other than wages as defined in paragraph 6 of the Schedule hereto, which sets out the principles to be followed for the purpose of the periodical ascertainments.

6. In arriving at the amount to be expressed as a percentage of the basis rates in conformity with Clause 4 hereof, the following items shall be treated as payments on account of wages, and not as costs of production other than wages:

   (a) The sums paid in wages to make up the subsistence wage.
   (b) The value afforded as the equivalent of wages by the provision of workers' houses and rates thereon.
   (c) The cash paid to workers in lieu of the provision of houses.
   (d) The value afforded as the equivalent of wages in the form of house coal allowances.

7. The methods to be adopted for ascertaining fair values to be placed upon workers' houses and coal and fair prices in regard to coal or other transfers to excluded activities or in regard to any transfers to the collieries from the excluded activities shall, failing agreement by the Joint Accountants, be determined by a sub-committee appointed by the District Board. The Joint Accountants to attend meetings of the sub-committee when requested by the sub-committee to do so.

8. If the rates of wages as determined in the district do not provide in any period a subsistence wage to low paid adult day-wage workers, such additions in the form of allowance per shift worked shall be made for that period to the daily wage of these workers, as, in the opinion of the District Board, may be necessary for the purpose, but from the commencement of this agreement until otherwise determined the amount shall be such as to make up the wages of the persons concerned to 6s 8½d per shift.

9. If in any period of ascertainment the percentage addition to basis rates ascertained as hereinbefore provided shall be less than 89, then 89 per cent shall nevertheless be paid as a minimum percentage, but the amount of the deficiency represented by the difference between the sum applicable to wages after giving effect to the terms of Clause 6 hereof and the cost of wages at the minimum percentage shall be deducted in the next subsequent ascertainment from any balance available in excess of the cost of wages at the minimum percentage. If there should be no balance available for meeting a deficiency, or any part thereof, the deficiency or such proportion thereof as may remain shall be carried forward to be made good in the subsequent period or periods.

In the event of the District Boards deciding under Clause 10 hereof to vary the periods of ascertainment, then in calculating deficiencies and their recoupment, regard shall be had by the Independent Accountants to the fact that the results of any one month enter the ascertainment figures which govern the wages payable in respect of two or more months, or that an ascertainment which includes the results of two or more months governs the wages payable in respect of any one month.

10. The period of ascertainment shall, until otherwise determined, be one month. The percentage payable for the month of March 1927, shall be determined by the ascertainment of proceeds for the month of January 1927; for the month of April 1927, by the proceeds for the month of February 1927; and so on. The periods of ascertainment may be varied by the decision of the District Board.

11. In ascertaining the proceeds and costs other than wages the accountants shall, unless and until otherwise determined, follow the principles set out in the Schedule attached hereto.

The following additional arrangements with respect to wages, hours and working conditions in the district shall apply:

12. The hours of coal hewers shall be $7\frac{1}{2}$ per shift, plus one winding time. For all other classes of underground workers except deputies the hours shall be 8 per shift, plus one winding time. The hours of deputies shall be $7\frac{1}{2}$ per shift, plus one winding time, it being understood that if required they shall stay longer and be paid an equivalent wage for overtime.

13. The county standard basis wage for hewers and fillers shall be 4s 8d per shift.

14. The $12\frac{1}{2}$ per cent addition to pieceworkers' wages, whether merged in the prices or not, which was granted on the reduction of hours in 1919, shall no longer apply.

15. The hours of men employed at the surface shall be 49 per week, exclusive of mealtimes.

16. Hewers and fillers shall, if required by the management, do the necessary stone and shift work at and about the face in all systems of working, and if required by the management, shall work together and pool their earnings.

17. Where machine mining is applied the persons employed on this method, whether machine men, drillers, fillers, pullers-up of conveyors, or canchmen, shall, when required, work in conjunction with each other and all or any of them shall do any necessary work when required although it may be outside their ordinary work.

18. All seams where the management require shall be cavilled separately.

19. The practice of sitting at the kist shall be abolished and the men shall go straight to their working places as soon as authorized to do so by the deputy, and remain for the full hours of the shift.

20. Machinery shall be set up without delay for the adjustment of piece-work rates and determination of other matters of dispute continually arising at the pits.

21. This agreement shall continue in operation for one year from the date hereof subject to one month's notice by either party given after the expiration of that period.[1]

---

[1] The Agreement was signed on 30 November 1926. The author has been unable to trace an original copy of the terms which provides details of the individual signatories.

Chapter VI

IN DEPRESSION, 1927–39

I

For the miners who returned to work during the early months of 1927 the reality of their defeat in the struggle for better wages and conditions soon became obvious. The increase in the length of the working shift aggravated the industry's problem of overproduction in an inelastic market. Keynes remarked:

> 'A temporary eight-hour day is a ludicrous plan. If all the miners were to work eight hours we could not sell the coal produced, even if we were to capture the entire export market of Germany and the United States.'[1]

Wages in the Durham coalfield were fixed at the minimum level of 89 per cent above basic rates until 28 February 1927 according to the terms of settlement but, despite the fact that thereafter they were determined by the monthly ascertainment of district proceeds, they never rose above the minimum level in any month in 1927 nor indeed in any year before 1939.[2] Continued depression in the coal industry reduced district proceeds to such an extent that the ascertained percentage addition to basic wages constantly fell below the minimum level. The percentage addition to basic rates in March 1927 stood at 69·31, fell to 34·83 in September and had risen to only 40·65 in December. The total accumulated deficiency in standard profits in Durham at the end of 1927 amounted to £2,778,994 owing to the continued necessity for the owners to make up the difference between the ascertained percentage and the minimum addition to basic wages. Unemployment, low wages and short-time working were widespread. In the June 1924 quarter 171,414 wage earners were employed in the Durham coalfield. By March 1927 the figure had been reduced to 129,148.[3] In 1928 a larger proportion of the total insured work force in the coal industry was wholly unemployed in Durham than in the country as a whole.[4]

[1] J. M. Keynes, 'The Need of Peace by Negotiation', *New Republic*, 19 May 1926, cited in Crook, *op. cit.*, p. 344n.
[2] The precise amount of the minimum addition to basic wages altered in later years as a result of mutual negotiations between owners and men. See below, pp. 236–9.
[3] *Miner*, 28 May 1927.
[4] See Chapter VII, pp. 268–9, and Appendices.

The situation was made worse by the unconciliatory attitude of the local coal owners. Almost immediately after the signing of the terms of settlement in 1926 the Durham miners' leaders approached the owners to discuss a number of matters arising from the working of the agreement. At a series of meetings during the period December 1926–June 1928 representatives of the Durham miners attempted to improve the conditions of Saturday working, the payment for over-time and the terms of employment of putters, surface workers and bankmen but only succeeded in obtaining minor concessions which fell short of their original demands. The miners' leaders were left in no doubt that the owners were determined to enforce their victory of 1926. After a meeting between the Executive Committee of the Durham Miners' Association and representatives of the owners on 7 February 1927 W. P. Richardson wrote to members:

'It is correct to say that no Committee has ever had a more difficult task than confronted us on this occasion. The attitude of the owners was relentless throughout and their determination to secure the changes they required [was] clearly demonstrated. . . . Unfortu-nately the general position of our members, plus the fact that we still have over 30,000 members who have not been restarted since the end of the struggle, makes it impossible to do anything, except to make the best arrangements we can until such times as we are in a position to effectively improve our position.'[1]

The owners' previous guarantee that no victimization would occur after the stoppage[2] was not readily adhered to. The Consett Iron Company was particularly condemned by the Association for its refusal to employ men engaged in the dispute.[3] W. Whiteley, M.P. for Blaydon, announced in the House of Commons on 27 April 1927 that a number of mining families in Durham had been evicted because of the need to house 'strangers' brought into the district to replace certain miners at the pit. 'Evictions of miners are going on in many parts of Durham County,' he said, 'their wives, children and furniture being put on to the street, although there is no possibility of alterna-tive accommodation being secured.'[4] The evictions were particularly frequent at South Garesfield. At Sacriston, Chopwell and Hylton it was reported that local Lodge officials were deliberately refused em-ployment because of their activities during the 1926 stoppage.[5]

[1] D.M.A., 10 February 1927.
[2] See Chapter V, pp. 224–5.
[3] *Miner*, 28 May, 4 June 1927.
[4] 205 H.C. Deb. 5s, 987–988.
[5] D.M.A., 8 July 1927.

II

The Durham Miners' Association's fight to maintain the loyalty of a membership openly disgruntled by the 1926 defeat sprang not only from the owners' efforts to split the local miners' movement but also from the activities of non-political trade unions. Based upon a movement which had its strongest hold in Nottinghamshire and Derbyshire, under the leadership of George Spencer, non-political trade unionism spread to Durham during the early months of 1927.

The first non-political union in the County originated amongst those miners at the Esh Winning Colliery who had returned to work before the general resumption in December 1926. Incensed at the conduct of the strike negotiations and conscious of the Association's announcement that men resuming work would be deprived of all trade union benefits,[1] they decided at a meeting on 3 December 1926 to form the Esh Winning Miners' Industrial (Non-Political) Society. The Society aimed to establish a means of settling disputes amicably or by independent arbitration without recourse to political activity. Union funds were debarred from use for political purposes.[2] It failed, however, to secure official recognition from the local colliery company, Pease and Partners Ltd, which was bound by the statutes of the Durham Coal Owners' Association to recognize no other union than the Durham Miners' Association.[3]

Several more local branches of the non-political trade union movement were established in the coalfield during January 1927 with memberships ranging from 40 at Eden Colliery to 500 at St Hilda Colliery.[4] Following meetings of representatives of local branches in January 1927 the Northumberland and Durham Miners' Non-Political Trades Union was established to which J. Edmondson, Lodge Secretary and checkweighman at St Hilda Colliery since 1916, was appointed President in February.[5] By the first week in February its membership was reported to be over 10,500,[6] and by April it claimed to support 40 branches and over 14,000 members, representing about 7 per cent of the total number of miners in Northumberland and Durham.[7] These figures are probably exaggerated since apart from the gradual reduction in the influence of the Union after 1927

[1] D.M.A., 18 October 1926.
[2] *Durham Chronicle*, 18 December 1926.
[3] *Ibid.*, 22 January 1927.
[4] *Northern Echo*, 17 January 1927; cited in Mason, *op. cit.*, p. 448.
[5] *Durham Chronicle*, 29 January, 12 February 1927.
[6] *Ibid.*, 12 February 1927.
[7] *Ibid.*, 22 April 1927.

its total membership as reported to the Chief Registrar of Friendly Societies in 1928 stood at only 3,911, in 1929 at 4,081 and in 1930 at 4,068, in every case smaller in number than either the Nottingham-shire and District Miners' Industrial Union or the South Wales Miners' Industrial Union.[1]

The strength of the newly-formed Union was concentrated in north-west Durham especially amongst the miners at collieries owned by the Stella Coal Company and the Consett Iron Company.[2] The Union failed to secure the support of the Durham Coal Owners' Association and faced bitter opposition from the Durham Miners' Association. In the absence of support from a nucleus of County miners' officials the Union was not able to exert an independent influence of the magni-tude achieved by George Spencer in Nottinghamshire and Derbyshire. Furthermore, as far as Durham was concerned, the local miners' trade union succeeded in emerging from the 1926 dispute with a large core of loyal supporters. The traditional loyalty of the Durham miners to their Association allowed its leaders to gain the support of the rank and file miners so necessary in the years after 1926. Never-theless, the Association took active steps to condemn the activities of the non-political trade unionists. The miners' leaders saw that such a movement, if successful, would disrupt the whole basis of trade union activity. Throughout the early months of 1927 the Association arranged local meetings throughout the County forecasting the early doom of the new organizations.[3]

Two County Court cases against the non-political unions helped to boost the counter-attack organized by the local miners' leaders. A hewer at Greenside Colliery refused to contribute towards the main-tenance of the officially-appointed checkweighman at the colliery on the grounds that he was already making a similar payment in support of a checkweighman appointed by the colliery's non-political trade union in December 1926.[4] The Durham Miners' Association took the issue to court in October 1927. The judge at the Newcastle County Court deemed that since the notice for the appointment of the 'non-political' checkweighman applied only to members of the non-political trade union and not to the majority of the workmen at the colliery then all hewers were bound to support the checkweighman officially elected by members of the Durham Miners' Association.[5] Leave of appeal was granted but an appeal was subsequently dis-

[1] Mason, *op. cit.*, p. 449.
[2] *Durham Chronicle*, 22 April 1927.
[3] *Ibid.*, 29 January, 12 February, 29 July 1927.
[4] *Miner*, 14 April 1928.
[5] *The Times*, 21 October 1927.

missed at the Newcastle County Court in April 1928.[1] At a second
case in Newcastle in October 1928 judgement was passed in favour of
two coal hewers from Chopwell who sued the Consett Iron Company
over a wages agreement it had made with the local non-political trade
union. The judge upheld the claim that the non-political union did
not represent the majority of workmen employed at the Chopwell
Colliery.[2]

The non-political trade union movement was only one manifesta-
tion of a wider movement aimed at disrupting the whole basis of
trade unionism. Other organizations worked to the same effect. The
Industrial Peace Union, founded by J. A. Seddon, an ex-president
of the T.U.C., and Havelock Wilson, leader of the seamen's union,
advocated peaceful coexistence between employers and employed,
which in effect implied the subjection of the workers to reductions in
wages. Early in 1927 Lord Castlereagh, son and heir of Lord Londonderry, one of the most prominent of the Durham coal owners,
attempted to foster a branch of the Industrial Peace Union within the
coalfield.[3] No evidence has, however, been found of the success or
otherwise of this venture. The Economic League on the other hand
began organizing weekly meetings in the market place of Durham
City during 1928 in order to preach its doctrine of non-political trade
unionism and industrial peace. The organization was fostered in the
County throughout the 1930s by the Durham Coal Owners' Association which appointed it to conduct propaganda on its behalf.[4]

The Durham Miners' Association realized that the policy of the
local coal owners and of the various organizations established to
attract membership from the traditional union was to 'divide and
conquer'. The Association, therefore, began an intensive campaign
to unite its forces from within. Conscious that those miners who had
started work before November 1926, albeit in a minority, provided
a convenient hunting-ground for disruptive organizations the Association appealed to its members to consider allowing the 'blacklegs' to
re-enter into membership. The numbers involved were small. Only
eight out of every 100 persons previously employed in the coalfield
(including colliery officials and safety men) had returned to work by
12 November 1926 and only 12 out of every 100 by 26 November.[5]
A County vote on the Executive Committee's recommendations for
re-admittance resulted in 756 votes in favour and 230 against—a

[1] *Miner*, 14 April 1928.
[2] *Durham Chronicle*, 2, 16 November 1928.
[3] *Miner*, 19 February 1927.
[4] Durham Coal Owners' Association, *Annual Reports*, 1927-39.
[5] D.M.A., 5 January 1927.

majority in favour of 526.[1] In view of the low level of wages the Executive agreed to allow such lapsed members an opportunity of repaying the arrears in their contributions over a period of eight weeks before they became subject to the penalties imposed upon unfinancial members. The period was later extended by a further six weeks.[2]

The Government provided one of the most powerful reminders of the defeat of the miners in 1926 by passing the Trade Disputes and Trade Unions Act of 1927[3] which aroused the opposition of the whole Labour movement. J. R. Clynes described the Act as 'perhaps the worst piece of vindictive and spiteful class legislation which our country has known'.[4] The Act was bitterly opposed by the Durham miners. In his New Year sermon in January 1927 the Bishop of Durham, Dr Hensley Henson, had already described peaceful picketing as 'a barbarous menace to individual liberty' and had called for its legal restraint.[5] When the Government announced in April 1927 its intention to introduce legislation along such lines local Labour M.P.s in Durham joined with the Durham Miners' Association in organizing a campaign of protest, demanding the withdrawal of a Bill aimed at 'the enslavement of the workers'.[6] The Association joined forces in May 1927 with the M.F.G.B. and the T.U.C. General Council in a national campaign against the Bill having already succeeded in expressing its stern opposition at a series of May Day meetings throughout the County. A conference was organized at the Durham miners' headquarters on 14 May at which Ernest Bevin and Dr Marion Philipps spoke against the Government's act in introducing 'a monument to blacklegs'.[7] Despite the national outcry against the proposed legislation the Government, by careful use of the closure, passed the Bill into law. Although its basic clause, making sympathetic strikes illegal, was never invoked the Act remained a symbol of the defeat and humiliation miners suffered in 1926. Durham submitted a resolution to the 1928 Annual Conference of the M.F.G.B. urging the Labour Party and the T.U.C. to seek to have the Act repealed at the earliest opportunity.[8] The Act remained on the Statute Book, however, until May 1946.

[1] *Ibid.*, 8 February 1927.
[2] *Ibid.*, 9 May, 30 May 1927.
[3] 17 and 18 Geo. v. c. 22.
[4] J. R. Clynes, *Memoirs: 1924–37*, London 1937, p. 92. See also M. C. Schefftz: 'The Trade Disputes and Trade Unions Act of 1927: the aftermath of the General Strike', *Review of Politics*, 29, 1967.
[5] *Durham Chronicle*, 8 January 1927.
[6] D.M.A., 19 April 1927.
[7] *Durham Chronicle*, 20 May 1927.
[8] M.F.G.B., *Report of the Executive Committee, June 1928*, p. 186.

III

In September 1927 Robson, Secretary to the Durham County Federation Board, received an invitation from the Durham coal owners for the miners' representatives to attend a joint meeting for the purpose of discussing the future of the agreement entered into on 30 November 1926. The agreement was terminable by one month's notice given by either party after 30 November 1927. At the meeting on 26 September the owners proposed reducing the level of the subsistence wage in proportion to the decline in the cost of living and of inserting a clause into the agreement such as that provided in Northumberland whereby either side would be free to propose an alteration in the minimum percentage addition to basic rates after the agreement had been in operation for one year.[1]

The County Federation Board decided to submit the owners' proposals to the M.F.G.B. to ascertain whether the Federation could assist Durham to maintain the existing wages agreement or whether, in the circumstances, it would be better for her to negotiate alone. A special M.F.G.B. conference discussed the situation in Durham on 27 October. Proposals that the Federation should support Durham financially or sympathetically by way of a national stoppage in opposition to the coal owners' intentions were rejected. Delegates from South Wales, where conditions of depression and poverty were as severe as in Durham, feared that similar attacks upon wages would occur elsewhere unless the Federation took a determined stand against the coal owners in Durham. The Executive Committee of the M.F.G.B. refused to recommend any direct assistance to be given, however, and contented itself in drafting a resolution protesting against the Durham coal owners' efforts to seek opportunities to further reduce wages and authorizing the Durham Miners' Association to continue negotiating for an extension of the agreement as it was drafted in November 1926.[2]

The first intimation of the extent of the proposed reductions in wages in Durham was published in the *Colliery Guardian* on 21 October. The owners sought a reduction in the subsistence wage of 1s 8½d per shift in ratio with the decline in the cost of living and to regulate piece rates and the minimum percentage addition to basic rates 'by the capacity of the industry to pay'.[3] The Durham Miners' Association appealed to the owners to defer taking action to modify

[1] M.F.G.B., 26 October 1927; *The Times*, 10 October 1927.
[2] M.F.G.B., 27 October 1927; For Cabinet reaction see P.R.O., Cab. 23/55.
[3] *Colliery Guardian*, 21 October 1927.

the agreement for at least two months so that there might be time for testing the possibility of a revival of demand and prices in the first months of the winter.[1] On 7 November the owners agreed not to make any application for a revision of either the minimum percentage or the subsistence wage prior to 15 January 1928 and that no resulting alteration in their amounts should take effect before 1 March 1928 if the miners would agree to empower the District Wages Board, on application of either party, to revise the minimum percentage from time to time.[2] The Durham miners eventually agreed by 1004 votes to 107 to accept the owners' proposals and the wages agreement was subsequently amended on 23 December 1927. It was to last until 31 December 1929 and thereafter be subject to three months' notice by either party.[3]

The owners lost no time in using their newly-acquired prerogative and on 16 January 1928 submitted an application to the District Wages Board for a reduction in both the minimum percentage addition to basic rates and the subsistence wage. The Durham County Federation Board responded by submitting an application for an increase in both items. Not surprisingly both sides failed to reach an agreement and the issue was referred to Sir William Plender, Independent Chairman of the Wages Board.[4]

The arbitration proceedings opened at the Coal Trade Offices in Newcastle on 3 February and continued during the following day. In submitting their case the owners' representatives drew attention to the fact that during the operation of the agreement in Durham from 1 January 1927 until 30 November 1927 the accumulated deficiency in standard profits amounted to £2,778,994. Furthermore a large part of the export trade had been lost to other countries as a result of the 1926 stoppage, especially Poland,[5] and the only hope of recapturing it was by competitive price reductions which demanded lower working costs, namely wages. The owners suggested establishing a minimum addition to basic rates of 41 per cent which represented the wages which would have been paid in January 1928 according to the ascertainments but for the operation of the minimum wage clause. The subsistence wage was to be reduced from 6s 8½d to 6s 1d on the basis of a reduction in the cost-of-living index from 86 per cent above its pre-war level in 1922 (when the 6s 8½d was decided

---

[1] *The Times*, 26 October 1927.
[2] *Ibid.*, 14 November 1927.
[3] D.M.A., 16 November 1927.
[4] *Minutes of the District Board for the Durham Coal Trade*, 16 January 1928.
[5] See Chapter I, pp. 37–8.

upon) to 68 per cent in 1928.[1] The proposed reduction in the subsistence wage was less than that previously announced in the *Colliery Guardian* but was justified by a procedure to which the miners had taken strong objection in 1922.[2]

In opposing the owners' application representatives of the County Federation Board attacked the contention that reductions in costs should necessarily mean reductions in wages and, believing that the miners had made sufficient sacrifices for the sake of industrial competitiveness, called upon Directors, General Managers and the ancillary trades to contribute towards alleviating depression.[3] Repeating long-standing grievances the Board claimed:

'It is well known that many Owners of large companies are closely associated with other Industries directly or indirectly depending upon the Mining Industry and there is a strong suspicion that in times of depression there is not the incentive to maintain a reasonable standard of revenue, because what they lose on the one they gain on the other investment: then, in any readjustment of the financial position of the Coal Industry, they come along and ask the workmen to accept a lower standard of life.'[4]

Furthermore, they claimed, the miners, and especially the hewers, had already suffered an increase in hours and a reduction in standard wages. Although the output per shift of Durham miners compared favourably in 1927 with that in other coalfields the level of average earnings per shift stood at almost 1s 2d below the national average yet the Durham miners were being asked to agree to a further reduction.[5] Since the resumption of work sixty-eight collieries had had to face local reductions in wages.[6] On these grounds the Board submitted a counter-claim for increasing the minimum percentage addition to basic rates from 89 to 97.[7] After a careful consideration of the evidence Plender announced his award on 9 February. From 1 March 1928 the minimum percentage addition to basic rates was to be reduced from 89 to 65 and the subsistence allowance from 6s 8½d

---

[1] District Board for Coal Mining Industry in Durham, *Revision of Minimum Percentage and Subsistence Allowance, Proceedings, February 3 and 4 1928,* pp. 115–17.
[2] See Chapter V, pp. 162–4.
[3] District Board for Coal Mining Industry in Durham, *Revision of Minumum Percentage and Subsistence Allowance, Proceedings, February 3 and 4 1928,* pp. 137–40.
[4] *Ibid.,* p. 128.
[5] *Ibid.,* pp. 132–3.
[6] *Ibid.,* pp. 133–5.
[7] *Ibid.,* p. 141.

per shift to 6s 6½d.[1] The reduction in the minimum percentage implied a reduction of over 1s 2d per shift in the case of hewers and fillers, of 1s per shift for piece-work stonemen and 1s 3½d in the case of deputies.[2] The Durham Miners' Association calculated that the reduction in the fillers' wage would bring it down to a level only 6½d a day greater than it had been in 1914.[3]

The 'Plender Award' was received amongst the Durham miners with alarm, disappointment and indignation. The County Federation Board arranged jointly with the Northumberland Federation Board to organize a series of public demonstrations against the attacks on wages.[4] Meetings were held at Newcastle, Sunderland, Durham and Chester-le-Street.[5] At Chester-le-Street Peter Lee observed dolefully:

'Some of us . . . thought we had reached a period when human life would be of greater value than profits but as far as these two counties are concerned we have been mistaken.'[6]

Local Primitive Methodist Churches openly condemned the reductions in wages[7] and the Council of the Durham Miners' Association resolved to press the Government to institute an enquiry into the living and working conditions of miners in Northumberland and Durham 'with a view to finding some method of increasing revenue and reducing costs other than by attacking wages'.[8]

Other organizations were more forthright in their criticisms of the 'Plender Award' and more specific in what they thought should be done about it. Ever since the resumption of work in December 1926 the Non-Political Unions, the Minority Movement and the Communist Party had been conducting extensive propaganda campaigns amongst members of the Lodges of the Durham Miners, Association.[9] The National Minority Movement, a Communist front organization designed to attract workmen dissatisfied with orthodox trade unionism but reluctant to join the Communist Party, gained much of its sup-

[1] *Ibid.*, p. 110; *Durham Chronicle*, 17 February 1928; *The Times*, 11 February 1928.
[2] *Miner*, 25 February 1928.
[3] *The Times*, 11 February 1928.
[4] The Northumberland miners had also suffered by the decision of the independent chairman of the District Wages Board, P. M. Dodds, to reduce the percentage addition to basic wages from 89 to 40 per cent although the level of the subsistence wage was unaltered.
[5] D.M.A., 14 February, 15 March 1928.
[6] *Durham Chronicle*, 24 February 1928.
[7] *Ibid.*, 24 February, 9 March 1928; D.M.A., 12 March, 2 April 1928.
[8] D.M.A., 25 February 1928.
[9] *Ibid.*, 25 May, 28–9 June 1927.

port amongst the Durham miners. In 1927 over 30 Lodges of the Association were reputed to favour N.M.M. policy.[1]

The frequency and tenacity of the attacks upon the Association by these organizations increased significantly after the announcement of the Plender Award. Rank-and-file miners were continually called upon to revolt against the existing union leadership. The Tyneside Communist Party, allegedly composed of 90 per cent of the members of the Durham and Northumberland Miners' Association,[2] played a leading role in this campaign urging miners to fight in defiance of their leaders and their seemingly ineffective and conciliatory policy and to support sectional stoppages and deliberate restriction of output. In an undated circular issued to miners in both Durham and Northumberland during February 1928, the Tyneside Communist Party vigorously condemned the leadership of Robson and Straker, leader of the Northumberland miners, called for a ballot for a stoppage of work throughout both coalfields, appealed to the M.F.G.B. to seek national and international action in defence of miners in Durham and Northumberland and asked:

'When are these so-called leaders going to get up from their knees, from grovelling and whining before the bosses, and fight to stop these reductions?

Do Robson, Straker & Co. think that the bosses take any notice of their prayers and whines? Not a bit of it.'

The circular ended with the commands:

'Refuse to honour the Agreement which means starvation.
Smash the Plender and Dodds Awards.
Kick out the Traitors of 1926, 1927 and now 1928.
Get a leadership of Fighters.'[3]

The document was headed 'Cook's "Call to Action" ' but A. J. Cook denied having any knowledge of his name being used.

On 19 March the Secretary of the Durham Miners' Minority Movement informed Richardson that a deputation would wait upon

[1] R. Martin, *Communism and the British Trade Unions 1924–1933*, Oxford 1969, p. 58.
[2] *Colliery Guardian*, 9 March 1928. The Communist Party had gained a strong hold within the coalfields during the period of the miners' lock-out. Albert Inkpin, the Party's Secretary, reported to the Executive in August 1926: 'In the whole of the Durham coalfield recruits are rolling in at a rate which creates an acute problem for the Party'. Cited in J. Klugmann, *History of the Communist Party of Great Britain, Volume Two: The General Strike, 1925–1926*, London 1969, pp. 345–6.
[3] D.M.A., March (?) 1928.

the Durham miners' Agents and Executive Committee on the following day to discuss the Plender Award. The deputation duly arrived but the Association's leaders refused to conduct any business with it.[1] By the beginning of April two further circulars characteristically entitled 'Manifesto to the Durham Miners' and 'Strike Bulletin' had been issued jointly by the Durham Miners' Minority Movement and the Communist Party.[2] Their propaganda was not without effect since, following the demands of 25 Lodges, the Association's Executive Committee was forced to call a Special Council Meeting on 28 April to discuss taking a strike ballot on the Plender Award. The suggestion was eventually rejected.[3] W. P. Richardson had always denounced the pronouncements of the minority groups as ineffective and totally unsympathetic to the conditions facing the coal industry. In a circular to members in April he wrote of these groups:

'They have two phrases that cover the gamut of their case, "Stop the pit or pits" and "Let's have an individual ballot". Both slogans lead nowhere, except to further disaster and they know it. The man or woman who would lead you to believe that there is some solution to hand in the present state of affairs, wherein nearly quarter of a million are unemployed—50,000 of whom are in one County, our own—and where whole districts, as well as individual pits, are working slack time, where stocks of coal are accumulating in an already overstocked market, and where selling prices are being ruthlessly cut under the soulless system of competition, is not only mocking you but adding insult to injury.'[4]

The indignation and opposition towards the Plender Award, whilst most vociferously expressed by the Minority Movement and the Communist Party, were most keenly felt by the miners who suffered its consequences. During the months after 1 March 1928, when the reductions in wages took effect, there was a series of disputes throughout the coalfield. On 8 March putters employed at the Thomas and Oswald pits at Craghead, and the William and Hedley pits at South Moor, all owned by the Holmside and South Moor Colliery Company and jointly employing over 3,000 hands, went on strike because of their dissatisfaction over the reduced wages paid according to the Plender Award.[5] Ryhope Colliery was laid idle on 22 March for the

[1] *Ibid.*, 4 April 1928.
[2] *Ibid.*
[3] *Ibid.*, 30 April 1928.
[4] *Ibid.*, 4 April 1928.
[5] *Colliery Guardian*, 16 March 1928.

same reason.[1] On the following day 18,000 miners at Harton Colliery stopped work in protest against the existing level of wages.[2] At a number of collieries notices were served to men and boys in cases of alleged restriction on output. On 14 March over 400 men at Horden Colliery, where normal daily output of coal had fallen from approximately 6,000 tons to between 2,000 and 3,000 tons, were served with a fortnight's notice.[3] On the following day 2,000 men and boys at Shotton Colliery received notices for similar alleged offences.[4] Previously on 9 March 200 men at Easington Colliery, where normal coal output had fallen by almost 50 per cent, received their notices.[5] Since the propaganda issued by the Minority Movement and the local Communist Party had called on occasion for deliberate restriction on output by miners in the coalfield local managers were quick to attach all blame to these influences. No evidence has been found to support the truth of such accusations but in the absence of an organized ballot through which dissatisfaction over the proposed wage reductions could be expressed many miners probably adopted a readily-available method of expressing their anger which, in the very short run at least, did not openly endanger their job. The supposedly direct influence exerted by minority groups was not an opinion held only by local colliery owners. The Board of Trade Advisory Council reported to the Government in April 1928 that in Durham 'a considerable amount of trouble' and 'a considerable loss of output' had been caused 'by the action of young men and boys under the influence of the minority movement'.[6]

The conditions in Durham resulting from this early attack upon wages after the defeat of 1926 achieved national consideration in April 1928. On 4 April representatives of the M.F.G.B. and the Durham County Federation Board met the Secretary for Mines. The Federation representatives claimed that the Umpire's award in Durham had 'left the workers in a hopeless position in seeking to maintain a standard of life that affords the bare necessities of food alone'.[7] Bemoaning the fact that the Durham owners seemed 'incapable of realizing any other method of reducing cost apart from attacking wages' the representatives appealed to the Minister to encourage a greater degree of voluntary amalgamation and unification

[1] Ibid.
[2] The Times, 23 March 1928.
[3] Colliery Guardian, 16 March 1928.
[4] Ibid.
[5] Ibid.
[6] Cabinet Papers, 24/194 C.P. 128(28).
[7] Durham Chronicle, 20 April 1928.

of the industry within the area such as had taken place in South Wales and the Midlands.[1] The only outcome of the meeting was an assurance by the Secretary for Mines that the Government would consider the issue further.[2]

The reductions in wages were most keenly felt at those collieries where, prior to 1 March 1928, coal owners had already succeeded in enforcing local reductions in piece rates. Local reductions in wages were agreed to at South Hetton Colliery in July 1927 in the face of the threatened dismissal of 1,200 miners.[3] Stoppages at the Harton, Boldon and Whitburn Collieries, all owned by the Harton Coal Company, were only averted at the end of 1927 by the men agreeing to accept piece-rate reductions.[4] Further trouble occurred at Boldon Colliery during February 1928 when the men struck in defiance of the owners' attempts to reduce tonnage rates.[5] Miners at the neighbouring Whitburn and Harton pits struck in sympathy and were eventually charged with breaches of contract. The 3,000 sympathizers at the two collieries had to pay 12s 6d each plus Court fees, the amount being deducted from their weekly earnings.[6]

IV

After 1926 the miners turned their attention increasingly away from industrial towards political action as a means of improving their economic and social well-being. With a general election due in 1929 the M.F.G.B. took an early opportunity to determine what designs the Labour Party had for the coal industry were the Party to be returned to power. At a meeting with Federation representatives, including W. P. Richardson, on 26 March MacDonald pledged that in order to meet the immediate needs of the industry his Government would regulate the supply of labour to mining by raising the school-leaving age, suspend the recruitment of adult labour from outside the industry, provide a superannuation allowance for mineworkers at the age of 60 and, most important of all, seek to repeal the Eight Hours Act.[7] Throughout 1927 and 1928 the Durham Miners' Association had waged an almost continuous attack upon the hours situation in the industry, holding it responsible, through its effects on

[1] See Chapter I, p. 44.
[2] *Durham Chronicle*, 20 April 1928.
[3] *The Times*, 14 July 1927.
[4] *Ibid.*, 3, 5, 13, 20 December 1927.
[5] *Ibid.*, 14, 24 February 1928.
[6] *Ibid.*, 22 March 1928.
[7] M.F.G.B., 12 April 1929.

overproduction, for low wages, most of the chronic unemployment and emphasizing its disruption of the miners' social life. By January 1928 there were 50,457 fewer men employed in the mines in Durham than there had been in April 1924 and between January 1924 and November 1928,128 pits affecting 17,730 men had closed, 71 of which, affecting about 8,000 men and boys, having been abandoned entirely.[1] The only comfort which could be drawn from the reduction in the minimum percentage on 1 March 1928 was the knowledge that it prevented wage rates from falling to the desperately low levels dictated by the district ascertainments. In May 1928 the ascertained percentage addition to basic rates was only 28·82 and by November 1928 had fallen to 16·2.[2]

As a prerequisite to formulating a policy on working hours in the coal industry MacDonald invited the M.F.G.B. on 19 July to estimate the probable effects of a shorter working day on wages and employment.[3] The employers had already intimated that a reduction in hours would force them to claim a 20 per cent reduction in wages. The miners decided to press for a six-hour day bank-to-bank. The Government aimed at securing the maximum reduction in hours which it felt the industry could bear without forcing a reduction in wages and at making reduced hours conditional upon the acceptance of schemes of reorganization. Its final proposals were discussed by the M.F.G.B. on 5–7 November. A Bill was to be introduced which would initially reduce the length of the working day by half an hour and provide for the reorganization of the production and sale of coal.[4] The miners were particularly anxious to secure concessions in hours before they were involved in negotiations for new district agreements. Most of the agreements reached in the districts in 1926 were due to expire in 1929. In Durham the agreement was terminable on 31 December. The Government's proposals left the Durham hewers, already working a seven-and-a-half-hour day, unaffected but were clearly advantageous to the remainder of the workers. A ballot of the miners in Durham in November showed 1,046 in favour of accepting the Government's proposals and only 28 against.[5] Lord Londonderry criticized the proposed measures as a means of increasing prices, especially of fuel supplied to industry, and of reducing the competitiveness of British industry in world markets.[6] The Durham Coal

[1] 222 H.C. Deb. 5s, 228.
[2] M.F.G.B., 23 July 1929.
[3] Ibid.
[4] Durham Chronicle, 18 October 1929.
[5] D.M.A., 16 November 1929.
[6] Durham Chronicle, 10 January 1930; The Times, 6 January 1930.

Owners' Association claimed the Bill would 'seriously impair the general industrial condition of the country, and of this county particularly'.[1]

The Government's proposals were eventually embodied in the Coal Mines Bill and introduced into the House of Commons in December 1929. During the discussions on the Bill the Mining Association approached the M.F.G.B. to agree to ask the Government to insert in the Bill a proviso enabling any district, upon agreement between the owners and the miners, to vary the rigid seven-and-a-half-hour day by fixing a weekly maximum of 45 hours, or a fortnightly maximum of 90 hours. The owners realized that under this agreement for a permissive 'spread-over' of working time it would be possible for pits either to retain an eight-hour shift on five days a week, working a five-hour shift on Saturday, or to work eight hour shifts on 11 days a fortnight, so that the miners would have every alternative Saturday as a holiday. The economic advantage from the point of view of production costs in retaining eight hours as a full day's shift was obvious. The Federation realized, however, that in most districts working an eight-hour shift hours on Saturdays were shortened by amounts ranging from $1-2\frac{3}{4}$ hours, while in Durham and Northumberland only 11 days per fortnight were being worked. The imposition of a seven-and-a-half-hour day upon the existing eight-hour districts meant, given the continuance of existing Saturday practice, a working week ranging from $42\frac{1}{2}$ to $44\frac{1}{2}$ hours. As the Federation explained:

'If these proposals were accepted it would mean that, in all probability, the workmen in those districts where an eight-hour day is now in operation, would find that, despite the Bill, they would still be working an eight-hour day on every day on which work was available to them. In short, the proposal negated the whole principle of the shorter working day.'[2]

By the time the Bill received the Royal Assent on 1 August 1930 it provided that the 'spread-over' of hours in any district could not become operative without the joint approval of the Mining Association and the M.F.G.B.[3] Part III of the Act,[4] which regulated the hours of work, became operative on 1 December 1930 and immediately abrogated all district agreements based on a working day of more than $7\frac{1}{2}$ hours.

[1] *Durham Chronicle*, 7 March 1930.
[2] M.F.G.B., 10 April 1930.
[3] *Ibid.*, 16–17 July 1930.
[4] For a discussion of Parts I and II see Chapter I, pp. 46–52.

Earlier in October the Durham coal owners attempted to persuade certain classes of workmen to accept a 'spread-over' system of hours. Their proposals were limited to those miners working 12 days per fortnight, namely stonemen, shiftmen and wastemen. These classes ordinarily worked eight hours per shift plus one winding with, at some collieries, one short shift of six hours bank-to-bank and, at others, two short shifts per fortnight of seven hours bank-to-bank. The owners suggested a 'spread-over' of 90 hours per fortnight whereby those men working a short shift of six hours per fortnight would have the length of their ordinary shift reduced from 8 hours to 7 hours 38 minutes and those working two short shifts of seven hours per fortnight their ordinary shift reduced to 7 hours 36 minutes. The reductions in time of 22 minutes and 24 minutes per shift respectively compared unfavourably with the reduction of 30 minutes contemplated in the Act. Furthermore those classes other than stonemen, shiftmen and wastemen who were working an ordinary shift of eight hours plus one winding with one short Saturday shift but who were working only 11 days per fortnight i.e. all other underground workmen except hewers would get no reduction. The hewers were working a daily shift of seven and a half hours plus one winding with either one short Saturday shift of six and a half hours bank-to-bank or of seven and a quarter hours bank-to-bank, the latter working alternate Saturdays only, and therefore only 11 days per fortnight.[1] The proposals were overwhelmingly rejected by the miners.[2]

Negotiations continued with the owners in an effort to formulate a new agreement on hours and wages. The employers submitted their final terms to the Durham Miners' Association on 24 November. The hours of all underground workers (except deputies) were to be seven and a half per shift plus one winding. The standard basic wages of piece workers other than hewers whose hours were thus reduced were to be adjusted *pro rata* to the reduction in hours. The system of of short shifts was to be kept intact. Datal wages were to remain fixed at the level ruling under a system of eight hours plus one winding. The lodges decided by 938 votes to 66 to accept the proposals.[3] The agreement was signed on 26 November 1930 and provided that except for the amendment in hours the provisions of the Agreement of 30 November 1926, as amended by the Agreement of 23 December 1927, were to continue to apply. The agreement was to last for three months from 1 December 1930. Durham, Northumberland and Somerset were the only areas to have reached an agreement

[1] M.F.G.B., 19 November 1930.
[2] D.M.A., 3–4 November 1930.
[3] *Ibid.*, 27 November 1930.

for temporary settlements on the basis of a seven-and-a-half-hour day with no reductions in wages. The only slight wages modification in Durham had been in the case of piece workers other than hewers whose hours were reduced. The datal hands who enjoyed a full half hour's reduction in working time maintained the same level of wages as under eight hours. The Durham miners had successfully resisted the owners' attempts to impose a 'spread-over' system of working. Many more months were to pass, however, before miners in other districts settled this issue.

In some districts, including South Wales and Scotland, owners attempted to enforce wage reductions and a 'spread-over' system without the consent of the workmen. On 3 December 1930 the Prime Minister announced that over 210,000 people were working the 'spread-over' on terms which were in direct opposition to the principles of the 1930 Coal Mines Act.[1] Since prosecution was obviously out of the question the Government suggested to the Federation that it agreed to approve the 'spread-over' applications for a temporary period subject to no reduction in wages and without prejudice to other districts[2]. The proposal was discussed by Federation delegates at a meeting on 3 December and eventually submitted to the districts for their consideration. Robson joined other Durham miners' leaders in violently opposing the adoption of the 'spread-over' and complained:

'If Wales is allowed to work more than we are in Durham—half an hour longer—it will be a very serious matter to Durham and Northumberland working $7\frac{1}{2}$ hours and South Wales 8 hours...
I want to suggest ... when talking about the spread-over please remember this aspect, the disparity in hours intensifies the competition in the districts, and especially in the exporting districts.'[3]

The Durham County Federation Board decided on 8 December to reject the proposals and to vote in favour of the withdrawal and prosecution of those connected with working the 'spread-over' against the will of the workmen. The decision was confirmed by the Council of the Durham Miners' Association on the following day. It was feared that at the end of a temporary period, such as that suggested by the Prime Minister, other districts like Durham could be faced with demands by the owners for them to work a 'spread-over' or suffer a reduction in wages. Inter-district competition in common markets would thereby be intensified and the movement towards a

[1] M.F.G.B., 3 December 1930.
[2] *Ibid.*, 4 December 1930.
[3] *Ibid.*

shorter working day in every district completely frustrated.[1] Nevertheless a narrow majority of the districts voted in favour of the Government's proposals and the Federation duly approved the scheme.[2]

The Durham miners' leaders feared the consequences of the Federation's decision. In a circular to members in January 1931 Robson wrote:

'We set out with a view to reducing hours, and we are offering now to set the Act aside so far as the hours are concerned as an alternative to a reduction in wages. . . . Instead of having uniformity of hours we have encouraged and agreed to a variation which must increase the intense feeling between owners and owners, and to inspire those who have complied with the Act with a strong desire to be placed upon an equal footing with districts where the longer hours have been retained.'[3]

The temporary arrangements of hours existed in districts only until the end of March 1931 for, despite the fact that ten districts were reported likely to suffer wage reductions were the 'spread-over' system to end after three months, the M.F.G.B. decided on 19 March not to approve any further temporary arrangements after 31 March.[4] All districts, with the exception of Scotland and part of North Wales, consequently made arrangements to work without the 'spread-over'.

V

As the depression in the coal industry deepened during 1930–1 and the compulsory restriction of coal output became operative throughout the country conditions in the coalfields worsened. In July 1930, 2,000 men and boys at Shotton Colliery received their notices owing to the slackness of trade.[5] Collieries at Seaham, Trimdon Grange and Dean and Chapter closed down temporarily in October of the same year.[6] The number of men and boys employed in and about the mines in Durham totalled 107,938 in December 1931, compared with 172,026 in May 1924.[7] Wages had remained at their minimum level since January 1927. In December 1930 the average earnings per shift

[1] D.M.A., 9 December 1930.
[2] M.F.G.B., 16 December 1930.
[3] *Durham Chronicle*, 19 March 1931.
[4] M.F.G.B., 19 March 1931.
[5] *Durham Chronicle*, 1 August 1930.
[6] *Ibid.*, 17 October 1930.
[7] *Ibid.*, 14 November 1930.

worked in Durham stood only 29 per cent higher than they had been in June 1914, compared with a national increase of 44 per cent above the 1914 level. In the South Derby, Leicester, Cannock and Warwick district average earnings per shift were 60 per cent higher than in June 1914.[1] Meanwhile local coal owners persisted in enforcing reduction in wages whenever the opportunity arose. A notable example occurred at Dawdon Colliery between March and June 1929 when almost 4,000 miners were locked out for refusing to submit to reductions in piece rates. The dispute was finally settled on 17 June after the intervention of W. L. Cook of the Mines Department. Piece rates were to be agreed upon by local negotiation or arbitration if necessary. Both Lord Londonderry, who owned the colliery, and local Lodge officials blamed the activities of the district Workers' International Relief Committee and the national Miners' Minority Movement, both of which helped provide relief to the men engaged in the dispute, for actively prolonging the dispute 'for the sole purpose of furthering their political aims'.[2] Despite the growth of a local branch of the Communist Party the majority of the Dawdon miners remained faithful to their leaders and neither the Party nor the Minority Movement made any permanent gains in the area.[3]

In the midst of industrial depression the Durham Coal Owners' Association applied to the local District Board on 23 February 1931 for a reduction of the minimum percentage addition to basic rates from 65 to 50 and of the subsistence wage from 6s 6½d to 5s 11d (in accordance with the fall in the cost of living) in order to provide for an immediate cut in working costs. The workmen's representatives, headed by Robson, urged that the existing level of wages should continue at least until July when, in the absence of further legislation, hours of work would be reduced to seven per shift thereby necessitating further negotiations regarding working conditions.[4] During the meetings which followed the miners submitted a counter-claim demanding increases in both the minimum percentage and subsistence wage.[5] Eventually on 27 April the owners agreed to defer their application for reductions because of 'the importance of maintaining the most friendly relations with the Workmen in the County in view

[1] M.F.G.B., *The Claim for Legal Minimum Wages for Mineworkers*, 1931, Appendix I, p. 12.

[2] *The Times*, 18 February, 26, 27 April, 11 May 1929. *Durham Chronicle*, 3, 10 May, 21 June 1929. See also J. Ancrum, 'The W.I.R. in the Dawdon Lock-Out' *Labour Monthly*, 11 September 1929. Ancrum was district secretary of the W.I.R. at the time of the dispute.

[3] Martin, *op. cit.*, pp. 129–30.

[4] *Minutes of the District Board for the Durham Coal Industry*, 6 March 1931.

[5] *Ibid.*, 1 April 1931.

of the important negotiations upon which the parties must enter shortly',[1] i.e. the question of hours. The owners urged the miners to do everything in their power to prevent any further reduction of hours of work after July and warned that whatever the outcome of the discussions on hours they could not continue to support the existing level of wages.[2]

The temporary agreement on hours entered into by the two parties on 26 November 1930 had by this time expired but had been extended by mutual agreement until the eve of the expiration of the 1926 Act in July 1931. In the national discussions on the question of hours of work after July the Mining Association made it clear that the introduction of a seven-hour day would involve drastic wage reductions. The Government refused to consider the question of hours except in relation to wages and invited the owners' and miners' representatives to meet to discuss the two issues. A joint sub-committee representing the M.F.G.B. and Mining Association subsequently met on 5, 11 and 19 June during which time the owners proposed an unlimited extension of the legislation permitting a seven-and-a-half-hour day with the maintainance of existing wage rates for a period of six months.[3] The miners' representatives refused to consider the proposals. The Government, anxious for the two sides to reach some settlement, took the initiative and met the owners themselves. In the negotiations which followed the employers refused to make any further concessions except to lengthen the period of guaranteed wages from six to twelve months. The Federation made it clear, however, that if it was to compromise on the question of hours and accept a seven-and-a-half-hour working day either the period of guaranteed wages would have to coincide with the period during which seven and a half hours was operative or that, after the twelve-month period proposed by the owners, no reductions in wages would occur thereafter save by mutual consent and under a system of national wage negotiation. The owners refused to concede the Federation's requests and the Government was called upon to suggest a basis for legislation.[4] The resulting Coal Mines Act, 1931, continued the statutory limit of seven and a half hours for a further twelve months or until the passing of an Act to ratify the Geneva Convention of 18 June 1931 (if this occurred within twelve months).[5]

[1] *Ibid.*, 27 April 1931.
[2] *Ibid.*, Durham Coal Owners' Association, *Annual Report*, 1931, pp. 3–6.
[3] M.F.G.B., *Report of the Executive Committee, June 1931*, pp. 179–80.
[4] M.F.G.B., 26 June, 3 July 1931; P.R.O., Cab. 23/67.
[5] Miners' Federation of Great Britain, *Hours of Work in British Coal Mines*, 1 October 1937. Hours of work under the Geneva Convention would have been 7¼ per day.

Many of the Durham miners were disappointed at not gaining a reduction in the length of their working day. Twenty-four delegates from various colliery districts and 'militant Lodges' in Durham assembled in Durham City on 20 June to protest against the conduct of the negotiations on hours. A resolution was passed urging a strike in support of a seven-hour day and which further read:

'Now, more than ever, it is clearly revealed that with mass un-employment, short time working, lower wages, and worse conditions as the order of the day, the bureaucracy of the Miners' Federation and the County miners' associations are agents of the coal owners in the sense that they facilitate and assist the employers to protect their profits at the expense of the wages and conditions of the workers in the industry. The return of the Seven-Hour Day, so far as the leadership is concerned, is a thing of the past.'[1]

The eventual outcome of further national negotiations on hours during 1932 did nothing to dispel such despair and mistrust amongst the miners. The 1931 Act regulating hours of work was to expire on 8 July 1932. The M.F.G.B. and the Mining Association met during April 1932 to negotiate the future length of the working day. The coal owners persisted in demanding a seven-and-a-half-hour day and re-fused to discuss wages. At a meeting on 29 April the owners proposed an unlimited extension of the seven-and-a-half-hour day, subject to the ratification of the Geneva Convention, and offered to guarantee wages for a year. The M.F.G.B. responded in a similar way to what it had done in 1931 demanding either an unlimited guarantee of wages or that the twelve-month guarantee should be followed by the establishment of national machinery to regulate district changes in wages.

On 25 May the Government announced its intention to introduce a Bill to meet the owner's demands on hours. Since the Federation had up till this time used the annual necessity of discussing the hours question to negotiate for a national wages machinery it now realized that it had to embark upon an independent campaign in favour of this ideal. The hardships being experienced in Durham at this time under the system of district bargaining and inter-district competition served only to intensify their support for the national wages cam-paign. Although productivity was increasing in the coalfield un-employment and short-time working grew as the continued depres-sion in export markets drove down prices and proceeds. The average net selling value of coal in Durham lagged behind the national

[1] *Durham Chronicle*, 26 June 1931.

average standing at 12s 2·46d in 1932 compared with 13s 3·11d for the country as a whole. The net trading loss in the County rose from 0·69d per ton in 1931 to 4·11d in 1932 while the total numbers employed above and below ground fell by over 9,000. During 1931–2 the Londonderry group of collieries dismissed 2,600 men.[1] By the end of 1932 almost one-third of the total number of persons employed in the Durham coalfield received only the subsistence wage of 6s 6½d per day.[2]

The Federation's campaign for a national system of wage regulation continued during 1933. On 1 March the M.F.G.B. called upon the districts to empower its Executive Committee 'to call upon all affiliated district organizations to terminate their agreements simultaneously, unless guarantees satisfactory to the National Executive are obtained before July 1933'.[3] A strike was never called and neither were any guarantees given. In Durham the agreement made on 30 November 1926, as amended by the agreement of 23 December 1927 and the award of Sir William Plender on 9 February 1928, was still in force. In no month in any year since 1927 had the proceeds been sufficient to provide for the payment of wages up to the minimum, the owners being continually called upon to make up the difference. In September 1932 the ascertained percentage addition to basic rates stood at only 18·23 and by April 1933 was still only 34·98.

The Government persistently refused to meet the miners' representatives to discuss the introduction of a national wages system. Peter Lee, then President of the M.F.G.B., continually warned the Government of the immediate possibility of a national miners' strike if the demands were not met. The combined forces of poverty, depression and district settlements had already seriously weakened the united strength of the Federation, but Lee reminded miners at Ferryhill in November 1933:

'War as a rule is a hard and cruel way of settling disputes, but there are times when injustice, poverty and hardship are worse to bear than to fight in endeavouring to remove those evils. We shall never rest content under district agreements; . . . if trouble comes I hope and trust that the miners of this country will join their strength in resisting the evil forces which are directed against them.'[4]

Conditions in the coalfields improved only slightly during 1934.

[1] *Durham Chronicle*, 30 December 1932.
[2] Durham Miners' Association, *General Secretary's Report*, No. 10, March 1933, p. 3.
[3] M.F.G.B., 1 March 1933.
[4] *Durham Chronicle*, 3 November 1933.

Durham's coal export trade benefited to a small extent from the stimulus given by the Government's bilateral trading agreements but not to an extent sufficient to offset the world decline in the demand for coal. Total coal output in Durham during 1934 was still over 8 million tons below the level reached in 1929. The inadequacy of the attempts to regulate output and prices under the 1930 Coal Mines Act provided little hope of any sudden improvement in conditions in the coal exporting areas.[1]

The Federation's attempt to secure national machinery for the settlement of wages had ended in failure. Joseph Batey, M.P. for Spennymoor, was told in answer to a question put in the House of Commons on 1 May 1934 that there was no possibility of introducing legislation to establish national wage regulation in the coal industry.[2] In the circumstances the Durham County Federation Board approached the local Coal Owners' Association in August demanding an increase in wages for all workmen and a reduction in hours for surface workers to 48 per week, inclusive of mealtimes.[3] It demanded the immediate restoration of the minimum percentage addition to basic rates from 65 to 89 and an increase in the subsistence wage from 6s 6½d to 7s per day.[4] The owners refused to concede any advance in wages or reduction in hours because of 'the present condition of the coal trade'.[5] On 15 December, at a united Council meeting of representatives of the Miners', Enginemen's and Mechanics' Associations, it was decided to tender three months' notice to terminate the existing wages agreement.[6] The owners immediately responded by suggesting the establishment of a Sub-Committee of nine persons from each side to deal with the whole question.[7]

The negotiations were eventually postponed as a result of the demand by the M.F.G.B. in August 1935 for a flat-rate advance of 2s per shift for adult workmen and 1s per shift for boys in all districts. In the meantime the parties agreed to continue the existing agreement pending the settlement of a new one at a later date. By the time the demand for a national increase in wages was made the economic position of the Durham miner had seriously deteriorated. The average wage per shift paid to Durham miners in 1935 stood at 8s 0·55d

---

[1] See Chapter I, pp. 46-9.
[2] 289 H.C. Deb. 5s, 123.
[3] D.M.A., 2 August 1934.
[4] *Ibid.*, 2, 26 November 1934; Durham Coal Owners' Association, *Annual Report*, 1934, pp. 3-4.
[5] *Durham Chronicle*, 30 November 1934.
[6] D.M.A., 15 December 1934.
[7] Durham Miners' Association, *Quarterly Report*, No. 14, February 1935, p. 4.

compared with 9s 3·15d for Great Britain as a whole and was 2s 0·79d below its 1924 level. Although output per man-shift in the Durham coalfield had increased during the period 1924–35 from 17·77 cwt to 22·07 cwt proceeds per ton of coal commercially disposable had fallen from 19s 10·9d to 12s 4·37d and the number of miners employed from 174,756 to 101,401. In comparison the total amount of rents, royalties and wayleaves drawn from the Durham coal industry during the period 1921–36 amounted to £11,730,467— equivalent to more than the amount received in wages by all the miners in and about the mines in Durham during 1935. Trading losses in Durham of 4·57d and 3·59d per ton in 1933 and 1935 respectively compared with profits of 2·82d and 6·26d per ton for the country as a whole.[1]

Average annual and weekly cash earnings in Durham during 1934 were lower than in any other district as the following table shows.[2]

District	Average no. manshifts worked	Average cash earnings in 1934			Average Weekly Earnings	
		£	s	d	s	d
1. Scotland	304	133	2	8	51	2½
2. Northumberland	282	109	14	7	42	2½
3. Durham	261	104	19	2	40	4½
4. South Wales and Mon.	264	119	7	0	45	10½
5. Yorkshire	225	114	9	7	44	0½
6. North Derbyshire and Nottinghamshire	216	112	16	3	43	0½
7. South Derbyshire, Leicestershire, Cannock Chase, and Warwickshire	228	110	7	7	42	5½
8. Lancashire, Cheshire and North Staffordshire	249	114	11	10	44	0¼
9. Cumberland, North Wales, Staffordshire, Shropshire, Bristol, Forest of Dean, Somerset and Kent	278	120	10	4	46	0½
10. Average for all Districts	253	115	11	6	44	5½

In response to appeals by the M.F.G.B. the Durham County Federation Board pledged its full support to the campaign for a national wages advance and immediately sought sympathetic support outside

[1] Durham Miners' Association, *General Secretary's Quarterly Report*, No. 5, December 1936, pp. 4, 10–11, 14–15.
[2] W. H. Williams, *The Miners' Two Bob*, London 1936, p. 17.

of the industry. A resolution calling upon the Government to establish for the miners a wage 'sufficient . . . to maintain . . . wives and families as human beings should be maintained in a civilized community' was forwarded to all local authorities and local Labour Party secretaries in the County.[1] By mid-October over 1,000 letters appealing for support had been addressed to Ministers of religion, local authorities and labour groups and over one hundred meetings organized around Durham and Tyneside.[2] On 4 October the *Durham Chronicle* reported: 'The Durham County miners' campaign . . . is in full swing. Meetings are constant and arguments are widespread.'[3]

The Bishop of Durham strongly opposed the campaign and advised his clergy to dissociate themselves with a movement which could result in 'immoral' strikes causing 'economic confusion' and 'lamentable social embitterment'.[4] The Bishop's attitude aroused strong protest in Durham and elsewhere despite the fact that many local ministers publicly announced their support of the miners.[5] The *Miners' Campaign Special*, a propaganda newspaper first issued by the M.F.G.B. in September 1935, emphasized the fact that the Bishop drew a salary of over £7,000 per year whilst many Durham miners earned less than £2 per week.[6] Indeed, the classes of workmen on a subsistence wage—horsekeepers, onsetters, rolleywaymen, sinkers, stonemen, shifters and wastemen—estimated to be one in every three miners in Durham in 1934, could earn only 39s 3d for six working days.[7] Although by 1935 the average number of days worked per week by the miner in Durham improved compared with the early thirties and relatively faster than the country as a whole[8] at its best it still only provided an average gross weekly wage for such classes of 32s 8½d.

A Special Conference of the M.F.G.B. decided on 18 October to take a ballot vote of its members on the question: 'Are you in favour of authorizing the Executive Committee to press the claim for an advance of 2s a shift for adults and 1s a shift for youths, even to the extent of tendering your notice, if necessary, to enforce the claim?' The delegates from Durham opposed the ballot fearing the possible repercussions of a national strike. Gilliland explained to the delegates:

[1] D.M.A., 23 August 1925.
[2] *Durham Chronicle*, 6 September 1935; D.M.A., 15 October 1935.
[3] *Durham Chronicle*, 4 October 1935.
[4] *Ibid.*, 27 September 1935. Cf. *The Times*, 24 September 1935.
[5] M.F.G.B., 17 October 1935.
[6] *Miners' Campaign Special*, No. 3, October 1935, p. 3
[7] *Durham Chronicle*, 19 December 1935.
[8] See Chapter VII, Appendix I.

'Our men are as loyal as anyone, and so far as I know there is no difficulty in taking the platform to prove that our men are the most shockingly paid so far as their labour is concerned. There are other aspects of this matter we ought to look at reasonably. . . . What about our men who are only getting three days a week? We have collieries where there are thousands of men working on an average four days a week. These people have got to live.'[1]

The Association's leaders and the rank-and-file miners in Durham decided, however, to remain loyal to the Federation. Indeed, despite their poverty and hardship, the miners in Durham voted in favour of strike action if necessary by 73,765 votes to 7,120. Nationally, the result of the ballot showed 409,351 for and only 29,215 against, a majority of 93 per cent.[2]

Attempts by the Secretary for Mines during November to find a basis for settlement between the two parties proved abortive. Eventually on 17 December the owners, frustrated in their attempts to derive extra revenue from increased coal prices under existing contracts, offered an advance in wages in each district as from 1 January 1936, the amount and method of payment being determined locally. The Government announced at the same time that no subsidy or loan from public funds would be provided to increase miners' wages. At the M.F.G.B. Conference on 18–19 December, called to decide on future action, the delegates decided by 278,000 to 28,000 votes that notices to cease work at midnight on 26 January 1936 should be tendered unless satisfactory wage proposals were received in the meantime. The owners' obvious determination to fix wages on a district basis ruled out any hope of an imminent settlement. Lord Londonderry in an article in the *Daily Telegraph* on 7 December expressed clearly the owners' policy in writing:

'The present demand for a return to the system of national agreements must be resisted because a national agreement, whatever its form, inevitably involves the impossible task of endeavouring to deal uniformly with conditions which are essentially different, and can only result in continual friction and strife.'[3]

Many of the Durham miners, restless at the drawn-out negotiations, welcomed the Federation's threat of strike action. 'The action of the [M.F.G.B.] Executive Committee is long overdue,' remarked J. E. Watson, Chairman of the Eppleton Lodge. 'We have everything to

[1] M.F.G.B., 18 October 1935.
[2] *Ibid.*, 20 November 1935.
[3] *Daily Telegraph*, 7 December 1935.

win and nothing to lose.'[1] The possibility of a national strike depended, however, upon the Federation's assessment of the owners'
wage proposals. On 8 January 1936 the owners offered increases in
wages varying between 1s and 5d a day in the various districts. The
miners' leaders rejected the offer but agreed to postpone the handing
in of notices to allow a further meeting to take place with the owners
on 23 January to consider amendments to the proposals.

Despite renewed negotiations the employers' offer to Durham
miners remained precisely the same as was proposed on 8 January.
Datal workers over 18 were to be granted an extra 6d per shift, those
under 18 3d per shift, and piece workers an agreed increase of percentage equivalent to these amounts.[2] Elsewhere increases were to be
granted ranging from 6d to 1s a day according to the ability of the
coalfields to pay. The offers made bore no relation to the relative
importance of the various coalfields in terms of output and employment and served only to increase the existing disparity between the
competitive position of each district which the 1930 Coal Mines Act
had aimed to reduce. Under the terms of the various district offers,
boys in Lancashire and Cheshire, North Wales, South Derbyshire,
Yorkshire, Leicestershire, South and North Staffordshire, Cannock
Chase, Warwickshire and Shropshire were to receive advances
equivalent to those offered to adult datal workers in Durham and,
in the case of adult underground workmen in these areas, would
receive increases amounting to twice as much per shift.[3]

The owners also agreed to co-operate with the M.F.G.B. in establishing a joint standing committee 'for the consideration of all
questions of common interest and of general application to the
industry, not excluding general principles applicable to the determination of wages by district agreements'. The miners were assured
by the Secretary for Mines that schemes for district selling agencies
with central co-ordination would be established not later than 1 July
1936. In the absence of any alteration in the ratio of the division
between wages and profits in the various districts the miners were
doubtful that such developments would afford any immediate relief.
In 1935 the M.F.G.B. estimated that coal prices in Durham could
rise by 1s 4½d per ton without a single penny going to wages.[4] Nor

---

[1] *Durham Chronicle*, 27 December 1935.
[2] Difficulty was found in arriving at an equivalent percentage and the owners
ultimately decided to offer all piece workers over 18 an extra 6d per shift and
those under 18 3d per shift. Durham Coal Owners' Association, *Annual Report*,
1935, pp. 18–19, 26.
[3] M.F G B., 23 January 1936.
[4] *Ibid.*, 13 December 1935.

did this estimate take into account the necessity to recoup accumulated deficiencies which in 1934 amounted to £16,238,157.

In view of the owners' offer of joint consultation and in an effort both to avoid industrial disturbance at a time of national mourning (following the death of King George V) and to prevent a sympathetic public from suffering loss through strike action, a conference of the M.F.G.B. decided on 24 January 1936 to accept the owners' offers 'as an instalment of the further improvement which will be rendered possible by the proposed selling agreements'.[1] Durham voted in favour of the decision.

The eventual wages settlement was severely criticized in Durham both by the Association's officials and the rank-and-file miners and brought forth the usual condemnation of district agreements. 'Instead of bringing the Durham miners nearer to a national uniform rate of pay', Swan said of the Durham owners' offer, '[it] has widened the margin between Durham and some other districts. It will certainly sow seeds of discontent. Even though the Durham miners live in what is an export district their needs are equal to those living in inland areas, and they should be paid an equal wage.' [2] The reaction of the Durham miners themselves was more hostile and their condemnation more specific. The Morrison and Chopwell Lodges issued circulars in February 1936 demanding a ballot vote on the terms of settlement, the resignation of the Executive Committee of the M.F.G.B. and deploring 'the dictatorship of agents of our Association'.[3] The Morrison Lodge described the Association's acceptance, albeit reluctantly, of the owners' offer as 'a spineless exhibition of leadership'.[4] Thirty delegates from Lodges throughout the coalfield attended a meeting at Annfield Plain in March 1936 and demanded that unless negotiations were reopened for a national wages advance of 2s per day a strike should be called in all districts in October.[5]

Answering the denunciations of the Lodges the Durham miners' Executive Committee repeated its belief that strike action in defiance of the owners' offers was out of the question in face of industrial depression and the economic and political power of the coal owners.[6] Furthermore they rightly claimed that the advance in wages, meagre though it was, was the first all-round increase won for the workmen since 1920. The promise of joint consultation offered

[1] Ibid., 24 January 1936.
[2] Durham Chronicle, 31 January 1936.
[3] Ibid., 21, 28 February 1936.
[4] North Mail and Newcastle Chronicle, 9 March 1936.
[5] Ibid.
[6] Durham Chronicle, 28 February 1936.

an opportunity for owners and miners to meet together formally for almost the first time since 1926. Nevertheless, although unemployment in the Durham coalfield fell during 1936–39, largely under the stimulus of the Government's armaments programme, neither the trade revival nor the provision of coal-selling agencies increased coal prices sufficiently enough to provide increased wages to miners. Wages as determined by district ascertainments never rose above the minimum level in Durham in any month before the outbreak of the Second World War.

The meagre advance in wages conceded by the Durham coal owners compared with other districts kept miners' wages in the coal-field below the national average and served to reinforce the County Federation Board's determination to seek a more equitable district wages agreement. In reformulating their proposals following the 1935 wages campaign the Board attacked long-standing grievances— especially in relation to the factors affecting costs of production and the treatment of accumulated deficiencies, both of which directly influenced the district's ability to pay increased wages to the miners. During meetings with the owners the Federation Board demanded that the standard wages in the County should consist of the basic rates operating in June 1936 plus the minimum percentage and 6d flat-rate advance awarded in January of the same year; that subsistence wages payable on June 1936 should be merged into a basic wage and constitute a minimum standard wage for all low-paid daywage workers; that deficiencies should not be carried forward and deducted from subsequent ascertainments; that surplus proceeds should be equally divided between wages and profits in the ratio 50:50 up to an agreed point where profits were regarded as 'adequate' i.e. 1s 3d per ton after which all increases in surplus proceeds would go to wages; that the cost of providing workers' houses and the cash paid to workers in lieu of the provision of houses and for coal allowance should be included in 'costs of production other than wages' and that the results from ancillary undertakings [1] be included in the ascertainments, the workmen being granted a definite voice in fixing the minimum transfer prices of coal to such concerns.[2] Under the existing method of fixing transfer prices at current market values the miners believed that coal could be sold at a price so far below the cost of production as to reveal a loss at the coal mine but be

---

[1] Brickworks, Coke-Ovens and By-Product Works, Smokeless and Patent Fuel Plants, Oil and Electric Power Plants, Gas and Selling Agencies and Merchanting Depots.

[2] Durham County Federation Board, undated circular outlining the proposals for a new wages agreement.

responsible for substantial profits accruing to the excluded concern receiving the coal. Such transfers made at below average price reduced the level of average pit-head prices in the ascertainment and materially affected the level of miners' wages.[1]

The Board's representatives were determined to improve the total amount of district proceeds out of which increases in wages might be met. They suggested further that the owners' contributions to the maintenance of pit-head baths and the penalties payable by colliery companies for evasion or breach of regulations under the terms of the central selling schemes might both be regarded as inadmissible items of costs of production.

The owners refused to concede any of the Board's demands but suggested an alteration in the ratio of wages to profits from 87:13 to 83:17 and a 25 per cent increase in basic rates.[2] Finally, on 15 May settlement was reached on the terms of a new County wages agreement. The basis of ascertainment in the agreements of 30 November 1926 and 23 December 1927 was to be continued. The ratio of 87 per cent of surplus proceeds applicable to wages, the subsistence wage of 6s 6½d and the minimum percentage of 65 were also to be continued. The basic wage of all adult workmen was fixed at 4s 3d and was increased by 3d per shift for all datal boys. As a temporary concession an advance of 5 per cent on basic rates was given 'in anticipation of proceeds justifying the advance'. The deficiency at 31 December 1936 (amounting to £19,791,023) was cancelled. Deficiencies occurring thereafter were to be carried forward and recouped at the rate of one-third of the surplus above the minimum percentage, such deficiencies to be cancelled annually one year in arrear. The hours of surface men were reduced from 49 to 48 per week, exclusive of mealtimes. The agreement was to continue in operation for three years and thereafter be subject to three month's notice given by either party.[3] Each section of the Federation Board agreed by a majority to accept the agreement.[4]

At the same time as signing the new County wages agreement the representatives of the miners' and owners' Associations agreed upon increases in the County basic wages for all classes of workmen, ranging from 4d to 1s 4d per shift. County basic rates of wages for particular grades of workmen had been established since 1872 and those prevailing in November 1879 had formed the 'standard' or 'basis' upon which future percentage additions or reductions in

[1] D.M.A., 22 May 1936.
[2] Durham Coal Owners' Association, *Proposed New Wages Agreement*, July 1936.
[3] Durham Coal Owners' Association, *Annual Report*, 1937, pp. 10–15.
[4] D.M.A., 21 May 1937; See Appendix I to this chapter.

wages, determined either by sliding scale agreements, conciliation, or by the system of 'profit-sharing' adopted during the 1920s, were eventually based.[1] By establishing new County basic rates the miners at last escaped from the '1879 base' which they had long felt did not provide a wage adequate enough to meet rapid changes in the cost of living. For the lower paid workers the new rates represented a substantial increase: in the case of adult datal workers, such as onsetters and horsekeepers, from 3s 5$\frac{1}{2}$d and 3s 0d per shift to the newly-established minimum basic wage for all adult datal workmen of 4s 3d per shift.[2] There had previously been changes in basic rates for particular classes within our period. It was agreed on 6 December 1918 that hand and pony putters over 21 years of age should receive the same basic rate as was then payable to hewers, i.e. 4s 2d per shift with equivalent increased rates for those under 21.[3] The hewers' and fillers' County basic rate had been increased from 4s 2d to 4s 8d per shift in 1926 as part of the terms of settlement of the General Strike.[4]

V

Despite their active participation in rallying district support for the national campaign for increased wages in 1935 and their efforts to secure a new County wages agreement during 1934–7, the Durham miners remained keenly aware of developments outside of their own coalfield. The dispute at Harworth Colliery, Nottinghamshire in August 1936 attracted the attention of miners in all districts for it epitomized the conflict which had been raging since 1926 between the Nottinghamshire Miners' Association and the breakaway Union headed by George Spencer.[5] The series of disputes which followed upon the alleged assault on two boys by colliery officials at Harworth resulted from the district employers exploiting the opportunities which the 'Spencer Union' provided for further dividing the loyalty of the workmen, by making membership of the rival union a condition of employment, and for weakening the influence and authority of the Nottinghamshire Miners' Association.

The M.F.G.B. eventually intervened in the dispute in an effort to enforce the principle of freedom of organization. The Federation also

---

[1] See above, pp. 22–3.
[2] The establishment of this minimum was written into the terms of the County Wages Agreement.
[3] Durham Miners' Association, *County Agreements*, Durham 1940, p. 64.
[4] See Chapter V, p. 224.
[5] For a full account of the Harworth dispute see A. R. Griffin, *The Miners of Nottinghamshire, 1914–1944*, London 1962, Chapter 15.

called upon the Government for support, but attempts by the Secretary for Mines during February 1937 to secure an amalgamation of the two rival unions ended in failure.[1] One of the major obstacles towards a settlement was the refusal by the 'Spenser Union' to guarantee that there would be no victimization or discrimination against the men at Harworth who had resisted the interference with their freedom to organize in an Association of their own choice. On 1–2 April the M.F.G.B. called for a strike ballot to be taken amongst the districts 'with the object of securing recognition of the Mineworkers' Federation of Great Britain and adequate assurances to prevent victimization at Harworth Colliery'.[2]

The Durham delegates supported the principle of a national strike and the Executive Committee of the Durham Miners' Association advised all members to vote in favour of the Federation's recommendation. The resulting ballot showed 70,337 in favour and 11,668 against.[3] The national figures were 444,456 for and only 61,445 against.[4] The M.F.G.B. Executive Committee failed to persuade the districts to allow further negotiations to take place amongst the parties 'for a reasonable period' and on 30 April it was decided that notices should be handed in to expire simultaneously in every district on 22 May.[5]

Swan urged the Durham miners to remain loyal to their previous decision to support strike action, 'as a determined protest against the unwarranted injustice that has too long been imposed on the gallant men at Harworth, who are fighting in the defence of liberty and freedom of Association.'[6] The strike never came owing to the intervention of Crookshank, Secretary for Mines, who eventually persuaded the M.F.G.B. to abandon its claim for direct recognition of the miners' Association in Nottinghamshire in favour of an amalgamation of the rival unions on satisfactory terms. The Federation agreed and a negotiating sub-committee, of which Lawther and Gilliland were members, met representatives of the Nottinghamshire owners and the 'Spenser Union' under the neutral chairmanship of John (later Sir John) Forster on 24 May. The Durham miners' Executive Committee had already empowered its officials to accept the principle of fusion of the two unions in the event of the Federation's

[1] Mineworkers' Federation of Great Britain, *Annual Report of the Executive Committee, 1936–7*, pp. 168–9.
[2] M.F.G.B., 2 April 1937.
[3] D.M.A., 19 April 1937.
[4] M.F.G.B., 20 April 1937.
[5] *Ibid.*, 30 April 1937.
[6] D.M.A., 4 May 1937.

failure to secure direct recognition of the district Association.[1] The result of the discussions was the establishment of a new organization, the Nottinghamshire and District Miners' Federated Union, with George Spencer as President. The officials of the Durham Miners' Association, many of whom had vigorously opposed the activities of rival unions in their own coalfield after 1926, welcomed the outcome of the dispute not only as a means of peace in Nottinghamshire but as a means of maintaining the unity and strength of the Federation upon which the poorer exporting districts had come to depend during the years of depression. 'One Union will be able to function in Nottinghamshire and negotiate on all matters common to the Miners' welfare,' wrote Swan. 'It ought also to absorb all conflicting elements which have been manifest since 1926, and preventing unity.'[2]

The Harworth dispute signified the dangers facing any district Association which allowed large numbers of workmen to remain outside of its direct influence only to be subject to the persuasions of sectional interests. In August 1937, therefore, the Durham miners' leaders organized a '100 per cent Union Campaign' in an effort to recruit the existing non-union labour and the boys entering the occupation for the first time. In the period immediately following the termination of the 1926 dispute the Association had made arrangements for the readmission of one-time non-political trade unionists and unfinancial members.[3] Throughout the period of depression, however, the need to maintain the loyalty of the existing membership and to increase its numbers attracted added significance. At a Council Meeting in March 1934 the Association's Executive Committee resolved to inaugurate an extensive campaign towards achieving 100 per cent membership, a resolve ultimately strengthened by the conflict at Harworth. In his appeal for support of the campaign Swan wrote on 18 August 1937: 'The non-union man not only brings reproach upon himself, but often brings shame and embarrassment to his wife and children by cold ostracism.'[4] Whether or not workmen were particularly influenced by such direct reproaches is difficult to assess, but whereas between 1934 and 1935 the net increase in membership of the Association amounted to only 168 and only 34 between 1935 and 1936 the net increase during 1937 amounted to over 2,500.[5]

The Durham Miners' Association's activity in negotiating for a

[1] *Ibid.*, 10 May 1937.
[2] *Ibid.*, 28 May 1937.
[3] See above, pp. 234–5.
[4] D.M.A., 18 August 1937. Cf. the comments of Lawther, *Durham Chronicle*, 6 November 1936.
[5] Durham Miners' Association, Balance Sheets, 1931–1940.

new County wages agreement and campaigning for increased membership coincided with a gradual upswing in the trade cycle, reinforced
by the rearmament programme. The recovery in Durham was not
as marked as elsewhere and did not completely overcome the problem
of large-scale unemployment, although in 1937 the proportion of the
total insured work force engaged in coal mining in Durham which
was wholly unemployed fell below the national average for the first
time since 1928.[1] Nevertheless the gradual recovery of the industry
provided a background against which further concessions were won
for the miners. Output of coal in Durham increased from 30·3
million tons in 1935 to 33·5 million tons in 1937, falling to 31·4
million tons in 1938—even then higher than any year between 1931
and 1936. The average net selling value of coal increased in Durham
from 12s 1·48d in 1935 to 16s 0·2d in 1938. The average declared
value per ton of coal (f.o.b.) exported at Newcastle and Sunderland
rose between 1935 and 1938 from 13s 1d to 18s 11d and from 13s 10d
to 18s 9d respectively. By 1938 the index of miners' average real
earnings (1914 = 100) had reached its 1914 level in Durham for the
first time since 1921 although an equivalent position had been reached
for the country as a whole in 1933.[2]

During 1936–37 the M.F.G.B., supported by the T.U.C., campaigned for holidays with pay for the miners. The scheme was first
introduced in those areas which could most easily afford it, Derbyshire and Nottinghamshire being the first coalfields to make such
concessions. In Durham during August 1936 the local Lambton,
Hetton and Joicey Collieries miners' Federation Board approached
A. Kirkup, a director of the colliery company, proposing the adoption of an annual fourteen days' holiday with pay for miners. The
Board suggested that one person for every twenty-five employed
should be brought from the ranks of the unemployed to enable an
equivalent number to take a holiday every fourteen days. The scheme
proved abortive.[3]

In November 1937 Swan, Secretary to the County Federation
Board, pressed the owners for an early meeting to discuss holidays
with pay but evoked little response.[4] By April 1938, however, the
Federation Board representatives had signed a holiday-with-pay
agreement with the owners at almost the same time as a government
committee, presided over by Lord Amulree, and called upon to

[1] See Chapter VII, pp. 268–9.
[2] See Chapter VII, Appendix II.
[3] *Durham Chronicle*, 28 August 1936.
[4] D.M.A., 19 November 1937.

investigate the holiday-with-pay movement, had reported in favour of its widespread adoption.

Under the terms of the Durham agreement all piece work and datal wage workers became entitled to an annual holiday of seven consecutive days, with a holiday allowance, to be taken between 1 April and 31 October in each year. The holiday allowance was provided at weekly rates ('credits') of 1s per week for married workmen, 7d per week for single workmen over 18 years of age and 5d per week for boys under 18. In the event of any employees' holiday coinciding with one or more of the recognized public holidays which fell within the prescribed period he would not be entitled to any extra days as a substitution. The agreement operated from 1 April 1938 and the first annual holiday with pay was fixed for between 1 April and 31 October 1939. Holiday allowance credits were treated as a wages cost under the terms of the 1937 wages agreement and debited to the cost of wages in each monthly ascertainment. The agreement was to last for five years [1] and was particularly welcome since the consistently low wages payable to miners during and before the outbreak of world depression made it virtually impossible, however careful they might be, for them to save for an annual holiday. For many the only time spent away from work was by virtue of ill-health, accident or unemployment.

However beneficial the changes in wages and conditions effected during the latter part of the 1930s were there were to be even greater benefits following the outbreak of war. After the experience of years of meagre earnings, short-time working and long periods of unemployment, more serious than ever in exporting regions where the extent of the collapse of markets and their slowness to recover were particularly emphasized, the urgent needs of war produced a market situation inherently favourable to the miner. The Durham miners who, through their Association, had pleaded in the mid-1930s for Government aid to assist their coalfield, suddenly found themselves members of an expanding, high-priority industry. The changes which the demands of war wrought went further than many of the miners and their officials envisaged, eventually culminating in the establishment of a national union and a nationalized industry.

---

[1] Durham Miners' Association, *County Agreements*, 1940, pp. 76–81.

Appendix I

Wages and Conditions of Employment
(*Agreement dated* 15th *May* 1937)

It is hereby agreed as follows:

1. The basis of ascertainment in the Agreements of 30 November 1926, and 23 December 1927, to be continued.

2. The ratio of 87 per cent of surplus proceeds applicable to wages, the subsistence wage of 6s 6½d and the minimum percentage of 65 to be continued.

3. The basis wage of all adult datal workmen whose basis wage is at present less than 4s 3d to be increased to 4s 3d per shift.

4. The basis wages of all datal boys to be increased by 3d per shift.

5. As a special and temporary concession an advance of 5 per cent on basis rates to be given in anticipation of proceeds justifying that advance, it being understood that for purposes of calculation the minimum percentage of 65 shall continue to apply in all respects as at present.

6. The deficiency as at 31 December 1936 (including trading loss) to be cancelled.

Deficiencies occurring after 31 December 1936, to be carried forward to be recouped at the rate of one-third of surplus about the minimum percentage, such deficiencies to be cancelled annually one year in arrear.

7. The hours of all underground workers (except Deputies) shall be 7½ per shift, plus one winding time. The hours of the Deputies shall be 7½ per shift, plus one winding time, it being understood that in accordance with the provisions of the Coal Mines Acts they shall if required stay longer, and be paid an equivalent wage for overtime.

8. The hours of men employed at the surface shall be 48 per week, exclusive of meal times.

9. This Agreement shall continue in operation for three years, and thereafter until it shall be terminated by three months' notice given by either party to the other party after that date.

For the Durham Coal Owners' Association,

REGINALD GUTHRIE, *Secretary.*

For the Durham County Mining Federation,

JOHN E. SWAN, *Secretary.*

Chapter VII

LIVING AND WORKING CONDITIONS, 1919–39

I

In a County such as Durham where the coal industry was of greater singular importance than in the country as a whole, it was inevitable that during a period of decline in the fortunes of the basic industries miners and their families should suffer acute distress. The miners as a class suffered the consequences of industrial depression to a greater degree than most sections of the working-class community and even amongst the miners the intensity of poverty varied between districts and was at its worst in the coal exporting areas.

For the greater part of the inter-war period the Durham miners suffered the hazards of unemployment, short-time working and low wages. Although their average earnings per shift (exclusive of allowances in kind) remained above the 1914 level they lagged behind the national average, with the exception of two years during the brief post-war boom. Taking 1914 as 100 the relevant index in Durham stood at 146·3 in 1922 compared with 154·0 for the country as a whole. By 1929 the indices for the two areas stood at 128·2 and 142·4 and in 1938 at 156·0 and 173·7 respectively. The disparity became particularly marked after 1927 once the impact of the immediate post-war economic dislocation, and especially the short-run influences upon the prosperity of the coal export trade, had largely disappeared, and once employers in mining areas were free to impose onerous working conditions to meet the needs of competition. The Durham miners were compensated to some extent by their higher-than-average level of payments of allowances in kind, which averaged 1s 1½d per shift between the wars, compared with only 4¾d per shift for the country as a whole.

Since wage rates in Durham, unlike the country as a whole, lagged behind the cost of living throughout the post-1921 period, the disparity in real earnings is especially apparent. Although the national level of miners' average real earnings per shift lagged behind its pre-war level during the twenties and early years of the thirties, by 1933 it had regained its 1914 level. In Durham on the other hand the pre-war level of average real earnings per shift was not reached until 1938.[1]

---

[1] See Appendix II to this chapter.

The miners' earning capacity depended in part upon the regularity of work. In Durham the average number of days worked per week by the miners fell from 5·16 in 1922 to 4·59 in 1932, a reduction of 11 per cent. Although wage rates fell during that period the cost of living was reduced by 21 per cent. As wage rates increased during 1933–8 by 16·95 per cent in Durham compared with 8·93 per cent in Great Britain as a whole, the average number of days worked per week increased by 6·7 per cent and 8·9 per cent in Durham and Great Britain respectively.[1] At the same time, however, the cost of living increased by 10 per cent and thus significantly reduced the real effect of improved wages and employment.

Percentage of the Total Insured Workforce in the Coal Industry Wholly and Temporarily Unemployed, 1928–38 *

	Wholly unemployed		Temporarily unemployed	
	Durham	Great Britain	Durham	Great Britain
1928	19·16	14·37	3·07	7·54
1929	13·00	11·77	8·08	4·26
1930	16·43	13·28	2·22	7·15
1931	25·40	18·06	4·74	9·91
1932	30·22	21·27	4·88	12·70
1933	29·28	21·92	4·92	10·73
1934	23·18	19·27	2·69	8·43
1935	21·48	18·37	3·79	6·46
1936	16·97	15·89	1·67	5·52
1937	10·32	11·20	0·62	3·36
1938	7·80	9·63	4·17	5·77

* Compiled from figures supplied in *Ministry of Labour Gazette*. Comparable figures are not available for the period 1921–7. In any event problems of post-war reconstruction were still paramount during most of those years.

Unemployment was a persistent problem between the wars. The average level of unemployment amongst the working population as a whole was at least twice as severe during the inter-war years than in the period before the First World War.[2] In Durham County the percentage of the total insured work force in all industries (excluding agriculture) wholly and temporarily unemployed rose from 21·78 per cent in 1928 to a peak of 40·52 per cent in 1932 and averaged 28·74 per cent during the period 1928–38.[3] The percentage of the total

[1] See Appendix I to this chapter.
[2] W. H. Beveridge, *Full Employment in a Free Society*, London 1944, pp. 72–3.
[3] Calculated from local unemployment exchange statistics prepared by the Ministry of Labour. T.U.C. Library, Congress House, London.

insured work force in coal mining wholly unemployed within Durham during the period 1928–38 was for the most part above the national average, the percentage temporarily unemployed,[1] with the exception of one year, remaining below the national average as the preceeding table shows. It was not until 1937 that the percentage of miners wholly unemployed in Durham fell below its 1929 level. By that time the total number of wage earners on colliery books in the coalfield had fallen to 114,480 from a total of 136,413 in 1929, compared with a peak of 170,181 in 1923.[2]

II

With the onset of industrial depression and growing unemployment after 1921 the miners became severely critical of the Government's inactivity in providing more generous relief to those out of work. The M.F.G.B. agreed in January 1921 to support a resolution before the National Conference on Unemployment, convened by the Parliamentary Committee of the T.U.C. and the Labour Party, calling for a basic maintenance provision of not less than 40s per week for each householder.[3] In the following month the Miners' Federation appointed a Sub-Committee, of which Whiteley was a member, to formulate a scheme for a district levy in aid of the unemployed.[4] The Committee recommended that every full member should donate 6d per shift worked to provide a weekly benefit of £1 per man and 2s for each dependent under 16 years of age. If a miner worked two days or less the benefits were to be reduced to 3s 4d per day and 4d per day respectively.[5] Nothing came of the scheme.

The 1921 dispute increased material hardship within the coalfields. The Courts ruled that the stoppage was an industrial dispute within the meaning of the Unemployment Insurance Act and that any miner involved forfeited his claim to benefit. The miners and their families were forced to seek aid from the local Board of Guardians. The total number of persons receiving outdoor relief from the Poor Law unions representing mining areas in Durham increased from 18,309 on 16 April 1921 to 92,436 by 18 June 1921.[6] Miners in Durham who resisted the coal owners' attempts to further reduce

[1] i.e. those temporarily stopped and suspended from work on the understanding that they were to return shortly to their former employment.
[2] See Appendix I to this chapter.
[3] M.F.G.B., 26 January 1921.
[4] Ibid., 24 February 1921.
[5] Ibid., 2 March 1921.
[6] 200 H.C. Deb. 5s, 23–4.

wages and increase hours after the stoppage were accused of entering a trade dispute and refused the benefit which many local Courts of Referees had already awarded.

The series of modifications made to the Unemployment Insurance legislation after 1921 caused further hardship. The 1920 Unemployment Insurance Act required the prior payment of contributions as a condition of benefit but in 1922 an emergency scheme was drafted on to the permanent one whereby large numbers of the unemployed were admitted to benefit having contributed little or nothing to the Unemployment Fund. The 1922 Unemployment Insurance Act provided for 37 weeks uncovenanted benefit to be paid between April 1922 and June 1923 but that from April to October 1922 the benefit should be available only in five weekly intervals. During that 30-week period, therefore, miners unemployed since the 1921 stoppage were only able to draw 15 weeks' benefit in three separate intervals.

W. P. Richardson appealed to the M.F.G.B. to call the Government's attention to the plight of the unemployed miners especially in areas where the Boards of Guardians were openly unsympathetic. In a letter to Hodges Richardson wrote of the situation in Durham:

'I need not assure you that the conditions in this area, where they [the miners] have never had the chance of employment since the stoppage, is exceedingly bad, and in this area there is a Board of Guardians who, to say the least, have no sympathy with our side, and, as a result, relief has been given in a very niggardly way, thus adding to the hardships of our people.'[1]

The Durham miners had received some local assistance in the period immediately following the end of the 1921 dispute but it proved insufficient to meet the distress of long-term unemployment. In September 1921 the working miners in the coalfield began to contribute 3s per man per fortnight to help aid the unemployed.[2] At Hebburn Colliery a 5 per cent deduction from each man's wages was made at the colliery office to encourage more systematic support.[3]

As the depression deepened, as coal owners in Durham succeeded in persuading workmen to accept lower wages and longer hours, especially by eliminating variations in working time between collieries,[4] and as the Unemployment Insurance Regulations became more stringent, conditions gradually worsened. By December 1925 91 pits, about one-fifth of the total, had closed throughout the

[1] M.F.G.B., 8 June 1922.
[2] *Durham Chronicle*, 9 September 1921.
[3] D.M.A., 17 October 1921.
[4] See Chapter V, pp. 166–7, 175.

Durham coalfield and over 34,000 miners were unemployed.[1] When the local coal company folded up at Trimdon Grange early in 1925, one writer noted: 'Almost the only men in employment were the few schoolmasters, the two policemen, the two scavengers, one road man and the odd railway employee.'[2] Those who had worked earned barely enough to maintain a family. During the week immediately preceding the outbreak of the 1926 dispute over 41 per cent of the 3,837 miners working at Dawdon Colliery earned £2 or less per week before deductions.[3]

Conditions naturally deteriorated during the protracted dispute in 1926. As in previous stoppages the local communities were quick to organize soup kitchens and to arrange the distribution of what gifts of food and clothing were made available. The feeding of children was undertaken by the local education authorities under the jurisdiction of the 1921 Education Act. The Durham County Education Authority alone provided 309 feeding centres for children[4] and provided 19,387,504 meals at a total cost of £283,781 between 1 May and 26 December 1926.[5] On 29 June 1926 the N.S.P.C.C. inspector for Durham claimed that children under his care were 'not up to the present adversely affected by the strike, except in the matter of clothing and boots' and that he was unable to quote any case 'where difficulty has been experienced in obtaining necessary food or milk where recommended'.[6]

Help was offered by outside bodies. Hunters' Bakers at Gateshead supplied 1,000 loaves of bread weekly free of charge to the districts of South Shields, Sunderland and Durham.[7] At the end of May 1926 J. S. Fry and Sons of Bristol agreed to distribute 7,500 quarter-pound tins of cocoa to mining families in the Durham coalfield.[8] The Co-operative Societies resumed their often-played role of feeding the unemployed and entered into credit arrangements with local miners' Lodges. By September 1926 the Ryhope and Silksworth Co-operative Society (with credit arrangements with Lodges in east Durham) was owed more than £44,000, The debt was not finally cleared until 1947.[9] The Northern Echo inaugurated a 'Shilling Fund' during June and July of 1926 in order to attract funds in aid of unemployed

[1] Durham Chronicle, 12 December 1925.
[2] Northern Echo, 26 February 1966.
[3] Colliery Guardian, 28 May 1926.
[4] Mason, op. cit., pp. 392-3.
[5] 204 H.C. Deb. 5s, 583-4.
[6] The Times, 29 June 1926.
[7] D.M.A., 19 May 1926.
[8] Ibid., 27 May 1926.
[9] Mason, op. cit., pp. 397-8.

miners but the scheme was disbanded in August after about £500 had been distributed.

Such local efforts to relieve distress proved inadequate as the miners' resistance to the owners and the Government dragged on until autumn 1926. The Durham Miners' Association, aware that the miners had been locked out by the employers, sought to institute a test case to establish the workman's right to receive unemployment benefit. The Courts ruled, however, that since the men had refused to accept terms offered by the owners they had entered into a trade dispute and thus forfeited their claim to relief.[1]

The persistent claims for relief made by members of the Association during the five years before 1926 so severely restricted its financial ability to withstand the protracted dispute that relief payments ended early in June 1926.[2] The M.F.G.B. thereafter provided support but in the absence of continuing aid from their trade union the majority of Durham miners and their families were at the mercy of their local Board of Guardians. On 15 May 1926 the total number of persons receiving outdoor relief from the eleven Poor Law Unions representing mining districts in Durham stood at 179,449. By 6 November it has risen to 338,851.[3] Even by the end of July 1926 the total sum of loans and current overdrafts sanctioned on behalf of these Unions amounted to £612,000.[4] The Ministry of Health had circularized all Boards of Guardians on 5 May 1926 outlining the scale and distribution of relief which could be granted during the crisis period. It was particularly emphasized that no relief was to be given to able-bodied men physically capable of work. The refusal of the West Ham Board of Guardians to economize on their relief expenditure in accordance with the Ministry's instructions led eventually to the passing of the Board of Guardians (Default) Act [5] on 15 July 1926. Under the terms of this Act the Ministry was empowered to replace representatives of recalcitrant Boards of Guardians by its own nominees.

Although the majority of the local Boards of Guardians in Durham operated in accordance with the Ministry's instructions, at Chester-le-Street the Board persisted in granting relief to unmarried, able-bodied men engaged in the dispute. For almost a year prior to the outbreak of the 1926 crisis the Guardians had increased the scale of relief to the point of indebtedness and despite warnings from the Ministry continued to make indiscriminate relief payments. Of the

---

[1] *Newcastle Daily Journal*, 5 May 1926.
[2] Cf. Chapter II, p. 87.
[3] 200 H.C. Deb. 5s, 23–4.
[4] 198 H.C. Deb. 5s, 2347.
[5] 16 and 17 Geo. V. 1926, Chapter 20.

59 members on the Board 47 represented Labour, of which 39 were either miners' officials, miners or miners' wives.[1] The Board's elected representatives were eventually suspended on 30 August 1926 and their powers placed in the hands of a Ministry Inspector. From that date the scale of relief was gradually reduced. The Board's total bank overdraft at the time Ministry control became effective stood at £78,908 and its total indebtedness at £178,732. By the week ending 27 November 1926 payments had been reduced to £5,728.[2] The local Boards of Guardians proved indispensable in relieving distress and preventing starvation. It has been estimated that 86 per cent of the married or widowed mineworkers in Northumberland and Durham applied for relief for themselves and their families during the period of the 1926 dispute.[3]

The years following the General Strike proved some of the worst the miners were to experience. By mid-February 1927, 38,123 miners were wholly unemployed in Durham—the highest number for all colliery areas except Wales.[4] Between April 1926 and September 1927 the total number of people employed in and about the mines throughout the country fell from 1,107,100 to 982,600. In the two counties of Northumberland and Durham the decrease amounted to 43,300 or over one-third of the total loss. As unemployment increased further pressure was put upon local Boards of Guardians. In the week ending 30 July 1927 alone the total number of Poor Law Unions in County Durham granted relief to 58,014 unemployed at a cost of £14,545.[5] Many of those miners who secured work had to repay out of meagre wages the emergency relief granted to them during the 1926 crisis. By April 1930 the Easington Board of Guardians had collected £50,000 from past recipients of relief by weekly repayments of up to a maximum of 2s.[6] The Durham correspondent of *The Times* had remarked in August 1927: 'Never were the Durham miners so impoverished as now through the debt incurred during the struggle and the consequence of under-employment, unemployment and low wages.'[7]

The hardships of unemployment and short-time working were

[1] Ministry of Health, *Chester-le-Street Union. Report of the Board of Guardians on the Administration for the Period 30th August 1926 to 31st December 1926* (Cmd. 2818), p. 7.
[2] *Ibid.*, pp. 4–6. Cf. *Miner*, 19 March, 2 April 1927.
[3] Ministry of Health, *Eighth Annual Report, 1926–7*, p. 262.
[4] 202 H.C. Deb. 5s, 271–2.
[5] *Conference of Northern Poor-Law Unions and Other Local Authorities, Deputation to the Minister of Labour, 27 October 1927*, pp. 17–18.
[6] Mason, *op. cit.*, pp. 385–8.
[7] *The Times*, 6 August 1927.

accentuated by the continual stern administration of the Unemployment Insurance Regulations. So varied and complex were they that
many local administrators found it increasingly difficult to assess
individual cases. Men could be refused relief because they were 'not
likely to obtain insurable employment', were not making reasonable
efforts to secure work or because on the basis of the amount of work
secured during the preceding two years their future prospects of
unemployment were particularly weak. These problems proved a
frequent source of distress in Durham, where thousands of miners
had been unemployed since before the 1926 dispute and where the
prospects of future employment in an area heavily dependent upon
the depressed staple industries were obviously weak. Having exhausted their statutory benefit, many miners and their families were
refused further assistance owing to their inability to satisfy the necessary requirements. As more and more workmen turned to the Boards
of Guardians for assistance the gulf widened between the numbers
registered as unemployed in Durham and in receipt of relief, and the
proportion of the mining population actually out of work.

During 1928 the situation grew even more serious. In March of
that year the unemployment rate in the Durham coalfield, as
measured by the total number of persons on the unemployment re-
gisters, stood at 19·7, compared with 9·4 for Great Britain. In only
four of the 28 administrative areas into which Durham was divided
for insurance purposes was there less than the national average
amount of unemployment.[1] Although these estimates do not refer
specifically to unemployment in the mining industry it is obvious from
the nature of the region's industrial structure, and the fact that many
of the administrative divisions were situated in predominantly mining
areas, that the miners were suffering to a greater degree than were
the majority of the occupied population in other parts of the country.

Under the terms of the 1927 Unemployment Act new regulations
came into force on 19 April 1928 governing relief payments. Dependant's benefit was increased by 2s whilst that for men between 18 and
65 years of age was reduced by 1s from 18s to 17s. Eligibility for
benefit rested on the payment of 30 insurance contributions during
the two years prior to the claim or, as a temporary measure, on proof
that either contributions had been paid in the preceding two years
(or 30 during any period of time) or that a reasonable period of employment had been undertaken over a two-year period. This latter
condition still proved a stumbling block to many long-term unemployed miners in Durham, although some did possess a total of

[1] *The Times*, 27 March 1928.

30 contributions, amassed over a number of years, and succeeded in obtaining relief. Following representations by Trotter, the Association's Treasurer, to the Chief Insurance Officer in London regarding the difficult employment prospects facing the Durham miners, it was agreed in June 1928 that local insurance officers should grant relief to those miners who had not worked at all during the two years prior to a claim providing that their failure 'was not due to lack of effort'.[1]

A correspondent of the *New Statesman*, on a tour of the Durham coalfield during 1927, was particularly struck by the suffering of many of the miners' families, and wrote:

'They are entering now upon the third year of acute suffering, without a gleam of hope. The miners' standard of living has gone. In the stoppage of 1926 the families were bared to the bone: savings exhausted, humble possessions sold, clothing worn out, debts incurred. The past year has brought nothing back. Even when the miner is in regular work his wages, on the standard basis, are below the acknowledged subsistence level. The victory of the owners in 1926 was disastrously complete.'[2]

In view of the limited opportunities available in an area geared to the success of a few staple industries the large number of juveniles in Durham faced the alternative of remaining idle or of moving to another district. The normal arrangements for securing employment for such groups via the Employment Exchange scheme and the Juvenile Employment Bureaux of the Local Education Authorities [3] proved particularly inadequate in conditions of long-term depression. Acting in co-operation with local education authorities the Ministry of Labour established a network of Juvenile Unemployment Centres throughout Durham and Northumberland in December 1927 aimed at maintaining the general 'employability' of boys. By the end of December 1928 533 boys had been transferred to outside districts, mainly to S.E. England but also to the North-West and the Midlands.[4]

Assistance was also given to all single and married miners (or widowers with dependant children) who had been continuously unemployed for not less than eight weeks. The Ministry of Labour guaranteed to contribute towards their lodging and/or removal expenses if they moved to another area outside of Durham in search of

[1] D.M.A., 20 June 1928.
[2] *New Statesman*, 31 December 1927.
[3] Exercising powers under Section 107 of the 1921 Education Act and Section 6 of the 1923 Unemployment Insurance Act.
[4] Ministry of Labour, *Memorandum on the Transfer of Juveniles from Distressed Mining Areas to Employment in Other Districts*, December 1928, p. 21.

work.[1] The Ministry also established preliminary farm training centres within Durham to encourage miners to train for work overseas.[2] The Durham Miners' Association, in conjunction with the Durham Labour Exchange, arranged in April 1928 to train 100 young unmarried miners for work on farms abroad.[3]

The plight of the coalfields and the degree of destitution to which mining families, especially in the exporting areas, were being subjected received particular public attention during 1928. In April of that year the Lord Mayor of London launched a fund to aid the distressed men and women in Durham, Northumberland and South Wales. The King contributed £500 and the Queen £250 to the fund in an attempt to encourage voluntary support.[4] The Lord Mayors of Cardiff and Newcastle were invited to become controlling trustees of the fund and arrangements were made to establish regional committees to help administer the scheme. The Committee eventually chosen for the northern coalfield consisted of the Lord Mayor of Newcastle, the Chairmen of the Durham and Northumberland County Councils, F. R. Simpson, representing the Durham coalowners, T. Eustace Hill, Medical Officer of Health for Durham, R. Warham, representing the Northumberland Coal Owners' Association, M. Meos from Newcastle and W. Straker and J. Gilliland as the Northumberland and Durham Miners' Association's representatives respectively.[5] Robson had been invited by the Lord Mayor of Newcastle in April 1928 to join the Committee but he declined the offer owing to pressure of work.[6] Local committees were established for each separate county, represented in Durham by the Chairman of the County Council (W. N. Smith), the region's Medical Officer of Health, the Director of Education, J. Gilliland, F. R. Simpson and the Chairmen of six Boards of Guardians and of the Chester-le-Street Rural District Council.[7]

Between the date of its inception and the end of September 1928 the 'Lord Mayor's Fund' accumulated a total of £88,770,[8] an amount

---

[1] Ministry of Labour, *Facilities Available to Unemployed Workers for Training and Transference including Migration Overseas*, April 1929, pp. 2–3.
[2] *Ibid.*, pp. 6–7. Cf. *The Times*, 13 September 1928.
[3] D.M.A., 12 April 1928; *The Times*, 10 December 1928.
[4] *The Times*, 3 April 1928. The fund was referred to as either the 'Mansion House Fund' or 'Lord Mayor's Fund'.
[5] Lord Mayor's Distress Fund 1928, CC/X, File No. 1, Durham County Record Office.
[6] *Ibid.*
[7] *Ibid.*
[8] Miners' Federation of Great Britain, *Report of the Executive Committee, June 1929*, p. 11.

which proved wholly inadequate to meet fully the demands made upon it. In Durham alone the Medical Officer of Health reported on 18 May 1928 that a total of 19,486 women and children were in need of boots and a further 10,382 in need of clothing, at an estimated total cost of £14,085.[1] Of the total disbursements made by 30 May 1928 Durham County had received only £6,000.[2] In Durham the local Committee gave first priority to providing footwear to necessitous schoolchildren but, despite these and other efforts, S. Easten, Lord Mayor of Newcastle, was forced to report on 3 August 1928:

'The operations in the two Counties ... have revealed that, notwithstanding the magificent response to the Appeal on behalf of the Mansion House Fund, the distress amongst women and children (to say nothing of the menfolk) is so appalling that only a comparatively small proportion of those in need is likely to be relieved.'[3]

A more determined public response to the needs of the distressed areas followed upon an intensive publicity campaign organized by the M.F.G.B., in conjunction with the *Daily Mail*, during November–December 1928.[4] Apart from increased cash subscriptions to both the Lord Mayor's Fund and the National Distress Fund established by the M.F.G.B. in September 1928, the appeal resulted in over 20,000 parcels of food and clothing being sent to miners' families in Durham during December.[5] On 17 December the Prime Minister announced a Government grant of £150,000 to the Lord Mayor's Fund and a promise to augment the Fund by adding £ for £ to every sum voluntarily subscribed.[6] From January 1929 the scope of the fund was also increased to include areas outside of the coal exporting regions.[7]

Apart from grants to help provide boots and clothing Durham also received assistance towards providing extra nourishment to families and to schoolchildren (over and above that provided by the local authority). By 11 December 1928 E. Percy, President of the Board of Education, had reported to the Cabinet that there was 'grave cause for anxiety' over the need for feeding schoolchildren in Durham.[8]

[1] Lord Mayor's Distress Fund 1928, CC/X, File No. 1, Durham County Record Office.
[2] *Ibid.*
[3] *Distress in Mining Areas: Mansion House Fund. Brief Statement as to the Administration of the Fund in the Counties of Northumberland and Durham,* 3 August 1928, p. 3.
[4] M.F.G.B., 13 September 1928; D.M.A., 17 December 1928.
[5] D.M.A., 17 December 1928.
[6] 223 H.C. Deb. 5s, 2607–2613.
[7] *The Times*, 27 December 1928.
[8] Cabinet Papers, 24/199, C.P. 388(28); Cf. Cabinet Papers, 24/207, C.P. 326(29).

Between 1929 and 1930 the number of families in receipt of extra nourishment within the Durham coalfield increased from 1,779 to 2,609.[1]

By April 1930 Northumberland and Durham together had received a total of £454,474 from the Lord Mayor's fund to help relieve distress in their regions.[2] The extent and duration of the depression within the northern coalfield was such, however, that the claims for relief continuously outstripped the resources to meet them. Even in November 1929 it was estimated that an extra £110,000 would need to be allocated to Durham to help meet the needs of winter.[3] Furthermore, up to January 1929 relief within the Durham coalfield was distributed not on an urban and rural district basis but according to the administrative divisions under the Poor Law scheme with the result that the claims met in shipbuilding and engineering districts deprived families in predominantly mining areas of some of the available funds.[4]

The vexing problem of the miners' claim to unemployment benefit again assumed importance during 1929. The difficulty miners in Durham had to prove, according to law, that they were 'genuinely seeking work but unable to obtain employment' was particularly stressed by the M.F.G.B. in its evidence to the Morris Committee, established to enquire into the functions of Unemployment Insurance Officers and Courts of Referees.[5] The subsequent Unemployment Insurance Act, 1930,[6] repealed the 'genuinely seeking work' clause and placed the onus upon local insurance officers to prove that applicants for relief had refused a suitable offer of employment. At the same time the scale of benefits for boys and girls between the ages of 17 and 21 was increased by varying amounts from 2s to 4s with an additional benefit from April 1931 of 6s for boys between 15 and 16 years of age.[7] The legislative changes were warmly welcomed in Durham. Trotter, whilst realizing that by no means all the anomalies of the Unemployment Insurance Acts had been removed, praised the abolition of the 'genuinely seeking work' clause:

'The old method of deciding whether or not a claimant was

---

[1] Durham County Council, *Annual Report of the Medical Officer of Health*, 1929, p. 41, *Ibid.*, 1930, p. 169.
[2] *Durham Chronicle*, 27 March 1931.
[3] Cabinet Papers, 24/207 C.P. 326(29).
[4] *The Times*, 2 March 1929.
[5] Miners' Federation of Great Britain, *Report of the Executive Committee for the Year ending June, 1930*, p. 12.
[6] 20 Geo. 5, Chapter 16.
[7] D.M.A., 12 March 1930.

genuinely seeking work was a most unsatisfactory one.' he explained in 1930, 'as it was left to the speculative opinion of men, many of whom had the foolish conception that a round of places visited each week, no matter how remote the chance of obtaining work at many of them, was the only proof of genuinely seeking work.'[1]

Whatever the benefits of the Act they were soon to be overshadowed by the hardships resulting from the Government's reorganization of the national finances in 1931. Seeking an immediate reduction in national expenditure the Government decided to reduce the amount of unemployment relief payments in view of the increasing indebtedness of the Unemployment Fund—in 1931 the Fund was borrowing £1 million a week. Ramsay MacDonald wrote to his Seaham constituents in August 1931:

'We were suddenly faced with a grave financial crisis which, unless averted, would have brought this country to a state of industrial chaos. . . . I want to tell you . . . that a small cut in unemployment pay is now absolutely necessary in order to keep unemployment pay going at all.'[2]

Weekly benefit rates, except for children's allowances, were reduced by 10 per cent while the working man's insurance contribution was increased by 3d per week. 'Such further withdrawal of purchasing power,' one writer notes, 'was like treating an anaemic patient with leeches.'[3] A dual scheme of unemployment benefit was introduced and provided for benefit drawn as a right plus a secondary scheme of 'transitional payments' made only after a means test. Local Public Assistance Committees were empowered to question applicants as to their private resources in order to assess eligibility for relief. It was the introduction of the family means test that ultimately aroused the stern opposition of the unemployed.

Protest meetings were organized by the Durham Miners' Association throughout the coalfield during February 1933. At every meeting a resolution was unanimously carried calling for the abolition of the means test and for the government to institute a vigorous national works programme 'thus enabling the workless to have what they so earnestly desire, useful employment, in place of their present hopeless inactivity'.[4] Miners at Dawdon Colliery demanded a 48-hour stoppage of all pits throughout the coalfield in protest at the means

[1] *Ibid.*
[2] *Durham Chronicle*, 4 September 1931.
[3] C. Cross, 'The Slump', *The Observer*, 6 February 1966.
[4] *Durham Chronicle*, 24 February 1933.

test but were reprimanded by the Executive Committee for proposing actions which 'may do harm to our Association'.[1] Other workmen were more active in their protest. On 10 April 1933 over 1,000 unemployed men, mostly miners, marched to Durham and demanded entrance to the offices of the Ministry of Health Commissioners, from where the means test was being administered. When police attempted to disperse the crowd it was alleged that miners, armed with sticks and bottles, attacked them as a band played the 'Dead March'.[2]

It is indicative of the extent of distress amongst the mining community that the number of claims for benefit which were disallowed within the Durham Administrative County during the period 12 November 1931 to 20 February 1932, because the needs of the applicants did not justify payments being made, was the lowest on record throughout the country. Only 1·3 per cent of the total claims were disallowed and 90·4 per cent were granted the maximum rate of benefit.[3] During 1932 the Durham Public Assistance Committee became increasingly critical of the Government's insistence upon a full enquiry into the unemployed's resources and on 12 September decided to ignore Parliament's instructions.[4] The Durham County Council supported the Committee in its action and eventually the Minister of Labour was forced to appoint a Commissioner to administer the means test in the area.[5] The lack of alternative employment opportunities for displaced miners in Durham had already accentuated the worst features of the Unemployment Insurance legislation, especially with regard to the 'genuinely-seeking' work provisions, whilst the administration of the means test amongst families whose degree of poverty and destitution had already attracted national sympathy only added insult to injury.

The cuts in unemployment benefit imposed in 1931 were restored by the 1934 Unemployment Act. At the same time the Unemployment Assistance Board was established and superseded the local Public Assistance Committees as the administrator of 'transitional payments'. 'It was, in fact, the nationalization of assistance for the able-bodied.'[6] Local branches of the Board, working under central Government control, supervised unemployment payment in the localities in an effort to establish uniform principles and equality of

[1] D.M.A., 22 April 1933.
[2] *Durham Chronicle*, 14 April 1933, Cf. 277 H.C. Deb. 5s, 1677, 1841.
[3] 263 H.C. Deb. 5s, 891–2.
[4] *Durham Chronicle*, 14 October 1932.
[5] 269 H.C. Deb. 5s, 6. Labour Party, *The Iniquitous Means Test*, London 1933, p. 10.
[6] A. J. Youngson, *Britain's Economic Growth, 1920–1966*, London 1968, p. 130.

treatment throughout the country. The balancing of resources against a household's needs still remained a central part of the scheme.

Despite frequent alterations to the Unemployment Assistance Regulations it became painfully obvious to the miners after 1934 that the means test was to remain a permanent feature of the unemployment situation. The agitation amongst the Durham miners against the scheme became particularly intense during 1934-6. Watson, the Association's Unemployment Officer, continually denounced the effect of the means test in destroying the harmony of family life and in 1936 called upon all miners to seek its abolition.[1] In February 1935 representatives of 175 miners' Lodges, acting on behalf of over 122,000 Durham workmen, met in protest against the Government's treatment of the unemployed.[2] During the summer recess of Parliament in 1935 Lawther addressed a letter to all Northern M.P.s attacking the operation of the means test .'Feeling is high,' he wrote, 'and women are well nigh driven to desperation by your Government's action.'[3] Earlier in the year the Durham Miners' Association was pressed by three of its Lodges to seek the support of the M.F.G.B. and the T.U.C. in inaugurating a 48-hour 'down tools policy' in protest against the Government's 'degradation of the moral standard of our people'.[4]

Despite the miners' determined opposition towards the U.A.B. Regulations the agitation within the Durham coalfield did not attain the violence experienced in some other parts of the country.[5] The Association acted as a liaison between its members and the U.A.B., helping to remove any possible sources of conflict. During 1935, for example, it quickly intervened to prevent miners, wrongfully believing that lump-sum receipts of compensation reduced their future prospects of unemployment benefit, from dissipating their resources. Cases arose where miners spent as much as £200 in the course of a few weeks.[6]

---

[1] Durham Miners' Association, *An Examination of the New Draft Regulations Submitted by the Unemployment Assistance Board to the Minister of Labour*, 15 June 1936.
[2] *Durham Chronicle*, 1 March 1935.
[3] *Ibid.*, 16 August 1935.
[4] D.M.A., 27 April 1935.
[5] *Report of the Unemployment Assistance Board for the period ended 31 December 1935*, June 1936 (Cmd. 5177), p. 129. In its survey of the unemployed during the thirties the Pilgrim Trust frequently contrasted the Durham miners' determination to make the best of their condition with the self-pity and perpetual sense of grievance amongst workers elsewhere. Pilgrim Trust, *Men Without Work*, London 1938.
[6] *Ibid.*, p. 132.

The depression in the coal-exporting areas became the subject of detailed Government investigation during 1934. D. Euan Wallace, Civil Lord of the Admiralty, reported in November 1934 that in Durham and Tyneside 27·2 per cent of the total number of insured workers were unemployed on 4 June compared with 16·1 per cent in the country as a whole.[1] In towns in the south-western part of the Durham coalfield the situation was much worse. At Bishop Auckland on the same date 50·4 per cent of the insured workers were unemployed.[2] Such was the extent of the depression within the coalfield that Wallace claimed in January 1935:

'I regard the return to the land as being the best hope for the mining villages of Durham, both as an immediate and interim policy and as a long-term policy. I am certain that the future of a large part of Durham county . . . must be a return to some form of agriculture.'[3]

Following upon the Government's investigation Durham was scheduled as a Special Area under the 1934 Special Areas (Development and Improvement) Act. Under the Act two Commissioners were appointed, one for the depressed areas of England and Wales and another for Scotland, charged with the 'initiation, organization, prosecution and assistance of measures designed to facilitate the economic development and social improvement of the areas'. The Commissioners were, however, subject to the general supervision of the Minister of Labour and to a financial control as orthodox as in any Government department and their powers remained so restricted as to be of little long-term value. The reorganization of industry, the provision of large-scale transference schemes for surplus labour and aid towards the establishment of new industries were all outside their scope of activity.

In Durham a particular stimulus was given to the development of small agricultural holdings for the unemployed. With aid from the Special Areas Fund the Durham County Council provided men with working capital and instruction in cultivation methods and in the care of stock.[4] The first scheme was begun in May 1935 and provided for the settlement of 19 unemployed miners over an area of 95 acres at Mount Pleasant, Crook.[5] Financial assistance was also offered to

[1] *Reports of Investigations into the Industrial Conditions in Certain Depressed Areas*, 1934 (Cmd. 4728), p. 106.
[2] *Ibid.*, p. 116.
[3] *The Times*, 17 January 1935.
[4] *First Report of the Commissioner for the Special Areas*, July 1935 (Cmd. 4957), pp. 40–1; 102–3.
[5] *Ibid.*, p. 41.

the County Council to help support improvements in local amenities, over £15,900 having been granted by September 1937.[1]

The North-Eastern Trading Estates Company was incorporated in May 1936 to help foster the development of a government-sponsored trading estate in the Team Valley at Gateshead [2]—the first clearly recognizable step towards a direct policy of industrial development—but even by the end of 1937 plans to secure a more balanced industrial growth within the north-east were still very much in their infancy. Efforts were also made to assist the population of the ageing south-western part of the Durham coalfield where seams of coal were either exhausted or so nearly worked out that to win coal from them was no longer an economic proposition. In 1936 the South-West Durham Reconstruction and Development Board was established,[3] and in the following year an Improvement Association developed to help promote industrial growth within the area.[4]

Not all the improvements in aid of the unemployed within the Durham coalfield were the result of Government activity although the publicity given to the Special Areas was often directly responsible for initiating voluntary efforts elsewhere. Organized groups in the South of England, ranging from villages and counties to government employees, undertook to 'adopt' particular Durham mining villages and to distribute money, clothing and equipment to help relieve poverty and distress. As a result of an appeal initiated by the High Sheriff of Hertfordshire £16,580 was raised during December 1934 and March 1936 and used to finance occupational, poultry and allotment centres throughout the Durham coalfield.[5] Staff of the Home Office, Patent Office, Ministries of Agriculture, Health and Labour, the Exchequer and Audit, Post Office, and Board of Education undertook voluntarily to accept reductions from their salaries to help provide financial aid to mining families in Durham.[6]

The Community Service Council for Durham, an organization inspired by the National Council of Social Service, helped promote Social Service clubs throughout the coalfield in an effort to maintain the morale and self-respect of the miners by providing them with opportunities for useful work e.g. shoe-repairing and woodwork.[7]

[1] *Report of the Commissioner for the Special Areas in England and Wales for the Year ended 30 September 1937* (Cmd. 5595), p. 193.
[2] *Third Report of the Commissioner for the Special Areas (England and Wales)*, November 1936 (Cmd. 5303), pp. 39–41.
[3] Cmd. 5303, *op. cit.*, p. 45.
[4] Cmd. 5595, *op. cit.*, pp. 79–80.
[5] *The Times*, 13 December 1934; 3 April 1936.
[6] J. Newsom, *Out of the Pit*, Oxford 1936, pp. 85–6.
[7] *Ibid.*, pp. 79–83; *The Times*, 21 May 1934; 28 March 1936.

Miners and their wives promoted their own schemes of self-help. Unemployed miners at Thistleflat, near Crook, transformed a pit-heap into a children's playground, tennis court and bowling green during 1935 whilst their wives organized fund-raising activities to help finance the venture.[1] During 1933 workmen at Lambton Colliery organized a scheme of 'employment by rotation', believed to be the first of its kind in the country, whereby they agreed to work three out of every four weeks, their ranks being filled by the unemployed.[2]

Despite the efforts of the Government and the public at large the effects of long-term depression upon the miners and their families were still evident by the late 1930s. Referring to the various schemes of relief initiated on behalf of the unemployed a Durham miner commented in 1936:

'They have commissions and inquiries and all that but what happens? A few chaps get temporary work on sewage schemes and roads, about fifty out of ninety thousand have been settled in these land schemes in the south, a good many kids have gone off into domestic work, and as cheap labour for factories; these social service clubs provide a few with occupation and somewhere to forget their troubles—but they haven't begun to deal with the real problem. . . . Don't they see that while they sit gassing and exploring avenues and talking up in the air conditions are worsening and men getting driven harder and harder until they are afraid of going stark staring mad.'[3]

A miner from Crook, unemployed since 1927, recalled his experiences of the depression in a similar mood of despair:

'It's just over seven years since I was stood off and we've lived on about thirty-six bob during that time, that's me and the wife and the six kids. The rent's not bad, eight and six, but it's replacing breakages, clothing, extra nourishment for the kids and furniture that we find it difficult to get. I've a bit of an allotment that brings us potatoes and cabbages but we don't often get meat and as for fruit you just can't buy it. The worst thing of all is that you get used to it. At first I used to feel bitter and want to do something violent. I got books from the County Library, Socialist books and works on Economics. I read a lot about Russia and Communism and joined some demonstrations. But it leads to violence and you can't take risks with the authorities when you've a wife and kids. That's

[1] *Durham Chronicle*, 15 November 1935; *The Times*, 9 November 1935.
[2] *Durham Chronicle*, 20 March 1933.
[3] Newsom, *op. cit.*, p. 26.

what makes a lot of us only armchair revolutionaries. . . . I suppose if conditions worsened we might risk it . . . but as long as you've got the dole regular, well, you think twice before doing anything militant.'[1]

Reports from the Medical Officers in Durham helped substantiate the claim that the general industrial depression and the working of the means test had led to a serious impairment in the health of the unemployed.[2] The Medical Officer of the Durham County Society for the Prevention and Cure of Consumption reported to a meeting of the Society's governors in 1934 that 75 per cent of the children's cases admitted to the sanatorium originated, not from tuberculosis, but from starvation.[3]

Equally serious was the waste in human resources and loss of self-respect inflicted by enforced and continuing idleness. Hensley Henson, Bishop of Durham, in a sermon preached at Durham Cathedral in January 1929 warned against the inherent dangers of charity as a possible solution to unemployment the scale of which was 'wrecking the homes and rotting the characters of so vast a number of our people'.[4] A Durham miner's wife confessed in 1936:

'I don't know which is the biggest anxiety, my husband or the children. He's still under forty but feels that he's no more use, they haven't begun to live yet and if we have to stick on here they'll never know what life can be, but there must be something better than this. Someone said the other day that we oughtn't to have such large families and that it was our own fault if it brought suffering. I should like to ask him how we ought to stop it, birth control appliances cost money and even with them you can't be certain. On our money food must come first.'[5]

The reductions in transitional payment imposed by the Unemployment Assistance Board from November 1936 aroused fresh opposition from the miners. The Durham Miners' Association organized a series of mass demonstrations throughout the coalfield during August 1936 when the proposed reductions were first announced,[6] and later

[1] *Ibid.*, p. 20.
[2] W. Hannington, *The Problem of the Distressed Areas*, London 1937, p. 52.
[3] *Ibid.*
[4] *The Times*, 7 January 1929. Cf. H. Henson, 'The British Lazzaroni', *English Review*, July 1930.
[5] Newsom, *op. cit.*, p. 43. Cf. Cmd. 4728, *op. cit.*, p. 76; M. Robb, 'The Psychology of the Unemployed from the Medical Point of View', in H. L. Beales and R. S. Lambert (eds), *Memoirs of the Unemployed*, London 1934, pp. 273 87.
[6] D.M.A., 20, 27 July, 7 August 1936.

appealed to the M.F.G.B. to call a one-day strike in every coalfield as a token of the miners' opposition to the Government's unemployment policy.

Some compensations were won. Largely through the efforts of Watson, the Association's Unemployment Officer, particular classes of miners secured increased unemployment allowances in November 1937 on the basis of the rising cost of living. Watson urged local mining communities to prepare reasoned statements of their particular plight regarding rising prices and low incomes which the Association eventually used to buttress its own efforts to persuade the authorities to grant minor concessions.[1]

In spite of the effects of trade improvement and armaments orders from 1937 onwards an enormous volume and degree of unemployment persisted in the Durham coalfield. This was due largely to the fact that even if the coal industry returned to full activity the loss of markets incurred and the degree of rationalization and mechanization already attained made it virtually impossible to absorb the large numbers of unemployed. Even in 1931 it had been estimated that a permanent surplus of 64,000 male insured workers for whom work could not be found would remain in the North-East coast area even if trade was restored to its 1929 level.[2] The situation remained particularly bad in the south-western part of the coalfield and affected most those elderly miners whose chances of re-employment after the thirties were very slim. Thus on 15 March 1937 the percentage unemployed amongst all insured persons in Bishop Auckland and Shildon, mining villages in south-west Durham, stood at 39·5 per cent and 38·8 per cent respectively.[3] In Durham and Tyneside alone during March 1937 24 per cent of the total number of workmen unemployed for three months or more were miners, the largest proportion of whom were between the ages of 55 and 64.[4]

III

In addition to the hardships of low wages and long-term unemployment the miners suffered during the inter-war years from a shortage of

[1] Durham Miners' Association, *A Prepared Statement . . . . to Seek Higher Unemployment Benefit Scales and Unemployment Assistance Board Allowances because of the Rising Cost of Living*, Samuel Watson, Unemployment Officer, D.M.A., September 1937.
[2] N.E. Industrial Survey, *op. cit.*, p. 121.
[3] *Durham and the North East Coast. Report of the Labour Party's Commission of Enquiry into the Distressed Areas*, April 1937, p. 4.
[4] D.M.A., 3 September 1937.

good-quality housing. The conditions within the Durham coalfield proved to be amongst the worst in the country. The cessation of building during the First World War caused serious shortages. It was estimated that over 46,000 houses were needed in Durham County in 1918 and still over 30,000 by 1925.[1]

The Durham miners' officials took an active interest in urging both national and local authorities to improve housing conditions within the coalfield. At a gathering of trade-union and co-operative societies' representatives on 20 July 1918 Robson and Cann urged the Government to take legislative action to make the preparation of house building and improvement plans obligatory upon all local authorities.[2] The Housing Act passed in the following year required the local authorities to survey the housing needs of their districts and, with the aid of national subsidies, to carry out building schemes accordingly. The situation improved only very slowly. Peter Lee reported to the M.F.G.B. in 1922 on the Durham housing situation:

'I have no hesitation in saying it is one of the worst districts in Britain as far as housing is concerned. . . . The local bodies in our County have attempted to do something so far as houses are concerned . . . but owing to the high cost of production the rents are very, very high.'[3]

Overcrowding was a serious problem. In certain mining villages in Durham in 1919 four out of every ten persons were living in overcrowded conditions, i.e. more than two in a room compared with only one in ten for the country as a whole.[4] Even in 1936 Durham ranked as the County with the highest percentage of working-class families over crowded in the country according to the standards laid down in the 1935 Housing Act. The incidence of overcrowding, by no means the worst, reached 8–10 per cent in the predominantly mining area of the Seaham Harbour Urban District and the Durham and Easington Rural Districts.[5]

With overcrowding went insanitary conditions. T. Eustace Hill, Medical Officer of Health in Durham, reported in November 1921 that in one colliery area he visited liquid excreta ran from the doors

[1] *Durham Chronicle*, 5 December 1925.
[2] *Ibid.*, 26 July 1918.
[3] M.F.G.B., 18 July 1922; Cf. Coal Industry Commission, 1919, II, QQ. 14,252; 14,261.
[4] Coal Industry Commission, 1919, I, Q. 8837. Cf. A. L. Bowley and M. H. Hogg, *Has Poverty Diminished?*, London 1925, pp. 170–1.
[5] Ministry of Health, *Housing Act, 1935. Report on the Overcrowding Survey in England and Wales*, 1936, pp. xviii, 9.

of ash-closets into the back street. 'Outside one house is a miniature cesspool round which young people play,' he noted. 'The houses are intended for two tenants, but there are three or four in most of them, and in one house there are eighteen people.'[1]

The miners were quick to blame the coal owners for the conditions which existed. The provision of free colliery housing or a rent allowance to those miners in private houses, both long-established customs in the Durham coalfield, helped to perpetuate the worst evils of the housing problem, they claimed, and reduced the local authorities' sense of responsibility towards providing and maintaining more houses. This accusation was not new. The Report of the Land Enquiry Committee noted in 1914 that in Durham mining villages 'there is a definite relation between the "free house" system . . . on the one hand, and overcrowding and insanitation on the other'.[2] Furthermore the wide discrepancy between the rent allowance awarded by colliery companies and the rent actually paid by miners created 'many evils', the most serious of which was that:

'There are always applications from men living in "rented" houses for the tenancy of a free colliery house, however old and worn out it may be. The proximity to the pit of the "free house" is one factor in this demand; but without doubt the principal factor is the desire to avoid the expenditure on rent of any part of the wage earned.'[3]

In a speech at Burnopfield in June 1919 Batey described the system of rent allowance as a 'huge blunder' since it was 'an encouragement to the owners to allow men to live in private houses, pay them a small rent, and escape their responsibility of providing houses for their own workmen'.[4] A correspondent of *The Times*, investigating the conditions in the Durham coalfield in 1928, wrote:

'The colliery house system . . . has merits, but it must be held largely responsible for the tradition of overcrowding . . . because families that could afford to pay rent for more adequate accommodation are tempted to remain where they can live for nothing and the will to progress is subtly stifled.'[5]

So long as houses were scarce and Council house rents high few miners were prepared to refuse the offer of a free colliery house. In

---

[1] *Durham Chronicle*, 11 November 1921.
[2] *The Land: The Report of the Land Enquiry Committee, Volume 11: Urban*, London 1914, p. 197.
[3] *Ibid.*, p. 199.
[4] *Durham Chronicle*, 6 June 1919.
[5] *The Times*, 11 September 1928; Bowley and Hogg, *op. cit.*, pp. 180–1; Cmd. 4728, *op. cit.*, p. 103.

1925 out of a total number of 147,022 miners employed in the Durham coalfield 54,639 received a rent allowance of 10d or 11d per shift. During the same year 48,942 houses were provided free to miners by, or on behalf of, colliery owners in Durham compared with a total of 67,150 for England and Wales as a whole.[1]

The coal owners were also accused of delaying capital expenditure for the provision of houses immediately after the First World War in face of the threatened nationalization of the mines. A number of owners and their representatives confessed to this although it is difficult to assess whether or not their estimates of the housing losses thus involved were made simply to discredit the notion of mines nationalization. J. Prest, General Manager of Horden Collieries Ltd, told the Sankey Commission that the Company had abandoned plans to spend about £275,000 in building an additional 600 houses at their colliery at Blackhall for fear of State ownership of the mines.[2]

Whatever factors were involved in influencing the rate of house-building in the short run there was still a great scope for the improvement of existing colliery houses. In July 1919 representatives of the County Council of Durham, headed by their Chairman, Peter Lee, and of the Local Sanitary Authorities met representatives of the Durham Coal Owners' Association and urged upon them the necessity for the coal owners to augment the work of Local Authorities in mining villages in improving existing houses. The Owners' Association replied that it had 'no power to make any arrangements on behalf of any of its members in connection with housing conditions' and expressed 'very much sympathy with the desire for improvement in the condition of dwelling houses for the miners'. It agreed, however, to recommend that 'every endeavour should be made to improve or replace, where necessary, houses which are not in satisfactory condition'.[3]

Conditions were slow to improve. During the period 1919–25 only 47 houses let at a rental were built by, or on behalf of, colliery companies in Durham.[4] During a tour of mining villages in Durham in 1924 one investigator wrote:

'In the mining villages of Ludworth and Haswell I saw no homes which were really fit for habitation but their defects were increased

[1] R.C. on Coal Industry, 1925, III, Appendix 18, Tables III, V, pp. 248–9.
[2] Coal Industry Commission, 1919, II, Q. 27,202.
[3] Durham Coal Owners' Association, *Annual Report*, 1919, pp. 51–3.
[4] R.C. on Coal Industry, 1925, III, Appendix 18, Table IV, p. 249. Cf. P. H. White, 'Some Aspects of Urban Development by Colliery Companies, 1919–39', *Manchester School of Economic and Social Studies*, XXIII, 3, September 1955, pp. 271–2.

by overcrowding. The pleasantest block of dwellings was that most remote from the slag-heap, from which the cinders and fine ash seemed to percolate into every door and window.'[1]

At Haswell nearly all the houses were reported to be 'dilapidated and falling to pieces'.[2] In 1925 the Samuel Commission, on the basis of the evidence of district Medical Officers of Health, reported:

'The condition of housing in Northumberland and Durham would appear to be bad. In Stanley and Hetton large numbers of houses are shown as being not necessarily fit for human habitation.'[3]

Houses at Framwellgate were described by the contemporary novelist Joan Conquest as 'evil-smelling infested rookeries'.[4] Even in 1934 *The Times* reported that in Durham:

'Housing conditions have remained as they were. Overcrowding, though mitigated by council houses and a falling birth rate, is still worse than in any other county in England.'[5]

Despite the magnitude of the housing problem local efforts were made to alleviate the situation in particular mining villages. In 1923 the South Hetton Coal Company inaugurated a scheme whereby its employees could become house owners. The Company supplied each interested workman with a freehold site and met all building and legal costs. A mortgage secured on the land and building was given to the Company by each purchaser who, in turn, could claim a joint subsidy from the Government and the local authority to the value of £89 per house. Each purchaser authorized the Company to deduct not less than 7s per week from his wages in repayment of the principal and interest on the money advanced. 159 homes were originally erected at South Hetton and an additional 153 were built later at the Company's Murton Colliery. The 1926 stoppage depleted the company's liquid assets and reduced the rate of building. The scheme aroused interest throughout the County and on the Continent. The Durham Miners' Association left the matter of purchasing houses

---

[1] *Coal and Power: the Report of an Enquiry presided over by D. Lloyd George,* London 1924, p. 130.
[2] *Ibid.*
[3] R.C. on Coal Industry, 1925, III, Appendix 35, p. 330.
[4] *Durham Chronicle,* 1 September 1933. See also *New Statesman,* 31 December 1927. B. S. Townroe, *The Slum Problem,* London 1928, p. 179; 'A National Disgrace: Plight of Miners' Houses', a report by a member of the Committee of the Winter Distress League, London, *Review of Reviews,* 470, 15 March 1929, pp. 201–3.
[5] *The Times,* 20 March 1934.

under the scheme to the individual discretion of miners in the districts concerned.[1]

The gradual impoverishment of local authorities during the long period of industrial depression prevented many of them from making the contribution from rates which the 1930 Housing Act determined to be a necessary prerequisite to receiving a housing subsidy from the Exchequer. With the aid of the Commissioner for the Special Areas, however, the North-East Housing Association was established in December 1935. This body was able to draw upon the Special Areas Fund to provide local authorities with the resources necessary to meet their housing obligations without making a charge upon the rates.[2] By September 1937 over 6,000 houses had been completed or reached near-completion under the scheme at an estimated saving in contributions from rates of over £400,000.[3]

The provision of free houses to superannuated miners had been undertaken by the Durham Aged Mineworkers' Homes Association since 1894. The movement developed under the inspiration of Joseph Hopper, born at Windy Nook in County Durham in May 1856 and supplied its first homes at Haswell Moor in October 1899.[4] Lord Joicey, a prominent coal owner in Durham, decribed the work of the Aged Homes Association as 'the most philanthropic done by any body of workmen.'[5]

The movement relied upon the voluntary contributions of workmen, coal owners, private individuals and organizations to help finance its work. Building activity was maintained until 1917 when the cost of materials finally proved prohibitive but was resumed in 1920. J. Adair, Secretary of the Association, reported during that year that 'there is a greater desire than ever to erect Homes for the Aged People in the Mine-Working Community'.[6]

---

[1] J. H. B. Forster ,'Model Homes for Mineworkers' Families' in *Daily Telegraph*, special supplement, 'The British Coal Mining Industry', 16 September 1930, p. 60; *Durham Chronicle*, 12 October, 1 December 1923; 16 August 1924; 3 October 1930; *The Times*, 11 September 1928; D.M.A., 24 November 1923.
[2] *Second Report of the Commissioner for the Special Areas (England and Wales)*, 1936 (Cmd. 5090), pp. 45–6.
[3] Cmd. 5595, *op. cit.*, p. 135. The housing situation between the wars in the Easington Rural District, a predominantly mining area, is described by W. A. Moyes, *Mostly Mining*, Newcastle-upon-Tyne, 1969, Chapter 11.
[4] For a full account of the early development of the Aged Mine Workers' Homes Association see J. Oxberry, *The Birth of the Movement: A Tribute to the Memory of Joseph Hopper*, Gateshead District Aged Mineworkers' Homes, 29 November 1924.
[5] Durham Aged Mineworkers' Homes Association, *16th Annual Report . . . for the Year Ended 31 December 1914*, p. 68.
[6] *Ibid.*, *22nd Annual Report . . . for the Year Ended 31st December 1920*, p. 1.

The Durham miners remained loyal to the movement throughout the difficult years of depression and continued to make their contributions even during periods of industrial dispute. The local coal owners were equally sympathetic. During 1920 Pease and Partners set aside £15,000 to build homes for disabled soldiers and sailors which afterwards were to be converted to become homes for aged mineworkers. In 1925 the Consett Iron Company undertook to meet the total cost of payments to workmen and contractors involved in erecting 40 aged miners' homes.[1]

Despite the encouragment given to the movement from various quarters it remained in financial difficulty for most of the 1920s. Finance proved the only major obstacle towards increasing the scope of building activity. In 1921 and 1922 the D.A.M.H.A. was forced to realize some of its National War Bonds in order to enable it to meet the liabilities incurred in building new homes.[2] A suggestion that all miners' Lodges should adopt contributions of 1d per week per member from 1923 failed to elicit much response.[3] By the end of 1927 the bank overdraft of the Aged Mineworkers' Homes Association had risen to over £32,500 but, as a result of a 'Million Shillings Fund Appeal' launched in March 1929, over £22,472 was collected from a multitude of sources to help restore finances.[4] The Fund closed in September 1933 and although it had failed to achieve its ultimate objective it allowed the D.A.M.H.A. to secure a credit balance at the end of 1932 amounting to £3,773.[5] The *Durham Chronicle* described the community's support for the movement as 'one of the most remarkable features of the social effort of the mining community in the County'.[6]

By the end of 1925 a total of over 1,200 houses had been erected throughout the coalfield,[7] and by mid-1930 the number had increased to 1,800.[8] Until 1930 the vast majority of the houses built by the D.A.M.H.A. were financed from its own resources but thereafter contributions were made available either from the Exchequer or, in exceptional cases, from the Special Areas Fund.[9] The achievements of

[1] *Ibid.*, p. 2.
[2] *Ibid., 24th Annual Report . . . for the Year Ended 31 December 1922*, p. 13.
[3] *Ibid., 25th Annual Report . . . for the Year Ended 31 December 1923*, p. 13.
[4] *Summary of Contributions to Durham Aged Mine Workers' Homes Association Million Shillings Fund*, Pelaw-on-Tyne, 1934, p. 4.
[5] Durham Aged Mineworkers' Association, *34th Annual Report . . . for the Year Ended 31 December 1932*, p. 11.
[6] *Durham Chronicle*, 1 June 1934.
[7] *Ibid.*, 17 October 1925.
[8] *Ibid.*, 13 June 1930.
[9] Cmd. 5090, *op. cit.*, pp. 46–7; Cmd. 5303, *op. cit.*, p. 94; Cmd. 5595, *op. cit.*, p. 136.

the Aged Mineworkers' Homes movement received widespread publicity. During a visit to Durham in January 1930 S. Lawrence, Under-Secretary to the Ministry of Health, claimed:

'There is not a working class organization in England and Wales that has done anything comparable to the miners' associations up and down the country for the housing of old people. Of all counties Durham leads the way. . . . When it comes to housing of the old folk, Durham has a great deal to teach not only London but England and the world.'[1]

The extent of the support given to the movement within Durham can be judged from the total amounts of money subscribed to the D.A.M.H.A. between 1919 and 1939. The total contribution made by private individuals and organizations and the coal owners together amounted during this period to £20,098 compared with £419,781 contributed by the workmen themselves.[2]

IV

The implementation in 1920 of the Sankey Commission's recommendation that there should be a welfare levy of 1d per ton of coal output resulted in a substantial improvement in the provision of amenities in colliery areas. The levy, originally imposed for a period of five years, continued in varying amounts throughout the inter-war years and was augmented in 1927 by a 1s levy in the £ on coal royalties. The levy on output was reduced to $\frac{1}{2}$d per ton in 1934 but restored to its original amount in 1939.

The Miners' Welfare Fund, the first and only statutory provision for the social welfare of workers in any industry, was administered by a Central Committee appointed by the Board of Trade and consisted of representatives of the miners and coal owners together with independent members. W. P. Richardson joined the Committee as a M.F.G.B. representative in 1926, Lee in 1932 and Lawther in 1934. Ad hoc joint committees representing local coal owners and miners were established in the districts to help administer the scheme. In Durham the District Welfare Committee, which first met in April 1922, was composed of T. Taylor, President of the Durham Coal Owners' Association as Chairman, W. B. Charlton, Chairman of the County Federation Board as Vice-Chairman and Guthrie and Robson as joint secretaries.

---

[1] *Durham Chronicle*, 24 January 1930.
[2] Durham Aged Mineworkers' Homes Association, *Annual Reports*, 1919–39.

Since the welfare levy was originally imposed for only five years the Durham District Welfare Committee decided in 1922 to retain two-fifths of its allocation from the Central Committee for 'general County purposes' so as to prove that 'at least some portion of it has been spent upon something of a County character, to which we could direct the attention of the public and the Government in urging our claim for the renewal of the contribution'.[1] The remaining three-fifths was to be spent on local schemes arranged between management and workmen throughout the coalfield. Contributions from the Welfare Fund were meant to defray the capital cost of any proposed scheme, the maintenance of which was the responsibility of the district committee. In 1925, when the welfare levy was renewed, the Durham District Committee increased the proportion of the Central Committee allocation devoted to 'County purposes' to four-fifths and reduced that of district use to one-fifth.[2]

The Miners' Welfare Fund helped reduce the coal owners' responsibility for providing such amenities as workmen's institutes and medical and nursing services and as such gained their ready support. Some colliery companies in Durham openly encouraged the workmen's participation in the welfare schemes and offered to help reduce overhead charges by a free gift of land or by promising an annual contribution towards meeting running expenses.[3]

A large part of the expenditure in Durham during the early years of the Welfare scheme was devoted to providing recreational facilities. Robson, reviewing the situation up to 1928, wrote:

'Some of the schemes sent forward were too ambitious, the estimated expenditure being far in excess of the amount they were likely to receive from the Fund. Others were of a character entirely outside the spirit and meaning of Welfare work. . . . We find that Recreation Grounds . . . have found great favour. . . . Institutes and Memorial Halls of a splendid and commodious type, catering for all indoor, and providing much needed meeting places for the villages, have been erected in many parts.'[4]

By the end of 1939, 154 recreation schemes had been developed throughout the coalfield including 33 combined institutes and halls, 85 recreation grounds and an enclosed swimming bath.[5] Despite the

[1] D.M.A., 31 May 1922; *Durham Chronicle*, 22 June 1923; Durham Coal Owners' Association, *Annual Report*, 1922, pp. 30–2.
[2] D.M.A., 20, 28 April 1925.
[3] Durham Miners' Association, *Report on the Miners' Welfare Fund*, February 1928, p. 5.
[4] *Ibid.*, pp. 5–6.
[5] *Miners' Welfare 1939, Annual Report of the Miners' Welfare Commission*, p. 47.

increasing opportunities such welfare schemes provided for social
intercourse within the mining villages they were not without their
critics. G. Salisbury, Vicar of Eppleton, wrote in his parish magazine
in 1931:

'Enormous sums of money are being spent on welfare schemes in
mining areas. They provide very cheap and satisfactory forms of
amusement for the butcher, the baker and the candlestick maker—
they do not . . . appear to make any great appeal to the miners
themselves. Institutes are erected with little or no organized social
or intellectual life in them. They become mere reading-cum-billiard
rooms, and like so many other rooms of the kind, under lax management, may degenerate into miners' casinos for the playing of "pink"
and "live" pool and other gambling games. So they may become
a demoralizing rather than a healthy factor in the life of the
miner.'[1]

To counteract such possibilities Salisbury advocated that lecturers
should be appointed to visit welfare institutes and that extra resources
be allocated to 'local organizations aimed at the higher interest of
the miner'.[2]

The provision of pit-head baths in Durham, potentially less
dangerous, was one of the most welcome features of the Miners'
Welfare Scheme. Under the Coal Mines Act 1911 colliery proprietors
had been required to provide pit-head baths only if a two-thirds
majority of the workmen demanded them. At the time the welfare
levy began there were no such facilities in either the Durham or
Northumberland coalfields.[3] Plans had been formulated during 1919
for building pit-head baths at Burnhope Colliery but were abandoned
owing to the 'unsettled state of the coal trade'.[4] 'It is a curious thing
that in a large mining County like ours an experiment of this kind has
not been made,' Robson wrote in 1922. 'On the very surface of it the
advantage must be very great to any locality; and the extent to which
it will relieve our womenfolk of the hard drudgery work in the homes
must be obvious.'[5] Not everyone agreed. Baron Gainford of Headlam,
Vice-Chairman of Pease and Partners, whilst not opposed to the
provision of pit-head baths, doubted even if the miners themselves
wanted them. In evidence before the Sankey Commission he claimed:

[1] *Durham Chronicle*, 4 September 1931.
[2] *Ibid.*
[3] Coal Industry Commission, 1919, III, Appendix 65, p. 198; R.C. on Coal
Industry, 1925, III, Appendix II, p. 89.
[4] *Durham Chronicle*, 27 June 1919.
[5] D.M.A., 31 May 1922. Cf. *Durham Chronicle*, 27 April 1923.

'Where men are exposed to all kinds of inclement weather they would much sooner go home than they would walk long distances in their dry clothes, which they have had put on at the pit-head, and then walk home in rain and sleet and snow, and reach home in their ordinary clothes, and leave their pit clothes behind them.'[1]

The majority of the pit-head baths eventually erected in Durham, except the first, benefited from the special fund created for the purpose by the Mining Industry Act, 1926. A levy of 1s in every £ of royalties derived from coal provided the bulk of the finance for the 31 pit-head baths built in the Durham coalfield by the end of 1939. The first baths to be installed at a Durham pit were opened on 5 February 1927 at Boldon Colliery. They were financed largely from the District Welfare Fund although contributions from the workers and the coal owners allowed the baths to open free of debt.[2] The first baths to be built by the Central Welfare Committee in Durham were opened at Mainsforth on 6 July 1929, as the last of the four experimental schemes to be started under the terms of the Mining Industry Act, 1926.[3] 'Pit head baths have revolutionized our village life,' Robson claimed at New Herrington in June 1932. 'To observe the men returning from their work dressed in their ordinary garb has changed the whole of our outlook and has given a social standing to the miners never previously dreamed of.'[4]

V

One feature of the social life of the Durham miner which remained unaltered by and large throughout the inter-war period was the annual miners' demonstration in Durham city. Commonly known as the 'Miners' Gala' or the 'Big Meeting' it was first held at Wharton's Park in Durham on 12 August 1871 when the Durham Miners' Association was almost two years old but still without official headquarters. The meeting was a demonstration of solidarity and a token of faith in the benefits which the miners believed could be achieved by combined action. When, after the interval of the First World War, the Gala was restarted in July 1919 it bore many of its old characteristics. Thousands of miners and their families thronged into Durham

[1] Coal Industry Commission, 1919, II, Q. 20,745.
[2] *Durham Chronicle*, 12 February 1927.
[3] Mines Department, *Miners' Welfare Fund, Sixth Report of the Committee Appointed by the Board of Trade to Allocate the Fund*, 1927, p. 24; D.M.A., 1 July 1929; *Durham Chronicle*, 12 July 1929.
[4] *Durham Chronicle*, 3 June 1932.

City to the sound of brass bands amidst a colourful array of colliery banners. After 1919 the annual demonstration became the means not merely for educating the miners as to the conditions within their own coalfield but of providing an opportunity for leading political figures to comment upon the national issues facing the coal industry as a whole. Among those invited to address the crowds were Ernest Bevin, Philip Snowden, George Lansbury, Ramsay Mac-Donald, Emanuel Shinwell, Oswald Mosley, Ellen Wilkinson, Arthur Greenwood, Clement Attlee, Stafford Cripps, Herbert Morrison, Harold Laski and Aneurin Bevan. The annual Gala was abandoned three times during the inter-war period: in 1921 owing to the national lock-out, in 1922 because of industrial depression and in 1926 owing to the national stoppage.

Even throughout the years of depression the miners remained steadfastly loyal to their tradition of demonstrating their solidarity and determination to better their condition. Often the gatherings offered little more than the hope of future prosperity but they helped remind each miner and his family of a common cause and of the strength that lay in unity.

Within the colliery villages the facilities for entertainment and recreation increased during the inter-war period. The coming of the cinema and the development of omnibus services helped relieve the tedium of colliery life. The Durham miners' leaders continued to encourage the coal owners to provide sporting facilities. Canvassing the owners' support for a football club in Durham City, Trotter claimed in 1920: 'There could not be a finer antidote to the prevailing unrest than the giving to the working classes full, free and unfettered opportunity of having their periods of relaxation at the end of their week of toil.'[1]

In addition to the relief provided in the depressed coal-exporting areas by schemes such as the Lord Mayor's Fund,[2] efforts were made to develop recreative work. In many parts of the Durham, Northumberland and South Wales coalfields the need for something to break the dullness associated with prolonged inactivity and privation proved hardly less urgent than the need for material relief. In 1929 the Carnegie United Kingdom Trustees allocated £5,000 to this form of work in those areas and a Distressed Coalfields Committee was established in London.

Robson joined the local committee established for the Durham and Northumberland region and helped organize the various educational

[1] *Durham Chronicle*, 21 May 1920.
[2] See above, pp. 276–8.

and musical activities provided by the scheme.[1] Such developments were further encouraged during the 1930s by the first Commissioner for the Special Areas through the auspices of the National Council of Social Service.[2] Adolescent welfare schemes were developed in mining areas and occupational clubs established, providing facilities for musical, choral and dramatic work, dressmaking, cookery and 'keep-fit' classes.[3]

The Durham Miners' Association had long recognized the importance of education for the benefit of its members and miners' movement as a whole,[4] and continued to promote its development after 1919. The north-eastern branch of the Workers' Educational Association had been established in 1909 and in 1911 joined the University of Durham in providing tutorial classes throughout the coalfield. The miners' union helped finance the work of the W.E.A. in the County,[5] and worked in close co-operation with the County Education Authority in promoting the development of adult educational facilities in colliery villages. A review of the adult education movement within the coalfield during the 1920s has concluded that the miners were 'the backbone of the Movement, both as students (exactly one-third of tutorial class students in 1924 were colliery workers) and as County Council representatives in helping to finance classes when they were organized'.[6]

The Association was particularly intent on extending the educational opportunities available to its younger members. In 1932 it organized a series of examinations throughout the Lodges as a means of selecting four miners to attend the Central Labour College for two years.[7] In August 1937, 18 young miners enjoyed a fortnight's expenses-paid holiday at the Workers' Travel Association Pannell Ash College, Harrogate after winning an essay competition promoted by their union. The success of the venture led the Association to encourage similar efforts at a local level in order to capture the enthusiasm for education shown by the younger members.[8] 'By doing so,' the union's Executive Committee claimed, 'you are not only

[1] *Report on the Activities of the Northern Committee of the Distressed Coalfields Committee under the National Council of Social Service*, 1929–33. T.U.C. Library, Congress House; *Durham Chronicle*, 3 May 1929.
[2] Cmd. 4957, *op. cit.*, pp. 53–4; Cmd. 5090, *op. cit.*, pp. 82–3.
[3] Cmd. 5303, *op. cit.*, pp. 139–45.
[4] Welbourne, *op. cit.*, pp. 204–5.
[5] D.M.A., 15 March 1919; 29 May 1920; 26 June 1931.
[6] *Workers' Educational Association, Northern District, 1903–1953, Jubilee Brochure*, 1953, p. 14.
[7] D.M.A., 24 November 1923; 28 May 1924.
[8] *Ibid.*, 20 May, 7 July 1937.

helping these young men but also strengthening the base of our movement.'[1] Following a conference of Durham miners' Lodge delegates
at Herrington in January 1938 a scheme was adopted for the publication of a monthly newspaper to provide scope for news coverage at
local collieries. The *Durham Miners' Monthly Journal* was issued
during the summer of 1938 and sold at 1d per copy.[2]

The imposition of a longer working day throughout the coalfield in
1926 aroused severe criticism from miners and educationalists alike
since it reduced the working man's leisure time and opportunity to
seek further education. Although shift-working was not new the
effects of the reorganization of working conditions upon social life
in the mining villages served to emphasize the worst effects of the 1926
defeat. 'Evening classes on Industrial History, Mathematics and
Ambulance have all been knocked on the head,' a Quarrington Hill
miner wrote in 1927. 'These hours and terms are the most inhuman . . .
ever imposed on any body of men.'[3] J. Batey, M.P. for Spennymoor,
expressed similar concern in the House of Commons in February 1927:

'Those bad employers have done everything they possibly can to
degrade and push down our men. They have taken the opportunity
of destroying the social conditions in our colliery villages. Where
we had a second shift of workmen prior to the dispute ceasing work
at 4 o'clock, those men cannot now cease work before 9 o'clock at
night. That prevents the younger man in the villages from attending
religious, political or educational classes, and is destroying the whole
social life of the villages and making the life of the miners' wife that
of a complete drudge from morning until late at night.'[4]

The establishment of the Miners' Welfare Fund helped extend the
educational facilities available to miners and their children. The
Durham District Welfare Committee approached the local branch of
the W.E.A. in 1928 and began negotiations towards providing a
series of non-vocational lectures in the various mining villages.[5]
Under the terms of the Miners' Welfare National Scholarship scheme
assistance was provided for miners' children to attend university.
The District Welfare Committee in Durham undertook in 1928 to
make special grants to deserving candidates and in 1938[6] established

[1] *Durham Chronicle*, 17 September 1937.
[2] *Ibid.*, 28 January, 18 March 1938.
[3] *Miner*, 8 January 1927.
[4] 202 H.C. Deb. 5s, 187. Cf. *Colliery Guardian*, 17, 31 December 1926; *Durham Chronicle*, 11 December 1926.
[5] Durham Miners' Association, *Report on the Miners' Welfare Fund*, February 1928, p. 8.
[6] D.M.A., 7 March 1928.

a local university scholarship scheme. One scholarship valued at £150 per annum became available for providing a three-year course in mining at King's College, Newcastle, part of the University of Durham.[1]

The development of technical education was similarly provided for by the miners' welfare scheme but was largely neglected in Durham. Before the establishment of the Welfare Fund the Education Committee of the Durham County Council, of which J. Lawson and J. Gilliland were members, had held discussions with representatives of the Durham Coal Owners' Association on the proposed establishment of a mining college in the County.[2] Nevertheless, despite the financial support which became available in 1920, no real progress was made by the County education authority during the inter-war period. In 1925 it applied to the Central Welfare Committee for a grant to help establish three senior centres for mining education,[3] but even by 1939 nothing had been done towards completing the project. When war broke out the grants which had then been promised to provide advanced mining centres were suspended in view of the retriction on building activity.[4]

More progress was made by the local university authorities. With assistance from both the Central and Northumberland District Welfare Committees a new mining department was opened at Armstrong College at Newcastle by the Prince of Wales in May 1929. Armstrong College, itself the oldest mining school in the country dating back to 1837,[5] formed part of the University of Durham. The new department provided a general laboratory and supported a Research Board for the purpose of investigating the physical and chemical properties of the coal seams in Durham and Northumberland.[6] The development of the new mining centre encouraged further educational activities. During 1929 Saturday afternoon lecture courses were organized for colliery officials in the north-eastern coalfield.[7] The growing interest in mining education led eventually to the establishment of the County of Durham Mining Society in May 1931

---

[1] *Miners' Welfare 1938, Annual Report of the Miners' Welfare Committee*, p. 45
[2] Durham Coal Owners' Association, *Annual Report*, 1920, pp. 58–9; *Northern Echo*, 31 July 1919.
[3] Mines Department, *Miners' Welfare Fund, Fourth Report*, 1925, p. 31; D.M.A., 22, 30 April 1925.
[4] *Miners' Welfare in War Time, Report of the Miners' Welfare Committee for 6½ years to June 30 1946*, p. 59.
[5] *Iron and Coal Trades Review*, 17 May 1929.
[6] Mines Department, *Miners' Welfare Fund, Eighth Report*, 1929, p. 17, Appendix IX, p. 48.
[7] *Reports of H.M. Inspectors of Mines (Northern Division)*, 1929, p. 53.

which aimed to foster lecture courses and discussions on all branches of mining technique and organization.[1]

VI

Owing to the particularly dangerous nature of the miners' calling the Durham Miners' Association was ever ready to support developments aimed at reducing accidents in the mine. Falls of roof, shaft accidents and coal dust explosions remained a constant threat to life and limb. The proportion of deaths and serious injuries per 100,000 manshifts worked in the northern area[2] caused by falls of roof remained below the national average during the inter-war period,[3] due in large part to the extended use of steel props, the low rate of mechanization[4] and the regular inspection of collieries by workmen's representatives.[5]

The need for more adequate support of working places was stressed by the Northern Division's Mines Inspector in 1922 and again in 1926. As the advantages of steel props and arches, by way of increased strength and resistance to atmospheric agencies, began to outweigh those of timber, more and more collieries brought them into use. In 1930 the Divisional Mines Inspector reported:

'At one colliery no less than 2,120 yards of roadway was supported with steel arches. . . . At this colliery arches erected 4 and 5 years ago in very faulty ground have not required repairing service, and the Manager is convinced that the usual props and girders would have resulted in heavy falls of ground.'[6]

By 1937, 28,982 steel props were in use at the working face throughout the Northern Division and almost one-third of all roadways fitted with steel supports.[7] Following an investigation by the Support of Working in Mines Committee into the support of underground working in Durham, Northumberland and Cumberland in 1930, the North of England Institute of Mining and Mechanical Engineers

---

[1] *Ibid.*, 1931, p. 59.
[2] Defined by H.M. Inspector of Mines to include Northumberland, Durham, Cumberland, Westmorland, North Riding of County of York.
[3] R.C. on Safety in Coal Mines, 1938 (Cmd. 5890), III, Minutes of Evidence, Q. 27,063.
[4] See Chapter I, pp. 52–4.
[5] See below, p. 304.
[6] *Reports of H.M. Inspectors of Mines (Northern Division)*, 1930, p. 21.
[7] *Ibid.*, 1937, p. 37.

began a systematic study of the means of preventing accidents from falls of ground which lasted throughout the 1930s.[1]

The adoption of stone-dusting as a means of preventing the ignition of coal dust was made obligatory in all mines by the Home Secretary during 1920-1 and received wide publicity through the Safety in Mines Research Board. The Board organized a special train in 1923 to take miners from Durham at a reduced fare to the Home Office's miniature mine at Eskmeals in Cumberland to witness experiments on coal-dust explosions.[2] The Durham Miners' Association purchased a film of the experiments in October 1923 and circulated it throughout the colliery areas.[3]

The danger from shaft accidents was emphasized in 1923 following an accident in the Busty Shaft at Medomsley Colliery in the Durham coalfield. Eight men were accidentally killed by falling out of an ascending cage when one or more of the cage shoes broke dislodging the cage from its guides.[4] In view of the conflicting evidence presented to the Coroner's inquiry at Consett early in March 1923, the Durham Miners' Association called for a public enquiry into the accident.[5] During the course of the enquiry, held during 20–23 June, Peter Lee, representing the Association, succeeded in convincing the Chief Inspector of Mines that the shoes on the north-west guide had become dislodged, and not those on the north-east guide as other witnesses attempted to prove, so that the cage was able to swing round whilst ascending and come in contact with the under-side of a metal girder which broke the detaching hook on the cage and caused the accident.[6] As a result of the investigation the Chief Inspector of Mines called for a stricter application of Section 66 of the Coal Mines Act, 1911 which required thorough examinations to be made of all items in use in the mine.[7]

The establishment by the Home Office of the Miners' Lamp Committee in 1919 marked the beginning of attempts during the inter-war period to improve the efficiency and design of safety lamps. Electric lamps became of increasing importance because of their easy handling,

[1] Ibid., 1930, p. 21; ibid., 1936, p. 31; Safety in Mines Research Board Paper, No. 61, 'The Support of Underground Workings in the Coal Fields of the North of England', London 1930.
[2] D.M.A., 22 June 1923.
[3] Ibid., 26 October 1923.
[4] Mines Department, Report on the Causes of and Circumstances Attending the Accident which Occurred in the Busty Shaft of the Medomsley Colliery, Co., Durham, on 24 February 1923, by Henry Walker, 1923 (Cmd. 1965).
[5] Durham Chronicle, 2 March 1923, M.F.G.B., 6 March 1923.
[6] Cmd. 1965, op. cit., pp. 16–26.
[7] Ibid., pp. 26–8.

superior light and greater resistance to structural damage. Between 1922 and 1938 the number of flame safety lamps in use in the Northern region declined from 88,467 to 40,663 while the number of electric lamps increased from 20,066 to 44,793.[1]

The obvious disadvantage of electric lamps was their inability to detect gas. In 1929 however M.W. Thornton, from Armstrong College, Newcastle, invented a firedamp detecting electric safety lamp,[2] and during the 1930s the Ringrose Firedamp Alarm Lamp received wide publicity. This lamp, which normally gave a white light, showed red in the presence of gas and was demonstrated in the Durham coalfield in May 1931 at the Association's request.[3] Nevertheless even in 1934 the Council of the Durham Miners' Association instructed all mines officials to provide at least one flame lamp at every working place and at all loading points where tubs were mechanically filled.[4] In 1936 Watson was appointed a member of a committee established by the Mining Association to advise on the preparation of a safety lamp which would incorporate maximum illumination with an automatic signalling device for detecting firedamp.[5]

The need for such a protective device was emphasized following an explosion at Murton Colliery on 21 December 1937 when four men died from carbon monoxide poisoning.[6] Moore and Watson, who represented the Association at the enquiry during December and January 1938, called for more research into the development of automatic detectors to register the presence of gas before the explosion stage was reached.[7]

In spite of the persistent dangers attached to mining the development of 'safety consciousness' amongst employers and employees alike in the Durham coalfield had only slow beginnings. The Mines Department sponsored a 'Safety-First' campaign throughout the coalfields during 1922 but even by 1927 the Divisional Mines Inspector in the North complained of the lack of co-operation between coal owners and workmen towards improving safety.[8] There were exceptions. In 1929 John Bowes and Partners established a Voluntary Safety Service whereby the company's agent and chief engineer met colliery officials to discuss the most effective means of reducing the accident rate at

[1] *Report of H.M. Inspectors of Mines (Northern Division)*, 1922, 1938.
[2] *Ibid.*, 1929, p. 50.
[3] D.M.A., 9 May 1931.
[4] *Ibid.*, 13 October 1934.
[5] M.F.G.B., 15 May 1936.
[6] Durham Miners' Association, *Report on Inquiry into Explosion at Murton Colliery on December 21 1937*.
[7] *Ibid.*
[8] *Reports of H.M. Inspectors of Mines (Northern Division)*, 1927, p. 56.

the company's group of collieries. At local level managers and colliery officials were encouraged to investigate together the various accidents which occurred in order to gain valuable experience for the future. 'Suggestion boxes' were provided at each colliery to develop the individual's interest in promoting greater safety.[1] Similar efforts at joint consultation were begun by the Dorman Long and Consett Iron companies during 1933 and 1934.[2]

Regular inspection of the mines proved a valuable aid to greater safety. Ever since 1872 workmen had had the right to appoint their own representatives to help inspect the mines and from 1911 provision was made for the appointment of full-time workmen's inspectors. Both liberties were freely exercised throughout the Durham coalfield. Of the 495 mines inspected throughout the country during 1937 114 were in Durham compared with 61 in the Yorkshire Division and only 33 in the districts of Derby (North), Nottinghamshire and Leicestershire.[3] By April 1923 Lodges in the Silksworth area had established a Philadelphia and District Mines Inspection Board employing its own fully-qualified inspector.[4] Payments to the inspector were met from workmen's contributions. At Holmside Collieries a 'safety inspector' was appointed in 1924 to pay surprise visits to the company's pits and report any defects to the manager.[5] By 1938 there were six full-time workmen's inspectors in the Durham coalfield.[6]

The question of safety could rarely be divorced from wages and conditions of employment. During September–December 1934 a dispute raged among the Harton Coal Company's group of collieries over a proposed change in the status of deputies. The dispute began at Boldon Colliery in September 1934 when the management suggested that deputies be paid a weekly instead of a daily wage. In effect the proposals gave the deputies a status equivalent to other mining officials. This aroused the opposition of the Durham Miners' Association which feared that the deputies, with a responsibility for ensuring the safety of working places in the mine, would be constantly harassed by the management to help increase output, with a possible disregard for safety.[7] In periods of long-term depression the desire to secure maximum output and reduce costs often threatened the adoption of adequate safety precautions by colliery management.

[1] *Ibid.*, 1929, pp. 46–7.
[2] *Ibid.*, 1934, p. 44.
[3] R.C. on Safety in Coal Mines, 1938 (Cmd. 5890), Report, p. 139.
[4] *Miner*, 29 October 1927.
[5] *Reports of H.M. Inspectors of Mines (Northern Division)*, 1924, p. 37.
[6] R.C. on Safety in Coal Mines, 1938, III, QQ. 27,134–27,141.
[7] Durham Miners' Association, *General Secretary's Quarterly Report, No. 13*, October 1934, pp. 7–8; *Durham Chronicle*, 21 December 1934.

Furthermore workmen were loathe to make formal complaints about working conditions for fear of dismissal. The issue was even more fundamental in Durham where, unlike other mining districts, the deputies assumed responsibility not only for general safety but for shot-firing and as a consequence became increasingly responsible for the lives of underground workers.

The failure to agree upon the payment of wages and status of deputies led to a strike at Boldon and sympathetic action by the workmen at the Company's other collieries. By the end of December 1934, nearly 5,500 miners had ceased work.[1] The dispute ended on 4 January 1935 once the management agreed to withdraw their plans for deputies. At the height of the conflict Peter Lee had remarked 'It is going to be a fight to the finish. We are not going to arbitrate on men's lives.'[2] The Durham Miners' Association had long canvassed for the abolition of piece-work as a means of ensuring greater safety in the mines and in 1936 pressed the M.F.G.B. to seriously consider the dangers of men compelled to work at top speed for meagre wages in order to increase output and reduce costs.[3]

The disaster at Wharncliffe Woodmoor Colliery in Yorkshire and the death of 101 miners in the Durham coalfield during 1936 increased the Association's determination to evoke a greater degree of 'safety consciousness' throughout the region. It called for more intensive safety propaganda and joint consultation between management and Lodge officials at each colliery; for increased repair work at weekends and for a County-wide inspection of pits.[4] A Safety Campaign was launched by the Association in February 1937. The full-time workmen's inspectors joined the miners' officials in addressing conferences throughout the County.[5] In September of the same year a Special Mines Safety Conference was held at the Miners' Hall in Durham to which deputies, chargemen, shot-firers and the workmen's inspectors were invited.[6]

The Durham coal owners proved exceptionally reluctant to engage in joint discussions on questions of safety. Individual colliery managers had succeeded in establishing Pit Safety Committees,[7] but the Durham Coal Owners' Association refused to consider the possible scope and constitution of such bodies despite persistent

[1] *The Times*, 29 December 1934.
[2] *Ibid.*, 31 December 1934.
[3] M.F.G.B., 23 July 1936. Cf. R.C. on Safety in Coal Mines, 1938, III, p. 1000.
[4] D.M.A., 14, 17 August 1936.
[5] *Ibid.*, 4 February 1937.
[6] *Ibid.*, 1, 22 September 1937; *Durham Chronicle*, 3, 23 September 1937.
[7] *Reports of H.M. Inspectors of Mines* (*Northern Division*), 1938, pp. 44–5.

appeals by the Durham miners' officials during 1937.[1] It was not until May 1939 that representatives of the owners and miners agreed upon a draft constitution for such committees.[2]

The Durham Miners' Association was particularly responsive to movements aimed at securing the safety of young miners in view of the coalfields' unfavourable record of fatalities and injuries amongst boys. The absence of a complete series of boys' accident statistics for either the Durham coalfield alone or the Northern Division as a whole during the inter-war period makes statistical comparisons over time difficult but does not invalidate the coalfield's position. Thus during the period 1927–32 the average number of boys under the age of 16 killed and injured per 1,000 persons employed below ground in Durham stood at 318 compared with a national average of 230. The corresponding figures for boys between 16 and under 18 years of age are 282 and 215 respectively. Between 1935 and 1938 the average number of boys under the age of 16 killed and injured per 1,000 persons employed above and below ground in the Northern Division as a whole stood at 500 compared with a corresponding national average of 366.[3]

In May 1927 the Executive Committee of the Durham Miners' Association undertook to ensure that adequate information and advice were supplied to boys starting in the mines.[4] The Mines Department, anxious to reduce the accident rate amongst boys in Northumberland and Durham, established a sub-committee in 1930 to confer with the Chief Inspector of Mines, the Northern Divisional Inspector and representatives of the Durham miners and coal owners.[5] Following the discussions, Sir Henry Walker, Chief Inspector of Mines, called for more adequate training of boys before they proceeded underground and for improvements in their conditions of work.[6]

The first surface training ground for boys in the Durham coalfield was inaugurated by the Lambton, Hetton and Joicey coal company in 1931.[7] The Miners' Welfare Fund helped towards providing safety instruction courses for boys during 1933,[8] and, after a series of discussions between local coal owners' and miners' representatives during 1938–9, agreement was reached to limit the employment of boys

[1] D.M.A., 21 May 1937.
[2] Ibid., 15 May 1939.
[3] Reports of H.M. Inspectors of Mines, 1927–38.
[4] D.M.A., 21 May 1927.
[5] Durham Coal Owners' Association, Annual Report, 1931, p. 13.
[6] Ibid.
[7] Reports of H.M. Inspectors of Mines (Northern Division), 1931, p. 54.
[8] Ibid., 1933, pp. 40–1; Miners' Welfare Fund, Twelfth Annual Report, 1933, p. 32.

underground to those over 15 years of age. Those starting work were to undergo a surface training course of not less than three months and thereafter be supervised for a further period of two months.[1]

There were other more diverse efforts made towards fostering greater safety in the coalfield. Ambulance and first-aid competitions were organized by individual colliery companies and the Durham District Ambulance League in an attempt to educate the miners in practical methods of medical care.[2] Individual miners and officials sought their own solutions to mining dangers. G. Lister, a surface official at a colliery in Consett, invented a safer device for the withdrawal of chocks in 1929. Two intermediate chock pieces each comprising two parts of wedge shape were arranged with their inclined faces in contact. By the use of a special withdrawing appliance the wedge members could be simultaneously forced into relative movement from a safe distance, thus enabling the chocks to be withdrawn.[3] In the same year J. Myers, an employee at Bowden Close Colliery, invented a safer method of raising heavy girders for the support of roadway roofs.[4] Earlier in 1923 F. P. Miles, a member of the Durham and Northumberland Fire and Rescue Brigade, had secured the approval of the Mines Department for his design of a new type of liquid air rescue apparatus.[5]

In spite of such technical advances the Durham miners remained slow in adopting more obvious safety precautions such as the use of protective clothing. Whilst progress was made at individual collieries —such as those belonging to the Horden Colliery company where from 1935 the cost of providing safety helmets was shared between owners and men[6]—W. Charlton, the Divisional Inspector of Mines for the Northern Division, reported in 1938:

'Workers interviewed individually almost invariably agree with the beneficial effect to be derived from the use of suitable equipment but the excuses advanced for not taking advantage of facilities offered are many and diverse.'[7]

[1] D.M.A., 15 May 1939.
[2] Ibid., 18 August 1934; Reports of H.M. Inspectors of Mines (Northern Division), 1925, p. 48; Ibid., 1924, p. 39; Durham Chronicle, 5 October 1923; 28 October 1932; 24 August 1934.
[3] Reports of H.M. Inspectors of Mines (Northern Division), 1929, p. 51.
[4] Ibid., pp. 51–2.
[5] Durham Chronicle, 26 January 1923.
[6] Ibid., 15 November 1935.
[7] Reports of H.M. Inspectors of Mines (Northern Division), 1938, p. 51. Cf. R.C. on Safety in Coal Mines, 1938, III, Q. 29,121.

VII

Both the miners' and coal owners' Associations in Durham had long taken an interest in providing adequate compensation to injured workmen. By the time the Workmen's Compensation Act, 1897, had come into force, which determined that employers met the cost of accidents to workmen, the two Associations had agreed upon the establishment of a Compensation Committee in an effort to avoid friction and litigation over the operation of the new act. Under Section 11, Clause 16 of the Act the Committee was endowed with all the powers given to the County Courts and the owners' and workmen's representatives agreed to assess mutually the amounts to be paid in compensation.[1] The possibility of establishing a system of State-supervised accident insurance was investigated in 1919 by the Holman Gregory Commission, of which R. Guthrie, Secretary of the Durham Coal Owners' Association was a member, but the Committee failed to evoke any legislation along such lines.

The Workmen's Compensation Act, 1923, failed to resolve the most important problems workmen had to face in obtaining relief and to provide for compensation payments equivalent to pre-accident earnings. The Compensation Committee in Durham, the only one of its kind in the country, had greatly accelerated the settlement of cases compared with the County Court system but the employers still retained the power to compel a workman to submit to a medical examination and to stop compensation payments at once if evidence was found of even a partial recovery from an accident.[2] Under the 1923 Act, however, workmen were allowed ten days to provide adequate medical testimony of their right to compensation. The Compensation Committee in Durham agreed to consider all cases where compensation payments were stopped after ten days but the miners' leaders remained dissatisfied with the extent of the powers granted to the owners. 'The Owners have displayed a great activity in having our injured members repeatedly examined,' Swan complained in 1924. 'At some firms few will have escaped being hauled up for medical examination by the Owners' doctors. . . . The reason is not a question why compensation should be paid but a search for a reason to stop it.'[3] The friction between owners and workmen over the payment of compensation increased markedly after 1926. The lengthening of the

[1] Wilson, *op. cit.*, pp. 291–2.
[2] Durham Miners' Association, *Review of the Work of the Compensation Department during the Year 1922*, p. 7.
[3] D.M.A., *Review etc . . . during the Year 1924*, p. 1.

working day added to the risk of accident at a time when the employers, in an effort to reduce costs, were demanding stricter medical examinations.[1]

In 1933 the Durham Coal Owners' Association proposed drastic changes in the procedure for dealing with compensation cases. For over thirty-five years the owners had dealt with all claims through their Association but now suggested to the Durham Miners' Association that all claims prior to July 1932 should be settled after consultation with local colliery managers or their representatives. The Durham miners' leaders feared that local colliery representatives might prove even less sympathetic to the needs of the injured than the Owners' Association and be more willing to evade their obligations. Nevertheless the scheme was eventually adopted with the promise that the owners would accept the full liability for compensation claims in the event of any of its local collieries going into liquidation.[2] The weekly rates of compensation fixed by the various colliery companies proved woefully inadequate. The Durham Miners' Association demanded that the outstanding claims should be brought before the Medical Referees to help discover any discrepancies in medical testimony, but the companies involved refused the request. The cases were consequently submitted to the County Courts for final assessment.[3]

Workmen who were not permanently injured but who suffered from the continuing effects of a disability presented an equally serious problem. Miners' representatives on the Compensation Committee constantly argued that men suffering from nystagmus, a recurring disease affecting eyesight, should be awarded full compensation as if permanently injured. Since the owners were not required by law to provide light work to men certified as partially recovered from an injury, many miners returned to their previous jobs and relinquished their right to compensation only to find themselves incapable for work after only a short period of time. At a test case at Seaham Harbour Court on 19 June 1933 a hewer from Dawdon Colliery succeeded in proving that but for the continuing effects of nystagmus he would have been able to obtain work in the same grade and class of employment as before his injury and was therefore due to full compensation under Section 4 (2) of the Workmen's Compensation Act, 1931.[4] The decision proved even more significant at a time when

[1] D.M.A., *Review etc . . . during the Year 1927*, p. 2.
[2] D.M.A., *Review etc . . . during the Year 1933*, pp. 1–2.
[3] *Ibid.*
[4] D.M.A., 28 June 1933.

nystagmus sufferers were finding extreme difficulty in obtaining work of any kind once certified as partially recovered.

The low rates of compensation payments and the lack of any provision to meet pre-accident earnings remained vexing problems throughout the inter-war period. The Executive Committee of the Durham Miners' Association urged the Government during 1938–9 to improve the financial plight of the injured but met with little success.[1] During 1939 Lawther gained the distinction of being the first member of the Durham Miners' Association to be appointed to a Royal Commission when he joined the investigation into workmen's compensation. During the Commission's proceedings R. Williams, the Association's solicitor, drew attention on behalf of the Miners' Federation to the persistent problem which miners faced in proving the credibility of their claim for compensation. 'I know of no cases where there is a doubt as to the accident having been reported,' he said, 'in which it has not been suggested that the man is telling lies and is coming along pretending that an accident has happened when in fact no accident has happened at all.'[2]

The Miners' Permanent Relief Fund movement had originated in the northern coalfield in 1862 and had long provided a means of social security amongst the mining community.[3] In Durham the movement continued throughout the inter-war period to provide a means of support in addition to that provided through compensation legislation. Funds were raised by subscription among the members to help finance accident benefit, funeral costs and maintenance to those unable to work because of age or infirmity.

The Durham Miners' Association was keenly aware of the need to investigate the nature of miners' diseases and to consider the miners' health in general if only to reduce to the minimum the number of workmen forced into idleness through no fault of their own. In May 1919 the Association's Council called for a full investigation into the best means of combating nystagmus.[4] The connection between nystagmus and inadequate illumination had been conclusively established in 1912 but still in 1923 A. S. Percival, referee in Durham and Northumberland for nystagmus compensation cases, argued that the disease was hereditary and aggravated by the working position of men underground, especially hewers.[5]

[1] *Ibid.*, 16 May 1938; 27 November 1939. Cf. J. Lawson, *Labour Fights for Workmen's Compensation*, Labour Party, 1939.
[2] R.C. on Workmen's Compensation, 1939–44, Minutes of Evidence, Q. 7038.
[3] Fynes, *op. cit.*, pp. 199–200.
[4] D.M.A., 3 May 1919.
[5] *British Medical Journal*, 5 May 1923.

The miners' welfare scheme provided invaluable aid in promoting health in the coalfields. During 1928 the Durham District Welfare Committee sponsored a series of lectures throughout the coalfield on behalf of the Industrial Health Education Council.[1] The Durham Miners' Association had already undertaken during the previous year to distribute amongst its members a leaflet published by the Council entitled *Health Hints for Miners*.[2] The total capital cost of establishing a cottage hospital in 1927 on behalf of the miners at Holmside and South Moor was met by the local welfare fund whilst the hospital's maintenance costs were financed by contributions from both the workmen and the coal owners.[3]

The first convalescent home in the Durham coalfield was opened in 1930. The Victoria Garesfield Lodge of the Miners' Association had called for the District Welfare Committee to establish a home for miners in 1924 but the suggestion was ignored.[4] Following negotiations between owners' and miners' representatives it was decided in 1929 to purchase the Conishead Priory at Ulverston at a cost of £35,000 for conversion to a convalescent home.[5] The Priory was originally founded by St Augustine monks in the twelfth century although the building which was acquired dated from the sixteenth century. The home, which provided accommodation for 170 people, was opened on 23 August 1930 by T. Taylor, President of the Durham Coal Owners' Association and Robson, Chairman of the District Welfare Committee.[6]

In view of rising costs after the First World War the Durham miners found their voluntary contributions to hospitals an increasing burden. In 1931 the Durham Miners' Association called upon the Miners' Federation to seek State grants for all hospitals in the country.[7] The Labour Party's resolution to seek a comprehensive State medical service led the Association's Executive Committee to reject a resolution submitted by a number of Lodges in 1939 calling for support from the District Welfare Fund for the building of a County Hospital within the coalfield.[8] In addition to the miners' voluntary efforts hospital services improved with assistance from

---

[1] Mines Department, *Miners' Welfare Fund, Seventh Report*, 1928, p. 12.
[2] D.M.A., 31 October 1927.
[3] Mines Department, *Miners' Welfare Fund, Third Report*, 1924, pp. 13–14; . . . *Eighth Report*, 1929, Appendix VIII, pp. 46–7.
[4] D.M.A., 23 August 1924.
[5] *Ibid.*, 30 September 1929.
[6] *Ibid.*, 2 October 1930; *Durham Chronicle*, 29 August 1930.
[7] M.F.G.B., 22 July 1931.
[8] D.M.A., 11 February 1939.

coal owners. In 1923 Lord Londonderry offered Durham County Council his property at Seaham Hall for the provision of medical treatment.[1] The building was officially opened in February 1928 as a tuberculosis sanatorium.[2]

[1] *Durham Chronicle*, 27 April 1923.
[2] *Ibid.*, 2 March 1928.

Appendix I

EMPLOYMENT IN COAL MINES, 1922–39

	Total number of wage earners on colliery books		Average number of days worked per week by the mines*	
	Durham	Great Britain	Durham	Great Britain
1922	154,837	1,095,186	5·16	5·17
1923	170,181	1,137,926	4·84	5·00
1924	169,142	1,171,896	5·09	5·26
1925	147,022	1,086,103	4·69	5·02
1926		National stoppage		
1927	128,283	999,941	4·94	4·80
1928	126,762	923,092	5·02	4·68
1929	136,413	932,330	5·30	4·73
1930	131,197	916,809	5·04	5·09
1931	112,968	848,455	4·98	4·85
1932	103,768	802,705	4·59	4·50
1933	101,129	790,868	4·75	4·56
1934	106,814	774,866	5·04	4·80
1935	105,698	758,587	5·09	3·91
1936	107,426	756,232	5·22	5·02
1937	114,480	777,791	5·39	5·26
1938	114,472	781,865	5·07	4·97
1939†	112,182	771,950	5·27	5·18

* The figures show the number of days (allowance being made for short time) on which coal was got from the mines included in the returns. It is not necessarily implied that all persons worked every day the mines were open. Mines not working are omitted in computing the average number of days worked.

† Average of eight months.

Source: *Ministry of Labour Gazette.*

Appendix II

COAL MINERS' EARNINGS PER SHIFT, 1920–1938*

	Index of average money earnings per shift (1914 = 100) (excluding the value of allowances in kind)						*Cost of Living Index (July 1914 = 100)†*	*Index of average real earnings per shift (1914 = 100) (excluding the value of allowances in kind)*	
	Durham			Great Britain				Durham	Great Britain
	s	d	Index (1914 (6s 2½d) = 100)	s	d	Index (1914 (6s 5¾d) = 100)			
1920 (Jan–Mar)	14	7½	235·6	15	1½	239·4	249·0	94·6	93·7
1921	15	4¾	248·0	15	11	245·5	226·0	109·7	108·6
1922	9	1	146·3	9	11¾	154·0	183·0	79·9	84·1
1923	9	11	159·7	10	1	155·6	174·0	91·8	89·4
1924	10	2	163·8	10	7¾	164·3	175·0	93·6	93·9
1925	9	11½	160·4	10	6	162·0	176·0	91·1	92·0
1926 (Jan–April	9	11¼	160·1	10	5	160·7	172·0	93·1	93·4
1927	9	2¼	148·0	10	0¾	155·3	167·5	88·4	92·7
1928	8	1½	130·9	9	3½	140·8	166·0	78·9	84·8
1929	7	11½	128·2	9	2¾	142·4	164·0	78·2	86·8
1930	8	0¾	129·9	9	3½	143·4	158·0	82·2	90·8
1931	8	0¾	129·9	9	2¼	141·8	147·5	88·1	96·1
1932	8	1	130·2	9	2	141·4	144·0	90·4	98·2
1933	8	0½	129·6	9	1½	140·8	140·0	92·6	100·6
1934	8	0½	129·6	9	1¾	141·1	141·0	91·9	100·1
1935	8	0½	129·6	9	3¾	143·0	143·0	90·6	100·0
1936	8	7	138·3	10	0¼	154·6	147·0	94·1	105·2
1937	9	1	146·3	10	8	164·6	154·0	95·0	106·9
1938	9	8¼	156·0	11	2¾	173·7	156·0	100·0	111·3

Appendix III

LIFE IN A DURHAM PIT VILLAGE IN THE 1920s

It is seven-thirty in a July morning in the 1920s. In a street typical of all in mining areas, mother makes preparation for the weekly wash, a task arduous enough without the merciless heat of an unclouded sun beating down upon her endeavours. For this reason she starts early, in the comparative cool of the morning, pausing only to get the children off to school before the wall-pendulum strikes nine. Meantime, she has paid repeated visits to the street tap in order to replenish a huge black pan on an equally huge fire, maintained at a stifling intensity of heat now that the gruelling task of cauldroning the 'boil' has begun.

Early Callers

Ten-to-nine, and the children are off, hopping over traces of patterned 'bays' and 'penker-holes' that scar the sun-baked surface of the street. Too early yet for the doctor who pays all his calls on foot, but the postman conforms to schedule, dispensing with quick strides his impassive distribution of enveloped pain and pleasure, passing early milk and midden-carts and coal loads already lying in the gutter. Sometimes these later marks of an earlier industry bar his entrance but his climb will be intercepted by the housewife with a ready 'good morning', curling-pinned or hair-pinned heads nodding recognition from taps and gates. He knows everyone and where he encounters the drawn blinds of bereavement can correctly assume the deceased's identity.

Meantime, it is after nine, and mother, with perhaps another addition to an already large family, has been temporarily obliged to enlist the services of a neighbour's daughter who will assist for 5s a week. Now, with laborious boiling and scrubbing over, they will double-poss the black pan's steaming contents, tipped with mutual perspiration into a tub placed near the door of the kitchen-cum-scullery-cum-wash-house-cum-everything. Sitting-rooms were notably absent but would have been museum pieces anyway.

Banishment

Jinny, the help, crosses the street to stretch the line to a hook in the stanchion of what would now be termed a 'toilet' but was called then, from however obscure an abbreviation, a 'netty'. The prominently exposed position of this row of conveniences like large sentry-boxes down the middle of the street dispensed with most false modesty, and to refer to them is to be reminded of the various roles they played. Apart from their initial function, they were often all a miner's child knew of a nursery, and children were banished to them on wet days to erect swings, blow pipe-bubbles from the steps, and to play shops and schools and sew dolls' patches.

Sometimes it became a theatre, the wide wood seat making an excellent platform. The wide wood seat would cover a week's ashes and worse, but provided nobody fell down the hole the 'pin-to-see-the-concert' was an assured success. With costumes made of tissue-paper much practice went into the production, so that considerate adults even refrained from 'interrupting' the performance, and would obligingly 'slip next door'. Not always, however; sometimes a decorative egression en masse was demanded, a slight often repaid by shooting the bolt to lock in the temporary intruder.

Today, however, mischief is at school, and Jinny pegs out the wash optimistic about its drying before the midden-cart's approach, and periodically propping it clear of fruit and other carts that seek passage up the street.

Ten o'clock, and mother with skilled precision propels the tub for emptying at the yard sink, while a cooper calls 'tubs to mend' in the distance. This is a process interesting to watch as he deftly encircles the barrel with flexible steel laths.

The heat is increasing and Jinny 'swills the doors', while Mary, the fish-wife, sings abroad that her new kippers are a penny a pair, Meggie, her fellow-traveller, informing us less musically that hers are the same. With sweat trickling down her genial countenance, she lowers her basket from its lofty perch to serve customers in friendly and familiar conversation. Then she retwists her head-towel and, basket on high, traverses the rows until it empties, when she retraces her steps to the mile away station to be train-borne back to Sunderland.

The Pot-Pies

Now, washing blowing in the warm breeze, mother proceeds with pot-pies for the men in 'first-shift'. The crake-man calls that there will be a Union meeting at seven o'clock—very important business. Jinny places heating-irons on a lowered bar before the fire. A skylark mingles its high notes with the purring sound of a hay-cutting machine, for fields and farms surround us, and the farmer passes up the street on his way to market with Wild Tommy harnessed to the trap.

Eleven-thirty, and tired, black-faced workers arrive, discarding dusty clothes at the door. With the pot-pies or 'cold warmed up' disposed of, the fireside mat is rolled back for bath-on-cracket ablutions. 'Douces' smoked, with the sun at its zenith, they depart for afternoon rest, all except dad, who remains glued to the Sporting Pink studying the form. When pit-clothes are 'dadded' and pit-boots greased, the children will next arrive for lunch. A hawker of four-a-penny caller herrin' leaves in his wake harassed housewives who, with no time for crossing to the midden, pitch fish-washings across the road, leaving patches of sparkling scales where the water is absorbed and fish heads instantly pounced upon by vigilant, scavenging cats.

Homely Sound

Much splashing and sloshing centres round the tap to the harmonizing notes of a practising trumpet-player anticipating Sunday's band concert. A tinker goes from door to door without a sale, and a pit-engine's whistle signals as it pants laden to South Hetton. Its puffing up the line has a welcome, homely sound, and for the time being at least, denotes industry, however the strike-anxiety develops. At a sink a neighbour is already trimming her lamp-wick. It is her night for the pictures and her children will mind the house, duly instructed not to light the lamp before dark. A pail of pig-swill is on its way to the allotments and a whippet-trainer steers his charge to the open fields.

Twelve-thirty, and I am sent for yeast to a neighbour's house-shop. Here I interrupt an argument re the potentialities of Mr Ramsay MacDonald, the daughter meanwhile applying polish to the fireplace, with brass and steel fender set aside for polishing. Back home, dad, dissatisfied with his own paper, dispatches me next door for the loan of theirs. I rebel, but a clip on the ear sets me in motion, and I commiserate on the way with a mournful mendicant's rendering of 'Jesus, Lord, I ask for mercy'. I reflect that mercy may be all he will get today since Friday's pay-packet is a long way off, but his supplication will elicit some return securing for him a night's lodge in a town doss-house.

Waiting for the paper whose owner is in a similar state of fixation I am sent up the street for jam by his mother. At this house-shop I interrupt the process of herb and ginger beer making, later to be sold at 2d a bottle. A candy-man outside is exchanging bath-brick and pipe-clay for jam-jars, and chasing off would-be riders from his cart. Dad will be fuming at the delay and, in accelerating, I almost collide with the chassis of a pram quitting a yard under its own steam, its squawling occupant tipped into the gutter and my progress impeded in restoring its equilibrium. Dad by now is agitatedly scanning the street, and I counter another clip as I eventually present him with the paper.

One o'clock, and I am delivering his note to a furtive watchful bookie at the corner-end, proceeding on to school to leave a now hushed and drowsy household in the throes of baking bread.

Evening Out

The product of this twice-weekly event will fill the square-table, and tea, with the ironing strung across the kitchen, will see the end of Jinny's assistance, her evening being spent watching Norma Talmadge at the Empire or Lillian Gish at the Olympia, Invincible bus-rides to the Harbour 'play' being left till Saturday.

Questa's ice-cream cart whistles its customers, the fly pestered horse whipping winged tormentors with its tail. The heat is overpowering, and with tea over, men make for the fields where walks to Cath Robins' Wood, whippet-training at the running-pitch, cooling-off in the bathing-hole, or merely lying relaxed in the grass are pleasures costing nothing, a common indulgence of this community.

The day draws to a close, and mother, too, at long last may relax. Darning done and the last patch applied, she puts up the 'first shift baits' by the light of a glimmering oil-lamp. On her way to the tap with pit-bottles, she welcomes the setting sun with weary relief. As one of many performers in a colliery's vast supporting cast, her day's last task is over, and with the rest of her household sleeping she will, perhaps, lean at the gate, watching the mackerel sky darken into dusk.

Pounding Pulse

Some special thrift has made possible the painting of doors and the coal-tarring of railings, and their pungency blends with the scent of new-mown hay wafting to her from the fields. The cutting-machine and the lark lie quiet, but the pounding pulse of pit-life is seldom still. Day activities may mute its voices, but the rhythmic orchestration of the colliery clamours louder as the quiet dusk accentuates its incessant accompaniment.

In sotto voce the pulley's whine is whirred into the night; the hiss of disgorging steam, the intermittent screech of timber-saws, the clang of shunting and the lumbering roll of wagon-wheels form the tempo of a tune to which her life is set. Surface sounds of an activity far below where humanity feeds the greedy grunt of an industrial monster, in sweating serfdom wresting a pittance out of all proportion to the labour and risk involved.

The orchestral concerto may not be sweet. The piercing whistle-signals may disturb those whose sickness is insomnia, but the woman at the gate recognizes it as the theme of her inheritance. In the shadow of pit-chimneys on a summer night in the 'twenties' she envisages no future variation regarding its symphony. Her heritage is accepted in unquestioning resignation, and while the buzzer's deep bassoon will sound too early a reveille no sedative or serenade is necessary for the sleep of duty well and willingly executed.

Source: N.U.M. (Durham Area), *Annual Report*, 1958, pp. 19–22. The original source is unknown.

Chapter VIII

POLITICAL ACTIVITIES, 1919–39

I

The miners were the first group of workers to send their own representatives to Parliament. In 1874 A. MacDonald and T. Burt were returned as Members of Parliament for Stafford and Morpeth repectively and paved the way for more direct working-class representation, particularly in mining constituences. It was in such areas that the most decisive use of the trade union vote could be made since a substantial proportion of the working population belonged to a single industry and were embraced by a single union or federation of unions. Union membership amongst adult males tended to be unusually high and the bulk of the labour forces concentrated in particular constituencies.

This exceptional political situation had been used with particular effect in Durham and Northumberland during the last quarter of the nineteenth century and the early decades of the twentieth. By 1904 the North-East, with less than 20 per cent of the total labour force in the coal industry, supported four miners' candidates and even in 1889 was responsible for three of the five seats held by miners.[1] In the absence of a distinct party of their own the miners aligned themselves with the Liberal-Radical element in the House of Commons. The Liberal tradition remained an important influence within the Durham Miners' Association in the period up to 1914, largely due to the dominant role adopted by John Wilson, a staunch Liberal supporter. It was largely through the support given by the North and South Durham Liberal Associations that W. Crawford and J. Wilson, both Agents of the Durham Miners' Association, were returned in 1885 for the Mid-Durham and Houghton-le-Spring divisions respectively. Wilson was eventually defeated in 1886 but succeeded Crawford as a member for Mid-Durham in 1890, remaining its representative until 1915.[2] Wilson remained the only official of the Durham miners to represent a predominantly mining constituency within the coalfield in the decades before 1914. Indeed during 1886–1904 only one of the

[1] H. A. Clegg, A. Fox and A. F. Thompson, *A History of British Trade Unions Since 1889, Volume I, 1899–1910*, Oxford 1964, p. 271.
[2] Wilson, *op. cit.*, pp. 195–6; R. Gregory, *The Miners and British Politics, 1906–1914*, Oxford 1968, pp. 68–9, P. P. Poirier, *The Advent of the Labour Party*, London 1958, p. 257.

seven County divisions in which the miners represented the largest proportion of the electors supported a miners' candidate. In 1905 J. W. Taylor, Secretary of the Durham Colliery Mechanics, was returned at Chester-le-Street and in 1904 J. Johnson, Financial Secretary of the Durham Miners' Association since 1896, had been elected in the County Borough of Gateshead, a working-class constituency but with relatively few miners.[1]

The Lib.-Lab. tradition within the Association did not go unchallenged. The North of England Socialist Federation, formed by Tom Mann, J. L. Mahon and James MacDonald, exerted considerable influence within the Durham coalfield during the 1880s.[2] The growth of socialist propaganda was enhanced in 1893 with the formation of the Independent Labour Party which established branches in the North East during the 1890s. The I.L.P. steadily gained the support of those miners who sought an eight-hour day and a floor to wages in opposition to the official policy of the Durham Miners' Association. The stubborn resistance of the union officials to Socialist aspirations forced recalcitrant members to seek political action, whether or not they regarded themselves as Socialists. During 1905–7 the number of I.L.P. branches in Durham increased from 16 to 60.[3] 'By 1910', one writer notes, 'the Durham and Northumberland coalfields had become hot-beds of socialist activity.'[4] The decision of the Durham miners to join the M.F.G.B. in 1907; the warm reception given to Keir Hardie and Arthur Henderson, recognized leaders of the Labour Party, at the miners' annual demonstrations; and the bitter attacks Wilson made upon all who refused to support official union policy indicated the growing strength of the Socialists within Durham in the period after 1905. 'At every half-yearly election to the executive of the D.M.A. the number of Socialists steadily increased until by 1910 they were probably in a narrow majority'.[5]

Liberalism was by no means dead. Wilson, already a Member of Parliament when the M.F.G.B. agreed to affiliate with the Labour Party in 1910, refused to sign the Labour whip and was never regarded as a Labour M.P.[6] The by-elections in Houghton-le-Spring and North-West Durham during 1913–14, at which Labour candidates sponsored by the Durham Miners' Association were defeated in areas where the miners represented a significant proportion of the

[1] Clegg, Fox and Thompson, op. cit., pp. 271–2.
[2] D. Torr, Tom Mann and His Times, I, London 1956, pp. 242 ff.
[3] Gregory, op. cit., p. 69.
[4] Ibid., p. 67.
[5] Ibid., p. 73.
[6] R. P. Arnot, The Miners, 1889–1910, London 1949, p. 369.

total electorate, testified to the strength of Liberal support still within the coalfield.[1] The success of the Association in gaining support for its official Labour candidates depended upon the union's propaganda and organizational work between and during elections and upon the readiness of the miners to regard direct Labour Party representation as the most effective means of political agitation. The changes in the composition and organization of the electorate in 1918, the adoption by the Labour Party of a socialist programme and the determination of the working class to seek a better world during peacetime combined to provide the opportunities for growing Labour support.

II

At the time of the passing of the Representation of the People Bill in 1918, which allowed for the first time in history women over 30 and all adult working men to use their combined votes to elect Members of Parliament, Labour Party organization within Durham County was sorely lacking. Officials of the Durham Miners' Association lost no time, however, in encouraging effective political organization within the coalfield as a means of capturing votes for Labour. Already, as a result of elections in 1913 and 1918 the Association had increased its number of prospective miners' candidates to thirteen. These included four of its agents Robson, Whiteley, Richardson and Batey, and eight local miners, R. Richardson (Ryhope), J. Neville (Birtley), J. Cullen (Marsden), J. E. Swan (Dipton), J. Herriotts (Windlestone), J. Ritson (Monkwearmouth), James Gilliland (Birtley) and J. Lawson (Chester-le-Street), seven of whom were checkweighmen. The remaining candidate was John Gilliland, Political Agent at Chester-le-Street.

In January 1918 Richardson, Whiteley, Batey and Trotter, all electors in the newly-constituted Durham division, which encompassed fourteen collieries, joined other Labour supporters in an attempt to establish a local Labour Party organization within the division.[2] Representatives of trade-union organizations, Labour bodies and co-operative societies met at the Miners' Hall on 9 February and agreed to establish a local branch of the Labour Party within the Durham division and to prepare for running a Labour candidate at the next general election.[3] W. Whiteley became the first President of the divisional party.

[1] Gregory, op. cit., pp. 79–81.
[2] Durham Chronicle, 1 February 1918.
[3] Ibid., 15 February 1918.

By May 1918 four nominations had been received for the Division's first Labour candidate. These included two of the Association's political candidates, Neville and Swan, together with C. Thompson, nominee of the Durham Cokemen's Association and R. J. Wilson, the nominee of the co-operative employees.[1] Neville, who for the previous twelve years had been a member of the Durham miners' Executive Committee, secured a clear majority of votes on the first poll and was elected as the division's prospective Labour Candidate.[2] R. J. Wilson was later appointed as prospective Labour candidate for the North Ward of the Newcastle division.

By the end of January 1918 local Labour Party associations had been established in all County divisions except Sedgefield and pre-election preparations similar to those in the Durham division were made in other areas. J. E. Swan, whom Neville defeated at Durham, was elected as the miners' candidate at Barnard Castle. The local Labour Association at Spennymoor decided in April 1918 to adopt Batey as their official Labour candidate.[3] During the previous month the Liberals had agreed to run S. Galbraith, an Agent of the Durham Miners' Association from 1900 until 1915 when he was elected as M.P. for the old Mid-Durham constituency, as their official candidate.[4] When John Wilson died in 1915, Galbraith, although a member of the Association's Executive Committee at the time when it was decided to nominate William House, another Agent, to succeed Wilson and thus maintain Mid-Durham as a miners' seat, agreed to stand in opposition to House as a representative of the Northern Liberal Association. However, in view of the political truce in force during the war the Labour nomination was eventually withdrawn and Galbraith secured the seat without forcing a head-on clash with the Durham miners' officials.[5] At both Spennymoor and Durham the Unionist, Liberal and Coalition candidates agreed not to oppose one another.[6]

When Parliament was dissolved on 11 November 1918 and a general election fixed for 14 December seven of the eleven County divisions in Durham supported official miners' candidates. In addition to those already mentioned W. Whiteley was selected to contest Blaydon, R. Richardson and J. Herriotts represented Labour at Houghton-le-Spring and Sedgefield respectively and J. Lawson was

[1] *Ibid.*, 22 March, 17 May 1918.
[2] *Ibid.*, 12 July 1918.
[3] *Ibid.*, 15, 22 March 1918.
[4] Metcalfe, *op. cit.*, pp. 456–7.
[5] *Durham Chronicle*, 4 October 1918.
[6] *Ibid.*, 15, 22 March 1918.

adopted in March 1918 as prospective Labour candidate for the Seaham division.[1]

Before the general election took place Labour representation in the Durham division changed. At a meeting at Ushaw Moor on 23 November attended by Neville, Batey and Swan, Neville, the elected Labour candidate, declared his support of the Labour Party remaining a part of the Coalition Government. His declaration was immediately rebuked by Swan and Batey who were intent on opposing a Government which they claimed, by calling a general election, had waged war upon the Labour Party. As a result of the meeting Neville withdrew his candidature and was replaced by J. Ritson, a checkweighman at Monkwearmouth Colliery and a member of Sunderland Town Council. Ritson had previously been invited to contest the Barnard Castle, Bishop Auckland and South Shields divisions but had declined for health reasons.[2]

The electioneering conducted on behalf of the Coalitionists during the political campaign was highly emotional popularizing such slogans as 'Hang the Kaiser' and 'Make Germany Pay'. The minority parties criticized the Government for calling an election so quickly after the armistice and deplored Lloyd George's use of a signed letter sent to approved candidates (known as the 'coupon') as open discrimination.[3] The Council of the Durham Miners' Association urged all working-class voters to secure the election of the Labour candidates, especially those nominated by the Association itself.[4] The results of the election, however, were disappointing only two of the seven miners' candidates being returned, J. Swan at Barnard Castle and R. Richardson at Houghton-le-Spring. At Barnard Castle Swan defeated the Coalition Unionist Candidate J. E. Rogerson, who had numerous business interests in Durham including connection with Wolsingham Steel Works, the Liberal A. E. Hillary, from Middlesex, but a native of County Durham, and the Independent candidate O. Monkhouse, the voting being 5,468, 3,837, 2,180 and 1,274 respectively. In a three-cornered fight at Houghton-le-Spring R. Richardson opposed the division's Liberal M.P. T. Wing, who had defeated William House in 1913 and who, prior to that, had been Parliamentary agent to the Commercial Travellers of Great Britain and Ireland and J. Lindsley, the official candidate of the British Workers' League. Richardson captured the seat by 7,315 to 6,626 votes, Lindsley receiving 6,185 votes. At Blaydon the Coalition Liberal

[1] Ibid., 15, 22 March 1918.
[2] Ibid., 3 December 1918.
[3] Taylor, op. cit., pp. 127–8.
[4] D.M.A., 7 December 1918.

candidate W. Waring, whose previous seat at Banffshire disappeared as a result of the reorganization of constituencies under the Representation of the People Act, defeated Whiteley and the Liberal Candidate T. A. Graham by 9,937 to 7,844 and 1,064 votes respectively.

The Coalition Unionist J. W. Hills defeated Ritson in a straight fight at Durham by 9,027 votes to 8,809, 'a majority of only 218. Hills had held the seat at Durham City from 1906 until 1918 when, as a result of the reorganization of constituencies, the City electorate was merged with that of a larger part of the surrounding district to form the new Durham division. This merger effected a notable change in local electioneering tactics and introduced an element of uncertainty as the outcome of the voting within the division. The City voters, notoriously Liberal in outlook, were now only subsidiary to the larger representation of the mining community following the addition of the Mid-Durham and Houghton divisions to the new constituency. Since the Liberals had already agreed not to oppose the Unionist candidate Ritson concentrated on securing the support of those voters outside of Durham City clearly susceptible to Labour's influence. His success in this respect can be judged from the fact that having replaced Neville in early December and being in the contest only a matter of weeks he was defeated by such a small majority.

Lawson defeated the Liberal candidate E. Hayward at Seaham by 13,754 votes to 8,988 despite the fact that the Wingate Miners' Lodge, representing the largest mining village in the constituency, had decided in November 1918 to support Hayward against Lawson on the grounds that Labour's opposition to the Coalition Government was without a mandate from the rank-and-file.[1] Hayward had formerly represented the South-East Durham division before it was incorporated in the Seaham Division in 1918.

At Sedgefield Herriotts lost to the Coalition Unionist R. Burdon, a native of County Durham who had previously contested the old South-East Durham constituency without success, by 6,627 to 5,801 votes. The Liberal candidate C. Sturmer, Managing Director of the *Birmingham Gazette, Sheffield Independent Press* and the North of England Newspaper Company Ltd., received 3,333 votes. J. W. Taylor, the existing Labour member for Chester-le-Street, was returned unopposed. At Spennymoor Batey, the official miners' candidate, was defeated by S. Galbraith, standing as a Lib.-Lab. Coalitionist, by 9,443 votes to 8,196. 'The defeat of the official candidate by the unofficial in the Spennymoor division,' commented the *Northern*

---

[1] *Durham Chronicle*, 29 November 1918.

Echo, '. . . raises the question of the equity of compelling the miners to pay for the exploitation of one man when by their vote they show a preference for another miner. It is an issue which cannot be long burked.'[1] Labour candidates in the County divisions of Consett and Jarrow and in the Borough divisions of Gateshead, the Hartlepools, Sunderland and South Shields were all defeated. A Labour candidate who was not sponsored by the Durham Miners' Association was successfully returned in the Bishop Auckland County division.

The general election proved a sweeping success for the Coalition Government. 339 Coalition Unionists and 136 Coalition Liberals were returned. Labour's representation in the House of Commons increased from 39 to 59, all but one of the candidates having been sponsored by a trade union. Only 26 Liberals were returned.[2] 'The election,' writes Somervell, 'provided Great Britain . . . with the wealthiest, the stupidest and least representative House of Commons since the Great Reform Bill of 1832.'[3] Cann claimed that in supporting the Coalition Government the electorate had 'not hesitated to mortgage their future well-being, by placing the policy of reconstruction absolutely in the hands of the party traditionally opposed to raising the standard of life of the common people from an educational, social and economic point of view.'[4]

The results of the Durham County Council elections held in March 1919 prevented a similar state of affairs occurring within local administration. For the first time in history Labour, as a distinct political group, secured a majority position on the Council under the chairmanship of Peter Lee. Of the 99 seats available Labour members (excluding aldermen) secured 56. The existence of local Labour Party organizations proved a distinct advantage to working-class candidates. Before 1914 the emergence of a definite programme of local reforms and the sponsorship of candidates had resulted largely from the initiative of local Lodges, albeit encouraged by their union. After 1918 the encouragement which the Durham Miners' Association continued to provide was linked with a determination by the Labour Party to secure adequate representation at all levels of administration. In addition to the obvious advantages of a Labour-controlled Council Cann hailed the results as a timely avengement of the outcome of the general election and wrote to members:

---

[1] *Northern Echo*, 1 January 1919.
[2] Taylor, *op. cit.*, p. 128.
[3] D. C. Somervell, *British Politics Since 1900*, London 1953, p. 123.
[4] Durham Miners' Association, *Monthly Circular No. 37, November–December, 1918*, p. 3.

'Removed from the glamour of the War and the dread that in-spired many people that to vote against the then Coalition candi-dates was equal to voting against the War . . . our people have come out in no uncertain way and voiced their discontent. . . . Many of the candidates who represent the capitalist system are now deplor-ing the fact that the subterfuge which exercised so potent a charm during the recent General Election could not be utilized on the present occasion.'[1]

III

Only six months after the general election J. W. Taylor, Labour M.P. for Chester-le-Street, decided to resign his seat for health reasons. Taylor had been returned unopposed in 1918 in an area where Labour controlled practically every district council within the division and had a majority on the urban council. The Durham Miners' Association officially sponsored J. Lawson as prospective Labour candidate in the by-election although the divisional Labour Party favoured Arthur Henderson. Henderson eventually decided to withdraw his nomination rather than split the Labour vote and supported Lawson throughout the campaign.[2]

By 13 November 1919, the date of the by-election, the contest had resolved itself into a straight fight between Lawson and the Coalition candidate D. Gilmour, General Secretary of the National Demo-cratic Party. With the support of Henderson, the Miners' Associa-tion and the M.F.G.B., and at a time when the deliberations of the Sankey Commission had popularized the miners' cause, Lawson's victory seemed inevitable. He was returned with a huge majority, de-feating Gilmour by 17,838 votes to 5,313.[3]

Meanwhile Labour's defeat in the general election had led to renewed attempts at both national and district level to strengthen political organization. In July 1919 the M.F.G.B. increased its annual political levy from 1s to 2s which enabled it to increase the amount returned to districts for local propaganda work.[4] Salaries payable to the Federation's M.P.s were increased from £350 to £600 per annum on 1 October 1919, allowing them for the first time to earn at least as much as the law provided. Previously, miners' M.P.s had handed their annual salary of £400, statutorily introduced in 1911, to the

[1] D.M.A., *Monthly Circular, No. 38, January–February, 1919,* p. 1.
[2] *Colliery Guardian,* 9 July, 8 August 1919.
[3] *Newcastle Daily Chronicle,* 13 November 1919.
[4] M.F.G.B., 18 July 1919.

Federation and received the £350 payment which almost twenty years previously the M.F.G.B. had decided to be an adequate return. The salaries were increased by a further £100 per year from 1 October 1920.[1]

The Durham Miners' Association strengthened its own political organization in August 1919 by appointing a further six Parliamentary candidates, one of whom, W. Lawther (the Victoria Garesfield Lodge nominee) had been defeated in the ballot held in January 1918 but who was destined to become one of the Association's most prominent officials. The others elected were H. James (Shield Row), J. Summerbell (Boldon), G. Harvey (Follonsby), R. Wren (Clara Vale) and H. Bainbridge (Political Agent, Sunderland).[2] Bainbridge had been elected in October 1914 with James Gilliland as a Political Agent to the Durham Miners' Association,[3] but had been able to offer only limited assistance, especially when the reorganization of constituencies in 1918 provided Durham with eight County divisions. In October 1919 therefore, the Association's Executive Committee agreed to appoint two further full-time Political Agents so that four men could assume responsibility for two constituencies each.[4]

IV

In view of its increasing dissatisfaction with the Coalition Government the Conservative Party decided at the famous Carlton Club meeting on 17 October 1922 to fight the next general election as an independent party. Lloyd George immediately resigned and was succeeded by Bonar Law. Parliament was dissolved and a general election fixed for 15 November.

In spite of the suddenness of the political crisis the party organization in Durham was not unprepared for the electoral struggle. There were, however, some changes in the representation of miners' candidates. J. Lawson's victory at the Chester-le-Street by-election in November 1919[5] left a vacancy in the Seaham division for a miners' candidate to oppose E. Hayward, the existing Liberal member. In view of the recent increase in the list of their prospective Parliamentary candidates the Executive Committee of the Durham Miners' Association was anxious that the position should be filled by a person

[1] *Ibid.*, 22 October 1919; 5 January 1921.
[2] D.M.A., 31 October 1919.
[3] D.M.A., 30 October 1914.
[4] *Ibid.*, 31 October 1919.
[5] See above, p. 326.

from its own ranks. J. Robson had decided in 1919 to offer himself as a prospective candidate in the division but withdrew his candidature in January 1920.[1]

In the autumn of 1919 a number of miners' Lodges in the Seaham division invited Sidney Webb, who had then distinguished himself in defending the miners' case before the Sankey Commission, to contest the seat.[2] Webb provisionally accepted the nomination in February 1920 but subsequently withdrew it when the Association's Executive Committee informed the Divisional Labour Party that they felt the selection should take place from amongst those miners' parliamentary candidates elected by ballot but as yet unplaced in constituencies.[3] The miners at Seaham persisted in their demand for Webb as their prospective candidate and, in spite of the opposition of the Durham miners' officials, he was unanimously chosen on 10 July 1920 to fight as Labour candidate in the next general election.[4] Despite the fact that Webb had previously intimated that he would remain financially responsible for the election and would neither ask for nor accept trade union funds to meet his expenses,[5] the miners in the division forwarded him cheques towards meeting the cost of the election once Parliament had been dissolved.[6]

Galbraith retired from politics in 1922 and T. Wing, who was defeated by the miners' candidate R. Richardson at Houghton-le-Spring in 1918, was elected to defend the Liberal seat at Spennymoor. J. Batey remained as the miners' prospective Labour candidate in the constituency but no longer had to contest the seat against a Liberal with strong local connections and a personal popularity amongst the miners. There were no other changes in the representation of the remaining miners' candidates except for the adoption of W. Lawther, an officially-sponsored miners' candidate, as prospective Labour candidate for the County Borough seat at South Shields. Lawther had been elected to the Executive Committee of the Durham Miners' Association in December 1918 and from 1919 to 1929 served as Secretary and delegate of the Victoria Garesfield Lodge.

Durham miners' candidates contested seven County divisions and one County Borough seat. The outcome of the general election proved an overwhelming victory for Labour. Labour secured victories in ten of the eleven County divisions in Durham, six of them

[1] M.F.G.B., 11 November 1919; 27 January 1920.
[2] M. Cole, *Beatrice Webb's Diaries, 1912–1924*, London 1952, p. 175.
[3] *Ibid.*, p. 176.
[4] *Ibid.*, p. 184.
[5] *Ibid.*, p. 176.
[6] *Ibid.*, p. 228.

being held by miners' candidates. J. E. Swan was narrowly defeated at Barnard Castle by the Conservative candidate J. E. Rogerson, who had lost to Swan in 1918, the result, only announced after a recount, being 8,271 votes to 8,052. Lawther fighting an election for the first time, was defeated at South Shields by the Liberal candidate E. A. Harney, a lawyer, by only 25 votes, the voting being 15,760 to 15,735. The National Liberal candidate, J. Havelock Wilson, leader of the Seamen's and Firemen's Union, secured 8,121 votes. It took eight and a half hours to determine the result of the election following a recount when it was understood that only two votes separated the Liberal and Labour candidates.[1] The result was even more encouraging for Lawther since Wilson had been returned at South Shields in 1918 with a majority of 13,000 votes. All other miners' candidates were successfully returned. At Blaydon W. Whiteley secured the seat against F. R. Simpson, head of the Stella Coal Company, whom the Blaydon Division Unionists had officially adopted as their candidate on 28 October,[2] and F. W. Cook, the National Liberal candidate, and chairman of the Midland Association of Local Authorities and of the Drapers' Chamber of Trade of the U.K. The voting was 14,722, 7,963 and 4,606 respectively. At Durham Ritson won the seat from the existing Conservative member, J. W. Hills, who in November 1922 had been appointed Financial Secretary to the Treasury, by 14,068 votes to 11,396. Herriotts secured the seat at Sedgefield by a majority of only 729 against the Conservative candidate E. Waddington, who had unsuccessfully contested the Bishop Auckland division in 1892, and the Liberal candidate C. H. Brown, Secretary of the North-East branch of the Free Trade Union, the voting being 9,796, 9,067 and 3,561. T. E. Wing failed to retain the seat at Spennymoor for the Liberals, losing to Batey by 13,766 votes to 7,567. The Conservative candidate A. Eden, whose career had been spent mostly in the Army and who in 1919 became the youngest person to hold the rank of adjutant, polled 6,046 votes.

At Houghton-le-Spring R. Richardson retained his seat with an increased majority polling 14,611 votes against 7,555 for the Conservative candidate, W. Shaw and 5,958 for the Liberal, J. E. Johnston, a local draper and urban councillor. Lawson retained his seat at Chester-le-Street against opposition from the Conservative candidate D. F. Todd, the voting being 20,296 to 9,335. At Consett and Jarrow the Labour representatives who were not miners' candidates successfully captured seats from the Liberals while at Bishop Auckland,

[1] *Newcastle Daily Chronicle*, 17 November 1922.
[2] *Ibid.*, 30 October 1922.

B. C. Spoor, the existing Labour candidate retained his seat against opposition from the National Liberals. At Seaham Sidney Webb secured a dominant victory, defeating the existing member E. Hayward by 20,203 votes to 5,247. Hayward polled 3,068 fewer votes than his Conservative opponent T. A. Bradford, a director of the Charlaw and Sacriston Coal Company.

The Labour victories in the general election were especially encouraging in Durham since, as a result of the County Council elections held in March 1922, Labour lost the majority position it had secured in 1919. Labour lost 18 seats and gained 4, the Council now being composed of 57 Moderates and 42 Labour representatives. Peter Lee was again elected Chairman of the Council.[1]

In an effort to maintain and strengthen Labour's representation on local councils the Durham Miners' Association agreed to conduct a ballot in 1923, in accordance with the 1913 Trade Union Act, to legalize the practice of Lodges setting aside weekly contributions per member for paying the expenses and wages of miners serving on Boards of Guardians, and county, rural, urban and parish councils. The Executive Committee recommended, however, that only half of the existing 1d per week contribution should be used for such political payments, the other half being used to support representatives to meetings of the Aged Miners' Homes Association and of infirmaries and hospitals. The miners agreed to support the amended scheme by 62,390 votes to 14,947.[2]

V

Only six months after Baldwin became Prime Minister he announced that he wanted a general election to be called on the issue of adopting a protective tariff to counteract depressed trade and growing unemployment. Baldwin felt unable to introduce a tariff without an election since Bonar Law had pledged himself not to consider such a measure during the current Parliament. The appeal to the electorate in autumn 1923 brought the Liberal and Labour parties out against protection and helped reunite the Liberal Party, although in Durham only one three-cornered contest occurred within the eleven County divisions. In the Durham division there were early hopes that the Liberal Party would contest the seat. By the time Parliament was dissolved the Conservatives had already chosen T. A. Bradford, who

[1] *Ibid.*, 6, 9 March 1922.
[2] *Durham Chronicle*, 16 November 1923.

had unsuccessfully fought the seat at Seaham against Sidney Webb in 1922, as their prospective candidate.[1] On 16 November the *Durham Chronicle* stated:

'Liberal opinion in Durham is . . . steadily developing in favour of the party seizing what is believed to be a unique opportunity of contesting the seat. In common with other parts of the country the Liberal cause in the constituency has suffered from party disunion, and now that complete unity has been achieved the feeling prevails that members of the party on this occasion would rally as one man in support of Liberal principles and in defence of Free Trade.'[2]

The Durham Liberal Association decided on 17 November to run a candidate,[3] but by the time the election had arrived no opposition against Bradford and Ritson, the miners' candidate already holding the seat, had been organized.

J. E. Johnston, who had fought the Houghton-le-Spring seat as a Liberal in November 1922, announced his decision not to stand for re-election early in November 1923. By 18 November A. C. Curry, a member of a Newcastle firm of accountants and auditors, had been adopted as prospective Liberal candidate.[4] The Conservative Party decided not to run a candidate in the division after W. Shaw, their candidate in the 1922 election, had accepted a nomination for a seat in the south of England.[5] R. Richardson defended the seat as the official Labour candidate of the Durham Miners' Association.

The Liberals decided against running a candidate at Blaydon in favour of reorganizing their party machinery in preparation for a future general election.[6] G. Denson, a native of Sunderland, had agreed on 17 November to contest the seat for the Conservatives against Whiteley, the existing miners' M.P. So clear did the opposition to protection appear in this mining constituency that the local political correspondent wrote on 27 November:

'There can be no doubt as to the result of the present contest. If there is any speculation, it's about the size of Mr Whiteley's majority'.[7]

The same candidates who were sponsored by the miners' Association and fought the County divisions in 1922 stood for election in the

[1] *Durham Chronicle*, 16 November 1923.
[2] *Ibid.*
[3] *Ibid.*, 18 November 1923.
[4] *Ibid.*, 17 November 1923.
[5] *Ibid.*
[6] *Ibid.*, 21 November 1923.
[7] *Ibid.*, 27 November 1923.

autumn of 1923 except at Barnard Castle. Following his defeat during
the 1922 election Swan, who had contested the constituency since
1918, was elected an Agent of the Durham Miners' Association.[1]
The political vacancy thus created was filled, not by a miners' candidate, but by M. Turner-Samuels, elected by the constituency's Labour
Party. Samuels, prior to being called to the Bar in 1922, had been a
solicitor in Newcastle and an ex-member of Newcastle City Council.
Lawther remained the only miners' candidate contesting a County
Borough seat having been relected to fight at South Shields.

The Durham Miners' Association continually urged its members
to support the Labour candidates by their votes and by their work
on behalf of local Labour Party committees.[2] In the *Durham Miners'
Manifesto*, issued on behalf of the miners' candidates by the Association's Executive Committee, the issue of protection received special
attention. Referring to the Conservatives the Committee wrote:

'They come before you now with the old dogma of Protection and
Tariffs. How will this affect you Northern Miners whose trade is
largely export? It will close markets against you and thereby cause
unemployment. It will send up the cost of timber and other materials
brought from abroad, add to your other costs, and thereby reduce
your wages.'[3]

That the majority of the voters within the County shared such doubts
about protection was revealed in the sweeping victories recorded
within the divisions for the Free Trade candidates. Five of the
miners' candidates were successfully returned whilst Labour secured
victories in nine of the eleven County divisions. At Durham Ritson
defeated Bradford by 13,819 votes to 10,530, increasing his majority
within the constituency. W. Whiteley retained the seat at Blaydon,
defeating Denson by 15,073 votes to 7,124, a majority of 7,949. At
Houghton-le-Spring Curry, the Liberal candidate, was defeated by
Richardson by a majority of 4,980, the voting being 15,225 to
10,445. At Chester-le-Street Lawson retained his seat against the
Conservative candidate C. R. S. Harris by a majority of 13,697, the
voting being 20,712 to 7,015. W. Appelby, the Conservative candidate
at Spennymoor, was defeated by Batey by 15,567 votes to 8,116. The
most surprising defeat occurred at Sedgefield where Herriotts, who
had secured the seat as a miners' candidate in 1922, was defeated by
the Conservative candidate L. Ropner, Director of Ropner Shipbuilding and Repairing Company (Stockton), Ltd., by only six

[1] See Chapter II, pp. 75–7.
[2] D.M.A., 19, 24 November 1923.
[3] Durham Miners' Association, *General Election 1923, Durham Miners' Manifesto*.

votes. The final voting, which gave Herriotts 11,087 votes to Ropner's 11,093, 110 papers having been spoilt, was only announced after three recounts and several scrutinies. Herriotts was bitterly dis- appointed with the result and told a *Durham Chronicle* reporter: 'We are not satisfied with the decision. . . . I am certain that I would have won the seat had not the unstamped ballot papers been re- jected'.[1] In the County Borough division of South Shields Lawther, the miners' candidate, was defeated by the Liberal candidate A. E. Harney by 22,912 votes to 15,717. Lawther's supporters publicly expressed their disappointment with the result and, according to one newspaper report, 'retired a broken chagrined . . . people'.[2]

As a result of the election the Conservative Party lost 87 seats, although by being returned with 258 seats was still the largest party in the House. The Labour Party, however, gained 49 seats and were returned with a total of 191 compared with the Liberals' 159. De- mands for a Liberal-Conservative Coalition were frustrated by the opposition of Asquith. The Labour Party refused to consider forming a coalition with the Liberals and MacDonald, as leader of the larger of the two opposition parties, was called upon to form the first Labour Government. Lawson, M.P. for Chester-le-Street, was appointed Financial Secretary to the War Office. B. C. Spoor, who represented Bishop Auckland, was appointed Parliamentary Secre- tary to the Treasury and Sidney Webb, who again had been success- fully returned at Seaham, became President of the Board of Trade.

VI

Labour's victory was short-lived. On 8 October 1924 the Govern- ment was defeated in the House in a vote on the Campbell case and resigned subjecting the country to yet another general election. The sudden decision to dissolve Parliament on 10 October found the political parties in Durham largely unprepared for a contest, although on the following day the *Durham Chronicle* reported that 'there has been much political activity during the last few months and arrange- ments are quickly being made to meet the emergency'.[3] During the following weeks the newspaper announced that 'campaigns are vigorously proceeding in all constituencies'.[4]

Earlier in September the Durham Divisional Liberal Association

[1] *Durham Chronicle*, 15 December 1923.
[2] *Newcastle Daily Chronicle*, 8 December 1923.
[3] *Durham Chronicle*, 11 October 1924.
[4] *Ibid.*, 18 October 1924.

had invited W. McKeag, a 27-year-old solicitor born at Belmont, near Durham, to contest the seat at the next general election. The Liberals had not contested the seat during the previous elections since, according to the secretary of the Northern Liberal Federation, they 'were without organization throughout the constituency'.[1] On 19 September S. R. Streatfield, who had served an apprenticeship as a mining engineer at Ryhope Colliery,[2] was unanimously adopted by the Durham Divisional Unionist Association to represent them at the next election. Ritson remained the official miners' candidate and the Durham Division entered upon the first three-cornered fight in its history.

At Sedgefield Sir Alfred Palmer, chairman of the local Liberal Association, agreed to support Ropner, the Conservative member with a majority of only six votes, despite the official pledge that the Liberals would remain strictly neutral.[3] At South Shields the candidate adopted by the Unionist Association eventually withdrew his nomination, leaving Lawther to contest the seat against the existing Liberal member E. A. Harney.[4]

The Durham Miners' Association's political candidates contested the six County divisions and the one County Borough division they had fought in 1923. The Association urged all members to secure victories for every Labour candidate fighting in the County [5] and made a grant of £100 from its political fund to help the national Labour Party assist candidates fighting in rural constituencies.[6]

At Blaydon the political situation had not altered since 1923, Whiteley being opposed by the Conservative candidate Denson. In 1924, however, Whiteley succeeded in increasing his majority defeating Denson by 27,670 votes to 10,549. Lawson held his seat at Chester-le-Street with only a slightly reduced majority against the Conservative candidate M. D. McCarthy, an under-manager at the local Ouston 'E' pit since 1912 and who previously had worked as a miner at Murton and Birtley.[7] Batey defeated his Conservative opponent H. C. Surtees at Spennymoor by 17,211 votes to 10,101. Herriotts failed to secure the seat at Sedgefield from the Conservatives, Ropner, the existing member, increasing his majority to 1,410 votes, the voting being 13,968 to 12,552.

[1] *Ibid.*, 6 September 1924.
[2] *Newcastle Daily Chronicle*, 20 September 1924.
[3] *Durham Chronicle*, 18 October 1924.
[4] *Newcastle Daily Chronicle*, 18 October 1924.
[5] D.M.A., 11, 21 October 1924.
[6] *Ibid.*, 28 October 1924.
[7] *Newcastle Daily Chronicle*, 15 October 1924.

At Durham Labour held the seat with an increased majority, the voting being Ritson 15,032, Streatfield 9,614, and McKeag 2,747. McKeag forfeited his deposit but held out strong hopes for the Liberal cause in Durham:

'I do not accept the result of this election as representing the voice of the people of Durham against Liberalism', he said. 'I believe that I am only the victim of the landslide which has happened during this election. The people have either voted to the left or to the right, and I have been in the unfortunate position of being in the middle.'[1]

Although the other Labour candidates in the County divisions of Bishop Auckland, Consett, Jarrow and Seaham held their seats the Barnard Castle Division fell to the Conservatives. Lawther was yet again unsuccessful at South Shields the existing Liberal member E. Harney defeating him by 23,171 votes to 16,852.

Nationally the election resulted in a resounding victory for the Conservatives who secured 419 seats (a gain of 161) compared with Labour's 151 (a loss of 40) and the Liberals' 40 (a loss of 119). The Conservatives came as near to an overall Conservative majority as was ever achieved between 1874 and 1931.[2] Five of the candidates sponsored by the Durham Miners' Association had been successfully returned and Labour secured nine of the eleven County seats. Nevertheless the Association, whose loyalty to Labour by this time was to a party as much as to a political philosophy, remained disappointed at the loss of Sedgefield and determined to intensify its future propaganda work in that division.

The County Council elections took place in March 1925 and had been preceded by the usual exhortations by the Durham miners' leaders appealing for increased Labour representation. As a result of the polling in the 74 electoral divisions Labour was able to regain a majority position on the Council securing 40 seats compared with 31 for the Moderates and 3 for the Independents.[3] Peter Lee was again returned for the Thornley division which he had represented since 1919. Six months after the elections the Association's Washington Glebe Lodge submitted a resolution to a Council Meeting requesting that the Agents should no longer be allowed to run as candidates in local elections.[4] This was due, in part, to the heavy demands being made upon the Agents by the growing industrial crisis in the autumn

[1] *Durham Chronicle*, 1 November 1924.
[2] Taylor, *op. cit.*, p. 221.
[3] *Durham Chronicle*, 7 March 1925.
[4] D.M.A., 5 September 1925.

of 1925 but in view of the successes which Labour members had already gained in helping influence the social and industrial conditions of their own environment there was little chance of such a restrictive measure being adopted. The Council described the resolution as 'the most retrogressive that has ever appeared on our ... programme' and 'fatal to the growth of democracy in this Country'.[1] It was subsequently rejected.[2]

The degree and strength of the future political representation of the miners suffered a more damaging blow with the passing of the 1927 Trades Disputes Act. The Government, intent on curbing the power of organized labour, not only made general sympathetic strikes illegal but sought to restrict the political activities of trade unions.[3] Miners now were required to 'contract in' as against 'contract out' of the payment of a political levy. In an effort to persuade as many miners in the County to continue paying their $\frac{1}{2}$d per week contribution for local political purposes together with the 2s per annum contribution to the M.F.G.B. the Executive Committee of the Durham Miners' Association organized a series of mass propaganda meetings between 29–30 October 1927 which were addressed by miners' officials and local miners' M.P.s.[4] Posters were issued for use at or near all local pits affording 'convincing reasons why all Durham miners should contract-in'.[5] The Trades Disputes Act came into force on 1 January 1928 and throughout the year the Durham miners' leaders urged members to support the political levies. The income of the Association's political fund fell sharply from £52,885 to £28,737 during 1927–8, the Association's total membership falling during the same period by over 9,000. During the period 1928–9 the total amount of the political fund rose to £38,542 as membership increased by just over 3,000.[6] By the end of November 1928, 120,348 of the Association's members (employed and unemployed) had contracted-in compared with only 6,980 who refused to pay the levies.[7] The Durham miners had expressed in no uncertain way their traditional loyalty towards political activity.

The County Council elections in March 1928 gave the miners the opportunity to express their political convictions. Labour's prospects were dimmed to some extent by the rule under which no person in

[1] *Ibid.*, 22 August 1925.
[2] *Ibid.*, 5 September 1925.
[3] Cf. Chapter VI, p. 235.
[4] D.M.A., 15, 20 October 1927.
[5] *Ibid.*, 14 November 1927.
[6] See Appendix I to this chapter.
[7] D.M.A., 16 January 1929.

receipt of unemployment relief could offer himself as a candidate at the local elections. The poverty and distress occasioned by the General Strike and its aftermath, whilst it may have reduced the number of potential candidates, intensified the determination of the miners to avenge their defeat in 1926. In addition the elections in Durham took place shortly after the imposition of severe wage reductions, amounting in the case of hewers to over 1s 2d per shift,[1] a fact which W. P. Richardson used with effect when he wrote in a circular to members on 23 February:

'By March 6th, the day on which the County Council Elections take place, you will have worked four shifts under the big reductions imposed upon you. It may be well for you to remember this as you go to the ballot box to record your vote. The opponents of Labour are, with some exceptions, the same people who have . . . associated with those who sought to reduce your wages and standard of life.'[2]

As a result of the elections Labour consolidated its control of the Council securing 46 seats to the Moderates' 25. The Independents failed to increase their representation retaining 3 seats. Thirteen Labour members, including Peter Lee, were returned unopposed.[3]

VIII

The Government returned in 1924 became the first to die a 'natural' death since quinquennial elections were introduced in 1911. The 1929 election, the first in which the complete adult electorate was allowed to vote, resulted in the formation of the second Labour Government. By the time the election took place on 30 May 1929 the Durham Miners' Association had increased the number of its Parliamentary Labour candidates to sixteen and in December 1929 added a further six.[4]

By the beginning of May 1929 all three political parties had selected their prospective candidates to fight the County divisions with the exception of the Liberals at Spennymoor and Sedgefield.[5] The Durham miners' officials invited all local Labour M.P.s to speak at the traditional May Day meetings as part of their election cam-

[1] See Chapter VI, pp. 236–9.
[2] D.M.A., 23 February 1928.
[3] *Durham Chronicle*, 2, 9 March 1928.
[4] D.M.A., 22 October 1923; 8 January 1924; 6 November 1928; 28 October, 27 December 1929.
[5] *Durham Chronicle*, 3 May 1929.

paign,[1] and issued appeals to all miners to vote solidly for Labour.

The Association again contested seven County seats, the only change in representation being the adoption of W. Lawther in January 1926 as the official miners' candidate for the Barnard Castle constituency, won by the Conservatives in 1924. The general election proved one of the least exciting of the post–1919 period.[2] On polling day the *Newcastle Daily Chronicle* reported of the Durham constituency:

'The campaign . . . ended as quietly as it began, and as serenely as it has been throughout its brief rather dull existence. Very little interest has been displayed in the city of Durham itself.'[3]

The same story of apathy was told in practically every constituency.[4]

However unexciting the various electoral campaigns were throughout the Durham County the electorate proved decisive in casting its votes. Labour candidates were returned in every County division and in six out of the seven County Borough seats, only the Labour candidate at the Hartlepools being defeated by the existing Conservative member. Whiteley, Lawson, Ritson and Richardson retained their seats and substantially increased the majorities secured in 1924.

In a three-cornered fight at Blaydon Whiteley polled 21,221 votes against the Conservative candidate R. C. White, a Newcastle businessman, who secured 7,847 votes and the Liberal T. W. Magnay, one of the founders of the National League of Young Liberals, who polled 6,878 votes. At Chester-le-Street Lawson defeated the Conservative candidate E. G. Payne, a barrister-at-law, and the Liberal J. W. Wright, a retired schoolmaster and member of the Middlesbrough Town Council, the voting being 26,975, 6,334 and 5,340 respectively.

At Durham Ritson again defeated McKeag, the Liberal opponent who had stood for the constituency for the first time in 1924, by 18,514 votes to 7,266. The Conservative candidate G. M. A. Hamilton-Fletcher, a Dorset magistrate, polled 6,820. The result was never really in doubt and, as the *Durham Chronicle* pointed out, 'the only point of speculation was as to whether the Conservative or Liberal standard bearer would occupy second place'.[5] The Liberal vote was surprisingly high considering the lack of Party organization in the

[1] *Ibid.*, 10 May 1929.
[2] Cf. Taylor, *op. cit.*, pp. 269–70.
[3] *Newcastle Daily Chronicle*, 30 May 1929.
[4] *Ibid.*
[5] *Durham Chronicle*, 7 June 1929.

constituency before 1924 and provided little hope for the future success of Conservative candidates.

R. Richardson retained his seat at Houghton-le-Spring against the Conservative opponent W. G. Pearson, the Mayor of Jarrow during 1928–30, and the Liberal candidate T. E. Wing, who had fought the Spennymoor and Houghton-le-Spring divisions in 1922 and 1924 respectively. The voting was 25,056, 8,545 and 10,267 respectively. At Sedgefield Herriotts captured the seat for Labour against Ropner, his Conservative opponent in both 1923 and 1924, and W. Leeson, a building merchant's warehouseman from Darlington and a member of the Thornaby-on-Tees Town Council, by 15,749 votes to 13,043 and 4,236. W. Lawther scored his first Parliamentary success in capturing the seat at Barnard Castle from the Conservatives. He defeated the existing member, C. M. Headlam, by 9,281 votes to 8,402. The Liberal candidate, E. Spence, a member of a Middlesbrough trading firm and a former Mayor of Middlesbrough, secured 4,402 votes. At Spennymoor Batey retained his seat against his Conservative opponent F. P. Gourlay, a London stockbroker by 20,858 votes to 8,202. The Liberals had initially decided to allow T. Magnay to contest the seat but he was later transferred to the Blaydon constituency.[1] The largest majority secured in the whole election was obtained by Ramsay MacDonald, who had replaced Sidney Webb as Labour candidate at Seaham, against Conservative, Liberal and Communist opposition. Both the Liberal and Communist contenders forfeited their deposits whilst Labour secured a majority of 28,794 votes.

As a result of the election the Labour Party became the largest party in the House of Commons but without a clear majority. Having captured 37·1 per cent of the total vote it secured 288 seats compared with the Conservatives' 260 and the Liberals' 59.

VIII

The advent of a second Labour Government failed to provide any effective cure to the country's industrial depression and rising unemployment. Its term of office has been described by one writer as 'an interlude of sheer futility'.[2] Nevertheless the collapse of the Government after only two years was directly caused, not by rising unemployment, but the financial crisis of 1931. In an effort to

[1] *Ibid.*, 24 May 1929.
[2] Somervell, *op. cit.*, p. 185.

balance the budget and prevent a 'flight from the pound' the Government believed that either unemployment benefit should be reduced or the gold standard suspended. The Cabinet was split over the necessary course to adopt, MacDonald favouring economy in government expenditure. In August 1931 MacDonald offered to resign but, in an effort to save the country from financial ruin, was persuaded to form a 'National Government' as an emergency measure. By 24 August MacDonald had become Prime Minister of a newly-formed National Government and on 7 October Parliament was dissolved. MacDonald pleaded for a 'doctor's mandate' in order that each political party might put forward its own programme to meet the crisis facing the country.

MacDonald's acceptance of a National Government aroused strong opposition in Durham. At the end of August 1931 the Executive Committee of the Seaham Divisional Labour Party recommended that MacDonald resign his seat being a leader of a government 'without ... Labour credentials'.[1] MacDonald refused to resign and in a letter to A. Coxon, secretary of the Seaham Labour Party, confirmed his decision to contest the seat at the coming general election.[2] Despite the support given by the local Labour Party's delegates to the Executive Committee's recommendation nothing was done to alter the Labour representation in the division.[3]

Nationalism spread throughout the North-East as the Conservatives and Liberals joined forces to oust Labour candidates. In the Durham division T. A. Bradford, who had been elected as prospective Conservative candidate in February 1931 and who had previously contested the seat in 1923, withdrew his candidature in October in view of McKeag's adoption as the National Liberal candidate.[4] At Chester-le-Street the Liberals agreed to support the National Conservative candidate R. G. Kellett, a 22-year-old stockbroker, in fighting perhaps the safest Labour seat in County Durham.[5] At their meeting at Crook on 13 October the Executive Committee of the Spennymoor Divisional Liberal Association decided unanimously to support the Conservative candidate M. D. McCarthy, who had unsuccessfully contested the Chester-le-Street seat in 1924, despite the fact that a candidate had already been invited to contest the seat as a National Liberal.[6]

[1] Durham Chronicle, 4 September 1931.
[2] Ibid.
[3] Ibid., 18 September 1931.
[4] Newcastle Daily Chronicle, 13 October 1931.
[5] Ibid.
[6] Durham Chronicle, 16 October 1931.

The general election, held on 27 October, proved a miserable defeat for Labour. The seven miners' candidates who had fought the 1929 election had again been elected to fight in 1931 but only two were eventually returned. W. Lawther was defeated at Barnard Castle by his previous opponent C. M. Headlam by 12,721 votes to 10,287. W. Whiteley, who had held the seat at Blaydon since 1922, was defeated by a narrow margin by the Unionist candidate T. B. Martin, a private secretary, by 18,927 votes to 18,431, a majority of only 496. In Durham, W. McKeag eventually succeeded in securing the seat from Ritson but by a majority of only 270 votes. McKeag, who had contested the seat in 1924 and 1929, secured 17,406 votes to Ritson's 17,136 and for the first time since 1922 the seat fell to the Liberals.

At Houghton-le-Spring the Unionist candidate R. Chapman, a member of the South Shields Town Council and a Deputy Lieutenant of Durham County, defeated R. Richardson, the officially-sponsored miners' candidate who had sat for the division since 1918, by 25,549 votes to 22,700. J. Herriotts lost his seat at Sedgefield to the Unionist candidate R. Jennings, a chartered accountant and a director of several companies associated with the mining industry in the North of England. The voting was 21,956 to 15,404, a Unionist majority of 6,552. J. Lawson retained his seat at Chester-le-Street against opposition from Kellett, the young Unionist candidate, with a majority of 8,539 votes. The voting was 24,373 to 15,834. The only other successful miners' candidate was J. Batey, who was again returned at Spennymoor defeating McCarthy by 18,072 votes to 14,072.

At Seaham Ramsay MacDonald succeeded in defeating the Labour candidate W. Coxon, a schoolmaster and divisional secretary of the Seaham Labour Party who had been adopted to contest the seat which MacDonald refused to vacate and the Communist candidate G. Lumley, a checkweighman at Ryhope Colliery and a member of the Executive Committee of the Durham Miners' Association. The Association agreed to support Coxon in his fight against MacDonald and protested against Lumley running against the officially-adopted Labour candidate.[1] Politically Durham County had become the cynosure of the whole country during the period of the general election by virtue of MacDonald's fight at Seaham. In a circular to the voters at Seaham Robson, who was unable to participate in the election campaign owing to ill-health, wrote:

[1] D.M.A., 20 October 1931.

'The Durham miner and his wife never had a greater responsibility
cast upon them than in giving their vote on this occasion. The
question is as to whether we should give a political home to men
who, to say the least, have turned traitors to the Labour movement.[1]

Despite the support given to Coxon he was defeated by MacDonald
by 28,978 votes to 23,027. Lumley, who secured only 677 votes,
forfeited his deposit.

In the three remaining County divisions the existing Labour candidates were all defeated and in the seven Borough divisions Labour
failed to secure a single seat. Nationally the Conservatives and their
allies the National Liberals and the National Labour candidates
together secured 521 seats. Labour held only 52 seats compared with
the Liberals' 33. Peter Lee believed the contest to be 'the worst fought
election of modern times for abuse and misrepresentation',[2] and
condemned the Conservatives and Liberals for uniting in opposition
to the Labour candidates. At a meeting in the Miners' Hall at
Durham following the declaration of the poll in Durham City Lee
complained:

'We are experiencing today what misrepresentation can do amongst
people who have no convictions. . . . The working people by this
election, will recognize that the Liberals and Conservatives are dead
against them and that they form one solid mass against Labour
being in power in this country.'[3]

At local level Labour had already suffered a net loss of two seats in
the County Council elections held in Durham during March 1931
although the Party retained a majority position. Forty-four Labour
members were eventually elected against a combined total of thirty
Moderates and Independents.[4]

The defeat of so many Labour candidates in the 1931 election
posed a serious problem in Durham since, unlike in most other coalfields, no provision was made for assisting M.P.s who lost their seats.
The former Union officials who were defeated in the elections in
Derbyshire and Lancashire returned to work as miners' agents. In
Yorkshire the three defeated miners' candidates were, according to
rule, employed by the miners' Association for six months at a salary
equivalent to a permanent official and thereafter at a retaining fee of

[1] *Durham Chronicle*, 23 October 1931.
[2] Durham Miners' Association, *General Secretary's Quarterly Report, No. 5*,
December 1941, p. 6.
[3] *Durham Chronicle*, 30 October 1931.
[4] D.M.A., 9 March 1931.

£150 per year for the period of the existing Parliament, providing they were readopted for their various constituencies. In Scotland five of the seven defeated miners' candidates were re-engaged within their trade union organization.[1]

The M.F.G.B. had decided in November 1931 that it was unable to make any provision from its central Political Fund for allowances to displaced miners' M.P.s.[2] The Executive Committee of the Durham Miners' Association rejected a resolution submitted by the Mainsforth Lodge in January 1924 calling for a scheme of financial security for defeated miners' candidates and when the Lodge put forward a similar request in January 1932 it was again rejected.[3] In May 1932, however, the Association's Council agreed that ex-miners' M.P.s should be engaged in propaganda work within the divisions for which they had been chosen and elsewhere and to be paid by the Association.[4] The salary, payable from the County Political Fund, was later fixed at £150 per year.[5]

Not only were the defeated miners' M.P.s in difficulty but many Lodges during the 1930s found that their local political funds quickly became exhausted owing to long-term unemployment amongst their paying membership. In October 1933 the Durham Miners' Association agreed to assist Lodges idle since June in financing Labour representation on local bodies providing that the unemployed members agreed to continue paying at least ½d per week into their local political fund. In addition the Association agreed to provide a quarterly payments to each Lodge idle according to the number of councillors supported and the number of meetings attended each quarter.[6] The scale of payments ranged from 1s per parish council meeting to 5s per meeting of County councillors.[7]

As the number of applications for assistance increased during 1934 the Executive Committee decided that any Lodge with not more than 50 per cent of its membership working and the remainder idle for at least three months should be paid only half the scale allowance.[8] In an effort to maintain their support to local councillors several Lodges throughout the County pooled their allowances and made payments from a central fund.[9]

[1] Ibid., 2 December 1931.
[2] M.F.G.B., 26 November 1931.
[3] D.M.A., 26 January 1924; 23 January 1932.
[4] Ibid., 14 May 1932.
[5] Ibid., 18 August 1934.
[6] Ibid., 17 June; 12 October 1933.
[7] Ibid., 20 November 1933.
[8] Ibid., 10 July 1934.
[9] Ibid.

344 THE DURHAM MINERS

The ability to support local Labour candidates assumed particular importance during 1934 since in March the election of the County Council was due to take place. Peter Lee had resigned as Chairman of the Council in 1932, having decided during the previous year not to stand for re-election as the representative of the Thornley division.[1] W. N. Smith, a member of the County Council since 1917 and a former secretary of the North-East District of the W.E.A., succeeded Lee as chairman in May 1932.[2] As a result of the elections Labour strengthened its majority position on the Council gaining an extra ten seats.[3] Not everyone was convinced of the ultimate benefit of the increasing participation of working men in local and national politics. In a radio debate between J. Lawson, M.P. for Chester-le-Street and C. M. Headlam, M.P. for Barnard Castle, in June 1924 Headlam proclaimed:

'It would be far better for the workers of this country if less of their money were expended on purely political purposes, and more were utilized for the provision of assistance when they were debarred from working from one cause or another. . . . In Durham and elsewhere there are many homes for aged miners; how many more might there be if only it were not deemed necessary to send so many socialists to the local Councils and to Parliament!'[4]

During the previous two years, however, arrangements had been made within the coalfield in preparation for the next general election. J. Ritson was again adopted as the prospective Labour candidate for the Durham division at a Labour Party meeting at the Miners' Hall in February 1932.[5] R. Richardson who had, until 1931, held the seat at Houghton-le-Spring for thirteen years, was defeated by six votes in a fight for the miners' candidature of the constituency in April 1932 against W. J. Stewart. Stewart, unemployed, and a former employee at Boldon Colliery, had served on the Executive Committee of the Durham Miners' Association, the Durham County Federation Board, the Durham County Council (since 1922) and had been Vice-President of the Divisional Labour Party since 1926.[6]

J. Herriotts, who had been elected as prospective Labour candidate for the Sedgefield division in April 1932, died in 1935 and was

[1] *Durham Chronicle*, 25 September 1931.
[2] *Ibid.*, 6 May 1932.
[3] *Ibid.*, 9 March 1934.
[4] *Listener*, 20 June 1934.
[5] *Durham Chronicle*, 19 February 1932.
[6] *Ibid.*, 15 April 1932.

succeeded by J. R. Leslie, General Secretary of the National Amalgamated Union of Shop Assistants, Warehousemen and Clerks and
chairman of the General Purposes Committee of the T.U.C. Leslie
defeated J. Kelly, H. Peacock and G. Bloomfield, all officially
sponsored by the Durham Miners' Association, in a vote for the
candidature.[1]

In March 1932 the Durham County Federation of Divisional
Labour Parties organized a mass demonstration at the Town Hall,
Durham, under the chairmanship of William Whiteley, to mark the
beginning of an intensive campaign to ensure increased Labour
representation at the next general election. Peter Lee represented the
miners and the defeated miners' M.P.s joined George Lansbury,
leader of the Parliamentary Labour Party, in addressing the gathering.[2] A similar meeting was organized at the Miners' Hall in June
1934.[3]

Though a resolution to enlarge the list of Parliamentary candidates
so that each Lodge of the Durham Miners' Association would have
one financial member upon the list was defeated in August 1934,[4]
the Association's Council decided in September 1935, that steps
should be taken 'to give the necessary attention to the perfecting of
our political machinery'.[5] Efforts were made to encourage the
development of study circles for the young members and to foster
discussion within the Lodges about 'those questions and subjects
which will be at issue in the election'.[6]

Such preparations were not without value for on 25 October Parliament was dissolved and a general election fixed for 14 November.
Foreign policy and the rearmament issue were gradually replaced by
housing and unemployment as the dominant election themes.[7] The
Durham miners' leaders had long sought to revenge the defeat of
Labour in 1931 and appealed to the union's membership to give unfailing support to the Labour candidates. In a circular to members
the Association's Executive Committee wrote of the election:

'No section of the community ought to welcome it more than the
Durham Miners. No area has been more stricken; and indeed none
paid for a bigger price than the Durham miner for our folly of 1931.

[1] *Ibid.*, 27 September 1935.
[2] *Ibid.*, 11 March 1932.
[3] *Ibid.*, 15 June 1934.
[4] D.M.A., 18 August 1934.
[5] *Ibid.*, 21 September 1935.
[6] *Ibid.*
[7] Taylor, *op. cit.*, p. 383.

Four valuable years have been thrown away by the National Government. They can take no pride for any decent improvement. Poverty has become more stark, distress has sunk deeper. . . .

We were vilely tricked and imposed on at the elections of 1924 and 1931. . . . We cannot be imposed upon for the third time. Further, Durham must take its legitimate place in the front of political democracy.'[1]

Immediately following the dissolution of Parliament local political party organizations made final preparations for the forthcoming election. At a meeting of the Houghton-le-Spring Liberal Association on 26 October it was decided to adopt E. Richardson, a Newcastle solicitor, to fight W. J. Stewart, the newly-elected miners' candidate.[2] At a further meeting four days later, however, the Liberals decided to postpone their fight until a later election. Undecided as to which of the remaining two parties to support (the Conservative having already decided to run a candidate), the Liberals invited both the Socialist and Conservative candidates to reply to a questionnaire covering the various election issues so as to provide a basis upon which Liberal supporters could be recommended to vote.[3] Both members succeeded in securing substantial Liberal support in favour of their nomination, whereupon the Executive Committee of the Liberal Association advised party members to vote according to their personal inclinations.[4]

At Spennymoor both Batey and McCarthy were again adopted as Labour and Unionist candidates respectively. During the last week of October the Independent Socialists decided to adopt C. Wilson, from Willington, Co. Durham, as their official candidate although it was found necessary to secure the support of local beneficiaries in order to raise his deposit. Local supporters organized a fighting fund and subscriptions were offered by unemployed miners from all parts of the division.[5] Wilson, who described the Labour candidates as 'a herd of careerists, opportunists, self-seekers, and position hunters', declared his intention to win the seat for the sake of 'pure unadulterated, uncompromising, four-square Socialism'.[6] Despite his determination and the promising financial support during the early stages of his campaign Wilson finally withdrew from the

[1] D.M.A., 1 November 1935.
[2] *Newcastle Daily Chronicle*, 28 October 1935.
[3] *Ibid.*, 31 October 1935.
[4] *Ibid.*, 25 November 1935.
[5] *Durham Chronicle*, 1 November 1935.
[6] *Ibid.*

fight, having failed to hand in his deposit within the specified time.[1]

At Seaham Ramsay MacDonald defended his seat against a new Labour opponent, E. Shinwell, who represented Linlithgow in Scotland at various periods during 1922-31. During the period of the first Labour Government he was Financial Secretary to the War Office and Secretary for Mines. The Durham Miners' Association, anxious to ensure Shinwell's success, granted him £100 towards his election expenses. A similar grant had been made in support of MacDonald's candidature in 1929 but the 1931 debacle and the deepening depression of the 1930s had wrought increasing disillusionment and an intense desire amongst the Durham miners to rid the County of all Coalition representatives.[2] MacDonald was not without support. At Shotton a temporary landing ground was developed to enable aeroplanes, bearing MacDonald's supporters, to land safely and quickly.[3]

In December 1931 Lawther had again been adopted as prospective Labour candidate for the Barnard Castle division but, having decided to devote his energies to industrial affairs following his appointment in 1935 as Vice-President of the M.F.G.B.,[4] he declined to fight the seat and was replaced by T. M. Sexton, a local schoolmaster. Sexton was not an official miners' candidate and the Durham Miners' Association relinquished its stand in the division.

Having failed to secure representation at Sedgefield,[5] miners' candidates fought seats at only five constituencies within the County, at Blaydon, Chester-le-Street, Durham, Houghton-le-Spring and Spennymoor. As a result of the election all the miners' candidates were successfully returned as were the Labour candidates within the remaining County divisions. With Labour's success in the Borough division of South Shields the Socialists gained control in twelve of the eighteen constituencies within the coalfield.

At Blaydon W. Whiteley succeeded in capturing the seat in opposition to C. E. Vickery, a retired Colonel, representing the Unionist party. The voting was 24,148 to 14,622. T. B. Martin, elected to the constituency in 1931, vacated the seat to fight the Camberwell North Division in London but lost to the Labour candidate C. G. Ammon. Lawson retained his seat at Chester-le-Street with a majority more than double that secured in 1931. He defeated C. R. Besley, assistant solicitor to the Newcastle-on-Tyne Corpora-

[1] *Newcastle Daily Chronicle*, 5 November 1935.
[2] *Ibid.*, 30 October 1935.
[3] *Ibid.*, 31 October 1935.
[4] *Ibid.*, 30 October 1935.
[5] See above, pp. 344-5.

tion, by 29,111 votes to 11,901. Batey, who with Lawson had been
the only other miners' M.P. to be returned in 1931, defeated his
former opponent M. D. McCarthy at Spennymoor by 21,473 votes
to 8,696, thereby increasing his previous majority. Ritson prevented
a second Liberal victory by defeating the existing member W.
McKeag by 21,517 votes to 14,910. McKeag openly criticized the
miners' union as being instrumental in his defeat complaining: 'The
machine of the Durham Miners' Association, with its affiliated
lodges, has been used for the dissemination throughout the division
of propaganda of the most scurrilous description'.[1] He later described
the fight as 'a filthy election'[2] although no evidence has been found
to support these accusations.

W. J. Stewart, contesting the Houghton-le-Spring division for the
first time, ousted the existing Unionist member R. Chapman by
30,665 votes to 22,990, a Labour majority of 7,675. At Seaham
Shinwell polled over twice MacDonald's votes, gaining 38,380 to
17,882. Nationally, Labour's representation in the House of Commons increased from 52 seats to 154, the Conservatives' declining
from 473 seats to 432 and the Liberals' from 33 to 20.

IX

Following the general election the Durham Miners' Association
turned its attention towards revising the method of selecting its own
Parliamentary candidates. Lodges were allocated votes according to
the number of their members paying into the local political fund and
were entitled to select a candidate for their division from the official
Association's list. The Lodge was thereafter honour bound to support
the nominee at the Divisional Labour Party Selection Conference.
At the same time the Association agreed to offer the selected candidates all necessary 'financial and moral support'.[3]

Until 1937 Durham miners were provided with a single document
upon which they could signify their willingness, or otherwise, to
contribute both to the M.F.G.B. and the Association's political
funds. To conform with the requirements of the Trade Unions and
Trade Disputes Act, however, it was necessary to supply separate
contracting-in forms for each levy. From 1937 the members' weekly

[1] *Newcastle Daily Chronicle*, 16 November 1935.
[2] *Durham Chronicle*, 22 November 1935.
[3] D.M.A., 28 December 1935; 23 May 1936.

political contributions were entered separately and the Association's contribution to each fund specifically indicated.[1]

Following the County Council elections in March 1937 Labour strengthened its majority position by securing 64 seats compared with the Moderates' 27. Thirty-two Labour candidates were returned unopposed.[2] The Executive Committee of the Durham Miners' Association had adopted its time-honoured role of encouraging all miners and their families to actively support the Labour candidates so that they could 'maintain their legitimate place in the vanguard of political democracy of Great Britain by retaining control of the County Council'.[3]

The approach of the Second World War turned the Association's attention increasingly towards the international situation. Various grants were made in support of the oppressed throughout Western Europe. In November 1937 the Durham miners granted £200 to German and Austrian political refugees.[4] In the previous year a similar amount had been given to the Spanish workers to support their fight for freedom,[5] and in October 1938 a fund was launched in support of the Czechoslovakian workers. Members of the Association were urged to establish committees within their localities under the auspices of the miners' Lodges and to arrange door-to-door collections in order to raise money.[6]

The Durham miners' officials played an active role in promoting the Labour Party's campaign for Peace and Security,[7] and protested vehemently against the Nazi treatment of the Jews. In November 1938 the Association's Executive Committee forwarded resolutions to the Labour Party, Foreign Secretary and the Prime Minister condemning 'the brutal and inhuman treatment meted out by the Nazi Government to the men, women and children of the Jewish race'.[8] Regarding the scheme of compulsory conscription introduced into Britain in 1939 as a direct threat to peace the Association appealed to the M.F.G.B. in May 1939 to help secure its withdrawal.[9] Despite its failure in this respect the Durham miners' Executive Committee determined upon further efforts towards fostering world peace but their activities were abruptly interrupted by the outbreak of war.

[1] *Ibid.*, 14, 17, 24 June 1937.
[2] *Durham Chronicle*, 5 March 1937.
[3] D.M.A., 1 February 1937.
[4] *Ibid.*, 2 November 1937.
[5] *Ibid.*, 12 August, 1 September 1936.
[6] *Ibid.*, 6 October 1938.
[7] *Ibid.*, 5, 12 March 1938.
[8] *Ibid.*, 14 November 1938.
[9] M.F.G.B., 10 May 1939.

Appendix I

DURHAM MINERS' ASSOCIATION POLITICAL FUND,
1921–1939

Year	Total £	Expenditure £	Balance £
1921	18,994	6,517	12,477
1922	41,215	17,863	23,352
1923	46,347	24,871	21,476
1924	75,156	47,958	27,198
1925	59,459	27,688	31,771
1926	39,348	7,580	31,768
1927	52,885	34,884	18,001
1928	28,737	13,111	15,626
1929	38,542	17,238	21,304
1930	36,032	12,370	23,662
1931	45,087	16,195	28,892
1932	44,162	11,585	32,577
1933	47,099	11,387	35,712
1934	50,812	12,563	38,249
1935	56,005	17,086	38,919
1936	56,160	12,646	41,514
1937	57,074	15,162	41,912
1938	57,250	17,958	39,292
1939	53,953	14,142	39,811

Source: Durham Miners' Association, *Financial Returns*, 1921–1939.

Chapter IX

THE SECOND WORLD WAR
AND AFTER

I

If the miners' experiences during 1919–39 differed considerably from those before 1914 the changing fortunes of the coal industry after 1939 provided an equally remarkable transformation. The priority position which the coal industry enjoyed during the difficult wartime period added considerably to its problems and at the same time increased its ability to secure long sought-after improvements. As old problems disappeared new ones emerged. Unemployment, poverty and long-term trade depression on the scale experienced during the twenties assumed less significance, whilst the difficulties of maintaining wages, output, employment, and productivity in accordance with the nation's needs and resources became increasingly apparent.

The coal industry entered the Second World War with most of its major problems unsolved. The demands of wartime production necessarily added a great strain upon what was already a depressed and contracting industry. The relative ease with which the industry could adapt itself to meet the abnormalities of war depended, to a large extent, upon the degree of co-operation between the coal owners, the miners and the Government. The Government, for its part, adopted a highly decentralized system of control in marked contrast to its use of direct statutory power during 1914–18. The supply and distribution of coal were controlled by officers of the Mines Department. The chairmen of the District Executive Boards of colliery owners, established under the Coal Mines Act of 1930, became the coal supplies officers in the various coalfields responsible for the maintenance of an adequate supply and distribution of coal at the pithead in accordance with wartime priorities. Divisional Coal Officers in each of the twelve regions into which the country was divided for civil defence purposes safeguarded the interests of domestic consumers. In each of the five coal-shipping districts coal export officers dealt with the certification of permissible coal exports under the Board of Trade licence scheme whereby the free export of coal was prohibited save by prior consent of the Board. Local fuel overseers were appointed by local government authorities to enforce

351

coal rationing.[1] In October 1939 the M.F.G.B. and the Mining Association agreed to a widening of the scope of activity of the Joint Standing Consultative Committee, established in 1936,[2] to allow it to consider all relevant problems arising from the abnormal circumstances of war.[3]

The most immediate problem facing the miners with the outbreak of war was the rise in the cost of living. In September 1939 the M.F.G.B. put forward a claim for an immediate flat rate increase of 1s per shift for men and 6d for boys in addition to what was being paid according to district ascertainments.[4] The owners offered increases of 8d and 4d per shift as a 'War Bonus' payable from 1 November to the end of December subject to a maximum of six shifts per week. The position was to be reviewed again in January 1940 in the event of a further rise in the cost of living. The M.F.G.B. accepted the terms on 27 October and the Durham County Federation Board, in consultation with local coal owners, on 6 November.[5] Some Durham miners, believing the offers to be inadequate, protested that their Association so readily agreed to the advances whilst the cost-of-living index continued to rise.[6] The M.F.G.B. was conscious of the need to establish an agreed formula to provide adjustments in wages in relation to unit changes in the cost-of-living,[7] but decided at its meeting on 20 December to consider instead the amount of the flat-rate advance which was to operate from 1 January 1940.[8] The Federation demanded an additional 7d a shift for adults and 3½d for boys, which the owners refused to consider. Eventually in January 1940 a formula was agreed upon for the automatic adjustment of wages which stated:

'That 0·7d per shift be the variation in the flat rate war additions to the shift wage of the adult worker corresponding to a variation of one point in the cost of living index number, subject to three-monthly reviews, and that there should be no change in the flat rates unless the index figure varies by not less than 5 points.'[9]

---

[1] W. H. B. Court, *Coal*, London 1951, pp. 40–3.
[2] See Chapter VI, p. 257.
[3] M.F.G.B., 27 October 1939.
[4] *Ibid.*
[5] D.M.A., 9 November 1939.
[6] *Ibid.*, 14 November, 2 December 1939; *Durham Chronicle*, 1 December 1939.
[7] Miners' Federation of Great Britain, *Wages and the Cost of Living*, 29 December 1939, p. 8.
[8] *Ibid.*, pp. 9–10.
[9] M.F.G.B., 25 January 1940.

The Federation recommended that districts accept the formula. The voting was 421,721 for acceptance and 166,600 against, Durham voting with the majority.[1] An additional 5d a shift for adults and $2\frac{1}{2}$d for boys was granted to cover the period 1 January to 31 March, the new agreement coming into operation on 1 April.

Not all miners received the total value of the flat rate advance in addition to ascertained wages, as in 1939, since the advances were made to include any percentage addition to basic rates above the minimum earned by districts in January 1940. In Durham wages had remained at their minimum level during October–December 1939 but, as a result of rising coal prices in November 1939, the percentage addition to basic rates had risen to 2·75 per cent above the minimum in January 1940, equivalent to an advance per shift of 2d for adults and 1d for boys. The net increase in wages payable to Durham miners, therefore, stood at only 3d and $1\frac{1}{2}$d. The anomaly did not last long, however, since in February 1940 the National Joint Consultative Committee agreed to grant the full value of all future wages advances made in compensation for the rising cost of living in addition to ascertained wages.[2]

In addition to these national concessions adult putters on piece work in Durham succeeded during 1940 in gaining a new standard basic wage of 4s 9d per shift compared with the rates fixed under the wages agreement of 15 May 1937[3] which varied from 4s 3d to 4s 8d per shift. The new standard was further increased to 5s per shift in October 1942.[4]

II

The dislocation of shipping during the early months of war seriously affected Durham's coastwise coal trade with public utility consumers in London. Attempts by the Mines Department during October 1939 to direct coal supplies to London from the Midlands proved disappointing and in January 1940 arrangements were made to rail coal from the Northumberland and Durham coalfield to the large electricity and gas works in southern England. The severe weather during that month eventually resulted in the complete stoppage of traffic and a spread of coal shortages to areas not normally dependent upon seaborne supplies.[5] The depletion of household and industrial coal

[1] *Ibid.*, 29 February 1940.
[2] D.M.A., 14 February, 18 March 1940.
[3] See Chapter VI, pp. 259–61; 266.
[4] D.M.A., 8 July 1940; 13 October 1942.
[5] Court, *op. cit.*, pp. 62–4.

stocks was aggravated by continuing bad weather and in February 1940 arrangements were made to send an extra 71,500 tons of coal per week by rail from collieries in the north-east and the Midlands.[1] By May 1940 the shortage of coal supplies to households and public utility undertakings had been overcome but only after the Ministry of Shipping and the Admiralty had eased the problem of distribution by supplying coal-carrying ships which, together with rail shipments, were expected to boost coal supplies to London to a rate of 100,000 tons a week.[2] The dislocation of trade and transport had immediate effects upon employment in the Durham coalfield. On 11 September 1939 a total of 18,372 miners in Durham were either wholly or temporarily unemployed and by 11 December the figure had fallen to only 15,087. Conditions improved as a result of the winter programme to increase coal supplies to the South and by 11 March 1940 the total number unemployed had fallen to 6,571.[3]

Coal production as well as distribution posed serious problems during the early war years. In September 1939 coal owners and miners were asked by the Government to raise the production of coal to 270 million tons per year, an increase of about 40 million tons compared with 1938. The achievement of such a programme largely depended upon the labour force available to the industry. The Government was anxious to meet the increasing demands of armament production and to maintain exports with the object of providing the greatest possible amount of foreign currency. Britain's ability to meet foreign coal demands was severely curtailed by shortage of shipping, such that between October 1939 and February 1940 coal exports to France fell short of expectations by almost 932,000 tons,[4] and by a level of home coal production insufficient to supply overseas consumers without danger to internal stocks.

In April 1940 a Coal Production Council was established to promote a substantial increase in the production of coal, especially in exporting regions. The Council, under the chairmanship of Lord Portal, consisted of an equal number of representatives of the coal owners, the Government, and the miners, of whom Lawther was one. Following a meeting with Portal on 18 April representatives of the owners and miners in Durham agreed to establish a District Production Committee.[5] The need for greater production became crucial following German action in the Low Countries during May

[1] *Ibid.*, p. 64.
[2] *Ibid.*, p. 65.
[3] 358 H.C. Deb. 5s, 731–2; 360 H.C. Deb. 5s, 39.
[4] Court, *op. cit.*, p. 73.
[5] D.M.A., 23 April 1940.

1940, and the Durham Miners' and Coal Owners' Associations jointly embarked upon an intensive campaign to increase coal output. Pits arranged to work double shifts on Saturdays; miners agreed to work during statutory holiday periods, for which the owners agreed to pay additional wages, and an appeal was made to reduce absenteeism to a minimum.[1] At many collieries miners agreed to working conditions which only during the previous month they had rejected as part of the Association's own attempts to improve coal output.[2] The campaign continued throughout June. Mass meetings were held throughout the coalfield and, following a recommendation by E. Bevin, Minister of Labour, the Association appealed to members to arrange with local colliery managers to suspend all holidays for the sake of increased output.[3]

The drive to increase coal production suffered a severe setback with the collapse of France on 18 June 1940. The desire to reconcile the British war effort towards meeting the extraordinary demands by France for coal exports had provided a major impetus behind the coal production campaign of April–June 1940. Indeed, on 6 May the War Cabinet had decided to embark upon a six-month coal export programme to feed the French steel industry.[4] The export market for Durham gas and coking coals was now completely disorganized. Cargo exports from the Durham and South Wales coalfields, totalling 750,000 tons, which had reached French ports at the time of the collapse, had had to be recalled for fear of falling into German hands.[5] The German occupation of the mainland of western Europe reduced the possibility of expanding coastwise coal trade to compensate for losses overseas. Whilst the Northumberland coalfield was able to help meet Lancashire's demand for extra supplies of industrial coal for work on war contracts[6] and South Wales to benefit from the relaxation of transport difficulties by September 1940, Durham found it increasingly difficult to dispose of its special-quality gas and coking coal, and the losses in coal exports, estimated at about 800,000 tons per month, caused immediate short-time working and closure of pits.[7]

On 25 June 1940 representatives of the Durham County Federa-

---

[1] *Ibid.*, 11, 20, 27 May 1940.
[2] *Ibid.*, 23 April, 20 May 1940.
[3] *Ibid.*, 3 June 1940; M.F.G.B., 4 July 1940.
[4] Court, *op. cit.*, pp. 76–81.
[5] *Durham Chronicle*, 28 June 1940.
[6] But not without opposition. Cf. J. E. Williams, *The Derbyshire Miners*, London 1962, p. 847.
[7] Court, *op. cit.*, pp. 83–4; Durham Miners' Association, *General Secretary's Review for the Year 1940*, p. 17.

tion Board met D. R. Grenfell, Secretary for Mines, and urged upon him the necessity of re-allocating the available inland coal trade by establishing for all districts a quota standard of tonnage so that collieries throughout the country could spread work during the period of dislocation.[1] The alternative, Swan argued at a Federation Conference on 16 July, was the re-emergence of price undercutting and a scramble for markets by exporting areas as occurred during the early thirties:[2]

'The policy we are putting forward is an economic policy, and as well as being economic it is a moral policy, that whatever amount of coal production is required it should be shared. No man in the Midlands or elsewhere can justify a system which allows some miners to be overworked while others are underworked.'[3]

The response of other districts was not encouraging. Delegates from South Wales and the Midlands emphasized at the same conference that they would never agree to a formula of trade-sharing until its total ramifications had been fully investigated.[4]

From August to December 1940 Durham miners' officials kept in close contact with representatives of the Mines Department. Watson continually urged the Government to allocate to Durham a definite share of the inland coal trade, to encourge the stocking of coal so as to provide increased employment and to transfer a larger proportion of the trade in coal by rail to the region.[5] The decision by the Minister of Shipping during December to advise shippers to avoid the use of Durham bunker coal in favour of large Welsh coal aroused a storm of protest from Durham miners' officials and mining M.P.s alike.[6]

Difficulties of haulage and distribution and of the variations in the quality of coals produced by different districts, to say nothing of the opposition of the coal owners, hampered the development of a scheme of trade-sharing whilst the disillusionment of miners in coal exporting areas, whose previous production efforts now appeared futile, gradually deepened. On 5 September 1940, J. Lawson, M.P.

---

[1] Durham Miners' Association, *General Secretary's Review for the Year 1940*, p. 17.
[2] During that period Durham sought to encroach upon markets normally supplied by Midland coal producers. See Chapter I, pp. 46–8.
[3] M.F.G.B., 16 July 1940.
[4] *Ibid.*
[5] Durham Miners' Association, *General Secretary's Review for the Year 1940*, pp. 17–18; *Durham Chronicle*, 22 November, 6 December 1940.
[6] D.M.A., 9 December 1940; *Durham Chronicle*, 6 December 1940.

for Chester-le-Street, reported in the House of Commons that some miners in his constituency had worked only eight days since June.[1] Between April and November 1940 the number of manshifts worked in the Durham coalfield fell by 811,419.[2] Whilst Durham and South Wales together produced 30 per cent of Britain's total coal output during the September quarter 1939 and the Midland (Amalgamated) region 32·8 per cent, the proportions had altered by the September quarter 1940 to 26·4 per cent and 37·6 per cent respectively.[3]

In face of the sudden reversal in the fortunes of the coal exporting regions efforts were made to assist those miners who had returned to the industry at the time of the production crisis and now found themselves unemployed. On 5 July 1940 the Undertakings (Restriction of Employment) Order,[4] which had been imposed upon the industry during the previous month in order to prevent what had up until that time been the free movement of mining labour to other industries, was relaxed to allow miners to engage in some other trade.[5]

As an alternative to work-sharing, with its waste of manpower, increased costs and reduced earnings, the Durham Miners' Association, in co-operation with the District Production Committee, actively encouraged labour transference. During August–September 1940 the Association sent four of its Executive Committee members as emissaries to the Midlands, Yorkshire, South Staffordshire, Cumberland and Leicestershire coalfields to investigate the possibilities of transferring Durham miners to those areas under a voluntary scheme.[6] The shortage of adequate housing proved a common drawback in most regions and the project proved only of limited success.[7] The decision of the Minister of Labour and National Service in October 1940 to release all miners under 30 years of age, whether employed or not, for the voluntary military service was thwarted to some extent by the reluctance of the local Ministry of Labour tribunal in Durham to advise miners to take such action, although many of the younger workmen volunteered of their own accord.[8]

Following the rejection of the proposal whereby coalfields hard

[1] 365 H.C. Deb. 5s, 48.
[2] Miners' Federation of Great Britain, *Report of the Executive Committee*, May 1941, p. 257.
[3] *Ibid.*
[4] S.R. & O., 1940, No. 877.
[5] Court, *op. cit.*, p. 134.
[6] D.M.A., 17 August, 2, 24 September 1940.
[7] *Ibid.*, 15 October, 6 November 1940.
[8] *Durham Chronicle*, 6 December 1940.

hit by restriction of foreign markets would have been allowed to participate in home markets, the Mines Department introduced the Coal Mines (War Levy) Scheme in December 1940 as an alternative measure of assistance. A levy, initially fixed at 3d per ton, subject to a limit of 4d, was put on coal sales, the proceeds of which were used to compensate collieries which had lost trade owing to enemy action. Compensation was at a rate not exceeding 3s 6d a ton in respect of the tonnage by which a colliery's sale of coal in any quarter fell short of that proportion of the national sales which it supplied in the corresponding quarter of 1939.[1] Since in its original form the levy permitted the payment of large amounts of compensation on lost trade to undertakings which were already making good profits, it was decided in January 1942 that no compensation payments should be made to an owner which would result in raising his credit balance above a specified level in relation to the average profit for the industry as a whole. Payment of compensation was conditional upon efficient maintenance of collieries for emergency production. At the same time it had become obvious that many collieries were suffering from financial need, rather than a specific loss of output, often in excess of what existing compensation payments catered for. A supplementary assistance scheme was thus evolved to help maintain the production of coal at such necessitous undertakings.[2]

The anger and opposition displayed by inland coal owners and trade union leaders alike to the levy roused the Durham miners' leaders to stern criticism of those in other producing areas. Swan blamed the necessity for the levy upon those coal owners and Federation delegates who had previously rebuked the scheme for trade-sharing.[3] J. Ritson, M.P. for Durham, believed with the Durham miners' officials that the levy was an inadequate substitute for a share in the inland coal trade and complained bitterly in the House of Commons in February 1941 of the unsympathetic response of inland coalfields—especially Yorkshire—to Durham's needs.[4]

III

With the fall of France Britain was freed from the restrictive influence placed upon her expanding coal stocks and by the autumn of 1940

[1] Miners' Federation of Great Britain, *Report of the Executive Committee*, May 1941, pp. 231–6.
[2] P.E.P. (Political and Economic Planning), *The British Fuel and Power Industries*, London 1947, pp. 102–3; Court, *op. cit.*, pp. 194–6.
[3] *Durham Chronicle*, 11 October, 20 December 1940.
[4] 369 H.C. Deb. 5s, 230.

stocks exceeded their autumn 1939 level by 1½m. tons. During the winter of 1940–1 coal shortages, although acute, tended to be local rather than general. Transport and distribution difficulties still existed. Efforts were concentrated upon reducing railway and shipping delays and the special coal trains introduced by the Mines Department during 1939–40 for moving coal from the northern coalfields to southern England continued to run from Northumberland and Durham in response to priority demands in certain areas.[1]

By the spring of 1941 a new problem had emerged: that of declining coal production. Coal output in Durham at the end of 1941 was 6 million tons below its 1939 level. The reasons for the decline are varied and complex. Up until mid-1941 the most important cause of falling output was not absenteeism, as many supposed, but the decline in the number of shifts worked at the coal face due largely to a loss of manpower. The number of manshifts worked at the coal face in Durham as a proportion of total shifts worked declined from 34 per cent in 1938 to 32·3 per cent in 1941.[2] In addition to the loss of miners to the Forces Durham suffered particularly from the competition of other industries for labour, especially after the fall of France. The average number of persons employed in the Durham coalfield during 1939–41 declined from 106,321 to 88,508. By the end of March 1941 at least 16,000 Durham miners had been lost to other types of work since the outbreak of war, 6,000 of whom had sought other employment after the fall of France.[3]

The coal industry also suffered from a high natural wastage through deaths and retirement among an ageing labour force and from the difficulty of attracting new entrants. In 1938 there were 2,402 boys under 16 years of age employed underground in the Durham coalfield. By the end of 1943 the number had declined to 750.[4] This was due, in part, to the reluctance of parents and school teachers to urge boys to enter the industry, the relatively poor wages and conditions offered and the sharp decline in the birth rate amongst mining communities during the years of poverty and industrial strife between 1924 and 1927. Taking 1923 as 100, the number of live births in England and Wales had fallen to 88 in 1928, while at Consett, in the south-west portion of the Durham coalfield, it had fallen to 82.[5]

[1] Court, op. cit., pp. 87–90; 95–7.
[2] National Union of Mineworkers, Durham Area, *Changes in Wages, Durham Coal Trade, 1871–1953*, Durham 1954, pp. 78–80.
[3] *The Economist*, 29 March 1941; *Durham Chronicle*, 15 August 1941.
[4] Durham Coal Owners' Association, Confidential Circular, *Reasons for Decline in Output*, 13 September 1943, p. 1.
[5] *The Economist*, 20 November 1943.

As the total number of workmen fell the tendency to transfer miners away from the coal face to perform other services not immediately connected with coal production, e.g. haulage and maintenance work, increased. In 1939, 25·8 per cent of the total number of miners employed in Durham were hewers and fillers compared with 20·1 per cent employed at the surface. By 1941 the proportions had altered to 24·0 per cent and 22·2 per cent respectively.[1]

From the third quarter of 1941 until the summer of 1942 the most persistent influence upon declining coal output was a severe fall in productivity, especially at the coal face. The decline in hewers' productivity in Durham had been taking place steadily since 1938. Output per manshift at the face had stood at 3·18 tons in 1938, 2·95 tons in 1941 and had declined to 2·89 tons in 1942. For the country as a whole the comparable figures were 3·00 tons, 2·99 tons and 2·91 tons.[2] The downward movement of productivity in the major exporting regions of Durham, South Wales and Scotland more than offset the upward movement of output at the face in high productivity districts such as Nottingham and Derby. This depressive influence upon the national trend would have been more pronounced had not the relationship between the various coal producing regions altered since the outbreak of war. Thus by January to June 1942 Durham was producing only 12·27 per cent of the country's total coal output compared with 13·84 per cent in 1938 while Yorkshire, a high productivity district, had increased her share during the same period from 18·67 per cent to 20·58 per cent.[3]

One reason for the decline in output per manshift at the face, apart from the fatigue of an ageing labour force, was the lack of sufficient nutritional food to sustain muscular energy. Commenting upon a deputation by miners' M.P.s to Lord Woolton, Minister of Food, on 6 March 1941 urging supplementary food rations Swan wrote:

'We can assure the Minister of Food that the miners' claim is a just one and that they will appreciate an increased allowance of necessary food such as meat, eggs, cheese, etc., which is so vital to sustain their health and energy. Further, the want is being reflected in their total production. If such increase can be organized and maintained it will be beneficial both to the miners and the nation in light of the urgent demand for coal.'[4]

[1] Durham Coal Owners' Association, Confidential Circular, *Reasons for Decline in Output*, 13 September 1943, p. 2.
[2] Central Statistical Office, *Annual Abstract of Statistics (1938–1949)*, London 1951, p. 127.
[3] Court, *op. cit.*, p. 121–2.
[4] D.M.A., 17 March 1941.

The outburst of strikes throughout the industry during 1942 had a more direct effect upon production. The stoppages were generally of short duration and reflected by and large the miners' discontent over wages, especially the disparity between their earnings and those of munition workers. During May 1942 disputes broke out at four separate collieries in Durham involving, directly and indirectly, a total of 5,615 workmen, as a result of dissatisfaction over wages. Similar disturbances occurred during June and July, whilst during May and November 1942 a total of over 5,000 workmen struck in support of the refusal by younger miners to work underground at the direction of the National Service Officer.[1]

The situation was aggravated by the return to the coalfield of those miners who had been drafted to remote parts of the country to take up ordnance work following the collapse of the coal export trade in 1940 and who were particularly conscious of the decline in the amount of their weekly earnings. During 1942 all classes of adult female daywage employees at ordnance factories in Durham earned more per week (exclusive of overtime) than did adult datal miners working six shifts, the disparity amounting in some cases to as much as £1 per week and, in the case of male ammunition workers on day rates, to as much as £2 10s 0d a week.[2]

During 1941-2 various attempts were made at national and local level to arrest the decline in coal output. Representatives of management and workmen established colliery Coal Production Committees throughout Durham and the miners' statutory holidays were suspended for the sake of increased production.[3] Admiral Sir Edward Evans, Regional Controller for Civil Services in London, addressed one of the mass meetings organized by the Durham District Coal Production Committee during July 1941 and appealed to every miner to exert greater effort towards expanding output.[4] Durham colliery officials pledged their full support to the production drive[5] and, at the invitation of the Ministry of Aircraft Production, six Durham miners toured a power station and armament factory on Tyneside during July 1941 to see how Durham coal was being used to aid the war effort.[6] On 6 September 1941 representatives of both the district and colliery coal production committees and of the coal owners met

---

[1] *Ministry of Labour Gazette*, 1942.
[2] Mineworkers' Federation of Great Britain, Board of Investigation into Wages and Machinery of the Coal Mining Industry, June 1942, Appendix 7, pp. 106-7.
[3] D.M.A., 25 April, 7, 14 June 1941.
[4] *Ibid.*, 23 June 1941; *Durham Chronicle*, 11 July 1941.
[5] *Durham Chronicle*, 1 August 1941.
[6] *Ibid.*, D.M.A., 11 August 1941.

jointly for the first time to discuss ways of increasing coal production.[1] As an inducement towards expanding the intake of youths
to the industry the Durham Miners' and Coal Owners' Associations
agreed in December 1941 to increase the basic wage of underground
datal boys by 6d per shift which, with the addition of the minimum
percentage addition to wages, was equivalent to an advance of 10·2d
per shift, the largest advance ever negotiated for this class in the
history of the Association.[2]

At national level the Government introduced the Essential Work
(Coal Mining) Industry Order[3] in May 1941 in an effort to stem the
depletion of the labour force. The order prohibited the free taking
on and dismissal of men by the employers; it gave the miner a
guaranteed wage, whether short time was being worked or not,
although not during an industrial dispute; and it gave the National
Service Officer power to deal with persistent absenteeism. From
December 1941 until September 1942 pit production committees
were empowered to report persistent absentees to the National
Service Officer.[4] Thereafter discipline of labour became a matter for
officials of the Ministry of Fuel and Power[5] and the Ministry of
Labour and National Service. An appeal by the latter Ministry on
23 June 1941 for the return of 50,000 ex-miners to the industry proved
disappointing. Although the Mines Department estimated in July
1941 that 3,500 men could be expected to return to the Durham coalfield from other industries in response to the appeal only 2,500 had
returned by September 1941.[6]

When the Essential Work Order was introduced in May 1941 it
was accompanied by an attendance bonus of 1s per shift payable to
miners who worked every day of the week but which was forfeited
for the whole week in cases of avoidable absenteeism. The bonus
involved a rise of 10d per ton in the price of coal.[7] The determined
opposition of the miners eventually led to the bonus being paid for
actual days worked, thus removing the financial incentive towards
good attendance and substituting instead a rise in wages.[8]

The miners' continued dissatisfaction with wages proved a persistent obstacle to the coal production drive. Apart from their

[1] *Durham Chronicle*, 29 August, 5, 12 September 1941.
[2] Durham Miners' Association, *General Secretary's Review for the Year 1942*.
p. 2, 4 December 1941.
[3] S.R. & O., 1941, No. 707.
[4] S.R. & O., 1941, Nos 2008 and 2096.
[5] See below, p. 363.
[6] D.M.A., 10 July 1941. *Durham Chronicle*, 5 September 1941.
[7] M.F.G.B., 30 May, 6 June 1931.
[8] *Ibid.*, 11 September 1941.

relatively low wages compared with ammunition workers the Durham miners were conscious of a substantial disparity in earnings between coal-producing districts. In 1939 average cash earnings per manshift worked in Durham stood at 9s 10d compared with 11s 7d for the country as a whole. By 1941 the situation had further deteriorated, the figures being 12s 11d and 14s 11d respectively.[1] The increase in average earnings per week and per shift in the coal industry since the outbreak of war, largely due to the operation of flat-rate bonuses, which by 1 July 1941 amounted to 2s 8d per shift, obscured important regional variations. Thus in May 1942 the average weekly wage (*including* the value of allowances) of piece-work coal getters in Durham stood at £4 14s 3d compared with £6 8s 3d in Nottinghamshire and £5 6s 3d for Great Britain as a whole and was the lowest in the country. The average weekly wage for all workers above and below ground similarly lagged behind the national average.[2] The percentage addition to basic rates rose above its minimum level in Durham in only one month during the first four years of war. In May 1942 representatives of the Durham coal owners and miners issued a joint appeal to the Board of Trade and the Mines Department to seek an increase in the selling price of Durham coal to allow higher wages to be paid but, despite a meeting with the Minister of Mines, the call went unheeded.[3]

IV

By mid-1942 the Government had become aware that some measure of direct control of the coal industry was necessary if the nation's demands for fuel were to be met. Consequently in June 1942 the Government assumed the general direction of coal mining operations, although not the day-to-day working of the mines, and established a new Ministry of Fuel and Power under the control of Gwilym Lloyd George. The Regional Organization of the new Ministry was divided into eight coal-producing regions and four non-coal-producing regions. Within each coal-producing region there was a Regional Controller assisted by Assistant Production Directors and Technical Advisers, a Regional Labour Director and a Services Director. National and Regional Coal Boards were established to advise the Controller-General and the Regional Controllers. T.

[1] D.M.A., 22 July 1942; Court, *op. cit.*, p. 221; see below, p. 373.
[2] Miners' Federation of Great Britain, Board of Investigation into Wages and Machinery of the Coal Mining Industry, July 1942, Appendix 9, pp. 109–110.
[3] Durham Miners' Association, *General Secretary's Review for 1942*, p. 2.

Hornsby was appointed in August 1942 as Regional Controller for Durham. Watson, Moore and Gilliland represented the miners on the Regional Control Board in Durham, whilst W. S. Hall of the Durham Mechanics' Association and Watson represented the County Federation Board on the National Coal Board.[1] The Coal Supplies Officers and Coal Export Officers in Durham remained outside of the new regional organization but continued to function, offering assistance whenever necessary.

Immediately after the institution of Government control of the coal industry the M.F.G.B. put forward a claim for wage advances of 4s per day for adults and 2s for youths, with a minimum weekly wage of £4 5s 0d.[2] The Government responded by appointing a board of inquiry under the chairmanship of Lord Greene, the Master of the Rolls, to consider the immediate wages issue and to inquire into the existing machinery for determining wages and conditions of employment. The Board of Investigation reported on 19 June and recommended an unconditional flat-rate addition of 2s 6d per shift for all workers over the age of 21 and all underground workers between 18 and 21; additions ranging from 1s 3d to 2s 3d a shift for underground workers under 18, and from 9d to 2s 3d a shift for surface workers under the age of 21 and a national minimum wage of 83s a week for adult underground workers and 78s for adult surface workers. The percentage addition to basic rates under the district ascertainment system was to be stabilized at its existing level. The Board also recommended the payment of an output bonus to encourage production.[3] The scheme eventually evolved by the Board provided for the payment of a bonus computed by a monthly comparison of the output of each district with a 'standard output' calculated from past performance. Bonus payments of 3d per shift were paid in accordance with a sliding scale for every complete 1 per cent by which the output exceeded the standard tonnage.

The burden of the flat-rate wage advances granted by the 'Greene Award' bore much more heavily upon low productivity and high cost districts such as Durham than elsewhere since they represented an addition to costs per ton above the average for the industry as a whole. To have met the cost of the awards by a national increase in coal prices aimed to meet the needs of high-cost undertakings would have meant subsidizing low-cost concerns whilst district price increases would have proved extremely uneven because of the varying

[1] D.M.A., 15 August, 24 December 1942.
[2] M.F.G.B., 5 June 1942.
[3] *Report of the Board of Investigation into the Immediate Wages Issue in the Coalmining Industry*, 1942, paras. 7–10, 13, 17.

incidence of the award on costs. The Government, therefore, arranged for the effect of the rise in costs to be averaged over the whole output of the industry. Under the Coal (Charges) Order of 3 June 1942 it discontinued the system of levies raised by the industry itself and introduced a system of charges upon all coal produced payable to a Coal Charges Account to be disposed of by the Minister of Fuel and Power, after Treasury approval, for any purpose connected with the production or marketing of coal. The new levy, originally fixed at 7d per ton of coal, was raised to 3s 7d on 3 July. Individual collieries were paid the actual cost of the Greene Award out of the Coal Charges Account. The price of coal was increased nationally by 3s per ton to allow the owners to meet the increased levy.

Of particular importance to Durham was the system of price allowances to districts introduced in July 1942. With increasing wages and declining output and productivity serious discrepancies in costs and profits had arisen among coal-producing areas as the following table shows:

Total Cost of Production and Profit Earned Per Ton of Coal Commercially Disposable, 1939–42*

	Durham		Nottinghamshire		Leicestershire		Great Britain	
	s	d	s	d	s	d	s	d
	(a)	(b)	(a)	(b)	(a)	(b)	(a)	(b)
1939	15·10	1·4	14·6	1·11	13·9	2·3	16·5	1·7
1940	19·1	0·9	16·1	2·5	15·5	2·6	18·11	1·7
1941	22·8	1·1	18·10	2·7	18·0	2·7	22·5	1·9
1942	25·5	0·9	21·8	1·8	20·2	2·3	25·4	1·2

(a) total costs of production per ton commercially disposable.
(b) profit per ton commercially disposable.

*Ministry of Fuel and Power, Statistical Digest from 1938, 1944 (Cmd. 6538), pp. 51–9.

In an effort to reduce such district disparities the Government allocated 6d of the increase in the price of coal for payments to districts where local price increases to meet rising costs of production, other than wages, were overdue. From 1942 any necessary increase in coal prices was on a national basis: the proceeds pooled and the high-cost districts aided by allowances from the Coal Charges Account and thus subsidized by low-cost districts. This new scheme eliminated competition between districts, but not between pits within a district, and was in accordance with the Government's desire to maintain standard district credit balances. In the summer of 1942 the Government agreed that the datum level for the national credit

balance in the industry should be 1s 9d per ton, with the provision
that if the profit became less than 1s 6d per ton or greater than 2s
there would be an adjustment of prices. District standard credit
balances were also determined, in the case of Durham at 1s 3d per
ton.[1] The price allowances paid in any district were equal in amount
to the difference per ton of the actual trading balance, as determined
for ascertainment purposes, and the standard district balances as
agreed upon.

The introduction of district price allowances marked the beginning
of a regular system of cross-subsidization within the coal industry
which was to prove of particular benefit to the Durham coalfield
during the later years of the war. This, in addition to the method of
payment of the Greene Award, also marked a distinct shift in the
degree of direct Government involvement in the finances of the
industry and provided the background against which future national
wage negotiations, so important to the miners, were to be won.[2]

The importance of the subsidies received by Durham is clearly
seen by a comparison of total costs per ton in 1938 with those at the
end of the war. Durham joined six other districts with the lowest
output per shift in the country in never contributing to the Coal
Charge Account but during 1942–5 drew from it contributions of
11d, 1s 6d, 3s 9d, and 3s 2d per ton of coal. By 1945 the total cost per
ton of coal in Durham had risen to 40s 2d, 25s 3d higher than in
1938, 4s 3d per ton higher than the national average and 15s 8d
greater than the lowest cost per ton in the country. Output per man
shift had declined in the seven years after 1938 by 4·47 cwt per shift
falling from 22·82 cwt per shift to 18·35 cwt per shift. Without the
aid of the Coal Charges Account Durham could never have com-
peted with the inland coalfields, whose costs of producing coal were
not only so much lower but sufficiently low to obliterate any advantages Durham might have possessed by virtue of her special types of
coal. As a result of the operation of the Coal Charges Account
Durham's credit balance of 2d per ton in 1942 was transformed into
a credit of 1s 1d per ton; her deficit of 6d per ton in 1943 into a
credit balance of 1s 0d per ton; a deficit of 3s 0d per ton in 1944 into
a credit of 9d per ton and a deficit of 2s per ton in 1945 into a credit
balance of 1s 2d per ton.[3] Rising costs and falling output from
1942–5 prevented the Coal Charges Account making such price
allowances as to establish the various standard credit balances

[1] Ministry of Fuel and Power, Coal Charges Account, April 1945 (Cmd. 6617),
p. 10.
[2] See below, pp. 370–2.
[3] *Ministry of Fuel and Power Statistical Digest*, 1945 (Cmd. 6538), Table 35.

among districts and provide a national average credit balance of
1s 9d per ton.[1]

Durham's ability to reap the benefits of assistance through price
allowances was increased to the extent that, compared with other
districts, only a small percentage of her total coal output was being
produced by necessitous undertakings in receipt of government aid.
Such receipts were added to district balances and thus reduced price
allowances. During 1945 the necessitous undertakings in Durham
receiving such supplementary aid from the Government accounted
for only 6 per cent of total coal output. In Northumberland 25 per
cent of total coal output was produced by necessitous undertakings
and in Lancashire and Cheshire 17 per cent.[2]

V

As a result of the recommendation of the 1942 board of inquiry
into the machinery for negotiating miners' wages a new National
Conciliation Scheme was introduced on 1 May 1943. A National
Board was established consisting of a Joint National Negotiating
Committee of twenty-two members, on which the owners and the
workmen were equally represented; and a National Reference
Tribunal of three members nominated and appointed by the Master
of the Rolls, whose decisions would be binding on both sides and
which had power to deal with all 'national questions' over which the
Negotiation Committee was in dispute. The provision of district
conciliation machinery was to continue on a model drawn up by the
Board and agreement was reached for the transfer of district questions to the National Board and, where necessary, to the Independent Tribunal.

During 1944 arrangements were made to effect a new district
conciliation system in Durham in accordance with the provisions of
the National Conciliation Scheme. From 1 March 1944 a new Conciliation Board was established to supersede the existing District
Wages Board and consisted of seven owners' representatives, five
representatives of the Durham Miners' Association and one representative from both the Durham Colliery Mechanics' Association
and the Durham County Colliery Enginemen's, Boilerminders' and
Firemen's Association. Three referees were also appointed of which
one was elected President and assumed the powers and functions of

[1] Court, *op. cit.*, pp. 337–8.
[2] *Ibid.*, p. 348.

the Independent Chairman of the District Wages Board. Any wages dispute arising within the district which affected the mutual relations of the Associations represented was to be referred in the first instance to the Conciliation Board and, if necessary, to the referees.[1] Arrangements were made by the Conciliation Board in the following November, under the powers granted by this new agreement, to establish a similar conciliation procedure at pit level. Disputes over wages and conditions affecting individual employers or workmen could thereafter be dealt with by any one of the four specialist Committees established to deal, for example, with questions relating to the Porter minimum wage or with issues requiring immediate attention in order to keep a pit working.[2]

The improved wages machinery did not absolve the industry of the problems of declining coal production. By 1943 total coal output in Durham had fallen by $6\frac{1}{2}$m. tons from its 1939 level and productivity from 22·43 cwt to 19·31 cwt per shift during the same period. Voluntary absenteeism amongst faceworkers in Durham during 1943 was only 2·7 per cent compared with the national average of 6·1 per cent and, with the exception of Bristol and South Derbyshire, was the lowest in the country.[3] During that year the Ministry of Fuel and Power's Regional Investigation Officer in Durham was empowered to impose a fine on the spot, up to a maximum of £1, for voluntary absenteeism. Offenders could reclaim their funds by working six weeks without losing a shift, forfeited money being paid to a charity such as the Aged Mineworkers' Homes Association.[4]

The Durham coal owners complained bitterly of the lack of discipline in the pits; of men arriving late and leaving work too soon; of an increasing amount of dirt being filled with coal thus demanding extra labour at the surface; that the guaranteed working week had removed the incentive to production and that the Essential Work Order had undermined managerial authority.[5] Spasmodic efforts were made locally to improve the situation—such as the miners' campaign to increase coal output during January 1943 in support of the Durham Light Infantry's campaign in North Africa[6]—but

[1] Conciliation Agreement for the District of Durham, 17 April 1944.
[2] Agreement for the Settlement of Pit Questions Arising in the District of Durham, 1 November 1944.
[3] P.E.P. Report, 1947, p. 80.
[4] The Economist, 20 November 1943.
[5] Durham Coal Owners' Association, Confidential Circular, Reasons for Decline in Output, 13 September 1943, p. 3.
[6] Durham Chronicle, 22 January, 19 February 1943.

were insufficient to arrest the decline in production throughout most
of the coalfield.

The Government's decision to direct youths into the coal industry
from December 1943 to allow more existing miners to be upgraded
to facework was warmly welcomed by the Durham Coal Owners'
Association. The expectation of voluntary recruits had proved disappointing. In September 1943 Hornsby, Durham's Regional Controller, had appealed for at least 5,000 men between the ages of 18
and 25 to work as 'coal getters' to compensate for the County's loss
of hewers from a total of 19,277 in 1939 to 16,401 at the end of 1942.[1]
By the beginning of November only about 180 youths had volunteered.[2] Two training centres were established in Durham at Horden
Colliery and Morrison Colliery, South Moor, aimed at supplying
surrounding pits with new government-directed recruits (known as
'Bevin boys') at the rate of 150 per week.[3] By the end of 1944 over
6,900 youths from all walks of life were in training or employment
in the Durham coalfield.[4] The first boys to arrive at the training
centre at Horden were a butcher's assistant and an accountant from
Stockton.[5]

The M.F.G.B. responded to the Ministry of Fuel and Power's
suggestions for increased production, which included mines working
a 12-day fortnight, the clearing of faces each day and working one
Sunday in every four, but implored the Government to assume full
financial and operational control of the mines. In its own post-war
programme for the coal industry the Federation proposed, among
other things, a national minimum wage of £6 per week for adult
underground workers; legislation governing hours of work; Government control of the disposal and price of coal, both inland and export, and the continuation of the guaranteed week.[6] The M.F.G.B.'s
insistence that the industry should be taken out of the hands of
private ownership received, if not immediate serious attention, at
least an undertaking by the Prime Minister on 12 October 1943 that
the Minister of Fuel and Power should open discussions with the
miners' leaders on the question of the post-war situation of the coal
industry.[7]

---

[1] *Ibid.*, 10 September 1943; Durham Miners' Association, Wages Ascertainments,
1939–44.
[2] *The Economist*, 6 November 1943.
[3] *Ibid.*, 20 November 1943.
[4] D.M.A., 2 March 1945.
[5] *Durham Chronicle*, 21 January 1944.
[6] M.F.G.B., 7 October 1943.
[7] 392 H.C. Deb. 5s, 932.

Meanwhile the miners sought an immediate improvement in their standard of living. The M.F.G.B. submitted a claim for higher minimum wages and for an adjustment of piece rates to maintain the wage differentials between one class of worker and another to the National Reference Tribunal, under the chairmanship of Lord Porter. On 23 January 1944 the Tribunal awarded a national minimum wage of £5 a week to adult underground workers and £4 10s 0d to surface men, an increase of 17s and 12s per week respectively on the rates settled by the Greene Award. Boys' rates were increased so that at the age of 20 those underground could earn £4 per week and those on the surface £3 10s 0d. The claim for an increase in piece rates was rejected as inconsistent 'with the granting of what is merely a minimum wage'.[1] The Porter Award caused a great deal of discontent in the poorer districts such as Durham since the rise in minimum rates upset existing wage differentials. The effect of flat-rate additions to wages was to reduce the proportion of the piece workers' wage which was dependent upon individual effort and to lessen the ratio between his wage and that of the daywage worker.

In Durham the miners' leaders hoped that the Government would finance such wage adjustments as would be necessary to maintain differentials from the Coal Charges Account. Negotiations to reduce the anomalies of the Porter Award were already under way between the Durham Miners' and Coal Owners' Associations when, on 11 February, the Government announced its refusal to finance re-negotiated piece rates from the Account.[2] The Durham miners' Executive Committee immediately forwarded a telegram to the Minister of Fuel and Power and to W. Whiteley, Chief Labour Whip and miners' M.P. for Blaydon, protesting against the announcement.[3] At its meeting on 12 February the Durham County Federation Board warned that 'no organization can take responsibility for circumstances that will inevitably arise where piece workers' rates and the rates of skilled craftsmen approximate to those of the day and unskilled men'.[4] Neither a deputation from the Association's Executive Committee nor one from the Executive Committee of the M.F.G.B. to the Minister of Fuel and Power during February succeeded in improving the situation whereupon piece workers in Durham took matters into their own hands. Between 24 and 29 February a total of 7,400 miners were involved in stoppages arising

[1] *National Conciliation Board for the Coal-Mining Industry, National Reference Tribunal,* Fourth Award, 22 January 1944.
[2] D.M.A., 11 February 1944.
[3] *Ibid.,* 12 February 1944.
[4] *Ibid.*

out of dissatisfaction with the minimum wage awarded by the National Reference Tribunal.[1] Throughout the coalfield underground coal getters resorted to restriction of output so long as the reward for earning above the national minimum wage remained unaltered.[2] By the beginning of March 1944 the output per shift of hewers at Easington Colliery had fallen by over four-fifths and the weekly coal output to less than 7,000 tons compared with an average weekly output during January 1944 of over 15,000 tons.[3] As a result of the fall in production at the colliery 450 miners were given two weeks' notice to terminate their employment in readiness for transference to collieries in other parts of the coalfield.[4] By the time the Association's Executive Committee met on 11 March 25 collieries were reported to be affected by deliberate restriction of output. The Durham miners' leaders appealed to the piece workers to abandon their protest for the sake of the war effort and tried to appease them by asserting their belief that the Porter Award provided a unique opportunity for a general overhaul of wages which could only result in an improvement of the hewers' relative wage situation.[5]

The National Wages Agreement signed on 20 April 1944 bore witness to such predictions and helped eradicate both the discontent over the Porter Award anomalies and the reluctance of the Government to view any change in the wage structure except in relation to output. The existing ascertainment agreements were suspended, the current percentage additions being merged into the day wages or piece rates payable under the new scheme. For piece workers all existing flat-rate additions, except the cost-of-living bonus of 2s 8d per shift, were merged into the piece-work rates by the addition of the percentage which the flat-rate allowances[6] bore to the effective district minimum shift rate. Flat-rate increases were to remain for daywage workers and the output bonus scheme was discontinued, special consideration being given to wages in districts which, unlike Durham, had regularly earned a bonus. The agreement was to operate until 31 December 1947 after which date it was subject to six months' notice.

In Durham the effect of the agreement was to establish a new district minimum rate for daywagemen of 11s 2·7d to which were added the war bonuses, the flat-rate additions and the amount necessary

[1] *Ministry of Labour Gazette*, March 1944.
[2] *Durham Chronicle*, 3 March 1944.
[3] *Ibid.*, 10 March 1944.
[4] D.M.A., 6 March 1944.
[5] *Ibid.*, 11 March 1944.
[6] Other than the cost-of-living allowance.

to establish a weekly minimum wage of £5. For piece workers the newly-established addition to basic piece rates was fixed at 153·3 per cent, to which was added the cost-of-living bonus of 2s 8d, providing increases in wages per shift varying from 1s 4·68d to 7s 3·24d and averaging 3s 3d.[1] A comparison of piece workers' earnings prior to and following the national wages agreement is given below:[2]

Class of piece worker	Average wage per shift during the 4 weeks ended 15 February 1944		Average wage per shift during the 4 weeks ended 10 June 1944	
	s	d	s	d
Underground	21	5·58	25	4·61
Surface	17	7·44	19	5·54
Total Underground and Surface	21	5·04	25	3·71

Whilst the absorption of the flat-rate increases into the piece-work rate provided a close link between potential earnings and individual effort and helped towards restoring customary wage differentials it did not lead to increased coal output, especially amongst piece workers at the face. Output per man shift as a whole in Durham continued to decline in 1944 to 18·42 cwt compared with 19·31 cwt in 1943. By 1945 it had fallen to 18·35 cwt whilst total coal production was 2m. tons below its 1943 level. Similarly output per manshift at the coal face in Durham had declined from 2·89 tons in 1942 to 2·22 tons in 1944.[3] At no time during the war, however, had wage increases brought forth increased productivity. Nationally the new wages agreement helped maintain production at a level sufficient to meet essential war requirements, including those of the civilian population, and at the same time demanded from the M.F.G.B. a method of negotiation for which its existing structure was particularly unsuited.[4] The establishment of a national minimum wage marked the climax of the miners' long struggle to rid the industry of the inequalities of district bargaining. The introduction of the wages ascertainment system in 1921 and the strengthening of district autonomy after 1926 combined to preserve, in its essentials, the power of the local employer. The success of the National Joint Standing Committee, set

[1] D.M.A., 21 April 1944.
[2] Durham Miners' Association, *Information Pamphlet No. 7*, August 1944, pp. 46–7.
[3] Central Statistical Office, *Annual Abstract of Statistics, 1938–1948*, London 1949, p. 127.
[4] See below, pp. 382–5.

up in 1936,[1] in encouraging both owners and miners to consider together all questions of common interest and general application to the industry had laid the foundation for the establishment in 1944 of a method of wage determination which was destined to alter the basic structure of the industry.

Over the whole period of the war the level of miners' money and real wages improved substantially and faster, for example, than those of engineering fitters and railway and cotton employees.[2] Within the coal industry the rate of improvement still varied amongst districts. The establishment of national minimum rates of pay and, later, of national wage advances could not obliterate the serious discrepancies in earnings produced under district bargaining. Thus for the whole of the wartime period cash earnings per manshift worked in the Durham coalfield lagged behind the national average. The higher than average value of allowances in kind paid in Durham did not compensate either for a similar lag in average weekly cash earnings as the following table shows:[3]

	Average cash earnings per manshift worked		Average weekly cash earnings (a) and value of allowances in kind (b)			
	Great Britain	Durham	Great Britain		Durham	
			(a)	(b)	(a)	(b)
	s d	s d	£ s d	s d	£ s d	s d
1939	11 6·8	9 10·2	2 19 6	2 3	2 10 3	6 4
1940	13 0·4	11 2·0	3 8 8	2 6	2 15 4	6 11
1941	14 10·9	12 11·2	4 0 0	2 9	3 9 9	7 5
1942	17 5·5	15 4·1	4 13 2	3 0	4 2 7	7 8
1943	19 1·2	17 0·8	5 0 0	3 3	4 9 11	7 8
1944	21 7·9	20 3·1	5 9 4	3 8	5 3 9	8 1
1945	23 1·0	22 2·0	5 12 8	4 3	5 8 3	8 7

VI

By the very nature of war miners and their families, like all other sections of the community, were forced to adjust their normal way of life and become subject to the endless uncertainties of a wartime existence. The rapidity with which conditions could change was quickly brought home to Durham miners with the collapse of

[1] See Chapter VI, p. 257.
[2] Court, *op. cit.*, p. 328.
[3] Ministry of Fuel and Power, *Statistical Digest from 1938* (Cmd. 6538), 1944; also *Statistical Digest 1944* (Cmd. 6639), 1945; and *Statistical Digest 1946 and 1947* (Cmd. 7548), 1948.

France in June 1940. Unemployment and short-time working re-appeared at a time when the urgent demand for coal seemed to assure the industry of, if not trouble-free growth, at least continued expansion. Fortunately the priority demands of war inspired quicker solutions to such problems than would probably have been forth-coming during peace time. In January 1941, Watson, the Association's Unemployment Officer, arranged in collaboration with the Welfare Department of the Ministry of Labour and National Service to acquire premises in each colliery area where large numbers of miners were out of work and to equip them as clubs or centres for social recreation in an effort to maintain the morale of the workmen.[1]

The miners shared those wartime inconveniences of rationing, fire-watching and restricted transport services which were common to most of the civilian population. Food rationing aroused particular opposition in the coalfields as miners sought extra rations by virtue of their strenuous work. The provision of colliery canteens, although not a new venture, was accelerated in response to such demands. Before the war most canteens provided only light meals and hot snacks. The decision of the Miners' Welfare Commission in August 1941 to defray the whole of the initial capital outlay on building and equipping canteens from the Baths Fund [2] encouraged wider development. By November 1941, 55 existing buildings in Durham had been adapted for providing canteen facilities and 28 new canteens had been erected.[3] By December 1942, 123 collieries in Durham were providing a supplementary food service varying from full meals to snacks.[4] By 1944, however, J. S. Rodger, District Welfare Officer in Durham, complained that the canteens were not being used sufficiently.[5] It is possible that many miners were reluctant to use the canteen service if its cost had to be borne from pocket money and that some were unable to stay at the end of a shift since transport arrangements allowed little or no time for taking meals.

The threat of coal rationing was particularly resented by the Durham miners since a coal allowance had long been an integral part of the workman's remuneration and standard of living. At a meeting on 4 May 1942, six days after the Government's White Paper on fuel

[1] Durham Chronicle, 17 January 1941.
[2] Miners' Welfare in War Time. Report of the Miners' Welfare Commission for 6½ years to June 30 1946, p. 21. Referred to hereafter as Miners' Welfare Report, 1946.
[3] Durham Miners' Welfare Fund, Minutes of Meeting of District Sub-Committee, 11 November 1941.
[4] Ibid., 8 December 1942.
[5] D.M.A., 28 August 1944.

rationing had been published but before any decision on coal
rationing had been made, the Association's Executive Committee
instructed three of its members to meet the Durham County Labour
M.P.s in London on 6 May to plead Durham's special case.[1] No
comprehensive rationing scheme for domestic coal consumers was,
in fact, introduced during the war years although the Government,
having decided not to withdraw miners' allowance coal, made it
illegal from May 1943 for miners to sell coal supplied to them free
or at a reduced rate.[2]

The anxiety expressed by the Minister of Fuel and Power in
September 1942 about the wastage of labour in the coal industry
prompted the Miners' Welfare Commission to encourage the establishment of rehabilitation centres for miners in the various coal-
producing districts.[3] In May 1943 the Hermitage at Chester-le-Street
was purchased from the family of Sir Arthur Wood, a former Durham mine owner, and converted to provide rehabilitation facilities
for 70 patients. A District Management Committee was appointed
consisting of an equal number of owners' and miners' representatives with Watson as its first Vice-Chairman.[4]

As the war years advanced grave concern was expressed about the
rate of accidents in the coal-mining industry, occasioned to a large
extent by the increased intensity of work, the growth of mechanized
mining, and the influx of inexperienced labour. The total number of
coal-mining fatalities in Durham increased by 22 per cent from 77
to 96 during 1939–40 and in the Northern Division as a whole from
124 to 165, representing an increase from 0·28 to 0·39 per 100,000
manshifts worked, during the same period. The situation was at its
worst during 1942. During that year 122 miners were killed in Durham compared with an average of 83 during the previous three
years. In the country as a whole the number of mining fatalities fell
from 925 to 877 during 1941–2 compared with an increase from 149
to 168 or from 0·37 to 0·4 per 100,000 manshifts worked in the
Northern Division.[5] Since miners throughout the country were subject to the same pressure for increased coal production and to a
potential disregard of matters of safety the reasons for Durham's
relatively poor record during 1942 must be sought elsewhere.

[1] Ibid., 4 May 1942. Cf. H. Dalton, The Fateful Years, Memoirs 1931–1945,
London 1951, p. 396.
[2] S.R. & O., No. 702, 13 May 1943.
[3] Miners' Welfare Report, 1946, pp. 45–8.
[4] D.M.A., 15 May, 10 August 1943.
[5] Ministry of Fuel and Power, Report of H.M. Inspectors of Mines for the Year
1947 (Northern Division), pp. 56, 59, Appendix V; M.F.G.B., Report of the
Executive Committee, May 1941, p. 208.

From 1939–42 the most important single explanation of the rise in mining fatalities in the coalfield was because of falls of ground. In 1942, for example, 56 of the 122 mining deaths were caused by falls of ground either at the working face or on roadways.[1] So predominant was this danger that a Durham Falls of Ground Advisory Committee was established, upon which the Association was represented, to investigate the hazard fully. 1942 also witnessed the first deaths from explosion since the outbreak of war, the most serious occurring at Murton Colliery. Thirteen men died from carbon monoxide poisoning and a further two were seriously injured following an explosion at the Back-over Flat of the Five Quarter Seam. The immediate cause of the disaster, which occurred at 8 p.m. on 26 June, was the ignition of a mixture of firedamp and air by a spark from a multi-shot exploder in use at the coal face. The exploder used by the responsible deputy at the time of the disaster was not an apparatus approved for coal shots under Clause 6(h) (i) of the Explosives in Coal Mines Order, 1 January 1934 and prompted R. Yates, the coalfield's Divisional Inspector of Mines, to demand that the use of unapproved exploders in any part of the mine where safety lamps were required should in future be prohibited.[2] It is an unhappy coincidence that it was the explosion and death of four men from carbon monoxide poisoning at Murton Colliery in 1937 that led the Association to demand the greater development of automatic gas detectors.[3]

The situation improved after 1942. By 1945 the rate of fatal accidents in the Northern Division per 100,000 manshifts worked had fallen to 0·26 or roughly the level reached in 1939. Sixty-eight fewer miners had been killed than in 1942 and 24 fewer than in 1939. The total number of miners suffering from non-fatal accidents and the rate of non-fatal accidents per 100,000 man shifts worked in the Northern Division both fell gradually during the war period except for a slight rise during 1944–5 but to a level still below that reached in 1939.[4]

The Durham Miners' Association continued throughout the war period the campaign for greater safety in the mine that it had embarked upon during the 1930s.[5] In May 1940 the Association pleaded

[1] M.F.G.B., *Report of the Executive Committee, June 1943*, p. 248.
[2] Ministry of Fuel and Power, Murton Colliery, Durham, *Report On the Causes of and Circumstances attending the Explosion which occurred on the 26th June 1942 at the Murton Colliery, Durham, by R. Yates*, 1943 (Cmd. 6413).
[3] Cf. Chapter VII.
[4] Ministry of Fuel and Power, *Report of H.M. Inspector of Mines for the Year 1947 (Northern Division)*, Appendix V; M.F.G.B., *Report of the Executive Committee*, May 1942, pp. 209–273.
[5] See Chapter VII, pp. 301–7.

for a greater use of protective equipment by miners[1] and in December of the same year agreed to supply all safety appliances free to workmen.[2] The importance which both Durham miners and colliery officials placed upon regular inspection of the mines made them particularly responsive to the scheme of compulsory partial inspection of pits introduced jointly by the M.F.G.B. and Mining Association in 1941. The scheme was meant to reinforce and not replace the periodic inspections made in accordance with Section 16 of the Coal Mines Act, 1911. During 1940 the number of pit inspections thus made in the Northern Division represented over half the national total.[3] Under the new scheme workmen were empowered to appoint additional inspectors to work with the district's full-time employees.[4] In April 1941 the Durham Coal Owners' Association and County Federation Board agreed to contribute an equal amount to that raised from a levy of 3d per workman over 18 (1½d for those under 18) to provide a fund for the payment of inspectors appointed under the new scheme. The existing full-time inspectors in Durham had until then been financed from funds supplied by the workmen. From June 1941 the cost of maintaining all pit inspectors in the coalfield was to be borne by both owners and workmen alike.[5]

In view of the concern over mining fatalities the implementation of the Workmen's Compensation (Temporary Increases) Act in 1943 was warmly welcomed by the Durham miners. The Act increased temporarily the allowances payable under the Workmen's Compensation (Supplementary Allowances) Act, 1940 and the maximum amount of compensation payable on the death of a workman under the terms of the Workmen's Compensation Act, 1925, in the latter case from £600 to £700. The minimum and maximum payments payable under the same Act to persons wholly dependent upon the earnings of the deceased were increased at the same time from £200 to £300 and from £300 to £400 respectively.[6] In addition to these changes in compensation law the Durham miners benefited from a revision of the method of paying allowances mutually agreed upon by representatives of the miners' and coal owners' associations in July 1944. The miners' leaders claimed that the calculation of compensation payments on the basis of average weekly pre-accident earning power did not make proper provision for the partially dis-

¹ D.M.A., 24 May 1940.
² Ibid., 21 December 1940.
³ M.F.G.B., Report of the Executive Committee, May 1941, p. 208.
⁴ D.M.A., 16 April 1941; Durham Chronicle, 2 May 1941.
⁵ M.F.G.B., 5 March 1941.
⁶ D.M.A., 29 November 1943.

abled miner employed at light work. As a result a new scale of average weekly earnings was agreed upon for each grade of worker to allow for the payment of a partial weekly rate of compensation (exclusive of supplementary allowances) to all men employed at surface datal work.[1]

VII

The first opportunity the Association had to fight a by-election during the period of the wartime electoral truce came in 1942 when Batey retired from the seat at Spennymoor which he had held since 1918. The political parties had agreed in the event of a by-election to allow a representative of the party to which the previous member had belonged to retain the seat without contest although independent candidates or representatives of minor parties were free to stand for election.

The selection of a miners' candidate to succeed Batey, then 75 years old, took place according to the new rules established by the Association in May 1936 whereby a Lodge's voting strength depended upon the extent of its paid-up political membership.[2] Five nominations were received from the Lodges, J. D. Murray, an ex-checkweighman from Meadowfield, finally securing the nomination from his closest rival W. Bourne, a miner from Willington, by 5,508 votes to 1,620.[3] Murray was returned unopposed at a by-election on 21 July.

The death in 1943 of D. Adams, Labour M.P. for Consett but not a miners' candidate, provided the Association with an opportunity to fight the division for the first time. J. E. Glanville, a miner from the Morrison Lodge, succeeded in capturing the candidature from N. F. Nattrass, an employee of the Ministry of Fuel and Power, by 4,004 votes to 3,455.[4] On 15 November 1943 he was returned unopposed as Consett's first miners' M.P. and as the first Durham miner to proceed to Parliament without being either a checkweighman or an Agent of the Association.

In 1944 W. J. Stewart and J. Ritson, Members of Parliament for Houghton-le-Spring and Durham respectively, decided to retire at the next general election. At Durham the contest for the miners'

---

[1] *Ibid.*, 31 July 1944.
[2] See Chapter VIII, p. 348.
[3] *Durham Chronicle*, 1, 15 May 1942; Durham Miners' Association, *General Secretary's Review for the Year 1942*, 8 January 1943, p. 12.
[4] D.M.A., 4 October 1943.

candidature resolved itself into a fight between C. F. Grey, a coal hewer from Elemore, and J. F. Watson, a checkweighman from Eppleton, Grey eventually being elected as prospective Parliamentary candidate by 5,108 votes to 2,729.[1] In September 1944 E. Pearson, a miner from Silksworth, succeeded in defeating H. Hodgson, a miner from Houghton, in the fight for the miners' candidature at Houghton-le-Spring by 5,261 votes to 3,360.[2] Pearson eventually withdrew his acceptance of the nomination for health reasons and forced a fresh election to select a miners' candidate for the division. W. Blyton, a miner from Harton, was eventually endorsed as the Association's prospective Parliamentary candidate at the next general election.[3]

The resignation of Churchill shortly after the end of the war with Germany in May 1945 brought the National Government to an end. A 'caretaker' government, composed predominantly of Conservatives, was established until the time of the general election in July. Labour, having decided to fight the election as an independent party, offered a convincing programme of social and industrial reform which appealed particularly to a public openly concerned with their future well-being. The Council of the Durham Area of the N.U.M.,[4] urging members to secure a Labour victory, proclaimed:

'A majority victory for the Labour Party will be an assurance to the electors that measures such as Housing, Full Employment, Social Security, Education, Pensions, Compensation and Public Ownership of Industry ... will be adequately implemented.'[5]

In confirmation of this declaration the Council unanimously agreed to donate £2,500 to the Labour Party general election Fighting Fund.[6]

The election proved a resounding success for Labour, providing it, for the first time, with a significant majority over all other parties. Every one of the 39 candidates sponsored by the N.U.M. was returned as a Member of Parliament. At Chester-le-Street J. Lawson, who had held the seat for Labour since 1919, defeated his Conservative opponent Viscount Lambton, heir to the Earl of Durham, by 33,788 votes to 10,228, a Labour majority of 23,560. J. D. Murray,

---

[1] *Ibid.*, 2 October 1944.
[2] *Ibid.*, 29 August, 5, 18 September 1944.
[3] *Ibid.*, 10, 24, 31 October, 13 November 1944.
[4] By this time district mining associations had been grouped into a new National Union of Mineworkers. See below, pp. 382–5.
[5] D.M.A., 26 May 1945.
[6] *Ibid.*

the only miners' candidate in Durham to fight a three-cornered contest, polled 22,587 votes at Spennymoor against his Conservative opponent F. D. Nicholson, Managing Director of a brewing company, with 7,510 votes and the Independent candidate C. F. J. Smith, Principal of the Durham Timber Company, with 2,222 votes. At Durham Grey defeated J. Bunyan, the Liberal National candidate, by 24,135 votes to 12,331 and at Consett the Liberal Nationalists were again defeated, J. Glanville polling 28,617 votes against J. A. McGilley, a former mineworker, with 12,198. W. Blyton retained the seat at Houghton-le-Spring for Labour by defeating his Conservative opponent T. B. Martin by 43,730 votes to 21,864, a majority of 21,866. Martin, who between 1937–40 had been political correspondent to the *Daily Telegraph*, had defeated W. Whiteley at Blaydon in 1931 by only 496 votes.[1] Whiteley regained the seat in 1935 and retained it in 1945 against Conservative opposition from E. C. Peake, a barrister, polling 29,931 votes to Peake's 11,842.

As a result of the election the Labour Party, with only 47·8 per cent of the votes, won 393 seats, the Conservatives and their allies securing 213, the Liberals 12 and the Independents 22. With the return of Labour to power the Durham miners' Executive Committee declared:

'We are rightly proud of the part played in the election by all labour workers in the County of Durham. To have won every parliamentary seat in the County is an outstanding distinction. Durham County solid for Labour is a proud record. That is Durham's contribution to the historic event of Labour's great national achievement. It is a fine testimony to the growing faith of the working class in social and political democracy.'[2]

VIII

The coal-production crisis which developed during 1945 was quickly viewed by the miners and the public at large as a test of the efficacy with which Labour could tackle the industrial problems of the postwar economy. In March 1945 it was estimated that the supplies of coal available to the country for the period May 1945 to April 1946 would fall short of requirements to the extent of 4 million tons. Similar deficiencies had previously been met from national coal stocks but, largely as a result of attempts during 1944–5 to balance

[1] See Chapter VIII, p. 341.
[2] *Ibid.*, 31 July 1945.

the nation's coal production and consumption, stocks in October 1945 were already 5 million tons below the level reached in October of the previous year.[1]

After a meeting with E. Shinwell, Minister of Fuel and Power, during August 1945 the Durham miners' Executive Committee agreed to convene special meetings between management and workmen at every Lodge in the County to help foster increased coal output[2] and thus, as they later claimed, 'expedite our claim for the nationalization of the industry'.[3] Determined to meet the nation's demand for an extra 26,000 tons of coal per week from every colliery in Durham, the County Federation Board urged that all workmen should work the full hours laid down in County Agreements; that all workmen engaged in machine mining should work overtime to complete a cycle of operations; that disputes should be kept to a minimum and speedily settled; that Pit Production Committees should encourage strict discipline in the pit and maintain a close liaison between officials and workmen; that the Minister of Fuel and Power should seek to recompense coal owners to the full extent of any capital expenditure aimed at increasing mechanization in the mines and that a system of fines should be instituted to help combat absenteeism and inefficiency on the part of the miners.[4] Despite ready exhortations no one assumed that the task of meeting the demand for coal would be an easy one. In September 1945 the 21,200 coal face workers employed in the Durham coalfield would have had to increase their weekly coal output by $1\frac{1}{2}$ tons each to satisfy the production target established for Durham by the Ministry of Fuel and Power.

Following a suggestion by the Special N.U.M. Sub-Committee on coal output, of which Watson was a member, Durham appointed an Area Production Officer in September 1945 to co-ordinate the work of the County's Pit Production Committee,[5] but soon found difficulty in fostering greater effort amongst younger miners. In an attempt to counteract this a special production conference for youths was organized in Durham during November 1945 to which three representatives between 16 and 20 years of age from each Lodge were invited to discuss 'Coal Production and the Future of the Industry under Public Ownership'.[6] There were other potential threats to

[1] Court, op. cit., pp. 388–90.
[2] D.M.A., 18 August 1945.
[3] Ibid., 20 October 1945.
[4] Ibid., 10 September 1945.
[5] Ibid., 10, 17 September 1945; N.U.M., 20 September 1945.
[6] D.M.A., 23 October 1945.

increased production apart from the indifference of younger miners. Lodges complained to the Association's Executive Committee during October 1945 'that the workmen are not receiving sufficient meats and other energy-building foods in order to sustain them for hard work throughout the whole of the shift'.[1] Coal owners in Durham also threatened to dismiss workmen of 65 years and over in accordance with the Essential Work (Permission to Terminate Employment) (Exemption) Order, 1945 and aroused the stern opposition of the miners' Association. Explaining their position the Council reported:

'We feel that the time is inopportune for dispensing with the services of these "stalwarts" of the industry, who are still capable and willing to do an efficient day's work, and who will if dismissed be enforced to exist, in these days of high cost of living, on their hard earned savings and an Old Age Pension which is, as yet, most inadequate.'[2]

Even those employed sometimes found difficulty in retaining enthusiasm for harder work. F. Malpas, Durham's Area Production Officer, reported to a national conference in February 1946 that there was a distinct impression in the coalfield that managers objected to workers making suggestions as to how to increase output with the result that the Pit Production Committees were not functioning efficiently.[3]

IX

The growth of national negotiations during the war and especially the establishment of the new conciliation scheme in the industry in 1942 necessitated a much stronger central trade union organization than that provided by the existing loose federation of district mining associations. The question of the reorganization of the M.F.G.B., which has been discussed throughout the inter-war period, again came into prominence as the needs of effective representation in national negotiations became more obvious. The Federations' Reorganization Sub-Committee, established in 1942 to draft proposals for a new miners' union,[4] was quick to appreciate the difficulties of incorporating the separate district associations, each with its own rules, procedures, and customs, into one union for all mineworkers.

[1] *Ibid.*, 1 October 1945.
[2] *Ibid.*, 20 October 1945.
[3] N.U.M., 14 February 1946.
[4] M.F.G.B., 20 July 1942.

Its proposals, submitted to the Federation's Annual Conference in 1942, were essentially a compromise between complete unification and district autonomy such as had been suggested in 1938. The new union was to assume complete central authority for all industrial issues whilst district associations were to retain independent control over matters of contributions and benefits. Each constituent association was to be required to pay a once-and-for-all capitation fee of £1 per head (women and boys under 18, 10s) in addition to a regular weekly contribution of 5d per member to help finance centralized industrial activity.[1]

The proposals for the reorganization of the Federation were submitted to the districts for amendment. The Executive Committee of the Durham Miners' Association failed to secure a 1d reduction in the members' weekly contribution for industrial purposes but succeeded in establishing that the new organization should, as one of its objects, 'seek the establishment of Public Ownership and Control of the mining industry'.[2] The determination of the Durham miners' officials to secure for the Federation a closer degree of central control over the various district associations sprang from their experience of the ineptitude and injustice of district bargaining during a period of world-wide depression.[3] This determination was reinforced once the miners' wartime experiences confirmed that the establishment of effective central authority would facilitate the nationalization of the mines. Watson told Federation delegates in 1943:

'Has not the war experience taught us, on wages, on holidays, on compensation or rehabilitation . . . that you have only been able to get satisfaction from a national angle and on a national basis? . . . The industry is tending not towards control by private enterprise, but towards public or State ownership. We happen to be the only industry in this country at the present time who have the assurance of Parliament that when this war is over they will discuss in Parliament the future of the mining industry and the organization necessary in the country for the mining industry. I submit to delegates that if when that discussion takes place in Parliament we are divided into districts, with district organizations and district Unions, we will not be able to bring to bear upon the people of this country, through our Members of Parliament, the force we could bring if we were organized into one Miners' Union.'[4]

[1] *Ibid.*, 22 July 1943.
[2] D.M.A., 7, 11 September 1943; M.F.G.B., 17 August 1944.
[3] See Chapter VI.
[4] M.F.G.B., 22 July 1943.

It was in an effort to ensure that a national miners' union succeeded in promoting such a lasting change in the ownership of industry that Watson joined Arthur Horner, from South Wales, in persuading delegates at the Special Federation Conference in August
1944 to make the negotiation of a national wages agreement with a
national ascertainment a first priority of post-war policy.[1] Whilst a
national ascertainment ran the risk of causing discontent by lessen-
ing percentages in certain districts and levelling them up in others,
such as Durham, it remained the only means of removing the disparity in the miners' standard of living throughout the districts for
which the Federation, and especially its representatives from coal-
exporting areas, had fought for so long. 'If the one union is not to
follow the line of National Wages Agreements and National Ascertainments,' argued Watson, 'we will have one union in name but
district organizations in practice.'[2]

According to the reorganization plan old district associations were
to become the administrative areas of a single national union, with
area officials' salaries paid and controlled by the national body, but
were to retain autonomy over contributions and benefits, retention
of real property, individual registration according to the laws
governing the activities of trade unions, the election of area officials
and the nomination of representatives to the national Executive
Committee. The new national union was to have a full-time President
and Secretary elected by the constituent membership and a part-
time Vice-President elected biannually by the national conference.

The ballot vote on the proposed rules of a single national miners'
union, conducted during October 1944, showed a 10:1 majority in
favour of acceptance, the voting being 430,630 for and only 39,666
against. Durham supported the change by 63,794 votes to 3,761.[3]
R. Williams, the Association's solicitor, worked on behalf of the
Federation in advising the district miners' associations how to partially amend their Rules to allow contributions and levies to be made
to launch the new union.[4] On 1 January 1945 the National Union
of Mineworkers was finally established, with the former Durham
Miners' Association becoming the Durham Area of the N.U.M.

Four nominations were received for the full-time position of
President of the new organization. Durham, Northumberland,
Bristol, the Midlands, Scotland, S. Derby and the Cokemen nomi-
nated Lawther, President of the former M.F.G.B., South Wales

[1] R. P. Arnot, *The Miners in Crisis and War*, London 1962, pp. 410–12.
[2] M.F.G.B., 16 August 1944.
[3] D.M.A., 30 October 1944.
[4] M.F.G.B., 14 December 1944.

nominated W. H. Crews, Kent J. Duffy and Yorkshire J. R. Machen. The ballot, conducted under the single transferable vote system, took place three times, no candidate receiving an absolute majority of votes during the first two elections. The final voting resulted in Lawther receiving 251,956 votes and Machen 129,611, Crews' and Duffy's votes having been transferred during the previous ballots. There were 14,125 non-transferable votes and Lawther, having received a clear majority, was appointed President of the N.U.M. from 1 April 1945.[1] R. Williams, the Association's solicitor, had previously been elected as the full-time solicitor of the N.U.M., the post having been offered to him by the unanimous decision of the National Executive Committee.[2]

[1] N.U.M., 8 March 1945.
[2] Ibid., 18 January 1945.

Chapter X

THE COAL INDUSTRY, 1947–56

I

The production crisis of 1945 and the advent of Labour to power once more brought coal nationalization to the forefront of public discussion. The report of the Technical Advisory Committee on Coal Mining (the 'Reid Committee'), issued in March 1945, had already drawn attention to the relatively poor record of mechanization in British mines compared with their Continental counterparts and to the manner in which the uncertainty as to the future structure of the industry delayed technical advance by restricting plans for long-term capital expenditure.[1] Whilst the Reid report was a timely reminder of the need to reorganize the industry it simply confirmed what the majority of miners had long felt and felt even more as a result of the experiences of the Second World War. The Sankey Commission's condemnation of private ownership of the industry appeared to them to be long-forgotten by the public at large; proposals for the amalgamation of colliery concerns had been sternly resisted and spasmodic attempts to gain support in the House of Commons for private members' Bills on coal nationalization had proved abortive. In November 1936 J. Batey, M.P. for Spennymoor, introduced a private members' Bill into the House 'to nationalize mines and minerals and to provide for the national winning, distribution, and sale of coal and other minerals; and for other purposes connected therewith'.[2] The Bill, which received a second reading on 12 February 1937, was finally defeated.

The coal owners themselves were not unmindful of the need to seriously consider the role of their industry in the post-1945 economy. In January 1945 Robert Foot, Chairman of the Mining Association of Great Britain, produced his *Plan for Coal* in which he suggested that a Central Coal Board could be established and manned entirely by employers. Every colliery undertaking employing more than thirty persons underground would be bound 'irrevocably to accept as binding every decision made by the Board' whilst District Boards, also drawn from within the industry, would act as outposts for the Central Board dealing with local questions. Compulsory amalgamation

[1] Cmd. 6610, *op. cit.*, p. 128.
[2] 317 H.C. Deb. 5s, 390.

of undertakings would be sacrificed in favour of amalgamation by agreement except where an undertaking failed to operate 'in an efficient manner'.[1]

The scheme, described by one writer as 'Bourbon self-Government—Government of the coal owners, by the coal owners, for the coal owners'[2]—made no provision for representation of miners' and consumers' interests or for safeguarding the national interest. The idea of providing a solution to the industry's problem by maintaining the *status quo* of owner-control exemplified the inability of the colliery owners to supply a feasible alternative to the miners' demand for nationalization and led Watson to draft a critical memorandum in reply to the scheme entitled *Coal Plan my 'Foot'*.

Within six months of Labour taking office a Bill was introduced to nationalize the coal industry. It provided for the establishment of a National Coal Board to which the assets, rights and liabilities of the industry were transferred, and for the payment of compensation to the former colliery owners. The Minister of Fuel and Power was empowered to issue general directions to the Board to ensure that coal supplies were made available in quantities and at prices calculated to further the public interest. The Bill received the Royal Assent on 12 July 1946, the eve of the first post-war Durham Miners' Gala.

The compression into a single entity of the colliery activities of more than 400 undertakings, varying greatly in efficiency, size and methods of administration, provided the N.C.B. with an unprecedented problem of industrial organization. To help overcome the task the Board developed a highly centralized administrative structure with a line of command running down from the N.C.B. through Divisional Boards and Area managers to colliery managers. Collieries, grouped into Areas, were to become the basic operational units for production whilst Areas, the units for commercial management,[3] were grouped into Divisions which acted as the intermediate authority between coalfields and national headquarters.

Durham, together with Northumberland and Cumberland, was grouped into the Northern Division which was subdivided into ten Areas. Within the Division a separate Board, collectively responsible to the N.C.B., was established to help advise in the formulation of policy. Four full-time divisional directors were appointed to deal with

---

[1] R. Foot, *A Plan for Coal*, London, January 1945.
[2] H. Wilson, *New Deal for Coal*, London 1945, p. 194.
[3] The Reid Report had earlier stressed the importance of adopting plans for reorganization on a coalfield basis rather than mine by mine. Cmd. 6610, *op. cit.*, paras. 705–9.

production, labour, marketing and finance.[1] H. O. R. Hindley, former Director-General of the British Air Commission, was appointed Chairman of the Northern Divisional Board, and S. E. D. Wilson, a Director of the South Derwent Coal Company, Deputy Chairman. N. F. Nattrass, the Ministry of Fuel and Power's Regional Labour Director for the Durham coalfield, became Divisional Labour Director and C. D. Marley, a member of the Durham Sales Control Committee established in 1936 under the terms of the Coal Mines Act 1930, was appointed Marketing Director. R. S. Barrett, Deputy Chairman of Londonderry Collieries Ltd., became Production Director, and S. J. Reid, Secretary of Pease and Partners Company Ltd., Finance Director. Below divisional level colliery managers became directly responsible to their Area general managers, who themselves were personally responsible to the Divisional Board. This 'line and staff' principle of management enabled responsibility for major decisions to be delegated to authorities in each link in the chain of command.

The responsibilities placed upon the Northern Divisional Board to control both 200 collieries and tackle the difficult economic and technical problems posed by West Durham and Cumberland led to the establishment of a new organization in the Division in 1949. New Divisional Boards were appointed, one for the Durham coalfield and the other for the Northumberland and Cumberland coalfields.

The N.C.B. and N.U.M. agreed to retain the Joint National Negotiating Committee and the National Reference Tribunal, established in 1943, for purposes of negotiating wages and conditions of employment. Collective agreements made between the N.U.M. and the Mining Association and between their constituent bodies were to continue, with modification, after vesting date. A National Consultative Council, established in 1946, was empowered to deal with all matters of mutual concern to miners, deputies and colliery managers other than those relating to wages and conditions of employment.[2]

On 1 January 1947, vesting date, the industry passed into public ownership. The Northern Divisional Coal Board became responsible for more than 200 collieries in Durham, Northumberland and Cumberland and a mass of ancillary and miscellaneous property including more than 44,000 colliery houses, 200 farms, c. 100,000 acres of land, 18 separate coking plants in Durham, numerous brickworks,

---

[1] National Coal Board, *Annual Report and Statement of Accounts for the Year Ended 31 December 1946*, London 1948, pp. 3–4; Appendix I.
[2] *Ibid.*, p. 16.

c. 100 local electricity networks and miscellaneous items including a mortuary, a fish-and-chip shop and a public house, all formerly owned by colliery companies.[1]

The nationalization of the mining industry was celebrated by nearly every Lodge in the County, in some cases with dances and socials. Parades with band and banner took place to the pits where the blue-and-white flag of the National Coal Board was unfurled. At each pit the seal of ownership was signified by a simple notice board which read:

THIS COLLIERY IS NOW MANAGED BY THE NATIONAL
COAL BOARD ON BEHALF OF THE PEOPLE

Implicit in the whole proceedings was the assumption that the Board's subsequent activities were at least destined to be implemented in a context psychologically favourable to the miner. The immediate problems of the post-war economy, especially the search for full employment, were in large part instrumental in effecting the change in industrial ownership for which the miners had campaigned for so long. It was in tackling those problems that the industry began its task of proving the worth of that campaign.

The Durham miners' bitter experience of private ownership of the industry served to increase their determination to make nationalization a success. To ensure that this determination proved more than a mere emotional commitment Watson felt it necessary to remind members on Vesting Day:

'Our Industry is now publicly owned. No longer are we working for Colliery Owners. No longer are profits being paid to absentee Owners. No longer is it "They and Them"—it is "We and Us". The Industry has passed from the propaganda stage to the administrative stage, and in place of political theorizing, slogans and alibis we have to put good, sound planning, real hard work based upon maximum co-operation and efficiency, and sound thinking reinforced with the acceptance of individual responsibility and self discipline, combining all three in a concerted effort to improve the productivity of the Industry.'[2]

II

The need to restore the efficiency and productive power of the staple industries and to expand exports as the basis of rebuilding the

[1] N.U.M. (Durham Area), *Annual Report*, 1956, p. 58.
[2] *Ibid.*, . . . 1946, pp. 10–11.

nation's economy after wartime hostilities placed a heavy burden upon the nationalized coal industry. A depleted labour force, a shortage of skilled engineers and an accumulated lack of maintenance and technical development had substantially reduced its ability to meet the demands of post-war reconstruction. The long period of stagnation between the wars had so gravely impaired the industry's productive capacity that at vesting date only one-sixth of total coal production came from shafts or drifts opened since the end of the First World War.[1] In 1948 the estimated net fixed capital per employee in coal mining, still a labour intensive industry, stood at £100 compared with £5,070 per employee in electricity and £1,080 per employee in manufacturing industry as a whole.[2]

The problem of expanding output and exports and of increasing technical efficiency was made more difficult by the pressure of the rising demand for coal. Whereas between the wars the mining industry had been capable of producing in excess of demand, the substantial energy requirements of the economy for most of the first decade of nationalization frustrated many of the efforts to sustain output at an acceptable level. Until the mid-fifties coal was virtually the only important source of energy available in Britain and supplies were allocated and rationed, with American imports making good some internal shortages.[3] Total internal coal consumption rose from 184½m. tons in 1947 to 218½m. tons in 1956, the major consuming sectors being electric power stations and gas and coke carbonization plants.[4] The increase in domestic consumption after 1945 was probably due to the expansion in the size of the employed population than to any increase in energy requirements per head.[5] The coal-export programme had often to be adjusted and cut back to meet the rising demands of inland consumers. Britain proved to be the only European country to experience a substantial and sustained

[1] National Coal Board, *Annual Report and Statement of Accounts for the Year Ended 31 December 1955*, p. 52; see also C. C. and W. Reid, 'The Reconstruction of the British Coal Mining Industry', Second Cadman Memorial Lecture, Royal Society of Arts, 16 March 1949.
[2] W. G. Shepherd, *Economic Performance Under Public Ownership: British Fuel and Power*, Yale University Press 1965, p. 14.
[3] See below, pp. 398, 407, 410–11, 413 and Appendix II to this chapter.
[4] National Coal Board *Annual Report and Statement of Accounts for the Year Ended 29 December 1956*, pp. 34–5. In the industrial sector from 1923 to 1957 the mean value of the rate of increase in the index of total fuel consumption over the rate of increase of the index of industrial production was ½. From 1948 to 1959 it was ⅔. A. S. Rodger, 'British Fuel Requirements and Investment to 1975'. Unpublished Ph.D. thesis, University of Edinburgh 1961.
[5] A. Beacham, 'The Coal Industry', in D. Burn (ed.), *The Structure of British Industry: A Symposium*, Volume I, Cambridge 1958, p. 122.

rise in internal coal consumption compared with pre-war trends.[1]

The period from 1947 to 1952 was one of 'coal at any price', when existing capacity at both Divisional and national level was more fully used. Output rose steadily in Durham until 1951 but thereafter, as the effect of diverting men, capital and management from current production into reconstruction became increasingly felt and as the rate of exhaustion of existing capacity kept pace with rising efficiency, production improved at a slower rate.[2] In older coalfields such as Durham the pressures to contribute towards meeting national fuel requirements and yet increase coal exports to boost foreign currency earnings proved enormous. To maintain let alone increase output at collieries 80 to 100 years old and with seams deeper, thinner,[3] and farther away from the shaft than in most other coalfields [4] required the keenest effort of every miner. The output of deep-mined saleable coal in the Durham Division [5] increased during 1947–56 by 5 per cent compared with a national increase of 12 per cent although the average number of men on colliery books fell by 6·5 per cent compared with only a 1·1 per cent decline in the country as a whole. Whereas in 1947 the Division required almost 109,000 men to produce 24m. tons of deep-mined saleable coal, in 1956 with 7,000 fewer men employed 1m. more tons was produced.[6] The rise in output per manshift overall during the first decade of nationalization in Durham was equivalent to that in the country as a whole (14·6 per cent compared with 15·0 per cent respectively) although productivity at the face rose much faster by 27 per cent compared with a national increase of only 16 per cent.[7]

Though it is difficult to calculate precisely production losses through absenteeism, partly because there is an unknown minimum of excusable absence and partly because differences in absence rates

---

[1] Sir A. Bryan, 'Prospects of the British Coal Industry with Particular Relation to Exports'. Address delivered at Jesus College, Oxford, 19 April 1952.

[2] See Appendix I to this chapter.

[3] In 1944 over 64 per cent of total saleable coal output in Durham was mined from seams less than 4 ft thick and only 2·7 per cent from seams over 6 ft thick. National Coal Board, *Plan for Coal*, October 1950, Appendix I, Table I, p. 51.

[4] E. F. Schumacher, 'Efficiency in Coal Production', *The Financial Times*, 31 December 1953.

[5] For details of the changing Divisional organization within the north-east see above, p. 388.

[6] Despite the fact that the *saleable* proportion of total output had declined by *c.* 6 per cent largely because of the deterioration in thickness and the dirt content of the seams being worked.

[7] See E. H. Sealy, 'A Statistical Analysis of Productivity Movements in British Coal Mining'. Paper read before the Manchester Geological and Mining Society, 12 April 1962.

can affect productivity,[1] the better than average attendance and absence rates in Durham for the greater part of 1957–56 at least suggest the extent to which output performance could well have been worse had Durham's absenteeism experience corresponded more closely to the national average.

Absence and Attendance in Coal Mining 1947–56

	Total absenteeism %		Average number of manshifts worked per man per week	
	Durham	Great Britain	Durham	Great Britain
1947	9·7*	12·4	4·8*	4·7
1948	8·5*	11·5	4·8*	4·7
1949	9·6*	12·3	4·8*	4·7
1950	9·9	12·0	4·8	4·7
1951	9·5	12·0	4·8	4·8
1952	9·1	12·4	4·8	4·8
1953	9·6	12·2	4·7	4·7
1954	9·5	12·5	4·7	4·7
1955	9·5	12·9	4·7	4·7
1956	10·1	13·8	4·7	4·6

* Northern Division

Source: National Coal Board, *Annual Reports*; Ministry of Power, *Statistical Digests*.

Notes: Both absence and attendance figures have been given since until 1954 the absence rate reflected the number of manshifts lost in a particular period expressed as a percentage of the number of manshifts thought 'possible' during that period. Should this latter figure be increased—for example through a change in the length of the working week—then the absence rate could rise unless there was a proportionate increase in the number of manshifts worked. See L. J. Handy, 'Absenteeism and Attendance in the British Coal-Mining Industry: An Examination of Post-War Trends', *British Journal of Industrial Relations*, 6, March 1968.

The impact of changes in the number of men on colliery books, in the average number of manshifts worked and in the average output obtained from each shift upon the rate of output was affected by changes in the industry's total capacity. Since the N.C.B.'s major schemes of reconstruction only got under way in 1948–9, and bearing in mind the inevitable delay in their effects upon production, the expansion of output from these sources could barely be sufficient

[1] See S. Moos, 'Statistics on Absenteeism in Coal Mining', *Manchester School of Economic and Social Research*, 3, 1951; R. B. Buzzard, 'Attendance and Absence in Industry: the Nature of the Evidence', *British Journal of Sociology*, 3, 1954; F. D. K. Liddell, 'Attendance in the Coal-Mining Industry', *British Journal of Sociology*, 5, 1954.

to offset the decline in production resulting from loss of capacity. An examination of the changing pattern of Divisional coal outputs during the first decade of nationalization emphasizes the severe effect of declining capacity in the Durham, Scottish and South-Western Divisions, especially the relatively small percentage change in output amongst those collieries scheduled for reconstruction or expected to continue without major reorganization, compared with say the East Midlands or North-West Divisions.[1]

Aggregate analyses of production and manpower trends over a ten-year period disguise the extent to which the industry was often forced to adapt to varying energy requirements at times when it was least able to do so. The necessity to promote steady industrial growth at home, to safeguard the nation's trading position by expanding exports and to appease labour in a period of full employment made effective co-operation between the miners, the Coal Board and the Government of paramount importance. The extent to which their interests combined and conflicted can best be judged by a close examination of the problems which had to be faced in the post-war era.

III

The pressure of demand and the inadequacy of coal supplies was no more apparent than during the fuel crisis of 1946–7. There had been fears as to the availability of coal as early as the spring of 1946 when in April of that year total national coal stocks were over 6m. tons fewer than in the corresponding period in 1945. The problem was not one of falling output but the inability to keep pace with rising consumption. In December 1946 the Government called upon industry to reduce coal consumption by 5 per cent and imposed a $2\frac{1}{2}$ per cent cut on industry's gas and electricity consumption.[2] By January 1947 national coal consumption was exceeding total production by more than 300,000 tons a week.[3] During the following month coal exports were prohibited and supplies to bunkers restricted. Severe weather and transport difficulties intensified the problem. 595 industrial premises consuming more than 100 tons of coal per year shut down during the month for want of coal supplies.[4]

[1] National Coal Board, *Annual Report and Statement of Accounts for the Year Ended 29 December 1956*, pp. 9–12.
[2] W. W. Haynes, *Nationalization in Practice: The British Coal Industry*, London 1953, p. 131.
[3] National Coal Board, *Annual Report and Statement of Accounts for the Year Ended 31 December 1947*, p. 2.
[4] 443 H.C. Deb. 5s, 53.

In the Northern Division [1] as a whole during 1947, 19,000 more tons of coal were lost through rail transport difficulties and shortage of wagons than in 1946.[2]

The N.U.M. representatives on the Joint National Negotiating Committee, conscious that Labour's opponents could readily exploit the fuel crisis for political ends, eagerly joined members of the Special Committee of Ministers, established by the Prime Minister at the height of the crisis, in London on 27 February 1947 to seek improvements in coal transport, the supply of mining machinery and equipment, and the conveyance of miners to and from their work. Whilst priority was naturally given to measures aimed at overcoming the coal shortage the representatives conceded that long-term improvements in miners' housing, welfare and earnings were also required to safeguard an adequate level of recruitment to the industry. Already between August and October 1946 an enquiry into the recruitment of boys in six coalfields, including Durham, conducted on behalf of the Ministry of Fuel and Power and the N.C.B., had emphasized the extent to which considerations of health, safety and welfare entered into boys' assessment of the attractiveness of mining as a career.[3]

The easing of the coal shortage by mid-March 1947 in no way reduced the need for a considerable expansion in production. In its *Economic Survey* for 1947 the Government had called for a coal production target of 200m. tons for the home market alone, almost 5 per cent. more than had been produced in 1946, and a manpower target of 730,000, over 36,000 more than were employed in mining on vesting day.[4] Furthermore the agreement reached between the N.C.B. and N.U.M. on 18 April 1947 to institute a five-day working week in the industry threatened future coal supplies. This measure, officially sanctioned by the Government in the House of Commons in June 1946,[5] had earlier received the recommendation of the Reid Committee on technical grounds [6] and had been incorporated in the

[1] In 1949 the Northern Division was subdivided into the Durham Division and the Northern (Northumberland and Cumberland) Division. See above, p. 388.

[2] National Coal Board, *Annual Report and Statement of Accounts for the Year Ended 31 December 1947*, Table 7, p. 226; *The Times*, 6, 7, 8, 12, 22 February 1947.

[3] G. Thomas, *The Recruitment of Boys to the Mining Industry. An Inquiry carried out in Six Coal Fields for the Directorate of Recruitment, Ministry of Fuel and Power and the National Coal Board*, August–October 1946, p. 2.

[4] National Coal Board, *Annual Report and Statement of Accounts for the Year Ended 31 December 1947*, p. 5.

[5] 424 H.C. Deb. 5s, 1321–24.

[6] Cmd. 6610, *op. cit.*, para. 743.

Miners' Charter, a document issued by the N.U.M. in 1946 listing proposals for easing the manpower crisis.[1] To help combat absenteeism and to promote productivity so as not to endanger the national fuel supply provision was made in the agreement for a bonus to be paid to miners completing five shifts and for an assessment of working tasks to be agreed upon at local level. Daywagemen were to be paid a bonus representing their average daily wage during any one week and piece workers 16 per cent of their earnings over a five-day period, excluding overtime. For piece workers, therefore, the bonus was an incentive not only to greater attendance but also towards greater effort. The more work performed the greater the bonus.[2]

The operation of the Five-Day Week Agreement, concluded during a critical period of fuel shortage, was estimated to entail a national weekly loss of coal output of 350,000 tons from Saturday working. The extra strain thereby imposed upon the industry soon became apparent. For the Government's 1947 coal target to be reached under the new working arrangements national daily output would have had to increase by more than 140,000 tons. A special N.U.M. Committee had already estimated in March 1947 that no fewer than 100,000 persons would need to be recruited during the year to produce the necessary coal.[3] Agreement had been reached between the N.C.B. and N.U.M. in January 1947 for the employment of Polish workers in the mines but only with the consent of local branches and on condition that the recruits joined the N.U.M. and were transferred or dismissed whenever their continued employment deprived a British mineworker from the opportunity to work.[4] The arrangement was later extended to other European volunteer workers.

Coal production during the first five-day week operation was not encouraging. Over 260,000 tons were lost owing partly to a minor dispute in Lancashire, two days statutory holidays taken by Scottish

---

[1] The shortage of miners after the Second World War led the Minister of Fuel and Power to seek aid from the N.U.M. in drafting proposals to increase the rate of entry of new recruits to the industry. The Union's Executive Committee responded with a list of twelve requirements, embodied in the *Miners' Charter*, which included demands for the modernization of existing pits and the sinking of new ones; adequate and careful training of young miners; improved social and welfare provision; the maintenance of average wage standards at a level at least equivalent to those of any other British industry; the restoration of the 7-hour day for underground workers and the continuation of the principle of the guaranteed weekly wage.

[2] National Coal Board, *Annual Report and Statement of Accounts for the Year Ended 31 December 1947*, p. 12.

[3] N.U.M., 2 April 1947.

[4] *Ibid.*, 13 February 1947.

miners and, most important of all, as a result of the Durham winding enginemen's dispute.[1] This unofficial stoppage accounted for all but 4,500 tons of the 91,000 tons of coal lost in the Northern Division during the first five-day week.[2] The implementation of a shorter working week was not expected to be attended with as many complications in Durham as elsewhere since the contribution made by the coalfield to the global Saturday output in the period prior to the five-day week agreement was the lowest in the country.[3] Nevertheless the Durham miners, who had voted by a large majority to implement a five-day week, were frequently reminded by their union of their obligations under the Agreement especially in co-operating with the reassessment of tasks and completion of the cycle of operations at individual collieries.[4]

Intensive working to meet the rising demand for coal continually emphasized the critical manpower situation in the industry. In April 1947, in response to appeals by the N.U.M. and N.C.B., the Government agreed to defer the call-up of those miners who pledged to stay within the industry, to release from the Forces men with previous mining experience, to speed up the supply of materials and equipment, to encourage local authorities to give priority to the housing needs of miners and to expand the capacity of Government training centres.[5] The success of the N.C.B.'s pioneering scheme to establish two juvenile residential training centres in the Durham coalfield during May and June 1947 led to similar centres being opened elsewhere.[6]

Throughout the majority of the collieries in Durham strenuous efforts were made during 1947 to make effective use of manpower. The only pits closed were those where most of the men could be immediately transferred to productive work. When Dunston Garesfield colliery was closed during 1947 all but three of the total number of men employed were placed at other collieries.[7] Watson also pleaded with Lodges to offer their full co-operation in accepting Polish workers.[8] 'The success of our Government lies in increased coal production,' he wrote in August 1947, 'and we should be willing

[1] See Chapter XII, pp. 462–4.
[2] N.U.M. (Durham Area), 19 May 1947.
[3] National Coal Board, *Annual Report and Statement of Accounts for the Year Ended 31 December 1947*, p. 31.
[4] N.U.M. (Durham Area), August, September 1947.
[5] N.U.M., 18 April 1947.
[6] N.U.M. (Durham Area), *Annual Report*, 1947, pp. 116–24.
[7] National Coal Board, *Annual Report and Statement of Accounts for the Year Ended 31 December 1947*, p. 40.
[8] See above, p. 395.

to carry out any temporary policy which the Government feels essential to the successful solution of our economic difficulties.'[1] By the end of January 1948, 324 Poles and 126 European voluntary workers had been placed in the Northern Division.[2]

In spite of the increased effort imposed upon miners by the five-day week operations and of the short-term expedients adopted to encourage increased coal supplies it was obvious by the autumn of 1947 that the production and manpower targets felt to be so important for national well-being were not going to be met. The Five-Day-Week Agreement was barely three months old when worsening economic conditions led the Government to appeal to all basic industries to extend their hours of work for the sake of increased production. An Extension of Working Hours Agreement, made on 29 October 1947 between the N.C.B. and N.U.M. and scheduled to operate for twelve months, invited Divisional Boards and Area Executives of the national Union to collaborate in arranging for an additional half-hour to be worked daily or, alternatively, that extra Saturday shifts should be adopted. The main provisions of the Five-Day-Week Agreement were to remain intact.

The agreement was accepted in Durham by an overwhelming majority. Only three Lodges voted against the proposals and were immediately called upon by local headquarters to convene special meetings to reconsider their decision.[3] Following discussions between representatives of the N.C.B. (Northern Division) and the N.U.M. (Durham Area) it was agreed on 8 November 1947 that underground miners at collieries adopting an additional Saturday shift should work six and a half hours plus one winding time and surface workers six and a half hours excluding meal times. Piece workers on Saturday shifts received in addition to their normal earnings a gross payment per hour at overtime rates. Provision was made for those collieries working an extra half hour daily, which in Durham amounted to almost half the total, to adopt Saturday working if from experience the arrangements were found to be unsatisfactory.

In the Northern Division it soon became obvious that the most successful results were being obtained from pits working an extra half-hour and that high absenteeism among face workers reduced Saturday output below what had been expected. Because of the long underground travelling time and difficult working conditions in many pits in the Division the costs of Saturday working often outstripped the value of the additional output thus achieved. The additional

[1] N.U.M. (Durham Area), 23 August 1947.
[2] N.U.M., 12 February 1948.
[3] N.U.M. (Durham Area), 22, 27 October 1947.

income the majority of miners themselves received put them into a higher tax bracket so that the *net* rate for the Saturday half shift worked out less than normal time. The not unnatural result was that the attendance on Saturdays soon fell below the level at which it was worth opening the pit at all.[1]

The estimated extra output obtained in the Division from Saturday working in the ten weeks ending 3 January 1948 amounted to 171,700 tons compared with 326,700 tons and 416,100 tons in the East Midlands and North Eastern Divisions respectively.[2] During the week ended 24 January 1948 the percentage of absenteeism amongst piece workers on Saturdays at Easington Colliery amounted to 68 per cent and at Horden Colliery to 55 per cent and had shown little alteration almost a month later.[3] On the other hand out of a total estimated increase in output throughout the country of 173,200 tons from extended hours the Northern Division was responsible for 163,000 tons.[4]

The support given by the miners to the coal production drive and to measures designed to increase manpower, especially the employment of volunteer European workers, helped ease the critical fuel situation which had existed at the beginning of 1947. By the end of that year coal stocks were almost double their 1946 level and coal exports had been resumed. During 1947 the demands of inland consumers had left little coal available for export and, in preparation for winter, over 700,000 tons of coal were imported from America and Poland during the summer at an estimated loss of more than 2d per ton on total saleable output.[5] Meanwhile the manpower situation slowly improved. The total number of wage earners on colliery books in December 1947 stood at only 12,000 short of the Government's projected total of 730,000, the numbers in the Durham coalfield having increased during the year by over 5,000.[6]

IV

As the need to expand coal output and exports increased during 1948 to meet the requirements of the Marshall Plan and to promote

[1] I am grateful to H. Hindley, former Chairman of the Northern Divisional Coal Board, for this information.
[2] National Coal Board, *Annual Report and Statement of Accounts for the Year Ended 31 December 1947*, p. 102.
[3] N.U.M. (Durham Area), 22 March 1948.
[4] National Coal Board, *Annual Report and Statement of Accounts for the Year Ended 31 December 1947*, p. 102.
[5] *Ibid.*, pp. 75–7.
[6] *Ministry of Labour Gazette*, December 1947.

economic recovery within the country miners were constantly urged to sustain their production efforts. In September 1948 the N.U.M. instructed Area Unions to seriously consider ways and means of implementing its pledge to the Government to secure a target of not less than 200m. tons of coal for that year. After a careful analysis of Lodge comment and opinion the Durham Area of the N.U.M. called for more frequent joint meetings between management and union representatives at each pit to discuss production methods; the establishment of new machinery for the determination of piece-rates; the provision of adequate spare parts for machinery; a drastic reduction in the amount of dirt filled; the provision above the normal ration of additional food supplies to those engaged in heavy work and the concentration of available manpower on the most productive seams in the pit.[1] Of particular concern to union officials in Durham was the lack of co-operation amongst the various grades of workman engaged on machine-mining faces. By virtue of the tasks they performed these miners negotiated separate piece-work rates and as a consequence were often accused of working for their own interest without real regard for the condition of those grades which followed on in the same cycle of operations.[2]

When production efforts did provide a surplus for export it was not always in the places most convenient for shipment. Traditionally the British coal export trade had mainly been built up in South Wales and the northern coalfields but in 1948 the output from these fields was insufficient to enable them to provide their pre-war share of the trade. Relatively more was supplied for export by the East Midlands and North-East Divisions.[3] Though after 1945 the pressures of internal coal consumption severely restricted the export performance of coalfields such as Durham it was imperative that every opportunity to compete successfully abroad was fully exploited. Watson, Secretary of the County Mining Federation Board, wrote to Lodges in 1948:

'In the past we had a considerable export trade, sometimes equivalent to 40 per cent of our output and with an employment equation slightly in excess, as many of our larger collieries on the East Coast were in the export market. . . . We need not stress the fact that our own export trade today is negligible. . . . It is important . . . that we do everything we can to produce good quality, clean coal at prices

---

[1] N.U.M. (Durham Area), *Annual Report*, 1948, pp. 34–41.
[2] N.U.M., *Information Pamphlet*, No. 22, October 1948.
[3] National Coal Board, *Annual Report and Statement of Accounts for the Year Ended 31 December 1948*, p. 64.

which will attract trade abroad, and in return secure the food and raw materials so essential to our prosperity. More and more we shall have to concentrate on the best pits and seams. Good wages and conditions cannot be maintained (short of subsidies) if 20 per cent of our pits are losing between 5s and 15s per ton.'[1]

The Extension of Working Hours Agreement, due to expire on 30 April 1948, was renewed for another year but, even in conjunction with the production campaigns so vigorously organized by Area Unions and Divisional Coal Boards, it failed to provide the means of adequately meeting minimum coal output requirements. In September 1948 Watson warned the N.U.M. Executive Committee not to rely too heavily on securing coal targets on the basis of extended hours. Drawing on experience in Durham he wrote:

'It is problematical whether the Extension of Working Hours in this Area, either on a Saturday or during the week, has given the desired results. In any case, the cost is prohibitive, especially for Saturday working, and very few Managements at collieries are in favour of its continuation.... The Divisional Coal Board has taken steps to cease working certain pits on a Saturday where the attendance has been poor and the cost high. The result has been a reaction at the pits which are working the eight-hour shift under the Extension of Working Hours Agreement, it being claimed by workmen at these pits that just as the Divisional Coal Board has the right to stop Saturday working, so has the Lodge the right to cease working the extra hours during the week, and we have reached a position where the National Agreement is in grave danger of being ignored altogether.'[2]

Appeals for a more systematic production drive did not go unheeded. A special Joint Production Committee, established by the N.C.B. and N.U.M. to make recommendations for meeting the coal requirements of 1949 and with Watson as a member, recommended in November 1948 that, in addition to seeking more effective implementation of the Extension of Hours Agreement, an intensive recruitment drive for face workers should be inaugurated and that committees be established at every pit to help reduce absenteeism.[3] The Northern Division's success in winning the Mitchell-Hedges Trophy in 1948 by securing the largest percentage advance in production above the best week's output of saleable coal during

[1] Durham County Mining Federation Board, *Annual Report*, 1948, p. 3.
[2] N.U.M. (Durham Area), *Annual Report*, 1948, p. 38.
[3] N.U.M. (Durham Area), 20 November 1948.

May and June 1947 (the 'target output') provided some recognition of the continuing local response to the nation's fuel requirements.[1] But the response was by no means unanimous. By 31 December 1948, 40 collieries in Durham had still not adopted extended working hours though 63 had agreed to adopt an extra half hour and 24 to work Saturdays.[2]

The rapidity and enthusiasm with which local Union and Coal Board officials in Durham responded to appeals for increased coal production sprang basically from a keen desire to help meet the needs of domestic and foreign consumers but was strengthened by the realization of the extent to which rising output was the key to substantially improving the coalfield's financial performance. Insufficient manpower, poor attendance, technical setbacks and the variable rate of increase of productivity rarely appeared as problems of equal intensity at all times. Nevertheless the existence of many old, relatively uneconomic pits near exhaustion and the technical difficulties of working deep, seaward sloping coal seams had traditionally made production costs in Durham and Northumberland not only higher than elsewhere but particularly susceptible to rapid changes in an upward direction. The degree to which higher than national levels of pithead proceeds per ton of saleable coal produced in Durham were eroded by rapidly rising costs during the first decade of nationalization and a tendency for persistent losses to develop can be judged from figures in Appendix III to this chapter. Certainly during the early post-war reconstruction years the losses would have been greater in Durham were it not for her ability to exploit the foreign demand for fuel and to supply non-substitutable classes of coal. While domestic coal prices were controlled by the Government export prices were allowed greater, though not unrestricted, scope for adjustment. It has been estimated that the premium from increased exports at preferential prices improved Durham's total pithead proceeds by over 8d per ton during 1948–9 and that, despite a slight reduction in total production costs, reliance on inland sales alone would have produced a Divisional loss not of 2s but almost 4s a ton.[3]

The export premiums would have been much higher if coal export prices had been allowed to respond to market forces, but prices were fixed with reference to what was being charged by other exporting countries. The adjustments made to the inland prices of different

[1] N.U.M. (Durham Area), *Annual Report* 1948, p. 28.
[2] *Ibid.*, p. 46.
[3] National Coal Board, *Annual Report and Statement of Accounts for the Year Ended 31 December 1949*, p. 23.

types of coal during 1948–9, providing better returns for higher-quality grades, reduced the export premium slightly. Whilst Durham was still able, therefore, to benefit from a ready demand for her first-class coking coal such adjustments could in no way compensate for the losses incurred in having supplies for export restrained by the demands of home consumption. The Durham County Mining Federation Board complained in 1949:

'Much of our coal is denied access to the Export Markets of Europe, and is utilized on the Home Market, thus bringing in lower prices than we would get if it was exported. There is a case for investigation into this question and it is not unfair to suggest that if, as a County, we are denied our natural Export Markets, due to Home demands, some compensation should be afforded by granting to us increased inland prices. The West of Durham produces some of the finest coking coal in Europe ... yet it has to be sold on the Inland Market at prices considerably below the cost of production. ... It is alright for Home Industry to secure this coal below cost price but it does not help Durham to become an economic coalfield. We could get at least a further 25s per ton for a large part of this tonnage if we were allowed to sell it in the Export Markets and this would enable us to show a profit and not a loss. ... The value of the coal should be related to the Selling Price. The customer cannot, or at least should not, have the best quality coal available in any country in Europe, at prices which enable him to make the very pits which provide his valuable fuel, uneconomic.'[1]

Conscious of the northern coalfield's weak financial position Divisional Coal Board representatives meeting in Newcastle in February 1949 called for increased output and a reduction in costs of at least 2s 6d per ton, to be achieved largely by the closure of uneconomic pits and a more efficient deployment of manpower. Two months later the Durham County Mining Federation Board were informed by local N.C.B. officials that steps would be taken to close pits working at an average monthly loss of at least £10,000 and with output per manshift less than 15 cwt.[2] Burnhope Colliery, which incurred a total loss of £123,851 during 1948 and where overall output per man shift averaged only 14·2 cwt, was subsequently closed in July 1949.[3] However much the individual workmen affected by pit closures might condemn such action local miners' officials realized

[1] Durham County Mining Federation Board, *Annual Report*, 1949, pp. 1–2.
[2] N.U.M. (Durham Area), 18 June 1949.
[3] *Ibid.*, 11 July 1949.

the problems an old coalfield faced in trying to sustain the levels of output and efficiency which were being demanded in the post-war years. Watson wrote to Lodges in January 1949:

'The next decade will witness many changes in the Durham Coalfield. . . . That more pits which are uneconomic will close as their losses mount cannot be gainsaid. . . . Concentration on the best pits will mean a gradual closing of the most uneconomic pits, and no amount of easy talking or easy thinking will hide the stark economic reality involved.'[1]

The persistent pressure of demand for coal constantly averted attention away from the legitimate concern over how best to reduce costs, at least on a long-term basis, towards adopting immediate expedients designed to increase output. In the autumn of both 1949 and 1950 the N.U.M. and N.C.B. encouraged Areas to support intensive coal production drives. In both cases the decision to continue the provisions of the Extension of Working Hours Agreement provided an integral part of the operations. The Minister of Fuel and Power calculated in April, 1949 that unless extended hours were maintained coal output for the year would fall to 24m. tons below national requirements and only 16m. of the necessary 23m. tons would be available for export.[2]

The Durham miners, having endorsed the decision to continue extended hours, joined wholeheartedly in the campaign for more coal. During the week ended 10 September 1949, 45 collieries in Durham were not working any extra hours for additional production.[3] By 31 December 1950 the number had been reduced to only one.[4] This movement was singled out by the Prime Minister in his radio broadcast to the nation on 24 October as an example of the encouraging response to the need for expanding production when he said:

'The need is for an all-out effort and you know this has not been forthcoming. . . . There are workers who only do the minimum, who don't care, who take days off because they know that in these days workers are needed. If all did as well as the best, or even as the good, we should be well on the way to getting through our difficulties. Example is better than precept. In some big steel plants and in a Lancashire wagon works all have decided to work longer

---

[1] Durham County Mining Federation Board, *Annual Report*, 1949, p. 4.
[2] N.U.M., 14 April 1949.
[3] N.U.M. (Durham Area), 3 October 1949.
[4] N.U.M. (Durham Area), *Annual Report*, 1950, p. 126.

hours in the national interest. In Durham a big campaign has been run by miners; thirty collieries have decided to operate fully an extended hours agreement and to encourage overtime working. . . . These are just some instances.'[1]

Special mass meetings of workmen and management became a regular feature of colliery village activity during 1949, characterized by the majority acceptance of resolutions calling for increased output, overtime working to help complete the cycle of mining operations and the elimination of unofficial strikes.[2]

Rising productivity and an increase in the number of shifts worked helped counteract the continuing tendency at both national and Divisional level for manpower to decline. The total number of workment effectively employed in the Durham coalfield fell during 1948–9 by over 9,000, the number engaged at the coal face having dropped from 43,362 to 39,373.[3] Overall output per manshift on the other hand increased slightly from 0·92 to 0·96 tons and at the coal face from 2·25 to 2·39 tons. High absenteeism at collieries implementing the Extension of Hours Agreement by Saturday working still created a problem. During the week ended 12 November 1949, for example, Saturday absenteeism amongst hewers at Brancepeth Colliery stood at 77 per cent and at Easington Colliery, where the problem was of long standing,[4] at 85 per cent.[5]

Improving the balance of manpower by recruiting *volunteer* faceworkers for Saturday shifts and providing a sufficient complement of datal workers was found at one Durham colliery to significantly improve output, raise attendance and, in spite of overtime payments, maintain production costs at a reasonable level. The experiment received the warm support of local Union and Coal Board officials, especially since a 1 per cent rate of absenteeism in the coalfield was estimated to lose more than 250,000 tons of saleable coal per annum.[6] The renewal of the Extension of Working Hours Agreement for a further year in March 1950 gave poignance to such efforts to obtain the full attendance of a balanced labour force but response at pit level during the ensuing twelve months proved dis-

[1] *Listener*, 27 October 1949.
[2] N.U.M. (Durham Area), *Annual Report*, 1949, pp. 54–8.
[3] Durham County Mining Federation Board, *Annual Report*, 1948, pp. 14, 16. *Ibid.*, 1949, pp. 14, 16.
[4] See above, p. 398.
[5] N.U.M. (Durham Area), 28 November 1949.
[6] Durham County Mining Federation Board, *Annual Report*, 1950, p. 7. This estimate must be regarded as extremely tentative since it is very difficult to calculate production losses through absenteeism. See above, pp. 391–2.

appointing. In the circumstances the Durham Divisional Coal Board proposed to terminate Saturday working at collieries which refused to accept balanced manpower teams and where the rate of absenteeism exceeded 30 per cent.[1]

The familiar appeals for lower costs, reduced absenteeism, closure of uneconomic pits and increased output were reiterated by E. H. D. Skinner, Chairman of the Durham Division of the National Coal Board, at a County Conference of Colliery Consultative Committees held at the miners' headquarters on 19 August 1950. Having reminded delegates of the extent to which the coalfield's future viability depended in a large measure upon increasing efficiency and effort, especially the capacity to export, Skinner concluded his address with a call for greater local initiative and responsibility saying:

'The Durham coalfield is today making heavy losses. This fact makes people critical of it. Most of its coals—say 75 per cent—are high class, but even high class coals can be too dear. A number of pits in the West and some in the East are becoming exhausted and must close and be regrouped before long. Others are marginal and their existence depends upon reducing costs to meet changes in economic conditions. Much improvement is undoubtedly possible through better mining technique, through greater attention by everyone to detail and efficiency . . . and evidencing a sense of responsibility on all sides. People in the position of final authority, i.e. the National Board, while sensible of our difficulties, must in the end look to overall results and will turn where they can get the right quality of coal at the lowest cost. We must help ourselves and do so quickly. We have got to make an extra effort to fill the gap until reorganization and technical improvement can give us a substantial advance. With any luck and by thought and determination we can probably take care of redundancy arising from normal decline, but excessive decline through inability to attain an economic level of activity would be outside the powers of this Division to control.'[2]

It was precisely the disappointing overall operating results to which Skinner had referred in his address that must have led Durham miners during 1949–50 to begin questioning the value of coal production drives. Since effective action to meet adequately the nation's fuel demands depended always upon a critical balancing of resources and a ready adaptability to meet short-run crises any sudden

[1] N.U.M. (Durham Area), *Annual Report*, 1950, p. 121.
[2] E. H. D. Skinner, *The Coal Industry in Durham Today—and Tomorrow*. Conference address printed for private circulation, 1950.

deterioration in circumstances could so easily retard what progress had been made. Thus the worsening manpower situation in Durham by the end of 1950 overshadowed the fact that output and productivity (both overall and at the face) had reached their highest levels since nationalization. The average number of men on colliery books in the Division fell by over 2,400 during 1949–50. In addition the number of average shifts worked per man each week remained constant at its 1949 level (4·76) being the lowest on record since 1947,[1] whilst the rate of recruitment of both adults and juveniles per 100 men on colliery books in Durham fell below the national average during 1950.[2] The loss of manpower in the industry as a whole during the same year amounted to over 20,500 men, representing almost 3 per cent of the total mining labour force.[3]

The relative importance of factors affecting the supply of labour to mining varied amongst the different coalfields, but one common influence must have been the removal in 1950 of the restrictions imposed by the Ministry of Labour upon the miners' freedom to seek alternative employment. Up to the end of 1949 it had been the practice of the Ministry to refuse permission to men between the ages of 18 and 50 normally employed in agriculture or coalmining to move into other kinds of employment unless there was some convincing reason for the change. They could move freely between jobs in their respective industries but had not the same freedom of choice of other employment as persons in other industries. These restrictions, known as 'ring fences', were abolished from 1 January 1950, whereupon miners desiring employment outside of their industry became subject like other workmen to the provisions of the Control of Engagement Orders, 1947–9.[4]

Thus they were unable to accept alternative employment otherwise than through a local office of the Ministry of Labour or an approved employment agency. These Orders themselves were revoked on 10 March 1950. The rise in military pay in the autumn of 1950 attracted into the Forces an estimated 1 per cent of the total mining work force in Northumberland and Durham although this leakage was later stemmed by subsequent national advances in miners' wages.[5]

---

[1] National Coal Board, *Annual Report and Statement of Accounts for the Year Ended 31 December 1951*, p. 92.
[2] *Ibid. . . . for the Year Ended 31 December 1950*, p. 9.
[3] *Ibid.*, p. 7.
[4] S.R. & O. 1947, No. 2021; S.I. 1948, No. 2608; S.I. 1949, No. 2251.
[5] G. B. Baldwin, *Beyond Nationalization: the Labour Problems of British Coal*, Cambridge, Harvard University Press 1955, p. 207.

Despite the fact that proceeds from inland coal sales in Durham (largely to coke oven and gas works) improved during 1950 the northern coalfields (Durham, Northumberland and Cumberland) were the only ones to incur a financial loss during the year. Durham's net loss (before charging interest and interim income) had increased by 3d per ton over its 1949 level to a total of 2s 3d per ton. Rising home consumption and the low level of stocks halted the recovery in exports which had slowly taken place since 1947. The reduction in coal exports ordered by the Government in August 1950 was unfortunate in as much as British supplies, already beginning to hold their own in European markets, would have been in ready demand with the outbreak of the Korean War.

V

The inclusion in the terms of the January 1951 national wages agreement[1] of measures to promote increased production reflected the persistent need for more coal and, more specifically, the urgency with which an impending winter fuel crisis had to be tackled. The now all-too-common demands for full implementation of extended hours of work and reduced absenteeism were to be reiterated with special force as miners were urged to produce an extra 3m. tons of coal by the end of April 1951. The pressures of internal consumption had already driven stocks so low that coal had to be imported during the 1950–1 winter. Altogether, between December 1950 and October 1951, 1,192,400 tons of coal, mainly for use in power stations, were imported from America at an average landed cost of £4 5s 5d more than the selling price of British coal of comparable quality.[2]

Neither patriotic appeals by the Durham County Mining Federation Board for all workmen 'to do service to save the people from unemployment, dislocation of industry and suffering'[3] during the winter months nor the persistent call for sustained effort throughout the year went unheeded. By the end of 1951 total deep-mined output had increased in the coalfield by 2·9 per cent, the contribution made by Saturday working having shown a distinct improvement. Eppleton Colliery received third prize in the *News of the World* competition to find the pits displaying the best individual performance in

[1] See Chapter XI, p. 437.
[2] National Coal Board, *Annual Report and Statement of Accounts for the Year Ended 31 December 1951*, pp. 32–5.
[3] N.U.M. (Durham Area), 9 January 1951.

meeting the demand for increased winter fuel.[1] The constituent members of the Durham County Mining Federation Board decided by a majority of over 600 votes to agree in April 1951 to authorize the N.U.M. Executive Committee to rescind a previous agreement whereby extended hours were to be suspended for the summer months. The Extension of Hours Agreement was therefore renewed for a further twelve months.[2]

In Durham the manpower situation and the problem of rising costs still remained critical. The Division was the only one to suffer a reduction in the number of wage-earners employed during 1951 although a secondary problem of a decline in the proportion of face workers to all workers (from 43 per cent in 1946 to 42·7 per cent in 1951 and contrary to national experience) was counteracted to some extent by rising productivity. Thus whilst in Durham in 1946 463 shifts were needed at the face to produce 1,000 tons of coal only 399 shifts were needed in 1951.[3] Despite this improvement, overall output per manshift in the coalfield in 1951 was the second lowest in the country while wages cost (including the value of allowances in kind) was the highest, standing at 36s 9d per ton compared with 29s 9d per ton nationally and only 22s 10d per ton in the East Midlands Division. The Durham Division was responsible in 1951 for producing the second largest share (24 per cent) of the least profitable coal output in that year.[4] The trading losses in the six Areas of the Division varied from 1s 3d per ton to 9s 8d per ton, only one of the six making a profit.

The persistent problems of manpower shortage and rising costs were prevented from impairing Durham's trading performance to a much greater extent than they did in 1952 by the fact that high export prices and the coalfield's ability to supply good quality coals to the home market improved total pithead proceeds to a much larger extent than in the country as a whole, especially compared with inland coalfields. Thus, although a rise in total costs per ton in the Durham Division of almost 10s between 1951–2 outstripped the increase in total proceeds and brought the loss for the year to 3s 5d per ton, the deterioration in financial results was less serious than in the majority of other areas. This situation was particularly fortunate since productivity, overall and at the face, took a downward turn in

[1] N.U.M. (Durham Area), *Annual Report*, 1951, p. 29.
[2] N.U.M., 5 April, 1, 26, July 1951.
[3] National Coal Board, *Annual Report and Statement of Accounts for the Year Ended 31 December 1951*, pp. 14–16.
[4] Sir H. Houldsworth, 'The Pits of Britain'. Paper read before the Manchester Statistical Society, 11 February 1953, p. 13.

1952 for the first time since nationalization and at a time when Durham remained the only Division in the country not to improve its manpower situation. Whilst the total recruitment rate per 100 men on colliery books stood at 11·1 and the total wastage rate at 7·9 for the country as a whole during 1952 the comparable rates in Durham were only 5·8 and 6·2 respectively.[1] By 1952 the total number of juveniles recruited nationally to the industry stood at almost double its 1949 level, though in Durham during the same period only 25 per cent more boys entered mining.[2]

Number of New Entrants Under 18

	Durham	Great Britain
1949	2,430	14,160
1950	2,530	15,120
1951	2,730	19,590
1952	3,040	27,110

In common with earlier practice the N.U.M. and N.C.B. agreed in February 1953 that the implementation of the newly-won national wages advance should be made conditional upon production campaigns being inaugurated throughout the coalfields. During the following month N.U.M. and N.C.B. representatives addressed meetings in Durham whilst the local Divisional Consultative Committee established a body, with Moore and Watson as members, to consider practical means of promoting increased coal output. By mid-1953, 11 pits in Durham were still not working on Saturdays,[3] whilst few had opted, as was their right, to work a limited number of Saturdays during the summer period when, by previous agreement, the extension of hours arrangements had been suspended. By the middle of June 1953, however, Colliery Consultative Committees in the coalfield had succeeded in persuading men at 46 pits to work extra hours during the summer which, as a consequence, provided sufficient extra tonnage to compensate for that lost during the Coronation Day holiday earlier in the year.[4] At the same time the inauguration of an extra week's paid holiday for miners had entailed an even greater loss of output, amounting in Durham alone to over 600,000 tons during 1953.[5]

---

[1] National Coal Board, *Annual Report and Statement of Accounts for the Year Ended 31 December 1952*, p. 11.

[2] Baldwin, *op. cit.*, p. 201.

[3] N.U.M. (Durham Area), 13 June 1953.

[4] *Ibid.*

[5] N.U.M. (Durham Area), *Annual Report*, 1953, p. 77.

In the country as a whole the fall in coal production during 1953 was matched by an almost equivalent increase in home demand, necessitating drawing on stocks and the authorization of coal imports. Though exports (excluding bunkers) increased from 11·6m. to 13·8m. tons nationally and from 1·9m. to 2·4m. tons in the Durham Division during the year,[1] ½m. tons of coal were imported from France, Belgium and Germany at a loss of almost £2 per ton.[2]

The campaigns for increased output undertaken during 1953 were intensified during the following year since, under the terms of the 1954 wages settlement,[3] the N.U.M. and N.C.B. had agreed to secure 2½ per cent more coal than had been produced during the previous twelve months, equivalent to an additional 5m. tons,[4] of which Durham's share amounted to 647,470 tons.[5] Neither the Divisional nor the national target was reached. Local union officials had tried hard in Durham to persuade more miners to volunteer for Saturday working during the summer period, when technically extended hours were suspended, but with little effect. The estimated increase in saleable output due to Saturday working throughout the whole year in the coalfield amounted to only 5,000 tons.[6] Nevertheless the speed and efficiency with which organized production drives could be inaugurated, no doubt due to the persistence of the fuel shortage, bore witness to the zeal of local Divisional personnel and the willingness of managers and workers alike to at least tackle the problem. When Horner appealed to Areas in December 1954 to take immediate steps to combat falling output Durham was able to report that, unlike most other Divisions, a production campaign had already been implemented with an emphasis placed upon regular meetings of Colliery Consultative Committees throughout the entire coalfield.[7]

Disputes and a worsening manpower situation severely restricted the industry's ability to meet home fuel requirements during 1955, so much so that coal exports were reduced and imports stepped up, the loss incurred on imported coal amounting in total to over 47s

---

[1] See Appendix II to this chapter.
[2] National Coal Board, *Annual Report and Statement of Accounts for the Year Ended 31 December 1953*, p. 29.
[3] See Chapter XI, p. 440.
[4] National Union of Mineworkers, *Report of the National Executive Committee May 1954*, pp. 12, 16.
[5] N.U.M. (Durham Area), 1 June 1954.
[6] National Coal Board, *Annual Report and Statement of Accounts for the Year Ended 31 December 1954*, Appendix I, Table 4, pp. 114–15.
[7] N.U.M. (Durham Area), 1 November 1954.

per ton.[1] The reduction in output and stocks during 1954 had led to an increase in coal imports from 0·5m. to 3m. tons during 1953–4 and by the end of 1955 imports had reached a post-war peak of 11·5m. tons.[2]

The N.C.B.'s deliberate subsidization of U.K. fuel consumption had involved losses totalling over £70m. on imported coal between 1951 and 1957 which seriously affected the financial performance of the industry. Though selective price increases had taken place since 1947 in an effort to reflect more adequately quality and cost differentials between the coalfields Ministerial restraint on raising prices during the fifties, for fear of encouraging similar increases elsewhere and possibly endangering the competitiveness of British exports, hampered the N.C.B. from capitalizing on the rising demand for coal. A review of the N.C.B.'s financial policy since nationalization has led one writer to conclude that 'Government restraint on price increases has been such that deficits are more an index of official attitudes to public industry than of an industry's own performance'[3]. Watson reminded delegates at the 1955 N.U.M. Annual Conference just how true this was of British coal when he claimed:

'Many of the faults that are laid at the door of this industry, including the National Coal Board, are due in themselves to the limitations placed upon the Coal Board by the Government's price policy. Indeed, I would go further than that and say this, that if the Coal Board was only permitted the same ordinary business latitude as other industries are permitted, we would make a bigger profit than I.C.I. or steel—aye, and anyone else.'[4]

A similar point was made by the Report of the Select Committee on Nationalized Industries in April 1858:

'If the Coal Board had not been subject to their statutory duties, and had been free from export restrictions, millions of tons of coal would have been exported at well above the price paid for it at home. . . . As a result, the Board would have shown tremendous profits.'[5]

[1] National Coal Board, *Annual Report and Statement of Accounts for the Year Ended 31 December 1955*, p. 17.
[2] See Appendix II to this chapter.
[3] M. Posner, 'The National Coal Board, 1947–62', *Annals of Collective Economy*, 33, October–December 1962, p. 347. See also M. Barratt-Brown, 'Coal as a Nationalized Industry', *Economic Studies*, 4, October 1969, pp. 111–12, 124.
[4] N.U.M., 6 July 1955.
[5] House of Commons, *Report of Select Committee on Nationalized Industries: Coal*, H.C. 187–1, April 1958, p. xxiii.

An unofficial strike of coal fillers in Yorkshire, which at one stage involved 84 collieries and almost 800,000 men, together with lesser disputes elsewhere, cost the industry more coal during 1955 than in any year since nationalization. The problem of insufficient manpower was a particularly crucial one in the North-Eastern, West Midlands and South-Western Divisions which were alone responsible for over 9,000 of the 13,000 miners needed in the industry at the end of 1955.[1] In Durham on the other hand the total manpower employed above and below ground showed a net increase of 220 during the year, with a proportionately greater number of face workers engaged, although total coal output fell during 1954–5.[2] The situation would have been worse had miners at 42 collieries not decided to volunteer for Saturday working during the summer.

Durham's particular manpower problem now was one of how best to organize and utilize the existing labour force rather than how to attract new entrants. Watson summarized the major difficulties thus:

'We have as many surface workers as we have coal face workers and a large percentage of our surface shaft transportation is still dependent upon handpower. Then there is the exploitation of our valuable coking coals in seams 20 in. to 14 in. thick. The roadways necessary to comply with the Coal Mines Act and the number of men employed to do this work throws the ratio of preparatory workers as against coal face workers out of proportion. But this coal is essential both to the industry and the country and cannot be abandoned.'[3]

In addition the uncertainty attached to modern machine mining in undersea coal seams that were highly faulted often hindered the most efficient deployment of men.

However much manpower difficulties might differ in degree amongst the coalfields they were sufficiently serious during 1955 for the N.U.M. to consider a suggestion from the N.C.B. that foreign workers should be employed. Polish workers had already been recruited to British mines during 1947–8 [4] and small numbers of Italians were similarly recruited during May 1951 and July 1952 under the National Coal Board/Ministry of Labour Bulk Scheme. The Durham miners' Executive Committee had always supported the N.U.M.'s acceptance of foreign workers and pledged its further

[1] National Coal Board, *Annual Report and Statement of Accounts for the Year Ended 31 December 1955*, p. 34.
[2] N U M. (Durham Area), *Annual Report*, 1955, pp. 306–9.
[3] N.U.M. (Durham Area), 15 August 1955.
[4] See above, pp. 395–7.

co-operation.[1] It refused, however, to succumb to requests for transfer labour from districts suffering manpower shortages because of their refusal to employ foreigners. 'We are not prepared to create pockets of unemployment in certain parts of Durham to fill vacancies elsewhere so long as we can employ our own people to advantage in our own pits,' wrote Watson.[2] Despite the fact that Durham had fewer foreigners working in its pits than in any other coalfield (on 2 April 1955 out of a total foreign mining force of 10,268 men only 110 were placed in the Division[3]) some Lodges were more hesitant than officials in welcoming non-British workmen. Chopwell, Blackhall and Thristington Lodges condemned the suggestion outright whilst the Wheatley Hill Lodge recommended acceptance on condition of a favourable vote amongst existing miners.[4] Eden Lodge called for an immediate investigation into why men were leaving the industry, a suggestion which was subsequently supported by the N.U.M.'s decision to defer action towards attracting foreign labour in favour of examining more effective ways of retaining and efficiently deploying the existing labour force.[5]

The increase in the number of wage-earners on colliery books in Durham during 1955–6 from 102·1 to 102·3 thousand was encouraging if only because it was the first increase since 1952. Compared with 1955 the number of manshifts worked per 1,000 tons (all workers) fell by 0·9 per cent to 979 whilst output per manshift increased only slightly from 2·77 to 2·8 tons at the face and from 1·01 to 1·02 tons overall.[6] Output remained almost constant though in general trends were encouraging. The productivity levels, overall and at the face, equalled the highest yet achieved since nationalization and the Divisional loss per ton of coal was the lowest on record.

Coal production was still insufficient to allow for an expansion in exports. The import of 5·3m. tons of coal during 1956, whilst much less than in the peak year 1955, was with that exception the highest post-war intake and especially disquieting considering that high transatlantic freight rates made British coal relatively cheaper in Europe than American supplies.

Considering the importance to Durham of its supplies of high-quality coking coals brief mention must be made of carbonization

[1] N.U.M. (Durham Area), 6 August 1955.
[2] Ibid., 12 August 1955.
[3] National Union of Mineworkers, Memorandum on the Situation in the Coal-Mining Industry, August 1955, p. 13.
[4] N.U.M. (Durham Area), 29 August 1955.
[5] N.U.M. Report of the National Executive Committee, May 1956, pp. 7–10.
[6] National Coal Board, Annual Report and Statement of Accounts for the Year Ended 31 December 1956, p. 5.

developments in 1956. The Northern Divisional Coal Board in-
herited 18 coking plants, the majority of which were over 50 years
old. One of them, at Bankfoot, was the oldest in the country having
been erected in 1882. By 1956 the Durham Division was carbonizing
more coal than any other industrial unit in the country, almost £10m.
having been spent since 1947 in improving efficiency and maintaining
supplies of high grade cokes. New coking plants were opened at
Fishburn in 1954 and at Lambton in 1955. Major reconstruction
and enlargement work was begun at the Monkton plant in 1956.
The Division supplied 60 per cent of all the foundry coke used in
Britain in 1956 as well as a large quantity of blast furnace coke.
The Northern Gas Board obtained about 40 per cent of its total
supplies from Durham's surplus coke oven gas in the same year whilst
the annual output of by-products amounted to 10·5m. gallons of
crude benzole, 160,000 tons of tar and 30,000 tons of sulphate of
ammonia.[1]

VI

The pressure for increased coal production immediately after the
end of the Second World War delayed the formulation of long-term
plans for the reconstruction of the industry. Already the Reid Report
had emphasized the need for improved methods of coal-getting,
haulage, lighting and ventilation; for the maximum employment of
coal-cutting and loading machinery and for a general reconstruction
of surface plant.[2] The modernization of existing collieries and the
sinking of new ones were undertaken in the early years of nationalization as a preliminary to the preparation of a co-ordinated national
plan for the industry. In the Northern Division during 1947, for
example, improvement work was in progress at 19 collieries and plans
were being formulated for the reconstruction of 15 more.[3]

It was not until 1949, however, that the N.C.B. formulated a
scheme for the reconstruction and development of the industry over
a 15-year period up to 1965. Its details, published in 1950 under the
title *Plan for Coal*, did not provide a finished blueprint but a programme subject to revision in light of accumulated experience. An
attempt was to be made to adjust the supply of coal to demand at the
lowest possible cost to the country and to determine the strategy of

[1] N.U.M. (Durham Area), 7 January 1957.
[2] Cmd. 6610, *op. cit.*
[3] National Coal Board, *Annual Report and Statement of Accounts for the Year Ended 31 December 1947*, p. 112.

long-term investment in the industry. Current reconstruction plans at individual collieries were to be grafted into the national scheme.

The *Plan* envisaged a reduction in the number of collieries, the employment of almost 80,000 fewer men by 1965 and a capital investment programme of £635m., of which *c*. £486m. was to be spent directly on colliery development.[1] The greater part of the planned production in the industry was to come from areas already explored and being worked, the emphasis being placed upon the reconstruction of old mines rather than upon the construction of new ones. The proposals for the Durham coalfield can be summarized thus:

	Planned output 1961–5 (m. tons per year)	Percentage increase or decrease on 1949 output	Planned capital expenditure on collieries 1960–5 (£m)	Manpower estimate 1961–5
Durham Division	27·0	+2	54·0	80,100
East Durham	16·0	+23	34·0	42,100
West Durham	11·0	−18	20·0	38,000
Great Britain	240·0	+18	486·6	618,100

East Durham pits with cheap 'leadage' to ports and a natural geographical advantage for supplying gas coals to London were scheduled for potential expansions in output. The estimates for West Durham were higher than would have been justified had the same criteria for determining the potential contribution of each coalfield to the planned increase in national output been applied as in other areas. The high tradition of skill and co-operation among the mineworkers in West Durham, the social costs of a drastic cut in mining operations and the area's natural endowment of first-class coking coals helped overcome the region's poor prospects for low-cost expansion.[2] Fortunately low-cost mining was by no means coincident with special-quality coal production. Thus whilst in the country as a whole in 1949 general coals accounted for only 45·5 per cent of the total output in the lowest-cost Division, the East Midlands, where costs were 20 per cent below the national average,

[1] National Coal Board, *Plan for Coal*, October 1950, paras 9–10.
[2] *Ibid.*, paras 28–32; For comments on the justification of continuing mining in West Durham see E. H. Brown, 'The Coal Fields of Great Britain and their Future Development', *Transactions of the Institution of Mining Engineers*, 114, 1954–5.

general coals made up 83 per cent of the output. In the three highest-cost Divisions, South Wales, South East and Durham, where costs were 17 per cent above the national average, general coals accounted for only 0·8 per cent of total output.[1]

Despite assurances from the Durham Divisional Coal Board that, given a continuation of the rising demand for coal, the rate of pit closures in the coalfield would be no greater than that ordinarily dictated by exhaustion, efficiency, or the need for amalgamation the Area Union constantly condemned the *Plan* as biased against Durham, especially in its readiness to wipe off West Durham as an economic liability. The Report of the Committee on National Policy for the Use of Fuel and Power Resources (the 'Ridley Committee'),[2] published in 1952, provided some encouragement inasmuch as it forecast a greater share for coal in the total inland fuel demand of the sixties than N.C.B. estimates had allowed for. The National Coal Board remained sceptical. By the autumn of 1955, after five years' experience of meeting the energy requirements of the nation, it confessed to a growing realization of the physical difficulties and costs involved in expanding output and of the problems arising from manpower availability and distribution in a period of full employment. More specifically an annual loss of capacity within the industry of at least 4m. tons had proved higher than originally expected. In addition the task of creating new capacity, both for replacement and expansion, whilst expanding current output, promised to strain severely the industry's resources. The 1950 *Plan for Coal* had to be revised.

Between 1950 and 1955 actual capital expenditure on collieries and ancillary activities, at mid-1949 prices, had fallen short of the *Plan*'s estimates by only £20m. Large schemes of reconstruction were taking longer to complete, however, and over half of the money being spent was being devoted to smaller schemes designed to secure an immediate increase in output or efficiency.[3]

By the time the national plan for coal was being revised all but nine of the total major schemes of reconstruction scheduled for the Durham Division had been completed or were in progress. According, however, to the new projections, published in 1955 under the

---

[1] E. S. Simpson, *Coal and the Power Industries in Postwar Britain*, London 1966, pp. 5–6. The extent to which capital expenditure was to be allocated to the working of high-cost quality coals did not escape criticism. See A. Beacham, 'Planned Investment in the Coal Industry', *Oxford Economic Papers*, 3, June 1951, pp. 132–3.

[2] Cmd. 8647, September 1952.

[3] National Coal Board, *Annual Report and Statement of Accounts for the Year Ended 31 December 1955*, p. 52.

title *Investing in Coal*, the planned output for Durham was to be scaled down from 27m. to 24m. tons by 1965 although manpower requirements were raised from 80,100 to 90,000.[1] National deep-mined output was estimated to reach 230m. tons in 1965 compared with the previous calculation of 240m. tons at a date in the period 1961–5. Even though the inclusion of an estimated 10m. tons output of opencast coal in 1965 brought the totals into equality the assumption contained in the original *Plan* that sufficient manpower would be available where needed was later abandoned with the expectation that Divisional deficiencies would occur.

Recognition of the economic facts of life prompted the Board to revise capital expenditure estimates not solely in relation to the expected gain in output but to account for the current loss of capacity suffered, especially in the older coalfields. By 1 January 1956 four of the 134 collieries producing in Durham in 1947 had closed down altogether. Although estimated saleable output in Durham in 1965 was expected to be over 1m. tons below the existing level total capital expenditure for 1950–65 was expected to reach £95m. compared with an estimated £58m.[2] in the *Plan for Coal*. £33m. of the revised total had actually been spent during 1950–5, the bulk of the remainder (£44m. of the necessary £62m.) being planned for the period 1959–60. This upward revision of the *Plan*'s estimates was smaller, however, than in any other Division except the Northern largely because the age of the Durham coalfield, the diminishing reserves on the western side and the uncertainties of undersea strata made it impossible to predict how far the expansion in the east would be able, in the long term, to offset the inevitable decline in the west.

Whilst it was generally acknowledged that West Durham was a declining sector it is interesting that the total output from the three Areas within its compass proved extremely consistent. Combined saleable output in 1947 was 12,264,000 tons and was still above 12m. tons in 1956.

The Durham miners' officials had recognized during the early years of nationalization that the search for more efficient low-cost mining would involve contraction in West Durham and rationalization elsewhere in the coalfield. Without accurate knowledge of the future trends in energy supply and consumption it is not surprising that the Area Union confidently expected that if only efforts were concentrated upon developing the best seams and working methods in east coast pits the coalfield would, given the state of demand for

---

[1] National Coal Board, *Investing in Coal*, April 1956, pp. 14–15.
[2] This figure differs from the estimate of capital expenditure in Durham given on p. 415 since that total refers to expenditure on collieries and associated activities.

coal, eventually reap compensation for the difficulties older and more technically deficient collieries were having to face. Thus Watson, Secretary of the County Mining Federation Board, wrote to Lodges in 1955 heartily supporting the need for greater investment and reorganization in the industry not only for the sake of its future viability but also for the sake of national well-being demanding:

'The nation must make up its mind to invest in the coal industry all the capital needed to enable the industry to meet industrial requirements and to keep a foothold in the export markets. It is nonsense to talk about "wasting millions" on the "nationalized coal industry". The plain fact is that our survival as a nation makes coal the most important single factor in our economy. The nation has no other alternative than to invest in the coal industry, not for the benefit of the industry and the miners but for the benefit of every man-jack in the country.'[1]

VI

Both increasing output in the short-run and formulating a long-term programme of development for the industry involved considerations of increasing the technical efficiency of mining operations. Greater mechanization was a pressing need. Although by 1947 the coal cutter had already replaced the pick in many collieries and face conveyors were in general use hand-loading was still predominant. The percentage of total coal output power loaded, conveyed and cut by machinery in Durham persistently lagged behind the national average during the first decade of mines nationalization. By 1956 there was still considerable room for improvement especially in the adoption of power-loading techniques.[2]

Power-loading at the working face offered the most obvious possibility for improved mechanization. Since at the time of nationalization the use of existing loading machinery, designed mainly from American prototypes, was limited to thick seams and generally favourable mining conditions, the N.C.B. devoted a great deal of effort towards developing types of machine for different conditions, especially for thinner and harder seams. This was particularly encouraging for Durham since the loading machine most widely used during the fifties, the Meco-Moore, generally best suited to seams over 3 ft thick, was not readily adaptable in a coalfield where in 1952 the estimated reserves of all seams less than two feet in thick-

[1] Durham County Mining Federation Board, *Annual Report*, 1955, p. 3.
[2] See the table opposite.

ness were 779 m. tons.[1] Effective mechanization for the economic exploitation of the very thin seams in West Durham was largely responsible for the relative popularity in the Division of 'coal ploughs'. These machines employed a wedge to force the coal out of the seam instead of a jib to cut it and became even more practical following the development of a water-infusion/blasting technique which pre-softened seams previously thought too hard for such extraction. This new technique was developed by the Safety in Mines Research Establishment and I.C.I. Ltd. and arose out of research initiated as a result of recommendations made by the Chief Inspector of Mines following the explosion at Easington Colliery in 1951.[2]

The low priority give to mechanization at the coal face during the immediate post-war years when reconstruction of existing collieries was of paramount importance and the subsequent time needed to develop power-loading machinery suitable for British mining conditions allayed a widespread application of mechanized loading until after 1956.[3] The degree to which it was adopted in the Durham Division and the extent therein of other forms of mechanization compared with national trends can be summarized thus:

Percentage of Output

	Power loaded		Cut by machinery		Conveyed	
	Durham	Gt Britain	Durham	Gt Britain	Durham	Gt Britain
1947	n.a.	2·5	70·1*	74·9	43·6	75·3
1948	n.a.	2·5	63·5*	76·2	52·0	78·4
1949	n.a.	3·2	49·0	77·5	52·0	82·0
1950	2·8	3·7	51·8	79·3	57·7	85·1
1951	3·6	4·7	56·6	80·9	65·0	87·6
1952	3·8	4·9	58·6	82·7	67·9	88·9
1953	4·0	5·9	59·9	83·3	70·9	89·2
1954	4·8	7·4	62·2	84·9	73·2	91·2
1955	5·4	9·8	65·2	86·0	75·2	91·3
1956	8·5	14·1	68·1	87·1	77·5	92·7

* Northern Division

Sources: N.C.B. *Annual Reports; Reports of H.M. Inspector of Mines*

[1] H. E. Collins, 'Coal Ploughs in the Durham Coalfield', *Transactions of the Institution of Mining Engineers*, 112, December 1952.
[2] *Report of H.M. Inspector of Mines* (*Northern Division*), 1953, p. 2. See Chapter XII, pp. 477–8.
[3] The introduction of power-loading in British mines and its effects on productivity, wages and efficiency are discussed in D. M. Kelly, 'The Process of Mechanization in British Coal Mining since 1945', *Economic Studies*, 4, October 1969. It was estimated at the end of 1956 that productivity at coalfaces in Durham collieries where power-loading machinery had been adopted was at least 25 per cent above the coalfield average. N.U.M. (Durham Area), 7 January 1959.

420 THE DURHAM MINERS

Improvements in technique were especially important in determining the future viability of the western portion of the Durham coalfield. The N.C.B.'s *Plan for Coal* envisaged little scope for big schemes of reconstruction in the region, having decided that the main improvement 'must come from technical changes on a smaller scale'.[1] In 1950 a start was made with the implementation of a scheme which had been under consideration for many years for the dewatering of the large areas of abandoned and water-logged workings in south-west Durham. As a result of centralized pumping carried out at West Auckland Colliery the level of the water table in the area was lowered by almost 20 ft during 1951, enabling Bildershaw Drift Mine to be reopened on a small scale by the N.C.B.[2] Other drifts were subsequently opened as the dewatering process continued.[3]

As efforts were made to preserve long-established sources of coal supply attention was also focused upon tapping new reserves. The proving of the seaward extensions of the Durham coalfield by means of underground boring was begun in 1949. A bore hole was put down from the pier at South Shields[4] and exploratory work continued during the fifties. In the south-east of Durham the base of the magnesium limestone was also checked to establish the levels at which it would be safe to have workings beneath it.[5]

The sinking of a new shaft at Hawthorn was begun in 1952 as part of a scheme to establish a combined mine to work the existing Murton, Elemore and Eppleton collieries.[6] By 1957 it had been sunk to a depth of 1,180 ft and finally began supplying coal in September 1959. A new shaft sunk at Wearmouth Colliery in 1956 'started coaling' in April 1962.

Improving the technical efficiency of the industry encompassed more than sophisticated coal-face mechanization. Haulage and handling, roof support and standards of maintenance[7] all came under the close

[1] National Coal Board, *Plan for Coal*, October 1950, para. 30.
[2] *Report of H.M. Inspector of Mines (Northern Division)*, 1951, p. 1.
[3] For more detailed consideration of these projects see G. Armstrong and S. Buchan, 'Dewatering Schemes in the South Durham Coal Field', Paper read before the North of England Institute of Mining and Mechanical Engineers, 4 June 1959.
[4] National Coal Board, *Annual Report and Statement of Accounts for the Year Ended 31 December 1949*, pp. 56–7.
[5] *Ibid. . . . for the Year Ended 31 December 1952*, p. 19.
[6] *Report of H.M. Inspector of Mines (Northern Division)*, 1952, p. 1.
[7] In this context see A. Young, H. A. Longden and B. L. Metcalfe, 'Post-War Developments in the Coal Mining Industry', *Proceedings of the Institution of Civil Engineers*, 6, 1957; F. Marsh, 'Haulage and Handling' in Sir G. Nott-Bower and R. H. Walkerdine (eds), *National Coal Board, The First Ten Years*, London 1956, pp. 17–23; H. L. Willett, 'Some Developments in Mining Techniques',

scrutiny of the Mechanization Branch of the N.C.B. With Area and Divisional assistance mechanization advanced from a system of limited application concentrated in particular regions to one of comparatively widespread use. The advance in coal-face technique, especially the development of armoured, flexible chain conveyors in place of the conventional belt conveyor, was well fitted to improve efficiency and offset potential manpower deficiencies in the future. Ironically, whilst 1956 saw the culmination or at least progressive development of so many technical, organizational and production schemes in the industry it also marked the beginning of an era when the demand for coal was to fall off sharply in face of the competition from other fuels.[1] Certainly much had been achieved within the industry during the first decade of nationalization. Reviewing the situation in 1957 E. F. Schumacher, Economic Adviser to the Coal Board, could write, 'The industry is back on its feet for the first time in forty years . . . the forces of decline have given way to the forces of expansion.'[2] Unfortunately the experience gained by the Board in trying to reconcile the aims of a public service with the rationalization of production during years of rising demand was destined to be applied under conditions hardly foreseen at the time of vesting-day celebrations.

VII

The conflicting pressures within the coal industry during the first decade of public ownership to expand output in the short-run and at the same time plan for large-scale co-ordination and operation increasingly brought into question the organization and efficiency of the National Coal Board. The highly centralized 'line-and-staff' procedure adopted by the Board for managerial purposes created Divisions and areas under its authority each with staffs rigidly placed in the line of command. Thus Divisional Boards were collectively responsible to the N.C.B., though functional officers appointed to serve as specialists to a specific Area were responsible to functional departments at Divisional headquarters and not to the Area General Manager.[3]

---

loc. cit., pp. 28–33; and for a detailed review of coal-face mechanization, R. F. Landsdown and F. W. Wood, 'Coalface Machinery Developments', loc. cit., pp. 39–44.
[1] See Epilogue.
[2] E. F. Schumacher, 'Britain's Coal', National Provincial Bank Review, November 1957, p. 10.
[3] See above, p. 387.

The Durham Area Union lost little time in reminding Coal Board officials of the responsibility shared by both management and men for creating a viable industry in the post-war period. In November 1947 when costs, efficiency and wages were central themes of argument and discussion Watson wrote to H. Hindley, Chairman of the Northern Divisional Coal Board, expressing the growing dissatisfaction amongst Lodges of the increase in number of surface and underground officials to undertake 'unnecessary and costly jobs' which added 'neither to efficiency nor production, but merely to cost'.[1]

The Area Union's charge of cumbersome and top-heavy management, and of its knowledge of the abuse of perquisites by local Board officials who organized workmen to do gardening or to run errands, met with stern reaction from the Divisional Board. The Board's Deputy Chairman pointedly replied that:

'Altogether, about 150 people, many of advanced age and nearly all drawing very high salaries, have left the industry in the Northern Division since the Vesting Date. . . . The number of clerical and administrative workers in the Northern Division is far below the average for the country in relation to the total number of workers employed.'[2]

The initial response of parties ever ready to defend their own position proved of limited satisfaction. Watson was empowered by the Area Union's Executive Committee in April 1948 to request that the N.C.B. should appoint highly-skilled business executives for each of the Areas in the country 'to investigate . . . the question of administration and personnel of the Coal Board and other allied matters calculated to give the mining industry the highest standard of efficiency and economic well-being'.[3] The resignation of Sir Charles Reid[4] from the N.C.B. in the same year attracted a growing amount of support for his basic contention that the Board was over-centralized[5] and led to the appointment of a committee under the chairmanship of Sir Robert Burrows, a part-time member of the Board and former coal owner, to investigate the organization of the industry. The Burrows Committee's recommendations for relaxing central

[1] N.U.M. (Durham Area), 31 January 1948.
[2] Ibid.
[3] Ibid., 12 April 1948.
[4] Reid had acted as Chairman of the Technical Advisory Committee on Coal Mining which reported in 1945.
[5] See Sir Charles Reid in The Times, 22–24 November 1948; H. A. Clegg and T. E. Chester, The Future of Nationalization, London 1953; Acton Society Trust, Nationalized Industry, a series of nine pamphlets issued during 1950–51.

control, for example by encouraging part-time members to join functional boards to help assist in the formulation of broad policy, were partly met by the provisions of the 1949 Coal Industry Act, though a proposal that Divisional Chairmen should serve on the N.C.B. was rejected by the Board.[1]

The pressure exerted upon the N.C.B. by outside experts, especially the Conservative Central Office, for greater decentralized control gained strength during the early fifties[2] and evoked favourable responses from the Board. Thus in 1953 all Divisional Chairmen received a directive the main aim of which was to achieve as much decentralization of decision-making at Area and Divisional level as was consistent with the Coal Board's statutory responsibilities. Apart from a few exceptions no instructions were to be issued by headquarters to individual members or officials of Divisional Boards and Area General Managers were to be free to decide which of the services and managerial functions provided at Divisional level should be used.[3]

In view of the mounting criticism against the Board's organization an official enquiry was launched in December 1953. An Advisory Committee on Organization was appointed under the charmanship of Dr Alexander (later Lord) Fleck, Chairman of I.C.I. and with ex-Durham miners' Agent Lawther as a member. If the N.C.B. Directive of 1953 represented 'a capitulation to the exponents of decentralization'[4] the Committee's Report, issued in February 1955, sought to undermine substantially that surrender. The Fleck Committee approved of the main structure of the Board's organization—Headquarters, Divisions, Areas and Collieries—and of the principle of 'line and staff' but regarded the special problems of the nationalized coal industry as making for centralization, submitting that:

'The British coal industry is different in nature from many other big industrial undertakings in that mining is an extractive industry in which, broadly speaking, the same job is being done in every part of it. The industry is not an amalgamation of manufacturing units of

[1] National Coal Board, *Annual Report and Statement of Accounts for the Year Ended 31 December 1948*, Appendix V.
[2] See for example Conservative Political Centre, *Inside Industry: Coal*, London 1948; *Facts and Ideas about Coal*, London 1948 and *Structure of the Coal Industry*, London 1951. For a review of some of the contemporary criticisms levelled against the N.C.B.'s administration see D. W. Kelly, 'The Administration of the National Coal Board', *Public Administration*, 31, 1953.
[3] J. Platt, *British Coal*, London 1968, p. 34.
[4] A. E. Thompson, 'Organization in Two Nationalized Industries: Fleck versus Herbert', *Scottish Journal of Political Economy*, 3, June 1957, p. 91.

different kinds. Coal production in any one part of the country can be sold in any other. For these reasons the amount of coal to be produced by any particular part of the industry, and the amount of capital to be spent on that part, are questions which must be settled by reference to the possibilities of the industry as a whole.'[1]

The N.U.M. supported the opponents of decentralization. Its representatives declared in verbal evidence before the enquiry that the Union would resist 'any measures which would result in a dissipation of the authority and central direction of the National Coal Board' on the grounds that the whole purpose of nationalization had been 'to establish a form of national organization for running the industry which would treat the coal industry as a national entity'.[2]

The Committee's main criticisms and proposals related to the constitution of the Board itself; general management policy; the Departmental organization at headquarters and below; Area management and the level of management between Area and Colliery. The most important proposal relating to the Board was to reverse the movement which had taken place since 1951 whereby Board members had become less 'functional', that is without specific responsibility for one or more Departments. From February 1955 the Board was reconstituted so that each full-time member, other than the Chairman and Deputy Chairman, took on such responsibilities.

The main emphasis of the Fleck Report was laid on general management policy. The Committee was not satisfied that policies and decisions emanating from the Board's headquarters were being properly carried out in the Divisions and Areas. Much of the blame for this was felt to stem from the Board's interpretation of decentralization. Whilst the Committee agreed in principle with the Board's decision to decentralize management it criticized it for failing to enforce policy decisions for fear of interfering with day-to-day management.[3] In doing so the Committee effectively challenged previous exhortations to reduce centralization in policy-making by strengthening the powers of local managements.

As a result of the Fleck Report's recommendations a new General Directive was issued by the N.C.B. on 5 July 1955, replacing that formulated in 1953, instructing that policy decisions were to be set down in more detail and with greater clarity. The technique of control by means of forecasts and budgets was to be substantially

[1] National Coal Board, *Report of the Advisory Committee on Organization*, February 1955, para. 36.
[2] N.U.M., 14 October 1954.
[3] National Coal Board, *Report of the Advisory Committee on Organization*, paras. 298–318.

developed without encouraging interference with the day-to-day work of each level of management.

The main criticisms of departmental organization were centred upon the inadequacy of the Board's headquarters in effectively discharging its personnel functions—labour relations, manpower and welfare and the recruitment and conditions of service of non-industrial employees. The recommendation that these personnel duties should be split between two new Departments entitled Industrial Relations and Staff (the latter to care for non-industrial employees)[1] was later adopted by the Board.

The Committee's concern over the responsibilities placed upon the Area General Manager led it to recommend the creation of a new post of assistant Area General Manager and the adoption of a standard pattern of Area organization. Where planning problems were large or difficult it was also suggested that Area Production Managers should have at least two deputies.[2] In its new 1955 Directive the Board subscribed to the notion of adopting a uniform pattern of organization in the Areas and maintained this allegiance, at least in theory, until 1962 when Divisions were encouraged to submit suggestions for streamlining the administration at Area level.[3] It also agreed to creating a post of assistant to the Area General Manager but, contrary to the implications of the Fleck Report's recommendations, warned that such a post would not be regarded as an essential step in the promotion ladder.[4]

The Fleck Committee's submission that major reorganization was needed at the level of management between the Area and the colliery prompted the Board to accept a recommendation to form collieries into Groups each under a Group Manager who was to be regarded as in the line of management and accountable to the Area General Manager. Colliery managers it was felt should also be assisted by the appointment of colliery administrative officers and personnel officers.

One of the basic principles underlying the Fleck Report was the belief that private enterprise should set the management standards for public undertakings. In a coalfield like Durham, where miners had foregone potential rewards by directing their efforts towards meeting home consumption at controlled prices instead of being free to

[1] *Ibid.*, paras. 107–30.
[2] *Ibid.*, paras. 217–54.
[3] J. R. Nelson, 'The Fleck Report and the Area Organization of the National Coal Board', *Public Administration*, 43, 1965, pp. 43–4.
[4] National Coal Board, *Annual Report and Statement of Accounts for the Year Ended 31 December 1955*, p. 30.

compete for the available foreign coal trade, the possibilities of sharing in the advantages of private enterprise administration without its commercial benefits were of little comfort. Doubting the validity of the Report's philosophical assumptions Watson succeeded in summarizing much of the contemporary unease in Durham towards the Fleck Report when he wrote:

'We are of the opinion that the Committee set up by the National Coal Board came to conclusions that the members considered to be in the best interests of the coal industry. We make no unjust criticism on these grounds against the Committee but we do claim that the task that confronted them was not to impose on a Nationalized Industry that has no right of price fixing without Government sanction, the administration of a private industry which has not only this right but can so fix prices as to be always in the "black" and employ on its pay roll many administrators not permitted in a public industry. . . . It would have been better for the Nation and the Industry if the Committee had never been appointed or when appointed had spent at least 12 months on the job before reaching any recommendations, for there is no evidence at all that it has improved the standard of organization and it is certain beyond doubt that coal production has not been affected one iota.'[1]

Of the 57 recommendations made in the Committee's Report which rested with the N.C.B. 50 were accepted without significant reservations, some of the results of which had already been indicated. The findings and recommendations met with 'widespread approval in nearly all sections of the press'.[2] Reviewing the official reaction to the Report the Secretary of the Board wrote in 1957:

'The results are not yet to be seen in increased output of coal or in reduced costs. But it is fair to say that steps have been taken in consequence of the Report which will have their effect in greater efficiency. The whole tone of management has improved; questions that have agitated the minds of senior officials for years have been authoritatively answered.'[3]

It was precisely the fear that the implementation of the Report's recommendations would not readily show itself in reduced costs or increased efficiency that evoked a hostile reception to the investigation within the Durham coalfield. Officials of the Durham Area

[1] N.U.M. (Durham Area), *Annual Report*, 1955, p. 3.
[2] Baldwin, *op. cit.*, p. 18n.
[3] C. A. Roberts, 'The National Coal Board and the Fleck Report', *Public Administration*, XXXV, 1957, p. 8.

Union had been severely critical of the N.U.M.'s attitude that the organization of the Committee's work and the implementation of its recommendations were properly the concern of the Coal Board. When members of Fleck's team visited Durham during their deliberations the Area Union was never consulted nor was any information sought from its officers.

The N.U.M. Executive had been pressed since 1948 to inaugurate a full-scale investigation into the Board's administration. A Sub-Committee began work in 1952 studying the precise nature of the Board's existing organization pending fact-finding visits to Areas.[1] For Durham union officials who were anxious that the industry should be efficient and productive such action was insufficient. Watson claimed at the N.U.M. Annual Conference in 1948 that 'any committee of investigation ought to fall equally in responsibility upon the Board, upon the Union, upon the management and technicians, and with representation from the British community'.[2]

The necessity to appoint more people in line of command in order to implement changes in management policy served in particular to resurrect Durham's prevalent concern over the number of personnel being recruited within the Coal Board's organization.[3] In November 1955 Watson invited the Divisional Coal Board to reply to rumours growing amongst Lodges that a large number of additional appointments were to be made on the administrative side of the industry. 'If half the statements which are being made . . . are correct it makes nonsense of our campaign for increased production,' wrote Watson. 'We shall have so many people watching other people that nobody will be producing anything.'[4]

Skinner, Chairman of the Divisional Board, responded to the challenge by elucidating the precise nature of the extended managerial practices necessitated by the acceptance at national level of the Fleck Report. The Durham Area Union remained dissatisfied and Watson returned to the subject in an address delivered at the opening of the Chester Moor Pithead Baths on 16 December 1955:

'We want to know what is happening in the mining industry, in this coalfield, so far as appointments are concerned. We want to know whether these appointments are justified, where they are going to be and what the cost is going to be, for we as a Union

[1] National Union of Mineworkers, *Report of the National Executive Committee, May 1952*, p. 293.
[2] N.U.M., 8 July 1948.
[3] See above, p. 422.
[4] N.U.M. (Durham Area), 21 November 1955.

cannot support any appointment arising from the Fleck Report to establish upon this coalfield costs which cannot be justified, by the creation of new appointments. . . . We ask nothing from the Board but to be taken into confidence, to be treated as comrades and partners in this industry and to be given the essential information.'[1]

Despite growing generalizations that the reconstructed Coal Board would become 'a paradise for pen-pushers',[2] the proportion of staff employed in the coal industry by the end of 1955 compared with the total number of industrial employees was much smaller than in most other industries and in comparable industries abroad, suggesting that there was some room for additional appointments. The proportion of 5 per cent for the British coal industry compared favourably with 17 per cent for British industry as a whole, and 10 per cent and 7½ per cent in the French and Ruhr coal industries.[3]

Nevertheless the N.C.B.'s acceptance of the Fleck Report induced the official implementation of most of its recommendations without further thought and inquiry—and with perhaps more concern over adopting those changes which could readily display to the public that action was being taken than with adopting those most required in the interests of increased efficiency. The Durham Area Union persistently poured scorn on the idea that administrative change within the industry was necessarily the best form of progress. Watson wrote in his *Annual Report* for 1955:

'Some folk have the idea that correct statistical information implies a well-ordered industry and if only we have proper pockets and duckets [sic] for every nail, nut and bolt, all is well. The fact that these essential cogs in the industrial rhythm may be "statistically taped" and by the time we have got them on the job we have lost hundreds of tons of coal, never seems to enter into the minds of "statisticians". . . . Then there is the other side to consider. Nearly every new administrative appointment means the setting up of an additional office together with staff and equipment. . . . So another wheel goes inside a smaller wheel . . . and the nett [sic] result is "paper" and not coal.'[4]

If the most significant short-term result of the Fleck Report was to remove the question of the N.C.B.'s organization from public enquiry it laid the basis for years of debating and questioning within

---

[1] *Ibid.*, 21 January 1956.
[2] N.U.M., 22 March 1956.
[3] *Ibid.*
[4] N.U.M. (Durham Area), *Annual Report*, 1955, pp. 2–3.

the industry itself. The post-mortem on the Fleck Committee may well have continued for much longer had the change in the industry's circumstances after 1957, especially the contraction of manpower, not called for specific organizational developments which themselves were to become subject to intense criticism and investigation.

Appendix I

OUTPUT AND EMPLOYMENT, 1947–1956

	Saleable output * (thousand tons)		Number of wage earners on colliery books (thousands)	
	Durham	Great Britain	Durham	Great Britain
1947	24,306	186,543	108·9	711·4
1948	25,604	195,807	110·9	724·0
1949	26,402	202,658	110·7	719·5
1950	26,509	204,124	108·2	697·0
1951	27,198	211,271	107·1	698·6
1952	26,464	211,853	107·2	715·8
1953	25,899	211,821	105·2	716·9
1954	25,914	213,561	102·4	707·2
1955	25,582	210,186	102·1	704·1
1956	25,586	209,925	102·3	703·4

Note: * Saleable output is the sum of coal sold commercially, consumed by the colliery, supplied to ancillary works and disposed of free and at concessionary prices, plus the increase or less the decrease in colliery stocks of saleable coal.

Source: National Coal Board, *Annual Reports*, 1947–1956.

Appendix II

EXPORTS AND IMPORTS OF COAL, 1947–1956

| | Exports (excluding bunkers) (m. tons) | | Imports (m. tons) |
	Durham	Great Britain	Great Britain
1947	0·2*	0·9	0·7
1948	2·6*	10·7	0·1
1949	3·5*	14·1	—
1950	1·9	12·8	—
1951	1·4	7·7	1·2
1952	1·9	11·6	0·3
1953	2·4	13·8	0·5
1954	2·3	13·6	3·0
1955	1·9	11·8	11·5
1956	1·0	8·1	5·3

* Northern Division

Sources: National Coal Board, *Annual Report and Statement of Accounts for the Year Ended 31 December 1956; Returns of Disposals, Stocks and Method of Transport.*

Appendix III

PROFIT AND LOSS ACCOUNTS (COLLIERIES), 1947–1956

	Pithead proceeds per ton saleable				Total costs per ton				Profit (+) or loss (−) before charging interest and interim income			
	Durham		Great Britain		Durham		Great Britain		Durham		Great Britain	
	s	d	s	d	s	d	s	d	s	d	s	d
1947	40	6·7	40	3	46	5·9	41	3·0	−5	11·2	−1	0·0
1948	48	2·5	47	2·5	52	1·9	45	6·6	−3	11·4	+1	7·9
1949	49	0·4	47	11·5	51	0·1	45	0·3	−1	11·7	+2	11·2
1950	49	3·6	47	9·6	51	6·4	45	4·9	−2	2·8	+2	4·7
1951	53	0·7	51	2·5	55	10·1	49	2·2	−2	9·4	+2	0·3
1952	61	11·9	57	3·0	65	5·2	56	8·5	−3	5·3	+0	6·5
1953	66	4·7	61	1·5	67	7·5	59	2·4	−1	2·8	+1	11·1
1954	69	4·4	63	5·9	70	6·6	61	11·3	−1	2·2	+1	6·6
1955	75	9·8	68	0·4	77	6·2	67	3·5	−1	8·4	+0	8·9
1956	86	1·2	76	11·9	86	1·6	74	5·2	−0	0·4	+2	6·7

Source: National Coal Board, *Annual Reports*, 1947–1956.

Chapter XI

WAGES AND INDUSTRIAL DISPUTES, 1947–56

I

Having succeeded in securing a system of national wage determination in 1944, thus transforming the entire collective bargaining procedure within the industry, the miners were resolute in their determination to obtain improved and sustained increases in earnings during the post-war period. The *Miners' Charter* incorporated the demand that '. . . average wage standards shall not be permitted to fall below those of any other British industry'[1] and sought 'the continuation of the principle of the guaranteed weekly wage'. All the collective agreements and settlements in operation in December 1946 were adopted by the N.C.B. and N.U.M. subject to an amendment of Clause 4 of the 1944 Wages Agreement[2] making it permissible to discuss pit questions after a period of six months from the date of the adoption of pit conciliation machinery.

The degree to which the post-war demand for coal accentuated the already critical manpower situation in the industry provided the miners with a ready means of justifying their claims for improved wages and working conditions. Unless the relative deterioration of earnings in coal mining compared with other industries, especially apparent since the Porter Award in 1944, could be halted there seemed little hope of attracting sufficient labour to expand output. It was against this background and shortly after the time when the country had endured the hardships of the 1947 fuel crisis that the N.U.M. and N.C.B. agreed to an increase in the weekly minimum wage[3] to £5 15s 0d for underground and £5 for surface workers and

---

[1] This principle had also been the basis of a resolution passed by the Coal Mines Committee of the International Labour Organization at its first meeting in 1945.

[2] Part of Clause 4 stated that until June 1948 'no application for alterations in wage rates at a pit shall be made other than those normally made in respect of changed methods or conditions of working in accordance with custom or Agreement existing in the District'. The absence of major national or district negotiations until the signing of the Five-Day Week Agreement in April 1947 was concomitant with a policy designed, not to prevent wages from rising, but to safeguard against some deflationary forces threatening wartime advances.

[3] Previously fixed by the Porter Award at £5 per week for underground workers and £4 10s 0d per week for surface workers. See Chapter IX, p. 370.

to an increase in day rates of 2s 6d for underground and 1s 8d for surface adults. The Coal Board refused any increases for piece workers in a hope, shared by the N.U.M., that the widening gap between their earnings and those of the lower-paid would be reduced. The extent to which the 1947 agreement had failed to establish this condition and/or the degree to which steady pressure on pit price-lists had further advanced piece workers' earnings so as to worsen the situation, was apparent in the unanimity with which delegates at the 1949 N.U.M. Annual Conference instructed the Union's Executive to seek 'a substantial increase in minimum rates for all lower-paid workers'.[1]

The method by which this advance was to be secured involved the consideration of one of the issues which had earlier served to empha-size the plight of the lower-paid. The N.C.B.s hesitation in deciding how best to apply the newly-constructed interim index of retail prices, introduced by the Government in 1947, to the 1940 cost-of-living wages agreement had provided the N.U.M. with an opportunity to consider departing from a literal application of the 1940 agreement so as to benefit lower-paid miners. Whilst an increase in the cost-of-living bonus under the terms of this agreement could raise the wages of those at or above the minimum it simultaneously reduced by an equivalent amount the 'make-up' wage—i.e. the amount necessary to bring the lower-paid worker's rate up to the national weekly mini-mum. Those workers, therefore, whose shift rate fell below the national minimum would not benefit from a cost-of-living advance so long as its amount was less than the former amount of 'make-up'. A formal interpretation of the agreement could increase differentials without providing a rise in the amount going to the lower-paid, both developments running counter to the N.U.M.'s wage objectives.

For its part the N.C.B. opposed the automatic regulation of miners' wages by reference to the cost-of-living index,[2] but was pre-pared to consolidate the 2s 8d per shift bonus granted according to the level of the index at June 1947 into existing wages if the 1940 agreement was abandoned and if an increase in wages for the lower-paid was considered only 'on its merits with due regard to all the relevant circumstances, including the cost of living'.[3] The N.U.M. was equally determined to revise the 1940 cost-of-living agreement

---

[1] Baldwin, op. cit., pp. 134–5; N.U.M., Report of the National Executive Committee, May 1950, p. 230.
[2] Durham miners had similarly opposed attempts by employers in the twenties to tie wages to automatic movements in the cost of living. See Chapter V, pp. 162–4.
[3] N.U.M., 4 April 1950.

so as to incorporate the newly-established index and to direct its benefits to the improvement of lower-paid miners in all districts. The Union could not easily defend a blunt demand for a substantial wage increase for all lower-paid workers since the publication in 1948 of the Government's White Paper on Personal Incomes, Costs and Prices[1] established a 'wage freeze' whereby, although there was to be no direct government interference with collective bargaining, further increases in money incomes were to be made dependent upon corresponding increases in production.[2]

Since there appeared little hope of joint agreement between the N.C.B. and N.U.M. on the plight of the lower-paid the matter was referred to the National Reference Tribunal in the autumn of 1950. By that time the contrast in average cash earnings per shift amongst the various classes of workmen in Durham and their comparison with national trends was as follows:

Average cash earnings per manshift worked in 1950

	All workers		All workers underground		All surface workers	
	s	d	s	d	s	d
Durham	33	4	36	6	23	2
Great Britain	34	0	37	1	24	4

Note: The disparity with national earnings per shift was reduced to some extent by the fact that allowances in kind averaged 1s 4d more per shift in Durham than elsewhere. Within the coalfield there was a differential of 7d per shift in the amount of allowances in kind paid to underground workmen compared with those on the surface.

The Tribunal's twenty-third award published on 7 October 1950 proved disappointing. A global sum of £3½m. was to be distributed to the lower-paid miners according to principles established by the parties themselves. Both the national weekly minimum wage of adult surface and underground workmen was raised by 5s to £5 5s 0d and £6 respectively; men underground earning under 23s per shift (21s 4d on the surface) were awarded 6d per shift or less if shift

---

[1] Statement on Personal Incomes, Costs and Prices (Cmd. 7321), 1948.

[2] Increases in wages and salaries could be justified when thought necessary to attract labour to undermanned industries or where incomes were being seriously eroded by marked rises in the cost of living. The decision of the N.U.M. to vote against the T.U.C.'s recommendation in January 1950 to continue to support the principle of wage restraint testified to the pressure placed upon the Union to improve the conditions of the lower-paid. See B. C. Roberts, *National Wages Policy in War and Peace*, London 1958, Chapter 4.

earnings would thereby exceed the ceilings just specified. The existing cost-of-living bonus of 2s 8d per shift was merged with the adult
daywagemen's shift rates but paid as a flat-rate payment to piece
workers (the '1950 Flat Rate'). Juvenile rates were also slightly raised.
The smallness of the increases and the fact that they were withheld
from those men above the newly-established ceilings hardly effected
a substantial improvement in the condition of the lower-paid or
promised to invigorate the industry's recruitment drive.

The Tribunal based its award among other things upon the capacity
of the industry to pay. Surprisingly the N.U.M. did not challenge the
importance attached to the industry's financial performance, though
it could well have claimed that coal prices were being held at an
artificially low level. Affirmations that a continuation of the rate of
profit already earned by the Board during 1950 without further wage
advances could clear the debt incurred in 1947 took no cognizance
of the contribution rising prices could have similarly made. It is
almost certain that had private colliery owners been operating in such
a seller's market for coal commercial considerations of this sort would
have attracted more sympathetic support. With his control over coal
prices the Minister of Fuel and Power had become a central figure in
wage determination. Since the industry was commanded by statute
to operate so as to break even, industry-wide over the long-run, and
since coal prices were set to provide low-cost coal to railways and
steel and power industries the bargaining criteria, in some measure,
became how best wage demands could be made consistent with these
national objectives. The N.U.M. failed both to emphasize the gap
which existed between the selling price of coal and market demand
and to point out that a policy of maximum output at minimum break-
even price could countenance wage increases in a period of rising
demand for coal so long as output expanded and the increase in total
costs did not exceed total revenue. Not until 1953 did the consideration that coal prices were too low enter into the Union's bargaining
criteria.[1]

The Durham County Mining Federation Board, recalling the
angry reception with which the Tribunal's award was greeted, noted
at the end of 1950:

[1] K. J. W. Alexander, 'Wages in Coal Mining since Nationalization', *Oxford Economic Papers*, N.S. VIII, 1956, pp. 171–8; F. Meyers, 'Nationalization, Union Structures and Wages Policy in the British Coal-Mining Industry', *Southern Economic Journal*, 24, 1958, p. 431; T. Nuttall, 'Changes in the Wage Structure of the Coal Industry since Nationalization', M.A. thesis, University of Leeds 1966, p. 99.

'The spirit in the coalfield was, to say the least, defeatist and there was sufficient evidence to show that production was likely to go down and men would leave the Industry rather than the contrary.'[1]

The coal crisis which developed during the latter part of 1950 added poignancy to such predictions. As coal production lagged under the impact of a continuing drift of men from the industry internal coal consumption rose rapidly. Fully recognizing the need to expand output to avoid a winter fuel crisis akin to that of 1946–7, representatives of the N.U.M. and N.C.B. met on 10 January 1951 to discuss the miners' claim for a general wage increase for all day-wagemen, a pension scheme, and a second weekly vacation with pay.[2] By this time the Government's policy of wage restraint, first intro-duced in the winter of 1948, had been officially abandoned, the Prime Minister having already assured the miners' leaders that their negotiations with the Board would be continued 'in a sympathetic atmosphere'. The need to placate workmen over the meagre terms of the Porter Tribunal's Twenty-Third Award had become a pressing one. After only one day of negotiation agreement was reached to increase the shift rates of adult underground daywage workmen by 1s 2d up to a ceiling of 24s 2d per shift; and juveniles by 10d per shift subject to the same ceilings. The national weekly minimum wage of adult underground workers was increased by 7s 0d to £6 7s 0d and for surface workers by 5s 0d to £5 10s 0d. Craftsmen and winding enginemen did better with a 2s 0d advance in shift rates and an increase of 2s 8d in the national minimum shift rate for winders. The claim for a second week's vacation pay was rejected for the sake of maintaining production although a contributory pension plan was agreed to in principle.[3] Piece workers were unaffected by the award but were expected to co-operate fully in an effort to increase output according to a plan agreed upon by the Union as an integral part of the terms of settlement.[4] The Durham miners accepted the award by 722 votes to 41.[5] As a consequence the shift rates of underground day-wage adults in the coalfield rose from 16s 11d to 18s 1d; of surface adults from 16s 1d to 16s 11d; of underground juveniles under 18 from 14s 5d to 15s 3d and of surface juveniles from 11s 11d to 12s 9d.

[1] Durham County Mining Federation Board, *Annual Report*, 1950, p. 3.
[2] N.U.M., 10 January 1951.
[3] See Chapter XII, pp. 485–6.
[4] *Ibid.*, 16 January 1952.
[5] N.U.M. (Durham Area), 20 January 1951.

II

Despite the fact that the Coal Board had secured from the N.U.M. a moral commitment not to put forward any new wage demands until June 1952 unless there was 'a substantial change in the value of money' delegates at the Union's Annual Conference in 1951 agreed to resolutions calling for wage advances for both daywagemen and piece workers. Negotiations were delayed by the appointment of new personnel to the N.C.B. and the general election in September. By November 1951 the Vane Tempest Lodge in Durham was demanding for all miners 'a general increase in wages . . . because of the increase in the Cost of Living'.[1] At almost the same time the N.U.M.'s Executive Committee submitted to the Board claims for 23s per week for underground workers, 20s for surfacemen and 3s per shift for piece workers. Agreement was reached one month later. Adult and underground daywage workers' shift rates were increased by 2s 3d per shift up to a revised ceiling of 27s 6d and those of adult surface daywage workers by 1s 11d per shift to a ceiling of 24s 1d. Craftsmen and winders were given equal advances. National weekly minima were raised by 13s 6d to £7 0s 6d for adult underground workers and by 11s 6d to £6 1s 6d for surface workers. Juveniles were granted even larger proportionate advances. Piece workers received their first national increase since nationalization amounting to 2s 3d per shift for those underground and 1s 11d per shift for surface workers. Thereafter changes in piece rates were frozen for twelve months 'except in respect of changed methods or conditions of working' or alternatively until a Joint Committee, appointed to consider the future regulation of piece workers' wages and conditions, had reported whichever period was shorter. This Joint Committee was entrusted to evolve a scheme for the remuneration of piece workers 'so as to achieve a more rational wage structure with greater uniformity in wages and emoluments for similar work and effort'.

The threatened increase in food prices following the 1952 Tory Budget instituted a series of wage demands in several industries, including coal mining. The N.U.M. decided to press for an increase of 5s per shift for all daywagemen and piece workers irrespective of ceilings, largely to provide higher-paid datallers the opportunity to participate in increases which previous advances *with* ceilings had denied them, and irrespective of the fact that the stabilization period for piece rates was still in operation. A claim was also included for an advance of 30s in the national weekly minimum wage of both

[1] *Ibid.*, 3 November 1951.

surface and underground adults.[1] The Board rejected the Union's demands and the matter was referred to the National Reference Tribunal. The miners had their demands turned down flat. The Tribunal, which published its findings on 27 October 1952, again proved particularly sensitive to the financial plight of the N.C.B., insensitive to the rate of increase in the cost of living as a sufficient justification for wage advances and anxious not to jeopardize the progress which was being made towards establishing a new national wage structure from which it was expected that wage increases would accrue.

The Durham miners were bitterly disappointed at the rejection of the wages claim. Watson, dispirited at the decline in coal output in Durham during 1952, sensed that part of the origin of the growing frustration and disillusionment within the coalfield lay in the effect which the rejection of the miners' wage demands had upon the workmen's sense of individual commitment, especially in view of the successful wage claims lodged by other of the industry's employees. Writing in 1953 he recalled:

'It is well known that nearly every Union, having members employed in the Mining Industry, sought wages increases in 1952, and the disparity in the claims (from £5 to 30s) per week and their subsequent settlement or rejection gave rise to deep dissatisfaction.

There were Managerial, Technical, Supervisory and Weekly Wage Staffs, Officials, Overmen, Deputies and Shotfirers, some of whom not only received considerable increases in wages, but were also safeguarded for sickness and accident on a basis hitherto unknown on such a wide scale in the Mining Industry.

On the other hand, the ordinary daywageman or piece worker had his wages claim rejected, and had no safeguard whatsoever so far as loss of wages were concerned when off work through sickness or injury.

Did these concessions, emphasizing as they did wages-status principles, cause a temporary sense of frustration among the great majority of the ordinary men employed at the pits, and cause the feeling—"Well, what's it matter?" '[2]

The N.U.M. was honour bound under the terms of the national conciliation machinery to accept the Tribunal's findings on the 1952 wages demand but immediately reopened negotiations with the Coal Board on the basis of a fresh claim. Discussions with the Board continued until February 1953 when it was agreed to increases the rates

[1] N.U.M., 14 May, 26 June 1952.
[2] N.U.M. (Durham Area), *Annual Report*, 1952, p. 3.

of adult surface and underground daywage workers by 1s per shift
subject to ceilings and to raise their national weekly minimum wages
by 6s. Piece workers were again unaffected by the award. Underground daywage adults in Durham were now entitled to a shift rate
of 21s 4d and those on the surface of 19s 10d.

Whilst for the time being piece workers could only rely upon
increasing productivity to gain a substantial advance in earnings the
N.U.M. persisted in its policy of securing wage increases for daywagemen. By the beginning of October 1953 the Coal Board was
faced with yet a further demand for an increase in daywage shift
rates of 2s 3d and 2s 1d and for a rise in the national weekly minimum
wage of 13s 6d and 12s 6d for underground and surface adults
respectively.[1] The Board subsequently rejected the Union's demands
insofar as they were based upon the rise in the cost of living since
October 1947,[2] but conceded that there was some scope for raising
daywagemen's wages inasmuch as coal was being sold to some
industrial concerns at too low a price.[3] The N.U.M. had finally
argued a case with regard to the selling price of coal and had secured
a sympathetic hearing.

The terms of settlement eventually agreed on 14 January 1954 were
made conditional upon the N.U.M. pledging its fullest co-operation
towards increasing productivity in the industry, especially by fostering extra Saturday working.[4] All adult daywagemen (including winding enginemen and craftsmen) were granted an advance in shift rates
of 1s 5d for those underground and 1s 3d for those on the surface.
The latter's national weekly minimum wage was increased by 7s 6d
to £6 15s 0d and that of male adult underground workers by 8s 6d
to £7 15s 0d. The Durham Area Union accepted the terms by 806
votes to 46,[5] but was later reprimanded by the Thrislington Lodge
for having voted favourably at a meeting where the Chairman had
'refused to allow any discussion of the new wages offer'.[6] The Lodge's
accusation that there had been 'an interference with the democratic
right of the rank and file' was immediately repudiated by local

[1] National Union of Mineworkers, *Report of the National Executive Committee*,
May 1953, pp. 9–12.
[2] Lord Porter had previously stated that the relevant period for considering wage
claims on the basis of changes in the cost of living should be 'that which begins
at the date when the last wage agreement between the parties or the last Award
of the Tribunal was made and terminates at the date when the claim is heard'.
[3] N.U.M., 6 January 1954.
[4] But with little success in Durham. See Chapter X, pp. 397–8, 400–1.
[5] N.U.M. (Durham Area), 30 January 1954.
[6] *Ibid.*, 15 February 1954.

miners' officials and by Lodge representatives who had attended the meeting.[1]

III

The emphasis put upon compensating low-paid miners for the degree to which their earnings had fallen behind those of piece workers had delayed the development of the new wages structure in the industry which the N.U.M. had long regarded as a priority of policy. Horner, addressing the N.U.M. Annual Conference on the Isle of Bute in 1947, had declared, 'Our aim and our desire is to institute on a national plane the same rate for the job from Lands End to John O'Groats.'[2] This aspiration was a natural development of the drawn-out struggle which had taken place between the wars to prevent earnings amongst the various coalfields being left to the mercy not only of the type of work performed or the physical effort of the miner but also of geological conditions, the efficiency with which coal was got from the face, transported to the pit bottom and wound to the surface and of the influence of many local and traditional practices.

The initial hope of the N.U.M. and the N.C.B. that a more rational wage structure within the industry would be developed at an early stage so that short-run wage problems could be settled in a manner which would not embarrass later attempts to formulate a new wages system was not fulfilled. In the event the structure which emerged was conditioned largely by the succession of *ad hoc* wage settlements made in the fifties which themselves helped reinforce the existing pattern of wages. Thus the awards of October 1950 and October 1952 conduced the industry to maintain existing differentials whilst attention could be focused upon improving the system of wages.

Other factors worked in a similar way to increase the complexity of wage determination in the industry. The introduction of pit conciliation machinery in January 1947 allowed piece-rate alterations at pit level, previously frozen for a minimum period of $3\frac{1}{2}$ years by the 1944 national wages agreement. Time workers continued to have their wages regulated by national agreements which, as it turned out, followed a common pattern of flat-rate increases limited at the upper end of the scale by 'ceilings' linked with increases in national weekly minimum wages. Such general advances failed to rationalize the occupational pattern of wage rates over the country as a whole whilst

---

[1] *Ibid.*, 22 February 1954.
[2] N.U.M., 8 July 1947.

the 'ceilings' caused compression at the upper end.[1] Since anyone earning a shift rate in excess of established maxima was excluded from each national increase in wages a narrowing of differences between highest and lowest paid workers in any one category, e.g. underground daywagemen, could occur without any reorganization in between. By 1955 only craftsmen and winding enginemen had national wage rates determined for them.

To discover how the prevailing pattern of wages within the industry could most easily be refashioned it was important to establish what different kinds of jobs were being performed and for what rates of pay. As a preliminary effort a joint committee of the N.U.M. and N.C.B. succeeded by the end of 1952 in reducing the existing list of almost 6,000 differently named jobs for daywagemen to a more composite list of about 300 distinct tasks, each accompanied by an agreed description of the duties and responsibilities of each job. On close examination many of the 'jobs' had been found to be only local names describing the same type of work performed elsewhere. As a next step the new job titles were fitted into 13 grades to cover 400 national jobs. A first assimilation of daywagemen working underground (except at the coalface) and on the surface into the newly-devised grade structure, each man placed according to the work he was doing into the appropriate national job classification, demonstrated that for almost every job performed there was a wide scatter of wage rates within the industry as a whole and in each wage district.[2]

The task of introducing established differentials throughout the industry without reducing the wages customarily earned by individual workmen involved eliminating thousands of accepted local differentials and carried with it the risk of creating widespread industrial unrest. Nevertheless on 20 April 1955 agreement was reached upon the first stage of the revision of the wage structure in the industry when standard grade rates were established for daywagemen. The standard grade rates opposite were to be applied to the newly-devised national schedule of occupations and job descriptions:[3]

Although the assimilation and grading process applied to all workers piece workers and task workers were unaffected by the

[1] W. H. Sales and J. L. Davies, 'Introducing A New Wage Structure Into Coal-Mining', *Bulletin of the Institute of Statistics*, 19, 1957. Nuttall, *op. cit.*, p. 51.
[2] National Coal Board, *Annual Report and Statement of Accounts for the Year Ended 31 December 1955*, p. 38.
[3] For a full discussion of the difficulties in formulating a new wages structure see Sales and Davies, *loc. cit.*, from whose article the table opposite has been taken.

The New Wage Structure, April 1955

Category	Grade	Standard rate		Limit	
		s	d	s	d
Underground	I	31	9	39	6
	II	30	9	36	0
	III	29	9	34	0
	IV	28	9	32	0
	V	27	9	30	0
Surface *	IA	31	1	34	0
	I	27	5	31	0
	II	26	5	30	0
	III	25	5	28	6
	IV	24	5	27	6
Craftsmen	I plus				
Underground		35	5	—	
Surface		32	1	—	
	I				
Underground		32	11	—	
Surface		29	7	—	
	II				
Underground		30	5	—	
Surface		27	1	—	

* For women (working on the surface in Grades I–IV) the standard rate was 4s 11d lower than the corresponding rate for men, the limit was 7s 6d lower in I and II and 7s lower in III and IV.

variation in wage rates except in special circumstances, for example when a piece worker was paid a guaranteed wage because his normal work was not available. The 1955 agreement provided not only for occupational grading and the consolidation of wage rates but also for a general wage increase. Consolidated wage rates were raised by a maximum of 1s per shift subject to grade limits, the actual amount being paid to an individual workman being determined by how much his consolidated wage rate fell below the appropriate grade limit. Any wage rates still found to be below the appropriate standard grade rate were raised to the new standard rate. At the same time the national weekly minimum for all underground workers irrespective of grade or occupation, which had stood at 25s 10d per shift before April 1955, was raised by 1s 11d per shift to form the lowest standard rate for underground workers in the revised structure. Inter-grade differentials of 1s were then established involving advances ranging from an increase in the lowest rate in Grade I of 5s 11d to an increase of only 1s 11d for the bottom grade, Grade V. Immediately after the new wage structure was introduced it was calculated that about 70 per cent of all daywagemen would be on standard rates, 25 per cent on 'personal rates' i.e. between the standard rates and the limits[1] and 5 per cent would have rates already above the limits.[2]

However much the new 1955 agreement was regarded as a triumph for careful planning and bold experimentation in the wages field, at least as far as the miners were concerned, the N.U.M. remained acutely conscious of the need to further improve wages if manpower was to be attracted to and retained within the industry. Acting upon the instructions of delegates at the 1955 N.U.M. Annual Conference, and partly in response to the threat to living standards introduced by the Government's supplementary Budget in October 1955, the Union's National Executive decided on 8 December to submit a claim to the Board for an increase of 3s 4d a shift in national grade rates and an advance of £1 per week in the national minimum wage. A demand was also made that the existing payment of an extra shift's wages for working five shifts in a week should be abolished in favour of incorporating one-fifth of that bonus into a new shift rate.[3]

Other demands for the restoration of a seven-hour day for underground workmen and the introduction of a forty-hour week, including mealtimes, for surface workers; for the introduction of three weeks' annual holiday with pay and the payment of full wages for periods of absence through sickness for up to six weeks in any one year were left in abeyance once early representations to the Board had made it clear how reluctant it was to negotiate such a composite claim, especially when certain provisions potentially threatened coal output.

Watson joined other N.U.M. representatives in opening informal discussions with the Board during the winter of 1956 to help widen the basis of agreement between the parties but failed to make any substantial progress. The negotiations were eventually terminated by an agreement made in February 1956 to increase the 1955 standard daywage grade rates for underground and surface workers (except Grade IA) by 2s 4d per shift up to prescribed limits. Craftsmen, winding enginemen and surface workers (Grade IA) received an advance on underground rates of 2s 8d per shift and juveniles increases ranging from 1s 7d to a maximum of 2s 4d per shift and averaging 1s 10d per shift. Some of the wage 'ceilings' established in

[1] Sales and Davies, *loc. cit.*, p. 219.
[2] Wage rates paid above standard were restricted to those miners who were paid such rates when the new structure was introduced and were countenanced only because reductions in rates were ruled out.
[3] N.U.M., 5 July 1955; 12 January 1956.

1955 remained whilst others were marginally increased but their function of acting, not as maximum wage levels but as a brake upon the amounts which workers could gain from successive general increases, was clearly underlined.

IV

The rate of improvement in miners' average money and real earnings per shift in Durham between the wars lagged behind the nation as a whole. Taking 1914 as 100 the relevant indices in Durham in 1938 stood at 156 and 100 respectively compared with 173·7 and 111·3 for Great Britain. Though this lag persisted during the first decade of nationalization the disparity between the two indices never reached pre-1939 proportions. The index of average earnings per shift (excluding value of allowances in kind) based on 1947 as 100 rose in Durham to 194·5 by 1956 compared with an increase to 206·6 for the country as a whole.[1] This relative improvement in Durham's position was even more significant considering that the average value of allowances in kind per shift during the first decade of nationalization stood at 3s 2d compared with only 1s 10d for Great Britain.

The miners also benefited from an improvement in real wages, the relevant index rising by 24·7 per cent from its 1947 level in Durham by 1956 compared with a national increase of 32·5 per cent during the same period.[2] The cherished hope that nationalization would reduce the differences in wages between the various coalfields was not completely realized as far as the experience of the first ten years is concerned, though the improvement in this respect was especially noticeable in areas like Durham where wage disparities with other coalfields before 1938 had long provided ammunition in the battle for public ownership of the industry. Thus whilst the percentage by which the average cash earnings per shift of all miners in Durham in 1930 fell short of the average shift earnings of miners throughout the country stood at 13·3 it had narrowed to 2 by 1950 and was only 0·3 in 1956.

The relative decline of miners' average earnings between the wars compared with other industries was halted during the Second World War and subsequently reversed during the fifties, as the following table shows:

[1] See Appendix I to this chapter.
[2] *Ibid.*

Rank in Average Earnings* by Coal-Mining Employees Compared with Other Industries

1921	9	1926	11	1931	10	1936	10	1942	2	1947	1	1952	1
1922	10	1927	9	1932	10	1937	10	1943	3	1948	1	1953	1
1923	9	1928	11	1933	10	1938	10	1944	2	1949	1	1954	1
1924	8	1929	11	1934	8	1940	6	1945	1	1950	2	1955	2
1925	8	1930	10	1935	8	1941	6	1946	1	1951	1	1956	1

Notes: * Average earnings include allowances in kind (greater in mining than in other industries) and overtime earnings (smaller than in other industries).

When comparing different years recognition must be made of the fact that the Ministry of Labour standard industrial classification was altered three times. Employees were grouped into 14 industries for the period 1921–38, 17 industries during 1938–47 and in 21 industries during 1948–58.

Source: C. E. Jencks, 'The Impact of Nationalization on Working Conditions in British Coal Mining'. Ph.D. thesis, University of California (Berkley) 1964, p. 57.

The extra benefits available to miners, such as a five-day week without loss of pay, a guaranteed weekly minimum wage and a supplemental injuries scheme which went beyond the provisions of National Insurance,[1] further improved their relative position compared with other industrial workers. Wage advances in the German coal industry between 1947 and 1956 outstripped those in comparable industries, though the French miners failed to substantially improve their relative earnings position compared with other workers. In Belgium the leading wage position achieved by coal miners in 1946 had been lost ten years later.[2]

Within British coal mining the widening differential apparent during 1945 to 1950 between face workers and all other workers had narrowed slightly by the mid-fifties.[3] Whilst the absolute cash differential between surface workers and face workers increased from 21s 10d per shift in Durham in 1952 to 25s 1d by 1956 the relative position of surface workers improved. Thus the average cash earnings per shift of surface workers in Durham as a percentage of face workers' average shift earnings in 1956 stood at 61·6 per cent compared with 57 per cent in 1952.

The number of wage agreements negotiated between the Divisional Coal Board and the Durham Area Union during the first ten years of nationalization are too numerous to treat in detail. The majority are concerned with the determination of rewards for specific tasks and

[1] See Chapter XII, pp. 482–4.
[2] Jencks, *op. cit.*, pp. 61–2.
[3] Alexander, *loc. cit.*, pp. 169–70. See H. A. Turner, 'Trade Unions, Differentials and the Levelling of Wages', *Manchester School*, 3, September 1952.

conditions of work in the pit. Of particular importance were the agreements safeguarding the terms and conditions of employment of workmen engaged in machine mining. A power-loading agreement was signed between the private coal owners and the former Durham Miners' Association in September 1945 providing a premium of roughly 10 per cent for men working on new equipment. Uniform day rates were established throughout the entire coalfield for four job categories providing shift payments 2s to 4s higher than the existing average earnings of face workers.

Not until eighteen months after nationalization, in June 1948, was an agreement signed for Meco-Moore work on longwall faces. Day rates were fixed at 5–8 per cent higher than the customary wage and as such provided greater rewards than were being paid to face workers operating under the 1945 power-loading agreement. The inequality was corrected two months later when a 'master agreement' brought the day rates fixed in 1945 up to the level of those agreed upon in 1948.

Many of the wage agreements established at local level reflected the extent to which improvements in technique so altered working conditions that fresh negotiations were required. Thus in 1955 Divisional wages agreements specified the terms and conditions of employment arising from Power (Pneumatic) Stowing, Longwall Wet Cutting, Wet Drilling, Wet Pneumatic Pick Hewing, Arcwall Wet Cutting and Water Infusion.

V

Those who hoped, rather idealistically, that mines nationalization, by ridding the industry of the private, profit-seeking employer, would inaugurate a new social spirit and an era of industrial peace must have been sadly disappointed during the first decade of public ownership. Certainly the established means of conciliation and arbitration available after 1947, theoretically providing for consideration of disputes from pit to national level, left no room for a union-supported official strike. The conciliation machinery evolved in 1943 established the National Conciliation Board, composed of the Joint National Negotiating Committee and the National Reference Tribunal, which handled disputes affecting the whole industry. District Conciliation Boards dealt with issues affecting their particular locality, though provision was made for matters concerning several districts to be referred to national level for consideration.[1]

[1] See Chapter IX, pp. 367–8.

In Durham a pit conciliation procedure had been developed in November 1944 to handle questions affecting individual employers or workmen as distinct from those affecting the mutual relations of the miners' and owners' Associations.[1] It was not until after nationalization that common machinery for subjecting unresolved matters in dispute to responsible bodies within a strict timetable was extended to every mine in the country. Thereafter a comprehensive scheme of joint consultation became available for use before recourse to the District Conciliation Board.

If disputes within the industry were subjected at every stage to the available means of settlement there could be no official strikes,[2] as the following chart shows:

Disputes Procedure in the Coal-Mining Industry

Stages	Maximum time limit before proceeding to the next stage
1. Discussion between men and pit officials	3 days
2. Discussion between men and manager	—
3. Discussion between manager and Union officials	3 days
4. Dispute discussed at pit meeting	14 days
5. Dispute discussed at Disputes Committee *	14 days
6. Dispute referred to Umpire	Final decision †
7. Dispute referred to District Conciliation Board as a District question	21 days
8. Dispute referred to a District Referee	Final decision ‡
9. Dispute discussed at J.N.N.C.	5 weeks
10. Dispute referred to N.R.T.	Decision final

Notes: * In Durham there was one overall Disputes Committee and three specialized Sub-Committees, one dealing with questions involving guaranteed wages and the 'Porter Minimum', a second, called the 'Urgency Committee', which met at quick notice when any dispute threatened to stop a pit and a third 'Approximate Committee' which dealt with the fixing and alteration of price lists.

† Unless it was decided that it was a district question.

‡ Unless it was decided that it was a national question.

The strength of the conciliation machinery lay ultimately in the respect each party had for each stage in the settlement procedure. What made the post-nationalization era so distinctive in this respect

[1] *Ibid.*

[2] Under the terms of the Government's Conditions of Employment and National Arbitration Order 1940 (S.R.O. 1940, No. 1305) strikes were illegal anyway until 1951. See below, p. 454.

was the suddenness with which workmen would break off negotiations and resort to unofficial action before a dispute had even exhausted the district conciliation procedure. An analysis of the total number of stoppages and restrictions in relation to the conciliation machinery available during the period 1949–56 has shown that in 1949 over 72 per cent of all stoppages occurred before stage 3 of the machinery had been reached and that 4·8 per cent occurred even before formal negotiations had begun. In 1956 the comparable figures were 68·3 per cent and 5·6 per cent respectively.[1]

As far as can be judged from available data Durham's record of the proportion of disputes resulting in a stoppage or restriction of work before any discussion took place with pit officials was particularly poor, standing at 11·5 per cent in 1953 compared with a national average of 8·6 per cent. The proportions in 1954 were 41·2 per cent and 8·3 per cent respectively; in 1955 16·2 per cent and 7·6 per cent and in 1956 12·8 per cent and 5·6 per cent.[2]

When local disputes were subjected to the pit conciliation procedure the results proved encouraging. From 1950 to 1956 the proportion of disputes thus referred which were settled at pit meetings remained remarkably constant despite fundamental changes having taken place in the wage structure, methods of working and in the rate of pit closures. The high proportion was maintained even over widely scattered coalfields with diverse structures and traditions. In these seven years an average of 95 per cent of all grievances which were referred to pit meetings in Durham were settled without recourse to the Disputes Committee compared with 94 per cent in the country as a whole.[3] No relation existed between the frequency of referral of grievances to pit meetings and the proportion of questions settled. Whether the rate was high or low the proportion settled at the mine remained high. The average number of disputes referred to pit meetings per 100 workers in the East Midlands Division from 1950 to 1956, for example, stood at only 0·2 compared with 2·1 in Durham, though its proportion of grievances thus settled was higher than in Durham.[4]

In one respect Durham's experience was at variance with the general trend inasmuch as those Divisions which had relatively high

[1] T. N. Hopkins, 'The Operation of the National Reference Tribunal in the Coal Industry since 1943'. M.A. thesis, University College of Wales, Aberystwyth 1961, p. 69.
[2] C. E. Jencks, 'British Coal: Labor Relations Since Nationalization', *Industrial Relations*, 6, 1966–7, p. 107.
[3] *Ibid.*, p. 104.
[4] Jencks, *op. cit.*, pp. 81–3.

rates of grievance referral to pit meetings, especially the Scottish, tended also to have the highest percentage of cases where there was *some* discussion with a mine official before a dispute began. In this sense the relatively high referral rate indicated a larger measure of confidence in the possibility of securing an adjustment of grievances. Durham's poor record of disputes occurring before the earliest stage of discussion had been exhausted [1] runs contrary to this explanation, although with the data for this calculation being based upon only three years' experience it is difficult to offer any plausible reasons for its peculiar situation in this respect.

Statistical comparisons of the number of stoppages occurring over time need to be treated cautiously since wide divergences in economic conditions and the varying aspirations of labour itself, to name but two factors, can seriously distort the picture. The propensity of British miners to strike had long remained high [2] and continued to be so after nationalization although the situation in Durham, in this limited sense, was not as serious as in most other coalfields. The proportion of total industrial disputes represented by mining disputes in the country as a whole rose from 33 per cent during 1928–36 to 40 per cent during 1937–43 and to 66 per cent during 1944–56.[3] 26 stoppages occurred in Durham during the first decade of public ownership compared with 27 in the decade before 1947 and 23 during the period from the end of the General Strike to the outbreak of the Second World War.[4]

Despite this secular increase in the number of disputes the stoppages themselves tended to be of shorter duration and/or involve fewer men. The proportion of total man-days lost by industrial disputes accounted for by those in coal mining throughout the country rose from 52 per cent in 1938 to 67 per cent in 1944 but fell

[1] See above, pp. 448–9.
[2] Professor Knowles has calculated a standardized industrial 'strike proneness ratio' (using as a weight the share of the country's various regions in total striking) for the period January 1911 to June 1945. The ratio for mining and quarrying stands at 3·7 compared with textiles (2·0); metals, engineering and shipbuilding (1·3); transport (1·1); building (0·4); clothing (0·3); and other industries (0·1). Knowles, *op. cit.*, pp. 195–209. The strike-proneness of mining was not confined to Britain. The results of a statistical investigation into the propensity to strike in the major industries of eleven countries during the early fifties have shown that, by relating man-days lost to industry employment, in every nation in which mining was a significant occupation it had the highest propensity to strike. C. Kerr and A. Siegal, 'The Inter-Industry Propensity to Strike: An International Comparison', in A. Korn-Lauser, R. Dubin and A. Ross, *Industrial Conflict*, New York 1954, pp. 189–212.
[3] Calculated from data published in the *Ministry of Labour Gazette*.
[4] N.U.M. (Durham Area), *Annual Report*, 1952, pp. 178–9.

to 37 per cent in 1947 and was only 24 per cent in 1956.[1] In no quinquennium between 1927 and 1956 did the average of days lost per worker involved in coal mining exceed the average for all industries in the country.[2] Within mining the record of man-days lost in strikes per worker employed during the first decade of nationalization in Britain compared favourably with the experience of France and especially with that of the U.S.A.[3]

Such widely-based calculations conceal important regional variations and underrate the grave consequences to national coal output of strike activity during the ten years after 1947. The amounts involved in this respect were not large but were often sacrificed at a time when the fuel situation was critical and coal was having to be imported from abroad.

The problem of loss of output was not one of equal intensity in all Divisions. The largest share of the total amount of saleable output lost through stoppages and restrictions [4] between 1947 and 1956 was accounted for in the main by three Divisions, the Scottish, North-Eastern and South-Western. In Durham the output of coal lost from such causes was very small. (See table overleaf.)

The outbreak of unofficial stoppages, seemingly as a form of local protest, could conceivably have been a result of frustration arising from the centralization of negotiation and the renunciation of the strike weapon so apparent since 1943. But this is unsatisfactory as a general explanation. Unofficial strikes were not new to the coal industry and a large proportion of disputes arose from workers' dissatisfaction over wages [5] and were therefore handled on a pit basis, although such jurisdiction, as has been noted, did not guarantee industrial peace. Furthermore in view of the rank and file's meagre negotiating power at the time when pre-war district agreements were being made there was little to lose at national level after

[1] Barratt-Brown, *loc. cit.*, p. 104; Hopkins, *op. cit.*, pp. 58–60.
[2] Jencks, *loc. cit.*, p. 109.
[3] G. V. Rimlinger, 'International Differences in the Strike Propensity of Coal Miners: Experience in Four Countries', *Industrial and Labor Relations Review*, 12, 1959, pp. 389–92.
[4] The remarks made in the preceding paragraphs about strike activity referred to stoppage of work only. The inclusion of data on restrictions on work does not invalidate any of the general statements made.
[5] Stoppages and restrictions caused by disputes over wages and price lists accounted for over half of the total tonnage of coal lost throughout the country during the first decade of nationalization. Jencks, *loc. cit.*, p. 108. It must be emphasized that strikes over basic issues such as wages may only reflect a deeper dissatisfaction with more general conditions such as the conduct or delay of negotiations.

*Percentage of Saleable Output Lost through Stoppages
and Restrictions*

	Durham	Great Britain
1947	0·30*	0·9
1948	0·05*	0·5
1949	0·08*	0·8
1950	0·07	0·5
1951	0·05	0·5
1952	0·18	0·8
1953	0·04	0·4
1954	0·24	0·4
1955	0·04	1·5
1956	0·06	1·0

* Northern Division

Source: National Coal Board, *Annual Reports*, 1947–56. The percentage figures found in the text of the Coal Board's *Annual Reports* relating to both the Northern and Durham Divisions differ marginally from those found in the Statistical Appendices to those *Reports* owing to the use of different output series. Cf. S. D. Spero, *Labor Relations in British Nationalized Industry*, New York University Press 1955, p. 51.

1943.[1] The reaction of the Durham Area Union to unofficial strike activity, whatever its overt cause, is best examined in the context of the major local disputes of the period.

VI

There were 27 unofficial stoppages in Durham during the first year of nationalization affecting altogether 36,817 men and involving an estimated loss of output of 115,952 tons of coal.[2] The most important of these, a strike of winding enginemen at 21 collieries during May, illustrated how disputes over seemingly basic issues such as wages could conceal deeper causes of dissatisfaction. Winding enginemen in the coalfield were normally organized by the Durham County Colliery Enginemen's Boiler Minders' and Firemen's Association, a constituent member of the N.U.M., but some agreed to join the National Union of Colliery Winding Enginemen, established in January 1947 and composed of several district unions, some of which had broken away from the N.U.M. The Coal Board refused to regard

[1] Baldwin, *op. cit.*, p. 77.
[2] N.U.M. (Durham Area), *Annual Report*, 1947, p. 56.

this new Union as qualified to negotiate on a national basis on behalf of the winding enginemen.[1]

Arising out of the efforts of the N.U.C.W.E. to seek recognition its supporters in Durham, organized by the Durham County Winders' Association, stopped work claiming, incorrectly, that the introduction of a five-day week meant a loss of £2 per week in their wages. The County Mining Federation Board immediately condemned the strikers:

'The action of the breakaway minority, i.e. 151 winding men out of a total membership of 4,000 in the official Area Union, is a stab in the back against the Five Day Week Agreement, is calculated sabotage, threatening the economic recovery of the country and is causing deep resentment among the members of the official Area Unions especially at those pits where work has come to a standstill.'[2]

The response of the miners' Area Union to the dispute typified the determined stand it was to take in the future towards unofficial strike activity. Lodges were reminded of the necessity to make full use of the existing conciliation machinery since a stoppage of work immediately precluded any possibility of negotiations proceeding on behalf of the workmen.

The difficulty facing the Area Union in trying to protect the miners' interests whilst they openly abrogated responsibility towards established means of conciliation was further demonstrated during the dispute at Whitburn Colliery during January 1949. An application by the local Marsden Lodge for an increase in the filling price paid in the East Yard seam was rejected though, the workmen claimed, with an implication that the fillers had been restricting their output. Work stopped at the pit on 13 January, although no written information regarding the dispute had reached the Area Union twelve days later when the General Secretary appealed by letter to neighbouring Lodges not to offer any sympathetic support. 'It is to say the least unfortunate that the services of the Area Executive Committee have been ignored,' wrote Watson. 'Every Lodge . . . is aware that so long as the stopping of work continues, no negotiations of any kind can be commenced.'[3]

Work was eventually resumed on 30 January, after which representatives of the Area Union joined Lodge members in seeking a settle-

[1] For a more detailed account of the organizational problems created by the N.U.C.W.E., see Chapter XII, pp. 462–4.
[2] N.U.M. (Durham Area), 5 May 1947.
[3] N.U.M. (Durham Area), *Marsden Dispute, 1948–1949*, p. 18.

ment of outstanding matters in dispute at Divisional level. Despite pleas by Union officials that claims for damages should be waived the Divisional Coal Board pressed ahead with claims totalling £12,000 or £11 17s 0d per person.[1] Skinner, Chairman of the Divisional Coal Board, reminded Watson that:

'We have no desire to punish anyone (in fact the offenders are only punishing themselves and the Nation) but in some way the gravity of the situation must be generally realized and the whole position improved.'[2]

Ultimately, however, the Board agreed to withdraw their claim to damages subject to the men taking no part in an unofficial stoppage for a specified period of time. This scheme of mitigated fines, whereby damages could be claimed immediately from those miners originally involved in a dispute should further trouble occur at the colliery during the enforced period of industrial peace, became a commonplace in the coalfield.

The introduction of a new Industrial Disputes Order in 1951 which revoked the prohibition on strikes and lock-outs previously contained in the Conditions of Employment and National Arbitration Orders 1940–1950 did not affect the rights of employers and workmen to take proceedings for breach of contract. Neither the theoretical risk of proceedings for damages nor the continuing pressure exerted by the Area Union upon Lodge members to reduce unofficial strike activity by exhausting conciliation procedures freed the coalfield from disputes during the fifties. The total losses in coal output may have compared favourably with other Divisions but even single acts of defiance appeared to local officials to prejudice the spirit of co-operation and responsibility being fostered throughout the region.

Ironically it was at Whitburn Colliery again, and later at Harton Colliery in 1954, that the conflict between workmen, Union and Coal Board officials over the operation of conciliation machinery was emphasized. A stoppage at Whitburn, based on the alleged 'tyrannical and bullying methods' of an overman named Pearson, was called by the local Marsden Lodge on 26 February 1954, after a single pit conciliation meeting had failed to clear complaints against the overman. By 7 March sympathetic support for the Whitburn miners had already spread to Harton Colliery before the Area Union had had any official notification of the details of the dispute. Boldon Lodge, represented with the Harton and Marsden Lodges on a local

[1] *Ibid.*, p. 30.
[2] *Ibid.*, p. 39.

Federation Board, refused to offer its support to the strike and to all intents and purposes was expelled from the Board, the first time in the history of the Union that a Lodge had been penalized by other Lodges for acting constitutionally.[1]

Instructions from the Executive Committee of the N.U.M. that the pits should resume work to allow a Committee of Inquiry to investigate the dispute were ignored by the two Lodges. Instead they decided to convene a County conference in order 'to urge Lodges to give active support by threat of strike action if necessary to the stoppage'.[2] Such action, besides constituting a breach of the Area Union's Rules,[3] was in open defiance of the directions of the national Executive and as such involved the risk of exclusion from the N.U.M.[4]

The recalcitrant Lodges eventually agreed to instruct members to return to work pending a private inquiry into the stoppage by the Area Executive Committee. Claims for damages by the Divisional Coal Board, amounting in total to over £63,000, were withdrawn on condition that all future disputes at the pits concerned would be settled by constitutional means and that every effort would be made to make good the loss in output caused by the strike, especially by increased Saturday working.[5]

The scope of unofficial strike activity was much wider, of course, than is indicated by the details of selected case studies, though it still remained relatively smaller in Durham than in most other coalfields. Nevertheless the determination of the Area Union to outlaw all such activity sprang from a clear appraisal of the dangers to the coalfield of declining output and reduced export opportunities.

Watson's call for increased coal production in 1952 aptly puts the concern over industrial relations in its proper context and helps explain the vehemence with which unofficial stoppages were attacked by Durham delegates at almost every N.U.M. Annual Conference:

[1] N.U.M. (Durham Area), *Marsden and Harton Dispute*, 1954, p. 5.

[2] N.U.M. (Durham Area), 17 March 1954.

[3] Rule 143 of the Durham Area Union read: 'No Lodge in this Association shall give any notice of a strike or a County alteration in the hours or conditions of labour until its case has been laid before the Council or Executive Committee Meeting for examination and approval.'
Rule 161 read: 'All resolutions made by the Lodge Committee ... shall be strictly in accordance with the Rules of this Association and in all cases of doubt or dispute the Lodge Committee shall be guided by the decision of the Executive Committee or the Council.'

[4] Part of Rule 40 of the N.U.M. read: 'If an Area or a Branch in an Area ... shall ... refuse to carry out the lawful directions, regulations and orders of the National Executive Committee such ... may be excluded from the Union by a resolution of Conference. ...'

[5] N.U.M. (Durham Area), 3 May, 12 July 1954.

'If we could export . . . we would inject a blood transfusion into our national economy which would give the country a new lease of life. Anything we in the Mining Industry can do to achieve this should be done, whether it is by securing labour from abroad, improving our methods of production . . . by concentrating on the development of better pits, by increased co-operation, and by the unqualified acceptance of the Conciliation machinery so as to entirely eliminate restrictions of output and strikes. Our very existence depends upon it, as indeed does our desire to maintain, and if possible improve, our standard of living.'[1]

[1] N.U.M. (Durham Area), *Annual Report*, 1951, p. 14.

Appendix I

COAL MINERS' EARNINGS PER SHIFT, 1947–1956
(ALL WORKMEN)

| | Index of average money earnings per shift (1947 = 100) (excluding the value of allowances in kind) | | | | | | Cost of Living Index (1947 = 100) | Index of average real earnings per shift (1947 = 100) (excluding the value of allowances in kind) | |
| | Durham | | | Great Britain | | | | Durham | Great Britain |
	s	d	Index	s	d	Index			
1947	27	2	100·0	27	8	100·0	100·0	100·0	100·0
1948	31	9	116·9	31	9	114·8	108·0	108·2	106·3
1949	32	7	119·9	32	11	119·0	110·5	108·5	107·7
1950	33	4	122·7	34	0	122·9	114·5	107·2	107·3
1951	36	8	135·0	37	3	134·6	125·0	108·0	107·7
1952	40	10	150·3	41	5	149·7	136·5	110·1	109·7
1953	42	9	157·4	43	5	156·9	140·5	112·0	111·7
1954	44	10	165·0	48	7	175·6	143·0	115·4	122·8
1955	48	2	177·3	52	11	191·3	150·0	118·2	127·5
1956	52	10	194·5	57	2	206·6	156·0	124·7	132·5

Sources: National Coal Board, Annual Reports, 1947–56. Ministry of Labour Index of Retail Prices.

Chapter XII

THE DURHAM MINERS UNDER NATIONALIZATION

I

Following the nationalization of the mines the N.U.M. became more involved in 'administrative' as distinct from 'protest' unionism as it sought to sponsor the new industrial order for which it was in large part responsible.[1] In doing so it allowed the Area Unions to retain a considerable measure of authority and influence. Issues of joint consultation, the administration of newly created welfare benefits and the inauguration of coal production campaigns, to list only a few examples, necessitated a close and continuing relationship being developed between the local miners' Union and its Divisional Coal Board if a similar desire to ensure the success of nationalization was to manifest itself outside of London.

As the number and scope of the issues in which the Durham Area Union and Divisional Board had a mutual interest expanded so did the frequency with which the miners' representatives could register their reaction to national policy, especially in emphasizing the special economic and social considerations arising from coal mining in an old high cost coalfield. The responsibility which the Durham Area Union thus shared with other miners' unions in fostering the development of their industry acted as a powerful force for decentralization, enhanced by the N.C.B.'s support for the greater autonomy of Divisional Boards, and as a counter-balance to the yielding of authority to the national union. A very significant bargaining authority was thus formally and actually exercised at Area level and, in lesser matters, at Lodge level.

The ability of the miners' organization in Durham to retain a specific and influential role under public ownership was also aided by the extent to which Area Union leadership could exert its influence upon the Executive Committee of the N.U.M. All but three of that body's members were Area representatives and not effectively responsible to the entire Union. Insofar as the National Executive exercised any authority it acted not as a single body but as an

---

[1] G. B. Baldwin, 'The Effect of Nationalization on Britain's National Union of Mineworkers', *Proceedings of the Fifth Annual Meeting Industrial Relations Research Association*, 1954.

aggregation of Area leadership. Though the National Union remained the bargaining instrument within the industry it was not the effective determinant of bargaining decisions. Rather than acting as a policy-formulating body the National Executive became the instrument for resolving the differences among Areas.[1]

Durham miners' officials between the wars had held responsible positions in the former M.F.G.B. and had established within their Union a tradition of close association with the activities of the central miners' organization. Watson was first elected to the miners' National Executive in 1935 and emerged in the post-1947 period as one of the industry's most influential and cogent spokesmen. Since in the context of national policy-making the autonomy of an Area was infringed only insofar as the political majority of the Areas imposed its will on the minority the claims of special interests within the industry had to be deployed with considerable skill. In this respect Durham was well served by Watson, and those of his colleagues who shared with him national representation, in the manner in which they fully exploited opportunities to plead the case of less fortunate Divisions. Public ownership emphasized the industry's national responsibilities. Thus so far as ability to pay remained a criterion for wage determination, for example, it was on a national basis and related to the total industry wages bill and all claims made upon the industry, including those arising from socially-orientated price policies directed towards providing low-cost energy. Watson in particular fervently believed that geologically inferior coal-mining regions producing mainly for the export market, such as Durham, should exert additional internal pressure towards greater wage uniformity and the subsidy of their Area by the more prosperous.

Those responsible for safeguarding the workers' interests within Durham therefore, whilst acutely aware of their differing tasks and responsibilities as members of a national miners' Union within a publicly-owned industry, rarely wasted opportunities to expound local interests at national level whenever it seemed likely to foster that greater sense of mutual interdependence amongst the coalfields for which the miners had fought for so long.

II

Apart from brief upsurges during the periods 1947 to 1948 and 1951 to 1952 the membership of the Durham Area Union during the first decade of mines nationalization continued a decline which had

---

[1] For further discussion of these points see F. Meyers, *European Coal-Mining Unions*, University of California, 1961.

become particularly noticeable in the former miners' Association during the mid-thirties. By 1956 total membership stood at 111,184 compared with 114,667 in 1947 and 124,783 in 1938. In money terms the union's financial position improved significantly aided especially by the absence of official strikes. Total investments rose from £498,353 in 1947 to £821,335 in 1956. The rise in investments per head from £4·35 to £7·39 during the same period proved less substantial in real terms. Allowing for changes in prices their value increased from £4·35 in 1947 to £4·83 in 1956.[1] Members' full contributions were increased twice during the first decade of nationalization, reaching a total of 2s 4d by the end of 1956. The Durham Area declined to operate the national agreement made in 1949 providing for the deduction of trade union dues from mineworkers' wages. It remained the only Area Union to collect contributions on a voluntary basis but felt justified in doing so for the sake of maintaining a personal link with its paying members. As Watson explained in 1955:

'The plain fact is that "The Union" in Durham never was merely a union contribution collecting machine. The local Lodge Officials and Committee members were and still are the men to whom the miner looks for advice and guidance. . . . There is nothing intimate and personal in a Colliery Office deduction. There is a link between the "family" and the Union and we have always prided ourselves upon the fact that it is this intimate and personal relationship that gives our Union its place and meaning in the lives of our people. When a members pays his "union money" voluntarily he accepts a responsibility and he considers himself to be a member of the "family".[2]

The efforts of the National Union of Mineworkers in 1948 to have union contributions deducted from wages were part of a general campaign to tighten its hold on those groups of workers it sought to represent at national level. The N.U.M. pressed the Coal Board in January 1948 to make it compulsory for mineworkers to be members of that union. The Board refused the request though it undertook to encourage union representation amongst mineworkers. The matter was of little direct relevance to Durham since trade union membership had already been made a condition of employment in February 1942 following a local agreement between the former coal owners' and miners' associations.[3]

[1] See Appendix I to this chapter.
[2] N.U.M. (Durham Area), *Annual Report, 1954*, pp. 1–2.
[3] See Chapter II, p. 92. For a discussion of the reactions of management to efforts to impose compulsory trade unionism in selected industries, including coal mining, see V. L. Allen, 'Some Economic Aspects of Compulsory Trade Unionism,' *Oxford Economic Papers*, 6, 1954.

Apart from Watson and Moore none of the Area Union officials who served in Durham after 1947 had been Agents before the end of the Second World War. Kelly, Foster and Joyce had been elected during 1945–6 following Lawther's adoption as President of the N.U.M. and the retirement according to rule of Gilliland and Swan. Unlike the inter-war experience the majority of new appointments to leadership within the Union after 1947 resulted not from the death of officials but from retirements.

Moore, the Area Union's President, reached 60 years of age during 1953 and, according to N.U.M. Rules, retired from official duty. Eighty-three nominations were received from Lodges for the vacancy, the eight nominees receiving the highest number of votes being subjected to a ballot under the single transferable vote system. No candidate secured an absolute majority vote on the first or second count. The process of eliminating the candidate with the lowest poll was continued throughout the third and subsequent counts until at the seventh final count C. Pick of Kibblesworth Lodge received 29,051 votes against 27,269 votes for S. Barratt of Dawdon Lodge, there being 6,176 non-transferable papers.[1] Pick was duly elected and began duty as Financial Secretary in January 1954, Kelly having become the Union's new President.

Pick was born in the Durham village of Eighton Banks on 22 June 1902. At 13 years of age he began working a ten-hour surface shift at Allerdene Shop pit moving underground a year later. For thirty years he worked for the same colliery company performing almost every class of pit work available. Elected Chairman of the Ravensworth Ann Lodge in 1940 he held the post until being appointed checkweighman at Kibblesworth Colliery in 1946. In the following year he became Secretary of the local Lodge combining this responsibility with his activities on behalf of Birtley Parish Council.

Until 1953 Watson, Kelly, Foster and Joyce had retained the offices they had held in 1946 namely General Secretary, Committee Secretary, General Treasurer and Financial Secretary respectively. Following Pick's appointment Kelly became President, Foster Committee Secretary, and Joyce General Treasurer. Watson continued as General Secretary, a post he held until his retirement in March 1963. In recognition of his services to the mining industry Durham University conferred upon him the Honorary Degree of Doctor of Civil Law in June 1955.

[1] N.U.M. (Durham Area), 11 January 1954.

III

The question of trade organization which most intimately involved the Durham Area Union, the National Coal Board and the N.U.M. during the early years of nationalization related to the representation of winding enginemen. The statutory duty imposed upon the Coal Board to enter into consultation with organizations appearing to represent substantial proportions of its employees touched off a scramble for recognition among several unions outside of the N.U.M. Conciliation machinery was established for example between the Board and the British Association of Colliery Management and with the National Association of Colliery Overmen, Deputies and Shotfirers.[1]

In January 1947 the National Union of Colliery Winding Enginemen was formed, a new organization outside of the N.U.M. consisting essentially of the independent craft unions for winders already existing in five districts, including Durham. Although the bulk of winding enginemen in Durham were organized within the County's Colliery Enginemen's, Boiler Minders' and Firemen's Association, a constituent body of the N.U.M., a minority subscribed to an unofficial organization called the Durham County Winders' Association. This body, joined in 1947 by members of Lynemouth Colliery in Northumberland,[2] became responsible for engaging support for the activities of the newly formed national breakaway union.

The N.U.M. repudiated claims by the new National Winders' Union that the interests of a specific grade of workman were not being adequately safeguarded by those representative bodies recognized at national level. The Coal Board rejected the breakaway union's request for official recognition, despite a strike threat from the winders, and referred the dispute to a special Court of Inquiry headed by Sir John Forster.

The Court reported early in 1948 and recognized that the formation of the National Union of Colliery Winding Enginemen could be traced back to the dissatisfaction of winders over their relative wage position compared with other grades of workmen. Nevertheless the Court decided that it would not be in the interests of the industry as a whole, or indeed of winding enginemen as a particular group in the industry, that an organization representing a section of them should

[1] For details of the conciliation procedures developed for most employees of the Coal Board who were not mine workers see W. K. Gratwick, 'Labour Relations in Nationalized Industries with particular reference to the Coal-Mining Industry', *Law and Contemporary Problems*, 16, 1961.
[2] N.U.M., 10 December 1947.

be recognized by the National Coal Board.[1] Feeling that there was some justification for the apprehension which had been felt by winding enginemen that their interests were not adequately represented, the Court suggested that:

'Within the existing organization of Craft Groups in the National Union of Mineworkers, means should be devised to ensure that, whenever questions affecting the rate and conditions of employment of winding enginemen are to be the subject of negotiations with the National Coal Board, at either district or national level, the Union shall include among their representatives persons regarded by the winding enginemen themselves as competent to represent their special interests.'[2]

The outbreak of a strike of breakaway winding enginemen in Durham during May 1947 in protest against an alleged loss of wages following the introduction of the five-day week[3] was seen by the Divisional Coal Board as no more than an effort to buttress the claim of the new national winders' union for official recognition. The Board's stern opposition to such direct action was founded on the knowledge that it:

'Could be held to ransom at any time by minorities who broke away from the Official Union. ... There would be no end to splinter breakaway unions if we permitted recognition to the so-called Winders' Union, and what is more important, no sense of trade union responsibility to collective bargaining.'[4]

Arrangements for a return to work were eventually made with the breakaway winding enginemen at each of the 21 collieries affected by the dispute on condition that the winders gave an understanding to rejoin the Durham County Colliery Enginemen's, Boiler Minders' and Firemen's Association, the official body recognized by the N.U.M. as responsible for caring for their interests. Not all men honoured this undertaking. By 14 July 1947, 57 winders had not paid contributions to the official trade union and even by the end of October 1949 two winders at Boldon Colliery were resisting pressures to honour their previous pledges of loyalty.[5] Trouble broke out at

[1] Ministry of Labour, *Report of a Court of Inquiry into a dispute between the National Coal Board and the National Union of Colliery Winding Enginemen, 28 January 1948*, para. 36.
[2] *Ibid.*, para. 38.
[3] N.U.M. (Durham Area), 5 May 1947.
[4] *Ibid.*, 14 July 1947.
[5] *Ibid.*, 29 October 1949.

South Hetton Colliery during November 1948 when nine breakaway winding enginemen refused to train any workmen for winding engine duties if they were members of the official union.[1]

The N.U.M. itself was not unsympathetic to the need to improve the wages of winding enginemen and, failing agreement with the Coal Board, submitted a claim to arbitration in 1948. The resulting Eighteenth Porter Award proved disappointing to both the N.U.M. and the breakaway groups since it did not ensure wage advances for all winders. The N.U.M., bound by the terms of the arbitration award, was immediately recognized by the breakaway minorities as powerless to achieve any further wage improvements for some time. The pressure to establish an organization independent of the N.U.M. and acceptable to the Coal Board grew. The Yorkshire Colliery Winders' Association, a N.U.M. affiliate which was severely critical of the wage negotiations conducted on its behalf, provided the necessary leadership and within three months of the Porter Award joined with breakaway groups in other districts to form the Colliery Winders' Federation of Great Britain.

The N.C.B. persistently refused to negotiate with an organization established outside of the existing conciliation machinery. Rather than allow the strike weapon to be used to force independent recognition from the Board, the dispute over organization and the new demands for improved winders' wages were referred to the National Arbitration Tribunal in 1949. The Tribunal refused to alter the terms of the enginemen's wage award as originally formulated by the National Reference Tribunal. When a further series of demands was made in 1950 aimed at the improvement of organization and working conditions of the breakaway winders the N.A.T. reasserted its determination not to consider any issue which fell outside of the existing conciliation machinery. A suggestion from the frustrated Winders' Federation that its members might be allowed to return to the N.U.M. in some new district organizations catering solely for winding enginemen, as distinct from a 'mixed' craftsmen's union such as existed in Durham, was vehemently opposed by officials of the National Union of Mineworkers.

The cancellation of the Eighteenth Porter Award in 1951 by a wage agreement which gave winding enginemen a larger advance than any other craft group, and the collapse in 1950 of one of the Winders' Federation's important district affiliates, eventually provided the opportunity for the breakaway section to rejoin the N.U.M. through the existing constituent associations.

[1] *Ibid.*, 16 November 1948.

One issue of trade union representation within Durham which aggravated more long-standing grievances than did the problem of the winding enginemen arose in 1952 in connection with membership of the Durham Deputies' Mutual Aid Association. Until May 1945 the deputies in the coalfield were, for membership purposes, roughly equally divided between the local Deputies' Association and the Miners' Association. The initial rights of trade union negotiation on all major questions up till that date lay with the Durham Miners' Association. In 1940 those deputies who wished to transfer their membership from the miners' to the deputies' Association had been allowed to do so. By 1945 the specific claims to membership of each of the rival organizations were finally settled when it was mutually decided that all those workmen who could rightly lay claim to the wages and status of a deputy should henceforth belong to the deputies' Association. All those remaining members of the deputies' union under 60 years of age and all members who subsequently were transferred to non-deputy work were required to transfer their membership to the miners' Association.[1]

On 3 October 1952 a new County wages agreement for shotfirers, a significant proportion of whom were members of the Deputies' Association, so altered their terms and conditions of employment that those who had by then become deputies could no longer rightly claim that status. Under the terms of the 1945 agreement, therefore, shotfirers were required to transfer their membership to the miners' Area Union which now had the exclusive right to negotiate on their behalf. At a special County meeting on 10 January 1953 the Deputies' Association rejected a resolution instructing its officials to transfer those shotfirers then in membership to the N.U.M.[2] The Durham Area Union pleaded with J. Crawford, the Deputies' General Secretary, to honour the terms of the 1945 agreement. A rejection of its provisions could have empowered the miners' Union to begin organizing deputies within the coalfield and thus renew the antagonisms which had bedevilled the relationship between the two organizations in the inter-war period.

The dispute was finally settled by mutual agreement on 10 October 1953 when those persons who had achieved deputy status before regrading in 1952 were allowed to remain within the Deputies' Association. All persons engaged within the deputies' union in 1952 as full-time shotfirers and all those workmen subsequently commencing as shotfirers were required to become members of the Durham Area Union of the N.U.M.

[1] See Chapter II, pp. 90–3.
[2] N.U.M. (Durham Area), 6 February 1953.

IV

Under the Nationalization Act the Coal Board was given a general instruction to secure the benefit of the practical knowledge and experience of its employees. More specifically it was committed to join with the trade unions in working out schemes for consultation on the safety, health and welfare of the people in the industry and also on the organization and conduct of the operations in which they were employed. Through this consultation, which covered everything affecting employer and employees except wages and conditions of employment, the Board hoped to foster a spirit of co-operation between management and men. The idea of consultation between workers and management in the mining industry was not new—it was suggested in 1917, envisaged in the Mining Industry Act 1920, and found some expression in the Pit Production Committees established during the Second World War.

A National Consultative Council composed of 27 members, nine of whom were N.U.M. nominees, was established in 1946 to discuss those matters of national interest which were properly the concern of consultative bodies. By July 1947 Divisional Consultative Councils, based on a 'model constitution' recommended by the National Council, had been established in all coalfields. The Northern Divisional Council was originally intended to consist of 20 representatives of whom six were allocated to the Durham, Northumberland and Cumberland miners, only as many as was provided for the Colliery Managers' Association alone. The miners, feeling that the proposed representation was totally disproportionate, succeeded in overcoming the difficulty of distributing membership of the Divisional Council among the separate coalfields by having three Sub-Divisional Councils established. Each of these organized a General Production Committee and a Safety and Health Committee, both of which met monthly. At each colliery in the coalfield there was a Consultative Committee under the chairmanship of a colliery manager. It consisted of three management nominees, two of whom were underground officials, the Divisional Board's mining agent, one deputy and six workers' representatives. The Area agent of the N.U.M. and the Colliery Lodge Secretary were *ex officio* members.

Despite early efforts to foster the development of effective consultation within Durham the adequacy of the machinery provided was soon brought into question. During 1948 an experiment, the first of its kind, was made in the coalfield to organize week-end schools for representatives of Colliery Consultative Committees. Arranged on a rota basis at the Miners' Rehabilitation Centre at

Chester-le-Street, the main purpose of the scheme was to encourage an exchange of ideas and experience so as to more adequately prepare representatives for the tasks facing them.[1]

It was soon appreciated that the principal difficulty in the system of consultation was that of communicating the decisions and spirit of the Consultative Committee to the workmen and officials in the pit.[2] 'We need a complete conveyor system of responsibility involving everyone employed in the industry,' declared Watson in 1949. To achieve this he suggested that a working party should be established at every pit charged with preparing comprehensive and detailed reports on matters which could be referred back to the Colliery Consultative Committee for further action. Membership of the Sub-Committee would be open to all grades of workmen except those elected to the Colliery Consultative Committee.[3] 'At some pits the consultative machinery is viewed mainly as an additional lever in the negotiating machinery,' Watson informed the T.U.C. in 1949, 'and the Committee is being used as an additional method of lodging complaints instead of devoting itself to the consideration and development of constructive ideas for the welfare of the miner.'[4]

The mere passage of time did not ensure that joint consultation would become so much a part of relationships at the pit that increased output or improved relations would depend upon its efficient functioning. The Durham Area Union reported in 1954 that there were pits within the coalfield 'where co-operation and consultation could not be bettered', and yet others where consultation had become 'as routine as washing day'.[5] Not that the Union was surprised as it explained:

'When the pits were under private control, and the Management so to speak had "all their own way" the difficulties of production, efficiency, safety, health and welfare and education were not eliminated. It is ... true if the pits were handed over to the men to work and manage themselves—the difficulties would still remain (maybe more so). We are in danger of mixing up industrial demo-

[1] N.U.M. (Durham Area), *Annual Report*, 1948, pp. 80–2.
[2] This problem was not, of course, confined to Durham. Two case studies of Colliery Consultative Committees in the Lancashire coalfield have suggested that many workmen were ignorant of the existence and functions of the machinery provided for joint consultation and that the Committees' work had been reduced to a merely ritualistic function. See O. Broadley, 'The Colliery Consultative Committee'. Ph.D. thesis, University of Liverpool 1959.
[3] N.U.M. (Durham Area), *Annual Report*, 1949, pp. 29–31.
[4] *Ibid.*, p. 32.
[5] N.U.M. (Durham Area), 11 January 1954.

cracy with Joint Consultation, and thereby expecting too much from men and management.'[1]

In practice the distinction intended to be drawn between wages and terms and conditions of employment on the one hand and matters not appropriate to collective bargaining but properly the concern of consultative bodies on the other, proved impossible to maintain. Thus important matters of safety and health escaped the consultative machinery and became the subject of negotiation between the Board and the N.U.M. Some indication must be given therefore of the formal progress made in fostering miners' welfare in the widest sense at both national and Divisional level.

V

The statutory duties imposed upon the Coal Board by the 1946 Nationalization Act ensured continuing support for the provision of welfare facilities for miners. This aspect of the Board's activity clearly overlapped the duties of the Miners' Welfare Commission which since 1920 had administered a welfare fund derived from levies on coal produced and, from 1926, on coal royalties.[2] To prevent duplication of effort the welfare activities of the Board and the Commission were co-ordinated from 1 January 1948 until 1952 through the National Miners' Welfare Joint Council. During these four years Sub-Divisional Welfare Committees with appropriate Area representation directed welfare activities in Durham. From 1952 onwards, under the terms of the Miners' Welfare Act, the Coal Board assumed responsibility for welfare at the colliery and a new body called the Coal Industry Social Welfare Organization (C.I.S.W.O.) became responsible for the 'social' welfare of all employed in the industry.

One of the most urgent welfare tasks facing the industry after vesting day was to build more pithead baths. The National Coal Board immediately assumed responsibility for meeting the full maintenance cost of baths, except for providing soap and towels, and thus relieved miners of the responsibility placed upon men during the Second World War of contributing a share of maintenance costs equal to that provided by colliery owners. Once the Board decided that baths should be provided at every colliery if its expected life was long enough to justify the cost then it became

[1] *Ibid.*
[2] See Chapter VII, pp. 293–6.

necessary to augment the funds already available to the Welfare Commission for this purpose. In 1949 the Board agreed to contribute £6½ million to a four-year building programme, the money being allocated to Divisional Welfare Committees in proportion to the number of men for whom baths had yet to be built.[1] Sixteen installations had been completed in the Durham coalfield by the time the organization of welfare activities was altered in mid-1952, bringing the total in operation throughout the Division to 42, providing full bathing accommodation for 65,150 men.[2]

The work of providing canteens at collieries, normally the task of the Welfare Commission, was taken over by the Ministry of Fuel and Power in May 1946 and entrusted to the Coal Board thirteen months later. The Board resolved to raise the standard of canteen service being provided at collieries and instructed the Catering Officers formerly employed by the Ministry to pay regular visits to canteens to inspect the quality of food served and the degree of cleanliness and hygiene. By the end of 1951, 101 canteens, providing breakfast, main meals, beverages and packed food, catered for 88,000 miners in the Durham coalfield.[3]

The improvement and extension of colliery amenities was not the only way in which welfare was fostered. The Miners' Welfare Commission, in co-operation with the Arts Council of Great Britain, arranged for a London drama company to tour the Durham coalfield during the latter part of 1947.[4] The restoration, maintenance and projection of institutes, halls and recreation grounds remained a constant preoccupation of the Divisional Welfare Committee whilst youth sections and games competitions involved personnel at local, Area and Divisional level alike. In 1947 the Coal Board began what was to become a regular activity of distributing a propaganda 'Mining Review' film to be shown in cinemas in pit villages.

The major improvements in social and colliery life followed the reorganization of welfare activities in 1952. The Miners' Welfare Commission and, consequently, the National Welfare Joint Council were both dissolved as the responsibility for 'colliery' and 'social' welfare came under the aegis of separate bodies. From 1 July 1952 pithead baths and the provision of canteen facilities came to be regarded officially as colliery welfare activities, the operation and maintenance of which became the sole responsibility of the Coal

---

[1] National Coal Board, *Annual Report and Statement of Accounts for the Year Ended 31 December 1949*, p. 101.
[2] N.U.M. (Durham Area), *Annual Report*, 1952, p. 381.
[3] *Ibid.*, 1951, p. 403.
[4] N.U.M. (Durham Area), 22 September 1947.

Board as a normal function of colliery management. By the end of 1956, 27 new pithead baths had been opened in the Durham Division although the number of canteens in operation had declined from a total of 101 in 1951 to only 88.

Whilst generally the range and quality of facilities available for social recreation and well-being increased as a result of the activities of the C.I.S.W.O., the allocation of funds for specific schemes varied amongst Divisions. It would be tedious to trace the development of even a sample of the many projects sponsored at Divisional level though a summary of the expenditure incurred in fostering the development of the most important of them in Durham down to the end of 1956 is instructive in indicating the predominance attached to providing recreation facilities.

Coal Industry Social Welfare Organization
Summary of Expenditure in the Durham Division

For the year ended	Recreation £	Social and cultural £	Youth and holiday schemes £	Convalescence and re-habilitation £	Education £
1952*	46,853	255	—	8,000	108
1953	44,934	511	—	28,378	375
1954	68,900	622	—	12,243	825
1955	86,004	812	123	7,524	946
1956	102,374	901	60	9,783	387

Source: *Annual Reports* of the Coal Industry Social Welfare Organization, 1952–6.

Notes: * Figures for 1952 relate only to the period from 1 July 1952 (the date from which social welfare was administered by the C.I.S.W.O.) to 31 December 1952.

The specific activities encouraged by the organization proved as wide as the interests of the mineworkers and their families themselves. Apart from the local events many activities came to be arranged competitively on a Divisional basis. These included drama, brass band and choral festivals, fishing, bowling, cricket and football competitions and, in Northumberland and Durham, pigeon racing competitions.

The shortage of professional engineers, surveyors and other technically qualified men in the mining industry, increasingly brought to light by the growth of mechanized mining and the demands of reorganization and reconstruction, prompted the Coal Board to join the trade unions in what to them was a traditional campaign for greater educational opportunities for the industry's employees. At national level the Board decided in 1948 to offer scholarships in mining and other technical subjects to boys leaving secondary schools and to boys and young men employed in the industry. A further three-year course of 'directed practical training', aimed at providing planned experience as a supplement to formal education, was offered to successful candidates after taking their first university degree or diploma.[1] Many responsible posts were to continue to be filled by men who had not been to university but who, by experience and part-time study, had qualified themselves for promotion. Miners in Durham who satisfied the colliery manager that they would be likely to benefit from further study were allowed by the Divisional Coal Board to attend part-time day classes in subjects related to their employment. Provision was made for the payment of class fees, half of the cost of essential textbooks and the appropriate day wage applicable to the student's age.[2]

Both the Holland Committee, set up by the Secretary for Mines in 1928, and the Report of the Royal Commission on Safety in Coal Mines had recommended that the standards of technical education of tradesmen (mostly mechanics and electricians) and under-officials in the industry should be raised. During 1949 the Board developed a plan—the Ladder Plan—to give every young recruit in mining a chance of systematic training for a career and to improve the standard of technical knowledge and skill in the industry. The plan was in three parts. The first part proposed to establish examinations to prepare students for a General Certificate and later for a Higher National Certificate. The second part of the Plan made provision for an oral and practical test for deputies to serve as an alternative form of qualification for men who were unable or unwilling to take a written examination. The third part proposed to establish a National Advisory Committee on Mining Certificates to suggest minimum standards of courses and practical training which might prove acceptable to the Ministry of Fuel and Power.

As a first stage in the implementation of the Ladder Plan in Durham special arrangements were made in 1950 to provide part-time courses in mining at Bishop Auckland, Easington, Jarrow and West Kyo.[3] In the following year a Divisional Apprenticeship Scheme was inaugurated by the Divisional Coal Board to help improve the skills of colliery mechanics and electrical engineers. It was formally re-

[1] National Coal Board, *Annual Report and Statement of Accounts for the Year Ended 31 December 1948*, pp. 60–1.
[2] N.U.M. (Durham Area), 22 August 1949.
[3] N.U.M. (Durham Area), *Annual Report*, 1950, p. 152.

placed in 1953 by a national scheme which followed closely the details of the Durham project. Approval was also given in 1952 for the Divisional Board to finance students who wished to embark upon the deputies' courses being sponsored by education authorities.[1]

The chief handicap in the development of mining education in the coalfield was the lack of technical colleges in the County Administrative Area. A total of 1,054 students were undergoing technical education in the County during 1949–50, 361 on a part-time basis,[2] but many plans for day-release courses were left unexecuted. Conditions were slow to improve. By 1955, even with two new technical colleges available at Stockton and Hebburn, the total number of students granted release from work for attendance at part-time day classes had only risen to 1,075.[3]

VI

One of the coal industry's most persistent social evils and one which particularly aggravated manpower shortages by discouraging labour mobility was that of inferior housing in mining areas. Some of the worst examples of overcrowding and sub-standard housing between the wars had been found within the Durham coalfield,[4] and local miners' officials needed little prompting after 1947 to seek immediate improvements in the situation. In one respect their task was eased by the creation, under the terms of the mines Nationalization Act, of Local Colliery Housing Advisory Committees representative of workmen and officials at each colliery. These Committees were mainly concerned with problems of house allocation, previously the prerogative of the colliery managers, and provision was made for matters in dispute to be referred to a similar body at Divisional level.

Conscious of the statutory obligations of the Coal Board towards its employees the Durham Area Union responded with alacrity to proposals for improving the conditions of colliery houses. Lodges demanded in 1949 that all miners' houses in the coalfield should be lit by electricity and not, as in most cases, by gas.[5] Earlier in August 1947 the Dean and Chapter Lodge had sought support for a widespread scheme for the modernization of colliery houses and especially for the provision of modern fireplaces which would 'lead to a big

[1] *Ibid.*, 1952, p. 227.
[2] *Ibid.*, 1950, p. 152.
[3] *Ibid.*, 1955, p. 292.
[4] See Chapter VII, pp. 286–93.
[5] N.U.M. (Durham Area), 28 May 1949.

saving in the consumption of coal'.[1] 'The standard of housing for colliery workers has not in all cases followed the general improvement in the standard of housing as illustrated by the modern colliery house,' reported the Durham Area in 1950. 'It is not unnatural that many of our members should expect some betterment in their living conditions.'[2] In the same year the N.C.B. authorized Area general managers to incur such expenses on the repair of colliery houses as was consistent with the life expectancy of the property.

One vision of social improvement which achieved particular support in the northern coalfield was that of creating fresh opportunities for community development in mining regions. It was in Durham County that the first step was made towards fulfilling the demand in the *Miners' Charter* for the building of new towns to provide an improved social environment for the miner and his family. Even before the Reith Committee[3] was established at the end of the Second World War to advise on the way in which new towns should be planned and built Easington Rural District Council had decided that their housing difficulties, concentrated in predominantly mining centres, could best be solved by the building of a completely new town on a site that would be centrally situated and easily accessible to the existing villages. This bold and original conception was planned in detail by the Council's Surveyor, C. W. Clarke, and published in a booklet entitled *Farewell Squalor*.

A site of over 2,300 acres was selected, bounded on the south by Castle Eden Dene, on the west by the main Stockton–Sunderland trunk road, on the north by the fringes of Easington and on the east by Horden and Blackhall. The new town was to be named after Peter Lee, at the time perhaps the best-known and well-loved of the former Durham miners' leaders. Peterlee Development Corporation was appointed in March 1948 to help create the first English new town for coal miners, the origins of which lay in the energy and initiative of the people living in the area in which the town was to be built. Apart from its Chairman Dr Monica Felton, who had been Vice-Chairman of the Stevenage New Town Project, all the members of the corporation had close connections with activities in the North. One of them, H. O'Neill, had at one time been Secretary of the Easington miners' Lodge and a member of the Executive Committee of the Area Union.

The objectives of the Peterlee project were to relieve the serious housing shortage in the overcrowded mining villages within Easing-

[1] *Ibid.*, 24 September 1949.
[2] N.U.M. (Durham Area), *Annual Report*, 1950, p. 273.
[3] *Interim Report of the New Towns Committee*, 1945–6 (Cmd. 6759).

ton Rural District; to provide an administrative, commercial and recruitment district centre for a heavily populated rural area and to establish new industry so as to provide the necessary diversification of employment to act as a bulwark against emigration from the coalfield. The problem facing the Development Corporation, therefore, was one which required a solution in many directions at once and not solely in terms of housing. A social survey of Easington's villages in 1948 indicated that 33 per cent of houses were overcrowded on the basis of one room per person, 30 per cent had no separate kitchen and 75 per cent had no indoor lavatory. Most of the villagers were miners who lived in colliery houses for nominal rents— 95 per cent paid less than 15s per week—and whose future prospects of alternative employment were poor.[1]

The Durham Area union warmly welcomed the Peterlee project. Writing in 1950 Watson claimed:

'It may well be that the concentration and co-ordination of urban building in the new town of Peterlee will represent one of the most important social contributions to the amelioration of living conditions in the North East Region, and will be a permanent contribution to the policy of making coalmining an attractive occupation. Thus Peterlee will play its part in arresting the drift from the mines.'[2]

The first major obstacle to progress was the need to reconcile the proposals for surface development with underground coal getting. Watson represented the Area Union on a working party designed to achieve the co-ordination of surface and underground planning between the Corporation and the National Coal Board. By 1950 considerable areas of land had been made available for immediate housing and town centre development with the minimum sterilization of coal.[3]

One year later the Development Corporation had let contracts for housing and engineering works and had acquired lands for development involving expenditure in excess of £2m. More important was the completion of a Master Plan which tackled the long term problem of correlating surface development with the coal extraction programme. Normally because of existing mining operations the areas for urban development only became available sporadically and rarely in the most suitable places. One task facing the Technical Officers of

[1] Moyes, *op. cit.*, pp. 164–7.
[2] N.U.M. (Durham Area), *Annual Report*, 1950, p. 271.
[3] See M. Felton, 'Britain's Model New Industrial Town: Peterlee', *Journal of the American Institute of Planners*, Spring 1949.

the Corporation, the Ministry of Town and Country Planning and the National Coal Board was to secure over the years a series of sites free from the treat of surface subsidence which could produce, when developed, a pattern of town development which adequately fulfilled the requirements of modern urban living.[1] The Master Plan for Peterlee was formally approved by the Ministry of Housing and Local Government in 1954.

By the end of 1956 the new town's population had reached a total of 8,346, almost half of whom were between the ages of 20 and 35.[2] Total capital expenditure by the Corporation had reached £5,983,000, of which £4,076,000 had been spent on house construction.[3] House rents in Peterlee were high compared with those charged by local authorities for equivalent accommodation, a factor which certainly reduced the importance of coal mining in the occupational pattern of the town's inhabitants. By the middle fifties miners' families living in the villages surrounding Peterlee increasingly came to associate life in the new town with the demands of high house rents. In 1956 Peterlee's actual population fell short of the estimates projected in the 1952 Master Plan and in every year thereafter the deficiency increased. By 1965 it had grown to a total of over 8,000 people.[4]

Industrialists who wanted to build their own factories in Peterlee were offered sites on lease from the Corporation or, alternatively, allowed to rent factories built by North Eastern Trading Estates Ltd. Industrial development in the new town was slow and when it did materialize provided employment opportunities better suited to women than to ex-coalminers. The first factory, built for the textile manufacturers Jeremiah Ambler Ltd of Bradford, was not opened until February 1955, and the second, for a Leeds clothing firm, until March 1956.

VII

The misery and suffering that death, injury, disablement and occupational disease inflicted upon the life of every mining family acted as a constant spur to improvements aimed at raising the standards of health and safety within the industry. The sensitivity of the Coal Board to pressures for legislation and its responsibilities to Parliament ensured that efforts in this direction were not only intensified after 1947 but were widely expanded. The erection of a memorial tablet

---

[1] *Ibid.*, 1951, p. 414.
[2] *Ibid.*, 1956, p. 409.
[3] *Ibid.*, p. 417.
[4] Moyes, *op. cit.*, p. 170.

within Durham Cathedral in January 1947 in memory of those who had lost their lives in Durham pits acted as a telling reminder of the human price of coal.

Coal mining will always be a dangerous occupation but during the first decade of public ownership there were signs that the situation was improving. In 1947 the number of fatal accidents in the Durham Division was 75 compared with 40 in 1956. The rate of fatal accidents per 100,000 manshifts worked in the Division also fell from 0·25 in 1949[1] to 0·16 in 1956.

Improvements in annual accident statistics could never reduce the need for greater safety-consciousness. The Safety Organization set up by the N.C.B. during the first year of nationalization did much valuable work in this respect. At national level a chief safety officer was appointed in addition to a Standing Committee of Board members to supervise the development of safety measures and to stimulate improvements throughout the industry. At Divisional level safety engineers were appointed in the Areas to work directly under The Area General Manager who in turn appointed at his discretion safety assistants, responsible in Durham to two or more collieries. At each large pit a colliery safety assistant worked under the direction of the colliery manager.[2] Questions of safety and health also came under the jurisdiction of the consultative machinery established at colliery, Area and national levels.[3]

Through bitter experience many of the basic types of colliery accidents were already well-known, and whilst human folly and negligence still played a large part in initiating them efforts still had to be directed towards developing adequate preventive measures. The Durham Falls of Ground Advisory Committee established in 1942[4] invited its Northumbrian counterpart in 1948 to join with Cumberland to form the Northern Divisional Falls of Ground Advisory Committee to help combat what was still the most predominant type of mining accident. Though the fatality rate for this hazard had been falling since 1942, there were still 23 such deaths in Durham in 1947 and an average of over 20 between 1947 and 1956. Much work was done at all levels to improve roof support, especially since power-loading techniques led to the development of large areas of unsupported roof near the coal face.

One of the most notable developments in improved working conditions was in the field of dust suppression. Dust suspended in the

[1] Comparable figures for 1947 are not available.
[2] N.U.M. (Durham Area), *Annual Report*, 1947, pp. 63–4.
[3] See above, p. 466.
[4] See Chapter IX, p. 376.

air increased the risk of fire and explosion and was largely responsible for the lung disease pneumoconiosis.[1] Divisional Dust Suppression Committees under the chairmanship of the local Inspector of Mines co-operated with the Coal Board in developing dust sampling techniques at pits in order to determine where suppression was most urgently needed. Spraying of roadways, wet cutting and water-infusion methods at the coal face were employed to reduce the potential risk of death, injury or disablement. The Scientific Research Department of the Northern Divisional Coal Board carried out a series of tests on wet cutting at Boldon and Silksworth collieries during 1949,[2] though the speed with which such measures were developed increased rapidly after 1951 following Durham's worst explosion disaster since 1909.

Eighty-one men were killed by an explosion in the Five Quarter seam in the 'Duckbill district' of Easington Colliery at 4.35 a.m. on 29 May 1951. Two rescue men were subsequently killed, bringing the total number of fatalities from this explosion to above that for the whole of the Durham coalfield during the period 1911–47. The timing of the explosion accentuated the tragedy since there were two shifts of men in the district when the disaster occurred, 38 belonging to a repair shift which was due to end at 5.37 a.m. The initial cause of the disaster was an ignition of firedamp due to sparks caused by coal-cutter picks striking pyrites. This in turn initiated an explosion of coal dust which swept through 16,000 yards of roadway killing all but one man almost instantly.[3]

The accumulation of firedamp in a seam in which gas was not normally regarded as a serious hazard resulted from inadequate precautions having been taken to ensure complete roof caving when adopting longwall retreating methods,[4] thus allowing cavities to form. At the same time, defects in the system of dust sampling and dust suppression and the adoption only days before the disaster of a ventilation system which effectively reduced the amount of inflow along the longwall face combined to magnify the dangers resulting from the initial explosion.[5]

Following the disaster the National Coal Board promptly initiated

[1] See below, p. 480.
[2] N.U.M. (Durham Area), *Annual Report*, 1949, pp. 165–6.
[3] *Ministry of Fuel and Power, Report and the Causes of and Circumstances Attending the Explosion which occurred at Easington Colliery, County Durham, on the 29th May 1951, by H. C. W. Roberts*, 1952 (Cmd. 8646).
[4] The longwall system of mining involved the progressive extraction of a rectangular block or panel of a coal seam. In retreating the face was opened up at the far end of the panel and was retreated backward.
[5] Cmd. 8646, *op. cit.*, pp. 24–38.

a special study into the causes of sparking and into methods of preventing dust formation.[1] A special committee reported in 1956 that so far as individual accidents were concerned the use of roadway conveyors such as at Easington, which were thought to intensify the danger from dust, were at least as safe as other transport systems, except locomotive haulage, although dust deposition in roadways would almost always occur.[2]

The Easington disaster prompted action of a more practical type. The N.C.B. decided in 1953 to install stone-dust barriers at strategic points in gate-conveyor roadways as an additional means of defence against the dangers resulting from dust accumulation. These barriers consisted of shelves containing stone dust which could be arranged to fall automatically in the event of an explosion and, by providing a barrier of incombustible material against the passage of flame, could help prevent an explosion.[3] The Easington Rural District Council joined representatives of the *Newcastle Journal* in establishing a Relief Fund for the care of bereaved dependants which, when it closed in August 1951, totalled more than £184,000.[4] Three dependant families also enjoyed a holiday in Yugoslavia in 1952 as the guests of the Yugoslavian Trade Union Confederation.[5]

The presence of coal dust on mechanized roadways had earlier swept the flames of a firedamp explosion throughout the Fourth North District of Louisa Colliery on 22 August 1947, killing nineteen workmen. The disaster was even more disquieting since the inflammable mixture was initially lit by a workman striking a match in order to light a cigarette. In his report to the Minister of Fuel and Power, R. Yates, Deputy Chief Inspector of Mines, noted that:

'Some members of the night shift were in the habit of smoking at their place of work. . . . It is difficult to avoid drawing the conclusion that there was connivance in this matter of smoking between deputies and the workmen.'[6]

Having emphasized the need to treat coal dust on conveyor roadways Yates called for a compulsory search for contraband to be made

[1] National Coal Board, *Annual Report and Statement of Accounts for the Year Ended 31 December 1952*, p. 27.
[2] *Ibid.,* . . . *for the Year Ended 31 December 1956*, pp. 21–2.
[3] *Ibid.,* . . . *for the Year Ended 31 December 1953*, pp. 21–2.
[4] Relief was also afforded from their Fund to dependants of men killed in the Eppleton disaster on 6 July 1951. See opposite page.
[5] N.U.M. (Durham Area), *Annual Report*, 1951, p. 270.
[6] *Ministry of Fuel and Power, Report on the Causes of, and Circumstances attending the Explosion which occurred at Louisa (including Morrison Old) Colliery Durham, on the 22nd August 1947 by R. Yates*, 1948 (Cmd. 7347), p. 17.

at all times in which safety lamps were in use.[1] The Coal Mines (Lighting and Contraband) Regulations 1949 provided for stricter searches to be made on all workmen even during the course of a shift.

Only excellent stone dusting at Eppleton Colliery prevented the firedamp explosion which occurred there on 6 July 1951 from spreading throughout the pit. A damaged power plug adaptor on a loading machine ignited gas in the Busty seam killing seven men and inflicting injuries upon two others who subsequently died. The disaster, following so shortly after that at Easington, prompted Watson to remind union members:

'There is one thing which is very difficult to describe properly in words and statistics when disasters such as these take place—that is the great personal and communal dignity which wraps itself around the womenfolk in the immediate agony of their trouble. . . . Our people may occasionally act wrongly and speak wrongly, but on major issues they think aright, and it is this deep instinct for right thinking and right conduct which in such tragic circumstances brings out the best in even the most unassuming men and women.'[2]

The research work which was so vigorously conducted at both national and Divisional level during the fifties to improve methods of water treatment, airborne dust surveying and dust suppression assumed even greater importance after the passing of the Mines and Quarries Act in 1954. This Act, which became operative from 1 January 1957, sought to improve safety regulations relating to shafts, roadways, transport and haulage systems, ventilation and lighting and made the prevention and suppression of dust obligatory at all collieries.

The basic unpleasantness of coal-mining as an occupation was intensified, not only by the constant danger to life, but also by the ease with which disease could inflict permanent disability and threaten future employment prospects. By the time of nationalization long-standing diseases such as nystagmus were still prevalent but increasingly coming under strict control. The imposition of the Coal Mines (Lighting) General Regulations in 1947 improved lighting standards in both fixed and portable apparatus whilst the Coal Board's experiments with fluorescent lighting promised to reduce further the risk to miners' eyesight.

The Nuffield Department of Industrial Health at King's College, Newcastle upon Tyne, began an investigation in 1947 of a sample of

[1] *Ibid.*, p. 19.
[2] N.U.M. (Durham Area), *Annual Report*, 1951, p. 16.

nystagmus sufferers in Durham and presented its report two years later. The results of the survey confirmed how difficult it still was for miners with this affliction to make a permanent return to work at the coal face and discredited the latest suggestion that nystagmus was essentially psychological in origin rather than due to lack of good light.[1] By 1953 the number of nystagmus cases certified in Durham had fallen to 20 compared with 215 in 1938 and 324 in 1943.[2]

The battle against pneumoconiosis, a lung impairment caused by coal dust particles surrounding the cell tissues of the lung and depriving them of air, was fought with particular vengeance during the fifties and became central to the Coal Board's Medical research activities. Miners' lung diseases had been recognized for over a century but specific research into their causes and means of prevention as well as the provision of compensation for sufferers had long remained sporadic and neglected. Increased mechanization of mining had accentuated problems of dust in mines and aggravated the danger to health and, as has been shown, to life itself.

During the fifties the Industrial Health Survey Team at King's College, Newcastle, co-operated with the Durham Regional Hospital Board in mass radiography work at pits in an attempt to determine the prevalence of pneumoconiosis disease in the coalfield. The number of new cases of the disease diagnosed per 1,000 workers employed underground in Durham rose from 4·4 in 1951 to 5·3 in 1956 compared with a rise from 5·6 to 8·8 per 1,000 workers in the country as a whole. This apparent worsening of the situation was less real than the statistics imply, however, since because of the operation of the Pneumoconiosis and Byssinosis Benefit Scheme (1951) and the inauguration of the N.C.B.'s Pneumoconiosis Field Research Project in 1952 a larger proportion of cases were being examined by the mid-fifties than had been possible years earlier.

If disease and injury were to be a commonplace of mining life it was essential that adequate medical services could be made available when most needed and that provision for rehabilitation should be organized on a large scale. Before the end of the Second World War the Durham miners had made their own provision for medical services and had encouraged the development of convalescent homes.[3] The scheme to provide colliery medical treatment centres, begun by the Ministry of Fuel and Power in 1945, was further developed by the Coal Board after 1947. The first of five such prototype centres to be

[1] R. C. Browne, I. F. Beck, E. G. Saint and R. I. McCallum, *A Study of Coal Miners' Nystagmus in Durham County*, Durham 1949.
[2] N.U.M. (Durham Area), *Annual Report*, 1953, p. 444.
[3] See Chapter VI, pp. 311–12; Chapter IX, p. 375.

completed by the Miners' Welfare Commission was opened in
Durham at New Herrington Colliery on 22 November 1947. A second
centre was opened later in the month at Vane Tempest Colliery.[1]

In 1950 the Durham Division pioneered a scheme to improve the
existing arragements for emergency medical services by appointing
a panel of doctors at each colliery whose duty it would be to meet
urgent calls for assistance in cases of accidents and sudden illness.[2]
During the same year the Government appointed the Dale Committee
to examine the relationship of industrial medical services to the
National Health Service. Its report, published in 1951, approved of
the provision of medical services by employers[3] and allowed the Coal
Board to recommence the building of treatment centres and the
recruitment of staff both of which had been temporarily suspended
whilst the investigation took place.

Rehabilitation facilities for Durham miners continued to be provided at the Hermitage centre at Chester-le-Street. With the introduction of the National Health Service and the acceptance of rehabilitation as a State responsibility negotiations began with the
Minister of Health to effect a voluntary transfer of such centres to
the N.H.S. on conditions which would preserve for miners the special
benefits obtained through their existing rehabilitation service.[4] Thus
the centre at Chester-le-Street was subsequently taken over by the
Ministry of Health on 1 April 1951. The Durham miners' convalescent home at Conishead Priory continued to function having admitted over 31,000 patients during the period from its opening in 1930
until 1947.

In July 1946 the miners' Association had accepted Lord Londonderry's offer of Dene House at Seaham for use as a rheumatic clinic.[5]
The clinic opened in June 1951, two-thirds of the capital cost having
been met by the Miners' Welfare Commission and one-third by the
Durham Area of the N.U.M. Lord Londonderry himself reduced the
total commitment by contributing £1,000 towards meeting capital
costs.[6]

It was imperative that miners were adequately trained to make
effective use of improved safety techniques and thus reduce the call

[1] N.U.M. (Durham Area), *Annual Report*, 1947, p. 76.
[2] *Ibid.*, 1950, p. 240.
[3] *Report of a Committee of Enquiry on Industrial Health Services*, 1950–51
(Cmd. 8170).
[4] *Miners' Welfare 1951–1952, Fourth Report of the National Miners' Welfare
Joint Council*, pp. 11–12.
[5] D.M.A., 27 July 1946.
[6] N.U.M. (Durham Area), *Annual Report*, 1947, p. 109.

made upon medical and rehabilitation services and that a sufficient number of juveniles were induced to enter the industry in order to gradually correct the unsatisfactory age structure of the labour force. In response to those needs and to its obligations under the Coal Mines (Training) General Regulations Order, 1945, the Coal Board in 1847 established Training Departments in each Division responsible for directing the work of Education and Training Officers in the seaparate Areas.[1]

To ease the problems of accommodation for boys from non-mining areas who were keen to enter the industry the Board established the country's first two Juvenile Residential Training Centres in Durham (at Easington and New Kyo) early in 1947. Courses lasted for 13 weeks with free board and lodging and were organized under the joint aegis of the Board and of the local education authority.[2] The coalfield was also served by seven non-residential centres which provided similar training instruction. The two residential centres were closed in 1950 and replaced by a Residential Training College at Dame Margaret Home, Washington at which further education tuition was provided for boys in addition to basic pitcraft training. In 1956, 2,354 juveniles were trained at residential and non-residential centres throughout the Division and over 1,000 adults also completed a programme of preliminary training.[3]

VIII

The miners had long recognized that activity on behalf of the widowed, injured or disabled, however well intentioned it might be, was incomplete without provision for financial assistance. Like all other workers pitmen benefited from the changes in the scope, amount and application of welfare and insurance provisions made during the post-war period but were also fortunate in being able to share in additional allowances provided for them within their industry.

The National Insurance (Industrial Injuries) Act, effective from 5 July 1948, superseded the existing Workmen's Compensation Acts. In coal mining the new benefits thus provided could be augmented by contributing to the National Insurance (Industrial Injuries) Colliery Workers' Supplementary Scheme, organized by the Coal Board under the terms of the new legislation. For every

[1] *Report of H.M. Inspector of Mines (Northern Division)*, 1947, pp. 34–5.
[2] *Ibid.*, p. 35.
[3] N.U.M. (Durham Area), *Annual Report*, 1956, p. 398.

week in which a colliery worker was liable to pay a contribution under the National Insurance Acts provision was made for a separate deduction of 4d (less for those under 18) to be made from his wage as his contribution to the Supplementary Scheme. The remainder of the money necessary to provide extra payments to men already in receipt of industrial injury benefit, an industrial disablement pension or death benefit was met by the N.C.B. from a charge of 4d per ton on all saleable output of deep-mined coal. A separate non-contributory scheme was developed for those miners injured or suffering disease on or before 4 July 1948 and therefore already in receipt of benefits according to the old Compensation Laws, and for those receiving benefit under the Pneumoconiosis Benefit Scheme, 1943. Such supplementary payments were financed out of the N.C.B.'s contribution to the Industrial Injuries Act scheme.

On 1 February 1952 Gaitskell, Minister of Fuel and Power, approved an agreement made in 1950 between the Coal Board and the N.U.M. to provide assistance to dependants of men killed through accidents on colliery premises or who died from natural causes on colliery premises. The scheme was intended to substitute 'a more practical mark of sympathy' for the custom of all miners ceasing work at a colliery where a fatal accident occurred, thereby reducing coal output. Both the Board and the N.U.M. contributed £25,000 to the Fatal Accident Fund, the Union's share being financed by workmen at collieries where the scheme was made applicable contributing 1d per week. Widows were to receive benefit of £150 and £25 for each eligible child up to a maximum of £250.[1] If the deceased left no widow but one or more eligible children £50 per child was to be paid to the person made responsible for their care. If there was no widow or eligible children persons wholly or mainly dependant upon the deceased miner could claim a sum not exceeding £150 to be divided amongst such dependants so that no one person received more than £100. Since the joint Fatal Accident Scheme applied neither to industrial diseases nor to cases of mineworkers dying as a result of an accident occurring before the operative date of the new agreement the N.U.M. formulated a separate scheme to cover such cases, the funds for which were to be provided entirely from workmen's contributions.

The Northumberland and Durham Miners' Permanent Relief Fund, established in 1862 following the Hartley pit disaster, had since then provided death benefits to the widows and dependants of those

[1] The limitation for this particular class of claimant was removed in 1952. In the same year, and again in 1956, the application of benefit payments was extended to cover other classes of labour.

miners contributing to the Fund. The inauguration of the new joint
N.U.M./N.C.B. accident scheme prompted the Durham Area Union
to appeal for continuing support for the Fund if only to provide
bereaved families with additional means of assistance and to warn
miners against mortgaging their families' future welfare for the sake
of saving contributions.

Very few Durham Lodges accepted the Fatal Accident Scheme
outright. Disagreements between management and men as to who
would be permitted to leave or be prevented from entering a pit in
the event of a fatal accident were rife. By 1955 six collieries still
refused to implement the accident scheme though 124 others had
done so, the total benefit payable during the year, covering 66 claims,
amounting to £10,625.[1]

The financial strain imposed upon families by the death, injury or
disablement of the bread-winner could rightly lay claim to compensation but a quite separate claim arising from redundancy achieved
growing importance during the fifties. The prospects of a sudden end
to regular employment for most miners caught up in reorganization
and reconstruction schemes within the coalfield grew more real as the
Coal Board's rationalization plans were implemented. On 22 December 1948 the N.C.B. and N.U.M. agreed to provide compensation in
addition to the benefits normally available under the National
Insurance Act for workers declared redundant 'as a consequence of
the implementation of reorganization and reconstruction projects'.
Surface and underground miners, providing they had served not less
than three years in the industry, became eligible for weekly rates of
compensation of £1 13s 8d and £2 3s 8d respectively for a maximum
period of 26 weeks. The existing procedure operated by the Durham
Divisional Coal Board to terminate the employment of workmen 65
years of age and over and to pay 12 weeks' guaranteed wage came to
an end. Workmen who received notice over the age of 65 years in
the ordinary way or who were declared redundant because of the
introduction of new methods of transport and machinery or by
virtue of a non-scheduled reorganization scheme were not entitled to
redundancy payment under the national agreement.

The possibilities of increased redundancy in Durham where many
old, uneconomic pits were past redemption by reconstruction made
these restrictive provisions appear especially pernicious. Of the
9,469 workmen involved in the 272 scheduled and non-scheduled
schemes of closure and reorganization of collieries in the Durham
Division between 1 January 1947 and 31 October 1955, 4,564 became

[1] N.U.M. (Durham Area), *Annual Report*, 1955, p. 212.

redundant of whom only 2,741 received benefits under the new national redundancy agreement.[1]

The formula for determining the amount of compensation payable to a redundant workman was altered in 1954. Thereafter they were to be paid the equivalent of two-thirds of the appropriate national weekly minimum wage for their class of occupation less the standard weekly rate of unemployment benefit, i.e. the amount a man would be entitled to if he had no wife or other dependants. The effect of this revision was to raise the rate of benefit payable to underground workers from £2 3s. 8d to £3 10s 10d and to surface workers from £1 13s 8d to £2 17s 6d. The maximum period of benefit remained unaltered until 1959 when it was increased from 26 to 41 weeks. Attempts by the N.U.M. to have the scheme applied to workmen declared redundant as a result of non-scheduled reconstruction projects were resisted by the Board, although an undertaking was given to apply a more liberal interpretation of the term 'scheduled project' in future deliberations.[2]

One of the important preoccupations of the former Mineworkers' Federation of Great Britain had been to ensure complete financial security for members in their old age as a reward for long service in the industry and the assurance that, in the event of their death, their dependants would be provided for. A demand for pensions for miners over 55 years of age had been included in the terms of the *Miners' Charter*. In the days of private ownership it had been customary to provide varying superannuation benefits for some of the clerical and administrative grades but these were, in the main, surface workers. In the early years of nationalization a cover scheme was introduced for these grades, but still the main body of the workmen in the industry remained without pension rights.

In 1951 an agreement was reached with the Coal Board to provide pensions to workmen on retirement at or after 65, to those obliged to retire before 65 because of ill health and to widows and dependant children. In return for weekly contributions deducted from wages mine workers could build up 'credits' to qualify them for benefits determined in relation to the length of service in the industry and the regularity of attendance at work. Payments ranged from 10s per week after 16 years' service to 30s per week after 45 years' service, paid in addition to the ordinary State pension. The Coal Board

[1] N.U.M. (Durham Area), 21 January 1956.
[2] N.U.M. (Durham Area), *Annual Report*, 1954, pp. 292–8. Earlier a resolution submitted by the Durham Area Union to the 1954 N.U.M. Annual Conference calling for redundancy of any kind to qualify for payment under the Agreement had been supported by the majority of delegates.

agreed to pay into the scheme 2s for each 1s 6d and 1s 8d for each 1s 3d weekly contribution made by workmen in addition to an initial payment of £2 million, granted in lieu of its refusal to accede additional paid holidays during 1951. For miners who had passed their 47th birthday at the inception of the scheme 'back service credits' were made freely available ranging from 58 units for one year's past service to 1,248 units for 16 years' service, the minimum number required to qualify for a weekly pension of 10s. Workmen were expected to 'contract-in' to the scheme, the first deductions from pay occurring during the first working week in January 1952.

Despite the fact that the majority vote recorded by members of the Durham County Mining Federation Board in favour of accepting the pensions agreement was the largest cast for any settlement during the previous 15 years, the miners themselves were slow to support the venture. By the beginning of December 1951 only 48 per cent of the Durham Area Union's membership had signed 'contracting-in' forms but twelve months later the scheme had 82,400 members, 83 per cent of all eligible persons employed by the Board in the Durham Division.[1] Nevertheless local union officials in the Division were concerned at the number of men unwilling to become members of the scheme and moved a resolution at the N.U.M.'s Annual Conference in 1952 calling for legislation to make such membership compulsory for all eligible mineworkers.[2] Though specific changes were made in the details of the pension scheme during the fifties, it was not until 1959 that membership was made compulsory for all new entrants to the industry. By April 1954, 81,000 of the 97,293 miners eligible for benefits in the Durham Division had agreed to make their individual contributions.[3]

IX

The financial allowances available to miners were not confined solely to payments in compensation for contingencies over which they had little or no control. In June 1952 the N.C.B., in an attempt to attract workmen to Areas deficient in manpower, introduced a scheme of payments to miners willing to undertake employment in other coalfields, which in Durham related mainly to the transfer of men to

[1] *Coal Industry 1952–53. Reports and Accounts, Mineworkers' Pension, Industrial Injuries Supplementary Benefits and Special Fatal Accident Schemes*, pp. 8–9.
[2] N.U.M., 10 July 1952.
[3] National Union of Mineworkers, *Report of the National Executive Committee*, May 1954, p. 297.

work in the West Midlands Division. A lodging allowance of 4s per day was payable to employees with dependants; a 'settling-in' grant of 24s 6d was to be paid on a man's arrival at his new place of work and provision was made for contributions to be made towards the cost of travel and household removal expenses. The arrangements, which were modified slightly in subsequent years, did not apply to new entrants to the industry who were entitled to similar allowances from the Ministry of Labour.

Altogether 230 miners were transferred from Durham to the West Midlands Division during 1952 of whom 119 finally settled.[1] Some miners soon returned because they were dissatisfied with either the lodging or colliery conditions. The Labour Director of the Durham Divisional Coal Board, in conjunction with representatives of the Labour Department of the West Midlands Division, arranged a deputation, consisting of a welfare officer of the Board and representatives of the Durham Area Union, to visit the West Midlands in order to investigate fully the miners' complaints. The deputation found that all the Durham miners they interviewed were satisfied with their work and that the majority of returning miners were men who had left the industry and were being recruited from the Durham Ministry of Labour Exchanges. It was recommended that future transfers should be arranged to provide a steady flow of migrant labour, and thus ease the pressure on housing, and that all workmen should be interviewed and made aware of the working conditions and customs prevailing in the West Midlands Division.[2]

Although Union officials in Durham were anxious to assist the transfer of miners declared redundant because of pit reorganization they refused to encourage indiscriminate emigration. Individual miners could not be prevented, of course, from working elsewhere if they so wished but the Area Union's Executive informed the Divisional Coal Board in January 1954 that:

'We cannot agree to any scheme of transference that will worsen the economic and productive efficiency of Durham. To provide manpower at the expense of our own coalfield is poor economics, for Durham coal is one of the most important high quality grades in the country and we cannot afford to lose the skills essential to the working of seams 18 to 20 inches thick. Once these skills die out it will be impossible to win coal in these seams.'[3]

[1] *Ibid.*, 1952, p. 213.
[2] *Ibid.*, pp. 214–19.
[3] N.U.M. (Durham Area), 18 January 1954.

Even when transfers received official Union blessing there were obstacles. The complaints of disgruntled miners who returned to Durham after only a short period of emigration received fairly extensive local press coverage. Some local authorities which had sunk capital into social amenities in colliery villages feared the results of widespread migration. Redundant miners in receipt of guaranteed compensation payments in excess of the amount of normal social security benefit were hesitant to move if there appeared to be some prospect of work in light industry, possibly as a result of the working of the Distribution of Industry Act. Durham migrants also forfeited concessionary coal and free house or rent allowances and often had to work in drier and warmer conditions than they were accustomed to, perhaps a surprising complaint to anyone other than those whose normal working habits were radically transformed.

The meagre prospects of improved employment opportunities in West Durham were sufficient to convince people that their best interests lay elsewhere. In the two years after 1954 nearly 4,000 miners left the area for work in other coalfields.[1] Contrary to some expectations social conditions in West Durham improved as a result of this migration since pressure on schools and hospitals was reduced and houses became more readily available.[2]

The decision of the Coal Board in 1954 to help to man the labour deficient areas of the West Midlands and South Yorkshire coalfields by advertising vacancies on a national scale angered the Durham Area Union. Though it supported the gesture in principle it was opposed, for reasons already made known to Divisional Board officials, to the pressure being applied upon the Area not to discourage labour transfers unless 'it would be impossible to continue the operation of a colliery, or there would be a serious threat to labour relations'.[3] Equally important in Durham's view was the potential threat of labour migration to the balance of manpower and stability of employment in the supplying coalfield. In February, 1954, in a letter to Skinner, Chairman of the Divisional Coal Board, Watson emphasized how important it was that decisions regarding labour transfer should continue to be based on the widest of considerations, warning:

'We cannot be expected to encourage men to go to the Midlands if investigation shows that by doing so we shall be faced with unbalanced manpower at our pits. . . . None had the right to determine

[1] C. S. Smith, 'Planned Transfer of Labour: with special Reference to the Coal Industry', Ph.D. thesis, University of London 1961, p. 73.
[2] *Ibid.*, pp. 86–8.
[3] N.U.M., 16 February 1954.

what is National interest and then by implication accuse those who have different opinions and ideas on the complex question of transfer that such opinions and ideas are "contrary to the National interest". Surely the well-being of Durham is as much in the National interest as the well-being of any other Area. If it is not then the sooner we know the better.'[1]

By the beginning of October 1954, 272 Durham miners had been transferred to the West Midlands Division and 288 to the North Eastern Division.[2] Since the number of houses available plus those which were expected to become available in these two regions would in the future be allocated to applicants from all receiving Divisions the Coal Board's Labour Director in Durham, hoping to allay fears such as those expressed by Watson, reported that as a consequence 'the offers of employment to Durham miners will not be excessive' and that 'no undue alarm need be felt in regard to the effect in Durham.'[3]

X

It was to be expected that the Durham miners' long-standing political commitment to the Labour Party would be even more firmly entrenched whilst the Party enjoyed power with a firm Parliamentary majority. The support given to the coal production drives of the post-war years, for example, rested in part upon a desire not to embarrass the Government in its handling of the fuel situation and thereby allow the critics of nationalization an opportunity to make political capital of the situation. The Durham miners were left in no doubt of how significant their local officials regarded the 1945 Labour victory. Watson wrote to members on Vesting Day:

'Opinions differ as to which is the most profound event of the last few years. Some claim it was in the field of medicine—the discovery of Penicillin. Others say it was the discovery of Radar, Jet propulsion, Gas turbines and Atomic Energy.
    We doubt very much whether the Atomic Bomb was as important as the ideological bomb which went off without fuss or noise on July 5th 1945, and placed in power for the first time in the history of our country a Labour Government. To us it represents the most

---

[1] *Ibid.*
[2] Between 1947 and 1955 at least 10,000 Durham miners were successfully transferred within and without the County in schemes of reconstruction and reorganization, or because of the closure of seams or pits.
[3] *Ibid.*, 25 October 1954.

profound change of all, A Labour Government in office and power.... A Labour Government which is trying... to bring under public control all essential services and wealth of the Nation, while at the same time rejecting the theory of dictatorship and safeguarding the essential freedoms of the individual.'[1]

At 21 years of age Watson had been elected in 1919 as Secretary of the Boldon Branch of the Labour Party, was appointed to the National Labour Party Executive in 1944 and subsequently became Chairman of the Party during 1949–50 and of its International Sub-Committee in 1953. He held the latter post for ten years.

When the economic and financial problems which the country had faced since the beginning of the 1945 Parliament led in 1949 to cuts in dollar imports, the devaluation of the £ and reductions in current spending and capital investment many observers felt that the Government would soon be forced to call a general election. The House of Commons debates increasingly developed into electioneering during the autumn of 1949 and by the middle of January 1950 the Prime Minister had decided to seek a dissolution. Polling date was fixed for 23 February.

During the 1945–50 Parliament a sweeping redistribution of Parliamentary constituencies had taken place and it was on this new electoral basis that the 1950 election was fought. Constituency boundaries were drastically revised and substantial transfers of voters effected from one electoral area to another. In the whole of the U.K. only 80 constituencies remained unchanged and the number of seats in the House of Commons was reduced from 640 to 625. The effect of the changes in Durham was both to reshape County and Borough constituencies in such a fashion as to include within their boundaries areas which had previously supported a separate Parliamentary division and also to create new constituencies.

Thus the urban and rural districts of Barnard Castle came to be included in the new Bishop Auckland county constituency, the urban district of Spennymoor in the Durham constituency and the Seaham urban district in the Houghton-le-Spring constituency. The rural districts of Lanchester and Weardale were joined with the urban district of Brandon and Byshottles, Crook and Willington and Tow Law to form the new County constituency of North-West Durham, whilst the rural district of Easington, which included most of the area in the former Seaham division, made up entirely the new Easington constituency.

The approach of the first post-war general election was accompanied

[1] N.U.M. (Durham Area), *Annual Report*, 1946, p. 9.

by repeated appeals by the Durham Area Union for members and their wives and families to ensure overwhelming support for Labour. Lodges not carrying out the Extension of Hours Agreement were urged to do so to 'better our chances of Victory in the Election'.[1] Sixty per cent of the voters in Durham County went to the poll.

The seven candidates sponsored by the miners were all successfully returned. W. Whiteley, who was first elected for Blaydon in 1922 and who was Chief Whip in the Labour Government, defeated an accountant, L. F. Lawson, the Conservative opponent in that division, by 28,343 votes to 12,772. P. Bartley, a former secretary of the Washington miners' Lodge, was elected at Chester-le-Street in preference to the Conservative H. J. Millican, head of a Newcastle firm of glass and paint manufacturers, by 35,348 votes to 10,379. J. E. Glanville, who had represented the Consett division since 1943, retained the seat in a three-cornered fight by defeating P. C. Goodhart, the Conservative candidate and a Cambridge University student, and the Liberal N. Dees, a lecturer, by 34,907 votes to 12,634 and 4,721 votes respectively. C. Grey, Durham's M.P. since 1945, defended the division against Conservative opposition from H. C. Haslett, a retired Lieutenant-Colonel from the Indian Army, defeating him by 36,024 votes to 16,903.

Mrs B. Bolam, who at 29 made local history in 1945 by becoming the youngest member to be elected to the Jarrow Town Council, fought the miners' candidate Blyton for the seat at Houghton-le-Spring but lost by 36,044 votes to 10,682. Murray, first elected M.P. for the former Spennymoor division in 1942, retained the North-West Durham seat for Labour by defeating the Conservative J. Quigley, a South Shields business man, by a majority of 17,554 votes, the voting being 31,084 and 13,530 respectively. At Sedgefield Slater, who succeeded J. R. Leslie as candidate in the area, defeated J. E. Watford, a Conservative and former Army Officer, by 27,946 votes to 16,782. The successes of E. Shinwell in the newly-constituted Easington Division, E. Fernyhough at Jarrow and H. Dalton at Bishop Auckland ensured complete victory for Labour in the Durham County constituencies. All 37 of the Labour candidates sponsored by the N.U.M. were returned by large majorities. The 3 per cent turnover of votes from Labour to Conservative in the country as a whole reduced Labour seats to 315 and increased those of Conservatives and their allies to 298.

Watson, Chairman at the Annual Conference of the Labour Party in 1950, suggested to delegates that the election victory was due to the

[1] N.U.M. (Durham Area), *Annual Report*, 1950, p. 284.

fact that: 'The one thing on our side was the greatest thing of all. It was truth.'[1] Continuing, he claimed:

'The Tories tried every device of misrepresentation, but without result. This time they could not tell the people about the horrible things which would happen if Labour achieved power. They had to try and convince the people that they had suffered in Labour's first five years. This time, however, the people knew the truth, because the truth was reflected in their own improved standards of life.'[2]

The Durham miners' leaders were fully aware of the difficulties which confronted Labour in view of its small Parliamentary majority. Shortly after the final results of the election were made known the Council of the Area Union unanimously passed a resolution expressing its loyal and faithful support of the Government, confessing:

'We recognize that nothing will be left undone by our opponents to secure an early defeat of the Government on ground of their own choosing.
    Nevertheless we are not dismayed. We secured the largest vote ever given to a single political party in the history of British politics, and it is indicative that millions of electors have faith in us and our policy. The Labour Government should proceed to govern and trust the people to support any reasonable measure calculated to improve the national position.'[3]

The survival of the Labour Government for twenty months after its 1950 victory proved longer than most observers expected. To some extent the burdens of governing with such a narrow Parliamentary majority were eased by the absence of a major legislative programme and by the extent to which both sides in this 'electioneering Parliament'[4] were reduced to scoring party points. Nevertheless the very restricted freedom of manœuvre prompted Attlee to call a general election in October 1951 so that the most important consequences of the Korean War and growing inflation could be tackled with greater effectiveness than the Labour Party could then achieve.

The disillusionment within the Labour Party during its uneasy period of office was increased to some extent by the loss of some of its strongest personalities. In October 1950 Sir Stafford Cripps resigned from the Chancellorship of the Exchequer because of ill-health and

[1] Ibid., p. 282.
[2] Ibid.
[3] Ibid., p. 291.
[4] D. E. Butler, The British General Election of 1951, London 1952, p. 16.

was succeeded by Gaitskell; Bevin abandoned his Foreign Secretary-
ship in February 1951 shortly before his death and two months later
Aneurin Bevan resigned from the Government as a result of his disagreement with the terms of the Budget and the scale of the rearmament programme.

The Durham Area Union's Executive Committee deplored Bevan's
resignation as 'an instrument in the hands of our opponents for
causing dissension in the Labour Movement'. In a circular to members the Committee claimed:

> 'The Tory Party is bereft of Policy and Programme; it is a first class
> tragedy that one of the ablest Ministers of the Labour Government
> should provide the Tories with political ammunition to hide their
> own bankruptcy and shoot their way out of a political cul-de-sac, by
> failing to appreciate that majority decisions, however much they
> might be disliked by individuals or minorities, should be accepted
> if the democratic texture of the movement is to be preserved.'[1]

Whether the general election should have taken place when it did
considering Labour's slight Commons majority and whether the
critics of party policy were justified in creating dissension on what
appeared to some as trivial matters soon became academic issues
quickly subordinated to the overriding need to defeat the Tories. In
view of the mounting difficulties facing the Government during 1951
Durham had moved a resolution at the N.U.M. Annual Conference
calling upon the membership to give full support to the Labour
Party 'in any steps it might take to ensure success in the next general
election'.[2] Fearing the consequences of a Tory victory J. Watson,
the Durham delegate, warned:

> 'We have no illusions as to what Tory control could mean if they
> were returned to power. Can anyone here imagine Mr Churchill
> being given full power or control over an industry and continuing
> to produce the same improved conditions for the worker as the
> Coal Board and the local people are bringing about today? Anyone
> with any knowledge of Socialism or trade unionism knows that
> the Tories have acted as the Executive Committee of Capitalism
> for so many years that there is only one word of importance in
> their vocabulary and that is the word "profit".... We cannot
> imagine any Tory control that will accept the responsibility of
> maintaining the conditions which have been achieved by the Coal
> Board.'[3]

[1] N.U.M. (Durham Area), 28 April 1951.
[2] N.U.M., 3 July 1951.
[3] *Ibid.*

Though the outcome of the electoral struggle resulted in an overall defeat for Labour only one constituency in Durham, at Darlington, fell to the Tories.[1] The size of some of the majorities recorded for Labour candidates in the County testified to the inbred opposition to Conservatism. At Blaydon the miners' candidate Whiteley, Parliamentary Secretary to the Treasury since 1945, defeated C. Satchwell, a solicitor and member of Morpeth Borough Council, by 28,337 votes to 13,223. Bartley retained the miners' seat at Chester-le-Street again defeating H. J. Millican by a majority of 24,879 votes. Glanville held his seat at Consett defeating G. Walker, a company director, by 19,844 votes, a lower majority than in 1950, the voting being 35,705 to 15,861.

C. Grey, the miners' candidate at Durham, increased his existing majority by defeating R. Fisher, a member of the executive committee of the Gateshead Conservative Association, by 35,597 votes to 17,447. Blyton again faced opposition from Mrs B. Bolam at Houghton-le-Spring but retained his seat by 37,718 votes to 12,042. A repetition of the electoral battle which had taken place in the North-West Durham constituency in 1950 resulted in another victory for Murray, the miners' candidate, when he defeated the Conservative J. Quigley by 30,417 votes to 13,885. At Sedgefield, the only other constituency contested by a miners' M.P., the existing member Slater faced new Conservative opposition from E. H. Harrison, a works manager and company secretary, but defeated him by 28,129 votes to 17,095.

The largest Labour majority recorded in the County was at Easington where E. Shinwell defeated the Conservative G. W. Rossiter by 37,899 votes to 9,025. H. Dalton, appointed Minister of Local Government and Planning in January 1951, retained the Bishop Auckland constituency for Labour and G. Fernyhough was again successfully returned at Jarrow by a majority of 16,746 votes against his former Conservative opponent J. Cox. Four of the five Borough constituencies within the coalfield, none of which supported a miners' candidate, retained Labour M.P.s.

Even though the Labour Party did relatively well in Durham its defeat nationally at once spurred the miners' Area Union to support a vigorous campaign for ultimate electoral revenge. Addressing members in his *Annual Report* for 1951 Watson wrote:

'We lost a good Government. We have to organize and work to get it back. There are, it is true, minor differences in policy . . . among

[1] For an account of electioneering tactics in one Durham mining constituency during 1951 see Butler, *op. cit.*, pp. 149–60.

party members, but there is nothing that cannot be overcome within the democratic processes of the Party. . . . therefore let us work and organize to make the Party ready for victory whenever the next election comes. Jackets off, shirt sleeves up, putting our policy before the electors with understanding and knowledge, encouraging youth to join the movement and pledging ourselves to WIN FOR LABOUR, AND TO DEFEAT THE TORIES.'[1]

Soon after the new Parliament was assembled in November 1951 it became plain that the Government had no intention of making an early appeal to the country. In October 1953 Churchill announced that he had no election plans for that year or, as far as he could see, in the next. By the end of 1954 there was a growing expectation that an election would be called in the autumn of 1955.

During the intervening period the Durham Area Union took steps to ensure that miners' candidates would be fully represented at the next general election. In 1955 both J. Glanville, M.P. for Consett and J. D. Murray, M.P. for North West Durham, decided to retire from politics. The Durham Area immediately organized a Lodge vote to select the candidate who would represent the miners at each local election committee of the Constituency Party. The Area Union's solicitor, I. E. Geffen,[2] allowed himself to be nominated for both vacancies whilst already a prospective Parliamentary candidate for the Newcastle North Division and without the consent of the Union's Executive Committee. Since Geffen had never been a miner nor a miners' representative within the Area Union for at least five years he could not be considered by Rule for the miners' nomination. His presumptuousness in offering himself as an opponent to the work-men's candidate angered local officials. In the event he failed to secure either nomination, being defeated at Consett by W. Stones, a mines inspector and Secretary of Stanley Labour Party, by 5,024 votes to 3,875 and in the North-West Durham division by J. W. Ainsley, a miner and Chairman of the Durham County Council, by 5,201 votes to 2,337.[3]

In just over a week after Churchill resigned his premiership Eden, his successor, decided to call an election on 26 May 1955 to seek the vote of confidence he felt his administration required. The Executive Committee of the Durham Area Union responded almost immediately by appealing for volunteers for 'doorstep' canvassing to ensure the success of every Labour candidate in the County. 'We in Durham

---

[1] N.U.M. (Durham Area), *Annual Report*, 1951, p. 19.
[2] Geffen had been appointed to the Area Union in 1947 to succeed F. Morris.
[3] N.U.M. (Durham Area), 23 November 1953.

have never deviated from our support and loyalty to the Labour Party,' the Committee reminded workmen. 'In the last three General Elections our voting has varied by less than one half per cent. This is the Labour stronghold of the Country and the movement as a whole recognizes our strength.'[1]

The essential truth contained in this statement was amply demonstrated when Labour candidates were returned in straight fights in every Durham County constituency. Whiteley retained his seat at Blaydon against new Conservative opposition from J. M. Reay-Smith, a solicitor and former member of Bishop Auckland U.D.C., the voting being 25,273 to 12,750. At Chester-le-Street Bartley defeated the Conservative D. A. Wright, a wholesale merchant, by 32,323 votes to 10,047, a majority of 22,276. C. P. MacCarthey, a manufacturing director and Conservative candidate at Durham, failed to win the seat from the miners' candidate Grey, who defeated him by 32,412 votes to 16,640. Blyton, who had represented the Houghton-le-Spring Division since 1945, retained the seat against his Conservative opponent J. E. Egerton, a Berkshire farmer, by 33,375 votes to 10,476. Slater defeated D. Appleby, Vice-Chairman of the Northern Area Conservative Party, at Sedgefield by 27,221 votes to 18,368.

In the Consett and North-West Durham divisions where the Labour candidature had altered since the 1951 election the two miners' representatives succeeded in securing substantial majorities against Conservative opposition. Ainsley defeated T. Hibble, a methods engineer, in the North-West Durham division by 27,116 votes to 13,110 and Stones polled 30,979 votes at Consett against W. F. Montgomery, a schoolteacher and member of the Hebburn Urban District Council. In the two County divisions which did not have miners' sponsored candidates, at Easington and Bishop Auckland, the existing Labour M.P.s were returned but with reduced majorities.

In the Borough constituencies the Conservatives retained the seat at Darlington which they won from Labour in 1951, whilst Labour candidates in three other divisions succeeded in preventing any further Tory gains. At Sunderland (South), where the only by-election in the 1951–5 Parliament had resulted in a Conservative victory over the existing Labour Member in 1953, the Tory candidate succeeded in retaining his seat, though in Sunderland (North) Labour was again returned by a majority of 2,836 votes.

After three and a half years of government the Conservatives

---

[1] N.U.M. (Durham Area), 21 April 1955.

became the first political party in office for nearly a century to be returned to power with a substantial increase in its majority, in this case from 17 to 60. This fact alone would have been sufficient to persuade the Durham Area to work steadfastly in support of Labour's future victory. That this determination was much stronger when the country next went to the polls in 1959 was due in large measure to the growing fears of redundancy and contraction within the coal industry in what by then had become an age of fuel competition.

Appendix I

MEMBERSHIP AND FUNDS 1947–1956

Year	Membership	Total investments £	Investments per head £	Investments per head at constant prices £ (at 1947 prices)
1947	114,667	498,353	4·35	4·35
1948	115,532	534,260	4·62	4·27
1949	114,410	561,623	4·91	4·42
1950	113,181	589,365	5·21	4·57
1951	112,449	616,045	5·48	4·38
1952	112,982	651,564	5·71	4·19
1953	111,885	688,641	6·15	4·39
1954	111,377	733,098	6·58	4·60
1955	111,364	777,442	6·98	4·68
1956	111,184	821,335	7·39	4·83

Source: N.U.M. (Durham Area), *Financial Returns*, 1947–1956. Ministry of Labour, Index of Retail Prices. The values of investments per head in real terms are not strictly comparable with those found on p. 96.

Appendix II

N.U.M. (DURHAM AREA) POLITICAL FUND
1947–1956

Year	Total £	Expenditure £	Balance £
1947	55,633	13,234	42,399
1948	57,371	15,486	41,885
1949	56,248	21,385	34,863
1950	48,618	16,005	32,613
1951	46,191	13,946	32,245
1952	47,081	12,227	34,854
1953	58,669	12,920	45,749
1954	69,648	13,025	56,623
1955	80,892	14,620	66,272
1956	91,135	13,542	77,593

Source: N.U.M. (Durham Area), *Financial Returns*, 1947–1956.

Epilogue

I

Much of the activity of the Durham Area Union during the first decade of nationalization centred upon the need to increase coal output as the necessary prerequisite to gaining improved living standards for miners. The sudden transformation in marketing conditions within the industry after 1957 ensured that in the following decade the Area Union adopted a distinctly different role. A fall of over 5½m. tons in the total inland consumption of coal during 1956-7 marked the beginning of an era of fuel surplus and a growth in the competition between coal and other energy sources, especially oil. Already the contribution made by coal towards meeting the total U.K. energy demand had fallen from 93 per cent in 1946 to 85 per cent in 1956 whilst that of oil had risen in the same period from 7 per cent to 15 per cent.[1]

The Coal Board's expectations that the demand for coal would continue to increase despite a falling share in the energy market were not to be fulfilled. After years of exhortation to its members to discourage any activities which might hinder coal production the Durham Area Union was forced to countenance an accelerated pace of colliery closure and a drastic redeployment of manpower as it became increasingly difficult to dispose of output at home and abroad. Though in 1957 the reversal in the demand for coal was attributed largely to 'exceptional circumstances', notably the higher than average temperatures for that year,[2] it became apparent in the following years that an entirely new situation had emerged. The pressure formerly applied to ensure maximum expansion within the coal industry was replaced by the demand for orderly retrenchment. Fears of an increasingly difficult future for coal were in Watson's mind when he wrote in his *Annual Report* for 1957:

'It is evident that the Coal Industries of Germany, Holland, Belgium and France are beginning to feel the effects of American and Polish competition, and while at the moment ... we are still maintaining our position there is no doubt that the economic sky

[1] C. Robinson, *A Policy for Fuel?*, Institute of Economic Affairs, Occasional Paper No. 31, London 1969, p. 12.
[2] National Coal Board, *Annual Report and Statement of Accounts for the Year Ended 28 December 1957*, p. 28.

is darkening and less and less coal (at least for a period) will be required.'[1]

Early in 1958 it became evident that if output continued at the current level there would be a growing surplus of some grades of coal even if there was no further fall in coal demand. In fact total coal consumption in that year fell by 13m. tons largely as a result of an industrial recession. But more fundamental changes were occurring in the energy field. The internal coal markets which showed the greatest contraction in the decade or so after 1950 both in relative and absolute terms were the industrial and railway markets followed by the gas-making market, all of which were traditionally the most prodigious consumers of coal. Of the markets which showed a contraction in coal consumption between 1950 and 1962 these three groups of consumers were responsible for 71 per cent of the tonnage lost.[2]

Watson felt obliged to dispel any misconception which delegates at the 1958 N.U.M. Annual Conference might have had that the trends in energy consumption were ephemeral, reminding them that:

'This industry of ours has no special dispensation. Whether we like it or not, this nation or any other nation will find fuel at the cost that is economic, whether it be oil, whether it be electricity or whether it be atomic energy. . . . I . . . am under no illusions, nor do I accept that atomic energy will be a slow, imperceptible process. Within 25 years, and that is a very short time, in my opinion atomic energy will be providing nearly one half of the power requirements of this country.'[3]

Marketing conditions worsened during 1958–9. Total inland consumption of coal during 1959 stood at 190,457,000 tons compared with 213,206,000 in 1957. The level of undistributed stocks on the other hand had risen from 8,570,000 tons in December 1957, the highest amount recorded during the century, to 35,637,000 tons by the end of 1959. The Coal Board embarked upon a policy of industrial contraction. Opencast production, one of the Board's most profitable activities, was cut back and the closure of high-cost collieries speeded up. The reduction in coal output proved insufficient to counterbalance the persistent decline in the demand for coal and the level of

[1] N.U.M. (Durham Area), *Annual Report*, 1957, p. 5.
[2] Simpson, *op. cit.*, p. 108.
[3] N.U.M., 10 July 1958. During the preceding year the Ministry of Power had published plans for expanding the country's nuclear power programme. See *Capital Investment in the Coal, Gas and Electricity Industries* (Cmnd. 132), 1957.

undistributed stocks continued to rise. With over 35m. tons in stock at the beginning of 1960 production was again deliberately kept below demand and pits were closed. By 1960 the total number of collieries in production at the beginning of the year in Durham had fallen to 114 from a total of 128 in 1957 and 134 in 1947.

The decline in manpower which this planned contraction in mining activity would entail was not a problem entirely new to an ageing coalfield such as Durham. During the interwar period the industry's labour force in the North-East had fallen by about 30 per cent and there was a further reduction of around 10 per cent between 1939 and 1957.[1] The N.C.B.'s policy of concentrating on low-cost pits in the years following 1957 brought reductions in coal output more closely to bear on old declining fields such as Durham and intensified fears of widespread redundancies.

Largely through the educative influence of the Area Union the Durham miners had learned to appreciate during the fifties that some pit closures and reductions in manpower were inevitable, especially in the western part of the coalfield, if costs were to be controlled and trading prospects improved. In the decade before 1958 there were 330 schemes of reorganization and mechanization in the Durham Division involving 11,957 men, of whom 5,572 became redundant.[2] In nearly all such schemes the introduction of new techniques and modern machinery, especially in the sphere of transportation, meant fewer men being employed. The experience which the Area Union gained in co-operating with workmen and officials in executing such reorganizations proved invaluable when the need for more drastic adjustments in mining activity became necessary.

One of the most remarkable features of the adjustment in manpower in Durham after 1957 was the way in which policies of industrial contraction were implemented without any serious stoppage or restriction of work or any high incidence of unemployment amongst the miners. The degree to which the labour force in the Durham Division was obliged to adjust to changed market conditions after 1957 can be judged from the table opposite.

An interesting feature of this adjustment over the four years in question is the relatively small proportion of workmen who were dismissed or who suffered redundancy compared with all other sources of decline. To some extent wastage of labour on medical grounds can be regarded as a form of early retirement and this, in combination with natural retirement, accounted for a large propor-

---

[1] W. Snaith, 'The Adjustment of the Labour Force in the Durham Coalfield— A Study of Redundancy', *Economic Studies*, 4, October 1969, p. 240.
[2] N.U.M. (Durham Area), *Annual Report*, 1958, p. 340.

Labour Wastage and Recruitment in the Durham Division
1957–60

	Wastage Involuntary (by cause)				Voluntary		Total wastage	Total wastage as a % of average number of men on books	Recruitment
	Deaths	Retirements	Medical	Dismissals and Redundancy	All other causes				
1957	452	1,143	499	599	3,482		6,175	6·1	5,673
1958	431	1,526	643	774	3,316		6,690	6·7	3,733
1959	431	1,097	787	1,358	3,324		6,997	7·3	2,152
1960	422	1,233	717	842	4,596		7,810	8·7	2,072

Source: National Coal Board, *Annual Reports*, 1957–60.

tion of the amount of involuntary wastage. Equally notable is the fact that over half of the rundown of the labour force was brought about by voluntary movement out of the industry. After 1957 work-men over 65 years of age were displaced on a strict one-for-one basis to enable younger men to be employed from other collieries. This scheme was followed in October 1959 by a national agreement which established compulsory retirement for miners at the age of 65.[1]

Whatever the severity of the decline in activity in the coalfield the Area Union remained constantly alert to the need to reduce hardship to a minimum. In 1958 it succeeded in persuading the miners' national Executive Committee of the N.U.M. to seek an amendment to the Compensation for Redundancy Agreement whereby all work-men who were declared redundant for any reason should become eligible for payment.[2] Two years later Durham joined South Wales and Scotland in demanding that the Government should intensify its efforts to direct industry into mining areas in order to widen the scope of alternative employment for redundant miners.[3]

In view of the depressing long-term prospects of the northern coalfield the Area Union wholeheartedly endorsed the N.U.M.'s plea in February 1959 for a national fuel policy based on the co-ordination of all energy industries. In a report to Lodges outlining the principles of this policy Watson demanded that:

'These industries should be under one umbrella, in charge of one Minister and Ministry , and the Minister should have Cabinet Rank. The "free for all" and "consumer choice" slogans of the Tory Government are mere palliatives. We are really facing a critical situation and the need is not for "atomizing" our energy industries, but co-ordinating them, thus enabling coal and all the associated fuel industries to make a contribution on a much bigger scale than at present to the energy needs of the Nation and enable Britain to maintain her place in the markets of the world, and her people to participate in steadily growing standards of living.'[4]

Nor was the Area Union the only party intent on minimizing the impact of contraction within the coalfield. The Divisional Coal Board, forced to quicken the drive for efficiency, sought to improve its marketing performance and sales development. A technical sales service manned by skilled engineers was developed to advise cus-tomers in the use of modern solid fuel equipment. The sale of such

[1] Snaith, loc. cit., pp. 241–2.
[2] N.U.M., 10 July 1958.
[3] Ibid., 7 July 1960.
[4] N.U.M. (Durham Area), Annual Report, 1959, p. 5.

equipment on hire-purchase was promoted by the development of a 'house-warming plan' in 1960. A sales development manager was also appointed to help extend the market for coal for domestic heating.[1]

II

The full extent of the reversal in the fortunes of the Durham coalfield during the late fifties compared with national trends can be judged from the table overleaf.

Estimates of the extent to which the decline in the comparative advantage of producing coal would affect future output and employment in Durham were contained in the Coal Board's *Revised Plan for Coal*,[2] published in October 1959. New projections were made of demand, investment and production within the industry for the remaining six years of the original 1950 plan in addition to proposals for more immediate restrictions on output. From a long-term point of view the *Revised Plan* sought to concentrate future production in the high productivity coalfields so as to increase coal's competitive position *vis-à-vis* other fuels.

The projected total demand for coal during 1961–5 of between 230m. and 250m. tons, originally made in the 1950 *Plan for Coal*, was revised in 1959 to an estimate of 206m. tons for 1965. Once it became clear that the demand for coal could no longer be expected to rise by 1965 to the level predicted in 1956 production plans were concentrated upon encouraging output in those coalfields where the new capacity created by investment since nationalization could most profitably be exploited. Thus in the *Revised Plan* the North-Eastern, East Midlands, West Midlands and South-Western Divisions were expected to produce more coal than in 1959; the Northern (Northumberland and Cumberland), Durham, North-Western and South-Eastern Divisions to produce less and the Scottish Division about the same.[3]

The contribution to total deep-mined output in 1965 expected to be made by the Durham Division was revised in 1956 to 24m. tons (10 per cent) from the 1950 estimate of 27m. tons (11·2 per cent) and was further reduced in 1959 to between 21·5m. tons and 23·5m. tons (9·2 per cent taking the mid-point of the estimate). This reduction in output allocation reflected the changing nature of the demand for coal, especially the fall in coal consumption in the London area

[1] *Ibid.*, 1960, pp. 229–31.
[2] National Coal Board, *Revised Plan for Coal*, 1959.
[3] *Ibid.*

Output and Employment, Durham and Great Britain, 1957–60

	Saleable output (over 52 weeks) m. tons		Wage earners on colliery books at the end of the year ('000s)		Total exports and bunkers (deep-mined and open-cast) ('000s tons)		Profit (+) or loss (−) per ton of coal commercially disposable			
							Durham		Great Britain	
	Durham	Great Britain	Durham	Great Britain	Durham	Great Britain	s	d	s	d
1957	25·0	207·4	100·9	703·7	777	7,110	−1	3	+0	7
1958	23·9	198·8	97·9	681·1	441	4,633	−0	10	+1	1
1959	23·3	192·6	93·0	634·0	525	4,266	−1	11	+1	0
1960	22·8	183·8	87·2	582·9	746	5,534	−1	7	+1	8

Source: National Coal Board, *Annual Reports*, 1957–60.

due mainly to a decline in the requirements of the gas industry. Since the Durham coalfield was one of the chief suppliers of coal to the North Thames and South-Eastern Gas Boards, providing 69 per cent and 80 per cent of total supplies respectively during 1961–2, expectations of falling demand from these consumers in the future were bound to have a direct adverse effect upon the region.

The Area Union was naturally concerned about the impact of the Board's new estimates upon manpower. To help ease the situation the Industrial Relations Department of the Divisional Coal Board drew up in 1960 the first of a series of Manpower Profiles which provided a basis for discussion between Coal Board officials and representatives of the unions on the Divisional Consultative Council. Collieries were placed in one of three categories depending upon the estimate of their future life expectancy. Those needing to recruit men in order to maintain or increase their manpower were placed in Category A; those at which normal labour wastage could be expected to reduce manpower in Category B and those destined to close and able to provide labour for transference to other pits in Category C. Once the Division became aware of what proportion of total national output it was expected to produce a general programme of closure and reorganization was decided upon and estimates made of the total demand for labour. Collieries and Areas with probable excess labour were then matched with recruiting collieries in order to effect a redeployment of labour with the minimum of hardship to the men involved.[1]

Such detailed analyses of the requirements for and the availability of various grades of workers throughout the coalfield did not obliterate problems of internal labour transference. Elderly surface workers, especially if disabled, were particularly difficult to transfer and low-paid daywagemen were reluctant to travel to other collieries or move home with little prospect of material improvement. Some redundant miners in Durham refused to accept vacancies at coke works because the wages available were below the minimum amount paid to surface workers and below the amount a married surface miner with two children could claim from redundancy and unemployment pay (including family allowances). At one particular pit in the coalfield where a scheme of reorganization and reconstruction had made 30 men redundant miners refused to respond to the need for 23 workmen at a coking plant only three miles away.[2]

The Coal Board's policy of planned reductions in output and

[1] Snaith, *loc. cit.*, pp. 242–5.
[2] N.U.M. (Durham Area), *Annual Report*, 1960, p. 2.

employment in the older mining regions was continued into the sixties and some measure of its continuing impact in Durham can be gained from the diagrams on pages 510 and 511.

In some respects the Area Union officials [1] who bore the responsibility for safeguarding miners' interests in Durham during the difficult period of transition after 1957 faced problems which were both more intense and more formidable than in most other mining districts. In the past many of the worst features of decline and dislocation within the industry had been focused within the Durham coalfield. During long periods of depression between the wars former leaders had had to battle to preserve even the most minimal standard of life for workmen in a coal-exporting district which was particularly sensitive to trade cycle fluctuations. Durham's traditional shorter working day for hewers, the coalfield's most numerous and dominant class of workmen, enhanced the power which autonomous district bargaining gave to employers to legitimately increase the length of the working day and/or reduce wages in order to sell cheaply at the expense of the miners' standard of living. Worse than average housing conditions, the lack of alternative employment opportunities in the north-east and the paucity of local coal owners' efforts at industrial reorganization and rationalization must have provided the Durham miners with a feeling, substantiated by their own experiences, that they were in the forefront of the battle against capitalism, repression and self-interest.

Though the pressing demand for coal for most of the first decade of mines nationalization dispelled, as the wartime economy had done, fears of lasting unemployment in the pits it also served to emphasize the technical backwardness and acute manpower problems within the industry. Older coalfields like Durham supporting costly, inefficient and inadequately mechanized pits and with the added burdens of a natural depletion of reserves were often hard pressed to fulfil the production requirements made of them. When the necessity for economy and competitiveness, especially after 1957, prompted pit

---

[1] By 1960 two new Agents had been appointed. A. Hesler was elected as Financial Secretary in 1957 following the death of Foster. Hesler had worked in the pits since the age of 14 and for the ten years prior to his election as Agent had been checkweighman at East Hetton Colliery and Secretary of the local miners' Lodge. He took an active part in public life and was a member of the Durham County Council and a past chairman of the Durham Rural District Council.

J. C. Robinson, elected as an Agent in 1958, began work at West Auckland Colliery in 1921 but moved to Easington three years later when the pit closed. He became Chairman of the Easington Colliery Lodge in 1948 and was elected to Easington Rural Council in 1955. In 1952 he was awarded the B.E.M. for his services at the time of the Easington Colliery mine disaster.

closures, labour transferences and colliery reorganizations Durham rarely escaped unaffected. Indeed one of the salient features of the Area Union's activity after 1947 was the continuous manner in which it involved its membership in a concern for the well-being of the industry as a whole and the way in which officials, especially Watson, sought to persuade workmen to identify themselves with the responsibilities a publicly-owned mining industry had towards the national economy, even when this called for planned reductions in the labour force.[1]

The annual Miners' Gala in Durham City provided Area Union officials with a unique opportunity to appeal to the workmen's common sense of dignity and loyalty, in the hope of establishing greater mutual trust and co-operation. Whatever else had altered under nationalization, the Gala still remained a day of boisterous activity with dancing and singing in the streets, uninhibited drinking and shameless nostalgia, but even this intense demonstration of unity and solidarity could not completely disguise the declining fortunes of coal. As the fifties wore on fewer and fewer Lodge banners adorned the City's old racecourse and by the early sixties the Gala began to emerge as a timely reflection of the pace of pit closures and as a constant reminder of the degree to which the Durham coalfield was being forced to bear the brunt of industrial change.

The return to Parliament of seven Durham miners' M.P.s in 1959 helped strengthen the Area Union's pleas for a reasoned and sympathetic response by the Government to the social implications of a planned contraction in the coal industry. At the same time the N.U.M. exploited every opportunity to improve workmen's living standards and succeeded in winning a 5 per cent wage increase for adult daywagemen in March 1957 (subject to a minimum increase of 1s 7d a shift in standard grade rates). Disputes with the Coal Board over subsequent claims led to three awards being granted by the National Reference Tribunal, a 1s 3d increase in daywage shift rates in September 1958, a 1s a shift increase in the national standard grade rate for the highest grades of craftsmen and for winding enginemen in November 1959 and an increase of 10d per shift in the national standard grade rates in September 1960.

[1] E. H. D. Skinner, Chairman of the Durham Divisional Coal Board during the first decade of nationalization, has written of the relationship between his Board and the Area Union: 'I believe that concern for the industry was the moving factor which governed or influenced, not overtly maybe or avowedly, the thinking and conduct of the majority of what is known as "both sides". . . . The common concern for the industry created a disposition to have regard for the difficulties and problems of the other side and to make allowances rather than create difficulties.' Letter to the author, 27 May 1969.

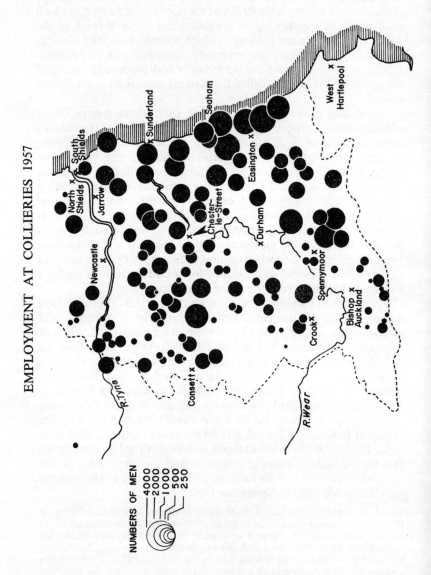

EMPLOYMENT AT COLLIERIES 1957

West Hartlepool ×

Seaham

Sunderland ×

South Shields ×

North Shields ×

Jarrow

Easington ×

Chester-le-Street ×

× Durham

Newcastle

Spennymoor ×

Bishop ×
Auckland

Crook ×

Consett ×

R. Tyne

R. Wear

NUMBERS OF MEN

4000
2000
1000
500
250

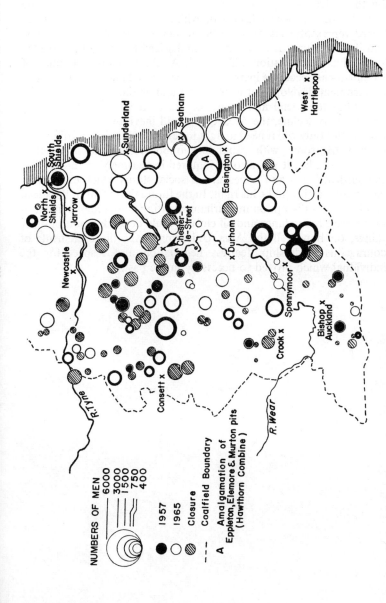

NUMBERS OF MEN

6000
3000
1500
750
400

● 1957
○ 1965
▨ Closure
- - - Coalfield Boundary

A Amalgamation of
    Eppleton, Elemore & Murton pits
    (Hawthorn Combine)

Source: Adapted from J. W. House and E. M. Knight, *Pit Closure and the Community*, Newcastle 1967. I am grateful to Professor House and to David and Charles (publishers) for permission to reproduce these diagrams.

For those whose task it was to provide leadership and courage during the quickening phase of mining contraction in the sixties the Area Union's post-war legacy of willingly co-operating with Coal Board representatives at all levels to develop an efficient and responsible industry could only have emphasized the important role the local miners' association still played. As the industrial complex of the north-east becomes increasingly more varied under the impact of Government development expenditure and as the dominance of the pit within the social and economic life of the mining community continues to decline, the Area Union will inevitably face new challenges. Not only will it need to fight to retain the loyalty and discipline of a work force with expanding opportunities for alternative employment, but it will also be required increasingly to safeguard a standard of living and a measure of social status which each miner vehemently claims to be his right. In the future the extent of the social and industrial disruption in Durham resulting from redeployment of manpower, redundancy and pit closure could depend, amongst other things, on how well the Area Union preserves those elements of courageous leadership, fearless negotiation and respect for the individual which proved so necessary in the past.

Bibliography

I: PRIMARY AUTHORITIES

1. *Trade Union Sources*

(a) The Durham Miners' Association: Minutes of Council and Executive Committee meetings, 1913–60, balance sheets, circulars, rule books, colliery agreements and miscellaneous documents.
(At the offices of the National Union of Mineworkers, Durham Area, Red Hill, Durham.)

(b) The Durham Coal Owners' Association: Minutes of Executive Committee meetings, annual reports and miscellaneous documents, 1919–46.
(At the Northumberland County Record Office, Melton Park, North Gosforth, Newcastle.)

(c) Miners' Federation of Great Britain: Minutes, circulars, reports and balance sheets 1914–44. Continued as National Union of Mineworkers, 1945–60.

(d) T.U.C. reports.

(e) Durham Aged Mineworkers' Homes Association, annual reports, 1919–39.

(f) *Account of the Proceedings of the Northumberland and Durham General Council Joint Strike Committee*, May 1926.
(At the offices of the National Union of Mineworkers, Durham Area.)

(g) Spen and District Trades and Labour Council, *Strike Bulletin* No. 1, 4 May 1926.
(At the Marx Memorial Library, Clerkenwell Green, London E.C.1.)

(h) T.U.C. Local collection on the General Strike, Congress House, London.

2. *Parliamentary and other Official Publications*

Reports of H.M. Inspectors of Mines and Quarries, 1918–56.

Coal Industry Commission, 1919.

Mines Department, *Report on the Causes of and Circumstances Attending the Accident which Occurred in the Busty Shaft of the Medomsley Colliery, Co. Durham, on 24 February 1923, by Henry Walker*, 1923.

Report by a Court of Inquiry Concerning the Wages Position in the Coal Mining Industry, 1924.

Report by a Court of Inquiry concerning the Coal Mining Industry Dispute, 1925.

Royal Commission on the Coal Industry, 1925.

Report of the Departmental Committee on Co-operative Selling in the Coal-Mining Industry, 1926.

Ministry of Health, *Chester-le-Street Union, Report of the Board of Guardians on the Administration for the Period 30th August 1926 to 31st December 1926.*

513

Ministry of Health, *Eighth Annual Report*, 1926–7.

Cabinet Papers.

Ministry of Labour, *Memorandum on the Transfer of Juveniles from Distressed Mining Areas to Employment in Other Districts*, December 1928.

Ministry of Labour, *Facilities Available to Unemployed Workers for Training and Transference Including Migration Overseas*, April 1929.

Report of British Coal Delegation to Norway, Sweden and Denmark, 1931.

Mines Department, Miners' Welfare Fund, annual reports.

Mines Department, Coal Mines Act, 1930. Working Schemes under Part I of the Act during the March quarter, 1931.

Coal Mines Reorganization Commission, Colliery Amalgamations, July 1931.

Board of Trade, *An Industrial Survey of the North-East Coast Area*, 1932.

Mines Department, Coal Mines Act, 1930. Working Schemes under Part I of the Act during the year 1932.

Agreement between the Government of the United Kingdom and the Government of Denmark Relating to Trade and Commerce, 24th April 1933.

Agreement between the Government of the United Kingdom and the Norwegian Government Relating to Trade and Commerce, 15th May 1933.

Agreement between the Government of the United Kingdom and the Government of Sweden Relating to Trade and Commerce, 15th May 1933.

Coal Mines Act, Durham District (Coal Mines) Scheme 1930, 1 August 1933.

Coal Mines Reorganization Commission, *Report to the Secretary of Mines*, December 1933.

Reports of Investigations into the Industrial Conditions in Certain Depressed Areas, 1934.

Reports of the Commissioner for the Special Areas, 1935–7.

Coal Mines Reorganization Commission, *Report to the Secretary of Mines*, January 1936.

Report of the Unemployment Assistance Board for the period ended 31st December 1935, June 1936.

Ministry of Health, Housing Act 1935, *Report on the Overcrowding Survey in England and Wales*, 1936.

Royal Commission on Safety in Coal Mines, 1938.

Royal Commission on Workmen's Compensation, 1939–44.

Report of the Board of Investigation into the Immediate Wages Issues in the Coalmining Industry, 1942.

Ministry of Fuel and Power, Murton Colliery Durham. *Report on the Causes of and Circumstances attending the Explosion which Occurred on the 26th June 1942 at the Murton Colliery, Durham, by R. Yates*, 1943.

National Conciliation Board for the Coalmining Industry, National Reference Tribunal Awards.

Ministry of Fuel and Power, Coal Charges Account, April 1945.
Ministry of Fuel and Power, *Coal Mining: Report of the Technical Advisory Committee*, 1945.
Ministry of Fuel and Power, *Durham Coalfield, Regional Survey Report (Northern 'B' Region)*, 1945.
Ministry of Fuel and Power, *Statistical Digest from 1938*, 1944.
Ministry of Fuel and Power, *Statistical Digest*, 1944.
Ministry of Fuel and Power, *Statistical Digest*, 1945.
Ministry of Fuel and Power, *Supplement to Statistical Digest*, 1945.
Ministry of Fuel and Power, *Report on the Causes of, and Circumstances Attending, the Explosion which occurred at Louisa (including Morrison Old) Colliery Durham, on the 22nd August 1947, by R. Yates*, 1948.
Ministry of Labour, *Report of a Court of Inquiry into a Dispute between the National Coal Board and the National Union of Colliery Winding Enginemen*, January 1948.
Statement on Personal Incomes, Costs and Prices, 1948.
National Coal Board, *Plan for Coal*, 1950.
Report of a Committee of Enquiry on Industrial Health Services, 1950–1.
Ministry of Fuel and Power, *Report on the Causes of and Circumstances Attending the Explosion which occurred at Easington Colliery, County Durham, on the 29th May 1951, by H. C. W. Roberts*, 1952.
Report of the Committee on National Policy for the Use of Fuel and Power Resources, September 1952.
National Coal Board, *Report of the Advisory Committee on Organization*, 1955.
National Coal Board, *Investing in Coal*, 1956.
Ministry of Fuel and Power, *Capital Investment in the Coal, Gas and Electricity Industries*, 1957.
Report of Select Committee on Nationalized Industries: *Coal*, 2 April 1958.
National Coal Board, annual reports and statement of accounts, 1947–60.
National Miners' Welfare Joint Council, annual reports, 1948–52.
Coal Industry Social Welfare Organization, annual reports, 1952–6.
Parliamentary Debates, fifth series.
Ministry of Labour Gazette.

3. *Newspapers and Periodicals*

(a) *Local*
Auckland and County Chronicle, Durham Chronicle, Journal and North Star, Newcastle Daily Chronicle, North Mail and Newcastle Chronicle, Northern Echo, Yorkshire Post.

(b) *National*
British Gazette, British Medical Journal, British Worker, Colliery Guardian, Colliery Year Book, Daily Herald, Daily Telegraph, The Economist, Iron and Coal Trades Review, The Financial Times, Listener, Miner, New Statesman, Stock Exchange Year Book, The Times.

4. Autobiographies and Memoirs

Lord Citrine, *Men and Work*, London 1964.
Clynes, J. R., *Memoirs: 1924–37*, London 1937.
Dalton, H., *The Fateful Years, Memoirs, 1931–1945*, London 1957.
Lawson, J., *A Man's Life*, London 1949, edn.
Thomas, J. H., *My Story*, London 1937.

5. Other Sources, Largely or partly Primary in Nature

A Durham Mining Engineer, 'The Position of the Durham Coalfield: Plain Facts and Figures', reprinted from the *Northern Echo*, June 1926.

'A National Disgrace: Plight of the Miners' Houses', A report by a member of the Committee of the Winter Distress League, London, *Review of Reviews*, March 1929.

Lord Aberconway, *The Basic Industries of Great Britain*, London 1927.

Earl Baldwin, *On England, and Other Addresses*, London 1938, edn.

Bowley, A. L. and Hogg, M. H., *Has Poverty Diminished?*, London 1925.

Browne, R. C., Beck, I. F., Saint, E. G., and McCallum, R. I., *A Study of Coalminers' Nystagmus in Durham County*, Durham 1949.

Coal and Power, *The Report of an Enquiry Presided over by D. Lloyd George*, London 1924.

Conference of Northern Poor-Law Unions and Other Local Authorities, *Deputation to the Ministry of Labour*, 27 October 1927.

Daily Telegraph, special supplement, 'The British Coalmining Industry', 16 September 1930.

Distress in Mining Areas: Mansion House Fund. Brief Statement as to the Administration of the Fund in the Counties of Northumberland and Durham, 3 August 1928.

Durham County Council, *Annual Reports of the Medical Officer of Health*, 1929–1930.

Durham District Committee of Investigation, *Complaints re: Coal Prices*, March 1938.

Durham and the North-East Coast, *Reports of the Labour Party's Commission of Enquiry into the Distressed Areas*, April 1937.

Final Report of the United States Coal Commission, 1922–3.

Foot, R., *A Plan for Coal*, London 1945.

Gibson, F. A., *The Coal Mining Industry of the United Kingdom, The Various Coalfields Thereof and the Principal Foreign Countries of the World*, Cardiff 1922.

Gibson, W., *Coal in Great Britain*, London 1927, edn.

Griffiths, J., *Between the Wars—Coal*, London 1939.

Harvey, G., *Capitalism in the Northern Coalfield*, Pelaw-on-Tyne 1918.

Labour Party, *The Iniquitous Means Test*, London 1933.

Lawson, J., *Labour Fights for Workmen's Compensation*, Labour Party 1939.

Londonderry Collieries Ltd., *History of the Londonderry Collieries Ltd.*, March 1946.

Lord Mayor's Distress Fund, 1928; deposited in Durham County Record Office, CC/X File No. 1.

Milne-Bailey, W., *Trade Union Documents*, London 1929.

National Union of Mineworkers (Durham Area), *Changes in Wages, Durham Coal Trade, 1871–1953*, Durham 1954.

Newsom, J., *Out of the Pit*, Oxford 1936.

Oxberry, J., *The Birth of a Movement: A Tribute to the Memory of Joseph Hopper*, Gateshead District Aged Mineworkers' Homes, November 1924.

Pease and Partners Ltd., reports and accounts, 1919–39.

Pilgrim Trust, *Men Without Work*, London 1938.

Report on the Activities of the Northern Committee of the Distressed Coalfields Committee Under the National Council of Social Service, 1929–1933.

Skinner, E. D. H., *The Coal Industry in Durham Today—and Tomorrow*, Conference address printed for private circulation, 1950.

Symons, J., *The General Strike*, London 1957.

Symon, Sir John, *Three Speeches on the General Strike*, London 1926.

Thomas, G., *The Recruitment of Boys to the Mining Industry. An Inquiry carried out in Six Coalfields for the Directors of Recruitment, Ministry of Fuel and Power and the National Coal Board*, London, August-October 1946.

II: SECONDARY AUTHORITIES

1. *Books, Articles and Pamphlets*

Acton Society Trust, *Nationalized Industry*. Nine pamphlets published during 1950–1.

Alexander, K. J. W., 'Wages in Coal Mining Since Nationalization', *Oxford Economic Papers*, VIII, 1956.

Allen, V. L., 'Some Economic Aspects of Compulsory Trade Unionism', *Oxford Economic Papers*, VI, 1956.

Ancrum, J., 'The W.I.R. in the Dawdon Lock-Out', *Labour Monthly*, II, 1929.

Armstrong, G. and Buchan, S., 'Dewatering Schemes in the South-West Durham Coalfield'. Paper read before the North of England Institute of Mining and Mechanical Engineers, 4 June 1959.

Armstrong College, Newcastle-upon-Tyne, *The Industrial Position of the North-East Coast of England*, London 1935.

Arndt, H. W., *The Economic Lessons of the Nineteen Thirties*, London 1963, edn.

Arnot, R. P., *The Miners, 1889–1910*, London 1949.

Arnot, R. P., *The Miners: Years of Struggle*, London 1953.

Arnot, R. P., *The Miners in Crisis and War*, London 1961.

Ashton, T. S., and Sykes, J., *The Coal Industry of the Eighteenth Century*, Manchester University Press 1964.

Baldwin, G. B., 'Structural Reform in the British Miners' Union', *Quarterly Journal of Economics*, LXVII, 1953.

Baldwin, G. B., 'The Effect of Nationalization on Britain's National Union of Mineworkers', *Proceedings of the Fifth Annual Meeting, Industrial Relations Research Association*, 1954.

Baldwin, G. B., *Beyond Nationalization: The Labor Problems of British Coal*, Cambridge: Harvard University Press 1955.

Barratt-Brown, M., 'Coal as a Nationalized Industry', *Economic Studies*, 4, October 1969.

Barry, E. E., *Nationalization in British Politics*, London 1965.

Beacham, A., 'Planned Investment in the Coal Industry', *Oxford Economic Papers*, 3, June 1951.

Beacham, A., 'The Coal Industry' in Burn, D. (ed.), *The Structure of British Industry: A Symposium*, Volume I, Cambridge 1958.

Bell, G. K. A., *Randall Davidson*, London 1935.

Bell, Sir Hugh, 'The Dispute in the Coal Trade', *Contemporary Review*, CXXX, 1926.

Beveridge, W. H., *Full Employment in a Free Society*, London 1944.

Bowie, J. A., 'A New Method of Wage Adjustment in the Light of the Recent History of Wage Methods in the British Coal Industry', *Economic Journal*, XXXVII, 1926.

Bowle, J., *Viscount Samuel*, London 1957.

Briggs, A., *History of Broadcasting in the United Kingdom*, I, Oxford 1961.

Brown, E. H., 'The Coalfields of Great Britain and their Future Development', *Transactions of the Institution of Mining Engineers*, 114, 1954-5.

Bryan, Sir A., 'Prospects of the British Coal Industry with particular relation to Exports'. Address delivered at Jesus College, 19 April 1951.

Butler, D. E., *The British General Election of 1951*, London 1952.

Buxton, N. K., 'Entrepreneurial Efficiency in the British Coal Industry between the Wars', *Economic History Review*, XXIII, 1970.

Buzzard, R. B., 'Attendance and Absence in Industry: the Nature of the Evidence', *British Journal of Sociology*, 3, September 1954.

Central Statistical Office, *Annual Abstract of Statistics, 1938–1949*, London 1951.

Clapham, J. H., *Economic History of Modern Britain*, Cambridge University Press 1932, 3 volumes.

Clegg, H. A. and Chester, T. E., *The Future of Nationalization*, London 1953.

Clegg, H. A., Fox, A., Thompson, A. F., *A History of British Trade Unions since 1889, Volume I: 1889-1910*, Oxford 1964.

Cole, G. D. H., *Labour in the Coal-Mining Industry (1914–1921)*, Oxford 1923.

Cole, M., *Beatrice Webb's Diaries, 1912–1924*, London 1952.

Collins, H. E., 'Coal Ploughs in the Durham Coalfield', *Transactions of the Institution of Mining Engineers*, 112, December 1952.

Communist Party, 'The General Strike in the North-East', *Our History*, 22, 1965.

Conservative Political Centre, *Inside Industry: Coal*, London 1948.

Conservative Political Centre, *Facts and Ideas about Coal*, London 1948.

Conservative Political Centre, *Structure of the Coal Industry*, London 1948.

Court, W. H. B., 'Problems of the British Coal Industry Between the Wars', *Economic History Review*, XV, 1945.

Court, W. H. B., *Coal*, London 1951.

Crook, W. H., *The General Strike*, Chapel Hill, University of North Carolina Press, 1931.

Cross, C., 'The Slump', *The Observer*, 6 February 1966.

Felton, M., 'Britain's Model New Industrial Town: Peterlee', *Journal of the American Institute of Planners*, Spring 1949.

Fynes, R., *The Miners of Northumberland and Durham*, Sunderland 1873.

Goodhart, A. L., 'The Legality of the General Strike in England', *Yale Law Journal*, XXXVI, 1927.

Gratwick, W. K., 'Labor Relations in Nationalized Industries with particular reference to the Coal-Mining Industry', *Law and Contemporary Problems*, 16, 1951.

Gregory, R., *The Miners and British Politics, 1906–1914*, Oxford 1968.

Griffin, A. R., *The Miners of Nottinghamshire, 1914–1944*, London 1962.

Hair, P. E. H., 'The Binding of the Pitmen of the North-East 1800–1809', *Durham University Journal*, LVIII, 1965.

Handy, L. J., 'Absenteeism and Attendance in the British Coal-Mining Industry: An Examination of Post-War Trends', *British Journal of Industrial Relations*, 6, March 1968.

Hannington, W., *Unemployed Struggles, 1919–1936*, London 1936.

Hannington, W., *The Problem of the Distressed Areas*, London 1937.

Haynes, W. W., *Nationalization in Practice: The British Coal Industry*, London 1953.

Heinemann, M., *Britain's Coal*, London 1944.

Henson, H., 'The British Lazzaroni', *English Review*, July 1930.

Houldsworth, Sir H., 'The Pits of Britain'. Paper read before the Manchester Statistical Society, 11 February 1953.

House, J. W., and Knight, E. M., 'Pit Closure and the Community'. Report to the Ministry of Labour, Papers on Migration and Mobility in Northern England, No. 5, December 1967.

Iremonger, F. A., *William Temple: His Life and Letters*, London 1948.

James, R. R., *Memoirs of a Conservative: J. C. C. Davidson's Memoirs and Papers 1910–37*, London 1969.

Jenks, C. E., 'British Coal: Labor Relations Since Nationalization', *Industrial Relations*, 6, 1966–7.

Jones, J. H., 'The Coal Mining Industry', in Jones, J. H. (ed.), *Britain in Recovery*, London 1938.

Jones, J. H., Cartwright, G., Guenault, P. H., *The Coal-Mining Industry*, London 1939.

Kelly, D. M., 'The Process of Mechanization in British Coal Mining Since 1945', *Economic Studies*, 4, October 1969.

520   THE DURHAM MINERS

Kelly, D. W., 'The Administration of the National Coal Board', *Public Administration*, 31, 1953.

Kerr, C. and Siegal, A., 'The Inter-Industry Propensity to Strike: An International Comparison', in Korn-Lauser, A., Dubin, R. and Ross, A., *Industrial Conflict*, New York 1954.

Keynes, J. M., *The Economic Consequences of Mr Churchill*, London 1925.

Keynes, J. M., 'The Need of Peace by Negotiation', *New Republic*, 19 May 1926.

Klugmann, J., *History of the Communist Party of Great Britain, Volume Two: The General Strike, 1925–1926*, London 1969.

Knowles, K. G. J. C., *Strikes—A Study in Industrial Conflict*, Oxford 1952.

Landsdown, R. F., and Wood, F. W., 'Coalface Machinery Developments', in Nott-Bower, Sir G., and Walkerdine, R. H., (eds), *National Coal Board, The First Ten Years*, London 1956.

Liddell, F. D. K., 'Attendance in the Coal-Mining Industry', *British Journal of Sociology*, 5, 1954.

Lawther, W., 'The Miners' Struggle in the North', *Labour Monthly*, 8, August 1926.

Lawson, J., *Peter Lee*, London 1936.

League of Nations, Economic and Financial Section, *The Problem of the Coal Industry*, 1929.

McCormick, B., and Williams, J. E., 'The Miners and the Eight-Hour Day, 1863–1910', *Economic History Review*, XII, 1959.

Marsh, F., 'Haulage and Handling', in Nott-Bower, Sir G., and Walkerdine, R. H., (eds), *National Coal Board, The First Ten Years*, London 1956.

Martin, K., *The British Public and the General Strike*, London 1926.

Martin, R., *Communism and the British Trade Unions, 1924–1933*, Oxford 1969.

Mason, A., 'The Local Press and the General Strike,: an example from the North-East', *Durham University Journal*, LXI, 3, 1969.

Mason, A., 'The Government and the General Strike, 1926', *International Review of Social History*, XIV, 1969.

Mason, A., 'The General Strike', *Bulletin of the Society for the Study of Labour History*, 20, 1970.

Meyers, F., 'Nationalization, Union Structures and Wages Policy in the British Coal-Mining Industry', *Southern Economic Journal*, 24, 1958.

Meyers, F., *European Coal-Mining Unions*, University of California 1961.

Middlemas, K., (ed.), *Thomas Jones: Whitehall Diary*, 2 vols, Oxford 1969.

Middlemas, K., and Barnes, J., *Baldwin: A Biography*, London 1969.

Mitchell, B. R., and Deane, P., *Abstract of British Historical Statistics*, Cambridge 1962.

Moggeridge, D. E., *The Return to Gold, 1925*, University of Cambridge, Department of Applied Economics, Occasional Papers: 19, Cambridge 1969.

Moos, S., 'Statistics on Absenteeism in Coal Mining', *Manchester School of Economic and Social Research*, 3, 1951.

Mowat, C. L., *Britain Between the Wars, 1918–1940*, London 1964.

Moyes, W. A., *Mostly Mining*, Newcastle-on-Tyne 1969.

Murray, J., *The General Strike of 1926*, London 1951.

Nef, J. U., 'The Progress of Technology and the Growth of Large-Scale Industry in Great Britain, 1540–1640', *Economic History Review*, V, 1934–5.

Nef, J. U., *The Rise of the British Coal Industry*, London 1932, 2 vols.

Nelson, J. R., 'The Fleck Report and the Area Organization of the National Coal Board', *Public Administration*, 43, 1965.

Neuman, A. M., *Economic Organization of the British Coal Industry*, London 1934.

Platt, J., *British Coal*, London 1968.

P.E.P., *Report on the British Coal Industry*, London, February 1936.

P.E.P., *The British Fuel and Power Industries*, London 1947.

Poirier, P. P., *The Advent of the Labour Party*, London 1958.

Pool, A. G., *Wage Policy in Relation to Industrial Fluctuations*, London 1938.

Posner, M., 'The National Coal Board, 1947–62', *Annals of Collective Economy*, 33, October-December 1962.

Postgate, R., Wilkinson, E., Horrabin, J. F., *A Workers' History of the Great Strike*, Plebs League 1927.

Redmayne, R. A. S., *The British Coalmining Industry During the War*, Oxford 1923.

Reid, C. C., and W., 'The Reconstruction of the British Coal Mining Industry', Second Cadman Memorial Lecture, Royal Society of Arts, 16 March 1949.

Rhodes, E. C., 'Output, Labour and Machines in the Coal-Mining Industry of Great Britain', *Economica*, XII, 1945.

Rimlinger, G. V., 'International Differences in the Strike Propensity of Coal Miners: Experience in Four Countries', *Industrial and Labor Relations Review*, 12, 1959.

Robb, M., 'The Psychology of the Unemployed from the Medical Point of View', in Beales, H. L., and Lambert, R. S., (eds), *Memoirs of the Unemployed*, London 1934.

Roberts, B. C., *National Wages Policy in War and Peace*, London 1958.

Roberts, C. A., 'The National Coal Board and the Fleck Report', *Public Administration*, XXXV, 1957.

Robinson, C., *A Policy for Fuel?*, Institute of Economic Affairs, Occasional Paper No. 31, London 1969.

Rowe, J. F., *Wages in the Coal Industry*, London 1923.

Safety in Mines Research Board, Paper No. 61, 'The Support of Underground Working in the Coalfields of the North of England', London 1930.

Sales, W. H., and Davies, J. L., 'Introducing a New Wage Structure Into Coal-Mining', *Bulletin of the Institute of Statistics*, 19, 1957.

Saville, J., 'English History, 1914–1945'. A review article, *Bulletin of the Society for the Study of Labour History*, 12, 1966.

Schefftz, M., 'The Trade Disputes and Trades Unions Act of 1927: the aftermath of the General Strike', *Review of Politics*, 29, 1967.

Schumacher, E. F., 'Efficiency in Coal Production', *The Financial Times*, 31 December 1953.

Schumacher, E. F., 'Britain's Coal', *National Provincial Bank Review*, November 1957.

Sealy, E. H., 'A Statistical Analysis of Productivity Movements in British Coal Mining'. Paper read before the Manchester Geological and Mining Society, 12 April 1962.

Sharp, T., *A Derelict Area: A Study of the South-West Durham Coalfield*, London 1935.

Shepherd, W., *Economic Performance under Public Ownership: British Fuel and Power*, Yale University Press 1965.

Simpson, E. S., *Coal and the Power Industries in Postwar Britain*, London 1966.

Snaith, W., 'The Adjustment of the Labour Force in the Durham Coalfield —A Study of Redundancy', *Economic Studies*, 4, October 1969.

Somervell, D. C., *British Politics since 1900*, London 1953.

Spero, S. D., *Labor Relations In British Nationalized Industry*, New York University Press 1955.

Sweezy, P. M., *Monopoly and Competition in the English Coal Trade, 1550–1850*, Harvard University Press 1938.

Tawney, R. H., 'The Abolition of Economic Controls, 1918–21', *Economic History Review*, XIII, 1943.

Taylor, A. J., 'Labour Productivity and Technological Innovation in the British Coal Industry, 1850–1914', *Economic History Review*, XIV, 1961.

Taylor, A. J. P., *English History, 1914–45*, Oxford 1965.

Thompson, A. E., 'Organization in Two Nationalized Industries: Fleck versus Herbert', *Scottish Journal of Political Economy*, 3, June 1957.

Torr, D., *Tom Mann and His Times*, I, London 1956.

Townroe, B. S., *The Slum Problem*, London 1928.

Trueman, Sir Arthur (ed), *The Coalfields of Great Britain*, London 1954.

Turner, H. A., 'Trade Union Differentials and the Levelling of Wages', *Manchester School of Economic and Social Studies*, 3, September 1952.

Webb, S., *The Story of the Durham Miners*, London 1921.

Welbourne, E., *The Miners' Unions of Northumberland and Durham*, Cambridge University Press 1923.

White, P. H., 'Some Aspects of Urban Development by Colliery Companies, 1919–1939', *Manchester School of Economic and Social Studies*, XXIII, 1955.

Willett, H. L., 'Some Developments in Mining Techniques' in Nott-Bower, Sir G., and Walkerdine, R. H., (eds), *National Coal Board, The First Ten Years*, London 1956.

Williams, J. E., *The Derbyshire Miners*, London 1962.

Williams, W. H., *The Miners' Two Bob*, London 1936.

Williams, W. H., *Coal Combines in Durham*, Labour Research Department, London 1939.
Wilson, H., *New Deal for Coal*, London 1945.
Wilson, J., *A History of the Durham Miners' Association, 1870–1904*, Durham 1907.
Workers' Educational Association, Northern District, 1903–1953, Jubilee Brochure, 1953.
Young, A., Longden, H. A., and Metcalfe, B. L., 'Post-War Developments in the Coal Mining Industry', *Proceedings of the Institution of Civil Engineers*, 6, 1957.
Youngson, A. J., *Britain's Economic Growth, 1920–1966*, London 1968.

2. *Unpublished Works*

Broadley, O., 'The Colliery Consultative Committee'. Ph.D. thesis, University of Liverpool 1959.
Hopkins, T. N., 'The Operation of the National Reference Tribunal in the Coal Industry Since 1943'. M.A. thesis, University College of Wales (Aberystwyth) 1961.
Jencks, C. E., 'The Impact of Nationalization on Working Conditions in British Coal Mining'. Ph.D. thesis, University of California (Berkley) 1964.
Johnson, W. A., 'The North-East Miners' Union (Hepburn's Union) of 1831–2'. M.A. thesis, University of Durham 1959.
Mason, A., 'The Miners' Unions of Northumberland and Durham, 1918–1931, with special reference to the General Strike of 1926'. Ph.D. thesis, University of Hull 1967.
Metcalfe, G. H. 'A History of the Durham Miners' Association, 1869–1915'. Library of the N.U.M. (Durham Area), Red Hill, Durham.
Nuttall, T., 'Changes in the Wage Structure of the Coal Industry since Nationalization'. M.A. thesis, University of Leeds 1966.
Rodger, A. S., 'British Fuel Requirements and Investment to 1975'. Ph.D. thesis, University of Edinburgh 1961.
Smith, C. S., 'Planned Transfer of Labour: with special reference to the Coal Industry'. Ph.D. thesis, University of London 1961.

Index

South-East Durham, 324
South Shields, 323, 325, 328, 329, 332, 333, 335, 347
Spennymoor, 322, 324, 328, 329, 332, 337, 339, 346, 347, 348, 378, 380, 386, 491
Sunderland, 325
Sunderland (North), 496
Sunderland (South), 496
redistribution of 1945–50, 490
Patent Office, 283
Patterson, W. H., 71, 72
Payne, E. G., 338
Peacock, H., 345
Peake, E. C., 380
Pearson, —, 454
Pearson, E., 379
Pearson, H., 76
Pearson, W., 79
Pearson, W. G., 339
Pearson and Dorman Long, 55
Pease, A. F., 32, 104, 175
Pease and Partners, 32, 54, 55, 57, 60, 104, 109, 152, 175, 232, 292, 295, 388
Pelaw Main Collieries, 218
Pennsylvania, 75
Pensions, 437, 485–6
Percival, A. S., 310
Percy, E., 277
Personal Incomes, Costs and Prices 1948, 435
Peterlee, 473–5
Peterlee Development Corporation, 473, 474, 475
Philadelphia and District Mines Inspection Board, 304
Philipps, Dr Marion, 235
Pick, Charles
biography, 461
Financial Secretary, N.U.M. (Durham Area), 461
Picketing, 199–200
Pit closures (see also Redundancies), 28, 35, 141, 155, 176–7, 191, 212, 244, 270–1, 355, 396, 402–3, 417, 502, 511
Pit-head baths, 206, 207, 260, 295, 296, 468–70
Pit Production Committees, 381, 382, 466
Pit Safety Committees, 305
Plan for Coal, Mining Association of Great Britain, 386
Plan for Coal, National Coal Board, 414, 416, 417, 420, 505
Plender, Sir William, 237, 238, 252
'Plender Award', 239–42
Pneumoconiosis, 477, 480

Pneumoconiosis and Byssinosis Benefit Scheme, 480
Pneumoconiosis Benefit Scheme, 483
Pneumoconiosis Field Research Project, 480
Poland, 37, 38, 41, 42, 44, 45, 49, 237, 395, 398, 412, 500
Police, 145, 199, 200, 218–19
Portal, Lord, 354
Porter, Lord, 370, 440n
'Porter Award', 370–1
Post Office, 283
Potts, J., 105
Powell-Duffryn Company, 59
Power, Ministry of, 501n
Prest, J., 289
Priestman Collieries, 59, 61
Prison, 195–6, 199, 218
Public Assistance Committees, 279, 280
Pugh, Arthur (afterwards Sir Arthur), 203

Quarrington Hill, 299
Quigley, J., 491, 494

Railway and Canal Commission, 50, 51
Railway rates, 38
Railways, 16
Rainton, 141, 212, 213
Colliery Employees' Thrift Fund, 218
Reay-Smith, J. M., 496
Reciprocal trading agreements, 42
Red Cross Fund, 90
'Red Friday', 183
Redpath Brown and Company, 55
Redundancies, 484–5, 502
Rehabilitation, 375, 480–1
Reid, C. C. (afterwards Sir Charles), 422
Reid Committee (see Technical Advisory Committee on Coal Mining 1945)
Reid, S. J., 388
Reith Committee 1945–6, 473
Retirement, compulsory, 504
Revised Plan for Coal, National Coal Board, 505
Richardson, E., 346
Richardson, R., 73, 148, 208, 219, 321, 322, 323, 328, 329, 331, 332, 338, 339, 341, 344
Richardson, W. P., 105, 108, 181, 189, 202, 243
biography, 73
Financial Secretary, D.M.A., 73
General Secretary, D.M.A., 77
death, 78